CHURCH AND CULTURE
IN THE MIDDLE AGES

Church and Culture
in
The Middle Ages

VOLUME I   350 — 814

Translated by
GEORGE J. UNDREINER, Ph. D.

Professor of Church History
Pontifical College Josephinum
Worthington, Ohio

From the German of
Gustav Schnürer

1956
ST. ANTHONY GUILD PRESS, PATERSON, NEW JERSEY

Nihil obstat:
BEDE BABO, O. S. B., Censor librorum

Imprimatur:
† JAMES A. McNULTY, Bishop of Paterson

September 12, 1955

Translator's Preface

In presenting this translation of the history of the relations existing between the Church and culture in the Middle Ages, the translator hopes to afford to English readers the opportunity of a personal acquaintance with an authoritative work on the subject. Comprehensive in scope and detailed in treatment, this work is based on sound scholarship and is the fruit of almost fifty years of research and teaching on the part of the late distinguished historian Gustav Schnürer.

Kirche und Kultur im Mittelalter consists of three volumes which trace the subject from its earliest beginnings to the rise of Spain and the Catholic revival in the sixteenth century. Each of these volumes, however, forms a unit by itself. Inspired, as he states in his foreword, by Frédéric Ozanam and Godfrey Kurth, the author resolved to attempt the realization of their unfulfilled desires as a means of rendering a permanent service to the Church he so profoundly loved.

At the urgent request, and with the full encouragement, of the Supreme Pontiff Pius XI, of happy memory, Professor Schnürer consented to continue his monumental labors. His researches resulted in two additional volumes entitled *Katholische Kirche und Kultur in der Barockzeit* and *Kirche und Kultur in der modernen Welt* respectively, thus completing the engrossing study and bringing the history of the relations of these two great world factors, the Church and culture, down to the present time.

The translator's aim has been to give a faithful English rendering of the German original, preserving as far as possible the constructions and the imagery of the author. A number of corrections and ameliorations sanctioned by Professor Schnürer have been incorporated in this translation. Finally, to the sources listed in the Third (and last) German Edition (Paderborn: F. Schöningh, 1936), other references have been added by the translator which the reader may find helpful. These supplementary titles are marked in the Bibliography with an asterisk(*).

Kirche und Kultur im Mittelalter has appeared in a French and in a Dutch translation. Unfortunately, the author did not live to see his work translated into English. His death occurred in 1941.

The preparation of this volume has been to the translator almost an act of filial piety, since the author was his esteemed teacher over a period of four years of historical studies at the University of Fribourg, in the medieval and modern fields.

Before concluding, the translator wishes to express his debt of gratitude to his former professor and colleague, the Reverend Herman C. Fischer (d. 1943). Dr. Fischer might almost be accounted co-translator, for he carefully scrutinized the entire manuscript and contributed many improvements in point of expression. Gratitude and appreciation are also due the Reverend Louis J. Puhl, S. J., who gave generous and willing aid in correcting the proofs.

GEORGE J. UNDREINER
Professor of Church History
Pontifical College Josephinum
Worthington, Ohio

October 28, 1955

Author's Foreword

The Middle Ages were the period in which the Church ruled almost without opposition. The relations of the Church and culture throughout this epoch do not present a new problem, but they do constitute the question which, in part unconsciously, in part explicitly, has lain at the root of the whole controversy over the evaluation of the Middle Ages. Individual phases of this question have been treated time and again during the past century and a half, not without prejudice and passion. In the manner of treatment, two extreme views have bitterly opposed each other: the one denying to the Middle Ages any mark of a cultural epoch, the other attributing to the Church all credit for culture and regarding the Middle Ages as the very apogee of cultural development. What has been lacking until now has been a comprehensive treatment of the problem, one that would take account of the development which the Middle Ages experienced in their various periods.

The problem suggested by the title of the present work will be understood, in general, without further ado. Upon closer consideration, however, a number of explanations concerning the object of the work will be seen as necessary even at this point. The idea *Church* needs no further elucidation; but it is quite in order to explain what we understand by the term *culture*.

The very history of the word opens up manifold points of view. It is derived from the Latin *colere,* which we translate by the colorless word *cultivate,* and which designates a human activity directed toward the most varied objects. Thus the Romans used the phrase *colere Deum* ("to worship God"), whence is derived the word *cult* to designate religion expressed by acts of worship. Though the word *culture* comes from the same root as *cult,* we clearly distinguish between them today, so that we speak and write of a relation between religion and culture.

The Romans also knew the word *cultura,* which to them was almost synonymous with *cultus* in the general sense, but which as a rule they applied to agriculture. Cicero does speak of *cultura animi*,[1] and Horace uses the word in the sense of moral ennoblement;[2] but these were isolated instances. It is likewise an exception when we read in a medieval poem of the *cultura Christi*, which could almost signify the Christian ideal of culture.[3] In medieval French the word *culture* was used only in the sense of agriculture. Not until the eighteenth century was the term generally applied to man's intellectual activity, to the cultivation of the arts and sciences, a meaning given it by the representatives of the so-called Enlightenment, d'Alembert, Voltaire and Rousseau.

A similar case is presented by the word *civilisation*, which is generally employed in the same sense in French, albeit a certain difference is early discernible, consisting in this, that *civilisation* is understood to imply a definitely superior degree of culture. The word was used for the first time in 1756 by the elder Mirabeau (1715-1789) and the circle of Voltaire, whence also we have the term "philosophy of history." These new formations and interpretations of words are related to the conception of history entertained by these circles, which see the end of historical development solely as a rational evolution of the human mind to the exclusion of all positive faith. That *civilisation* was long regarded as a new, unusual word is clear from the fact that it was incorporated in the *Dictionnaire de l'Académie* only in 1835.[4]

In England the word *civilization*, in its present meaning of the opposite of *barbarity*, had been admitted to a dictionary with some hesitation in 1772.[5] In Italy it was still harder to decide on naturalizing the word *civilizzazione*,[6] for medieval Italian already possessed the words *civiltade, civiltà* (derived from the Latin *civilitas*), which Dante used to designate the common ideal of human culture.[7]

The words *culture* and *civilization* arose, then, in the Age of Enlightenment, and originally they had a quasi-polemical character,

---

1. *Tusc.*, 2, 13.
2. *Epist.* 1, 1, 40. Cf. *Thesaurus Linguae Latinae*, IV, 1323.
3. Amarcius, *Sermonum*, II, ed. Manitius (Lips., 1888), V., 818.
4. Littrée, *Dictionnaire*, s. v. "civilisation," "civiliser."
5. Murray, *Dictionary*, s. v. "civilization."
6. Tommaseo-Bellini, *Dizionario*, s. v. "civiltà," "civilizzazione."
7. Convivio, IV, c. 4, *Le opere di Dante*, teste crit. (Fir., 1921), p. 250.

like that which also applied to the expression *Kulturkampf*. That character has now wholly disappeared, and we use these words generally as an intellectual measure for man's mental life and activity, for the products of such activity, and for the situation generated by it. The measure is taken from man's pursuit of material happiness and from the progress of man's intellectual mastery of the goods at his disposal.

The question we propose to ourselves is, How did the Church conduct herself as regards this pursuit and the intellectual progress of mankind?

Pondering the significance of the name of our chosen period, the Middle Ages, we observe that the question touches on some very controversial problems. The name itself was coined at the time when Humanism foretold the dawn of a new era. In a eulogy composed in 1469 by John Andrew de Bossi, Bishop of Algeria, the German cardinal Nicholas of Cusa was spoken of as a connoisseur of the Middle Ages (*media tempestas*). As designating a period of history, however, the term became current only in the seventeenth century in the works of Protestant authors of the Netherlands and Germany. Christopher Cellarius (1634-1707), professor at Halle, popularized our current division of history by his manuals of universal history, which distinguished ancient history (*historia antiqua*), medieval history (*historia medii aevi*), and modern history (*historia nova*). This division, opposed, indeed, at the time, is still criticized today, and not without cause, for the terms "Antiquity," "Middle Ages" and "Modern Times" tell us little. Taken by themselves, they express scarcely more than the chronological succession of three eras, a middle one between an earlier and a later. We might just as well supplant the terms with numbers and speak of a first, second and third period — in fact, this would be preferable, for the idea contained in the traditional designation is a fallacious one. The expression "Modern Times" presupposes that the third period will be the last. Were we to add a fourth period to the third, we certainly would not designate the third "Modern Times." But who can say that universal history must end with the period following the middle one? Are we to rule out the possibility that we may sometime have to make a dividing line in this third period much deeper than that now separating the Middle Ages from Modern Times, and that thus a fourth period will begin?

Even now there are some who demand that such a break be made at the so-called Age of Enlightenment, which they propose as the sign of a new stage in mankind's evolution; the preceding years they then naturally add to the Middle Ages. The purpose of this demand is to signify that positively revealed Christian faith has been definitively disavowed on all sides. This view, however, may certainly be questioned. A more justifiable reason for making a new dividing line appears to be the extensive diffusion of culture. We see how the culture of Western Europe, gradually matured, has become in our time more and more a world culture.

This viewpoint permits a positive characterization of the Middle Ages. After the crumbling of the Roman civilization which had flourished in Mediterranean lands, there gradually arose in Western Europe a new culture, which, progressing slowly, is today conquering the whole earth. The beginnings of this culture we find in the Middle Ages, which decidedly represent the origin of our own Western civilization rather than, as some historians have scornfully asserted, the decadence of the previous Roman culture. The characterization of the Middle Ages as the period of the decline of classical Latin — an implied criticism which gave rise to the name of the period — is very one-sided.[8] The rise of the modern nations, their languages and literatures, their cities and institutions of learning, is more significant than the decline of classical Latin; moreover, in place of classical Latin, the Middle Ages continued to develop Latinity in a unique manner.

The characteristic feature that we discern in all the special accomplishments of a particular group of new nations in medieval times is this: that religion, the Catholic Church, is the dominating factor. Thus it seems most fitting to designate the Middle Ages as the ECCLESIASTICAL PERIOD of Western civilization.

The tendencies associated with the creation of the words *culture* and *civilization* manifest themselves also in the conception attached

---

8. Translator's note: In literature this was disparagingly designated as the period of Middle Latin, which then led to naming the historical epoch the Middle Ages.

during the Age of Enlightenment to the expression *Middle Ages.* Not only did men condemn the Middle Ages, as the Humanists had done, as a period when classical Latin was no longer spoken and written; they went even further than the Protestants, who saw in the Middle Ages a degeneration of Christianity, and regarded them generally as a period of barbarism.

But a powerful reaction from this conception soon appeared in Romanticism, which gave a most productive impulse to the study of the Middle Ages. Catholic writers praised the medieval time as the age of faith, and in this praise no one outdid the English convert Kenelm Henry Digby. In his eleven books, *Mores Catholici, or The Ages of Faith,* Digby intended to show, by examples drawn from the various centuries, how the virtues commended in the eight beatitudes of the Sermon on the Mount were practiced in the Middle Ages. However, he took no account at all of another significant fact: the internal development historically manifested by these ages side-by-side with their external solidarity. It was a French scholar, the sympathetic Frédéric Ozanam, professor of foreign literature in Paris, who first grasped our problem, and essayed the task. Him we here gladly acknowledge as our precursor.

Ozanam's premature death in 1853, at the age of forty, unfortunately prevented the carrying out of his great design, evidences of which are furnished us, however, by some very noteworthy specialized studies. He was a sponsor of that young, enthusiastic movement which attempted to bring back to the Church the educated classes of France, drawn away during the Revolutionary period by the triumphant spirit of rationalism. In his student days he founded the Conferences of Saint Vincent de Paul, enjoining the personal visitation of the poor in order to show that social and fraternal charity was not dead in the Catholic Church. And later, in his researches in literature, he endeavored to demonstrate that the Church has been the founder of Western culture. Unlike the representatives of a dechristianized civilization, he did not see the Church and civilization as antitheses; they were intimately bound together. Joy grew in him as he reflected on the progress of civilization, especially in view of the proofs that that progress has been possible only through the Church. "Dans l'histoire des lettres," he wrote, "je cherche surtout la civilisation, et dans l'histoire de la civilisation je vois surtout le progrès par le christianisme."[9]

He planned a gigantic work which would survey civilization from the passing of the ancient culture and the first manifestations of the Christian genius to the end of the thirteenth century.[10] Brilliant fragments of this work are extant in his posthumously published lectures, *La civilisation au Ve siècle*, in the *Études germaniques*, wherein he treats of the Germans prior to the introduction of Christianity and Christian civilization among the Franks; in the especially mature work, *Dante et la philosophie catholique au XIIIe siècle*; and in the *Poètes franciscains en Italie au XIIIe siècle*, which reveals the whole warmth of his religious feelings. Finally, additional materials were gathered during a journey through Italy, in the *Documents inédits pour servir à l'histoire littéraire de l'Italie depuis le VIIIe siècle jusqu'au XIIIe siècle*.

The Liége professor, Godfrey Kurth, who died in 1916, followed in Ozanam's footsteps with his widely read study, *Les origines de la civilisation moderne*. But he, too, treats only of the earlier centuries of the Middle Ages, the above-mentioned work breaking off with Charlemagne. It is regrettable that Ozanam and Kurth could not have carried through their interpretation to the end of the medieval period. As that period continues, the problem takes on another aspect. In the last centuries of the Middle Ages, the civilization founded and fostered in the West by the Church becomes dangerous for the very servants of the Church. To a great extent they succumb to the temptation of overindulging in the mere enjoyment of that civilization, and in serving it, forget their higher, supernatural mission. Only after having viewed this final period does one grasp the problem in its whole extent; only then does one understand the Middle Ages with their lights and shadows. The inquiry thus covers not merely the fostering of civilization by the Church, but also the secularization of the Church as the fostering became more and more one-sided. The great antithesis between the world and the Church, between natural and supernatural aims, that has always existed though asserting itself in various degrees, was

---

9. *Oeuvres*, I, 16.
10. Jordan in *Ozanam, Livre du centenaire*, 231.

perceived and felt in the Middle Ages. Their historian must therefore take this antithesis into account in order to preserve himself from a partisan and unhistorical idealization.

The problem which confronts us in thus contemplating the Middle Ages in their entirety affects us perhaps in no period so much as our own. Today there are not a few who fear that the whole civilization of the West is beginning to totter; and the best minds are laboring to re-establish it once more on the foundation which furnished it its earlier superb growth. The longing for a new league of nations in the West bids us be mindful now more than ever of the commonwealth constructed by the Church, in which medieval Western Europe is revealed to us with its merits and its defects.

The magnitude of the task which we propose to ourselves might justly raise the question whether it can be undertaken by one person. Only too often has the writer of these lines himself realized this. Detailed studies, advancing steadily, will always reveal the imperfections of a comprehensive presentation. Still, it may be worthwhile, at least to a relative degree, that a single individual in his declining years should undertake to summarize the results of historical research, and thus leave a basis on which others may advance the work. More than a survey cannot be attempted because of the unfavorable bookmarket. The material must, therefore, be compressed into three volumes. But for those who desire to penetrate more deeply, a bibliography is added to serve as a guide and at the same time to indicate the special studies on which the presentation is based.

GUSTAV SCHNÜRER

Acknowledgment for permission to use quotations in this book is made as follows:

BURNS, OATES AND WASHBOURNE, LONDON:

The Rule of Saint Benedict: A Commentary, by Paul-Henri Delatte, O. S. B., translated into English by Justin Gilbert McCann, O. S. B.; quoted in this book in Book I, chapter IV, *passim,* and on pages 263, 299-300, 412.

BURNS, OATES AND WASHBOURNE, LONDON, AND HENRY REGNERY COMPANY, CHICAGO:

The Confessions of Saint Augustine, in the English translation of Sir Tobie Matthew, as revised and emended by Roger Hudleston, O. S. B.; quoted in this book on page 68.

All other renderings into English throughout these pages are the work of the present translator. Those few cases in which Professor Schnürer quoted German translations of original texts, are indicated in the footnotes.

Contents

CHURCH AND CULTURE
IN THE MIDDLE AGES

INTRODUCTION

FROM the time when historians began to consider the study of the genesis of events as the highest task of historical science, they have felt impelled to give an exposition of that "fullness of time" spoken of by the Apostle Paul in the Epistle to the Galatians: "But when the fullness of time came, God sent His Son. . . ." We venture to set out from this point, not with the intent to demonstrate the existence of a mechanical law in history divorced from the human will and from any lawgiver, but rather to discover the signs of a law which man, without ever completely understanding it, yet recognizes and honors as the direction of divine Providence. By "the fullness of time" we understand those circumstances under which the seed sown by the Incarnate Son of God was to develop. For us, this means chiefly the spread of Greco-Roman culture along the shores of the Mediterranean.

Attention has been rightly directed to the uniformity within the Roman Empire where one law obtained, where the Greek language was the medium of expression for the educated, where the Latin tongue, even where not spoken, was at least generally understood by officials everywhere, where peace and tranquillity reigned, and where a serious danger from without could not even be imagined. In the soil thus prepared, the new teaching, the "glad tidings," would find favorable conditions for its growth.

If, however, we wish to understand the earlier background of this development, it is necessary to consider in some detail the relations of Judaism to the Roman Empire. For Christianity was to manifest itself first in the most distant corner of the empire, a corner which had received but little attention. Thus was made possible Christianity's real and independent internal development. The belief of the Jews in one God had given them a unique position for centuries, and they were accustomed to go their own way. Yet set apart as their homeland was, the very peculiarity of its geography offered them commercial opportunities in all directions. The narrow strip of land, flanked by desert and sea, was to some extent a land-

3

bridge between two continents, between the oldest cultural centers of mankind, Babylon and Egypt. Palestine thus had the character of a corridor-state, like that which Switzerland would have later, on a smaller scale. Their location on the Mediterranean, the home of civilization at that time, gave the Jews access to all the favored shores of this sea. They were confined still more to these shores when they were dispersed throughout the world after the destruction of their city. A spirit of isolationism upheld by their strong will to preserve national independence existed side by side with an urge, increased by the needs of the age, to go forth into the vast expanse of the Roman world.

These contrasting impulses corresponded closely to those two poles of Christian teaching which together embrace the secret of Christianity's strength — the interior life that seeks a kingdom not of this world, and the divine mandate given the Apostles to carry the new teaching to all nations. In both the opposition and the harmony of these tendencies are mirrored the relations of the Church to civilization. For what else is civilization, the totality of material achievements of the human mind and will, but the "kingdom of this world"? But did the Divine Founder of the new institution for man's education wish to place it on the same level?

The question is not asked in a spirit condemnatory of civilization. The purpose is rather to forestall a distortion of its values — on the one hand, to warn against the danger of becoming absorbed in it, and on the other, to point to the loftier goal. For this reason the Saviour came, not as a worldly ruler nor as a brilliant scholar, not as a captivating artist nor as a magnetic orator, not as one seeking any place among those whom civilization might acclaim leaders. At no time did He specify learning and wealth, always considered the external marks of worth, as a requisite for the acceptance of His teaching; instead He held them a hindrance. He preferred and preached that simplicity and innocence usually scorned by those who boast of their culture. In contradiction to the pride, the selfishness and the blinding splendor so characteristic of the flourishing periods of mankind's development, He taught His followers to seek retirement. He designated humility as the virtue most in conformity with

His teaching, and related it to His greatest commandment, which enjoined the love of God and the love of neighbor.

The external effect of such a doctrine among His followers was at first a negative attitude toward civilization. Following the example of their Master, they withdrew from all that the world had to offer them. They became the more confirmed in this line of conduct since an active cultural co-operation with the pagans was likely to expose them only too easily to a denial of their faith. Gradually, however, the positive forces of that faith also manifested themselves in the social sphere. The practice of fraternal charity, the magnanimous disregard of class distinctions and differences of race and nation, and the willing acceptance of all men as brothers, very early stamped Christianity with the seal of a world-religion. These practices made it possible to bridge over differences between peoples and nations. At the same time they demonstrated that the new doctrine was able to create the basis for a more profound and complete human civilization.

A new spirit was infused in human culture by educating men to foster the culture of the soul with the help of divine grace. In becoming children of God, men were lifted up anew and ennobled. Where could a better guaranty of order and tranquillity be found than in a doctrine which inculcated in its followers the need of both social equality and subordination to an ordered authority, which gave no one preferential rights before God, and obliged all to show consideration for their neighbor? Through the worship of one God, every relationship of men with one another was given a new dignity. God, who compelled recognition as Ruler and Master, yearned above all to be known as the God of Love to whom men were to turn as their Father and in common fraternity as His children render to Him an account of their dealings with each other. The germ-cell of society, the family, was sanctified; the father could no longer expose his children to neglect or death, the husband must regard the wife as a companion, not a slave. Christian teaching also provided a new basis for the renovation of the State by subjecting it to God and at the same time defining the obligation of its citizens to obey; the while it safeguarded them against encroachment by placing divine commandments above human. Thus it rejected both state absolutism and self-seeking individualism.

In the face of the existing and officially fostered culture, these new, idealistic views of life and social relations inevitably provoked only antagonism. The sole bridge over this dividing gulf was the injunction upon the disciples of Christ to preach the new creed to the whole world, to speak to men in their own language, to enter into their thoughts and ideas in order to set them right and influence them to become recruits in the new dispensation. The apologists were the first who saw themselves constrained to challenge the culture and the aspirations of their era in order to transform them.

Christianity first came into contact with this culture which it was destined to oppose, in its Hellenistic form characterized by many Oriental elements. Preparation for this contact had been made by the Alexandrians when they translated the Jewish writings of the Old Testament into Greek and supplemented them. The Jewish spirit was thereby broadened; so, too, among the Apostles, it was Paul, the product of a Hellenistic education, who became the Apostle of the Gentiles. It was he who made the greatest impression upon the non-Jewish world, and who broke through those earliest restrictions which its Jewish surroundings imposed upon Christianity.

Later, when efforts to convert the educated and religiously receptive classes increased as the new religion spread, Christians were forced into discussion of those profound questions centering on the origin of all things — the beginning and end of the universe, the destiny of man, and the problem of evil in the world. These speculations and theories had occupied and tormented humanity for a long time. In the Greek world, and in the more or less Hellenized Orient, the desire for a solution was particularly strong at precisely the time Christianity appeared. Although worship of the ancient Greek gods still continued, belief in their reality had already been shaken. The increasing momentum of the religious urge, a longing for expiation and purification, prompted many to greet hopefully the new mystical ideas sweeping in from the Orient.

This movement, while indeed it proved advantageous to Christianity, at the same time exposed it to the grave danger of losing its distinctiveness in the maelstrom of pagan mystery cults and wild

Oriental mysticism. The peril became most threatening when an alliance with Christianity was sought by the Gnostics, whose variegated spiritual "experience," taught in many systems, promised the vision of God and sought to purify the souls of men. When the first impulse of Gnosticism, which produced a variety of entanglements, showed signs of exhausting its force, it rose anew in the dualistic doctrine of Mani, the Babylonian. In this form, by claiming to offer a higher, more religious view of life, Gnosticism continued to inflict many injuries on Christianity until late in the Middle Ages.

Pride in the culture of their era kept the Gnostics from accepting the simple practice of faith. They attempted to set up, with many variations, a different theory of redemption and a philosophical-religious system they proclaimed as superior. The result was an empty subjectivism, which gained a temporary following in certain circles, generally in the cities, cultural centers of the period.

Christianity recognized the danger implicit in involvement with the dominant culture, and from the vigorous reaction of many Christians there arose a tendency toward the opposite extreme. This was the rigorism which, while justly emphasizing simplicity and withdrawal from the world, insisted on them too exclusively. Its main proponents were the Montanists of Phrygia, who ruthlessly rejected everything civilization had to offer — jewelry, finery, all objects above essential needs. They forbade any contact with the world, whether by holding public office, accepting military service or even practicing the arts and sciences.

In the midst of these aberrations Christian apologists had to point out the correct way between extremes. Hermas, the brother of Bishop Pius of Rome, devotes the greater part of his *Shepherd,* that valuable portrait of the culture of the first half of the second century, to warning the Romans against worldliness. Justin, the Christian philosopher of the second century, tried to reconcile philosophy and Christianity by remaining a philosopher even after his entrance into the Church at Ephesus. He publicly taught Christian philosophy, making withal broad concessions to the pagan systems. Still another apologist of the second century was an adept in pagan philosophy — Saint Irenaeus, bishop of Lyons, who opposed Gnosticism in Gaul. On the other hand, Tatian, the Assyrian, who proudly boasted of being an Oriental barbarian, treated Greek poetry, philosophy and learning with scorn in his *Discourse to the Greeks.*

Both the points of contact between Christian teaching and Hellenistic learning, and their differences, showed even more plainly in the third century, and in connection with this very development the foundations of theological science were laid. Alexandria, the ancient seat of Hellenistic learning, became a center of Christian theological study. There, in the bishop's catechetical school, not only theology in its various branches, but the profane sciences as well, were followed. One of its teachers was the great traveler, Titus Flavius Clemens, disciple of the former Stoic Pantaenus. He was the first to apply the profane learning of the Greeks extensively to the defense of Christian truth, especially of Christian ethics, and to discover in Greek philosophy the initial step in the approach to Christianity. He met with sharp opposition on this point, and once complained that many feared Greek philosophy as children fear ghosts.[1] He was succeeded by Origen, under whom the school gained a wide reputation. With a complete knowledge of literary forms at his command, Origen was the first to attempt a systematization of Christian dogma. He repulsed the severe attack which the philosopher Celsus directed against Christianity by a comprehensive refutation that emphasized in particular the pre-eminence of the Bible over the teachings of Plato.

The philosophical system on which these Christian teachers leaned, and to which at times they too closely adhered, was Neo-Platonism. From it they borrowed their dialectic reasoning — and also, to an inordinate degree, their allegorical explanations. Philosophical terms and ideas played a great role in those controversies on the Trinity which at that time began to divide Christian scholars. Yet we encounter in the same period Tertullian, Roman jurist and first Latin ecclesiastical writer; Tertullian, the representative of practical rigorism, who had no use at all for pagan philosophy. In precise, juridical terms and elegant diction he gave expression to Christian truths, and agitated against the stage, art and literature.

---

1. *Stromata,* ed. O. Stählin (Leipzig, 1906), Bk. VI, c. 10, no. 80, 5).

Indeed, he went so far in his excessive and inflexible demands that at last he broke with the Church entirely.

Neo-Platonism was the form in which pagan philosophy confronted Christianity for the last time. This pantheistic-idealistic system attempted to revive paganism, to present the various pagan cults as so many forms of revelation of the one God, to fuse them together, and to preserve and dignify the pagan myths by giving them an allegorical interpretation. Its actual founder, the Egyptian Plotinus, who labored in Rome, did not himself adopt a position hostile to Christianity, but his pupil, Porphyry, wrote fifteen books against it in which he strove to exhibit its teachings as self-contradictory. Thus, after having served Christianity for a time as a positive support, Neo-Platonism became the philosophy of those intellectuals who accused Christianity of being a falsification of ideas originally Platonic, and who conformed in practice to paganism in all its external manifestations.

During the era of persecution the differences between Neo-Platonists and educated Christians necessarily assumed the aspect of irreconcilables, since the Christians refused to make concessions to paganism under any circumstances. This development, one of the first fruits of the persecutions, was indeed a blessing. It safeguarded the purity of doctrine and imbued its adherents with that fearlessness so necessary to them if they were to be steadfast in seeking the supernatural goal set for them. Actually the long duration of the persecutions afforded young Christianity the security that a thorn-hedge gives a seedling against violations from without.

The allurements of ancient culture, with all its pleasures and temptations, manifested themselves as soon as the intervals between persecutions lengthened. Such was the case in the first half of the third century and also at its end. Even in this early period, we read of the pomp-loving, extravagant and haughty Paul of Samosata, who occupied the episcopal see of Antioch while retaining the office of civil treasurer, with its substantial emoluments. If many had walked in this path, Christianity equally as creed and code would have degenerated: infected with paganism, it must have lost its inherent vigor. This was reason enough for Christian leaders to continue their severe strictures upon participation in theatrical performances, gladiatorial games, dances and public festivities. Since in these pastimes a lapse into idolatry was difficult to avoid, such warnings were necessary. Christianity, in order to preserve its own cultural vigor for the future, was forced to reject pagan culture.

This attitude was still supported at the end of the persecutions by the Latin author Lactantius, who had lived for a time as a rhetorician in Diocletian's palace in Nicomedia. His most interesting work, the *Divine Institutions,* is a compilation intended to wean educated unbelievers from their anti-Christian prejudices. Filled with a conviction of the dignity of Christian philosophy, and of the high standard of Christian ethics, he makes no secret of his low estimate of the worldly wisdom and worldly life of the pagans. He reverts so far to the earlier rigorism as to oppose all participation in commerce and war. Capital punishment also is condemned, for he argues that man is forbidden to shed blood. Lactantius even holds it below man's dignity to take pleasure in art, in flowers, in pleasant odors. In other matters he is, of course, less intolerant; and, in imitating the models of classic style, he shows at least how much he appreciates formal training. He is not a consistent thinker, not a theologian, but he is a very valuable witness to the attitude of mind prevailing both during the last persecutions and at the period of sudden change that came with Constantine, whose rise he viewed with amazement and admiration as an act of Providence.

By the favor of this emperor, the position of Christians in public life was rapidly transformed. In the process of adjusting themselves to the new and wholly changed conditions, it was only after many and serious digressions that they found the right path, that enjoined upon them by their faith. The first feeling animating them upon the sudden and happy change was one of exultation at the victory of the Cross. There followed naturally an impulse of gratitude to him who had not only ended the persecutions but invited the victims to collaborate in public life and moved to protect them against their numerous, still powerful and active adversaries.

From a human standpoint it is easy to understand that in their manifestation of gratitude the Christians failed to observe a proper restraint. They forgot or took no account of the fact that, though the mighty emperor was convinced of the power and value of the

Christian religion in the external world, internally he had accepted but little of its teaching. They all lived under the spell of the happy turn of events and the brilliant opportunities offered for the spread of Christian truth. The State now took Christianity's part and guaranteed it the right of a public corporation, for the time being alongside the pagan religion; but soon it went even further, opposing paganism and declaring Christianity to be the state religion. The change, to all then living, must have seemed like a dream. We can understand the origin of the legend of the Seven Sleepers, who closed their eyes during the severe persecution of Decius and awoke under Theodosius II to behold the wonderful transformation the world had undergone while they slept — the cross resplendent over the city gates and the faithful crowding into the splendid churches.

Now the organization of the Church could proceed openly. On the model of the administrative divisions of the Roman Empire, ecclesiastical jurisdictions were created, a diocese generally coinciding with the urban district of a *civitas*. The jurisdiction of the bishops was recognized not only in the purely spiritual sphere, but in civil affairs as well: an appeal to the bishop's court, as an episcopal court of arbitration, was permitted by a law of the year 321. Bishops could be judged only by a bishops' tribunal. Heresy was regarded as treason against the Divine Majesty, and punished accordingly. Just as the pagan temples were formerly regarded as places of asylum, so now were also the Christian churches; their confiscated properties were returned to them; and they were empowered to hold and dispose of property and to accept legacies. Constantine himself set the example of rich donations.

Christian priests were exempted from the laws imposing disabilities on the unmarried and childless. The clergy were also relieved of the burdensome obligation of assuming municipal offices and rendering personal services, and they acquired partial immunity from taxation. The great esteem enjoyed by the bishops, the precedence conceded them over civil officials, their influence at the imperial court, greatly enhanced their authority in public. They were not required to take oaths nor to appear as witnesses in the courts, and were even charged with supervision of the public domain. Consideration of Christian moral views resulted in proceedings against immoral theatrical presentations, and in the outlawing of the practices of exposing and murdering children. In criminal law many actions objectionable to Christians were forbidden, such as crucifixion, branding on the forehead, the breaking of the legs of condemned criminals. Broad powers facilitated the helping of the needy and the persecuted. The care of widows, orphans and the poor was regarded as an honor and a right. Bishops might intercede for prisoners and visit them. The ceremony of the freeing of slaves might take place in church. Jews were forbidden to hold Christian slaves. Constantine had early declared Sunday a general holiday.

Much as the Church benefited by these new regulations, it was only gradually realized that they all suffered from one defect, which could be remedied only by a slow process. These laws had come into being, not as a natural response to the general wish of the people, but by an edict of the emperor, who wanted to use the Church — a factor to be reckoned with — as an instrument in the internal administration of the empire.

The regeneration of the empire was only too sorely needed. While the reorganization by Diocletian and Constantine had brought back to it a measure of stability, their reforms did not remove the chief evil afflicting its constitution. This evil lay in the excessive accumulation of power in the hands of the emperor, who could rule with an absolute will. Moreover, the succession was in no wise regulated and thus, despite all precautions, the struggle for the throne went on endlessly. Members of the reigning families fought for it with one another, with usurpers, with the army, and with civil functionaries. The misery attendant upon these conditions naturally affected the Church much more keenly now that she was united with the State.

The supreme power of the emperor, who was the Church's protector, became for her a set of shackles whose weight she was soon to become aware of; for the emperors, still believing themselves the successors of the *pontifices maximi,* wished to extend their absolute authority over the province of religion. The antagonism became immediately apparent when there arose the momentous disputes about the person of Christ, and the emperors sought to interpose their authority to preserve peace in the empire, if not actually to decide the issues. The Church appreciated Constantine's generosity in putting public conveyances at the disposal of the bishops who attended the First Ecumenical Council at Nicaea, and in financing their maintenance in that city; but she felt this external dependence painfully when the emperor tried to direct the course of the deliberations as he wished, and planned to bring pressure to bear upon the Fathers of the Council to that end. The extent to which such pressure could go is revealed by this declaration of Constantius at Milan in 355: "What I will must have the force of ecclesiastical law." A natural corollary of such an attitude was the emperor's attempted interference in the filling of vacant bishoprics, which would then be determined simply by the emperor's nomination instead of by election on the part of the clergy and the people.

There ensued a series of ecclesiastical quarrels which, because the external unifying force of persecution was now absent, became very much more serious than in the earlier era. Fundamentally, these were a struggle for the Church's independence. If she did not want to perish with the Roman Empire, she had to carry on the war against caesaropapism to the very end. This conflict brought the faithful rallying in ever-closer ranks around the successors of Peter on whom the Saviour had conferred the pastoral office.

Without suspecting it, Constantine himself abetted this development by establishing his residence in the new capital in the East which bore his name. In Rome, thus abandoned by the emperor, there were daily occasions for the Pope to stand forth more and more clearly as the independent head of the Church. Rome thus became the center of a spiritual authority which was to have equal freedom with the civil power. There was no question of supplanting that power, for the welfare of the Church and the assured continuation of her ideal culture lay, not in the union of civil and religious power under one head, but solely in their separation. The fact that the churches of the two divisions of the empire adopted different attitudes in the Trinitarian controversies of the fourth century was to prove the necessity of the separation. It was also destined to produce other changes of world-wide historic importance.

When, under the influence of Philo's philosophy, the Libyan Arius, broadening the Origenist trends, denied the divinity of Christ, and thus attacked the central Christian doctrine, his unflinching opponent, the Alexandrian Bishop Athanasius, found his support mainly in the West. For a time, it is true, the despotism of Constantius even succeeded in bringing the Western bishops, assembled in Milan and Rimini, to the point where they no longer dared to reject Arianism openly. Upon the death of that emperor, however, it immediately became evident that Arianism could never take firm root in the West. How different from the course of events in the East! The accession of Julian to the throne sufficed to deprive Arianism of the imperial favor and to rob it of all support. Thereafter Rome and the Occident became for the storm-tossed Church of the Orient the mainstay in the defense of orthodoxy and ecclesiastical independence. This gave the West a superiority which was soon to make itself more strongly felt.

In addition to the Trinitarian disputes, which we need not follow here, the conflict with the still powerful remnants of paganism continued throughout the fourth century and led to one other episode which demands our attention. At this time paganism still had authoritative representatives among the rhetoricians and philosophers as well as among the conservative aristocrats. It was a proof of Constantius' short-sighted zeal that he believed he had proceeded far enough against paganism when he closed its temples and prohibited pagan sacrifices under penalty of death, meanwhile leaving the higher schools and the education of the upper classes in the hands of pagan sophists and Neo-Platonic philosophers. This merely surrounded the intellectual exponents of paganism with the glamour of intellectual martyrs and prepared the ground on which Julian could attempt the revival of paganism as representing ancient civilization and superior mental culture.

Thus, shortly after the death of the brutal and tyrannical Constantius, Julian initiated the first *Kulturkampf* in which Christians were persecuted and ridiculed as hostile to culture. The exponents of ancient pagan learning had long since centered on him, the pride of the Athenian school of philosophy, all their hopes of advancing Neo-Platonism, the systematic exposition of their teachings, to a new position of prestige. Therefore as soon as Julian could ascend the imperial throne, vacated by the sudden death of Constantius, he began to fulfill the expectations of his teachers.

He not only severed his connection with Christianity and restored pagan feasts and idols, but he also strove to stamp a pagan character anew upon public life. His ambition was to surround the ancient civilization with all possible splendor, while excluding Christians from its affairs. By a law of June 17, 362, he denied them the right to teach the classics, exposing them to the contumely of the educated. On the other hand he strove to endow paganism with those characteristics which he recognized as excellent in Christianity. He wanted the pagan priests to function as moral teachers and through them planned to introduce a system of penitential discipline; he contemplated establishing a hierarchy among them after the Christian pattern; he also founded charitable institutions so that even in this field the pagans might not be inferior to the "Galileans." But, despite the fact that he personally took up the pen against Christians, what he accomplished was negligible. With his death these attempts quickly collapsed. They resulted only in a more potent stimulus to the Christian efforts to foster what was positive in the ancient intellectual culture.

The attacks which the period's foremost writers, steeped in the old culture and training, unleashed against Christian teachings served as an impetus in this direction. If Christians were to convince the intellectual classes, they could not allow such attacks to go unanswered.

The leaders of these literary adversaries of Christianity were still the Neo-Platonic philosophers, seeking to restore paganism to favor by idealizing it. Their ranks were swelled by brilliant rhetoricians, teachers of elocution — an art that only too often achieved more importance in the religious controversies than it deserved. Preeminent among them were Libanius, the court rhetorician, who enjoyed the particular favor of Julian; and Himerius, who had been summoned from Athens to Constantinople by the same emperor. The rhetoricians were assisted by distinguished historians. Of these, the moderate Ammianus Marcellinus deserves particular mention because, although a pagan, he could not but disapprove Julian's religious policy.

Christians perforce, if they wished to fight for their teachings with like weapons, had to study under these contemporary purveyors of culture. Thus Saint John Chrysostom, endowed with profound spirituality, strength of character and rare eloquence, and Saint Amphilochius, one-time advocate, later bishop of Iconium, had both been pupils of Libanius. Saint Basil the Great, the patriarch of Greek monasticism, and his student-companion, Saint Gregory Nazianzen, the "Theologian," were the pupils of Himerius. To counter the pagans, proud of their ancient ancestry, in their assault on Christianity as a recent doctrine, Eusebius, the "father of ecclesiastical history," composed his *Chronicle* — a synchronistic survey which the whole Middle Ages adopted as the basis for the study of ancient history. Saint Cyril, the archbishop of Alexandria and the opponent of Nestorianism, wrote a polemic against the writings of the Emperor Julian. Another of this group, Bishop Theodoret of Cyrus on the Euphrates, impelled by the circumstance that the State under the Emperor Theodosius was sponsoring the cause of the Christians, defended Christianity against the charge that it flourished only because of the emperor's protection.

Just as the general intellectual movements of antiquity had always been inspired and furthered by the culture of the Greeks, so until this period had Hellenism been the determining factor in the intellectual movement within Christian groups. It was in Hellenized Asia Minor that Christianity had first won over the entire population — an achievement not duplicated anywhere at the beginning of the fourth century. Hellenism furnished the first formulas in which theological science took shape, and thus until the end of that century the Orient, the teacher of the West, determined the development of theology; and the ecclesiastical literature of the West advanced only through its recourse to the theology of Greek writers.

This is seen clearly for the first time in the case of the adversary of Arianism, Bishop Hilary of Poitiers, surnamed the "Athanasius of the West." He wrote his principal work on the Trinity between 356 and 359 while in exile in Asia Minor, where he was in close touch with Greek theologians. In both Saint Jerome and Rufinus the fact becomes still more apparent. These were the very men who, by translating and continuing the works of their Greek models, laid the solid foundations in the West for the general culture of the Middle Ages. Rufinus, born in the vicinity of Aquileia, and Saint Jerome, a Dalmatian, whose paths frequently ran parallel but also at times counter to each other, were the West's pioneer writers in the field of Christian historiography. They translated into Latin the great historical works of Eusebius, and extended these to include their own day.

Eusebius had written his *Ecclesiastical History* under the immediate influence of the triumph which the Church owed to Constantine and concluded it with a panegyric on that emperor. Rufinus wrote his translation and its sequel in 403, when his native land had just been invaded by Alaric's hordes. His purpose was to provide some consolation in that calamity by presenting a review of the past. Saint Jerome translated and supplemented the *Chronicle,* in which Eusebius refuted the charges of the ancestor-loving pagans against the "newness" of Christianity, by showing the great age of Jewish culture and the recent origin of the pagan States. By translating these chronological tables Jerome supplied the chroniclers of the Middle Ages with the material they needed to summarize the history of the past as introduction to their own writings. At the same time he determined that use of the annalistic method in history which became the norm during the first period of the Middle Ages.

But this work of Saint Jerome is far surpassed by his other translations, which include that of the Sacred Scriptures from the original text. This achievement establishes the author's greatest claim to fame; it justifies his being designated as the true intermediary between East and West. Although the irascible and contentious scholar laid himself open to many attacks, he nevertheless was uniquely distinguished in his day for his great erudition, his thirst for research, his knowledge of languages (he alone in that age had command of Latin, Greek and Hebrew), and the diversity of his literary productions. Even as a monk in Bethlehem he maintained that devotion to the Latin classics he had acquired in Rome, which later earned for him the veneration of the Humanists. But during his lifetime also, the West was grateful to Jerome for the cultural material he furnished it. In what high regard he was held we learn from the fact that a certain Lucinius sent six copyists from Spain to Bethlehem to obtain reliable editions of all the esteemed author's works. His great concern to make the West conscious of the material which the Orient had to offer is evident in his biographies of famous Oriental monks — *Vita Pauli, Vita Malchi* and *Vita Hilarionis,* works which introduced the lives of saints into Latin literature. In his most important historical work, *De viris illustribus,* Jerome made the first attempt to produce a history of Christian literature as proof that there was no dearth of men of learning among the Christians — an attempt often repeated in later eras.

We know, too, that Jerome's heart was most intimately involved with the destinies of Rome, over whose language he had a mastery equaled by few of his contemporaries. This we conclude from those touching lamentations which he uttered in Bethlehem upon receiving the news of Alaric's conquest of Rome in 410. "My voice fails me and, while I dictate, sighs cut off my words," he writes in one instance; "the city which vanquished the world is vanquished."[2] In another passage he describes how the terror spreading in all directions had affected his sensitive soul; and his words reveal that he already took the fall of the Roman Empire for granted: "After the brightest light of the world was extinguished, after the head of the Roman world was severed, and, to speak even more plainly, after the whole empire disappeared with one city, I was speechless and cast to the earth."[3]

This point had not then been reached, yet the events to come cast their shadows ahead and heralded the approach of that epoch in which the Roman Church was to contribute her share in laying the foundations of Western civilization.

---

2. Hieron., *Ep. 127:* Migne, *P. L.,* XXII, col. 1094.
3. Hieron., *Prolog. in lib. 1 in Ezechielem:* Migne, *P. L.,* XXV, 16.

BOOK ONE

THE ROMAN EMPIRE AND THE CHURCH: PILLARS OF WESTERN CIVILIZATION

THE ROMAN EMPIRE AND THE CHURCH:
PILLARS OF WESTERN CIVILIZATION

ROMANS who had the imperial destiny at heart and who knew how to appreciate the value of their civilization, noted with anxiety and fear the ever-increasing signs of the weakening of the empire. They realized only too well that the imperial regime was nearing its end, and under the pressure of terrible events they expressed this freely. Yet they clung to every shred of hope, denying as long as possible what the sober appraisal of contemporary facts taught them. The Christian thinkers among them, following the trend so dear to them, sought in their own way to fortify their courage for final perseverance.

Since Christian emperors held the reins of government, the Roman Empire was the Christian Empire; beside it there was no other, and beyond its confines there was little prospect of the Christian tenets ever taking root. The Roman Empire supplied the external forms within which the Church grouped and organized itself. The Church had grown great in the midst of the ancient culture, and the more Christians participated in the furtherance of that culture, as far as this was still possible, the more they valued it. With the fall of the old order it was natural that they should expect nothing less than the end of the world. They called to mind the interpretation given by Daniel the prophet to King Nabuchodonosor's dream, in which a statue with head of gold, breast and arms of silver, loins of brass, legs of iron, and feet of iron and clay, was ground to pieces by a stone that, loosened without the aid of hands, became as a mountain filling the whole earth. Daniel had read in this vision the succession of four world-monarchies, decreasing more and more in power until they finally were replaced by the Eternal Kingdom. He had explained a second dream, this time his own, in the same manner.[1]

---

1. Dan. 2: 29 sqq. and 7: 1 sqq. Cf. F. Düsterwald, *Die Weltreiche und das Gottesreich nach den Weissagungen des Propheten Daniel* (Freiburg i. B., 1890).

The patristic writers and notably Saint Jerome[2] had seen pro-phetically foretold in the four world-kingdoms the four great Empires, Babylonian, Median-Persian, Macedonian, including that of Alexander's successors, and finally, Roman. Thus it was popularly assumed, on the one hand, that the Roman Empire would last until the end of time, and on the other, that the Kingdom of the Saints would begin with its collapse. This opinion dominated the Middle Ages and thus sustained belief in the continued existence of the Roman Empire; but in the fourth century its effect was rather to cause people to see in the signs of the empire's dissolution the imminent end of the world.

Additional support was given this idea by the approach to world history often found among the first Christian writers, and still more prevalent in the Middle Ages: namely, a division of the record of mankind into six eras in accord with the allegorical interpretation of the six days of creation. The sixth era had begun, it was said, with Christ, and was to be followed by a final period, an era of the peace of God in His community, corresponding to the sabbath of creation in Paradise and preceding the last judgment.[3] Many believed that chapter 20 of the Apocalypse referred to this era of peace since it mentioned the chaining of Satan for a thousand years. Thus arose those chiliastic ideas so widespread in the fourth century, and so often the cause of skepticism and opposition when the millennium, looked for immediately upon the ceasing of the persecutions, failed to dawn.

Although the people of the Roman Empire were still divided in opinion on these details at the end of the fourth century, the beginning of the fifth found all minds in a state of universal tension.

---

2. Hieronymus, *Comment. in Danielem*, cap. II (Opp. Francof. et Lips., 1684, T. V., p. 486): Regnum autem quartum, quod perspicue pertinet ad Romanos, ferrum est, quod comminuit et domat omnia: sed pedes ejus et digiti ex parte ferrei et ex parte sunt fictiles, quod hoc tempore manifestissime comprobatur. Sicut enim in principio nihil Romano imperio fortius et durius fuit, ita in fine rerum nihil imbecillius, quando et in bellis civilibus et adversum diversas nationes aliarum gentium barbararum indigemus auxilio. — Ibid., c. VII (p. 497i): Quatuor regna, de quibus supra diximus, fuere terrena. Omne enim, quod de terra est, revertetur in terram. Sancti autem nequaquam habebunt terrenum regnum sed coeleste. Cesset ergo mille annorum fabula.

3. Cf. Hipler, *Die christliche Geschichtsauffassung.* 2. Vereinsschrift der Görres-Gesellschaft für 1884, S. 9 sqq.

This was all the greater in Christian circles the more conscious they were of the breadth of the world-view and the historical outlook now bound to triumph with Christianity. Viewing mankind, created by God, as one great unity, for which the Redeemer had died, and which had the sole aim of making God's kingdom a reality, men conceived of history as the portrayal of the education of the human race by God. Hence, God's plan with regard to the Roman Empire necessarily became a burning question.

The question was actually settled at that time. For us, of course, the meaning of that period, long since closed, is clear; but it was not so for its contemporaries. They merely suspected that Alaric's descent upon Italy, together with the sack of Rome, the invasion by the marauding bands of Radagaisus in 404, and the breaking through of the Rhine boundary by the barbarians in 406, might be the beginning of new, unprecedented events. No one surmised that the descendants of the Romans were to develop a new civilization in union with these hordes, so uncivilized at their first appearance. Little significance was attached to the separation of the East from the Western Roman Empire; on the contrary, the looser the connection became in fact, the more did the West cling to the East in sentiment. Lactantius had actually prophesied that the name of Rome would perish, the empire return to the Orient, and the West be subject to it.[4] In 506, after the fall of the Western Roman Empire, Pope Symmachus could still write to the Eastern Roman emperor, Anastasius — in a passage, frequently cited, which treats of the respective dignity of Emperor and Priest — that these two seemed destined to rule the human race forever.[5] From this may be seen how firmly the idea of the continuation of the Roman Empire was still rooted in the ecclesiastical circles of Italy.[6]

Nothing is more unjust than the accusation launched against the Christians of the fifth century, that they had no interest in the

---

4. *Inst. divin.*, VII, 15, 11.

5. Thiel, *Epist. Rom. Pontif.*, 703: His praecipue duobus officiis [sc. imperatoris et pontificis] regitur humanum genus et non debeat aliquid eorum exsistere quo valeat offendi Divinitas, maxime quum uterque honor videatur esse perpetuus, atque ita humano generi ex alterutro consulatur.

6. Cf. Nik. Reitter, *Der Glaube an die Fortdauer des röm. Reiches im Abendlande während des 5. und 6. Jahrh.* (Münstersche Diss., 1900).

Roman state, or the charge that they were actually responsible for the fall of the empire. Naturally they conceived of their earthly life, as every Christian should, as something merely transitory, the preparation for an everlasting life, which they valued more than the temporal one. Since such thoughts are always brought home more strongly to the community as a whole when troubled times lessen their material well-being, so the Roman Christians of that age generally turned their attention more seriously perhaps than would otherwise have been the case, to the life of the hereafter, to an eternal kingdom of peace and joy. But that love of self which would have striven to escape the duties of this earthly life in order to seek something easier or more agreeable, was certainly foreign to them. The Roman state did not disappear because the Christians failed to fulfill their duties; on the contrary, it was due to the Christians that whatever Rome possessed of permanent value was preserved.

The causes which doomed the Roman state to destruction were recognizable much earlier. There were grievous faults in the body politic, in the constitution, in the military system, and in the economic situation, which could no longer be remedied and the consequences of which became ever more apparent. The Roman state had become a bureaucracy in which everything was regulated in the interest of the administration. For the factors which were of primary importance no regulations existed. No provision was made for the rights of the citizens, for their participation in political life. The authority of the chief ruler was absolute; and this inordinate increase of the imperial power was the more serious since the succession to the throne was not fixed. Except for some generals who could urge their demands with the power of the sword, only favorites were able to maintain themselves near the emperor. While externally the court took on more and more the marks of an Oriental despotism, within, it became the arena of intrigues and the scene of clique-governments, which usually ended miserably within a short time, only to make room for others no better. The influence of the East, making itself felt first and foremost at Constantinople, created that spirit which we always observe as closely associated with despotism and which we have been accustomed ever since to brand with the term "Byzantinism." In the final issue it was usually the army or the general controlling the troops who decided the succession to the imperial throne. Yet the troops themselves were in an ever greater degree foreign mercenaries (at that time predominantly Germans), interested only insofar as their prestige and welfare were bound up with the cause of their general.

Hence the personalities of the great military commanders interest us more in the fifth century than the minor, insignificant bearers of the imperial title, who succeed each other with ever-increasing rapidity — set up and removed by the leaders in command of troops. The Roman masses in general viewed the changes with indifference; whatever the issue, they could become no more than the sport of wrangling usurpers.

The economic conditions were as unsatisfactory as the political. The flourishing peasant class from which, in the days of the republic, the Roman state had recruited its best forces, had disappeared, destroyed by the wealthy senators whose only concern was returns from the land cultivated for them by slaves. With the cessation of the wars of conquest, slaves in turn became scarce and costly; hence there was a growing lack of man power to till the land, and wide tracts were converted into pasturage or left uncultivated. An irrational and unmethodical working of the soil also contributed its share toward this development. And lastly, where the remnants of an economically sound middle class still existed, they were destroyed by a foolish system of taxation which made each class collectively responsible for the tax returns of its individual members, and each higher class responsible for the returns of the class next below it. Thus the decurions, extensive landowners and members of the town council of a tax-collector's district, were made liable by the state for the full payment of the land taxes imposed upon the landowners of that district. And as the economic strength of the landlords weakened because of the unfavorable times, the depopulation, the political disturbances, and the barbarian incursions which were repeated with ever greater frequency, the load imposed upon the decurions grew heavier until it finally crushed them. The desperate efforts of many to escape the burden connected with their rank by ascent or descent in the social scale — by moving up into the class of senators, or marrying slave girls, or even entering the clerical state — were countered by the foolish measure prohibiting the decurions from leaving their class: a measure invoked likewise against other groups, and one which condemned the social life to stagnation.

Thus, to make sure of the tax which the *colonus* (peasant) had to pay for the landowner from the acres he cultivated, the state bound the peasant and his posterity to the property. Besides these taxes, the peasants were forced to supply the army with provisions. Thus hard-pressed, they gave vent to their discontent in uprisings (such as also played a role in the Donatist movement in Africa), or they succumbed to despair, greeting the invading barbarians as liberators. In the same way the artisans, especially those engaged in producing army supplies, the shippers, and the tradesmen who had to pay for a trade-license, were bound to their class. Birth determined the social status of the citizen. Children were not allowed to step out of their parents' class, that its tax-paying ability might not be curtailed. This coercion stifled all independence and initiative; the individual, forced to work for the state machine merely as one of its cogs, lost all interest in public life.

Under such conditions it is easy to understand that an increasing number of noble-minded Romans who had whole-heartedly embraced the Christian faith, saw only one satisfactory field of action for the common welfare, namely, the service of the Church. Here all the excellent qualities of the old Romans could once more assert themselves without restraint: their practical sense, their organizing ability, their energy, and their art of ruling men. These activities could now be exalted by the Christian virtues; cynical pride, lust for power, licentiousness, could not be reconciled by a true Christian with Christian moral principles. It was this group of Romans, ennobled by Christianity, who laid the foundations of the Western civilization which was to rise anew on the ruins of the Roman Empire, the civilization destined to conquer the whole world. To assert that all Romans were degenerate and therefore doomed to destruction is to overlook these pioneers of the order to come. It is true that there was no longer any vigor in the political and social life drawing its nourishment from pagan principles, no prospect of successful activity for men of creative impulse; that the old Roman Empire and its social order were ripe unto decay. Yet it was important to preserve from impending catastrophe those cultural elements which, as valuable germs, were at a later time to find development in a new civilization. That they were preserved we owe to Christianity and the Church of Rome.

Nor would Christianity and the Church have been able to do so if the fossilized Roman Empire and corrupt Roman society had continued to exist. The old, dried-up trunk with its spongy branches would not have allowed the new germs sufficient light and air. The old forms had to be destroyed so that it would become essential to create newer and better ones. The ancient cities, with their over-developed culture, their ruinous financial system, their paralyzing restraints upon the social classes, and their unprincipled officialdom, had to disappear in order to bring about a restoration to social health by a back-to-the-land movement natural only to an age of agrarian economy. Family life, too, robbed of its sanctity and dignity by the public immorality of decadent pagan society, could hope for regeneration only through the disappearance of an urban culture oversaturated with intellectualism. The healthy families of the German warriors must be given lands so that they might spread out and teach in their ingenuous way a return to natural morality. Though they were uneducated they were capable of education; and only in this way would Christianity find a soil everywhere adapted to its doctrines of the dignity of womanhood and the blessing of children to the home. The land, too, which the pagans had wanted merely to possess, but not to cultivate, was provided again with laborers willing to work it. But above all, the fall of the Roman Empire brought about the end of the enthroned despotism with its enslaving imperialism and corrupting Byzantinism, while providing the necessary freedom for the operation of new moral forces within a group of new nations.

If anyone still harbors a doubt that the disappearance of the Roman Empire was really necessary, let him cast a glance at the Eastern Roman Empire. Here, too, healthy peoples, members of the Slavic race, living in a natural state, had a partially rejuvenating influence upon society, but the despotic caesaropapism of Constantinople, the antagonism between the civil authorities and the military party so characteristic of ancient civilizations, and the capital's unhealthy passion for sport, with its factions and intrigues, prevented a complete recuperation of society and the free operation of Christian moral forces. That is why the cultural leadership of the world came to Western Europe and not to the Orient, despite the fact that the former had been backward for centuries in every domain of external culture. The prerequisites for the free development of new nations, and for that wholesome balance between ruler and people that allows the individual sufficient scope for independent growth, were lacking in the Orient.

Hellenism had already fulfilled its historical mission by bringing Christianity and the intellectual culture of antiquity closer together. Now, to complete the fusion of Christianity and antiquity, after Judaism and Hellenism had made their respective contributions, it was Rome's turn to donate the best it had, namely, its talent for organization and its manly straightforwardness, its fortitude and perseverance. To the form of this cultural leadership, Christianity gave a definite character.

As organized Judaism had to pass away that Christianity might not be confined within its narrow boundaries, so, too, Rome had to disappear; not only must freedom of action be given that community which had its headquarters in Rome at the tomb of the Prince of the Apostles whom the Saviour had commissioned to feed His lambs, but Rome itself must be freed from its pride and lust for power, must be led from by-paths into the road which could be followed safely by those engaged in the spread of Christ's kingdom.

The period in which Rome faced this task was one of the most stirring in the world's history. Proud of its rule over the Mediterranean countries, its fame seemed to grow when its rulers became Christian and accepted the faith that was conscious of its mission, of the power within itself to spread to the ends of the earth and embrace all peoples. At the same time, however, Rome realized its weakness when confronted by the German might pounding on the portals of the empire until they sprang open. Woe and anxiety spread among the Romans as the invading barbarians overrun the imperial territory. Only the most courageous among them perceive where duty calls them to give aid. Imbued with their new spiritual mission, these accomplish great things; their only strength their faith in Christ and His kingdom, they create, without really knowing it, works of lasting value while the Roman Empire nears its end.

We have a literary monument which bears witness to this attitude of the Romans of the fourth and fifth centuries — and perishing Rome could not have produced a worthier tribute. It is the *Te Deum*, that hymn of praise wherewith the Catholic Church on solemn occasions expresses her joy, her thanks, and her humble devotion to the Ruler of Destiny. For power and majesty, delicacy and tenderness, nothing can be ranked beside it. This solemn chant of laudation resounding in our high-arched cathedrals will affect the historian all the more if, while listening to it, he can recreate in his mind the mood and sentiments of the Romans of those times long past. It is still debated whether Bishop Nicetas of Remesiana (Palanka near Nisch) in Dacia, who lived between 335 and 414 and is mentioned in eleventh-century manuscripts as the author, is really to be regarded as the first editor; but this much is certain, that the entire hymn was gradually made up from separate parts and existed in its present textual form as early as the beginning of the fifth century.[7] The sequence of the parts corresponds evidently to the chronological order in which they were composed. First we have the mighty hymn of praise to the Lord God and Eternal Father, whom all things praise in heaven and on earth: the angels, the apostles, the prophets and the martyrs. This reflects the triumphant mood of Christendom after the era of persecution. Victorious, the Church believes herself, under the first Christian emperors, sure of her eventual conquest of the whole earth: "The Holy Church throughout all the world acknowledges Thee." To this verse is added as a fitting conclusion a doxology, or solemn invocation of the Blessed Trinity. Then follows, as part two, an invocation of Christ, the *Patris sempiternus Filius*, which reminds us of the period of sorrow the Catholics of Rome had to pass through soon after the triumph under Constantine, when his son Constantius tried to introduce Arianism by force in the West as well as in the East. This invocation, remote from all terrestrial thoughts, ends with the

---

7. Cf. Morin in *Revue Bénédict.* XI (1894), 77 sqq., XXIV (1907), 180 sqq.; P. Wagner in *Gregor. Rundschau* VI (1907) and IX (1910), 572 sq.; A. E. Burns, *The Hymn Te Deum and Its Author* (London, 1926).

petition that the Saviour in whom they have recently learned to put their sole trust, may cause these His servants to be united with His saints in everlasting glory. The following prayer, composed of Psalms 27:9 and 144:2, implores the Lord still more urgently to save His people, who look up to Him day by day; it reminds us of the apprehension felt throughout the empire when the Visigoths arose to harass Italy under Alaric. To this prayer was finally added a separate psalmlike versicle, possibly used at one time as a morning prayer, which, full of contrition, beseeches God for mercy and ends with the hope that oppression will not be eternal. These were the sentiments prevailing after the first capture of Rome by Alaric, when many felt that the end of the empire was inevitable. The hope expressed was to be fulfilled: Rome was not to be crushed underfoot completely; it was to flourish anew, rejuvenated, in the Catholic Church.

This powerful canticle of thanksgiving is still called the "Ambrosian hymn," and an early tradition has it that Saint Ambrose alone or Saint Ambrose and Saint Augustine together composed it. Though this cannot be maintained, it expresses the truth in one sense, for Saint Ambrose and Saint Augustine were the first to prepare Rome explicitly for its new mission.

CHAPTER ONE

SAINT AMBROSE AND HIS SCHOOL

S AINT AMBROSE, son of a praetorian prefect who later was
governor of Gaul, was born in Treves, but at the age of fourteen, after his father's death, came to Rome with his mother. Here
he grew up in patrician circles, imbibing their ideas. A thorough
Roman in mind and heart, he nevertheless was also imbued with
the strong Christian convictions which ran in his family. One relative, the saintly virgin Sotheris, had suffered martyrdom under
Diocletian. His own sister Marcellina received the veil of a consecrated virgin at the hands of Pope Liberius. After her mother's
death, Marcellina came to Milan and assumed direction of a convent
founded by her brother, over whom she always exerted a profound
influence.

The ideals of Rome and Catholic Christianity were thus intimately united in his heart. When the peril of the empire resulting
from the Gothic invasions weighed upon him, he besought God in
earnest prayer to have mercy on the imperial realm[1] and to protect
the emperor Gratian.

The destinies of the empire necessarily affected Saint Ambrose
the more since the sphere of his activities was Milan. Here he
labored, first with the title of consul, as governor of Liguria and
Emilia, and later as bishop. Milan had been, from the end of the
third century, the first city of the West after Rome. It was in Milan
that Constantine issued his famous Edict of Toleration in 313. Here
resided one of the two governors (*vicarii*) charged with the administration of Italy, the other residing in Rome. The importance of the
city was even greater after the partition of the empire (in 364)
between the two brothers Valentinian I and Valens, a division which
henceforth remained permanent, though its final determination was
made by Theodosius. Valentinian I took the West for himself and

---

1. *De fide*, II, 141-143.

chose Milan as his residence; there, too, we find most of his immediate successors.

Valentinian I was followed at his death, in 375, by his son Gratian, who was forced by the German contingent in the army to accept his younger brother, Valentinian II, as co-regent. When Valens, the ruler of the East, was slain in the memorable battle of Adrianople (378) whereby the Visigoths forced an entrance into the Roman Empire, Gratian chose as regent for the East the able Spanish general Theodosius, who for a time gave the empire a measure of stability. Theodosius finally defeated the usurper Maximus, who had had Gratian murdered and planned to supplant his brother, Valentinian II, in the West. A second, more dangerous usurpation, which was connected with a pagan reaction, was ended when Theodosius marched against the Frankish general Arbogast, who in 392 had ordered Valentinian II strangled and put the pagan rhetorician Eugenius in his place. By his victory over Arbogast and Eugenius on the Frigidus River in the vicinity of Aquileia, Theodosius became sole ruler. Unfortunately, the victor, justly called the Great, died soon thereafter (395). At his death the two empires were separated once more, since he had appointed his son Honorius ruler in the West, while another son, Arcadius, governed the Eastern Empire.

These were the great events that occurred during the lifetime of Saint Ambrose, who was personally and intimately connected with all the emperors named. And nowhere were these events so vividly experienced as in the imperial city of Milan, which became his episcopal see. The dramatic scene in which he, the consul of Milan, was elected its bishop, is known, yet it bears brief repetition here, since it furnishes us with just those details that conduce to our purpose by sharply characterizing both him and his age.[2]

The episcopal see having become vacant in 374 by the death of an Arian bishop, Catholics and Arians opposed each other in a heated electoral contest. The Emperor Valentinian I gave the bishops conducting the election to understand that they would do best to choose that candidate whose life of itself would be an example. The

---

2. Theodoret, *Hist. Eccles.*, 4: 6, 7.

practical Roman sense which here found expression was in fact to determine the sensational outcome. Ambrose entered the church where the election was to take place, with the purpose of urging peace and order as the representative of the civil authority. A child in the crowd shouted: "Ambrose, the bishop!" — and the contesting parties came to terms: the consul, respected for his impartiality and righteousness, was forced to accept the office. The observation that he neither was baptized (a long catechumenate was the practice of the times) nor had received any orders, availed him nothing. He submitted, recognizing finally that here was a higher call: higher especially because he believed, with his contemporaries, that he was facing the end of the world. He felt called to act in that most difficult time as a guide and consoler of hearts, as a preacher of the imminence of the heavenly kingdom to the noble and the humble, and as the representative everywhere of right and truth, responsible only to the Supreme Master. "We are nearing the end of time," he wrote in 386, "and therefore certain diseases of the world presage its impending destruction."[3] Hope could be found only in Christian ideas. He thought of Noe, from whom a new human race went forth when everything appeared to have been destroyed by the deluge, and in thus picturing the patriarch to himself as the model of spiritual shepherds, he interpreted, as we see, the signs of the age correctly.[4]

Knowing himself the exponent of an idea broader and loftier than that of the empire, he proceeded unfalteringly against those of high and even the highest stations. Against aristocratic senators who, by setting up the Victory statue in the Senate chamber at Rome, defended the last citadel of official paganism, he represented at the court of the Christian emperors of his time the rights of the Christian religion, which had now become the state religion. He had no intention, however, of submitting to the ruler in the matter of religion. The frankness and genuine Roman dignity with which he opposed the emperors in this, ready as he otherwise was to support them, makes him the precursor of those great-spirited popes and bishops who in later centuries defended Christian morality and the

---

3. *Exposit. Evang. sec. Lucam*, 10, 10.
4. S. Ambros., *De Noe et arca*, 1, 2.

rights of the Church against the powerful rulers of the world. Thus he refused to hand over to the dowager empress Justina, who favored Arianism, and to her son, the young emperor Valentinian II, a Catholic church in Milan for Arian services. On the other hand, with equal courage, he declared for the legitimate emperor, Valentinian II, against the usurper Maximus, who as a protector of the Catholic faith wished to supplant Valentinian. With the high moral authority which the Milanese bishop acquired through his unswervingly courageous defense of his convictions, he even dared to demand that the emperor Theodosius, who gave the Catholic Church in the Roman Empire final victory over paganism and Arianism, should submit to the laws of the Church and accept penitential discipline for the massacre which, with undue severity, he had caused to be perpetrated on the rioters at Thessalonica. By imposing certain moral restrictions upon the bearer of supreme power and achieving the recognition of these restrictions, Saint Ambrose was the first firmly to lay down that basic principle of the separation of the temporal and spiritual powers which was to be of such great importance for the reconstruction of civilization. "In matters of faith," wrote he, "it is the bishops who are the judges of the Christian emperors, and not the emperors who are the judges of the bishops."[5]

How little the dignified and reverential bishop's personal relations with the emperors suffered despite such incidents is shown by his funeral oration for the murdered emperor Valentinian II, who shortly before his death had desired to have the bishop baptize him. This oration and the one for Theodosius the Great are the first funeral orations of the Christian West that have come down to us. The second of the two (delivered February 25, 395), in which Saint Ambrose, following ancient models, praised the departed Theodosius in the presence of the army and of the young emperor Honorius, who was to convey the remains of his late father to Constantinople, interests us in a particular way. Touchingly, Saint Ambrose professes his love for the departed ruler:

> I have loved the man, so compassionate, so full of humility on the imperial throne, so candid by nature and gentle of heart. . . . I have loved

---

5. *Ep.* XXI, 4.

the man who agreed more with the fault-finder than with the flatterer. He laid aside all the royal ornaments he was wont to wear, wept publicly in church over the sin to which he had succumbed through the deceitful words of others, and implored forgiveness with groans and tears. What common people are ashamed to do, the emperor was not ashamed to perform: public penance. . . . I have loved the man who in his last moments asked for me with his last breath. I have loved the man who, when very close to death, was more concerned about the fate of the Church than about his own dangers. I have loved him, I confess, and therefore has grief penetrated into my innermost soul; and I felt myself in duty bound to allay it by honoring his memory with a longer speech. I have loved him, and I have complete trust that the Lord will accept the voice of the prayer which I am offering for his pious soul.[6]

Nor is there any reason to doubt that the friendship, founded on strong convictions, was as genuine and profound as the speaker claimed. "The name of the One and Most High God should be glorified in all places," was written into one of the laws of Theodosius.[7]

But no bishop had ever spoken thus about an emperor in the Roman language. Centuries later a bishop in Spain, the native land of Theodosius, might possibly have uttered such words about his king. The oration marks the intimate union that had now been established between Roman life and the Church. Given such a frame of mind, the orator obviously felt himself called upon to invoke the blessing of heaven upon the sons of the deceased and to exhort his hearers to loyalty toward them:

To Thee, O Lord, ascends my petition: deign to let him [the deceased] rise again in his sons. Thou, Lord, who dost preserve also the children [the eighteen-year-old Arcadius, who had remained in Constantinople, and the eleven-year-old Honorius there present] in this humility, grant them, who trust in Thee, good fortune and salvation. . . .[8]

Pay to his sons the debt that you owe to the father! You owe him more after his death than when he was alive. For if the minority rights of children of ordinary people may not be violated without committing a grave crime, how much less can this be done against the children of an emperor![9]

---

6. Translator's note: Here Schnürer uses Niederhuber's rendering into German, which appeared in "Bibliothek der Kirchenväter": *Des hl. Ambrosius ausgewählte Schriften*, III (Kempten, 1917), S. 411, *Nr. 33, 34, 35*.
7. *Cod. Theodos.*, XVI, 5, 6.
8. *Funeral Oration for Theodosius*, 36.
9. Ibid., 11.

Saint Ambrose's anxiety for the imperial dynasty as well as for the welfare of the Roman Empire was certainly linked in the most intimate manner with his concern for the kingdom of God on earth. The past of the Roman Empire interested him only insofar as it was represented by Christian emperors and insofar as it corresponded to God's designs. In the funeral discourse he praises Constantine as the first emperor who embraced the faith and bequeathed it as a legacy to the rulers following him. He lauds the Roman rule only insofar as it is united with the faith. He perceives a symbol in the nails with which the Saviour was affixed to the cross (these were found in Jerusalem, together with the cross, by Saint Helena, Constantine's mother, who caused one of them to be inserted into the imperial diadem, and another into the reins of the favorite imperial charger):

> Saint Helena acted wisely when she set the cross upon the head of kings. The cross of Christ was to be venerated in the kings. It is not an unseemly act, but one of piety, to pay homage to the sacred Redemption. This nail in the bridle of the Roman rule is a blessing. It governs the whole universe and adorns the forehead of the emperors, so that they are now preachers who so often were persecutors.[10]

Once again we hear the echo of the triumphal hymn about the Christian ascendancy in Rome, as intoned in the first part of the *Te Deum.* But the human phase of this domination was to decline more and more and in its stead the spiritual to become more pronounced. With Theodosius there passed away the last emperor who would forcefully rule the whole Roman Empire. In the West from now on, children and weaklings succeeded one another on the imperial throne. Great Romans, exerting a deep influence on posterity, are found only in those ranks in which Saint Ambrose stood as a foremost leader.

We can clearly perceive how the great bishop of Milan diffused his spirit — a spirit in which Roman ideas and culture were to become profounder and more noble through Christian thinking — among his contemporaries and bequeathed it to succeeding generations. This was effected primarily in the field of morals, which lay closest to the practical sense of the organizing and lawgiving

---

10. Ibid., 48.

Roman. Saint Ambrose was the first in Christian antiquity to attempt a systematic presentation of Christian ethics, and the manner in which he did so is exceedingly significant. The work wherein he made the attempt is still the best known and most esteemed of his various publications. It is entitled *The Duties of the Clergy,* and was composed about 389.[11]

The treatise is connected with Cicero's work by more than its title; the whole disposition of Cicero is a determining factor for Saint Ambrose. Not only are many thoughts the same, but there is also no little verbal borrowing. However, it is not our intention to praise Saint Ambrose particularly as an original writer; there is general agreement that his greatness is not to be sought in that direction. It lies rather in his dominating moral personality, through which he shows the Romans new ways in the field of religion and politics. In this connection it is easy to understand, too, why he chose as model a work which every educated Roman knew and of which all were proud. It was not any sense of lack of originality on his own part that led him to seek as a pattern that work which lay closest at hand. On the contrary, the former high official was evidently fully convinced that here was the best the Romans, and especially the educated, the honorable, the dignified Romans, could point to as a description of those personal ideals to which they ascribed the origin of Rome's world hegemony, of Rome's greatness. And the former official, determined as bishop to go his own ways, wanted to set up something higher, something better, over against this work.

No one in the Christian ranks who occupied himself with the mental or ethical culture of the Romans could ignore Cicero. He was not only the unsurpassed master of the Latin language but also, for the Romans, the medium of Greek philosophy and practical wisdom. Then, too, it was he who had spoken most respectfully of religion and the moral principles which should govern the state and society. Whoever would speak to the pagan Romans as a Christian writer needs must address himself to them in the language and

---

11. Ed. Gilbert (Lips., 1839). Translated by Niederhuber in "Bibl. der Kirchenväter": *Des hl. Ambrosius ausgew. Schriften* III.

thoughts of Cicero. Thus Minucius Felix, the author of the oldest extant Christian Latin prose composition, the *Dialogue of Octavius,* cherished a particular regard for Cicero. For Lactantius, Cicero served as both point of departure and model to such a degree that from the age of the Humanists onward, the title "The Christian Cicero" has been given to him. And Cicero was so much the favorite author of Saint Jerome that he reproached himself for this predilection.

Hence, we should not be surprised that Saint Ambrose leans on Cicero — not, indeed, as one accepting him indiscriminately, but as a practical spiritual shepherd and preacher who would offer his priests, for their instruction, Cicero's universally esteemed book on duty in a revised edition which enters more deeply into the problem. He desires, by expounding Christian principles, to give the doctrine of moral obligations a deeper foundation; at the same time he proposes to meet objectively a reproach of the pagans, who are acquainted only with their own examples of high moral standards, by replacing the paragons of virtue adduced by Cicero from Roman history with examples from Holy Scripture. Saint Ambrose draws with particular preference upon the Old Testament; he can thus produce older models and refute (like Eusebius with his chronological tables) the objection that the Christian teaching is something new, unworthy of comparison with the tested practical wisdom of ancient Rome. He purposes to present in Christian ethics the source of pagan ethics; as "our ancestors" he therefore cites, not the pagan Romans, but the prophets and God-fearing men of the Old Testament.[12] For him the patriarchs surpass the jurists and the philosophers, the lawmakers of the pagan world; it is the former, not the latter, whom he holds to be intellectual leaders and models. Thus Cicero furnishes him merely the external form into which he endeavors to pour a new content in conformity with his own world-embracing concept. Little though he denies his Roman character outwardly, as a Christian he wishes to think independently and be free from all pagan tradition. Therein he is an example of the new Roman type, which as a spiritual force in the Church was to take

---

12. Cf. Lib. III, c. 17, § 98.

over the leadership of the new civilization then being formed. In contrast to the book written by Cicero for the Roman nobility about the morals conducive to the welfare of the Roman state, the Milanese bishop composed a book for the use of Roman Catholic priests dealing with those duties which flow from Christian ethics and are so important for the salvation of all human society. Just as he, the bishop, believed he was serving a greater and higher kingdom than when, as consul, he served the Roman Empire, so the moral order emanating from Christian teachings appeared to him — and rightly so! — far superior to and more comprehensive than the order represented by Cicero and the old pagan aristocracy, moving as it did in the atmosphere of Stoic philosophy.

Stoic philosophy, with its doctrine of moral obligations drawn from natural reason, was certainly the moral mainspring to which the Roman state owed its greatness, but it lacked a deep foundation. It is, and remains, the morality of an unbelieving rationalism which can answer the question "Why?" only with "Because"; or, to use the colloquial language of our time, can point in answer only to man's "confounded duty" or the state's command. This did not satisfy those who thought more profoundly. Saint Ambrose supplied the missing foundation in the very first chapter by teaching his spiritual sons that the fear of God is the basis of all obligation. According to Saint Ambrose the Christian's ultimate purpose in fulfilling an obligation is not the virtue in itself, as the Stoics taught, but the thought of eternal life: "We, however, measure exclusively only what is becoming and honorable, and we do so more by the standard of the future than by that of the present, and we designate as expedient only that which furthers the supreme happiness of eternal life, not that which favors the desires of the present life." But eternal life implies the knowledge of God and the fruit of good works.[13] Though this thought is not carried out very systematically, being interrupted at times by digressions and the interweaving of sermons, which results in a loosening of the logical processes involved, still we can easily see that Saint Ambrose's doc-

___

13. Lib. I, c. 9, § 28; II, c. 2, § 5.

trine of moral obligations goes deeper and is far more comprehensive than the doctrine we find in Cicero.

The four cardinal virtues — prudence, or, perhaps better, understanding, justice, fortitude, and temperance — he treats, in general, like Cicero and the Stoics. As a Roman, he was thoroughly familiar with everything these virtues taught, and by passing on the classification as well as the appreciation of these virtues to the following centuries, he transmitted the best in the practical wisdom of the old Romans, a contribution that in no small measure fitted the West to take over the leadership of the world's civilization. Above all should be emphasized that moderation based on self-control to which the medieval educators and moralists, like the Romans, attached such great importance that they regarded education as consisting, not in the eradication, but rather in the regulation, of the passions and the desires. There followed from this not only that reasonable organization in the religious and ecclesiastical life which distinguishes the West from the Orient (bent more on ecstasy and the cultivation of sentiment), and especially from Islam, but also the tendency toward striking a balance between political and social differences. This tendency aimed rather at the internal composition of these differences than at their removal. It favored the freely organized co-operation of various factors in contrast to paralyzing forced labor.

In connection with his treatment of the cardinal virtues, Saint Ambrose considers that external conduct which the aristocratic Romans so greatly stressed: the ideas of *decorum,* that which is becoming, and of *honestum,* that which is moral; to which two qualities he compared the beauty and health of the body: *gravitas,* dignity, and *verecundia,* modesty.[14] On these points the former high official felt himself completely in accord with the ancient Romans and their spokesman Cicero, and his teachings could only enhance the authority with which the Christian Romans, as teachers, were to face the new cultural world already shaping in the West. It is particularly through Saint Ambrose, whose work, as the many manuscripts prove, was circulated widely in the following centuries, that the Roman form

---

14. Lib. I, c. 50, § 256.

of Stoicism continued to exert in no small measure its influence on the West. But aside from the ideas borrowed by Saint Ambrose, because of his Roman viewpoint, from Cicero, there is no lack of original conceptions in what Saint Ambrose offers. These conceptions often reveal themselves in new applications of old designations and categories. Like Cicero, Saint Ambrose speaks of relative and absolute duties, but the meaning which he puts into the distinction is entirely different from that presented by the treatise of his pagan exemplar. The bishop separates the two groups, in accordance with the words of the Saviour, into commandments on the one hand — the observance of which is demanded of all — and evangelical counsels on the other, after which those seeking perfection are to strive.[15]

We must keep in mind here that he is writing for priests, in whom he would like to see realized the ideal of Christian feeling and conduct, but upon whom he also imposes particular duties as leaders of the people and almoners for the poor and oppressed. To them especially does he propose to point out higher aims, higher both in form and in content. Regarding the form, he recommends to them plainness and simplicity of speech, criticizing the affectations of ancient rhetoric, and therefore Cicero's also — a salutary admonition for the restoration of a degenerate superculture.[16] More important still are the ideals, largely new in substance, which he keeps before their eyes (outwardly following the plan of Cicero) and illustrates with examples from Sacred Scripture and the words of the Saviour.[17]

The Christian conception of life, with its upward glance to God and its hope of eternal life, gives a new form to the virtues transmitted by the Stoics, which had something arid and cold about them. What was formerly portrayed in mere lines appears now in warm coloring. Love of God and love of neighbor, in which all the obligations of a Christian life culminate, are presented in such a way that the old practical wisdom of the Stoics is elevated and revivified. For Saint Ambrose, prudence is the insight of the be-

---

15. Lib. I, c. 11, § 36 sq.
16. Ibid., c. 9, § 29; c. 25, § 116.
17. Cf. for the following the fine and delicate treatment by Thamin, *St. Ambroise et la morale chrét.*, 250 sqq.

liever, who desires to judge and see everything in the light of faith — in the last analysis, it is simply faith; justice is not so much insistence on one's own right as that consideration for one's neighbor which is demanded of the members of a community; temperance is inculcated especially in the form of meekness; and fortitude, in the patient bearing of sufferings. Examples of this virtue from the age of the martyrs were at that time still fresh in mind.

More memorable still are the new virtues Saint Ambrose teaches. Pre-eminent among these is humility, which stands in such sharp contrast to that desire for glory, that contempt for the humble and for slaves, which were entertained by the pagan philosophers. Not only is the Christian humble before God, he is also anxious to be eclipsed by his neighbor. That is why Saint Ambrose places great stress upon silence as a fruit of humility: "If anyone be careful in his speech, he will become mild, gentle, modest."[18] Thus his mildness, and in a wider sense his concern for the preservation of purity, link themselves to humility.

Next to humility, it is the virtue of fraternal charity, practiced particularly by the Christians of the persecution era, that Saint Ambrose praises. In speaking of charity he expressly inculcates a benevolent disposition and compassion: "Your disposition gives your work its deserved name: its worth is determined by you."[19] This places Saint Ambrose far above Marcus Aurelius, who conceived the disposition only in the sense that he said to himself: "I have done something useful for society, therefore have I done something which is useful to myself."[20] Saint Ambrose becomes still more explicit when he writes the sentence: "The strongest motive for mercy is compassion for the misery of others and the desire to relieve their destitution according to our ability, sometimes even beyond our ability." To this he appended a justification for the melting down of the church-plate ordered by him for the ransom of captives — an order for which the Arians had reproached him.[21]

Love for the poor induced in Christians such a high regard for poverty that they took the vow of poverty, a thing incomprehensible

18. Lib. I, c. 4, § 14.
19. Ibid., c. 30, § 147.
20. Marc. Aurelius, XI, 4.
21. Lib. II, c. 28, § 136.

to pagans. Fraternal charity leads, further, to forbearance and forgiveness, and finally to the highest rung of Christian perfection, love
of one's enemies: "But if I am perfect — I speak thus by way of
example, for in truth I am a weakling — if I am perfect, I bless the
reviler, as Paul also blessed him, who declared solemnly: They revile
us, and we bless them."[22] Self-abnegation culminates finally in this,
that Saint Ambrose refuses to know anything about a right of self-
defense: "A just and wise Christian ought not to save his life at
the price of another's destruction. Even when he falls into the hands
of an armed robber, he may not return the blow to the assailant, in
order not to fail against love while defending his life."[23]

In the joy of the early Christians at being able to climb to the
highest rung of perfection and self-abnegation, we see the great
ardor with which the new teaching imbued its confessors and their
consciousness of having a belief far above that of the ancient pagan
philosophers. There is something stirring about the manner in
which Saint Ambrose, while retaining the old Ciceronian plan, gradually penetrates in thought the limits of his model and goes far beyond
them — and that despite his own literary insufficiency. It brings
home to us how the ancient ideas of Rome were destined to be
vanquished and surpassed, even though it was as yet impossible to
dispense with the form in which they found expression. This
burning devotion of Saint Ambrose to Christian ideals from the
time of his becoming bishop explains, for the most part, why, in
his discussions on money and property, he allows himself to be
swayed only by the highest religious and moral considerations. It
must be especially borne in mind that he is attempting to set up a
norm for priests and wishes to place before them the ideal pastor
of souls, who ought not to be tainted by anything, least of all
by selfishness and ambition for material gain, in conformity with the
words of the Lord: "Possess not gold, nor silver, nor money."[24]

With Cicero[25] (who, to be sure, draws no further conclusions
from the Stoic conceptions, but simply lets them speak for them-

---

22. Lib. I, c. 48, § 235.
23. Lib. III, c. 4, § 27.
24. Cited in Lib. II, c. 25, § 128.
25. *De off.*, I, c. 7.

selves), he denies that private property is founded in nature: "God commanded all products of the soil to grow, to the end that every man might partake of the common property. Nature thus ordained a common right of possession for all. Usurpation has made a private right out of it."[26] This assertion is not far removed from the modern socialistic tenet that private property is theft. Saint Ambrose, following the teaching of the Saviour, uses some hard words concerning riches and money, such as we find later in Saint Francis of Assisi: "Corporeal and external goods are not only of no advantage to eternal life, but in truth a disadvantage."[27] To heap up treasures is for him a vain enterprise; it is like the labor on a spider's web, which has neither value nor use.[28] His language, otherwise calm, becomes vividly excited here as he gives expression to a deeply felt loathing:

> If riches flowed in streams, they would avail nothing; they rather divest you of the image of God and clothe you with the image of material things. If one wears the image of the tyrant on his person [we recall in this connection that honor was paid to an emperor through his statue or medal], does he not expose himself to condemnation? Do you desire to lay aside the image of the Eternal Ruler and wish for yourself the image of death? Away rather with the image of the devil out of the city of your soul!

He emphatically does not wish the priest to play the role of broker in money matters, and above all he condemns "legacy-hunting under the mask of disinterestedness and gentility, so repugnant to Christian sensibilities."[29]

What appears most odious to him is "to direct all one's thoughts and wishes restlessly and anxiously and systematically toward the acquisition of filthy lucre from vulgar commerce. He who does this degrades his soul."[30] Contempt of money is for Saint Ambrose simply a form of justice.[31] We see how closely connected this view is with the social duties he especially wishes to recommend to his clergy, always insisting on fraternal charity, so that, as we have already said, justice becomes essentially consideration for one's neighbor, not

26. Lib. I, c. 28, § 132.
27. Lib. II, c. 5, § 16.
28. Lib. I, c. 49, §§ 242, 245.
29. Lib. III, c. 9, §§ 58, 59.
30. Ibid., § 57.
31. Lib. II, c. 27, § 133.

the vindication of one's own right. That is why Saint Ambrose lauds poverty while disparaging riches. In conformity with Catholic doctrine of the present, Saint Ambrose does not preach hatred of the rich or urge an attack on them as a class. Rather, he concludes that they should see in their wealth, not a right, but the duty of helping the poor; they should not regard their riches as the means of enjoyment in this world but by giving away their super-abundance secure for themselves the enjoyment of heavenly blessings. The poor man should be a debtor of salvation to them. On the day of judgment they would then obtain salvation from the Lord, since they would have him as a debtor of His mercy.[32]

Taken in detail, we do perceive here a certain distinction in Saint Ambrose's condemnation of property and riches. He knows how to appreciate labor on a moderate-sized rural estate. However, it is not so much the possession of property he intends to sanction (unlike Cicero, who represented the ethics of an aristocratic land-owner) but rather the labor that is expended on it. He turns all the more sharply against the unjust grain trade, "the usurious grain business," which he brands as an economic canker in the Roman Empire of his time.[33] And because he sees so much injustice and fraud in the wholesale and retail trade about him — false weights and short measures — and only usury in the loan business, he has nothing at all to say in favor of that trade which recognizes a just standard. For the debtor who is imprisoned because he cannot pay, he is full of compassion, and demands mercy.[34] He is very reluctant to admit the justification of interest-taking: "Would it not be impious to demand under the cloak of humanity a greater sum from a person who was unable to pay a smaller one?"[35]

We must bear in mind that Saint Ambrose lived in the days of the economic collapse of the Roman Empire, when reorganiza-tion was hopeless, and a cure could be effected only by replacing the whole economic system based on money with a system of natural economy; by transforming a highly complex urban civilization into

32. Lib. I, c. 11, § 39.
33. Lib. III, c. 8, § 49 sq.
34. Lib. I, c. 30, § 148.
35. Lib. III, c. 4, § 20.

a primitive rural economy under patriarchal management. Christianity had in its ideal teachings the assurance that it could survive such a complete revolution; but even aside from this, he who fully appreciates ideal values will regard it as a blessing that Christian principles served as a check to the constant abuses of the monetary economic system. These, indeed, have been more dangerous to the Church at all times than to any other institution. If we compare the eloquent admonitions Saint Ambrose addresses to his clergy with the picture that the clergy of the waning Middle Ages presents to us, we can fully measure the decline which took place in the West in that thousand-year span.

Even the enthusiasm with which Saint Ambrose addresses his priests on fraternal charity and draws his uncompromising conclusions thereon from Christian teachings is surpassed by the sublimity of feeling he displays elsewhere in speaking of virginity and chastity. These he supremely extols; for the practice of these he desires especially to inflame men's hearts. Keen observers of the development of Christian thought have pointed out that in the fourth century there is noticeable a certain shifting in the appreciation of the various Christian virtues.[36] Until that time, fraternal charity had been cultivated pre-eminently; now the practice and praise of chastity began to compete with it for first place. This was due to the changed circumstances of those times. The age of persecution brought the Christians close together, and their loyalty to the faith translated itself into brotherly love for one another, which more than compensated them for the hatred they were exposed to everywhere from their pagan contemporaries. When Christianity enjoyed the protection of the state, this union naturally became looser. The Christians emerged from their seclusion; their ranks were joined by many who in reality accepted their teachings only halfheartedly. This involved new dangers, from which new impulses arose. The worldly spirit which some of their number had not yet laid aside, threatened also to infect the more idealistic adherents. These sought to protect themselves by insisting more strongly than before upon the loftiest standards for themselves, and by creating the possibility

36. Thamin, 356, 341.

of living up to them. Hence the emphasis on asceticism, on rigid discipline for the spiritual life, the rise of monasticism, and the enthusiasm for a life consecrated to God by the vow of virginity.

We shall take occasion to speak of monasticism later. Here we shall treat only of the impulse that manifested itself strongly in the fourth century among the women of the West to consecrate themselves to God. We can follow the movement in two groups. While the members of one group united into monastic communities, the others remained as consecrated virgins in the world, constituting, however, a distinct state in the Church, since they placed their vow in the hands of the bishop and received from him the consecration or blessing. Though the transition from one group to the other was easy, still in this period we can follow them clearly side by side.[37] As the Church fostered convents for women and the institution of consecrated virgins living alone, so we also see in these female circles an extraordinary interest in religious and ecclesiastical affairs. This interest lifted them out of their surroundings, liberating them to a certain degree, and gave the movement the character of an intellectual emancipation somewhat like the trend of women in our own day toward university studies.

We can recognize the strength of the movement particularly in Rome, where it had its center in the aristocratic classes, and where we find it sharply drawn in the correspondence of Saint Jerome with Roman matrons. It is not to be regarded as something transient, but as a movement which had effects of lasting consequence. The most important and most conspicuous of these was that women also felt themselves called to be custodians of the Christian culture. In the period of the conversion of the Germans it was generally women who, as wives of the Germanic chieftains, opened the doors in their husbands' realms to Catholic teaching. We have the earliest indication of this in the biography of Saint Ambrose composed after the holy bishop's death by his secretary Saint Paulinus. We read there that Fritigil, queen of the Marcomanni, who had been told about Saint Ambrose by a Christian from Italy, sent envoys to

---

37. Cf. Sr. Iniga Feusi, *Das Institut der gottgeweihten Jungfrauen: Sein Fortleben im Mittelalter.* Freiburg, Schweiz, 1917.

him with presents for the Church and begged for written instruction in the Christian faith. The saint complied with her wish and composed a set of directions for her, in which he advised her to induce her husband to keep peace with the Romans. The queen followed the instruction. Later she came to Milan in person, but the teacher she sought was no longer among the living.[38]

This event falls, therefore, in the last days of Saint Ambrose. But it was soon after the start of his episcopal labors that he began devoting special care to the direction of women's souls. He is not the first of the ecclesiastical writers, nor even the only one among Latin authors, to stand out in this way, for Saint Cyprian and Tertullian precede him, and the trend of their thoughts is, as may be easily understood, frequently the same. But one may, nevertheless, designate Saint Ambrose as among the very earliest apostles of Christian virginity, and because of the importance attained by his personality and his writings, his words had great influence in the course of time. This was also due to the fact that they were expressed with sublime enthusiasm and fiery eloquence, and clothed in rare poetic form — probably because they were committed to writing at the wish of his sister Marcellina, who embodied the family characteristic of ardent faith no less than the brother who finally recognized in its service his own high vocation. Marcellina had preceded him with her example. She came as a consecrated virgin from Rome to Milan, and there during their lifetime she and Ambrose were united by a common spiritual bond, a bond as ideal as can be imagined to exist between brother and sister. Marcellina directed a convent founded by Ambrose, whither came virgins from far and near, from Milan, Piacenza, Bologna, and Mauretania; under the spiritual guidance of Saint Ambrose the establishment in truth developed into such an attraction that the saint had to defend himself against the reproach made by his relatives, of being a fisher of souls; a reproach he accepted with a light heart.

Four treatises in praise of the virginal life are certainly his. The first, dedicated to his sister and composed in the third year of his episcopate, is entitled *Three Books Concerning Virgins, to My*

---

38. *Vita s. Ambrosii a Paulino notario*, c. 36.

Sister Marcellina. There followed the treatise *Concerning Virginity,* in which he justifies his recruiting for the virginal state; then the instruction to a virgin, Ambrosia, who is about to take the veil. The instruction is preceded by a dedication to Ambrosia's grandfather, Bishop Eusebius of Bologna, wherein the author refutes the attacks against the perpetual virginity of the Mother of God. The fourth work is a sermon preached in Florence on a particular occasion; in it Saint Ambrose exhorts his hearers to virginity. To this number may be added *Concerning Widows,* a treatise based on sermons, in which his intent is to show that widowhood is preferable to a second marriage.

In glowing colors borrowed from the Canticle of Canticles, Saint Ambrose paints the glory and the honor of those who desire to be the brides of Christ. Side by side with this he discusses, in a rather prosaic vein, the advantages of virginity in contrast to the burdens of marriage and motherhood altogether too soberly, according to our modern point of view, for he has no words for the poetry of motherhood. Seemingly he is aware how marked is his own attitude, for he feels himself obliged to declare that he does not, and may not, disapprove of marriage: "I do not then disapprove of marriage, but merely wish to enumerate the fruits of virginity consecrated to God. This is the vocation of the few; the other, the vocation of the many; and virginity itself necessarily presupposes entrance into life by birth."[39]

It will be easily understood that the dignity of woman in general was raised as a result of the particular esteem accorded virginity by Christianity, and the words of Saint Ambrose are especially suited to bring this clearly before us. The maiden who does not marry is no longer looked upon as one who has missed her vocation. She can achieve an even higher calling if she consecrates her virginity to the service of God. Those maidens of the upper classes who followed the encouraging words of the Milanese bishop felt this instinctively. His invitation possibly appeared to many in the light of a declaration of independence for them. Indeed, he openly advances such considerations in his exhortation that widows should forego a

---

39. *De virginitate,* Lib. I, c. 7, § 35.

second marriage. Woman has no need of man's protection, he says. A woman can protect herself, and men are not the only ones who can practice courage.[40] Thus woman is placed by the side of man as his equal. Actually, in this period it almost seems as if woman were leading man, hastening on in advance of him in the longing for Christian ideals. By her nature she more easily than man grasped the peculiarly Christian virtues of humility and modesty. And as a Marcellina influenced Saint Ambrose, so a Monica led Saint Augustine into the paths on which he advanced to become the greatest doctor of the Western Church.[41]

But to guard her independence, woman needed especially the protection of a life of modesty and retirement. With biting sarcasm Saint Ambrose speaks of the petty and degrading passion of women for finery, in order to lift the minds of those entrusted to his guidance above such things. Inwardly strengthened in this way, woman would then not need the mistrustful external guardianship by which she was degraded and secluded in the Orient. Thus Christianity laid the foundation for the greater external freedom which the woman of the Christian West was to obtain.

Woman, elevated to the position of an independent personality, also becomes quite a different being in marriage from what she was in pagan antiquity. There marriage was considered from the standpoint of the interest of the State more or less only as an institution for increasing the number of citizens. Less importance was attached to the mutual understanding and affection which should be the foundation of a lifelong union. Because of the part which she now took in religious and intellectual life, not only did woman as such rise in the esteem of all, but the relations between husband and wife grew also in dignity and spirituality. Love, which as sensual attraction was only an object of jest and contempt to the pagan philosophers, is spiritualized. By virtue of her modesty, woman renders herself at once more desirable to man and more worthy of esteem. Man pays homage to woman as the companion he wishes to gain, but he also pays homage to her as a person whom he respects and

40. *De viduis,* c. 8.
41. Cf. Thamin, 359.

honors in a special way. Thus romantic love, unknown to paganism, rests on a foundation first laid by Christianity, which taught man to court woman in a nobler way.

This elevation of woman to a higher position, which was now becoming characteristic of Christianity, was to have still further consequences. It lay in the character of Stoic ethics to prefer the masculine virtues.[42] At the head of the list of such virtues stood strength and courage. When a woman stood out among women, like the mother of the Gracchi, it was because she manifested masculine rather than feminine virtues. The old, robust virility of the Romans had few authentic representatives among the officials and officers of Rome in Saint Ambrose's time. Saint Ambrose sketches a picture of Roman army officers that seems satirical to us, and almost reminds us of those caricatures in certain comic journals before the Great War which ridiculed abuses in the army. We must, of course, take into account that the passage occurs in a treatise on fasting and that Saint Ambrose's purpose is to deride the kind of virility which displays itself in drunken carousals. He paints the imperial officers, adorned with precious shoulder-straps, golden neck-bands, belts and scabbards; allowing young barbarian slaves to fill the drinking-cups for them; and then challenging each other courageously, not to contests of arms, but to drinking-bouts.

> Toward the end, though, the young heroes, so formidable to the enemy, are seized by the laughing servants and carried out of doors. In this condition they reel like ships without a pilot, and, unless the servants support them, sink to the ground as though mortally wounded. Others, in mockery, are carried about on shields. Early in the day we see them as warriors, resplendent in arms and with threatening mien; in the evening we can see them ridiculed by children with impunity, when they are wounded without weapons, vanquished without a battle, confounded without an enemy, when, standing in the flower of youth, they tremble like decrepit old men.[43]

Christianity, which desired virility to find expression particularly in moral self-conquest, could not but doubly abhor such distortions of virility.

---

42. Seneca, *De constantia sapientis,* 1: Tantum inter stoicos, Serene, et caeteros sapientiam professos interesse, quantum inter feminas et mares, non immerito dixerim.
43. *De ieiunio,* c. 13.

But not alone masculine virtues are fostered by Christianity. Faith, trust, devotion, humility and chastity are demanded, and thus feminine virtues also are raised to an equal position of honor. The virtues as defined by the ancient Stoics automatically become a rational norm for progressive and just men. But to overcome the egoism which in the last analysis always underlay these virtues, God had to become man. The emulation of His example through the practice of the new virtues He taught, gave mankind new and higher aims. As a result of His self-abasement in becoming man, human nature was endowed with a new nobility, the human mind provided with a new breadth of view, and a new depth plumbed in the human soul.

A much more diversified culture is thus introduced, not based solely on strength, right, might and state law, but seeking to establish a superior type of organization, rooted in the expiatory death of the Divine Sufferer on the cross. It is a culture aspiring to a higher kingdom, the kingdom of God, and seeking its highest ideals in forgiveness and humility, in renunciation and confident prayer. The so-called active, masculine virtues almost seem less important than the passive, feminine virtues; just as the kingdom founded on force must in the long run yield to the more exalted kingdom of God, based on sacrifice and resignation.

These were the thoughts which so consoled the contemporaries of Saint Ambrose that, in the face of all the misery in the Roman Empire, they could rejoice in praise of the Most High despite their sorrow over the tribulations of the times. They esteemed His kingdom the more as the external and temporal empire of Rome began to totter. To spread the kingdom of God was accounted by them a higher cultural activity than the furtherance of the ancient culture which was part of their tradition. It is true that, although they did not intend it directly, they continued to occupy themselves with this culture; not to imitate it slavishly, but to use it insofar as it could supply them with forms for the expression of their new thoughts and sentiments. These latter, rooted in Christian teaching, were to become in time the basis of the new civilization in the West. Christian matter, in ancient but independently treated form, would be a characteristic of the new Western civilization. The person in whom we can clearly perceive the beginnings of this development is Saint Ambrose. Therein, chiefly, lies the attraction which the study of his writings has for us; they are filled with that freshness of enthusiasm which the independent expression of new ideas bestows upon superior minds.

This feeling also explains Saint Ambrose's attitude toward what he considered the trivial results of pagan learning. Very significant in this regard is an observation in his work *Concerning the Duties of the Clergy,* which begins with Ciceronian ideas but at once appends to them rather scornful criticism:[44]

> In the investigation of truth, therefore, we are taught thus: we must hold as becoming, that which is true; hold not what is false for true, obscure not what is true, occupy not the mind with idle or confused or doubtful problems. What would be so unbecoming as the worship of wooden blocks, which those teachers scrupulously practice? What so obscure as the astronomical and geometrical researches of which they approve? What so obscure as to measure the depths of space, to enclose the heavens and the sea within a system of numbers, to set aside the matter of salvation and become addicted to the cause of error?

Saint Ambrose cannot hide his classical training and his knowledge of the ancient authors, particularly of Cicero, though he is hardly attached to them. The poets are possibly an exception. Among these he is especially fascinated by Virgil, from whom he borrows numerous passages and allusions. And we note that, like Saint Ambrose in his own time, it was Virgil who in the Middle Ages became the connecting link between the pagan and Christian cultures.[45] The poets taught Saint Ambrose the language of the heart, and this he most delighted to cultivate, for he was a man not only of firm convictions but of deep feeling. It was to this latter gift that he owed the great influence he exerted upon his own and later generations. The emotional power evident in his funeral oration for Theodosius, already quoted, is displayed in an especially vivid manner in another funeral oration, this time for his dearly beloved brother Satyrus. His fondness for allegorical-mystical interpretations, through which his influence was projected for cen-

---

44. Lib. I, c. 26, par. 122.
45. Cf. Thamin, 316 sq.

turies — indeed up to the time of the mystics of the school of Saint Victor in Paris — shows us how his imagination and heart clung to religious truths.

Above all, evidence of this is found in his hymns. With these — himself a master — he inaugurated in the Latin West the modern trend in poetry, specifically Christian lyric poetry.[46] The patterns for such songs, used in religious rites, already existed in the Orient; it was Saint Ambrose who introduced them at divine services in the West, perhaps following the example of Saint Hilary. These activities of the Milanese bishop were determined (apart, of course, from his native endowments and inclinations) by practical apologetical needs, in the recognition of which his Roman character asserted itself time and again. The Arians had from their earliest days attracted followers by means of their hymns. And when the conflict with Arianism was at its height in Milan, and the anxious congregation spent the night in church with Saint Ambrose, then being persecuted by the empress Justina, there resounded for the first time the antiphonal chant of the hymns and psalms introduced by the saint. Christians remained so conscious of his work in embellishing the Western liturgy with new artistic and poetic beauty, that later, hymns sung at divine services in the West were called "Ambrosian" as a matter of course.

Actually, we cannot with certainty attach his authorship to many more than a dozen hymns, but these are sufficient even today to reveal his mind and heart. In form the hymns are constructed entirely on the pattern of ancient pagan poetry and conform to all the norms of art. The careful observance of the meter — that is, the measurement of syllable quantities, not rhythm and accent — still insures the authority of these compositions as models. They are written in the iambic dimeter then widely in use, with four lines to a stanza and eight stanzas to each hymn. Hence they could easily become fixed in the memory and popular. Entirely new ideas and emotions, however, are infused into this framework through which Christian spiritual life begins freely to unfold itself in the art of song.

---

46. Cf. Ebert, *Liter. des Mittelalters,* I, 147, 172 sqq.

One of the best-known of these hymns is *Deus Creator omnium,* an evensong in which there are offered to God gratitude for the day ended and a prayer for protection during the dark. A second one, *Aeterne rerum Conditor,* is a poetic morning prayer which should lift up the believing soul to God at the first crowing of the cock. Another, *Iam surgit hora tertia,* commemorates the death of the Redeemer at the third hour. A fourth hymn, *Veni Redemptor gentium,* has the intent of combating Arianism, hence it is dogmatic in content and extols the Incarnation of the Son of God, consubstantial with the Father. Its emotion is clothed in a certain vividness, yet we observe that moralizing and reserved Roman manner so typical of the character of Saint Ambrose and his Christian community. Thus while the Roman forms still prevail, a new spirit begins to expand them, which later will break through them completely. This spirit was that which fortified itself with the triumphs of martyrs and found ample recompense for the decline of Roman life in the blessing of faith.

A joyous and enthusiastic mood, inspired by faith, will always delight in expressing itself in poetry. Hence the art of poetry has constantly been favored by Christianity. At the end of the fourth century, conditions were more than propitious for such poetic expression. The Roman State under the pious emperor Theodosius had definitely destroyed paganism. The Roman Christians gladly believed that the Church would now be able to fulfill her mission to glorify God, unhampered in or beyond the Roman Empire. This is implied in the triumphant conclusion of the first part of the *Te Deum.*

Yet among many members of Roman society, particularly in the aristocracy and the leading literary circles, there still survived a sympathetic interest in the culturally proud paganism of antiquity. This interest manifested itself in a worldly spirit (to say the least) which led men to rank the ancient culture above Christian ideology and Christian feeling and to look down on the Church with condescending pity. But such an attitude served only to stimulate men of ideals to elaborate Christian thoughts and sentiments in poetic form as an expression of pious spirituality — not by state command but because of a personal conviction, won after a severe struggle. The old art of poetry still lived on, handled by brilliant new masters. Thus, among the contemporaries of Saint Ambrose, two poets stand out who, although they are on his cultural level, considerably outstrip the Milanese bishop in talent and emotional power. These two must not be passed over here.

The first of these illustrious poets was Saint Paulinus of Nola, scion of a senatorial family of Bordeaux, a family wealthy, aristocratic and Christian. This city, where his father had been praetorian prefect, offered at the time exceptional opportunities for literary training. There Paulinus was taught by the poet Ausonius, classical representative of Latin rhetoric and author of *Mosella*. Although it is true that Ausonius had become a Christian outwardly, in his method of thought he still inclined to paganism. A deep friendship bound teacher and pupil. This Paulinus sacrificed after a painful inner conflict, when he entered upon ways that Ausonius would not approve.

Paulinus married a noble Spanish lady, Therasia. The career of a public official, for which he was destined by birth and education and in which he rapidly attained the post of governor of the province of Campania, contented him for only a short time. He wanted to be at leisure to devote himself to literary pursuits, a mode of life made possible by the revenues from his rich possessions near Bordeaux. But this arrangement did not satisfy him either. Vicissitudes, especially the early death of his only child, turned him to more profound thoughts and taught him to seek the assurance of happiness solely in the way pointed out to him by pious friends like the Apostle of Gaul, Saint Martin of Tours, and Bishop Delphin of Bordeaux. Paulinus also had some association with Saint Ambrose. About 390 he received Baptism, which he had postponed for a long time, from the bishop of Bordeaux. Thereupon he sold a large portion of his property for the benefit of the poor, and went to Spain, where the bishop of Barcelona ordained him a priest. But he found peace only at Nola, in Campania, to which he was drawn less by his family possessions than by the tomb of the holy confessor Felix, whom he had early chosen as his patron saint. Paulinus lived with his pious spouse in an almshouse which he founded, and was happy to devote himself in self-chosen poverty to prayer and poetry. At the death of the bishop of Nola, the pastoral office was forced upon him. This he discharged in an undaunted spirit of sacrifice during the difficult times when the Visigoths were surging through Italy. He died on June 22, 431.

Before settling in Nola, Paulinus in poetic letters to Ausonius had announced his farewell to the pagan muses so that he might consecrate his heart wholly to Christ and seek his happiness in the expectation of eternal life. His poetic soul was then turned completely to religious subjects. He particularly glorifies Saint Felix, in compositions written for the anniversary of his death — his birthday in heaven — January 14. These poems describe in detail the basilica of the saint, which Paulinus had restored and enlarged, and its pictorial adornment. Other works laud the Christian faith in contrast to pagan folly; and still others, signalizing various occasions, are dedicated to like-minded associates. His attachment to old friends is revealed in certain of his prose letters which have been preserved. A gentle and contemplative disposition appears everywhere, which rejoices especially in the beauties of Christian faith, and in the house of God. It was his pleasure to compose metrical inscriptions for the decoration of church buildings, a custom which betrays his practical Roman turn of mind, just as the Roman national consciousness finds clear expression in his works.

The beauty of the psalms likewise attracted him. In several poems consisting of paraphrases of them, he offers a new type of Christian poetry, one which was to be cultivated later in the Middle Ages. His infusion of a new spirit into the poetical forms of the ancient school, his gentle character, the happiness he found in everything that breathes an ecclesiastical spirit, his joy in the veneration of saints and relics, all mark this pious poet as the bearer of that new, transitional civilization which the Romans bequeathed to the succeeding generations.

In his letters and poems, and in his association with friends, Paulinus shows us how widespread at that time were culture and refinement of social intercourse in the aristocratic circles of Romanized southern Gaul. After the disturbances occasioned by the migration of nations, these qualities again came rapidly to the fore in the classes which had been little influenced, comparatively speaking, by foreign elements, and which were destined to create the chivalrous conventions of the period of the Crusades.

Another author, not a poet, who can be cited as a witness to these facts was a friend of Paulinus, Sulpicius Severus. Following the death of his wife, a woman of gentle birth, he lived as a monk at Eauze, in his native province of Aquitaine, where he continued to occupy himself with the production of literary works for the instruction of his contemporaries. In the style of the great Roman historians Sallust and Tacitus, he wrote a historical reader for the use of educated Christians. He also composed a biography of the holy monk and bishop, Martin of Tours, in whom Gallic Christians of that period saw the realization of their ideals, and who became in the succeeding centuries of the Merovingian Age the patron saint of the Frankish kingdom. This biography of Saint Martin had been written as a devotional book for the general public and quickly met with extraordinary approval. The author charmingly expresses his enthusiastic fondness for the saint, who had encouraged him to follow the example of Paulinus and flee the world. He does not, however, steer clear of credulousness or an inordinate hankering after the miraculous. But the dialogues treating of the miracles and virtues of Saint Martin, which are appended to the *Vita,* have attracted the attention in particular of literary historians because in them is shown for the first time that flair, so peculiarly French, for the narration of personal experiences which was later splendidly developed in the literature of memoirs. Thus we observe the beginnings of those divergences which became so apparent when the Roman Empire split into its several parts and made possible the development of individual characteristics in every nation.

Even clearer than the French traits which appear in Sulpicius Severus is the Spanish strain, determined by the Celtiberian element, in Aurelius Prudentius Clemens of Saragossa, the greatest poet of this age in the West. His local patriotism is very evident in his praise of Spanish martyrs and in the high regard he expresses for his great countryman the emperor Theodosius — who, after Prudentius had held several governorships in Spain, admitted him to the highest class of court officials. Studying the development of his many-sided poetic talent, we intuitively perceive the Spaniard in his ardor, which exhales something of the hot desert whence the Iberians came to the peninsula named for them. That ardor, indeed, reminds us of the African, Tertullian, upon whom Prudentius often leans. A closely related trait is his predilection for dramatic and realistic description which almost repels at times. This shows itself especially in the scenes of martyrdom depicted in that very peculiar poem *Peristephanon,* which we are instinctively tempted to place side by side with the paintings of "Lo Spagnoletto" — Jusepe de Ribera, the seventeenth-century Spanish artist and copperplate-engraver. The rhetorical pomp and glorification of the martial virtues in Prudentius also run true to Spanish form.

But these tendencies work as it were subconsciously in the soul of the poet. He has lived and labored long in the world, and now his deliberate purpose is to use his intellectual powers to exalt the Christian faith and bring the doctrine of the Saviour closer to the minds of pagans, still numerous among the educated classes. To this end he utilizes all the tones of his many-stringed lyre — the dramatic and the narrative, the lyric and the epic, the didactic as well as the polemic and the humorous. In his pages artistic form and depth of feeling often unite in the purest harmony.

Like Saint Ambrose, he composed poetic prayers for different hours of the day; but his were not destined, nor are they suited, for liturgical use. They are too long, for one thing, and also too subjective. The whole body of Prudentius' poetry is less popular and practical than Saint Ambrose's; it is rather a studied work of art. But the depth of conviction is the same and the warmth of feeling perhaps even greater and more penetrating. We see this particularly in his polemical poem *Against Symmachus,* where the subject matter coincides with that used by Saint Ambrose. The latter had opposed the attempt of the pagan senatorial party to restore the old state religion, in letters which bear witness to his rhetorical style. Prudentius expresses the same opposition in poetry, often leaning on Saint Ambrose for his material, but far surpassing him by using every form of the art whereby feeling and mood can be expressed.

Confronting the educated pagans engaged in defending their tradition and culture, he feels himself to be the herald of a new, profounder and more comprehensive culture. He enters the arena as a champion of civilization and employs all the weapons the ancient culture has offered him in order to renew it in the spirit of Christianity. He has only scorn for the favorite argument of the opposition, namely, the worth of the age of paganism, refuting, as Minucius Felix and Tertullian have done before him, the claim that Rome owed her triumphs to the gods. At the same time he extols, in his own way, Rome's destiny to rule. He probably wrote these poems in Rome itself on the occasion of his visit there at the time (402) when the Roman soldiers under Stilicho had conquered Alaric at Pollentia and Rome could still be considered invincible. His heart beats joyously at the triumph of Roman arms, although for him Rome's world-mission consists only in having established an empire of peace and concord in which Christ's teaching may be spread without difficulty. The triumph of Christianity is more important to him than Rome's temporal rule, and his poetry reaches great heights in those passages that praise the potency of Christian teaching in its dominion over the minds of men. A splendid passage in point is contained in another polemical work, the *Apotheosis.* Here, defending the Catholic teaching on the Trinity against the heretics, he gives the strongest proofs of his mastery of form despite the unyielding character of the subject matter. We quote a few verses in English translation:

> Where is there a library of writings which is not replete with the praise of Christ? Where is there a collection of books which is not constantly extolling His miracles anew? The Jewish stylus, the rich language of Greece, and the eloquence of a third tongue, Latin, proclaim Him. Unwittingly Pilate issues his command: "Go, scribe, and explain in verses thrice written the Power which is crucified; threefold shall be the title on the Cross, and in three languages." Judea, Greece and venerable, glorious Rome, reading, shall acknowledge, know and examine in Him the Divine. The sounds of the trumpets filling the ethereal realms, the human aspirations rising from the depths of men's bosoms, the pure tones given off by the lute and the lyre, the harmonious message from the divers pipes of the organ, and the resounding echo of the shepherds' voices: all praise Christ, glorify Christ; and even inanimate Nature, vivified by the sacred strains, professes Christ. O Name so sweet to me, my light, my glory, my hope, and my protection! O sure haven after trials! Sweet delight, fragrant odor, life-giving fountain, chaste love, beautiful vision and sincere joy!...[47]

---

47. Cf. C. S. E. L., LXI: Prudentius, *Carmina,* ed. by J. Bergmann, pp. 96-97.

The verses of Prudentius rush upon us like a mighty oratorio-chorus. Here speaks a poet whose heart senses the cultural force of the Christian religion in its very essence. Thus, too, beyond almost any other writer of his day, he divined the mission the Roman Empire was called upon to fulfill for the new Western civilization then in process of formation. In the *Crown of Martyrdom,* dedicated to Saint Lawrence, which has been cited as the first example of a modern popular ballad, he has the martyr prophetically announce Rome's mission in a prayer:

> Grant to Thy Romans, O Christ, that their city may become Christian, through which Thou hast vouchsafed that the other cities become united in things sacred. From here as a center, all the members are bound together in one faith; the subject empire was mastered, may the head, too, be so mastered. . . . We already hold the surest pledges for this hope, for here reigned the two princes of the Apostles: the one the Apostle of the Gentiles, the other who holds the highest teaching office and unlocks the gates of heaven entrusted to him. . . . I see the future prince who, as a servant of God, will no longer permit Rome to serve the hideous impurities of the temples.[48]

Our poet thoroughly understands also where the cultural force of Christianity should manifest itself first of all; namely, in the social and moral field. When Saint Lawrence is ordered to yield to the avaricious prefect of the city the treasures of the Roman church assigned to his keeping, the poet has the saint gather all the infirm, the blind, the crippled, the lame, the lepers, and group them in the atrium of the church. "These are," he says, "the golden vessels and the hoarded-up treasures of the Church."

Prudentius knew how to use ridicule and scorn in castigating the moral evils of his day, which he was able to discern only too clearly in Rome. The opportunity presents itself in his polemical work against Gnostic dualism entitled *Hamartigenia* (The Origin of Sin), in which he enters into the question of the source of evil and its place in the divine plan of the universe. Here he treats the decadence of Rome with biting sarcasm, scoring the exaggerated luxury, the passion for finery on the part of women, and of men who were ashamed of being men, as well as the frenzy for brutal

---

48. *Peristephanon* II, 432 sqq.

circus-games, fights between wild beasts and gladiatorial combats. This condemnation of the blood lust which delights in gladiatorial games, he repeats in other passages, imploring the emperor Honorius in due form to abolish the disgrace: in the imperial city, no one should die for the mere purpose of providing mob recreation.[49] Prudentius composed these verses some years after the heroic death of Telemachos (or Almachius), a monk from the Orient, who during the pagan Roman festivals in the amphitheater on January 1, 391, rushed between the gladiators shouting that these pagan abominations must end. He was condemned as a disturber of the popular feasts by Alypius, the prefect of the city, and killed by the gladiators.[50]

In the poem *Psychomachia* (The Spiritual Combat), which extols the moral force of Christian culture, Prudentius confronted pagan vices with Christian virtues, ideally personified. This poem made the greatest impression on the Middle Ages, alike by its subject matter and by its form — the allegorical style of art. Artists later were fond of depicting the allegorical figures and scenes of combat in miniature, as many medieval manuscripts of the *Psychomachia* show; and they loved to imitate the Spanish poet, whose partiality to combat and moral idealism they shared.

For in the allegorical figures of the virtues Prudentius praised the new cultural forces of Christianity, destined to battle with the moral depravity of paganism. It is significant that Faith, dressed like a peasant, with uncovered shoulders and unkempt hair, with bare arms and no weapons, trusting only in her strength, opens the combat against the blindfolded figure representing the cult of the ancient gods. Then comes Modesty, a virgin in brilliant armor, who is attacked with a pitch-torch by the worst of the Furies, Unnatural Lust; but she disarms her adversary by hurling a stone, and kills her with a sword. The third figure to enter the arena is Patience, calm and serious of mien and clad in a triple coat of mail. Anger storms in against her, and when all her weapons glance off

---

49. Lib. II, C. *Symmach.* 1125; cf. lib. I, vs. 379 sqq.
50. Theodoret, *Hist. eccles.*, V, 26; *Martyrolog. Hieronym.*, ed. De Rossi-Duchesne (Paris, 1894), p. 4; Kirsch, "Das Ende der Gladiatorenspiele," *Römische Quartalschrift*, 26 (1912), II, 207 sqq.; Delehaye, "St. Almachius ou Télémaque," *Analecta Bollandiana*, XXXIII (1914), 421 sqq.

Patience's impervious armor, Anger throws herself upon a spear. A new pair of combatants follows. Seated upon a horse which is unbridled and caparisoned with a saddlecloth of lion's skin, Pride, in flowing mantle and high-towering headdress (she was later portrayed with similar magnificence in the pleasure-garden of the Abbess of Landsberg), rides at full tilt against a small army led by Humility and followed by Justice, Honesty, Sobriety, together with Modesty and Simplicity. Pride scoffs at Humility, who, as a naked combatant, proposes to drive out the old kings and deprive them of their rule. But Pride falls into a trap which Deceit had prepared for her. Next, in a four-horsed chariot, appears Sensuality, an intoxicated dancer, who carries no weapons but scatters violets and rose leaves to deceive the senses with perfume. Sobriety advances against her with the standard of the cross. The horses shy at the cross and Sensuality is thrown out. Avarice, with her daughters Care, Hunger, Fear, Anxiety, Insomnia, Perfidy, Bribery, Deceit, Falsehood and Impurity, attempts to gather up the spoils covering the ground. At first the army of virtues is at a loss to know how to conduct itself, since Avarice poses as Frugality. But charitable Solicitude recognizes the enemy and strangles her, while Concord leads the victorious army back to camp. Then Concord in turn is saved by Faith from a treacherous attempt upon her life by Discord, who bears the surname Heresy, and all celebrate the victory. A temple is built to Christ, in which Wisdom is to reign.

In this manner, with the help of the Christian virtues, mankind, general and individual, was to obtain peace of soul and the kingdom of God. A new civilization was to be established through the influence of Christianity, but only after a struggle in which every man must take part. Are we wrong in naming Prudentius a champion of civilization, a protagonist of the new Christian culture?

As a poet, we must call Prudentius an optimistic idealist. Though he knew that victory can come only to those who do battle, he imagined the triumph of Christianity and its culture as near at hand, and easier and simpler than history shows it to have been. He probably believed the kingdom of God on earth would be secured by Theodosius' absolute prohibition of pagan sacrifices, and looked to the Christian rulers of Rome to act as God's instruments in the spiritual transformation of the Roman people. His thoughts did not go beyond the confines of the Roman Empire. The conversion of the barbarian tribes beyond its border did not come within the range of his prophetic vision, for between the Roman and the barbarian there was a difference greater "than between the quadruped and the biped, between a speechless and a speaking man, between the Christian and the pagan."[51] When Prudentius thought of barbarians, he could only assume their subjection to Roman power and discipline as something self-evident. That the empire with its advanced civilization, to which by his own training and poetic art he was so proud a witness, must be destroyed by these very barbarians in order to realize the designs of Divine Providence; and that this was to be accomplished in the immediate future — for such an eventuality he was in no wise prepared. A kind fate spared him the foreknowledge, for he appears to have died soon after the victories of Stilicho over Alaric, in which he saw the cultural mission of the Roman Empire confirmed.

Many were not disillusioned until Rome was actually taken by Alaric. Painful as was the prospect this event presented to the Romans, it broadened their mental horizon in a quite extraordinary way. It was the experience that urged the greatest thinker of this transitional period, the teacher of the newly rising Western civilization, to set his pen to that work of his which has fascinated men's minds in unique degree to this very day. We refer to Saint Augustine's *City of God,* which has given the world the most intelligent system of Christian cultural ethics.

---

51. *Contra Symmachum,* II, 815 sq.

CHAPTER TWO

THE CULTURAL ETHICS OF SAINT AUGUSTINE

SAINT AUGUSTINE rightly belongs to the circle of Saint
Ambrose, since he was impelled by the great Milanese bishop's
apostolic dignity and impressive sermons to search his mind and
soul and to amend his life. Like Saint Ambrose, he desired to win
over to the ideals of the Christian faith the Roman world — that
world whose intellectuals numbered so many pagans proud of their
education and culture. In his literary achievement and enduring
influence, the African bishop of Hippo, however, far surpassed the
bishop of the imperial court. While the life and practical career
of Saint Ambrose were more directly integrated and consistent in
character, the history and development of Saint Augustine show
sharply contrasted lights and shadows. Such contrasts were in keeping with his age, which included not only the last triumphs of
Rome's imperial power but also the initial stages of its collapse.
Amid the ruins of the ancient world empire, he manifests a spirit
which looks far beyond all things temporal. In the plan under
which we have been treating some of the guiding intellectual leaders
at the end of the fourth and the beginning of the fifth century,
Saint Augustine, then, has his place.

Just as the mother-country is represented by Saint Ambrose,
scion of the old Roman nobility, Gaul by Paulinus and Sulpicius
Severus, and Spain by Prudentius, so is the special character of the
province of Africa typified by Saint Augustine. This character,
earlier distinctly revealed by Tertullian, is demonstrated both in the
storm-and-stress period of Augustine's youth and later, in the spiritual struggles so closely connected with the social and political
crises during his activity as bishop. In these conflicts he eventually
became the one voice to which all those hearkened who still, in the
ruined empire of the Roman West, retained some understanding of
the problems of the mind. He it was also who handed on to succeeding centuries all those elements from which Christian thought
and speculation were to obtain nourishment.

65

By his writings he gives us — and more fully than any of his contemporaries — an insight into the interior life of those intellectuals of the waning fourth century who, while superficially touched by Christianity, were still dominated by their pagan education, by worldly impulses and ambitions; vacillating thus until a profound desire for truth impelled them to find firm ground. To this firm ground of truth Saint Augustine, with rare fortitude and keenness of mind, resolutely advanced, never again to leave it. He points it out to numbers innumerable of his own and future generations as the only one on which spiritual tribulations can be met and problems of the human mind solved.

Augustine, the son of the pagan Patricius, a decurion (a position analogous to that of a modern councilman) and the Christian Monica, was born November 13, 354, at Tagaste, a small city in the province of Numidia. Had he continued in the ways of his youth, history would hardly have preserved his memory. His name would have vanished together with the splendor of that Roman culture in which, despite its marked decadence, he sought personal enjoyment and intellectual renown. What could he have offered us? Not much more than any of the company of rhetoricians who earned their livelihood in Carthage and Rome by teaching the art of the spoken word according to the affected taste of the times. Indeed, we understand that Saint Ambrose did not manifest any particular personal interest in the professor who had been called to the municipal chair of eloquence in Milan upon the recommendation of Symmachus, the pagan prefect of the city of Rome. The then thirty-year-old Augustine was rated at least technically as a catechumen among the Christians. But neither in morals nor in convictions had he given any noticeable sign of the spiritual comprehension of Christian truths. Only one person, his devout mother Monica, divined that he would soon be a different man. She had followed him from Africa and at Milan finally saw her beloved son in an atmosphere which favored the fulfillment of her ardent prayers.

It is probable that Augustine at first attended the preaching of the staunch Milanese bishop only out of curiosity; but he could not long resist its profound stimulation. Saint Ambrose's explanations of the Old Testament freed him from many of the prejudices he had imbibed from the Manicheans. Their teaching, which had once fascinated him as it fascinated so many intellectuals of his time, no longer satisfied him. Especially unsatisfactory was the principle which posited a world of dark, evil matter against the divine kingdom of light. This had practically nullified his own personal sense of moral responsibility, and he had for a time become a skeptic. However, he could not remain one. The reading of Cicero's *Hortensius* had, as early as his nineteenth year, instilled in him a passionate longing for truth, which drove him to seek through the medium of philosophy a positive solution for the riddles of life.

Those Neo-Platonic ideas, or more accurately, Platonic doctrines, with which he had become acquainted through the translations of the rhetorician Victorinus, were the means by which he rose to higher things. They directed him to the idea of God as the perfect, the absolutely good, Being. Evil could not then be something enjoying a separate existence. Thus he solved the problem of the origin of evil. Moral evil could have its foundation only in the depraved will of the creature. He was carried to a further stage of enlightenment by his own healthy introspection. The longing for truth which he felt so powerfully within himself led him to presuppose one eternal truth as the source of knowledge: wherefore a special proof of God's existence was not necessary for him. Though later, Scholasticism, based on Aristotle, contradicted him in this, Saint Augustine, through his deeply penetrating expositions on God, creation, and the human soul, exerted an extraordinarily inspiring influence on the Christian philosophy of succeeding ages.

In his interior development, the energetic grasp of eternal truth had this effect, that he was intellectually ready to accept Christian teaching and submit to the authority which divine revelation proposed to him in Sacred Scripture, even before he was morally ripe for it. Great difficulties in this regard had yet to be overcome before Augustine entered with his whole being upon those paths pointed out by his intellect. His mind was still bent on advancement in public life. The impediment to his conversion, an African girl who had borne him a son out of wedlock, he removed by separating from her. But he did not at once abandon his wild and morally reckless life. It threatened rather to grow worse, since he seriously considered with his friends whether lust, according to the teaching of Epicurus, might not be the highest good for man.

However, his spiritual development had already progressed too far to be halted in its stride. Suppose, he reasoned, there is an after-life for which we must contend, according to Christian teaching? He seized upon the Epistles of Saint Paul, and saw that the sole barrier which separated him from Christianity was the demand it made upon his moral conduct. When he heard of the ascetical austerity of the Egyptian monks and of imperial officials at Treves who had forsaken the world, he was so affected that he collapsed in his garden, weeping. The words in the Epistle which met his eyes — "Not in revelry and drunkenness, not in debauchery and wantonness, not in strife and jealousy; but put on the Lord Jesus Christ" — appeared to him as a divine admonition. He followed it forthwith, a man completely changed. Now he was prepared in mind and heart to give himself wholly to Christ and to live solely for supernatural ends. In the rural quiet of Cassiciacum, near Milan, where a friend's villa had been put at his disposal, Augustine recollected himself and prepared at once for Baptism. He received it at the hands of Saint Ambrose on April 24, 387, together with his highly talented son Adeodatus and his faithful friend Alypius.

> Thus were we baptized together, and instantly all solicitude for our former life fled away from us. Nor was there any end in those days to the unspeakable delight wherewith I considered the depth of Thy counsels concerning the salvation of mankind. How plentifully did I weep in those hymns and psalms, being touched to the very quick by the notes of Thy Church so sweetly singing. Those words did flow into mine ears, and the truth which was contained therein distilled melting into my heart, and from thence the affection of piety did overflow, so that my tears ran streaming down, and happy did I find myself therein.[1]

Thus vividly, thirteen years later, did Saint Augustine describe the deep impressions of his baptismal day, in those *Confessions* wherein he recorded his own aberrations as truthfully as he acknowledged

---

1. Translator's note: This English rendering of *Augustini Confessiones,* ed. Knoell (Lips., 1898), Lib. 9, c. 6, is that of Sir Tobie Matthew, as revised and emended by Dom Roger Hudleston; London, 1954, p. 241.

God's mercy and the effect of His grace on him: "In my pride I wandered about and was driven hither and thither by every wind, but in perfect seclusion Thy hand guided me." This is the basic thought of Augustine's most widely read work.

Although in form the *Confessions* can correctly be traced to Stoic and Neo-Platonic models,[2] the work stands alone as a candid exposition of the inner workings of the soul. In a manner similarly unique it reveals how Saint Augustine succeeded in terminating the spiritual conflict within his soul with perfect harmony and how in the Christian faith his restless heart found that complete happiness for which it thirsted. Here is tangible proof of how much nobility of thought and intellectual power existed in moribund Rome, which is frequently represented only as depraved. Though Saint Augustine, animated by profound humility, might never tire of ascribing everything to divine grace, it remains evident that this grace found in his soul predispositions favorable to its workings. One is astonished to note springing forth from the heart once racked by sensual passions and buffeted by the violent forces of his time, those tender emotions to which he gave expression in his last conversation with his mother Monica at Ostia before her death. The very fact that his heart remained responsive to the influence of this simple and pious woman, enabling him to speak as he did, is proof of his indestructible buoyancy of mind. The portrait of Saint Augustine's soul is at the same time a gauge by which to measure the great difficulties which Christianity then faced in conquering, in the hearts of the educated laity, the skepticism of the Academicians as well as the oriental mysticism advocated by the Manicheans; and in attaining its own inner clarity by means of the subtle theosophy of the Neo-Platonists.[3] Speaking to us as a convert, as one who has passed through the labyrinth of error, and as an intellectual who has attained perfect peace of soul, Saint Augustine offers us in his *Confessions* a work which to this very day makes a profound impression because it is so personal in its native simplicity, and because it rises above all stereotyped productions.

---

2. Kurfess, "Heidnisches Milieu in Augustins Bekenntnissen," *Histor.-polit. Blätter*, 160 (1917), 573 sq., 657 sqq.

3. Thoughts taken from Ebert, I (2 ed.), 222.

In 388 Saint Augustine had returned to his native city of Tagaste in Africa, an entirely different man from the one who had left it years before. Here he sold what little he had inherited from his father and planned to lead in his parental home a communal life with his like-minded friends — a life corresponding in part to his cherished dream of an association of Christian philosophers; in part, to a monastery. As in an Apostolic community, no one had any separate possessions. Prayer, spiritual exercises and literary activities constituted their occupation. Augustine desired to realize in his own way the ascetical ideal which had so forcibly appealed to him when he first heard about the life of the Christian hermits in the East. But it was never possible for him to detach himself completely from worldly occupations for any length of time.

During a visit to Hippo he was ordained a priest upon the urgent demand of the faithful, and in 395 he was consecrated co-adjutor-bishop by the aged Valerius. The latter died soon afterward and left to Augustine the sole care of his spiritual flock. A great amount of secular business was thus imposed upon him as a judge and as an administrator of the Church's possessions. Though he continued to live with his clergy in monastic brotherhood, sharing only in their common property, his office placed him in the midst of mundane affairs, and into these he was particularly drawn by his sharp opposition to the Manicheans and the Donatists. The controversy was not simply denominational in character but also political and social, often degenerating into rabid violence.

The greatness of Saint Augustine is manifest in his way of life. He was never engulfed in the varied professional tasks of his small diocese nor in his struggles with the sects; and always he regarded internal and basic differences from a high vantage point and defended the truth of Catholic teachings with unparalleled literary zeal. In 427, three years before his death, when he reviewed his whole previous literary activity in the *Retractations,* he counted ninety-three works in two hundred and thirty-two books, not including letters and sermons written at his dictation. Through these works he exerted an influence far beyond the African province, much like a journalist and missionary of our age. He has achieved an important place in the history of the world. His writings not only defend

Catholic doctrine for his contemporaries, but have developed it for later generations in western Europe, and beyond. Thus, even today, both Christian political philosophy and Catholic theology possess in Saint Augustine's work a still unexhausted source from which to draw knowledge.

It is especially by his ideas of God and God's relation to the world, of the Trinity, Providence, and free will and grace, that he established for the future those guiding principles which are always respectfully approached among Catholic theologians as coming from a Father of the Church. In the Middle Ages Scholasticism and mysticism continued to build on the foundation of his teachings. His authority was so great that one of his letters, addressed on a certain occasion to nuns who had become disunited, later furnished the material for a monastic rule which served the Canons Regular of the Middle Ages as the basic statute of their religious life, whence they were called Augustinians. Many other religious congregations have adopted this Augustinian Rule as the basis of their monastic constitution.

That striving for a harmonious conception of the world which inspired him in his youth while reading Cicero's *Hortensius,* and which later attracted him to Saint Ambrose, is now evident in his desire to probe with his reason the Christian dogmas which he embraced with his whole soul. It was this same yearning that had driven him to a more and more searching criticism of the Manichean teachings which he had accepted at that time. Since he wrote in Latin, he has become the chief founder of the science of theology for the West, and has stimulated the Western mind to treat those great questions which in a Christian philosophy will always be among its foremost problems. In addition, his interior experiences determined his activity in one very specific direction. That Augustine regarded his conversion and his deep understanding of Christian truth as an effect of divine grace, every page of the *Confessions* shows. This conviction led him in particular to define his position regarding the teaching of the Briton Pelagius, who was at that time questioning the doctrines of original sin and the necessity of grace. It was preeminently the mystics of the Middle Ages who took up the ideas of

Saint Augustine, the man taught by his own spiritual experience to comprehend God intuitively and to behold Him with his mind's eye.

Besides attracting theologians and philosophers, Saint Augustine captivated yet other circles by a work which merits our special attention. This, the best-known of all his writings, is *The City of God,* on the twenty-two books of which he worked from 413 to 426. He was impelled to such an undertaking to meet the charge, often raised by the pagans and as often denied by the Christians, that the weakening of the Roman Empire had resulted from the abandonment of pagan traditions, which were considered the foundations of the Empire. This reproach had grown even more emphatic when Rome was captured for the first time by the barbarians under Alaric (August 24, 410).

The event had been wholly unexpected, since Honorius, emperor of the Western Roman Empire, the son of the great Theodosius, had only a few years before celebrated the victories of Stilicho over Alaric's Gothic hordes by a brilliant triumphal procession in Rome. At the time of this jubilation (January, 404), the Romans did not foresee the disaster so soon to overtake them. But when, in 408, the jealous emperor had this same Stilicho, his best general, executed, Rome's doom became inevitable. There were other contributing factors: the Rhine frontier, which had been broken through in 406 by the Germanic tribes pushing westward, could not be repaired; Gaul and Spain had been definitively abandoned to the barbarians. From there the havoc was soon to reach the African province also. But at first Africa did not envisage danger from that direction. It feared rather that Alaric, who had moved from Rome toward southern Italy, would himself cross over to Africa, the rich granary of Rome. Although any such design was terminated by Alaric's sudden death, the terror which had taken hold of men's minds in Africa continued to grow. They no longer could ignore the fact that the foundations of the Roman Empire had been shaken, and that its destruction was a shocking possibility.

Among the Christians (who from the time of the Christian emperors had believed the kingdom of God to be intimately bound up with the Roman Empire), there were some who lost their faith in divine Providence. On the other hand the pagans, still numerous in the ranks of the educated and aristocratic classes, murmured that the cause of the present evils lay in the persecution of paganism by the Christian emperors. It was at this juncture that Saint Augustine wrote *The City of God*. Out of his own deep faith he wished to provide the distressed minds of the Christians with an answer to the questions crushing their hearts, and to reduce to silence the charges of the pagans. His friend, the illustrious Marcellinus, imperial tribune and notary at Carthage, who very likely sensed the mental confusion and spiritual anxiety there even more acutely than Saint Augustine did in Hippo, had begged him to undertake this task. Appropriately, Saint Augustine dedicated it "to the most beloved Marcellinus." The work is by no means systematic in form. Because the books were issued singly, it was difficult to carry out a unified plan of composition. Often interrupted by external circumstances, Saint Augustine labored on it for fourteen years. Frequently he yielded to the temptation of digressing from the main thought to indulge in detailed treatment of special questions. Hence one is justified in considering *The City of God* as a great arsenal of apologetic arguments — a work in which the author intended to answer all the objections raised in his time, to subdue his adversaries with his answers, and to strengthen Christians in their faith. But despite this external lack of proportion, a unified idea of prodigious magnitude informs the whole work, which even today continues to attract the noblest thinkers. Aside from the fact that it constitutes an imposing monument to the intellectual life of that period in which Christian ideas alone preserved vigor amid the decay of the ancient world, it deals with problems which will never lose their interest.

Entitling the work *The City of God,* Saint Augustine gives "city" a meaning of which the comprehensiveness has been fully understood only in recent times. During his own period, nevertheless, such usage was not new. The Donatist Tyconius had employed the figure a short time before, placing the City of God in juxtaposition to the city of the devil. For Saint Augustine the City of God is the communion of all devout, believing Christians of all parts of the world. It embraces not only the living but also the departed, so that the City of God extends beyond the earth into eternity and also includes those blessed souls who, after a pious life, are serving

God in heaven with the angels and who anticipate the resurrection of their bodies. To put it better, the City of God is the object of our humble petition: Thy kingdom come.

The train of thought embodied in *The City of God* is explained to us by Saint Augustine himself in his later *Retractations.* In writing the former work he was often compelled to restate his topic in order to recall the guiding idea, sometimes obscured or shunted aside by digressions. The twenty-two books can be divided into two principal groups. The first, comprising ten books, is essentially polemical in tone. Books One to Five reject the opinion that the worship of the many gods whom the heathens honored was necessary for material happiness, and that the current evils had resulted because the practice of the pagan religion had been prohibited. Books Six to Ten are directed against those who admit indeed that such evils never were and never will be far removed from mortal man, and that they appear in varying degrees according to local, temporal and personal circumstances; but who insist, on the other hand, that the worship of many gods, and especially sacrificial worship, is useful because of the life after death. The second group, in contrast to the first, is positive in tone. Books Eleven to Fourteen deal with the origin of the two cities — the City of God and the city of the world which contradicts and stands opposed to it. The next four books treat of the course or progress of the two cities, and the last four are concerned with the ends proper to them. The work might more appropriately have been titled *The Two Cities;* however, it was named for the superior city, the one which alone should exist.

The city of the world, or the terrestrial city, is the communion of those who have not God before their eyes. Founded in pride by the fallen angels, it has propagated itself on earth by original sin. Its characteristics are pride and a worldliness of thought. Its end is the eternal torment of hell, while the end of the other City is the blessed happiness of the beatific vision. The City of God is not synonymous with the Church, since it existed before her establishment and, moreover, the Church includes some worldly-minded among her members; nor is the city of the world the State without qualification, for the State corresponds to the natural state of man and is not, therefore, evil in itself. But, of course, the actually existing State has become evil largely through sin and often converts authority, legitimate in the sense of conscientious solicitude, into tyranny, justice into injustice, freedom into bondage.

The Roman state, insofar as it did not correspond to the highest aims of Christian civilization, became an example of the city of the godless by its alliance with pagan worship, by its deification of natural forces or cultural values, and by its immorality. Yet Saint Augustine no more failed to recognize the old Roman virtues which God rewarded with political power and grandeur, than he ignored the faults of Christian emperors. He did not consider the Roman state as yet so corrupt that its imminent ruin must be deemed inevitable. Though he regarded his epoch as the last of the traditional six periods of the world's history and, by comparison with the periods of man's life, the old age of the world;[4] and though he shared the prevailing opinion that the end of the Roman Empire would coincide with the end of the world,[5] he forebore to compute the time of that end[6] and did not despair of the empire:

> For all that, the Roman Empire has really only been terribly shaken; it has not changed hands; this has befallen it also in pre-Christian times, and it has recovered from such shocks; hence we must not despair now either. Who can know what God has decreed in this instance?[7]

As we see from this statement the vital question for him was not the fall of Rome, but the defense of Christians against the accusations of heathen contemporaries so that the Christians might not begin to falter. The same thought is powerfully stated in his sermon on the scandals of the world. There we simultaneously observe the preacher of faith striving to prevent the confusion of Christians living among pagans, and the preacher of morals aiming above all to make Christians better men:

---

4. *De civ.*, XX, 7: sexto annorum miliario, tamquam sexto die, cujus nunc spatia posteriora volvuntur.
5. Ibid. 19, 23.
6. Ibid. XVIII, 53.
7. Translator's note: Ibid. IV, 7. Here Schnürer uses Schröder's German rendering, found in *Bibliothek der Kirchenväter*, August, I (1911), p. 196.

The world is being afflicted, the wine-presses are set in motion. Come, ye Christians, children of heaven, strangers on the earth, who are seeking your kingdom in heaven and desire to be united with the holy angels, understand that you have come only in order to go away. Let not the lovers of the world confuse you, they, who want to remain on the earth and who are forced to migrate whether they want to or not; let them not deceive you nor seduce you. Those tribulations are not scandals. Be you just, and there will be occasions for practicing justice. . . . Answer the man who says to you: Behold, in the Christian era there are great tribulations, the world is afflicted; give the answer: Christ has foretold us this before it came to pass. . . .

You wonder that the world is declining? You ought rather to wonder that the world has grown old. Man is conceived, born, develops, and grows old. When old, he has many complaints. He is troubled with coughing, with phlegm, running of the eyes, paroxysms of fear, and exhaustion. Thus, when he has become old, man is full of complaints; and the world, which has become old, is full of tribulations. Has God offered you too little in sending you Christ in the world's old age, to strengthen you when all things decline? . . . Do not attach yourselves to the old world, but tend to become young in Christ, who says to you: The world is passing away, it is getting old, it is declining, it breathes heavily like an old man; but do not fear, your youth will be renewed as that of the eagle. . . . Behold, it is said, the world comes to an end in the Christian times. But perhaps Rome will not perish. Perhaps Rome is only scourged, not mortally wounded; perhaps Rome has only been punished, not destroyed. Rome will not perish, perhaps, if the Romans do not want to perish. But they will not perish if they praise God; they shall perish if they blaspheme Him. . . . Heaven and earth shall pass away. Why is it astonishing, therefore, if the State shall one day pass away? And perhaps the end of the State is not even now at hand; but some day, though, the State will have an end.

He concludes this sermon, which strikingly expresses the salient thought of the *Civitas Dei,* with the words: "What Christ commands, let the Christians do, and then may the pagans alone blaspheme over their evils."[8]

Saint Augustine argues against the same sentiments from another point of view in a sermon on the Scripture text: "Lay not up to yourselves treasures on earth":

One cannot get up, one cannot go out, without its being said by all in one voice: Woe betide us, the world is perishing! If it is perishing,

---

8. *Sermo* 81, 7-9.

why do you not wander away? If the architect were to tell you that your house will collapse, would you not rather leave than murmur? The Architect of the world tells you that the world will perish, and you believe it not? Hear the word of Him who has prophesied it, hear the counsel of the Admonisher! The voice of the Prophesier says: "Heaven and earth shall pass away." The voice of the Admonisher calls out: "Lay not up to yourselves treasures on earth."[9]

But it is no idle pessimism that Saint Augustine would encourage. In illustration, a passage from another vigorous and intense sermon on prayer may be cited:[10]

> Pray, brethren, as much as you can. The evils are increasing, and God willed that the evils increase. If only the wicked did not multiply so and the evils did not increase so! Bad times, hard times! — thus do men speak. Let us live well and the times will be good. We are the times; as we are, so are the times. But what are we doing? We cannot convert the multitude of men to a good life. May the few who hear, live well, and the few who live well, tolerate the many who live wickedly.... The evils increase in the world, so that the world may not be loved. Great were the men and saintly the faithful who have despised the glamorous world; we, we cannot even despise that which is defiled. Evil is the world; yes, it is evil, and still it is loved as though it were good. But what does it mean that the world is evil? Evil is not heaven, nor the earth, nor water, nor what is in them: the fish, the birds, and the trees. All these are good, but evil men make the world evil.... Let us not find fault with the Father of the house, for He is good. He sustains us, not we Him. He knows how He should rule, what He has done: do what He has commanded, and hope for what He has promised.

This was the spirit which the Church engendered in the best of her sons in the Roman world. It qualified them to fulfill the mission they inherited when the empire perished, and to promote that cultural program to which we owe the salvaging of all the finest in ancient civilization. For this Saint Augustine, without suspecting that any other dispensation would succeed the empire, worked, as no other. Yet it is precisely to him and his exhortations that we owe it that the Christian Romans laid that solid foundation on which alone the Christian culture of the West could rise. Many pastors of the Church followed his direction, and, like him, fearlessly held out during the upheavals caused by the migration of

---

9. *Sermo* 60, 6.
10. *Sermo* 80, 8.

nations, preserving the precious traditions of the first Christian centuries until they could again germinate and flower in a new culture.

A truly great fortitude of mind and a deep-rooted Christian conviction were required not to succumb in those times to the paralyzing influence of cynicism and the inaction of quietism. Saint Augustine was safeguarded by keeping his ardent gaze fixed on heaven. His example not only inspired his contemporaries, but has consoled and uplifted many generations since then, and still continues to do so. The reality of eternity and the connection between this world and the world to come are, of course, Christian truths, but no one has placed them before mankind so impressively or in such powerful language as did the bishop of Hippo in the period of the declining empire. Therein lies the greatness of that Christian philosophy of history which we encounter in *The City of God:* for if in the philosophy of history those factors are to be treated which determine the course of history, then the questions on the end of man deserve first place. At no time do these questions become more vital than when all material aims fade and everything inviting worldly aspiration threatens to collapse. For the hearts of his contemporaries, confronted by such a possibility, Saint Augustine found soul-stirring replies in the rich experiences of his own spiritual life and in his great store of knowledge which included the wisdom of the ancient philosophers.

In comparison, other ideas adduced as parts of a philosophy of history recede into the background, though on the surface they may have had a more marked after-effect merely because they were externally formulated and more easily intelligible. We have in mind Augustine's division of the history of the world into six periods.[11] This division is not especially original nor profoundly based, for it is frequently found in earlier patristic literature and rests upon that type of allegorical interpretation of the six days of creation which for generations was probably handed down in catechetical instructions. The first five periods are borrowed from a division of the history of the Old Testament. The sixth and last period begins with the Incarnation of Christ, which Augustine makes less historically

---

11. Principal passages: *De Genesi contra Manichaeos* I, 35-45; *De civitate Dei,* Conclusion.

dominant than does Dionysius Exiguus. The latter, writing a hundred years later, begins to reckon the years with Christ and thus makes the Saviour the central figure of the whole history of the world, while in the Augustinian division His birth only inaugurated the last period. How closely Saint Augustine followed the traditional division here is still more clearly seen if we observe that he also combines the interpretation of historical periods, compared to those of man's life, with the allegory of the six creation-days; and thus for him the last period of the world's history is the old age of mankind. This interpretation goes back far into antiquity and is linked with the symbolism of the number seven,[12] for Saint Augustine also further speaks of a seventh day, on which the Saviour of the world will return as judge, and eternal peace will begin.

But weak as the basis of the division was, it rested on the great concepts of the unity of the human race and its education by God, and these concepts are the only foundations on which historico-philosophical considerations can be constructed. They had to lead to a genetic view of history, on which we now lay such great stress, with the difference, of course, that today a mechanistic physical necessity is frequently accorded the place which a Christian philosophy of history can concede only to God. The history of the Jewish people naturally led Christians to such an evolutionary view of history, and Saint Augustine expresses it in concise form with the words:

> As the proper education of the individual advanced in certain periods or stages of life, so, too, in the same way did the education of the human race advance, insofar as God's chosen people are concerned, in order that we might soar from things temporal to an understanding of the eternal and from the visible to the invisible.[13]

The idea of the education of the human race furnishes Saint Augustine the frame for his great ethical expositions, for his magnificent synthesis. This synthesis, which of course is not presented in any precise arrangement and must be constantly supplemented by

---

12. Boll, "Die Lebensalter," in *Neue Jahrbücher für das klass. Altertum,* XVI (1913), 89 sqq.

13. *De civ.,* X, c. 14.

excerpts from other works of Saint Augustine, mainly determines the meaning of *The City of God*. It is based on the ideal rules of conduct set up by Saint Augustine for man's actions, and thus may be regarded as a cultural program for humanity, valid for all times.

Only from this angle will we fully appreciate the author of *The City of God;* from this point of view the work acquires its value for the centuries. For his own era, the pivotal point of the work may well have been its polemics. These were directed against the state's pagan theologians and philosophers because the sole determining factor for them was the surface glamour of the state; these polemics were likewise directed against society, still essentially pagan, because Saint Augustine feared the Christians would be thrown into confusion by its influence. On these two adversaries his work also had a decided effect. But for us, who regard that danger as long overcome, Saint Augustine is above all conspicuous as a moralist. In any case he concerns us chiefly in this role, since we are primarily interested in considering the attitude of ecclesiastical writers on those great, universal problems of civilization which always ultimately resolve themselves into questions concerning moral principles.[14]

A special danger for the Christians of that time — a temptation which will always recur in such circumstances — was the possibility of their succumbing to the inactivity resulting from pessimism, which might lead them to an attitude of apathetic isolationism. The Manicheans might easily exploit such pessimism to promote their contention that the celestial kingdom of light is an eternal substance, partly spiritual, partly sensible, to which is opposed the kingdom of darkness — an eternal, material substance. The earth and man they regarded as a mixture of both substances. It stood Saint Augustine in good stead that he had successfully struggled through this error with its extreme dualism; his former internal conflicts were now made to bear fruit for all Christendom. In this also he was aided by the realistic character common to the

---

14. We have here an excellent guide in the work of Joseph Mausbach, *Die Ethik des hl. Augustin,* 2 vols. (Freiburg i. B., 1909), especially I, 264 sq., II, 260 sq. See also Ernst Troeltsch, *Augustin: Die christl. Antike und das Mittelalter* (Munich, 1915); O. Schilling, *Die Staats- und Soziallehre des hl. Augustinus* (Freiburg i. B., 1910).

Latins, which kept him from yielding to quietism, a companion of pessimism to which the more mystically endowed Orient easily inclined. But this entirely vanishes before the great Principle of all knowledge and all feeling, to which Saint Augustine traces all things, to which he knows how to subordinate all things, and with which he uniformly solves the most profound problems. From it he was able to formulate such consolations that pessimism was silenced before them; he was able to assign to all men a program of action which could never become a mere dead letter, in the face of either prosperity or misfortune, and which offered every man, if only he were prepared to follow the Church's teaching, a spiritually satisfying vocation.

Saint Augustine maintained that the Christian law of morality rests on the commandments of love of God and love of neighbor; the latter is the proof of the former and the first step toward it. Virtue is simply the highest love of God, the Highest Good, in whom all things culminate. Of the many passages which can be adduced in proof of this, we will emphasize only one from *The City of God*:[15]

> Our final good, about whose nature the philosophers dispute so ardently, is none other than union with Him who, solely by His incorporeal embrace, if we can so speak, endows the perceptive soul with real virtues and fructifies it. This Good, so runs the commandment (Matt. 22:37-38; 39-40), shall we love with our whole heart, with our whole soul, and with all our strength; to this Good must they lead us who love us, and to it must we lead those whom we love. Thus will be fulfilled those two commandments on which dependeth the whole law and the prophets: "Thou shalt love the Lord thy God with thy whole heart, and with thy whole soul, and with thy whole mind"; and "Thou shalt love thy neighbor as thyself." That man may learn to know true self-love, an end was appointed him, to which he is to direct all his actions in order to be happy; for everyone who loves himself wants to be happy and nothing else. But the end is complete union with God. Hence, if the commandment to love one's neighbor as oneself is given, then to him who understands real self-love, the purport of this commandment can only be that he love God with all his strength. That is worship of God, that is true religion, that is genuine piety, that is the service due God alone.

Those who think thus are the members of the City of God. But they must act accordingly, for love cannot be passive. All

---

15. *De civ.*, X, c. 3.

morality is thus reduced to a uniform viewpoint. Man's whole life becomes a divine service. Humanity can always console itself with the knowledge that it always has the opportunity and the ability to praise God incessantly by means of moral conduct. "Not only thy voice should sing praises to God, but thy works should be in harmony with thy voice. . . . Hence, if thou wilt praise, praise not only with thy voice, but accompany it with the harp of thy good works."[16] In this sense Saint Augustine teaches the citizens of the City of God step by step the proper use of the things of the world. This especially merits our attention here.

Man's fundamental attitude toward civilization depends upon the question of man's conduct toward the goods of the world. Saint Augustine, who had found his happiness in the knowledge of the highest Truth, in the love of the highest Good, and in the humble worship of the omnipotent Creator and Preserver of all things, answers the question innumerable times by placing before our eyes the goods of the world as the creations of the good God. Hence they cannot be evil in themselves; they are good in themselves.

> Thus Divine Providence admonishes us not to criticize thoughtlessly, but to search studiously for the usefulness of created things, and where our acumen or better, our weakness of intellect, fails, to assume a hidden usefulness, as so many other things were hidden to us upon which we came only with much effort.[17]

Things of the world become evil only through the attitude man adopts toward them. They must be used, not enjoyed for their own sake, which makes them become evil for us. We should use them well, so that we become good and acquire eternal and spiritual things by means of temporal and corporeal ones.[18] Thus for the whole work of civilization, Saint Augustine establishes a moral end which, superior to worldly ends, leaves all transitory things behind. This does not lessen the relative value of these transitory goods. It is merely a question of that proper use of them which, just as it

---

16. *En. in ps.* 146, 2.
17. *De civ.*, XI, c. 22.
18. *De doctrina chr.*, I, 3, 4.

gives individual man interior harmony, binds the whole progress of civilization to the harmony of progress.[19] The harmony consists in referring everything to the Highest Good and to the final end of the other world; the disharmony, the opposition to God, consists in being captivated by temporal things, in the deification of worldly culture and its cultural ends. The regard for the supernatural also preserves man from morbid pessimism.

> Thus the whole train of servants of the highest and true God has its consolation, and this is indeed not a deceptive consolation, nor one which builds its hope on unstable and vacillating ground; life on earth is for these servants by no means an object of disgust, but the school for eternal life, in which they use the goods of the world in the manner of a pilgrim — a figure often employed by Saint Augustine — without attaching themselves to them. On the other hand, they experience in the evils their trial of probation or purification.[20]

The distribution of the goods of worldly culture cannot serve as a standard for man's worth. That depends rather on the use he makes of whatever has fallen to his lot:

> Temporal goods and evils fall to the share of the good as well as of the wicked, so that one will not strive too passionately after these goods, seeing that the wicked also possess them, nor evade these evils in a cowardly way, since the good also are for the most part affected by them.[21]

In the face of prosperity and misfortune the good man conducts himself differently than the wicked man, but even he is not spared misfortune. We understand that Saint Augustine, at a time when the Roman Empire was overrun by barbarians, had to elucidate in detail why the Christians needs must suffer:

> For as in the same fire gold glitters and dross smokes, as in the same threshing-machine the straw is broken to pieces and the grain is cleansed, and as the dregs are separated from the oil by the action of the same press, so one and the same destiny tries, purifies and refines the good and damns, destroys and disperses the wicked. Hence we have the

---

19. *De civ.*, XV, c. 22.
20. Ibid. I, c. 29.
21. Ibid. c. 8.

phenomenon that in the same affliction the wicked curse and blaspheme God while the good invoke and praise Him. It is not the type of suffering that is important, only the mettle of the sufferer. The same breath of air passing over filth sends forth terrible fumes; passing over oil used for anointing, it dispenses a sweet aroma.[22]

The personal disposition of the individual determines whether misfortune as well as prosperity contributes to man's salvation. This disposition alone is the standard for the value of civilization. Man should control and turn to account whatever good or evil comes his way. Thus Saint Augustine characterizes worldly perfection not as repose, but as personal, progressive activity. Men are pilgrims who, journeying toward the summit, may not rest here; only in the next world will there be complete repose. Man must earn this spiritual rest for himself by never allowing himself to be spiritually fettered while on earth, and by dominating that which is here offered him.

According to Saint Augustine, the intellectual goods, artistic intuition and intellectual cognition, clearly stand foremost among the goods of the world. Possessing these assets, he himself, inspired by Platonic ideas and joining them to the Christian faith, had achieved that internal harmony which as bishop he desired to communicate to others; and which was to find its completion in beholding the highest Truth and in enjoying the highest Beauty and Good. But wisdom and beauty in this world are to be ascribed to God alone. He who fails to do this does not belong to the City of God, which includes only those who love God and acknowledge Him in humility.

> There is good reason for impressing humility, above all, upon the members of the City of God who sojourn in this world; it is equally advantageous to glorify it above all in the person of Christ, the King of the City of God. Arrogance, the vice opposed to this virtue, is again and again mentioned in Sacred Scripture as the chief fault of His adversary, the devil. Herein lies the great difference which separates the two cities of which we are speaking: the company of pious men from that of the godless. Each of these estates has its own group of angels in whom first appeared the love of God and the love of self respectively.[23]

---

22. Ibid.
23. Ibid. XIV, c. 13.

Susceptible as Saint Augustine, the great literary artist, is to beauty and art, he can only see a turning away from God in those who praise beauty for itself without relation to God.[24] The sages of the world, among whom Saint Augustine very highly esteems the Stoics and especially the Platonists, also fail through pride: the first because they do not trace virtue back to God;[25] the second because, although they acknowledge God, they do not thank Him, and because they despise faith.[26]

The second great cultural group we call social goods, in which the commandments of love of God and love of our neighbor are one. For a long time Christians had been aware that social relations had assumed a practical aspect under the commandment of fraternal charity; the Church, as the great teacher of brotherly love, had inculcated this. In a work composed soon after his Baptism, Saint Augustine praised the comprehensive social activity which at that time the Catholic Church practiced everywhere, employing the following excellent antitheses:

> Thou dost take all under discipline and instruction: in a childlike way the little ones; outspokenly the men; calmly the aged, as is required not only by their physical but also by their intellectual maturity. Thou dost make women subject to their husbands, not for the gratification of their lust, but for the engendering of life and for domestic companionship in chaste and faithful obedience. Thou dost accord men precedence in marriage, not to mock the weaker sex, but according to the laws of sincere love. Thou dost subject the children to the parents in voluntary bondage, thou dost set the parents over the children in loving and reverential authority. Thou dost unite brethren with brethren by the bond of religion, which is firmer and more intimate than the bond of blood. Thou dost wind a new bond of mutual love round every relationship arising from birth or marriage, while preserving withal the duties of nature and contract. Thou dost teach the slaves to cleave to their masters, not so much because of the pressure of legal force as through the joy of fulfilling their duties. By the thought of God, the highest and common Master, thou dost inspire the masters with a gentle disposition toward their slaves, inclining more to solicitude than to severity. Thou dost unite citizen with citizen, nation with nation — indeed all men, through the faith in a common ancestry, so that they become not only companions but brothers. Thou dost teach the king to provide for the nation; thou dost exhort the nation to

---

24. *Confess.*, X, c. 34.
25. *Epist.* 155, 2, 4, 6.
26. *De civ.*, VIII, c. 19; X, c. 29. Cf. Mausbach II, 279 sq.

submit to the king. Thou dost impart conscientious instruction as to whom honor is due, to whom affection, fear and consolation, to whom discipline, blame or punishment, by showing that we do not owe every individual everything, but love to all, injustice to no one. But after this human love has so nourished and strengthened the soul which thou dost carry at thy breast, that it will be capable of attaching itself to God, when His glory begins to reveal itself as far as this is profitable to the pilgrim on earth — then will there spring up and arise such a fervor of devotion, such a conflagration of divine love, that all the vices will be burnt out, man will be purified and sanctified, and the divine utterance will be fulfilled: "I am a consuming fire" and "I am come to cast fire on the earth."[27]

This exquisite passage not only reveals to us the happiness of its author because through his recent Baptism he had become a fully accredited member of the Church, but also permits us to recognize in it his great synthesis, which now constituted his permanent happiness: fraternal charity flows into love of God and finally disappears in it. The synthesis is further revealed in Saint Augustine's proposition concerning another field — that of the philosophy of law. Here he goes considerably beyond Saint Ambrose by combining Stoic and Platonic ideas with the Christian viewpoint. Saint Ambrose had contented himself with the practical application in a wider Christian sense of borrowed Stoic views on natural law. Saint Augustine also took the natural law, the *lex aeterna,* from the Stoics, principally from Cicero, whom he esteemed very highly; and he brings this eternal law at once into relation with the eternal Creator and Ruler of all things. It is for him God's eternal world-plan, the moral world-order ordained by God. His famous definition coincides with this view: "The eternal law is the divine wisdom or the will of God, which commands that the natural order be preserved, and forbids that it be disturbed."[28] The divine order is mirrored in the ideas implanted in the human soul; these are necessarily in harmony with the divine order. Thus are Platonic ideas utilized, and rules of justice derived from the relation of created things to God. The objective moral order of the world, the *lex aeterna,* becomes natural law in the subjective sense in the con-

---

27. *De moribus eccl.,* 63 sq.
28. *C. Faust. manich.,* XXII, c. 27.

science of rational man; it becomes the basic rule of his moral judgments and efforts. As the love of our neighbor is merged in our love of God, as the finite goods are all referred to the Highest Good, so natural right is fused with the world-order of the Creator, to whom Saint Augustine refers all thought and sentiment.

Another point worthy of note is that Saint Augustine excels Cicero, Lactantius and Saint Ambrose, because they did not distinguish between the concepts of right and morality. The *lex temporalis,* the civil-juridical order, pertains to worldly matters. It is the regulation of living conditions in this world secured by the state or the people through threats of coercion; whereas the moral order of the world, the *lex aeterna,* to which we submit voluntarily out of love for God, is concerned with the attainment of eternal life. The latter provides for punishment of sin, the former for punishment of a violation of right, a violation of the constitutional order. Naturally, in its principles, the *lex temporalis* should not contradict the *lex aeterna,* although it overlooks many things which are punished by the divine law. The state, therefore, cannot be the final standard for virtue, and consequently state-absolutism cannot be advocated by Christianity.

The germ-cell of all society, the first natural form of the community, is the family, which is older than the state and hence entitled to claim certain prerogatives as against the state. Saint Augustine accorded the family particular attention because he realized how the undermining of social order had resulted from the disorganization of the family by paganism. The family is based on the propagation of the species in accord with the law of nature and reason, and also in strict conformity with the law of God. Monogamous marriage is the only relationship for propagation in accord with man's dignity. The opinion that marriage is only an evil to be tolerated has been unjustly ascribed to Saint Augustine; he speaks his mind on this matter unequivocally in *The City of God:*

> We do not doubt in the least, however, that to increase and multiply and to fill the earth according to the benediction of God is a gift of marriage, and that God instituted marriage from the beginning, before the sin of man, by creating them male and female.[29]

29. *De civ.,* XIV, c. 22.

But unregulated sensuality, concupiscence, a consequence of original sin, is an evil, as Saint Augustine sharply emphasizes in contradicting the Pelagian, Julian of Eclanum, who denied original sin.[30] Concupiscence is an evil because it seeks to destroy the balanced order between the spirit and the senses, but at this stage it is not sinful; it leads to sin insofar as man consents to this disorder. But man can also make good use of this concupiscence in marriage in a deliberate, licit and virtuous manner. The first end of marriage is the procreation of children, but this is not the sole end. It is well deserving of particular emphasis that Saint Augustine, here again excelling Saint Ambrose, values the spiritual bond of marriage. He also acknowledges fidelity, the spiritual communion of marriage, as a blessing of marriage, and rejects as unworthy the proposition of Julian of Eclanum, that lust, and not love, is the essence of marriage. As an illustration of the love man ought to have for God, Saint Augustine points to the mutual love of those betrothed as well as to conjugal love. If husband and wife love each other unselfishly with a chaste love, how greatly then must God, the true and real spouse of the soul, be loved.[31] That men might know how to keep sinful passion apart from true love with its pure flowering, Saint Augustine reminds them of the chaste love they hold for daughter, mother, sister.[32] He emphatically exhorts husbands regarding their obligation to observe the same fidelity toward their wives that they demand of them.[33]

As the third and highest good of marriage Saint Augustine mentions the sanctity of the sacrament, mindful of the indissolubility proper to the matrimonial union as such.

Because of these three goods which Saint Augustine ascribes to marriage, we are able to mark how much more firmly the family was grounded in the Christian era than in pagan times. We also observe this in the family's relation to the state. On this point Saint Augustine rises far above the concepts of the Greeks, who envisaged the family as completely overshadowed by the state and destined to

---

30. For details cf. Mausbach, *Ethik Augustins* I, 178 sq., II, 319.
31. *En. in ps.* 55, 17.
32. *Sermo* 343, 7; 349, 4.
33. *Sermo* 224, 3; 260; 132, 2.

be absorbed in it. He builds instead upon the healthy Roman concepts, especially those of Cicero which designated the family as
the beginning and the nursery of the state; Saint Augustine himself calls it the root, or molecule, of the state. Every social order
in human society corresponds to a natural order foreseen by the
Creator. God had the human race descend from one man in order to
foster concord among men by means of their common descent and
the resultant relationship.[34] The family, as the germ-cell of the state,
shows by what means concord is to be attained. "Domestic peace is
the ordered concord among the persons of a household in regard to
authority and obedience."[35] The same holds for the state, which
ranks above the family as an organically higher order. "Since man's
household must be the beginning, or molecule, of the body politic,
and since every beginning stands in relation to an end corresponding
to its kind, and every part stands in relation to the integrity of that
whole of which it is a part — it then follows clearly enough that
domestic peace has a bearing on the peace of the commonwealth;
the ordered concord among the members of a household with regard
to authority and obedience has a distinct analogy to the concord
among citizens in respect to authority and obedience. That is why
the father of the family is supposed to take from the laws of the
commonwealth the authoritative precepts according to which he
should so rule his house that it will conform to the peace of the
commonwealth."[36]

Thus the whole social order is a natural organism, in which
one component part proceeds from the other and the lower is subordinated to the higher. The fundamental element is individual man
with his social aptitude. The first group is the family; from the
family develops the state. Speaking of the influence of domestic
peace, Saint Augustine says: "Family solidarity is so much within
the natural order that the term *paterfamilias* is derived from it — a
term so universally spread that even those who rule unjustly like to

---

34. *De civ.*, XII, 22, 23.
35. Ibid. XIX, c. 14.
36. Ibid. c. 16.

be so called."[37] This natural order, as well as the power to command, in particular, comes from God.[38]

The state is a natural social organism; and since it is willed by God, it is not by nature evil, but good. Saint Augustine defines it in a very general way as a multitude of men "united by some bond of association," "by a common law,"[39] with the power to command. It is an error occasioned by the polemical character of *The City of God* to ascribe to Saint Augustine the view that the state in itself must be regarded as a work of the devil. We must not forget that in *The City of God* Saint Augustine was waging a controversy against his pagan contemporaries, who deified the Roman state and Roman culture and who, in praising both as the works of their gods, wanted to draw Christians away from their faith. Therefore one should never, without having carefully examined the context, cite individual passages of *The City of God* to illustrate Saint Augustine's conception of the state.

The *civitas terrena* which Saint Augustine opposes to the *civitas Dei* is no more to be unreservedly identified with the state as such than is the *civitas Dei* with historic Catholic Christianity. The *civitas terrena* is, in the first place, the communion of the godless, of the children of the world, who have not before their eyes the true God; it is the communion of the proud, who in their self-love despise God. In contrast to these stand the citizens of the City of God, who, humbly putting aside their selfish interests, love God. To this communion of the godless, founded by Cain the fratricide, belongs, to be sure, the pagan state insofar as it represents paganism; and Saint Augustine views the actual, historical Roman state as identified with the *civitas terrena* to the extent that it is built on idolatry. But neither to the state as such, nor to the Roman state in particular, is the right of existence or moral worth denied.

Saint Augustine did not say that sin had created the state and made it necessary. But he did say that sin has frequently corrupted

---

37. Ibid.
38. Ibid., V, c. 1; II, c. 21.
39. *Quaest. evang. lib.*, II, c. 46: est enim civitas non quorumlibet animantium, sed rationalium multitudo legis unius societate devincta. *De civ.*, XV, c. 8: civitas, quae nihil est aliud quam hominum multitudo aliquo societatis vinculo conligata. Cf. Reuter, *Augustin-Studien* (Gotha, 1887), 139 sq.

political order and the state; and first of all the sin of injustice, with which are connected despotism and the lust for power. The state should be built on justice. Its most important obligations comprise a due solicitude to foster security abroad, order and peace at home, and regard for the material welfare of its citizens. But the state must not be satisfied with this, since material things are not the highest good, nor is supreme happiness contained in them. Supreme happiness consists for the state, just as it does for the individual, in the service of the true God. Therefore, the state should not tolerate the cult of idols; it has the duty of promoting worship of the true God and observance of the moral order prescribed by Him. By no means may it restrict itself merely to the task of carrying out the obligations of a purely constitutional state; it must concern itself also with public morality. The state must not be its own end, for the terrestrial state is not the highest entity. It is precisely in this act of attaching itself to material things and ignoring the spiritual that perversity and wickedness manifest themselves in the *civitas terrena*:

> If we covet material things as if they were the only ones, or love them more than those known to be better, while at the same time we disregard those better goods appertaining to the Superior State where victory will be secured by eternal and profound peace, then misery will be the inevitable consequence, and the misery already existent will be intensified.[40]

Thus was the state reduced, indeed, from the supreme importance it had enjoyed in antiquity. But, in compensation, it was assigned loftier and more ideal ends. It was incorporated in the great, divine plan of the universe wherein God Himself is the Highest Good; the state also must contribute its part toward the education of men for their supernatural destiny. And Christianity, thus ennobling the conception of the state, also makes the individual freer by setting him a goal for the attainment of which, since it transcends the state, he must be allowed complete liberty of action. The individual person, in virtue of this higher end, has an inherent

---

40. *De civ.*, XV, c. 4.

dignity which the state neither gives him nor is permitted to take from him. Limits are set to the power of the state, for it is no longer omnipotent, as in heathendom. Society is not unconditionally incorporated into the state, nor does man lose his independence in it, for every individual is a free element, an integral part of the state, "just like the individual letter of a speech."[41]

Man is something more than a citizen. Not civilization nor civic virtue is the highest thing, but the fact and condition of being a child of God. By man's having assigned to him not only the right, but even the duty, of rising up against religious intolerance on the part of the state, human liberty is elevated to its highest dignity. But for what the state surrenders in the new Christian order, as Saint Augustine comprehensively explains, it gains in internal strength. Like the individual, it acquires a firmer basis for right and morality. Civic loyalty is guaranteed not merely by external coercion, but, what is better, by the consciences of the citizens, who are ultimately responsible to the great Judge of all. Those who command in the state have their authority from God; but they too are urged to fulfill their duties more conscientiously, since they too must think of eternity and fear God. For them, as for others, humility before Him is a sign of belonging to His kingdom, which embraces all the just. And, even as others, they too must do all things incumbent upon them out of a desire for eternal happiness rather than out of thirst for vainglory; they must bring to God the offering of their humility, their mercy and their prayers.[42] Here the author has sketched that program which was to be presented so often in the Middle Ages in the *Fürstenspiegel*.[43]

Saint Augustine has also extended his vision beyond the individual state to examine the relations between several co-existing states, thus suggesting the foundation of international law. This deserves all the more recognition since only the Roman Empire existed in his time and it was not even conceived that other civilized governments might come into being. In a theoretical manner, how-

---

41. Ibid. IV, c. 3.
42. Ibid. V, c. 24.
43. Translator's note: literally, "Mirror of a Prince." This was a work describing a sovereign as he should be, with general rules on governing.

ever, Augustine views the possibility that another political system could supplant the powerful Roman state. And there is present in his mind as the ideal, in this connection, something which appears to many in our time to be precisely the remedy for all international conflicts. Like the Stoic Marcus Aurelius, who had already entertained the thought,[44] Saint Augustine pictures many small states which might have existed side by side in harmony and peace, like so many families in the city, and expresses his conclusion with a certain reserve:

> It would seem perhaps unbecoming for well-disposed men to rejoice over the extent of the empire, since it has grown only through the injustice of those with whom just wars have been waged; it would certainly have been small, had peaceable and just neighbors taken care not to provoke war by any wrong. All kingdoms, then, happily for the world, would have been small, rejoicing in harmonious neighborliness, with the result that there would have been a large number of national kingdoms in the world similar to a large number of citizens' families in the city.[45]

In other passages Saint Augustine openly blames Rome's imperial policy, which was bent on the conquest of other nations, just as he condemns the policy of conquest of the Assyrian king Ninus and of Alexander the Great as a system of spoliation based only upon the lust of glory and power. In this connection, indeed, we find a sentence such as this: "What are governments after all, if justice is lacking, other than great bands of robbers?"[46] Quite unjust, however, is the conclusion drawn by some, that every political organism was for Saint Augustine simply a band of robbers.[47] We must remind ourselves again that he is disputing here with adversaries who point triumphantly to the expansion and duration of Roman power as achievements of the pagan gods. In his rebuttal of such claims, he first puts the question whether, from the viewpoint of true wisdom or happiness, the expansion of power is to be accounted a blessing, since it can be attained only through wars.

---

44. Cf. Schilling, *Staatslehre Augustins,* 91.
45. *De civ.,* IV, c. 15.
46. Ibid. c. 4.
47. Sommerlad, *Wirtschaftsprogramm der Kirche im Mittelalter* (Leipzig, 1903), 211; Mausbach, *Ethik August.* I, 336; Bliemitzrieder, *Theolog. Quartalschrift* 95 (1913), 101 sq.

He rightly answers that it is scarcely reasonable and prudent to boast
of the growth and extent of power, since it cannot be proved

> ... that those men are happy who live constantly in the midst of the
> disturbances of war; where they wade in blood, be it the blood of
> citizens or enemies, but still in human blood; where they are surrounded
> by fear and unrestrained blood-lust. The result of all such endeavors is
> a joy of splendor fragile as glass, and one cannot rid oneself of the
> horrible fear that it might unexpectedly break.[48]

At the same time Saint Augustine does not deny that a state
can be forced into war by the injustice of the opposing party, which
war then becomes for that state a just war. The Christian religion
in no wise forbids every war as a sin, though all wars are the consequence of sin. The ideal is peace, for which we should thank God
as a great blessing. Peace and tranquillity are indeed a part of
eternal happiness, which consists "in the perfectly ordered and
harmonious companionship in the enjoyment of God and in the
enjoyment of one another in God."[49]

Saint Augustine does not expect the ideal to be realized in
this life. He knows the misery of the world too well for that.
On the other hand, he knows that the true citizens of the celestial
city on earth try by every means in their power to promote peace
here and to do justice to special national characteristics which, if
suppressed, might so easily cause dissension to arise:

> During its earthly pilgrimage the celestial city calls its citizens out
> of all nations and gathers its company of pilgrims out of all languages,
> unconcerned about the difference in customs of life, laws and institutions;
> thus is worldly peace established or maintained. Instead of denying or
> annihilating any of these institutions, the celestial city rather treasures and
> protects them, for despite all national diversity, they are nevertheless
> adapted to one and the same end of worldly peace. It does so, provided
> that these institutions are not obstructive of religion, according to whose
> doctrine one supreme and true God is to be worshiped.[50]

In this passage we are made aware of several principles important
in respect to international law, which are of special consequence in

---

48. *De civ.*, IV, c. 3.
49. Ibid. XIX, c. 17.
50. Ibid.

our own time, since they define the consideration to which the language, habits of life, laws and institutions of every nation can lay claim. These principles furnish the only solid basis for any league of nations which promises a lasting peace.

Thus we see how Christianity gave the ancient cultural program not only a greater depth and nobility, but also a greater extension. To this enlargement must be reckoned, first of all, the legal status which had to be accorded to the Catholic Church after she had achieved the position of an independent organism.

In Saint Augustine's *City of God* the Church appears as the visible embodiment of the kingdom of heaven on earth, while on the other hand, the pagan state is the embodiment of the kingdom of the world insofar as it deifies created things and refuses to worship the true God. However, it must always be clearly understood that the kingdom of the world and the kingdom of God are broad terms because in the Church there can be and are some persons who should be numbered among the members of the kingdom of the godless; and in the pagan state there can be some who are "citizens of the spiritual Jerusalem."[51] The Church is the visible communion of the baptized, instituted by Christ and bearing the marks of catholicity, unity, holiness and infallibility. What attitude was this visible communion to adopt in principle and in detail toward the visible state, in which Saint Augustine lived? These are questions to which men, especially in the Middle Ages, but even today, have sought answers in Saint Augustine's works, finding them (as they have believed) now in this sense, now in that. We see that these problems, in their earliest stages, began to make their appearance in the time of Saint Augustine. In actual fact the bishop of Hippo accepted, for the most part, conditions as they were — a course of action demanded by the exigencies of his practical ministry. But we clearly perceive that the Church, as the independent institution of salvation possessing her own aims and prerogatives, transcends the limitations of the pagan state with its ancient *ius sacrum,* a part of the *ius pub-*

---

51. Ibid. XVIII, c. 47; XXI, c. 25. Cf. Romeis, "Das Heil der Christen ausserhalb der wahren Kirche nach der Lehre des hl. Augustin," *Forsch. zur christl. Literatur- und Dogmengesch.,* hrsg. von Ehrhard und Kirsch, VIII, 4 (Paderborn, 1908).

licum, and lays claim to an authority which even the emperor must acknowledge in religious affairs.[52]

Saint Augustine takes pains to give a rational foundation to that which had developed before his time. Negatively this was of the greatest consequence for the development in the West, difficult as it was there for the Church to escape being treated as a state institution as long as the Roman Empire endured. Saint Augustine personally had no difficulties in this regard. During his era the Church continuously needed civil protection, and the Christian emperors granted it willingly. State and Church lived in perfect accord, each supporting the other. Saint Augustine, by always reverting to the uniform starting-point of all his arguments, pronounces such a relation good:

> The celestial city, or rather that part of it which sojourns in this mortal life and lives by faith, must use this peace (aspired to also by the earthly city) until mortal life, for which such a peace is necessary, reaches its end. As long as it leads, so to speak, the life of an imprisoned pilgrim side by side with the earthly city (having already received, to be sure, the promise of liberty and as a pledge thereof the gift of the Spirit), it naturally observes the laws of the earthly city without hesitation. These laws served to regulate everything suitable to the maintenance of mortal life here below. They were necessary because this mortal life is common to both cities, and that harmony might exist between them regarding the things pertaining to the transient life.[53]

Saint Augustine calls the Christian emperors happy, "who put their power in the service of God's majesty."[54] Henceforth, these emperors regarded it as their task, in particular, to combat heresy and schism. The acts of violence on the part of rigoristic Donatists and rebellious peasants (Circumcellions) against African Catholics had confronted Saint Augustine with the grave question of whether or not to invoke state force in favor of the Church. At first he had rejected the idea, unwilling that anyone be compelled to join a religious group. But when all his efforts to reach an understanding were fruitless, and his bishopric in particular was harassed by the Circumcellions, he gave up this viewpoint and demanded that

---

52. Gierke, *Genossenschaftsrecht,* III, 111 sq.; Schilling, *Staatslehre Augustins,* 269.
53. *De civ.,* XIX, c. 17.
54. Ibid. V, c. 24.

the state protect the persecuted Catholics. He went further, and attempted systematically to justify state coercion in bringing the delinquents back into communion with the Church. Himself firmly convinced of the truths which he proclaimed, he simply could not believe it possible for a heretic to remain in error sincerely. Hence he abandoned the idea of tolerance in practice, though he personally always espoused the cause of mildness, declaring at the same time the death penalty to be inadmissible, since the reform of the delinquent must be kept in view.[55]

It is to be regretted that in the principle of allowing force in the treatment of heretics Saint Augustine was followed so precisely—for his position is comprehensible only in relation to the turmoil of his era. On the other hand, this time element explains why he furnished no basic solution of another, more important question which interested the Middle Ages: the question of the superiority of the Church over the state. Augustine knows nothing about the imperial authority deriving from the Church, as was taught in the Middle Ages; nor do the emperors proceed against heretics by order of the Church, but by virtue of their own authority. These were problems which came up for discussion only after the fall of the Roman Empire. The Church, as we meet her in Saint Augustine's writings, exercises essentially a spiritual authority. This is the spiritually militant Church which extends her hand to the triumphant Church in the world beyond, where she becomes entirely one with the City of God.

Since Saint Augustine insists mainly upon the spiritual character of the individual person, upon the motives of action which determine the attitude man assumes toward the things of the world, he does not give us any program for changing human institutions. He accepts things as they are and awaits improvement from the disposition and the will of the individual. We see this with especial clearness in his attitude on the economic questions which were being agitated violently all about him. In Africa he found himself in the midst of an agrarian socialistic revolution, whose supporters (the Circumcellions) were roving bands of plundering peasants. This

---

55. *C. Litteras Petiliani* 2, 215.

outburst, only one of the many consequences of the frightful oppression to which the *coloni* of the Roman Empire were then universally subjected, revealed the economic collapse running parallel to the political and military breakdown. But just as the peasant revolutions at the end of the Middle Ages and the beginning of the modern era took on a religious character, so did the movement of the Circumcellions. The Numidian and Mauretanian peasants voiced their economic demands in the name of religious equality. They banded themselves together against the ruling classes and against the government, which protected these classes and was concerned only to preserve public order. The rebels made common cause with all who were dissatisfied and who stood in opposition to the government, especially with the uncompromising sect of the Donatists, which had arisen in the year 311 on the occasion of an episcopal election in Carthage. Anarchistic elements probably also joined the movement when it became openly revolutionary.

Acts of violence increased to such an extent that at times the whole public order was at stake and the courts were powerless. Landowners who refused to remit debts were driven out and maltreated by their debtors. There were instances when the proprietor was forced to get out of the sedan chair in which he was being borne and compelled to carry his assailant. Slaves rose up and forced their masters into servitude; and landowners, believing themselves unsafe in the country, fled to the cities. At the instigation of the Donatists the landed estates of the Catholic Church were especially subjected to pillage and ruin.

Amid these evils there came forth from Pelagian circles in Sicily a treatise which rejected wealth and sought to justify the rejection by the teaching of the Saviour and the Apostles. Its salient proposition was: "Remove the rich, and you will find no poor. No one should possess more than is necessary, and then all will have as much as is necessary." If we recall the severe words of Saint Ambrose concerning wealth, we can understand how such communistic ideas, corresponding to the contempt of the Christians of the first centuries for riches, could make headway precisely among zealous Christians.

Some have maintained, but without any foundation, that Saint Augustine's writings also seem communistic and socialistic. Such a comparison is unjustified by the very fact that all Saint Augustine's thoughts are directed toward a life hereafter, a subject which neither Socialists nor Communists care to explore. But there is no lack, either, of clear passages in which Saint Augustine acknowledges the right to earthly possessions, even riches.

> The riches of the rich man are in no wise rejected, nor is the poverty of the poor man in any way lauded, but only the godlessness of the former is condemned and the piety of the latter praised.[56]

Riches are among the gifts of God to man, and man should make the proper use of them. Augustine emphasizes this last point in a very particular manner, since it coincides with his main thought regarding earthly goods: the difference between using (*uti*) and enjoying (*frui*). The Christian must not attach himself to his possessions; he must not be avaricious or miserly; above all he must not succumb to pride, which is so often associated with riches. When the Apostle declares, "Those who seek to become rich, fall into temptation," he does not take exception to riches as such, but to the desire for them, for in another passage he speaks commandingly:

> Charge the rich of this world not to be proud, or to trust in the uncertainty of riches, but in God, who provides all things in abundance for our enjoyment. Let them do good and be rich in good works, giving readily, sharing with others, and thus providing for themselves a good foundation against the time to come, in order that they may lay hold on the true life.[57]

Saint Augustine does not criticize the rich man, but he exhorts him to the correct use of riches:

> Preach to them that they too have become members of the Poor One (the Crucified Saviour).... The rich man shall be humble; he shall rejoice more in being a Christian than in being a rich man. He shall not exalt himself; he shall not be puffed up; he shall esteem the poor man as his brother.[58]

---

56. *Aurelii Augustini tractatus inediti*, ed. G. Morin. Tr. XXX, p. 130.
57. I Tim. 6, 17-19; cf. *De civ.*, I, c. 10.
58. *Sermo* 36, 5. 7.

He urgently recommends the giving of alms to the needy for God's sake and as an obligation of fraternal charity; and by his teaching on almsgiving he provided the Middle Ages with far-reaching impulses for works of Christian charity. He compares the donation made for the salvation of one's own soul — the bequests for pious causes of a later time — to a peculiar Roman business practice: the contract of bottomry. According to this procedure a loan was made on a ship going to sea with the agreement that the money would be regarded as lost if the voyage was unfortunate, but repayable with high interest if it was successful. Thus by way of allusion Saint Augustine says:

> Do as some avaricious people are wont to do. Advance a maritime loan. Give the earthly pilgrims something (for their material welfare), which you will receive again (with high interest) in your home in the next world. Here you give perishable things; there you will receive imperishable things.[59]

In a later period another passage from the sermons of Saint Augustine served especially as a guiding rule:

> In the disposition of your legacy give Christ a place beside your sons; let your Lord enter into your family. If you have two sons, remember Christ as the third; if you have three, include Him as the fourth; if you have five, let Him count as the sixth; if you have ten, He shall be the eleventh. I will not say more: reserve to the Lord a son's share.[60]

It was only consistent, then, for Saint Augustine to teach that alms in the Church, especially Masses, could be offered not only for the future of one's own soul after death, but also for the souls of those already deceased.[61] But he also knows that there are wrong forms of charity, and declares there are some of the poor so proud that, compared to them, a humble rich man is the better person. He criticizes indiscreet donations to churches with unreserved frankness: "Whoever wants to disinherit a son and desires to make the

---

59. *Sermo* 86, c. 11; *Sermo* 42, c. 2.
60. *Sermo* 86, c. 13.
61. *Enchiridion ad Laurentium*, c. 110; *Sermo* 172, c. 3.

Church his heir instead, should seek not Augustine, but someone else who will accept it; may it please God that he find no one!"[62]

Saint Augustine's attitude toward riches was similar to the one he took toward slavery, which in antiquity actually constituted the social question. Here, too, he follows the positive law, but not without a certain reservation in principle. However, he is not led to make any further deductions. Like the Stoics — and in contrast to Aristotle, who maintained that slavery was based on natural law — he held that originally all men had been free. Seneca had expressed this earlier in beautiful words:

> All men have the same origin and beginning; no one is nobler than another except it be by right disposition and good works. . . . only consider that he whom you call your slave has come forth from the same seed, that he enjoys the same sky, breathes, lives and dies like you! You could see in him then a freeman, and he in you a slave.[63]

But this did not prevent Seneca from speaking very disdainfully on certain occasions about the state of slaves. He called the slave a chained dog, whom his master could rightfully torture, mutilate and crucify.

Here we clearly perceive how Christianity with its new concepts helped to bring about a change in the treatment of slaves. Constantine, under the influence of Christian morality, had declared the intentional killing of a slave to be homicide. He also gave the Christian churches the right to effect the emancipation of slaves in a formal manner. In Saint Augustine's time this right was extended to the African churches, after the bishops had petitioned for it. Augustine weaves the Stoic theories and the Christian practices into his great synthesis. According to the natural order, he argues,[64] God did not create man to rule over his own kind, but only over irrational beings, as animals. By sin alone was slavery introduced among men. As a result of sin, men have been forced in conformity with God's justice to submit to slavery either to correct their faults or to pay the penalty for them. Thus the originally abnormal order became

---

62. *Sermo* 355, 5.
63. Seneca, *De beneficiis*, III, 28; *Ep. 46*.
64. *De civ.*, XIX, c. 15.

a legal institution in accord with divine justice. Slaves have no right to emancipation; but Augustine exhorts his friends who desire to share the communal life with him to give their estates to the Church, and not to sell their slaves but to liberate them.[65] Above all, he insistently impresses upon masters the duty of treating their slaves only in such a manner as becomes just men, citizens of the City of God, who should command "not out of love of power . . . but out of readiness to serve, not out of haughty ambition for pre-eminence, but out of solicitude fraught with mercy."[66] The masters should also show themselves to be true fathers, leading all the members of their household as children to the worship of God. The slaves, on the other hand, are admonished after the manner of the Apostle to be devoted to their masters and to serve them heartily and with good will,

> so that, if they cannot obtain their freedom from their masters, they themselves can make their slavery, in a certain sense, free, by serving not in crafty fear, but in faithful love, until wickedness shall pass away and all domination and human power be abolished, and God be all in all.[67]

Thus we see that Saint Augustine does not aspire to change the legal order, but attempts to remove its harshness by uniting the wills of the individuals involved until all things shall be adjusted in the next world.

As in the theoretical attitude toward the slave question, so, too, in the fundamental discussions regarding the obligation to work, we note that the Stoics had preceded Saint Augustine. Epictetus enunciated the principle that, as labor is in itself moral, no labor can humiliate man. Others, indeed, had not been able to renounce their aristocratic viewpoint and had regarded the occupations of hired laborers, shopkeepers, artisans and merchants as degrading. Even Cicero had expressed himself in similar terms. We have already seen that Saint Ambrose improves on Cicero in this manner. The progress is still plainer in Saint Augustine, who also shows himself,

---

65. *Sermo* 356, 3. 7.
66. *De civ.*, **XIX**, c. 14.
67. Ibid. c. 15.

as in so many other cases, more moderate in making distinctions between occupations. These distinctions were difficult to overcome because they were ancient prejudices. In his book concerning the work of monks he takes occasion to treat the question in some detail. Among the African monks there were certain ones who, regarding their own duty to be only prayer and meditation, wanted to assign all work to the laity. Saint Augustine opposed them and branded such a position as an apologia for idleness which might actually lead persons loath to work, to enter the monastic life. He teaches that work is a duty which indeed has become a bitter duty since the fall of man.[68] But he describes as hypocritical pride the viewpoint of those who feel it beneath their dignity to work. "A truly honorable disposition does not find fault with that which the pride of those criticizes who would like to be called honorable, but do not strive to be such in reality."[69] To show that work is not debasing, Augustine points to the foster father of Jesus and to the Apostle Paul. He turns with admiration to the great achievements of labor, to the trades, to agriculture, to the building of cities and the works of architecture; to the productions of literature, of music, of painting; to what has been deposited in books and monuments for transmission to posterity, to what has been achieved in the various offices in Church and State, to the fruits of intellectual research in poetry, music and mathematics. "All this," he concludes, "is great and certainly in conformity with man's nature."[70]

Naturally, he measures these occupations by his own ethical standard which, as his treatise on the labor of the monks, composed as early as 400, shows, was still influenced by Platonic ideas. In this treatise seven stages of spiritual purification are recognized. The three highest stages are concerned with contemplative thought on human society, the divine order and authority. Hence Saint Augustine esteems intellectual activity as a higher form of work: "To work only corporally and not intellectually produces no advancement, even when it appears good." But, no doubt having in mind at the time the monks of lower rank who wanted exemption from manual

---

68. Ibid. XXII, c. 22.
69. *De opere monach.*, 14.
70. *De quant. animae*, 72.

labor in the monastery, he immediately adds: "To work only intellectually, not corporally, is a characteristic of lazy men."[71]

To people of the world, if their wealth permitted it, he did not deny leisure. They were to spend it, however, in the search for truth and for the good of their fellow men. If an office was imposed on them, they were to accept it out of love for their neighbor. Thus the duty to co-operate for the common good was inculcated in the minds of all. We must here take into consideration the peculiar circumstances of the time. As the Roman Empire waned, there really was no outlet for individually chosen work, since the different classes, determined by birth, were organized into categories for purposes of taxation. Saint Augustine comments as a moralist on the various occupations primarily to determine whether or not they involved anything morally illicit. In themselves, all occupations arising from the needs of daily life and necessity are honorable.[72]

Following the inherent good sense of the Romans as well as the examples of the Old Testament, Saint Augustine accords agriculture first place among the forms of livelihood. This was, indeed, the occupation of Adam in his original state in Paradise, and Saint Augustine marshals charming words to depict the relation, ever present to his mind, between agriculture and God, the Creator and Dispenser of all things good and beautiful:

> Where is there a greater and more wonderful spectacle, or where can human reason better converse with nature, than when questioning it? While sowing, while planting in the furrows, while transplanting and grafting trees, one may inquire about every potentiality of the seed and the young plant, what it can do and what it cannot do; why it achieves certain ends and fails with others. Where can human reason commune better with nature than when it asks what the invisible, internal power of typical conditions can effect, what external cultivation can do; when it realizes simultaneously with this observation that neither he that planteth nor he that watereth is anything, but God that giveth the increase? . . . For the labor from without comes finally from beings, whom God has created and whom He guides and rules invisibly.[73]

---

71. *Sermo* 37, 5. 6.
72. *En. in Ps.* 83, 8.
73. *De Gen. ad litt.*, 8, 16.

But the trades, too, receive words of praise from Saint Augustine, because they do not so enslave the mind that it cannot turn to higher things. Hence they also are recommended to the members of monastic institutions.[74]

Commerce is viewed with suspicion, although Augustine does not condemn it completely, like other ecclesiastical writers. Agreeing that unjust practices not absolutely forbidden by civil law, frequently creep in, he demands that the dealer conduct his transactions fairly, that he not exceed a just price in his sales, and that he avoid lying and perjury.[75] According to general Christian opinion, interest-taking is condemned as a wicked practice, and Saint Augustine advocates its prohibition in favor of the poor.[76] He views it, indeed, as a particularly outrageous form of avarice and as an unfeeling exploitation of the most needy; accordingly he admonishes the rich to give the poor a loan rather than an alms.[77] We shall be able to appreciate these passages fully only if we remember that usury was widespread at the time and that the rich man in most instances left the collection of this income to his freedmen and slaves. The unhealthy economic and financial situation in the declining Roman Empire, after annihilating the sound middle class, had created extremely distressing conditions by a most ill-judged system of taxation. A recovery was no longer possible, and Saint Augustine no doubt sensed this. Hence, since he could not reform the institutions, he had to try at least to reform individually all those who cared to listen to him. This is the objective toward which all his admonitions as a writer on moral subjects are directed. Nor could anything else be expected at that time from a bishop.

In this, as in many other expositions, Saint Augustine merely advocates the viewpoint already adopted in practice by Christians long before his time. His greatness lies in this, that he not only gives information on almost all the questions about which the Christians of the Roman Empire were expected to take a definite attitude, but treats them from the highest point of view and reduces them to

74. *De op. monach.*, c. 15, 16; c. 25, 33.
75. *De Trin.*, 13, 3. 6. Cf. Schilling, 251 sq.
76. *Ep.* 153, 6. 25.
77. *De Serm. Dom. in monte*, 1, 67 sq.

their ultimate principles. Therefore men constantly resort to him and seek his guidance even under entirely changed conditions. Formerly, perhaps, too little attention was paid to the circumstances of the era in which Saint Augustine lived, circumstances which frequently colored his utterances; and the apologetic-polemical character of *The City of God* was especially slighted. But it is also true that these very circumstances cast him into bold relief. Standing on the brink of the abyss into which the Roman Empire of the West was to plunge, his figure was clearly visible to all who would review the past. It assumed gigantic proportions because he united in himself all the culture which antiquity had been able to offer. He combined the idealistic Platonic views of the true, the good and the beautiful with the sober but healthy ethics of the Roman Stoics. And what was more important, he fused these superlative bequests from antiquity with that burning Christian conviction which can never fail in its action upon Christian hearts. He was the Christian thinker on whose ideas succeeding centuries in the West nourished themselves. By his use of the Latin language, which he handled with a consummate skill that only a cultured rhetorician of his day could command, he supplied the technical terms in which difficult theological and philosophical problems could be speculatively discussed.

No doubt there were tasks which Saint Augustine left undone because he had no opportunity to accomplish them. Writing according to the requirements of the problems that assailed him, amid an absorbing and practical activity as the shepherd of a distressed diocese, he lacked the leisure to present the various questions in a systematic manner, to consider all objections and harmonize all random opinions. Thus it has happened that Saint Augustine could frequently be invoked as an authority by opposing factions in controversies involving important principles. This is clearly a sign that occasional utterances of his can be variously interpreted; perhaps, they were even biased.

What Saint Augustine was unable to achieve in the way of a universal and coherent system, was later accomplished by the Scholastics. They possessed a leisure and tranquillity denied to Saint Augustine for meditating upon the problems, treating them in systematic Summas on the basis of Aristotelian philosophy, adjusting them in every respect. This was at a time when Christian teaching held undisputed sway in the higher schools of theology and philosophy — schools completely imbued with the Christian spirit. Thus Saint Thomas Aquinas has above all supplemented Saint Augustine and in some instances corrected him. But just as Saint Augustine could not do what Saint Thomas accomplished, so neither did such a task fall to the lot of Saint Thomas as that which Saint Augustine so brilliantly performed. It was Augustine who recapitulated the spirit of antiquity in order to transmit it to posterity, after having given it greater depth and ennobled it by infusing into it a Christian philosophy of life and conception of the world.

Although Saint Augustine did not give us a ready system — it must be laboriously extracted from utterances scattered throughout his many works, which often require detailed commentaries — still his writings possess today rather an increased than a diminished power of attraction. This power lies not only in the magnificent synthesis, but even more, in the personal enthusiasm and persuasive force with which Saint Augustine propounds his views. One constantly feels how much for him religion is a matter of experience; how doggedly he fights his way through hard battles to the truth of the Christian teaching, to the harmonious union of ancient learning with Christian faith. One tastes with him the happiness which the promise of heavenly peace and rest in God holds out to the Christian, a thought which, especially in the last part of *The City of God*, he has painted with glowing enthusiasm for his contemporaries and the whole of posterity. Tradition has correctly expressed this feeling created so powerfully by Saint Augustine's literary activity, by representing him with a flaming heart in his hand as the symbol of his burning love for the Highest Good, while Saint Thomas is given the illuminating sun as the symbol of that speculation which clarifies all things. Harnack has voiced the same thought in his own way: "To this very day the inherent and living piety of Catholicism and its expression are essentially Augustinian."[78]

---

78. Harnack, *Das Wesen des Christentums* (Leipzig, 1905), 161. Cf. Harnack, *Lehrbuch der Dogmengesch.* III⁴ (Freiburg i. B., 1920), 59 sq.

In reality Saint Augustine teaches that

> there exists in the City of God no other human wisdom save piety, which worships the true God in the proper manner and so, in the communion of saints embracing angels as well as men, expects as its reward that God may be all in all.[79]

Especially, too, by the glowing allusions to the heavenly kingdom and to the habit of mind of the citizens of the City of God who live here on earth only as pilgrims — a habit of mind which rises above all earthly things and leaves all misery of sin far behind — does Augustine prepare the hearts of his fellow Romans to endure the troublous times awaiting them and to make ready for the cultural mission assigned them. Only as Christians could they weather the storm and become the agents of Divine Providence in protecting everything worth preserving in the ancient culture, and in transmitting to posterity in a nobler form the best of the Roman spirit. The pessimism with which Saint Augustine condemned the defilement and moral corruption stemming from pagan times and affecting ancient culture, was only too well justified, and this justification was soon made clear to all. No new, free and lasting Christian civilization could be erected on such a foundation.

Proof of the impossibility was the Empire of the East, where the old foundation was retained, essentially unshaken and unchanged. Caesaropapism continued to flourish there, and it would also have endured in the West had the Christian emperors of Rome been able to continue unbroken their line of rulers. In the case of Saint Augustine, therefore, we can understand why he refrained from making any positive recommendations for the betterment of the corrupt economic, political and social conditions, other than those which devolved upon him as a shepherd of Christian souls. But side by side with this pessimism, which Saint Augustine, Roman patriot that he was, did not wish to apply without qualification to the actual political situation, he preached a theoretical optimism. This was bound continuously to inspire new bands of Christian hearers and readers, trusting in God's Providence and grace, to courageous action and deeds.

---

79. *De civ.*, XIV, c. 28.

Everything that God has created and ordained is good; to work with confidence in Him assuredly brings success: perhaps God's blessing even in this world, or certainly the attainment of one's last end in the next world. Nature and all the goods of the earth are only waiting for men to make proper use of them to produce benefits for those who use them and for those for whom they are used, out of Christian charity founded on the love of God. There was no better doctrine to keep the Romans, accustomed to realistic action and intellectual supremacy, from folding their arms and becoming a prey to oppressive despair. And, all things considered, Saint Augustine was right: the Roman Empire fell, but its vigorous and practical spirit was preserved for the West and continued to exert its influence — but only in co-operation with a Christian philosophy of life and conception of the world. Thus the bishop of the Roman province of Africa performed for a new civilized society a most valuable service in transmitting the intellectual culture of antiquity, Roman realism, and the Roman's delight in productive work.

His attitude and his admonitions have encouraged the bishops and priests of the Catholic Church to remain bravely at their posts, whatever tribulations might befall. In a sermon which Saint Augustine preached on the occasion of an episcopal consecration he described the ideal bishop in these words:

> He who rules over the people must first know that he is the servant of many. Nor ought he to be ashamed of that, since neither has the Lord of Lords deemed it below His dignity to serve us. . . . We are servants through Him through whom we are also free. . . . We are both rulers and servants, but we rule only if we know how to serve. . . . It is easy to imagine splendors, to enjoy honors, and to lend one's ear to flatterers; to suffer reprimands, to accept insults calmly, to pray for the reviler — that is the chalice, the repast of the Lord.[80]

Once while Augustine was absent, his priests, paralyzed with terror over the approaching enemy, interrupted their care for the poor. Learning of this he wrote to them:

> I exhort you not to allow yourselves to be overcome by the disturbances of this world, for you see those things have come to pass which

---

80. *Aurelii Augustini tractatus inediti,* ed. G. Morin, Tr. XXXII, pp. 142 sq.

our Lord and Saviour, who cannot lie, has foretold. Not only must you refrain from curtailing your works of mercy, but you must do even more than ordinarily. Just as, when one sees the walls of the house shaking, one flees in all haste to the place which affords a firm support, so ought Christian hearts hasten to stow away goods in the heavenly treasury instead of amassing them on earth where they foresee the imminent collapse of this world from the increase of tribulations.[81]

When the Vandals invaded Africa and no one could stem their advance, bishops and priests asked the bishop of Hippo to indicate their course of action: whether they should remain, or flee as some Spanish bishops had done. Saint Augustine earnestly exhorted the petitioners to persevere in their communities under all circumstances, to implore God, who alone could avert the danger, and to keep themselves equally prepared for life as well as for death:

> If it be not possible that this chalice pass from you, may the will of God be done. God cannot will anything evil. The shepherds ought to save themselves with their faithful or endure with them what it pleases the Father to send them.[82]

Such manly words were not spoken in vain; rather, they were universally followed, for they came from him who, as the greatest Latin Doctor of the Church, was accorded a unique authority in the West.

When the seventy-five-year-old Saint Augustine breathed forth his soul on August 28, 430, without fear as he had taught others, the Vandals were besieging the city of Hippo and it was doomed to destruction. His mission had been fulfilled a hundredfold, and through it was firmly established the intellectual and cultural mission of Rome.

---

81. *Ep.* 122.
82. *Ep.* 228.

CHAPTER THREE

THE PAPACY UNDER LEO THE GREAT —
FALL OF THE WESTERN ROMAN EMPIRE

ALL the seeds sown by Saint Augustine, Saint Ambrose, and other Christian writers would have perished but for custodians who advocated and transmitted unadulterated to new generations the thought of these spiritually-minded men in the same sense in which it had been expressed.

At no time was it so urgently necessary that Christian traditions be preserved in their purity as in the period from the middle of the fifth century to the eighth century. The end of the fifth century, in particular, might have seen these traditions discarded, together with the vestiges of the culture of antiquity, had not Christianity been represented by an organized institution, the Roman Catholic Church. The first requirement of stable organization, a unifying bond and a governing authority whose transmission is based on fixed norms, was supplied by the Church with her head, the pope in Rome. Upon the collapse of the Western Roman Empire, the pope represented the supreme authority amid the chaos resulting from the violent onslaughts which attended the migration of nations and threatened to obliterate everything. This authority alone was able to maintain itself in the West, and instead of diminishing, it increased and was strengthened by the storms. The pressing need for a rallying point where some support could still be found, naturally induced the Romans to do their utmost to preserve and augment it.

The papal authority has its indestructible foundation in the words of the Saviour: "Thou art Peter, and upon this rock I will build My Church." Thereby, the authority of a ruler was conferred upon Saint Peter and the office of the supreme government of the Church vested in him. This figure of speech used by the Saviour is followed by a second: "And I will give thee the keys of the kingdom of heaven." Proof of the veritable transmission of the power conferred upon Saint Peter to those who regarded themselves as his

111

successors, depends first of all upon the historical evidence of Saint
Peter's presence in Rome. This latter is now admitted by Protestant
scholars.[1] Though the primacy has an intrinsic foundation and is in
no wise exclusively the product of an evolution connected with Saint
Peter's labors in the capital of the Roman Empire, still the historian
is wholly free to point out how the authority established by Christ's
words unfolded itself only gradually and how it was favored in its
development by external circumstances. Any Catholic interested in
tracing this development may legitimately do so; just as the early
Christians pointed out the external circumstances at the time of
the Saviour which favored the spread of Christian teaching.

As early as the end of the fifth century Pope Gelasius entertained such thoughts when he wrote: "Christ led the Prince of the
Apostles to Rome, the mistress of nations, in a marvelous manner
in order that He might guide the first and greatest Peter in the city
which excelled all other cities."[2] The working of Providence is apparent when we ask the question whether or not the development of
the primacy would have been equally promoted had Saint Peter not
gone to Rome but remained in Antioch. In that case, the bishops
of Rome, without being able to lay claim to the succession of Saint
Peter, would have contested (to say the least) the precedence of his
successors at Antioch. They would have acted with the same lack of
intrinsic foundation as did the bishops of Constantinople against
ancient Rome. Indeed, they undoubtedly would have done this
even more emphatically, for no city of the world could vie with
Rome. The poet Horace had given classic expression to this in the
famous lines:

> *Alme sol, curru nitido diem qui*
> *Promis et celas aliusque et idem*
> *Nasceris, possis nihil urbe Roma*
> *Visere majus!*[3]

1. Lietzmann, *Petrus und Paulus,* Bonn, 1915.
2. Gelasius, *Tractatus II: De damnatione nominum Petri et Acacii,* c. 10, ed., Thiel,
Epistolae (Braunsberg, 1868), p. 529.
3. *Carmen sec.* 9-12.

In the event we are supposing, the great advantages which the ancient mistress of the world offered through her splendor and her geographical position as the center of the Mediterranean countries, which contributed so much to the development of the Christian community in Rome and quickly carried every authoritative word throughout the Roman Empire, could not have been utilized. And, on the other hand, the martyrs who here remained loyal to their faith against the despotic orders of the pagan state shone brighter than anywhere else.

The vast population of Rome soon made its Christian community the largest and most noteworthy. From a letter of Pope Cornelius we are able to make some estimate of the number of the faithful, since we find therein the statement that the clergy together with the bishop numbered 154 persons, among whom were 46 presbyters. Besides the clergy, 1,500 widows and needy persons were supported by the community. This was about the middle of the third century, during the persecutions. The Roman community at this time, accordingly, has been computed to have already numbered from 30,000 to 50,000 members. In the year 419 we read of 70 priests. At a synod in the year 499, 74 priests are recorded by name as being present and we learn that there were at that time 29 titular churches — that is, churches which were the centers of regular pastoral activities — 15 or 20 of which we can assume existed as early as Diocletian's reign. These older *tituli* were Roman private mansions donated by wealthy owners for ecclesiastical purposes. This again permits us to draw an inference regarding the civic status of the community's members. If the Christian community was already a factor in the persecution era, we can argue that it grew tremendously from the time of Constantine, who, through his munificence in erecting the basilica over the tomb of Saint Peter and in donating the Lateran palace to the pope, gave the successors of the Prince of the Apostles a position of external splendor. When later the emperor transferred his seat to the new capital on the confines of Asia, the pope took up his residence in an imperial palace of ancient Rome.

This last incident tended to show, even to those incapable of perceiving the internal causes of events, in what direction the development in Rome was moving. The authority which was to be the representative, not only of Rome, but also of Western culture, was clearly unfolding itself. If what can easily be discerned in the cases of Saint Ambrose and Saint Augustine was true of all bishops — that after Christianity became the state religion they acquired great influence in civil affairs through their jurisdiction over disputes between clerics and laymen, through their judgments in all civil lawsuits voluntarily submitted to a bishop for decision, and through their protection of the indigent and those without rights — it was pre-eminently true of the Roman bishop. Everywhere he was called upon by the state to supervise the local government and the administration of justice, both departments standing only too much in need of such control. His external position became a matter of importance especially for the poorer inhabitants of the city, because the maintenance of the poor had devolved almost entirely upon the pope. Landed estates about Rome, in Italy, and beyond, in ever-increasing numbers, were placed at his disposal for this purpose.

On the other hand, for the papacy and the Church there was increasing danger from the possession of external power in the midst of such a strangely mixed population, accustomed to all the pleasures of a refined and decadent culture. That conception of Rome which led Saint Peter to call it Babylon, endured for a long time.[4] Tacitus had said of Rome: "All the crimes and all the outrages of the world flow together here."[5] And indeed, all the evils of a metropolitan culture were manifest. Public immorality and superstition necessarily infected the weaker Christians, and the number of these increased when, in the fourth and fifth centuries, many pseudo-converts were enrolled who had become Christians only because of the external change in public life and the pressure from above. Questionable characters also entered the clerical state: their ambition was to cultivate relations with the prominent and wealthy classes, to imitate them by dressing in the latest fashion, to please women, and to acquire gifts or legacies, if not even more dubious favors. Saint Jerome caustically described, possibly with some ex-

---

4. I Petr., 5, 13. Cf. Euseb., *Hist. Eccl.* II, c. 14.
5. *Ann.*, 15, c. 44.

aggeration, a number of these clerical confreres in a letter to the virgin Eustochium:

> They are concerned with their dress, whether it is scented with perfume, and whether their footwear is supple and fits well. Their hair is curled with hot irons, their fingers glitter with rings, and they walk with a mincing step lest possibly their soles get wet from the somewhat damp ground. Seeing them advance, one would sooner take them for suitors than for clerics.

He then sketches a satiric picture of a certain clerical personage who was especially typical of such gentlemen of the period:

> He rises with the sun and has his program of visits submitted to him. He ponders how he may shorten the distances and then sets out on his way at an unusually early hour. He advances almost as far as the sleeping apartments. If he sees a small cushion, a beautiful towel or any household utensil, he praises and admires it until it is given to him, for everyone is afraid to offend the town crier. Chastity and fasting do not appeal to him. He judges his breakfast by the rich odors and calls it a sacred agape. One sees him everywhere with his unmannered and impudent stare, his mouth forever ready for abusive speech. Wherever any news is heard, he magnifies and exaggerates the rumor. He changes horses every hour, and they are so dashing and fiery that one might well take him for the brother of the king of Thrace.[6]

Even the papacy could not always escape the danger of worldliness of spirit and the desire for power and honor. Who will be surprised at this? Only he who does not know human nature. One can only be surprised at the fact that the papacy could always be restored to the exalted mission assigned it. But it will ever remain Peter's bark, cast to and fro on a stormy sea. When the Roman Empire was vanishing, the danger was not yet so great that the incumbents of the papacy would allow themselves and their dignity to be absorbed in the enjoyment of power, in luxury, and in devotion to culture. This occurred only at the end of the Middle Ages. The ideal conception of the sacerdotal and pastoral dignity, such as a Saint Ambrose and a Saint Augustine had acquired and further devel-

---

6. Hieron., *Ep. 22 ad Eustochium, De custodia virginitatis,* n. 28: Migne, *P. L.,* XXII, 414.

oped, was too lofty to tolerate such things. Above all, the contrast between the worldly and ecclesiastical attitudes of mind was then far too vivid, because it coincided largely with the gulf that separated paganism and Christianity. But soon after the favor of the State and the court had externally exalted the Church, it became apparent that the papal office could become at times the object of ambitious efforts, leading to public scandal.

An occasion for this was provided by the papal elections, which then took place in the same manner as the elections of the other bishops. The papacy was an elective monarchy. According to human calculations, this furnished the best guarantee for safeguarding authority and permitting the free choice of the best-qualified candidate. It borrowed the best element from monarchy by entrusting the supreme direction and power to one man for life, yet was able to exclude the evils inherent in a secular elective monarchy. With worldly sovereigns the elective monarchy always tends to become a hereditary monarchy, because the father naturally desires to procure the succession for his son, although he thereby weakens the institution of monarchy, making birth and not fitness the determining factor.

This weakening tendency was of course eliminated in the sacerdotal elective monarchy. We do see cases similar to those occurring in a hereditary monarchy, in which well-meaning bishops and priests sought toward the end of their lives to determine their successors by designation. Thus did Saint Augustine solemnly constrain his community to accept the successor he had proposed. But the danger connected with designation was soon realized, since the elections could then be suppressed completely; and, with the establishment of a hereditary monarchy the transition to a purely temporal power would finally have been effected, as was done, for example, in Montenegro. Designation was consequently soon forbidden in Rome as well as in the other episcopal sees.

With freedom of election, on the other hand, one had to accept the concomitant abuses. The clergy and the populace took part in the election in the presence of the neighboring bishops, who had to give their assent and consecrate the person elected. Among the laity the high officials naturally took precedence, just as the higher clergy played a more important role than the lower. Under such conditions it was almost inevitable that at times ambitious members of the clergy should find a way, by means of factions which they fostered, to swing the election to themselves and acquire the position which they chiefly desired for its power and influence. The reaction which necessarily set in against such attempts, provoked in turn double elections and schisms. And such dissensions unhappily afforded the latent passions of the populace the opportunity of breaking out into open violence and of lowering the prestige of the Roman Church. Thus in 366 Ursinus began a schism against the duly elected Pope Damasus, which was accompanied by bloody street battles. The election of Pope Boniface I in the year 418 was also attended by acts of violence, when the archdeacon Eulalius procured his own election in the Lateran basilica with the support of Symmachus, the prefect of the city. In both instances the emperors had to intervene and remove the intruders. These were the first schisms, but they were not to be the last.

Such occurrences could only temporarily obscure the high mission which belonged to the popes as the bearers of the primacy, and which unfolded itself more clearly from century to century through the decisions emanating from Rome in matters of ecclesiastical teaching and discipline. The papal letters composed in this period, though they have come down to us in mere fragments, testify how often the popes were engaged in such matters and how many-sided was the activity which they exercised as the supreme custodians of doctrine and morals. Though there was no lack of contradiction and disobedience against their decisions, the chain of expressed acknowledgments of the primacy forged its links ever more strongly. Saint Ambrose wrote: "Where Peter is, there is the Church";[7] and from a passage of one of Saint Augustine's sermons we can justly derive the saying: "Rome has spoken, the case is finished."[8]

Even though the Orient, after the bishop of Constantinople was forced to serve the interests of imperial despotism, jealously

---

7. *Enarr. in psal.* 40, c. 30.
8. *Sermo* 131, c. 10: Iam enim de hac causa duo concilia missa sunt ad sedem apostolicam; inde etiam rescripta venerunt. Causa finita est. Utinam aliquando finiatur error!

strove to create its own ecclesiastical center, this move did not result at the time in more than an elevation in rank of the bishop of the new imperial city. The Council of Constantinople, in the year 381, wished to accord him the second place in the series of patriarchs — a design which Rome could legitimately reject. But the more such efforts manifested themselves in the East, the closer did the Western part of the Roman Empire unite itself with the papacy. Here the pope was not only primate, but patriarch and metropolitan of the principal country, Italy. Above all, he was bishop of the unique center for which people felt the greater concern as the political government (which no longer dared reside there) began to show signs of instability.

Though the terror of Alaric soon passed, the year 410 was to be the beginning of the end for Rome. To later ages, the Roman sepulchral inscriptions of the period speak a plain language. Up to that year, particular attention had been paid to their composition. They are suddenly interrupted, and those which gradually reappear are only a laborious and faltering imitation of the old models.[9] Rome no longer afforded a sanctuary for the peaceful pursuit of culture and learning, because no one any longer felt himself secure. But where in the West did there remain security or any power able to protect the individual?

Emperor Honorius, son of the great Theodosius, was a weakling to whom the West had fallen by partition. When, out of petty jealousy, he beheaded his father-in-law, the Vandal Stilicho, who had been victorious in encounters with Alaric and Radagaisus, he robbed himself of his sole support. He could only look on helplessly at Alaric's march on Rome, and contented himself with insuring the safety of his own person in the fortified city of Ravenna, which was protected by swamps. When he died in 423, Rome gave him no honor other than burial in the mausoleum at the tomb of the Prince of the Apostles. His sister, Galla Placidia, widow of the general Constantius who died a premature death, governed for her son, Valentinian III; but with all her prudence she was unable to accomplish tasks which in a particular degree demanded masculine

---

9. De Rossi, *Inscriptiones christ. urbis Romae,* I, 250.

energy. Under Valentinian III Africa was lost to the Vandals, Britain to the Anglo-Saxons; in Gaul alone was the honor of the Roman Empire upheld for a time by the general Aëtius. Yet he was able to repel the invading Huns under Attila at Châlons-sur-Marne, near Troyes, only with the aid of the Germanic tribes which had already entered Gaul.

This weakness of the political power drove the Romans in the West to seek their religious and moral support in the papacy. Thus they might have at least a spiritual bond which would hold them together. There, in times of danger, they sought at least moral help and support. In Rome itself the people flocked to the pope, the only authority which did not fail nor falter, but rather gained in strength. Here was the one remaining office which upheld the reputation of the Roman name. The incumbents of the papal dignity had risen from among them; they were men of their own blood. Almost all the popes of the first four centuries came from Rome or the vicinity of Rome. Rare exceptions were Damasus (366-384), who was Spanish in origin, and Zosimus (417-418), forerunner of the Greeks, whose numbers would markedly increase in Rome when she fell under the domination of the Eastern Roman Empire. In these men who had come forth from the Roman clergy could the ancient wisdom of the Romans in governing and directing the nations be perpetuated. They possessed also practical sense and a strong feeling for justice, which were to be supported by those ideal principles upon which their spiritual power rested. It was not easy to unite these two elements, for the passions still surviving despite all the distress, and the worldly spirit of the great mass of the Roman population, only too often touched even members of the clergy. For all that, there was no lack of popes who realized in themselves the ideal of a highpriest and a good shepherd; as models to succeeding generations, they kept the lofty mission of the papacy from lapsing into oblivion and permitted it to shine forth again and again.

Such a pope was Leo I (440-461). The first to be given the surname of "Great" as an expression of the people's admiration and gratitude, he signifies for us the high point of the papacy in Christian antiquity. It is incorrect to regard Leo I as the originator of the Roman primacy or to place its inception in his period. The truth is this: that the primacy, which is founded on the words of the Saviour, developed slowly under the influence of external circumstances and emerges into the light of the world's history fullblown at the time of Leo I.

The great luster which now surrounds it is produced chiefly by the contrast between the Orient and the Occident. In the Orient contrary to expectation, the imperial power had been newly strengthened, thanks mainly to the wisdom of the illustrious granddaughter of Theodosius the Great, Saint Pulcheria. At first she reigned for and with her pious but weak brother, Theodosius II; after 450, when she decided to marry the aged senator Marcian, she ruled as empress. All this time she determined the destinies of the Eastern Roman Empire. The internal consolidation of that empire can be gleaned from the collection of general constitutions issued from the time of Constantine. This codification of Roman Law, completed in 430 and known as the Codex Theodosianus, was to become important for the West also, including the regions governed by Germans.

Parallel with this internal and external political consolidation, which provided even the Western Roman Empire of Valentinian III with some support, we see the Orient divided religiously and disrupted by profound dissensions. No remedy could be found but an approach to the pope in Rome, that he might by his intervention save the unity of the strife-torn Church. Thus the pope, as the supreme religious head, helps the East, while the Eastern Roman emperor supports the Western Roman emperor on his tottering throne. What a consolation this must have been to the Western Romans in those dark times!

Leo I expressed that satisfaction in his clear and forcible language during the course of a famous sermon which compared the Rome of old with the new Rome and praised this latest mission she was fulfilling. He delivered this sermon on June 29, the feast of the Apostles Peter and Paul. "These are the two saints through whom the Gospel was made known to thee and through whom thou, once the teacher of error, hast become a disciple of truth." Thus he addresses his city, which is now serving him in the spiritual direction of the world.

They, thy saintly fathers, thy true shepherds, have founded thee anew; they have left behind them a creation destined for heaven — a creation much better and happier than the one of those two who built thy first earthly walls; of whom the one who gave thee thy name defiled thee with the murder of his brother. Through them thou hast attained great fame and become a chosen, a priestly, and a kingly city; as the seat of Saint Peter thou hast become the capital of the world, and by means of thy divine religion thou couldst subject wider territories than formerly through thy worldly power. Adorned with many victories, thou hast once wielded thy scepter over lands and seas; and still thou hast not conquered so much in war as thou hast now by means of the peace of Christianity.... Divine Providence has guided the destinies of the Roman Empire. The many states were united into one empire and were bound to one another that the preaching of the Gospel should find the ways prepared ... and the light of truth, which was revealed for the salvation of all nations, diffuse itself more effectively from the head through the whole body of the world.... What an aftergrowth the two Apostles, like divine grains of seed, have brought our city by their sacrificial death is shown by the thousands of martyrs whose tombs surround the city; a whole nation of martyrs, whose splendor attracts everything to itself and constitutes a true diadem of precious stones for Rome.[10]

No craving for power grew up in Leo's heart from this joy of his over the new splendor and mission of Rome, for he himself kept in mind that of which he reminded other bishops: that they must represent the teaching of Him who said: "Learn from Me, for I am meek and humble of heart; and you will find rest for your souls. For My yoke is easy and My burden light." Characteristically, Leo concludes a deeply earnest letter addressed to his vicar in Illyricum, Archbishop Anastasius of Thessalonica, with these words:

> But we will certainly not experience this in ourselves unless we also take to heart what the Lord said: "He who is greatest among you shall be your servant. And whoever exalts himself shall be humbled, and whoever humbles himself shall be exalted."[11]

He knows that his power is different from that of the temporal ruler; that it is spiritual, hence the emperor need not regard it with

---

10. Translator's note: Here Schnürer uses, in the main, Grisar's free German rendering of *Sermo* 82, from *Gesch. Roms,* 70-71.

11. *Ep.* 14.

jealousy, and that it proceeded from a poor fisherman. For this reason he could freely express such thoughts before the emperor without fear of being misunderstood. He did so on an occasion which epitomizes the change of the times better than anything else.

The emperor Valentinian III had come to Rome in the year 450 with his wife, Eudoxia, his mother, Galla Placidia, and a great retinue. His purpose was to express his veneration of the Prince of the Apostles by presenting himself in the pope's own basilica on the feast of the Roman primacy, then celebrated on February 22. In the presence of the emperor the pope addressed to the Romans a homily (discovered only in modern times) in honor of Saint Peter:

> Behold, to a poor, insignificant man like Peter was given by Christ the first and greatest city of the world for guidance. The scepters of kings have submitted themselves to the wood of the Cross; the purple of the court is subject to the blood of Christ and of the martyrs. The emperor, crowned with brilliant jewels and accompanied by innumerable warriors, comes to ask for the intercession of the fisherman. In his merits the ruler recognizes a greater adornment than in the precious stones which bedeck his own garments. What a mystery of wisdom, what a wondrous working of God's justice! The rich desire to benefit by the merits of the poor; noble and prominent people prostrate themselves before the tombs of the saints of humble rank.[12]

This was the proper spirit for uniting the whole Church and guiding it amid rending political changes; but besides this, it constituted the new bond which was to embrace the territory of the Western Roman Empire when its several parts threatened to split away. Rome was to become the intellectual center of a new society in the West; she provided the models for everything that still held the common framework together.

But these were all ecclesiastical matters, both externally and internally. We see this in ecclesiastical art — a field for which Rome naturally furnished more models than any other city in the West, since her traditional art experienced a revival following the accession

---

12. Morin, in "Anecdota Maredsolana," I (1893), 409, according to Grisar's German rendering (315). [Translator's note: Morin does not here subscribe to Pope Leo's authorship of this sermon. Cf. *Etudes, Textes, Découvertes,* I ("Anecdota Maredsolana" — Seconde Série, 1913), 35 and 515.]

of the Christian emperors. Although this revival merely followed the decadent trend, it was nevertheless capable of original expression. The basilican style became the established type for church edifices in the West. It had developed spontaneously in Rome from those stately private mansions which Christians used as assembly rooms during the persecution era. In Italy and beyond, indeed throughout the whole West, during the first millennium of Christianity, this style remained the standard for buildings of Christian worship and for assembly halls. This is one obvious demonstration of the influence Rome was now exercising in the West. Again, the still highly polished documents emanating from Leo I's chancery retained their metrically constructed conclusions of sentences. This style was imitated in the West in liturgical formulas of prayer as well as in other selected forms of writing; hence we speak of a *cursus leoninus*. Though later the knowledge of this art was partially lost, it did not die out completely. In the eleventh century it again experienced a revival in Rome, particularly in the papal chancery; and gave the ecclesiastical language a peculiar charm and warmth that compensate for certain defects from the viewpoint of correct classical style. This embellishment of the language, which men continued to cultivate, and to which they added rhyme, a usage just coming into vogue, enables us to recognize medieval Latin as an enduring language, capable of richly expressing diverse emotions in musical accents.

With her liturgy, Rome naturally served as a model in all places where the Sacred Mysteries were celebrated in the Latin language. The need for making the Mass prayers of the Roman priests available in their entirety was answered by the Roman sacramentaries. The oldest of these has been ascribed to Leo I, but erroneously so, for it originated in the sixth century and records the Roman liturgy of that day. The next sacramentary in the series bears the name of Pope Gelasius (492-496), but it actually dates from the seventh century.

The measures of organization undertaken by individual popes had an even more direct effect than these general impulses which in the course of time emanated from Rome as the ecclesiastical center of the West. Leo I gave evidence of the broad view of the ruler of the Roman world on such questions of organization. He was intent on systematically carrying through the institution of metropolitan sees whereby the bishops of an ecclesiastical province were placed under a metropolitan. Next above the latter were the patriarchs. Himself the patriarch of the West, the pope had a special vicar at Arles (which had replaced Treves as the administrative center for the temporal affairs of Gaul) and another at Thessalonica for Illyricum. Leo clearly defined the authority of all of these, stressing the fact that the powers of metropolitans and patriarchs are based on the statutes set up by the Holy Fathers, but that the primacy is of divine institution. Through the intermediary members the responsibility for the whole Church was to be concentrated in the one chair of Peter and no part was to be separated from the head.

There was one deed in particular, however, for which Leo the Great was always gratefully remembered and which the popular fancy soon shrouded in legend. This was his effective intercession in behalf of Rome with Attila, who was advancing on the city.

The leader of the Huns, alternately menacing the Eastern and the Western Roman Empire, had become the terror of all Europe. Neither the diplomacy of Byzantium nor the might of the Germanic peoples seemed capable of driving the wild hordes back toward the East. The "Scourge of God" threatened all peoples without exception with complete annihilation or enslavement. To be sure, the strategic ability of Aëtius in league with the Visigoths, succeeded in arresting his progress in Gaul by the battle of the nations on the Catalaunian Fields. But although this defeat forced Attila to retire to the Plain of Theiss in Hungary, his force was by no means exhausted. In the winter of 451-452 he mobilized once more and invaded Italy, where there was no one to offer him resistance. The important seaport of Aquileia was taken, plundered and destroyed so completely that the few surviving inhabitants despaired of rebuilding it. Instead they sought shelter in the protecting lagoons — a migration which resulted in the founding of Venice. Then Milan and Pavia were destroyed and the road to Rome lay open to the Huns.

The Roman senate took counsel with the emperor Valentinian III, who felt himself secure only in Ravenna whence he could very easily flee by ship to Constantinople. The senators knew but one expedient. They hoped an impressive embassy might persuade Attila to turn back — if necessary, by offering concessions which the delegation was fully empowered to grant. As its head they chose Pope Leo, the man to whom all ascribed the greatest authority and dignity, and associated with him the consul Albienus and the former praetorian prefect Trigetius. The delegation met Attila in his camp not far from Mantua. We do not know exactly what inducements the pope laid before the leader of the Huns. Prosper the Aquitanian, who wrote his *Chronicle* while Leo was still alive, says very briefly that everything was fulfilled "that Leo had expected in his trust in heaven, which never forsakes the pious in their hazards." There are indications that Attila feared to lay hands on Rome, remembering that sudden death struck down the Visigothic chieftain Alaric soon after his capture of the city. It is very possible that Leo induced the thought by referring to the mighty princes of the Apostles, who could invoke God's punishment upon Attila if he seized Rome. Certain it is that after the pope had spoken Attila left Italy, and Leo was hailed as the deliverer of Rome. Later — from the eleventh century — it began to be related that during the interview the Apostles Peter and Paul had appeared in the heavens over the pope and threatened Attila with drawn swords. This legend has been repeatedly depicted in art; its most famous representation is that by Raphael in the Vatican Stanze.

On another occasion the pope had the task of interceding for Rome in terrible days the affliction of which he was able to curtail and mitigate. Valentinian III had, with shortsighted jealousy, censured Aëtius, the only general on whom Rome could still rely; and when the accused defended himself, the emperor, beside himself with passion, personally murdered Aëtius, with the aid of the eunuch Heraclius. In retaliation the emperor himself was killed afterward in the streets of Rome (March 16, 455). The usurper Maximus, who had instigated the assassination, enjoyed the imperial authority only briefly. Within three months the Vandal king Genseric crossed over from Africa with his plundering hordes, and Maximus, attempting to flee, was dragged from his horse by the embittered mob and torn to pieces. Genseric rushed into the city, now bereft of its emperor and left without defense. Only Leo, accompanied by his priests, courageously approached Genseric and through his petitions obtained from him the promise that the inhabitants would be spared fire and sword.

This sack of Rome (455) was much more terrible than that of Alaric, which had lasted only three days. For fourteen days, from the fifteenth to the twenty-ninth of June, the feast of the Apostles, the Vandals pillaged Rome. Probably Leo had succeeded in having the looting cease on this day, as he probably also contrived that the two basilicas of the Apostles, as well as the Lateran, the principal church of the Bishop of Rome, should escape spoliation. While the Vandals dragged off the widowed empress Eudoxia to Africa, together with many captives and an immense amount of booty, they allowed the pope to remain in Rome with the treasures of his principal churches intact.

The Romans now realized what they possessed in the pope and in the tombs of the Apostles — all that had survived the catastrophe. The courage with which the Pontiff had twice intervened for the unhappy city had tremendously increased the prestige of the papacy throughout the whole of Christendom. Only a very few pagans still scoffed at Christianity; a Saint Augustine would not have been forced in the days of Attila and Genseric to write in defense of Christian doctrine against the charge of having caused the fall of Rome. Henceforth Rome had but one meaning: it was the city of the popes, the successors of Saint Peter.

This was a very important outcome. It was brought about partly by the circumstances of the time, partly by Leo the Great's own firmness of principle, his powers of quick decision, and his practical judgment, qualities above all necessary for a man who would rule. Yet it was hardly able to produce a feeling of triumph in the supreme ruler of the Church. Even if Christian humility, which he also possessed, had not forbidden this, a survey of the Roman world about him would have prohibited it. Only a few gave evidence of a true ecclesiastical and Christian spirit. Leo's own utterances tell us that the great masses had become Christian merely in name, without real inner conversion. One of his sermons complains that the horrors of the sack of Rome by Genseric had been forgotten only too rapidly and that few attended the services of reparation and thanksgiving instituted after those terrible days:

I am ashamed to say it, but I dare not keep it secret: greater zeal is shown in serving the spirit of the world and the demons than in serving the holy Apostles; mad spectacles attract more people than the shrines of martyrs. Was it indeed the circus games which preserved you from death by the sword, or was it not rather the prayers of the saints? Had we not deserved the full anger of God? And have we not been spared only that we might repent and seek forgiveness?[13]

From the same sermon we gather that there were not lacking those who ascribed the departure of the Vandals to the influence of favorable stars, and thus still strove to propagate pagan superstition. Leo also condemns a practice borrowed from the Manicheans whereby many, after climbing the steps before Saint Peter's and before they entered the basilica, would turn and greet the risen sun with ceremonial bows. He reminds these ignorant creatures that the radiant solar disk is a reflection of the Creator who is adored in the churches.[14] He earnestly warns the nominal converts that they must not be content with their renunciation of service to pagan gods.

There is no advantage for us in feeling secure in the freedom of the faith unless we resist immoral desires. The heart of man betrays itself in the character of his works, and the nature of his disposition becomes recognizable by the variety of his actions.[15]

It is true that moral reform was particularly difficult amid the continual convulsions that marked the last phase of the perishing empire. The assassination or deposition of emperors rapidly followed their elevation; thus, the Germanic general Ricimer, at the head of the Germanic mercenaries, after he had deposed Avitus in 456 controlled the imperial throne for sixteen years. Finally the German troops balked at shedding their blood to protect emperors who were such in name only, and when the Roman general Orestes placed his youthful son Romulus Augustulus on the throne, they declared they would henceforth serve only their own interests. They demanded that the quartering act be reformed and their maintenance guaranteed by enjoining the Roman proprietor to relinquish one

---

13. Translator's note: *Sermo* 84, according to Grisar's rendering (79, n. 1).
14. *Sermo* 27, c. 4.
15. *Sermo* 36.

third of his house to them, no longer as usufruct but as their own property. On rejection of the demand, the Herulian Odoacer placed himself at their head to enforce it. He defeated Orestes in 476 and compelled Romulus Augustulus to resign the imperial dignity, while he himself claimed all power in Italy as king. Thus the line of the Western Roman emperors came to an inglorious end. After Syagrius had also been defeated in northern Gaul by Clovis in 486, no Roman general remained in command within the limits of the Western Roman Empire. Kings of the Germanic race reigned everywhere.

In Rome itself they were hardly conscious at the time that a great period in history had ended with the ending of the Western imperial line. The kingship of the military leader of the Germanic troops was considered to be transitory, and those among the senators who played power politics looked to Eastern Rome which, they hoped, would sooner or later expel the Germans from Italy. The Roman administration naturally still continued to maintain itself, above all in Italy. The situation was otherwise in Spain and Gaul, where the Germans had already been established for a considerable time. There the first efforts to reach an understanding with the Germans had already been made, since a lasting association of the two races was no longer deemed impossible. We see this in the case of two clerics who, like Saint Augustine, began to write in order to bring home to the Roman Christians thoughts which would keep them from erring in their faith and continuing to live as pagans.

One of these writers is the Spaniard Orosius, a priest of Lusitania, who twice came to Hippo to consult Saint Augustine. During his second visit he received the inspiration from Augustine to write a historical work which would treat in detail an idea not fully developed in *The City of God.* Christians, in the face of the tribulations of the time, might come to doubt God's solicitude for man. Orosius had designed to provide them with a historical record showing that in former ages also men fared badly — frequently even worse than in the present. This work, entitled *Seven Books of History against the Pagans,* never wholly completed, was composed in the years 417-418, when the Visigoths were spreading over Spain.

Formally considered, the work is very remarkable as a first attempt at a Christian history of the world, and it enjoyed a high reputation in the Middle Ages, giving impetus to the writing of similar works. A great step forward was certainly taken in the plan followed by Orosius, for ancient historiographers had always treated history from an exclusively national standpoint and with a nationally limited outlook. Orosius himself writes with a definite tendency, but his is of a different type; it is bound up with his apologetic ideas. He exaggerates the consolations which history can furnish in dismal times by assembling all the miseries into one compilation which is often superficial, and magnifying the former misfortunes while minimizing present ones. But though his judgment is sometimes biased, there is no dearth of stirring and new ideas — ideas never before advanced. Referring to the uninterrupted wars by means of which the Romans forged their world empire, he suggests an absolutely sound verdict condemning Roman imperialism:

> Behold, while Rome happily conquers, everything outside of Rome is miserably conquered. Is this drop of painfully acquired good fortune, to which a single city owes its bliss, to be so highly valued in the midst of the vast flood of misery which overwhelms the whole world?[16]

He appreciates, indeed, the cultural unity of the Roman Empire, which has made it possible for him on his journeys to be understood and contract friendships everywhere. But there is no longer any trace of the nationalistic Roman pride. It is the unity of the Romano-Christian cultural world that Orosius praises, because as "a Roman and a Christian" he was everywhere readily welcomed "by Christians and Romans."

> Among the Romans it is as a Roman, among the Christians it is as a Christian, and among men it is as a man, that I appeal to the state on the strength of the laws, that I appeal to conscience on the strength of religion, and that I appeal to nature on the strength of the common unity. For a time I regard every country as my own because the native land which is truly mine and which I love, is not on this earth.[17]

It is the finer cultural world, based on Christian convictions and customs, that he appreciates as a benefit. One cannot say on this

---

16. Lib. V, c. 1, 3-4.
17. Ibid., c. 2, 3 and 6.

account that Orosius was devoid of patriotism. His heart also beat for his home — home, in a narrower sense, meaning the land of his birth. Thus we see in him the rise of a new national feeling, quite compatible with a universal culture, but having nothing in common with an authoritarian state like that of the Romans, which ignored the individualities of nations. Sadly he reminds his countrymen how for two hundred years the Romans warred upon their forefathers, destroying their independence. He even suggests the hope that perhaps better times will result for them from the present tribulation.

This explains, too, why Orosius regards the barbarians with different eyes than the other writers of the period. He takes pains — of course his only purpose is to comfort his contemporaries — to scrape together all the good things, and all the less bad things, that he can find to say about the barbarians. They are not nearly so barbarous and inhuman as they are represented to be. They are beginning to cultivate the fields. They let him depart in peace who does not wish to remain among them. They treat the Romans who remain as their allies and friends,

> so that many Romans, indeed, are found among them who prefer freedom in poverty under the barbarians to the anxiety occasioned by the payment of tribute under the Romans. If, however, it were true that the barbarians had been permitted to enter the Roman domain for the sole purpose that the churches of Christ generally, in the East and the West, might be filled with Huns, Suevians, Vandals, Burgundians, and diverse innumerable nations of believers, then the mercy of God should be extolled and praised, because so many nations would thus acquire a knowledge of the truth which they could find only in this way, be it even through the medium of our own upheaval.[18]

Thus Orosius recognizes a new mission for the Romans, a mission on which people had hardly cared to reflect before; namely, to bring Christianity to the nations waging war against them. He then pictures to himself a commonwealth of Christian nations, which he designates *Romania,* having a common Christian culture arising upon a Roman foundation.[19] We have here another noteworthy sign

---

18. Lib. VII, c. 41, 7-8.
19. Lib. III, c. 20, 11; VII, c. 43, 5.

of how Christian thought could broaden the mind; of how Christianity alone was capable of carrying the Romans safely through the chaos of the empire's collapse, meanwhile enabling their cultural mission to continue its function. The author of this earliest world chronicle was the first to interpret the signs of the times correctly and to have a true presentiment of the future.

These thoughts, which Orosius interspersed only casually throughout his work, doubtless received little immediate attention, being accepted merely as general expressions of consolation offered to relieve anxiety in current distress. They were not examined in detail. In later times, however, and especially in more recent times, men have noted the universal viewpoint which Orosius adopted as his point of departure, precisely to reproach him. They have blamed him for taking a pessimistic view of history because he observes everywhere only miseries and wars, a view which found many adherents in the Middle Ages. This accusation against Orosius was extended by some to the Christian conception of history and life in general. It is not erroneous to see the roots of Orosius' conception of history springing from the universal Christian conception of life. Since the Christian's end lies in the world beyond, he cannot seek his happiness in this world. That it is never completely found in this world is a fact of practical experience which Christians were not the first to discover. But they have the advantage: they do not in practice combine an embittering and self-tormenting pessimism with their religiously grounded pessimism, since they accept as their lot everything from God in grateful resignation — blessings as well as misfortunes. This explains the fact that we find in the representative of the pessimistic conception of history a remarkable hope at the same time for betterment within his own period, which distinguishes him from all his contemporaries. This hope is rooted in the assurance of victory given by Christian faith.

Another clerical writer of the fifth century pursued objectives similar to those of Orosius by urging Christians to look upon the trials that befell them as a merited punishment. This was the priest Salvian, who probably came from northern Gaul, for he had relatives in Cologne and speaks highly of Treves, which may have been his birthplace. In youth he had married Palladia, the daughter of a pagan, and later persuaded her to accept Christianity. After several years of marriage Salvian and his wife, like many others at that time, decided to embrace an ascetical life and to live together merely as brother and sister. Salvian attained a great age; he was still living about 480, when the Western Roman Empire was already extinct. He is designated as a priest of Marseilles.

About the middle of the fifth century he composed the work that is of interest to us here, *Eight Books on the Government of God,* which he dedicated to his former disciple, Bishop Salonius. The original title of the work seems to have been *On the Present Judgment of God,* but this perhaps was thought to be too harsh and consequently was replaced by another. The discarded title, however, indicated the contents better. Salvian wants to show how God judges men in his epoch. Here and there in his work Orosius had already touched upon the thought that we must not complain of evil fortune because it is a punishment for the injustices which we have committed. This is the only idea Salvian develops, but he does so more to accuse than to console. He is carrying on a controversy, not against pagans (at that time there were few pagans among the Romans about him), but against Christians unwilling to recognize God as the director of human destinies because He does not help the good nor punish the wicked. This was a conception which threatened to let down every moral barrier; men said there was no use, after all, in living a good and pious life since God does not care about man. Incensed, Salvian took up his pen to combat this lack of faith:

The Christian Romans murmur against God because He permits the barbarians to oppress them. But do not the Romans deserve this? They do not want to believe in God as they should, and still less do they want to live according to the faith. This affords Salvian the opportunity, while refuting these false and foolish objections, to sketch for us a terrible picture of the immorality and injustice still obtaining among the Christian Romans as a heritage from pagan times. The licentiousness, he declared, has even increased and deserves God's punishment. If anything, God is too lenient!

Expressing himself in passionate rhetoric, the controversialist may often have made his condemnations too harsh, but he does give us an extraordinarily graphic, though gloomy, portrayal of the moral conditions then prevailing. We see how these conditions had developed and how the realization of their seriousness had progressed. Salvian speaks about his time in an entirely different manner than Saint Augustine spoke of his. The bishop of Hippo wrote under the old Roman government which still protected him; whereas in Gaul when Salvian's picture was drawn, everything was at the actual point of collapse.

He makes no secret of the fact that all the power and material culture of the Roman Empire are gone. Rather, he expressly desires to show his readers this in order to expose their folly:

> We have learned to know religion; we are not excused by ignorance. We no longer enjoy the peace and wealth of former times. Everything that once existed has been taken away or changed; only the vices have grown. Nothing of the former peace and well-being has survived — except the crimes, which have not produced well-being. Where are the old treasures and dignities of the Romans? Once the Romans were strong, now they have no strength. The old Romans were feared, now we do the fearing; formerly the barbarian nations paid the Romans tribute, now we are tributaries to the barbarians. The enemy sell us the very enjoyment of the light of day; our whole welfare rests on our skillful dealing with them. How deep is our misfortune! What has become of us! And for this we even thank the barbarians, from whom we ransom ourselves with money. Could anything more abject and miserable befall us? And do we, who are in such a plight, believe that we are still living? In addition, we even make ourselves ridiculous. The gold which we pay we call gifts. We say that is a present which in reality is a price, the payment for our extremely hard and shameful social status. All prisoners enjoy their liberty once they have redeemed themselves; we redeem ourselves continuously but never become free.[20]

In the same way, without any hesitation, he frankly says: "The Roman state is already dead or in the last throes although it still appears to live."[21] This was about 450, before Attila's invasion of Gaul. Salvian had seen the truth with the penetrating observation of an impartial judge.

Beholding the somber picture of morals which he unveils, we too are brought to understand why the Roman Empire was ripe for

---

20. Lib. VI, c. 18, 98 sq.
21. Lib. IV, c. 6, 30.

destruction and had to fall. With justifiable disgust he describes how Christians retained a pagan infatuation for the disgraceful circus-games and immoral theatrical productions against which Pope Leo in Rome was likewise strongly complaining. Salvian writes:

> I ask you in conscience: which place shows greater crowds of Christian men, the arena of the public games or the sanctuary of God? . . . On every day of the Feralia [in February] they who call themselves Christians do not come to church, regardless of what holyday it is, or if they have really come not knowing there would be games, . . . they leave the church when they hear that they are taking place.[22]

Not all the misery could quell this rage for degrading entertainment. The few prominent citizens who survived the third capture of Treves demanded circus-games from the emperors as the best means of relief for the ruined city.[23] Revelry and the insane lust for pleasures did not cease to exist in the midst of the greatest distress. Salvian himself had witnessed banquets where elderly dignitaries lay full of meat and drink, bawling like madmen in their drunkenness, while the destruction of the city impended; in Cologne the enemy had entered the city while its officials were attending a wine party.[24]

He turns a searing light upon the worst sore afflicting Roman society: slavery, which has been called the great school of immorality. All too clearly we are brought to see what social misery was inextricably bound up with it. The slaves, he says, are accused justly, almost without exception, of being thieves. But why? Because they are not adequately remunerated or nourished. They are also charged with continually contemplating flight. But, considering the manner of their treatment, can one blame them for that? They are beaten by everyone, even by their fellow-slaves; they are rebuked as liars, but they are driven to deceit by the torture which awaits them.[25] Masters in most cases give slaves a bad example; if the

22. Lib. VI, c. 7, 37 sq.
23. Ibid., c. 15, 85.
24. Ibid., c. 13, 73 sq.
25. Lib. IV, c. 3.

latter are generally regarded as wicked and detestable, we must not forget that the former use their liberty to behave even worse. The master will kill his slave, believing he has a right to do so; the slave will beware of committing murder, because he realizes that then he will be sure to die. The rich allow themselves every shameless act against their women slaves, yet they consider themselves far superior to them; the slaves, however, have no concubines nor do they practice polygamy.[26]

Salvian also describes the existing economic abuses and the injustices connected with them. He excoriates, in particular, the arbitrary and unjust system of taxation which had caused an ever-increasing impoverishment. He complains, very reasonably, that the taxpayers have no voice in the voting of expenditures and that no control is exercised over tax assessments. He characterizes the officials as corrupt: they buy their offices and then exploit the populace in order to recover the purchase price and more. As a spokesman for the oppressed lower classes, Salvian protests against the pressure exerted by capital — the rich using their wealth to make slaves of the weaker. On this point, perhaps, he too sharply attacks the *curiales*. These, bound to their class, had been made responsible for the tax returns and in their turn were equally the victims of the unfortunate system of taxation which crushed all classes — some sooner, some later. Nevertheless, it redounds to Salvian's credit that, following the tradition of the Church, he thus used his influence especially in behalf of the lower classes; and also that he spoke in defense of the rebellious *coloni* who, driven to despair, overran the country, plundering and destroying. "We call them rebels and reprobates, whom we have driven to crime. What has made them Bagaudae if not our injustices and the unfair sentences and extortions of the judges?"[27] Besides severely condemning injustice and calumny in the officials, Salvian accuses the merchants of fraud and perjury.

Indulgence in unlimited pleasures, the unscrupulous pursuit of money and profits, and the exploitation of the lower classes, had,

---

26. Ibid., c. 5, 6.
27. Lib. V, c. 6.

as we see clearly, corrupted Roman society past remedy; and an unreasonable system of taxation, together with the corruption of officials, made any improvement in the state impossible.

There was another obvious reason for the fall of Rome, which Salvian failed to mention because it lay outside his theme: the Romans, with a few exceptions, had given up the bearing of arms, the waging of wars with their own soldiers, the defense of themselves with their own hands. Until the fall of the Roman Empire there were, indeed, Roman generals, like Orestes, the father of Romulus Augustulus, but these were dependent on Germanic troops who imposed their own will upon their commanders. This repugnance of the Roman populace to the profession of arms, however, had its moral reasons also: it plainly was related to the fact that the Romans did not want to separate themselves in any degree from the pleasures which their cities so profusely offered them. That is why they gladly permitted military service to be taken over by the barbarians, who flocked to it. This was, in the last analysis, the decisive factor which made it possible for the Germans under their own leaders to seize political power and retain it.

Salvian certainly sensed the moral causes that had brought about the new situation in which subjected Romans had to obey Germanic masters; and he misses no opportunity to cite these causes in his attempts to prove this to his Roman fellow-Christians. Placing the degenerate Christian Romans over against the Germanic pagans and Arians, he concludes from this comparison that the Romans deserve a far harsher condemnation than the Germans, who moreover are not wanting in natural virtues and are in fact less corrupt than the Romans:

> In comparison with all these we are, because of our possession of the divine law, certainly better; but considering our manner of life and our actions, I must admit with great distress that we are worse. To be sure, we do not exactly wish to assert this of the Roman people without exception — I exclude in the first place all religious, then also some laymen who are as spiritually developed as the religious, or if that is saying too much, are like them in a certain uprightness and honorable way of

acting; but all the others, or almost all, are more to blame than the barbarians.[28]

Of the pagan tribes the Saxons are ferocious, the Franks unfaithful, the Gepids inhuman, the Huns shameless, the Alamanni given to drink, and the Alans rapacious. But the Roman Christians have all these vices and are more at fault, because they are Christians. They go so far as to call upon the name of Christ when committing their crimes; many are accustomed to swear: "By Christ, I will take this," "By Christ, I will strike him," "By Christ, I will kill him."

Of Arian Germans, Salvian knows especially the Goths and the Alans. Here the comparison is still more unfavorable to the Romans, for these tribesmen evidently possess some excellent qualities which are wanting in true orthodox Christians. We observe how the members of the tribe love one another, whereas the Romans almost universally envy and persecute one another; they are unwilling to extend mutual help, each one seeking his own advantage at his fellow's expense, with the result that many of the oppressed seek refuge with the Germans. At this point we find that oft-quoted passage:

> Therefore do the oppressed flee on all sides to the Goths or to the Bagaudae or to other barbarians, who rule everywhere, and they feel no remorse whatever since they would rather be free under the guise of captivity than be prisoners under the appearance of freedom. Thus is the name of a Roman citizen, which once was not only greatly esteemed but also purchased at a great price, now voluntarily rejected; one flees from it — it is considered not only base but loathsome.[29]

In particular, he compares the Goths and Vandals with the Romans as regards the vice of impurity, and here again the comparison proves most unfavorable to the latter:

> Among chaste barbarians we are unchaste. I will say even more: the barbarians themselves are scandalized at our impurity. . . . Among the Goths impurity is a crime. . . . Here I will question those who think that

28. Lib. IV, c. 13, 61.
29. Lib. V, c. 5, 22.

we are better than the barbarians; let them say what in this regard is done by only a few Goths, and what all the Romans, or almost all, do. And then we are surprised when the lands of the Aquitanians and of us all have been given by God to the barbarians who, by their chastity, are now purifying those territories which the Romans have polluted with their immorality.[30]

In the same way Spain and Africa were given over to the Vandals, because they had proceeded against the houses of ill fame: the Roman cities of Africa, especially Carthage, had been steeped in impurity and immorality; the Vandals had purified them. The Germans deserve divine assistance for the added reason that before their battles they implore God for victory and put their trust in Him, which we have not done. Thus the Romans may infer from the event how God judges them and how He judges the Goths and Vandals: "They increase daily and we are dying off; they advance, we are humiliated; they flourish and we are withering."[31]

Salvian is thus resigned to the fact that the Germans will remain the masters, and he regards this as a just judgment of God. He says all this, of course, to reproach the Romans with their lack of faith: because they had been taught the true faith and still were unwilling to believe in God's Providence, He was forced to punish them more severely. If the Romans amended their ways, then their cause would be the only one which God would advocate. The author, too, who was censuring them so sternly, would support them, for he knew, after all, that the Goths and Vandals were only barbarians.

It is a terrible sermon, intended to affect its hearers profoundly. For this reason the picture is painted as black as possible and the contrasting side is allowed to appear in its brightest light. We do find some instances of evident partiality. The morality of the Vandals after they settled in Africa no longer deserved this high praise. Within a few generations, they showed such depravity — the result of mixing barbarian primitiveness with Roman decadence — that

---

30. Lib. VII, c. 6.
31. Ibid., c. 11, 49.

they were unable a hundred years later to offer any resistance whatsoever to the Byzantine forces. In condemning his countrymen,
Salvian also failed to make sufficient allowance for the internal
political and social disintegration, which considerably hastened the
relaxation of morals. However, despite all that may justly be dis-
counted, much still remains to show that the Roman people no
longer had the vigor to maintain their position against the Germans, and that the moral strength especially was lacking to accomplish this. On the other hand, the Germans, not corrupted by
overcivilization, still manifested the moral strength of a primitive
race. By means of this — thanks to the essential co-operation of the
Church — they were destined to work among the Roman people as
a rejuvenating force.

But that which most strikes us in Salvian's description needs
particularly to be emphasized at this point. From his words we see
that the Church in her struggle against the decadence of Roman
society would have been doomed to impotence if new and healthy
institutions had not been gradually brought into being by the fall
of the Roman Empire — on the one hand by the passing of the
depraved social conditions and the corrupt economic situation, and
on the other by the infusion of fresh blood. Some prominent
Romans, deeply imbued with Christianity, were able to achieve this
renovation in themselves or in a small circle; men like Saint Ambrose
and Saint Augustine could conceive of the ideals of Christian
thought and life as a standard and give them a form which would
be remembered through the ages. The masses, however, were unable to follow their lead; and the members of the Church who
were forced to live in the world as it was, ran the risk of being
dragged into the decadence of the period. We noticed signs of this
in the dissensions which sometimes accompanied the papal elections.
The blunt words of Salvian exhibit them to us still more clearly.
Frightful phrases are these which he pens:

> The Church herself, which ought in all things to be the appeaser of
> God, what is she but one who must incite God to anger? Except for the
> few who flee from the evils, what are almost all Christians but the dregs
> of vice? How many do you find in the Church who are not drunkards
> or gluttons, adulterers or fornicators, robbers or rakes, thieves or

murderers? And what is worse, is the sight of all this without being able to foresee an end of it. I question the conscience of all Christians: Who is not a part or the whole of these things? It would be easier to find one who is all of them than one who is none. . . . Almost the entire population of the Church has sunk into this moral depravity, so that in the entire Christian people it is to some extent a species of sanctity to be less vicious.[32]

If we place this picture side by side with those dealing with the Church's activity that we meet in the writings of Saint Ambrose and Saint Augustine, we sense a sharp difference, which cannot be explained alone by the vehemence of the moralist. A change must indeed have taken place in the first half of the fifth century; and it must have been worked by the influx of the great mass of pagan society into the Church. Saint Augustine in *The City of God* was writing to meet pagan accusations; Orosius likewise still carried on the controversy. In Salvian's time there is no further need for this. He writes against the reproaches of bad Christians. Outside the Church, there were no longer any pagans. Now they were in the Church, with their old mentality, their lust for pleasure and power, their immorality and base desire for profits, and permitted themselves to be numbered among her members. The reason for this was that a Roman and a Christian was now one and the same thing. This entry of the great masses into the Church had been brought about by their antagonism to the Germans, who had penetrated into and dominated the Roman Empire. Those aristocrats and rich landowners who had dared to defend pagan traditions had disappeared. Everything associated with Roman officialdom was tottering.

Only the servants of the Church remained steadfast, and the barbarians occasionally still showed them some measure of respect and considerate treatment, since the better elements among them were really Christians already, even though of Arian persuasion. Thus the Church's prestige mounted. Salvian could write of the Church's servants — secular priests and ascetics — that they wear the cross of Christ in such a manner that they have a greater share in the dignity of the Christian name than in the punishment for

---

32. Lib. III, c. 9, 44 sq.

Christ's sufferings.[33] Which of the Roman pagans would have tolerated being placed on an equal footing with the most uncivilized of those Germans who still were pagans? Thus it seems that the mass of the population first entered the Church under the pressure of the Germanic invasions into Gaul, after Saint Martin had already solicitously devoted himself to the conversion of the country folk in that land. The upper classes, the brutal slaveholders as well as the unjust officials and the dishonest tradesmen, who thus entered the Church, constituted a grave test of her powers of endurance; her innate strength, her spirit, suffered thereby.

This explains why zealous and idealistic representatives of Christian teaching and life felt themselves ever more strongly impelled to flee the world, and, far removed from its corruption, to live either as monks in a group of kindred spirits or as ascetic hermits. To these circles Salvian himself belonged, and he regarded them as furnishing the only bright aspect of his era. Monasticism had been introduced into Gaul principally by Saint Martin. At his death in about the year 400, approximately 2,000 hermits came together from all parts of the country to be present at his burial. Thereafter monasticism spread gradually throughout Gaul.

The religious, as Salvian calls the monks, were in his opinion the only true Christians (he did include a few laymen whose mode of life resembled the monastic).[34] We must appraise this judgment, based on sharp hostility to a corrupt society, in relation to the circumstances then prevailing. Without doubt, his hostility occasionally led Salvian too far — a fact we notice particularly in his earlier books, *Ad ecclesiam* and *Adversus avaritiam*.[35] In these works, which excoriate avarice, he generally demands that laymen, no less than priests and monks, bequeath their fortunes to the Church, which then had complete responsibility for the relief of the poor. On this point Salvian naturally met with opposition; indeed, the great Saint Augustine had not wished that anyone obligated to care for dependents should designate the Church as his heir.[36] But despite Salvian's

---

33. Ibid., c. 3.
34. See above, pp. 136-137.
35. *De gub.*, Lib. IV, c. 8, 43 sq.
36. See above, pp. 100-101.

one-sidedness he was essentially right, for it was chiefly the monks who were to be called upon to labor for the renewal of Christian society. Among them were found the best workers, those who had the objective clearly before them and possessed the spirit of sacrifice necessary for the task.

Although nothing was to be achieved in the face of the depraved culture of the cities — for instance in Gaul — the monks nevertheless demonstrated even at this early time, in another lost corner of the Roman Empire, at least their capacity for sacrifice. For this, our only source of information is a biography of Saint Severinus — without it we would know nothing of what an unselfish monk did in pious devotion for his fellow-men. The scene of his apostolic activity was the frontier-province of Noricum, then half abandoned by the Romans and hard pressed by the Germans. It still embraced several Roman cities, but soon all of these vanished, leaving only their name. Whence Severinus came no one knew, nor did he care to tell. From his speech it could be surmised that he was Latin by birth. Otherwise it was possible to worm out of him only that he had gone to the Orient, where he had learned to know, and embraced, the monastic life; that there God had commanded him to repair to the forsaken regions on the Danube.

Here he lived as an austere ascetic and soon gathered a number of disciples about him. He preached penance and imparted consolation to the Roman Christians who, on the brink of despair, were leading a wretched existence in the scattered villages. He also gave them what practical aid he could, being the only one who still had enough courage to undertake any enterprise. Everybody willingly obeyed him. He ordered the collection of tithes to assist the poor and redeem prisoners. Sometimes he encouraged the Romans to offer resistance to the Germans advancing across the Danube from the north; again, as an advocate, he used his influence with the invaders to liberate prisoners or conclude an armistice.

Once, Odoacer, then only a common soldier scantily wrapped in skins, entered the saint's cell; at his departure Severinus told him: "Go to Italy; soon you will have great gifts to distribute to many." Odoacer remembered the occasion when he became king, and sent Severinus the message that he might ask a favor. The saint asked for the liberation of an exile. Severinus died on January 8, 482. Six years later Odoacer invited the few survivors of the Roman population from this region to Italy, where he granted them a safe abode. In accord with the injunction of their deceased master, his disciples took the body of the saint with them; it was finally buried in the new settlement they were able to found in Castellum Lucullanum, near Naples. Eugippius, the abbot of this monastery, a former disciple of Severinus, composed a simple biography of this apostolic monk which serves as a precious testimony of his unselfish labors.

About the time that Saint Severinus ended his earthly career (apparently fruitless, but showing the forces latent in the monasticism of the Catholic Church), there was born in Nursia in the Sabine territory, close to Rome itself, the man who mobilized those forces — until then operating only disjointedly and confusedly. They were destined to conquer the West — not as the legions did, for the Roman Empire, but for the new Christian civilization; to transform it into a new cultural home which, with Rome as its center, would assume the leadership and determine the culture of the whole world. In the tracing of this development a particular fascination attaches to the fact that he who laid the foundation for it never thought of these things at all. And yet the little booklet of Saint Benedict bears within itself all the germs of the future growth.

CHAPTER FOUR

SAINT BENEDICT AND HIS AGE

WHILE the Church was receiving into her fold a constantly increasing multitude after the end of the persecutions, and thus coming into ever closer contact with the world, the deserts of Egypt and Syria were being peopled with ascetics. The life of the saintly hermit Anthony, around whose cell in the Thebaid disciples gathered as hermits, became a model and example for many. Numerous associations of hermits were formed, the movement spreading to Palestine. Pachomius, a former soldier, gave the societies of ascetics a fixed form by building at Tabennisi on the Nile a monastery and church surrounded by a wall, where the monks led a community life. Thus Pachomius became the father of the cenobitic life (*koinobion*). A second foundation soon followed the first. In all, he established nine monasteries for men, and through his sister, two additional ones for women. He gave to all a common rule. An abbot or an abbess headed each monastery, and an abbot-general presided over the entire group.

This monastic life, cloistered and disciplined, had an extraordinary attraction. During the lifetime of Pachomius his principal monastery counted some three thousand monks, and this number increased after his death (346). In the first half of the fifth century the society was said to embrace 50,000 members. The rule provided for a rigid examination at the time of reception, together with a period of probation (novitiate) and a solemn vow to observe the rule. The monks earned their living by agriculture and by manual work, according to which they were divided into various trades. The life spread first from Egypt to Asia by way of Palestine and Syria and then to Mesopotamia, Persia and Armenia. About the year 360, Saint Basil, who later became the brilliant archbishop of Caesarea and a Doctor of the Church, transplanted it to the shores of the Black Sea, and evolved new rules which provided for a combination of the hermitical and the monastic. By his insistence on obedience for the monks he imparted stability to his rule, which became the norm for monachism in the East. It was also spread in Italy by Rufinus.

But the West had already become acquainted with the marvelous growth of monastic life in the Orient through Saint Athanasius the Great, bishop of Alexandria. In 340, seeking refuge in the West, he had gone to Rome accompanied by two monks, Isidore and Ammonius. Monastic communities indeed existed there and elsewhere; but the Oriental prototypes, as they became known in the West, gave a new impetus in many localities. Bishop Eusebius of Vercelli, upon his return from exile in Asia and Egypt, was also active in spreading the monastic life with which he had become acquainted by personal observation. As a result, the end of the fourth century saw monasteries for men and women established in Rome, Milan, and other places in Italy and Dalmatia. Saint Ambrose, Saint Jerome and Saint Augustine contributed not a little by word and example to the spread of monachism.

The first monastery in Gaul was founded about 360 at Ligugé near Poitiers by Saint Martin, the son of a Roman military tribune and himself a former cavalryman. The authority of the saint as bishop of Tours (where he resided in the monastery of Marmoutier) and, after his death, the fascinating story of his life written by Sulpicius Severus — a counterpart to the life of Saint Anthony, the father of the hermits, composed by Saint Athanasius — were important factors in spreading the new monastic life through Gaul. In addition to this, a direct impulse from the Orient was transmitted to the maritime territories of southern France. Between 400 and 410, Saint Honoratus, the future bishop of Arles, established on the island of Lérins (known today as Saint Honoratus) a sanctuary for monastic life after the pattern he had gone to seek in Egypt. This foundation became a seminary for the clergy of all southern France, and through Saint Patrick it served as a model as far beyond this region as Ireland.

An even greater influence was exerted by the writings of John Cassian. These handbooks and devotional manuals on monastic life, later recommended by Saint Benedict, were deeply admired and devoutly read throughout the whole Middle Ages. Cassian had informed himself in the greatest detail on the life of the hermits and monks in Egypt. It is still disputed whether he was born in southern Gaul or in the Dobrudja. Together with an older friend, Germanus, he received his first religious instruction in a monastery at Bethlehem; hence he grew up as a monk. The desire to visit the home of monastic life and the most renowned exponents of its traditions drew him, like so many others, to Egypt. He arrived there with Germanus about 385 and remained a long time — at first seven years and then, after a return to Bethlehem, three additional years. Later, in his writings, he would utilize to the utmost this extended association with the holy anchorites and monks. The two friends next repaired to Constantinople, where Cassian was ordained a deacon by the bishop, Saint John Chrysostom. When Chrysostom suffered his second banishment from court, Cassian proceeded to Rome (405), where he implored Pope Innocent I to intervene for the exiled bishop. While in Rome he was probably ordained priest. Ten years later we meet him at the head of two monasteries, one for men and one for women, which he founded in or near Marseilles. Here, about 435, he died, highly revered as a teacher of the monastic and ascetical life.

Cassian had acquired this reputation especially by two works, written between 419 and 429 at the suggestion of the saintly Bishop Castor of Apt. In them, he transmitted to the West the teachings he had received in the cradle of monachism. The first deals with monastic institutions and with protective measures against the eight principal vices. Cassian gives full particulars of the external institutions and rules which were in force in the monasteries in the East, in Palestine, and in Bethlehem. He speaks of the apparel, the prayers and reading of psalms (to which the monks applied themselves by day and by night), the reception and probation of candidates, and the fundamental obligations of humility, obedience and poverty. Then follows the characterization of the eight vices against which the monk has to fight: gluttony, impurity, avarice, anger, dejection (*tristitia*), listlessness (*acedia* or *taedium,* which besets the hermits and itinerant monks particularly at noon and hence is called the noonday devil), vanity and pride. As the best remedy

against vanity Cassian recommends the systematic labor so much
favored by the Egyptian monks. It was thus that they provided
food both for their own sustenance and for others, and produced
whatever else was necessary. Although Cassian mentions only once
in this connection the transcribing of books (relating that a monk
from Italy took it upon himself because he knew no other occupation), this must not be stressed too much, for Palladius, a contemporary, in his history of the Egyptian monks also includes the copying of books among their occupations.[1]

The second work of Cassian is closely connected with the first
and forms a supplement to it. It is entitled: *Twenty-four Conferences with the Fathers.* Herein are repeated conversations which
Cassian and his friend had had with the most esteemed hermits
during their sojourn in Egypt. These discourses are to serve as an
introduction to a higher degree of ascetical life by presenting
the interior spiritual and contemplative life of the hermits as a
sequel to the active life of the monastic communities described in
the first work. Thereby, monks and hermits are to be edified, and
guided to a deeper interior life. The thirteenth conference, be it
remarked, gave rise to a great controversy. The author was accused
of opposing Saint Augustine on the doctrine of grace, and of being
the father of semi-Pelagianism; not without cause, for he had expressed the opinion that the beginning of good works and also the
preparation for grace can proceed from human nature alone. This,
however, did not prevent men from appreciating the many good
points contained in the work, which contributed unquestionably to
the particularly high esteem accorded to intellectual activity later
in the monasteries of the West.

At the end of the fifth century Saint Caesarius, as abbot of a
monastery in southern Gaul, composed a rule which served the
monasteries of the region for a long time. Later, as archbishop of
Arles and papal vicar, he strengthened the life of the Church, and
also gave a rule to the convent of nuns directed by his sister Caesaria.

The variety of rules and norms governing monastic life gradually gave rise to certain abuses. There were monks who moved

1. Palladius, *Historia Lausiaca,* c. 39: Migne, *P. L.,* LXXIII, 1139.

from one monastery to another, sometimes remaining only as long as suited their caprice or their desire for food and drink. Among such vagrant monks some questionable characters easily gained place who could only degrade the religious life, otherwise so highly esteemed. Then there were others called Sarabaites (from an Egyptian word), who like the ascetics of old lived in cities or hamlets alone or together in groups of two or three as it pleased them, without having superiors or binding themselves by any rule. The monks living in cloister and by a fixed rule could justly say that such as these, by wearing the habit, dishonored the religious state.

After the Rule of Saint Basil had attained almost universal observance in the monastic communities of the East, the need for a uniform and fixed norm was even more manifest in the West, where, following the collapse of the Western Roman Empire, complete disintegration threatened on all sides. This norm, however, had to proceed from the Western spirit; it could not consist of that external imitation of Oriental monastic customs which, beyond doubt, was a frequent cause of the worldliness creeping into monachism. And such a desirable expression of the Western spirit could not find a better place to take root in than Rome — indeed, that very Rome whose worldly power had disappeared. When the city had come under the control of the Germans, the time was ripe for Saint Benedict.

Born during Odoacer's reign, Saint Benedict died before the Ostrogothic rule in Italy had been abolished. Theodoric the Great, who had founded the Ostrogothic kingdom in 493 by usurping power through the bloody removal of Odoacer, was at his zenith when Benedict entered upon the course which led to his becoming the legislator of Western monasticism. The Romans of this epoch felt themselves exposed to a grave crisis — a crisis we can clearly follow through its various manifestations in the lives of three great men of the period: Boethius, Cassiodorus and Saint Benedict. They were born about the same time, between 480 and 490. All three have exerted a lasting influence on the culture of future ages, but Saint Benedict far surpassed the other two — thanks to the institution which he founded and which has endured to this day.

Anicius Manlius Severinus Boethius descended from the noble family of the Anicii. His father had been consul in 487; hence he was destined for the lofty career of politics — a career more dangerous at that time than ever before. Theodoric hoped to use him in promoting the royal policy, for Boethius was distinguished both by his exalted birth and his extraordinary learning. On one occasion he was commissioned to select a zither-player, whom Theodoric wished to send to Clovis, the Frankish king, as an expression of royal friendship. Again, Boethius was delegated to procure a water clock and a sundial, which Theodoric intended for Gundibald, king of the Burgundians. In making such gifts, Theodoric delighted to pose as the ruler of a highly cultured kingdom, and his choice of Boethius as an expert in these matters showed that he recognized the learned patrician as one of the most distinguished representatives of ancient Roman culture.

The letter authorizing the second commission justly praised Boethius for his translations of Greek masterpieces. Boethius had undertaken the translation of Aristotle; and eventually he planned a systematic synthesis of the doctrines of Plato and Aristotle. Of these projects he finished little more than the translation and a commentary on the logical treatises of Aristotle. Had his plan been realized, Aristotle's influence on the West would undoubtedly have begun as early as the Carolingian period instead of being postponed to the twelfth century.

Nevertheless Boethius' influence itself was important as being that of one of the last representatives and transmitters of ancient learning. Especially did his *Commentary* on the *Introduction to the Categories of Aristotle* by Porphyry the Neo-Platonist serve the Middle Ages as a manual of logic. Other writings of his — excerpts from the works of Nicomachus of Gerasa, the Pythagorean, and of Euclid — became basic for medieval knowledge in mathematics and the theory of music. In addition he wrote shorter theological tracts, two of which, on the Trinity, enjoyed great esteem in the Middle Ages.

But his scholarly activity was suddenly interrupted. In the year 510, he himself had obtained the consulate; in 522, his two sons, still youths, had been appointed consuls by Theodoric; and shortly afterward, he had been honored with the title of *magister officiorum*: surely he might have believed his position with Theodoric sufficiently firm to permit him to intercede on any occassion in the interest of his Roman friends. Nevertheless, when he attempted this in behalf of the former consul Albinus, accused of treasonable connections with Byzantium — Boethius declared before Theodoric that he himself and the entire senate would have to be arraigned if Albinus were regarded as guilty — he was subjected to an inquiry and condemned to death without trial.

He was executed near Milan about 524; a year later his father-in-law Symmachus met the same fate.

While in prison Boethius wrote the work which particularly won him the esteem of posterity: *On the Consolation of Philosophy*. In these five books, composed in dialogue form, the consoling thoughts that come to Boethius while he is awaiting death are all purely intellectual and based on Neo-Platonic philosophy; but we must not conclude from this that there is any doubt of his having been a Christian. The Middle Ages found nothing strange in the fact that he did not seek his consolation in faith also — this lack of criticism being bound up, no doubt, with the fact that he was regarded a victim of the Arian ruler, and was even honored in some localities as a martyr. From this viewpoint, his last work was judged. During the Middle Ages it was translated and commentated more often than any other work of antiquity.

The proud courage displayed by Boethius does him credit in point of character and as a philosopher; but it spelled his doom, for it led him to expose himself politically at a time when Theodoric's mistrust was not without foundation. Boethius undoubtedly sympathized with those senators who strove to establish relations with the Eastern Roman emperor as a means of terminating the barbarian rule in Italy. This group, to oblige Byzantium, had even provoked a schism in the Roman Church, following the election of Pope Symmachus in the year 498. The Byzantine party, led by the senator Festus, wanted the pope to yield in the Acacian schism, which at that time temporarily separated the East and the West; it sought a capitulation in Rome at the expense of the pope's authority in matters of faith. Against him, it set up an antipope, the archpriest Laurence, and thus provoked the Laurentian schism. The pope was able to maintain himself only through the intervention of Theodoric, who acted in the belief that he could earn the gratitude of the Romans by his tolerant attitude and his constant endeavor to reconcile Romans and Goths. When the Acacian schism had been healed and the ecclesiastical rift between East and West repaired, the senators strove to draw closer to Byzantium politically. Theodoric, his suspicions quickly awakened, cast Pope John into prison and pitilessly delivered Boethius and his father-in-law to their death. For proud Romans of this time, high politics was a dangerous field of activity — and one, moreover, in which there was very little chance of success.

The statesman Cassiodorus attempted to work politically in the opposite direction from the group led by Festus. Born at Squillace (Scylacium) in Bruttium, he too came from a distinguished family. His father had been active in the state under Odoacer and Theodoric, hence it was natural for him also to enter the service of the latter. As secretary and minister he abetted Theodoric's policy, which was to effect a reconciliation between the Romans and the Goths and to found a state on the basis of their peaceful cohabitation and cooperation. The two national groups were to remain distinct, however: the Goths, being the rulers, were to render military service and provide for peace and protection at home and abroad; the Romans, being the exponents of economic enterprise and intellectual culture, were to apply themselves to the arts and sciences. Though the execution of such a program proved to be impossible, its formulation is comprehensible in view of the fact that the Romans for generations had shirked military service, while in the fifth century Germanic troops, unaided, had very nearly secured the safety of Italy.

However, if Cassiodorus, who should have known better, believed he could achieve anything by this plan, he gave no evidence of a very profound grasp of either cultural problems or religion, for the idea was based on a superficial conception of the first and a neglect of the second. It was in harmony, however, with that superficial approach of Cassiodorus which we encounter not only in the opportunistic tendency of his politics, but also in his pedantic literary activity.

If Cassiodorus was not the originator of the royal policy, he was a highly welcome tool in its carrying out. He established his position with the king by a eulogy on Theodoric and planned to follow it with others on kings and queens. His appointment as *quaestor* brought him into intimate association with Theodoric, for it was his duty, as a kind of cabinet secretary or minister, to prepare the proclamations which were issued in the name of the king. He was personally so proud of these proclamations that he published them under the title *Variae* as a collection of formulas designed to serve others for models. For us they no longer fulfill this purpose, yet they are a valuable historical source, though difficult to use.

It was not possible for Cassiodorus to escape any or every honor, since his position with the king never weakened. In 514 he obtained the consulate, and when Theodoric died in 526, Cassiodorus was Master of the Offices — a dignity he retained even after the death of the king. In 533 he had himself appointed praetorian prefect, thus indicating that he was still unreservedly serving the kings of the Goths.

His literary works of the period also show this. He dedicated a bald chronicle to Eutharic, Theodoric's son-in-law and prospective successor, for whom it was written to provide a survey of Roman history. From the eleventh century onward it was used by German historians for the same purpose. By Theodoric's own orders, Cassiodorus wrote twelve books on the history of the Goths with the design of proving to the Romans (as the Christians had once attempted to prove to the pagans) that the Goths were not inferior to the Romans in the matter of ancestry. In this work his servility led him into gross falsifications: he identified the Getae with the Goths and applied to the Goths the existing historical information on the Scythians. Nevertheless we must regret that this work is no longer extant in the original; its precious information is preserved to us only in the excerpts of Jordanes, who continued, in a strongly modified form, the political program of Cassiodorus. Jordanes still sought a reconciliation between the Romans and Goths, but this seemed possible to him only through a fusion of the two. Cassiodorus himself was to live to see his program doomed to failure. When the war between the Romans of the East and the Ostrogoths broke out, in which the Romans of Italy had great difficulty in concealing their sympathies for Justinian's generals, he withdrew to a monastery, disappointed with the world.

Shortly before the year 540, following the suggestion of friends who were familiar with his sentiments, he wrote a philosophical treatise on the soul. This elaborates for the general reader the thoughts of others, for example those of Saint Augustine. He treats also the contrast between the good and the wicked — but how superficially! How far he lags behind Saint Augustine here! The wicked are those whose look is overcast despite all their bodily perfections; who are sad in all their joy, since remorse soon follows in its wake; whose glance wanders restlessly about, betraying fear and suspicion, anxiously asking the judgment of others, since they have lost their own. In seeking material life, they run the risk of falling victims to eternal death. Opposite these are placed the pious, the ascetics, who combat the flesh, who praise others, who despise and always accuse themselves, who displease themselves when they please everyone else. They are, though still in the flesh, stronger than the fallen angels whom they command. They are joyful amid constant weeping, and, although uncultured, are entirely pure. Their countenance is serene and calm, emaciated and graced with pallor; their long beards give them a venerable appearance; their glances are virtuous, modest and winning; their voice is moderate and gentle, and their gait neither too slow nor too quick.[2]

Before he retired to the monastery, this active man, gifted with the qualities of an organizer, entertained a plan which undoubtedly corresponded more closely to his own preferences. It reflects great credit on him, although it shows how incorrectly he judged the signs of his times. He had proposed to Pope Agapetus (535-536) the founding of a Christian university, which was to cultivate in particular the exegetical branches. He regretted that there were no public teachers for these sciences in Rome, whereas profane literature

2. *De anima,* c. 10, 11. Opp. ed. Garetius, II, 602 sq.

and science were well provided for. In support of his plan he pointed to the importance which Alexandria had formerly enjoyed as a center of Christian learning, and to the then flourishing university at Nisibis, the academy of Nestorianism in Persia.[3] The execution of the project seems to have been seriously contemplated in Rome, and Pope Agapetus, no doubt for this purpose, founded a library on the Clivus Scauri on the Caelian Hill. But the outbreak soon afterward of the Gothic War buried the plan for a long time to come.

The monasteries were to constitute in the beginning the only safe retreat of learning, and to have foreseen this fact remains the merit of Cassiodorus. In order to carry out his plan, at least on a small scale and as far as he could, he founded, at the age of sixty, the monastery of Vivarium on his estate in Calabria in the vicinity of Squillace. There, with like-minded companions, he devoted the remainder of his life to piety and studies.

For their guidance in the study of sacred and profane literature, he dedicated to his monks two books entitled *Institutiones divinarum et saecularium litterarum.* In the first he gives an introduction to theological study, by acquainting the monks with those authors who might profitably be read by them, after Holy Scripture itself — nor does he forget the works of the ancients on medicine! The second book is intended as an introduction to the branches of general secular learning and enlarges successively on each of the liberal arts: grammar, rhetoric, dialectics, arithmetic, music, geometry and astronomy. Rhetoric and dialectics are treated more fully because of their importance to the Romans in their practical application to governmental and judicial affairs.

The writings he cites here are those which were frequently transcribed in the monasteries. His suggestions became particularly important for this type of work. Cassiodorus personally impressed on the monks of Vivarium the importance of copying manuscripts. Proof of this is found in a sentence from the *Institutiones,* in which he writes:[4]

---

3. *Inst. div. litt.,* Praef. Garetius, II, 508.
4. *Instit. div.,* 30. Garetius, II, 525.

Much as you can accomplish by manual labor, I cannot refrain from expressing the opinion that the toil spent in copying ancient manuscripts is indeed more pleasing — provided they are copied correctly — and rightly so, because the copyists cultivate their own minds in a wholesome manner by reading the sacred writings again and by spreading far and wide the precepts of the Lord through their transcriptions.

Writing this passage with the transcription of theological works particularly in mind, he extols the merits of the copyists: "Satan receives as many wounds as the scribe copies words of the Lord." The three fingers of the copyists, he said, stood in the service of the Blessed Trinity. In addition he also composed, at the age of ninety-three, an instruction manual for good copying — a book on orthography which was a collection of extracts from the orthographers in his own library.

Cassiodorus commanded considerable attention as the last literary authority of antiquity; and, by his manuals and instructions, he is chiefly responsible for the transmission of the knowledge of many works to the Middle Ages through the medium of the monasteries.

Finally, he deserves credit for several theological works; among them, a comprehensive commentary on the psalter was widespread in the Middle Ages. He likewise inspired the translation of two large historical works. He had the Greek continuations of Eusebius' *Church History,* which Socrates, Sozomen and Theodoret had written, translated into Latin, and thus passed on to the Middle Ages by means of this so-called *Historia Tripartita* the ecclesiastical record from the Council of Nicaea to the year 439. He was also responsible for a translation of the *Antiquities* of the Jewish historian Flavius Josephus, which met with great approval in the Middle Ages.

His friendship with the learned Scythian Dionysius Exiguus — this monk resided in Rome in the first half of the sixth century and, through his translations, made valuable treasures of Oriental literature accessible to the West — certainly had a stimulating influence on Cassiodorus in this field. Other important examples of the work of Dionysius Exiguus as a translator are the great collections with which he established the historical basis of Western Canon Law — that is, his assemblage of the decrees of the Greek and Latin Councils and the first comprehensive collection of papal decretals. A more commonly familiar association with the name of Dionysius Exiguus is that of the new computation of time which he introduced with the transmission and continuation of the Alexandrian Easter Tables. By his method, the years are counted no longer from Diocletian, but from the birth of Christ. Thus he gave the whole world an example of how Christ should be exalted as the central figure in all history.

The preoccupation with the production of collections, translations and surveys, inspired by Cassiodorus and encountered again in Isidore of Seville, corresponded to a then present need. The era doubtless felt itself less and less able to create anything original, and so in duty bound to preserve and transmit what yet remained of organized knowledge. The recession of culture which led to such needs was bound up, in turn, with the decline of urban civilization. In the cities men devoted themselves almost exclusively to the simplest problems of self-preservation. There was no longer the intellectual alertness nor the tranquillity necessary for the cultivation of learning. That probably is the reason why Cassiodorus selected the monastery as the asylum of learning, the depositary for books, and the workshop for the patient copying of manuscripts. Therein he was undoubtedly correct, although the realization of this avocation in the monasteries could not have been brought about by his foundation of Vivarium alone.

Thus, when Cassiodorus founded his monastery, he was more concerned with creating a scientific institute than with establishing a monastery. He intended the monastery to be a sanctuary of literary culture rather than a society for ascetical life and prayer. His aims were similar to those pursued later by Charlemagne and others who thought as he did. They are highly praised — and who, that values literary culture, would not echo the praise? Who begrudges the monasteries their well-merited fame? To claim, however, as some have done, that the existence of monasteries is justified only if they foster literary culture, is to praise mistakenly. It is to fail to recognize the work for which monasteries were primarily destined. From the viewpoint of their historical mission as companies of monks associated for a common spiritual life, the fostering of literary culture must not occupy first place, but must be subordinated to the main purpose even where it is a special ornament of a monastery.

Here again Cassiodorus showed that he did not penetrate to the core of the spiritual problems of culture, for apparently he was chiefly intent on engaging the monks in his literary projects. And that is the reason why we do not hear of Vivarium having affiliated monasteries or expanding in any way. Had the program which Cassiodorus urged for the monasteries been restricted in execution to Vivarium, it would never have been carried on. Vivarium had no independent and active monastic spirit which it could transmit to others. Neither did it create the type of monastery that corresponded to the new needs and could maintain itself in the face of them. This was achieved only by the monasteries of Saint Benedict, which were able to take up and carry out the program of Cassiodorus.

Only against the background of the times, and in comparison with Boethius and Cassiodorus, can we understand the development of Saint Benedict and the importance of his monastic foundation.

He was a member of the Sabine nobility, a representative of that select race of the Roman people whose men Cicero described as being especially austere and strong. His native city, Nursia, was proverbial in Rome for its hardiness. The conservative character which was at home there, found expression in a noble family spirit. We know enough about Benedict's tender affection for his sister to infer this even though we hear nothing of his parents. In turn Saint Scholastica, who early in life dedicated herself as a consecrated virgin to the service of the Lord, preserved a most loyal attachment to her brother. When he was abbot of Monte Cassino, he visited her once each year. The touching scene of his last visit is familiar to us. Three days later she died and the abbot had his beloved sister buried in the grave he had destined for himself at Monte Cassino.

Vigorous uprightness and integrity, united with devotion to family, were the natural virtues by which the Romans had grown great, and these were the virtues on which Saint Benedict so built that he became the great founder and teacher of Western monachism. As a boy he took these virtues with him when he went to Rome to study the liberal arts and to prepare the way, no doubt, for a public career. But how depressing must have been the prospects for the future of a young Roman at that time! Rome had lost her supremacy and existed by the favor of Odoacer, a barbarian king. The senators were divided into parties, one group hoping and intriguing for the overthrow of the foreign domination, the other eager to use its talents and organizing ability in the service of Odoacer. With one faction the fate of Boethius was in store for a young Roman; with the other, the long and futile activity of Cassiodorus as an aide to the barbarian kings.

We can understand that a political career could not attract Benedict. It was, doubtless, more natural for him, following the pious sentiments he brought with him from home, to enter the service of the Church. But here, too, many things probably repelled him at the time. As we have seen, the political contentions among the senatorial parties had provoked a rift in the Church itself, which upon the death of Pope Anastasius, in 498, led to the Laurentian schism. In the face of this division, since Benedict saw no ideals anywhere which could move him to imitation, one thing only and above all was certain to him: that Rome was unable to offer him anything.

After a short stay with the priest of Enfide, in the Sabine mountains, he resolved to renounce the world. For the next three years he lived as a hermit near Subiaco in a cave beside the ruins of one of Nero's palaces — a site which reminded him only too well of the luxury and corruption of ancient Rome. After the death of their abbot the monks of the small monastery of Vicovaro in the vicinity prevailed upon him to preside over them as their director. There, however, a new disappointment awaited him. The austere direction of the young abbot did not suit the willfulness of the monks, who lived completely isolated from one another. Their antipathy to him increased to such criminal hatred that they attempted to poison him. Benedict returned to his hermit's cave.

But he did not long remain alone. Disciples gathered about him, full of trust in his ability to lead them. A monastic community grew up, then a second and a third, until he stood at the head of twelve groups of monks, each with its own superior, but all honoring Benedict as their superior-general. The life of these monastic communities does not appear to have been strictly regulated as yet; seemingly the eremitic life was still conceded a place alongside the demands of cenobitic organization. Yet these monasteries enjoyed such good repute that their attraction made itself felt even among the upper classes of Rome, and patricians entrusted their sons to Benedict to be reared for the monastic state. Among these young Romans, the cultured Maurus and the youthful Placidus came into especially close association with the abbot.

The hostility of Florentius, a neighboring priest, caused Benedict to leave Subiaco suddenly. In 529, he selected a new site at Monte Cassino, on the Via Latina between Rome and Naples, where he would build his institution from the ground up, utilizing the experience acquired at Subiaco. Here he erected the monastery that was to become the motherhouse of Western monachism. Here, too, he composed that monastic constitution, the Benedictine Rule, which even today remains the guiding norm for his sons. And here he concluded his life as a highly venerated and saintly father on March 21, presumably between the years 550 and 555.

Comparing the Benedictine Rule with the earlier monastic constitutions of the West, one is astonished to find that almost all the regulations declared to be distinctive in the Benedictine Rule were contained in one or the other earlier Rule. From this it might be hastily concluded that only external circumstances can explain the fact that the Benedictine Rule displaced all the other monastic constitutions in the West. External circumstances played a great role in this matter, certainly, but not the only role. The Rule itself in no wise lacked merits, extrinsic and intrinsic, which are essentially due to the practical and prudent sense of the divinely illuminated lawgiver, who combined most intimately the Roman science of government with a profoundly Christian spirit. The very fact that the Rule is so extraordinarily concise and brief has given it an advantage over much more comprehensive constitutions of monastic life such as those of Cassian. But above all, the determining factor was the whole spirit that the Rule breathes forth, a spirit which, proceeding from the personality of the founder, endured as a living tradition. It bears witness to a rare innate balance as well as to a pedagogical gift approaching genius; at the same time, it reveals the extraordinary experience and psychological knowledge of the author. Pope Gregory the Great, in his *Dialogues* written two generations later, has reared a literary monument to Saint Benedict's personal authority, a monument which has been received with the highest acclaim.

In the Benedictine Rule we miss, indeed, a systematic order, which we have also found lacking in the writings of Saint Ambrose and Saint Augustine; in point of fact, it is generally absent from men who exert influence through their personality. What was advanced was not a theory discovered by subtle reasoning nor a mere product of the mind; instead it was a wisdom lived and tested, certain of success because confirmed by many experiments. The Rule does not resemble the statutes of a modern society in which the duties and rights of every member are perfectly and precisely detailed. Fundamental regulations, such as the obligation of a life of virginity, are passed over as self-understood, or are treated only incidentally, from the same viewpoint as, for example, the renunciation of private property. The Rule clearly presupposes the external features characteristic of monastic life.

There is hardly any mention, either, of the highest degree of monastic life: that rising above all visible things, in which the Orientals took especial delight. Saint Benedict only briefly refers to it as the summit of perfection. This reference occurs at the end of his Rule, where he recommends Sacred Scripture, the lives of the Fathers, the books of Cassian, and the Rule of Saint Basil as guides to its attainment.

The Rule, with all its regulations and admonitions, is in the main devoted to the daily life of the monastery, which is to be based on monastic virtue. It is a guide and exhortation to the monk to improve himself morally. What has given the Rule its great importance is precisely the force with which this practical and moral direction is briefly and surely presented and the ideal conception of community life emphasized. The Rule was flexible and given the character of a norm applicable wherever similar aspirations existed. It appears less as a norm for a new foundation which intended to be different from others than as a regular guide for the life, prayer and work in a monastery.

The purpose of monastic life is constantly and keenly kept in view or, better, is seriously brought home to the monks. It consists in this, that the monastic community consider itself a *schola dominici servitii*. We do not translate this entirely correctly when we render it as "school of the Lord's service." *Schola* in late Latin signifies an association having regulated service, a troop; thus the men on guard in the imperial palace were also designated as a *schola*. The *schola dominici servitii* is to be regarded as a troop which, voluntarily submitting itself to a fixed discipline, renders service day by day in all reverence, loyalty and punctuality, not to a worldly lord but to the Majesty of God. There is no possibility here for the contemplative life of the hermit; that is considered a form suitable only for the well-tried.

The society stands in sharp contrast also to the vagrant monks and those living together in groups of twos or threes without a superior. He has hard words for these Sarabaites and gyrovagues. In order to exclude this cancerous sore from contemporary monachism Saint Benedict demanded of his followers — and this was something new — the *stabilitas loci,* that is, permanent residence in one monastery. To that requirement monks about to be received had to bind themselves in a solemn manner. This is still characteristic of the constitution of the Benedictine Order today: the individual does not pledge himself to the Order but to the particular monastery.

Besides permanent residence, he who desires admission must vow a life and obedience in accord with the Rule. Very particular emphasis is placed upon this obedience; it corresponds to that military relationship which was to be the rule of conduct for the society. In the novitiate, at the conclusion of every instruction period, the novice was addressed three times with these words: "Behold, this is the law under which you are to render military service; if you can keep it, enter; if you cannot, freely depart." Military obedience is demanded toward the abbot. Disobedience is severely punished, especially in the cases of boys and younger monks; even the rod could be employed, a provision also found in other monastic rules. In this connection we must bear in mind that by vicarious profession, as it were, minors offered to God by their parents could also be received into the monastery. Parents of means then had to promise in writing and under oath that the youth would never again be permitted to dispose of any property lest the oblate allow such a prospect to lure him back into the world.

A serious and almost harsh note runs through the Rule: it is the old, rigorous Roman discipline that we encounter. It is tempered, however, by the circumstance that in his severity the abbot is like the strict *paterfamilias*, who nevertheless always remains a father. Here we come upon the trait that without doubt reveals most notably the Roman concepts and family traditions which Benedict brought with him from his home in Nursia. In the discussion of Saint Augustine, we have already referred to the fact that the position of the *paterfamilias* served as a determining norm in every organization, even in the organization of the state. The Roman *paterfamilias* enjoyed an extraordinarily high authority in his family. He could dispose of his children without restriction — a power which enables us to understand the otherwise strange custom of the oblation of adolescents in the Rule. The Roman authors have spoken of "a paternal majesty." This paternal authority is fully vested in the abbot according to the Rule. He is for life the absolute master in the monastery, the ruler in the house; therefore he is to be called "master" and "father" by all. Compared with the later monastic rules of the West, the Benedictine Rule is conspicuous for the stress it lays on the idea of authority.

But in Rome the father was particularly revered as the loving father, and no title of honor was more beautiful than that of *pius pater*. In characterizing the abbot, the Rule devotes even more space to these qualities. Thus the abbot is designated as *pius pater* in the very first lines of the preamble. It begins with the characteristic words: "*Ausculta, O fili:* Hearken, O my son, to the precepts of your master, and incline the ear of your heart: willingly receive and efficaciously fulfill the admonition of your loving father." The abbot must be a faithful provider for all his sons in order to give them that happiness which should flourish in an ideal family, where all are devoted to one another and find their enjoyment in the father's house, from which no one as long as he lives desires to be absent. One of the finest passages of the Rule is found in the second chapter from the end, in which Saint Benedict describes this pious family happiness in terse words:

> Let monks in honor prevent one another. Let them most patiently endure one another's infirmities, whether of body or of character. Let them obey one another with rivalry. Let no one follow what he judges good for himself, but rather what seems good for another. Let them tender the charity of brotherhood with chaste love. Let them fear God, and love their abbot with sincere and humble affection. Let them prefer nothing whatever to Christ. And may He bring us all alike to life everlasting.[5]

Thus prudent severity, which should manifest itself in moderation, and mildness combine to form the essential qualities of the abbot, who has unlimited authority and makes all appointments to monastic offices on his own unhampered decision. Since the happiness of the family lies in his hands, it should consist in this, that he is loved as a father. The working of the Rule depends on his personality, whence it is understandable that Saint Benedict should so often speak of his qualifications. The abbot should not simply rule but should above all rule well. "It behooves him rather to profit his brethren than to preside over them (*prodesse quam praeesse*)."[6]

Everything depends on the abbot's pedagogical wisdom. Hence, to give him wise counsels in this direction is the chief concern of Saint Benedict. In the Rule, he has embodied a veritable treasury of educational wisdom. He cannot repeat often enough the fundamental principle of all pedagogy: that, in enforcing regulations, one must have regard for the individuality or peculiarities of each person. The second chapter especially is filled with such advice:

> Let the abbot take cognizance of the peculiarities of many; let him direct one with mild and kind words, another with sharp reproof, but a third by attempted persuasion. Thus let him suit himself to the peculiarity and the education of each, accommodating himself to all.

---

5. Translator's note: This English rendering is taken from Delatte-McCann, *The Rule of Saint Benedict: A Commentary*, pp. 487-489.

6. Ibid., p. 448 (C. 64). This play on words is to be found in Saint Augustine; cf. above, p. 109.

The monastic family seeks its end only within itself, and does not desire to project itself beyond its walls. That is why the lawgiver, who so strictly prescribed permanence in the same monastery, desired to see contact with the outside world avoided as much as possible. "Let not the brethren that return from a journey presume to relate what they have seen or heard outside the monastery, for that causes much harm."[7] For the site of his monasteries Saint Benedict chose remote mountain summits; he wanted them away from the large cities with their decay, and from the noise of battle which filled them at the time. We never hear that Benedict himself returned to Rome, even for a transient visit, after he had left it as a youth. But the seclusion from the outside world was to put no limitation upon hospitality. This was to be practiced as a part of Christian brotherly love, and the regulations pertaining to it point to a lofty trait of magnanimous courtesy.[8]

According to Saint Benedict's instructions, the monastery was to constitute a complete economic unit and produce as far as possible everything needed for the maintenance of the monks. The regulation reads as follows:

> The monastery ought to be so constructed that all things necessary, such as water, a mill, a garden, a bakery, and the various crafts may be contained within it; so that there may be no need for the monks to go abroad, for this is altogether inexpedient for their souls.[9]

In seclusion from the world the abbot was able to train his monks to become what he wanted them to be — the incarnation of the natural virtues once taught by the Roman Stoics and now ennobled by the Christian conception. Saint Benedict with his own serious and reserved personality is thus clearly reflected in the Rule. He was still influenced by the ancient Roman ideal of the *virtus,* that genuine virility which is foreign to everything effeminate and does not concede excessive influence to the imagination and the emotions, but entrusts the domination of man's mind to the will and intellect. *Honestas,* or the sense of justice, which together with

---

7. Delatte-McCann, p. 470 (C. 67).
8. C. 53, 56, 42.
9. Delatte-McCann, p. 466 (C. 66).

aequitas or fairness, should especially distinguish the judge, ranks high in his estimation. There are, in fact, several indications in the Rule that the juridical sense was particularly developed in Saint Benedict himself. External forms did not appear unessential to him, nor did he shrink from severity when it was necessary. The formulas by which the novice on his admission into the order binds himself to the society in an unequivocal contract, are prescribed with legal exactitude. The language of the Rule has all the terse explicitness of the Roman lawgivers and judges.

It reflects, too, that external dignity, *gravitas,* which is accorded to the monks by the Rule according to their rank. The insistence on *moderatio* and *discretio* — the prudent moderation which Saint Gregory the Great stresses so particularly — reminds us above all of the teachings of the Stoics. Had Saint Benedict remained in the world and gained prominence as a public servant, history would perhaps have described him as a proud official like Boethius, whose Roman dignity, if it came into conflict with another such Gothic ruler, would have cost him, too, his head. But his deep understanding of Christian ideals of virtue had taught him to practice strict self-discipline in order to temper the harshness and anger to which he perhaps inclined, with sincere love and forbearance for God's sake, and thus to practice the patience and humility which says: "By the grace of God I am what I am."[10]

Saint Benedict reveals himself to us as the perfect and authentic noble Roman, but not as a Roman of Cicero's time. On the contrary, he is a representative of that Rome whose aspirations for external power are shattered and whose heart has been freed from the curse of pride by the practice of the Christian virtues. He is a saintly Roman; his humble life, held up to millions as a model by his sons, enables us to understand why the new Christian culture could not have developed amid the proud monuments of the empire as once existing, but only in its ruins. A Roman living before the fall of the empire could hardly have written such a Rule, with its fundamental ideas of moderation and mildness. This was the spiritual harmony in which a Roman could find consolation for the fall

---

10. Prologue.

of Rome and which he was called upon to continue to teach in the empire now as before in the capacity of spiritual master of the nations.

Not as a Boethius, who accepted in proud and Stoic resignation the death sentence of Theodoric, nor as a Cassiodorus, the ever-obliging councilor of the Ostrogothic kings, who self-complacently looked back upon his elegantly couched governmental edicts — not thus did Saint Benedict meet the Goth Totila, who had been proclaimed king in 541. He met him with a dignity that craved nothing and feared nothing, that forced the man to his knees. Totila had achieved some temporary successes in the war with the generals of the Eastern Roman emperor Justinian — a war that lasted almost twenty years. It had even been possible for him to regain a foothold in Naples, and as he proceeded thence toward Rome, he came to the vicinity of Monte Cassino. Hearing of the miracles of the saintly abbot, he decided to test Saint Benedict's gift of prophecy. Riggo, Totila's swordbearer, was ordered to array himself in his master's purple while the king himself remained behind. But even from a distance — thus relates Pope Gregory the Great — the abbot called to the one approaching in royal disguise: "Lay aside, my son, the things you are wearing, for they do not belong to you." Dumbfounded, Riggo reported the experience to his master, who, immediately convinced of the abbot's sanctity, went to Saint Benedict and knelt before him. The abbot ordered him to rise, while he addressed him in a serious tone: "You have done much evil, and are still doing it. Desist from your wickedness. You will, indeed, enter Rome. You will cross the sea. Nine years more shall you be king, but in the tenth you shall die."[11]

We are not in a position to verify by any other evidence the prophetic words, with which the later events coincided, and thus to establish the absolute certainty of the scene; but that Totila came to Monte Cassino and paid his respects to the abbot is hardly to be questioned. Neither can anyone doubt that the attitude the story attributes to Saint Benedict is entirely consistent with the image we have in mind of the serious and saintly Roman. Similarly we can

---

11. S. Gregorius, *Dialog.*, II, c. 14, 15.

fairly assume that he saw little more in Totila than an Arian barbarian, and that he had to control himself in order not to show this by his expression. But he was a Christian, and so able to rise above the difference of race.

Among the wise lessons Saint Benedict gives the abbot is found the beautiful admonition:

> Whether bond or free, we are all one in Christ, and bear an equal burden in the army of one Lord: for "with God there is no respecting of persons." Only for one reason are we to be preferred in His sight, if we be found to surpass others in good works and in humility. Let the abbot, then, show equal love to all, and let the same discipline be imposed upon all according to their deserts.[12]

The portals of his monastery stood open also for the Goths. A second scene has been described for us by Saint Gregory the Great showing the profound impression that the quiet dignity of the pious abbot made upon a Gothic chieftain. A Goth named Zalla, doubtless engaged in collecting taxes, had demanded of a Roman peasant the surrender of his possessions, and to expedite delivery had the peasant tortured. In an effort to save himself in this extremity, the Roman declared he had willed his fortune to Saint Benedict. Desiring to establish the truth, Zalla mounted his horse and had himself led to Monte Cassino by the bound Roman. Saint Benedict sat before the monastery portal, reading. Not at all disconcerted by the strange visit and the haughty address of the Goth, he looked with compassionate eyes at the unfortunate peasant. Immediately the ropes fell from the man's hands. Perplexed and unnerved, Zalla threw himself on the ground and recommended himself to the holy man's prayers. After he had given orders that the Goth be taken into the monastery and had charged the brethren to wait on him with food and drink, Saint Benedict resumed his reading. When the guest was refreshed, he admonished him not to be so cruel in the future.[13]

The scene is symbolic of the position which the Benedictine monasteries were to occupy in the following centuries, when Ger-

---

12. Delatte-McCann, pp. 42-43 (C. 2).
13. S. Gregorius, *Dialog.*, II, c. 31.

mans and Romans would be brought together to form a common-wealth of nations, and rulers and subjects would be reconciled by Christianity. The representative of the ruling Germans mounted on horseback, the Roman bound, the two reconciled by the Roman monk steeped in spiritual reading. The scene also shows how sus-ceptible the Germans were to the calm and visible dignity which the founder of the Order so often imparted to his disciples.

Having examined the ideal of personality built up on the nat-ural disposition of the Roman, which Saint Benedict had realized in himself and held up to others for realization, we will next con-sider the occupations devolving upon the monks, individually and collectively. The *schola dominici servitii* — the troop — which felt itself placed before the throne of the Most High, was to render its service by praising God together in the Church's way: solemnly reciting the Office in choir punctually at the old appointed canonical hours, thus rendering Him homage in common prayer. Since this liturgical service of prayer was to constitute the principal occupation of the community, Saint Benedict devotes particular attention to its regulation. The monastic family is obligated to accompany the advancing and declining day with prayers and chants in the tradi-tional manner. The number twelve is retained for the nocturnal office of Matins as Saint Pachomius had introduced it in the monastic communities. But even here Saint Benedict does not exclusively adopt the Oriental custom. For the canticles of Lauds he follows the Roman model. And he shows by the little appended note, "As the Roman Church chants," that, in addition to the general monastic norms, the practice of Rome was finally decisive in the matter of details. Saint Benedict's family considered itself a monastic com-munity composed of Rome's own sons. The Divine Office, the daily service which the community offered to God, with its solemn gravity corresponded in particular to the character and tempera-ment uniting Benedict's sons. The saint further inculcated gravity by expressly stating that the monks designated by the abbot to chant or read the Office in choir should do so with humility, dignity and reverence.[14]

---

14. C. 47.

The time left free after the completion of the Office in choir — over which nothing was to take precedence[15] — was devoted to work, lest idleness creep in. In accord with the prescriptions given by Saint Augustine in his treatise concerning the work of monks, this work was to be a combination of the intellectual and the manual.[16] The intellectual labor, the *lectio divina,* was essentially the study of Sacred Scripture, clearly a necessary preparation for chanting the psalms. "But if anyone be so negligent and slothful as to be unwilling or unable to read or meditate, he must have some work given him that he be not idle."[17] Some have attempted to deduce from this passage that a great difference existed between the Benedictine monastery of Monte Cassino and Cassiodorus' monastery of Vivarium, the charge being that very little in the field of the systematic pursuit of knowledge was done at Monte Cassino. But what Cassiodorus says about work in his *Institutiones* is essentially the same as what Saint Benedict prescribes.[18] From the very Benedictine Rule itself we can collect allusions to not a few books which Saint Benedict consequently must have known, and which must have been in the monastery library. Besides the works of Cassian and Saint Basil and the biographies of the Oriental monastic Fathers which are explicitly named, we find references, more or less distinct, to various writings of Saint Augustine and Saint Jerome, Saint Cyprian and Saint Leo the Great, Saint Caesarius of Arles and Sulpicius Severus. Reminiscences of Sallust and Terence also appear. The truth is, Saint Benedict's difference from Cassiodorus lay in the fact that he did not make study the main purpose of his monastery. It was first and foremost a society formed for the purpose of praising God, an ordination whereby he secured for his communities that firm religious basis which alone could render them steadfast in the storms of the time.

Nor was physical labor in any wise disparaged by him. In this connection it is significant that we have no special chapter in the

---

15. C. 43.
16. Compare the passages parallel to chapter 48 of the Rule (ed. by Dom Cuthbert Butler, Freiburg i. B., 1912) in Saint Augustine's *De opere monach.*
17. Delatte-McCann, p. 316 (C. 48).
18. See above, pp. 154-155.

Rule dealing with scholars or writing rooms, but we do have one concerning artisans.[19] This does not cast any reflection on the Rule.

That the Benedictine Order should interest itself in the pursuit of learning was inevitable when the Church became the only institution to survive the disruption of ancient culture. Whatever could be saved of the latter's treasures was brought for safekeeping into the only edifice left standing; and the monasteries, that revered a Roman as their founder, gladly took charge of the heritage of antiquity. But since the trend of the times pointed to a decline of the cities and of all the activities associated with them — the financial system, as well as the urban accomplishments and urban organization — the Church also had to accommodate herself to this. Whereas formerly she was acquainted almost exclusively with urban cultural centers, now she had to consider establishing such centers in the open country; parishes had to be erected for the country folk who avoided the cities. The monasteries, which led the way in giving an inspiring example in both the economic and the intellectual sphere, were a blessed means of raising the religious and general intellectual level of the rural populations engaged in agriculture — especially of those in the kingdoms governed by the Germans.

In this regard Saint Benedict's monasteries were opportune foundations. They were usually established in spots far removed from cities, and constituted compact economic centers, similar to schools of household management, where intellectual and physical labor were simultaneously cultivated in an exemplary manner. Thus the monasteries arising in the wilderness north of the Alps became not only mission centers and outposts of religious life and intellectual culture in general, but also model institutions of economic culture for the development of agriculture and the various crafts. The Cistercians, who in the twelfth century undertook to reform the Benedictine Order, could justly refer to the oldest traditions of the Order in stressing physical labor.

Following the empire's disintegration, when the mission devolved on the monasteries of becoming the nurseries of a new cul-

---

19. C. 57.

ture in which energetic Christians came together according to the ideals of perfection, a series of advantages concurred to assign this task pre-eminently to the Benedictines. In accomplishing it they became an essential factor in the process of fusion whereby the emerging nations of the West united into a new cultural community. They were not the first monasteries of the West, as we have seen, and even after their rise other monasteries continued to work beside them in a commendable manner. But all these would eventually withdraw in favor of the Benedictine Order, whose Rule became from the eighth to the twelfth century the sole determining norm for monastic life in the West.

The advantages which gave the Benedictines this superiority did not lie in a greater zeal in striving to realize the Christian ideal. They are to be sought rather in the fact that the Benedictines had a particularly high value for the coming age; they were uniquely suited to the condition of Western society of that period, and they adapted themselves to the needs, the weakness and the forces of that society. And there were external circumstances, too, which did much to enhance this superiority.

We have just given an example of the advantages of the Benedictine method: the simultaneous interest in intellectual and physical labor, which does not neglect one type of work at the expense of the other, nor, above all, sacrifice that highest and primary purpose, transcending all human activity: the glorification of God in prayer. By tracing the harmony manifest here, as it appeared in all the regulations of the community, we can show how the basic appeal of the Benedictine Rule was increased and supplemented.

Apart from the detailed regulations concerning the Office in choir and the very emphatic demand of permanent residence in the same monastery, the Rule manifests a considerable latitude and elasticity. Thus the subordination of the unessential to the essential, to the main purpose, appears upon the whole one of the chief merits of the Rule. Everything pedantic is excluded and the way is kept open for the exercise of pedagogical insight and consideration, as well as for adjustment to particular conditions. In the various regulations concerning the material life it is mentioned more than once that these matters could just as well be regulated otherwise; or that these points can be carried out differently in the individual monasteries.

> Let clothing be given to the brethren suitable to the nature and climate of the place where they live: for in cold regions more is required, in warm regions less. It shall be the abbot's duty, therefore, to consider this.[20]

Its subordination of all that is unessential and rigidly fixed, and its adaptability to particular needs, made it easy for Saint Benedict's Rule to gain admission into older monasteries, which had been established originally according to other rules. The danger of arbitrary action and instability which might possibly have been the result of this, was removed by the fact that the monks were held together in virtue of their vow of permanent residence by an abbot who was elected for life. This official, moreover, guided by sincere solicitude, prudent judgment and firm purpose, could interfere in those matters not regulated once for all by fixed prescriptions, judging each case on its own merits and according to the circumstances. The secret of the power of the Benedictine Rule consists, therefore, in the union of a firm central principle with the greatest possible freedom in matters of detail; a freedom administered, not according to the judgment of the individual members of the society, but by a permanent commander invested with vast discretionary powers. In this way regard could be had for the weaknesses of the individual without the general discipline of the monastery suffering thereby, just as a single monastery could accommodate itself to the particular conditions of a region and not offend against the general spirit of the Rule.

The old Roman philosophy of life united with the self-control acquired by rigorous asceticism enabled the founder to strike that keynote in his Rule which has been justly designated as moderation and mildness. We encounter it in many of the regulations, those for the abbot as well as those for the lower superiors and the brethren in general. It is seen too in the directions for moderation and

---

20. Delatte-McCann, p. 346 (C. 55).

reserve which are to find expression in external conduct, and are so plainly reminiscent of Cicero's *De officiis*. Moderation, *moderatio*, was taught to the Middle Ages in particular by the Benedictines as the final goal of education and the finest ornament of man. Hence, we find a poet like Walther von de Vogelweide praising it in the beautiful words:

> *Aller werdekeit ein füegerinne*
> *das sît ir zewâre, frouwe Mâze.*
> *er saelic man, der iuwer lêre hât!*[21]

The many precious seeds which Saint Benedict planted in the soil of Monte Cassino did not begin to fructify for the masses, especially north of the Alps, until external circumstances led the Benedictines to labor outside their monasteries.

Nowhere is there any mention of a pastoral office to be exercised outside the monastery. The monastic community is, even in the opinion of Saint Benedict — as was the case with all the older monasteries — merely a community of lay brothers, in which ordinarily only one priest, the abbot, is found. The reception of a priest or the ordination of a monk to the priesthood is treated as an exceptional case. To such a one shall be accorded, indeed, the place after the abbot for his priestly functions, but he is to exercise these only so far as the abbot shall command him; for the rest, he shall receive, like the others, the place due him according to the time of his entrance into the monastery, unless the abbot and the wish of the community elect to promote him. In all things he is subject to the Rule, and he is forcefully admonished not to presume to be otherwise.[22]

All this, however, soon took a different turn because those who had acquired the necessary training were also ordained priests — a practice which became especially urgent when the Order was assigned missionary activities. The impulse to this move came from without, through Pope Gregory the Great, who sent the Roman

---

21. Walther von der Vogelweide. Edition of Pfeiffer (5th ed. Leipzig, 1877), 25, 1 sq.
22. C. 60, 62. Cf. Delatte-McCann, pp. 415-416, 427.

Benedictines to the Anglo-Saxons. The external circumstances which afforded the Benedictine Order its great cultural mission are certainly clearly present here. Yet it would surely be a one-sided, we might say a mechanical, conception of history to try to explain the great activity of the Benedictines as missionaries and promoters of culture solely by these circumstances. It is certainly very doubtful whether they would have accomplished such great results had not Saint Gregory directed them to missionary work (originally far from their thoughts), in particular to a mission field which was especially fruitful. But neither would Saint Gregory the Great have acted thus had he not recognized the Rule of Saint Benedict as an excellent one — his own words vouch for this — and had he not himself taken the habit of the Order and made the Benedictine spirit his own.

That the sons of Saint Benedict achieved such splendid results in this mission work is attributable in large part to their special character and the efficiency resulting from it. The point which originally militated against such work — their restriction to one monastery — even became a factor to promote it. In a secluded monastery, even in a foreign country, they could best preserve the spirit which they had taken with them from the motherhouse. The very fact that they lived aloof from the affairs of the world in accord with this spirit, secured for the Order that peaceful character which has remained peculiarly its own to this day. It was this same character which the Cluniac monks endeavored to preserve at the time of the Investiture Conflict.

The period from the fifth to the eighth century placed a particular obstacle in the path of the nascent culture of the West; this was a great national and cultural inequality, which had to be removed. Uncouth, rough, even savage Germans ruled over cultured Romans. Side by side with saints animated by a profound and pure idealism as well as a spirit of the greatest renunciation and sacrifice, we find, especially in the Frankish kingdom of the Merovingians, those who seem in comparison almost monsters with their repulsive mingling of sensuality, brutality and superstition.

It was not easy for monks not to overstress that moral opposition to such elements which the Christian ideals demanded; not easy to have patience, and to adapt themselves to diversified conditions so far as this was allowed and prudence admitted. But it was least difficult for Saint Benedict's disciples, for they had only to apply to the new conditions the wise pedagogical admonitions contained in their Rule. And when Pope Gregory I directed them to their first mission, among the Anglo-Saxons, it was the authority of the supreme head of the Church which inculcated in them individually the greatest consideration for the harsh dispositions and popular customs of that pagan people. Saint Gregory would not be the biographer and eulogist of Saint Benedict unless he had also instructed Saint Benedict's disciples in this very matter entirely in accordance with the mind of their founder. This is a point at which we see clearly how external circumstances, in their influence on the development of the Order, allied themselves with the internal advantages and with the directive ideas proceeding from the Rule itself. The pope who assigned the Order a field of activity promising such success, and who outlined the regulations for the monks, drew his own instructions from the spirit of the Rule.

For the adjustment of the differences between the races, the Church kept the admonition of the Epistle to the Galatians before her eyes — that we make no distinction between Hebrews and Greeks; and the Benedictines from the very beginning had been ready to serve as an instrument to this end when it was a question of uniting Romans and Germans in their own midst. We know that even in Saint Benedict's time there were Goths among his disciples. The manner in which King Totila and the Goth Zalla were received by him during the wars between the Goths and the Eastern Romans shows that only temporary obstacles remained, not such as tended to a permanent separation.

From the narration of these two visits we can also gather that the monastic community of Monte Cassino, although it was formed almost exclusively of Romans, attracted the Germans. We see this even more clearly when the Benedictines begin to establish monasteries in the Germanic kingdoms themselves. Several reasons can easily be advanced to explain this. Did not the organization of a Benedictine monastery agree essentially with the constitution the Germans had given their kingdoms? At the head of a Germanic kingdom stood an elective king, corresponding to the abbot elected by the monastic community. According to the Germanic theory every free member of the nation was eligible; according to the Benedictine Rule every member of the society, even the youngest, was eligible. The nobles of the kingdom surrounded the king as his councilors. So, too, in more important affairs the abbot was to call the community together and hear the advice of all the brethren; in less important matters he consulted with the older brethren, the decision, however, resting in his hand. Montalembert has ingeniously referred to the remarkable parallel.[23] Grisar, in his beautiful work on the history of Rome and the popes, adduces another: he represents the monastery as a "family under the fatherly government of the abbot," and recalls that the Germans were especially susceptible to family feeling, which was highly cultivated among them.[24]

We may point to other similarities between the Benedictines and the Germans. What impressed the Germanic warriors most was authority and dignity. Saint Benedict's personality made so great an impression on Totila and Zalla that they fell down before him, stirred to the depths. The solemn Office, performed with the greatest reverence as a service to the Divine Majesty, and the profound solemnity which was its dominant characteristic, must certainly have attracted the Germans in a special manner. We are also entitled to assume that the alternate chanting of the verses of the psalms, rendered with dignity by the Benedictine monks, was bound to touch the hearts of the Germans especially at a time when the Germanic imagination principally fed itself with the moving recital of epic themes.

If we follow the progress of the conversion of the Germans, we will notice a remarkable difference from the conversion of the Greco-Roman world. There, in the beginning, the lowest classes were the first to accept Christianity; in fact, the new teaching advanced so slowly in the highest circles — the last to cling to paganism — precisely because it was despised as the religion of the scum of society and devoid of all tradition. With the Germans, the peo-

---

23. *Les moines d'Occident*, II, 51.
24. Grisar, p. 563.

ple's acceptance of the Christian religion was usually brought about through the example of the princely houses embracing the faith. This was the case with the Goths, the Franks, the Bavarians, the Anglo-Saxons, the Thuringians and the Alamanni. The explanation is simply that Christianity was accepted by the Germans as a part of the superior Roman culture, and the princely houses were the first to come into contact with that culture.

These facts had to be taken into account by those who had been commissioned to influence the Germans. Is it saying too much to express the opinion that the Benedictines, with the importance they attached to external form, which the brethren were to observe even in their relations with each other, were particularly fitted for this task? According to the Rule, a hierarchy appointed by the abbot was to obtain among the brethren, and its determining factor was usually the date of entrance into the monastery. This order was to be observed at the kiss of peace, at Holy Communion, at the intoning of the psalms, and when standing in the choir. The younger brethren were commanded to reverence their elders. No one was permitted to address another simply by name, but the elder must address the younger as "frater" and the younger must address the elder as "nonnus," the equivalent of "reverend father." Wherever two brethren met, the younger was to ask a blessing of the elder in the customary form of salutation. When the elder passed by, the younger should rise; and the Rule continues: "The younger shall not presume to sit unless the elder bid him."[25]

Saint Benedict was led to formulate these instructions not only by the ideal of paternal authority in the old Roman family, but even more by his profound concept of the monastic community as a palace-guard in the service of the Lord. At Office in choir his society was to stand as before the throne of the Most High and to comport itself accordingly with all reverence. This could not but have its effect on the demeanor of every individual, and such dignified behavior was bound to make a great impression first and foremost upon the Germanic princely houses. We see its results in the considerable number of rulers among the German tribes who

---

25. C. 63. Cf. Delatte-McCann, pp. 431-438.

entered the Benedictine monasteries in the seventh and eighth centuries. The most renowned of these royal monks were Rachis of Lombardy and Carloman, the uncle of Charlemagne.

If Christianity was accepted by the Germans as a part of Roman culture, then the best missionaries were those who had absorbed Roman culture most profoundly. What other monastic group could compete with the Benedictine Order on this score? Everything that gave the Benedictine Order the external distinction it enjoyed everywhere among the Romance peoples had a still greater effect on the Germans. The founder had come from Rome, the mistress of the old world, from Rome which had understood so well how to impose her rule on the most diversified nations and peoples. In the period of her greatest splendor was accomplished the fullness of time, in which the Son of God had become man. Even though Saint Benedict only appeared as a son of Rome at a time when she had been stripped of her might and glory, she still, as if by a magical force, influenced her conquerors through the afterglow of her extinct worldly power.

In this Rome, then, there appeared more and more distinctly the center of the new spiritual power which alone was to unify the West. In the vicinity of Rome were established the first Benedictine monasteries. Rome's aristocratic circles furnished Saint Benedict his best disciples. Soon the Order gained a foothold in Rome itself. From the beginning he was guided by the customs of that Church which surpassed in authority all the other churches in the West. It was the authority of the papacy that caused the new Order to let its light shine, since no less a personage than Saint Gregory the Great had sketched in his *Dialogues* a reverent biography of the Order's founder. By the order of this pope, Saint Benedict's sons went on their first missionary venture — sent from the monastery which Gregory had established in his father's palace on the Caelian Hill, to the pagan Anglo-Saxons in England. When they began to labor there, they soon shone forth as perfect representatives of the high ancient culture. Intellectual and scientific pursuits were cultivated on so grand a scale under the direction of learned monks that the Frankish clergy soon were surpassed, even in the field of learning, by the disciples of Bede. What they taught the Anglo-Saxons in the economic and technical spheres, while teaching them agriculture and horticulture, cannot be proved by much detailed evidence. But the words borrowed from Latin which the German language still retains for designations of this kind, may fairly serve as a clue.

Benedict had chosen a time neither too early nor too late. The issue would hardly have been so fortunate if he had written his Rule when Rome was still exercising her worldly power. The fact that Rome had been freed from the spirit of pride, the unavoidable companion of worldly power, had led the best son she then possessed to outline and realize that ideal of an ennobled life which we meet in his Rule. Not the glory of Rome but the honor of the Most High is sought; every thought and desire is directed, not to Roman domination, but to the cultivation of a truly Christian personality. Thus Saint Benedict's disciples were not trained for a material reconquest of the world, but as missionaries of Christian culture who would spread a Kingdom above all racial and national differences. At the same time their training had another purpose: to preserve the best of the Roman *virtus* and transmit it to those peoples who had recently overthrown the Roman rule.

The foundation of Monte Cassino could not well have taken place later, for during the Gothic rule the whole Roman administrative system still continued in existence, and though it was under a Gothic ruler instead of a Western Roman emperor, his minister was the Roman Cassiodorus. And though this situation changed through the victories of the Eastern Romans in Italy, they made the conquered territory a province of the Byzantine Empire, where Greek officials ruled and, by their despotic orders, caused grave difficulties for the Holy See.

The dominion of the Eastern Romans was soon hemmed in by the advances of the Lombards. This still largely pagan people adopted an entirely different attitude toward the Romans than did the Goths. They swept the Roman administration wholly away, and only with their conquest does all that misery begin to come over Italy which earlier had attended the barbarian invasions in Gaul and Spain. Only now did the decline of Roman culture truly begin. Now ensued that chaos which separates antiquity from the Middle Ages, but which also binds the two periods together.

After Monte Cassino was destroyed by the Lombards, about 581, the monks took refuge with him who alone at that time could still give protection to Catholics and Romans — the bishop of Rome. Bringing with them only their most precious single possession, the original copy of the Rule, they secluded themselves near the Lateran Palace of the pope. Not until a century and a half later would Monte Cassino be rebuilt.

With the establishment of the Benedictine Order, it may be said that Christianized Rome had completed its preparation to become the basis for a new common culture in the West. Christianity could not save the empire, nor delay its fall any longer. In truth, as we have already seen, the empire *had* to pass away in order to make room for a free development of Christian culture. The broad masses of Roman society, locked in a rigid economic paralysis, oppressed by a suffocating system of taxation, and driven by senseless lust for pleasure and unbridled individualism, furnished that spectacle of a defunct and depraved culture so shockingly described by Salvian. It deserved to perish. That it did not disappear absolutely was due to those noble Romans whom we have been considering. Having absorbed the spirit of Christianity, they not only cast its profound concepts into the enduring form in which they would become the basis for a new culture, but also served as the connecting link between the new and the best part of the old, immortalized as it was in their own personalities. This was the service which Saint Ambrose performed, together with his contemporaries and successors, Sulpicius Severus, Saint Paulinus of Nola, Prudentius Clemens, and, surpassing all of them in genius, Saint Augustine. With the clarity of mind sometimes granted the dying, he compiled before the fall of Rome his grand synthesis of Greek speculation and Roman-Stoic philosophy with the faith and ecclesiastical teaching of Christianity.

The institution called upon to take over this spiritual legacy, not as a dead thing but as a living force, was the Church of Rome; and it was only by the collapse of the political empire that her supreme head, the pope, obtained the freedom to point the way as spiritual leader. The ministers who were to take charge of the legacy of ancient culture, were found ready at hand in the ranks of Saint

Benedict's sons. And when, by papal command, they were entrusted with the even higher mission of carrying the Christian teaching to the Germans, they became also messengers of civilization and peace spanning the chasm between the two races. Now the time was ripe for a common culture to be born. To bring this about would be, of course, no easy task. New obstacles continually arose. More than once the prospect seemed hopeless, and the West threatened to remain permanently in the chaos of the sixth century. But finally, in spite of all, the undertaking succeeded. And that it succeeded is the merit of the Church.

BOOK TWO

FORMATION OF THE CULTURAL COMMUNITY OF THE WEST BY THE CHURCH

FORMATION OF THE CULTURAL
COMMUNITY OF THE WEST BY THE CHURCH

THE idea of erecting a new community in place of the Western Roman Empire arose inevitably from the circumstances of the time, soon after the dethronement of Romulus Augustulus. Its first expression was, however, peculiar. Theodoric, the Ostrogothic king, conceived such a plan when with his warriors he set up his rule in Italy to replace that of Odoacer. One might, indeed, be inclined to question whether the credit for the idea should not be given rather to his prudent minister Cassiodorus, who composed his documents and who, being a Roman, desired to see a restoration, in some form at least, of Italy's rule over the West. The plan was supported by the sober political consideration that Theodoric's rule in Italy was threatened from the very beginning by the East. The military resources of Byzantium were far superior to those of the Ostrogoths, since the Byzantine fleet controlled the Mediterranean. It was only a question as to when the emperor of Byzantium would set these resources in motion. Actually the Ostrogothic kingdom did succumb to them later, when Justinian dispatched his generals Belisarius and Narses to the West, following his destruction of the Vandal kingdom in Africa. But the plan of Theodoric was not only political in character — it is precisely this fact that leads us to assume its author was Cassiodorus. As ruler of the country enjoying the cultural leadership in the West, Theodoric desired to achieve a Western hegemony, that is, to unite the rulers of the West into a commonwealth with himself as their suzerain. Since Germans were everywhere in power, the new commonwealth was to be built up on a union of the Germanic rulers and their tribes: the Franks in northern Gaul, the Burgundians in Sapaudia (Savoy), the Visigoths in southern Gaul and Spain, the Vandals in Africa, and the tribes north of the Alps — the Heruli, Thuringians and Alamanni. In his opinion, the means to the union lay in the establishment of personal relations and matrimonial ties with the kings of the Germanic tribes.

185

What kind of inducements he advanced in this connection is seen in his letter to King Hermenefrid of Thuringia, whose kingdom extended to the Danube. This letter was delivered by Amalaberga, Theodoric's niece, whom he sent to the Thuringian ruler to become his wife:[1]

> You, who are of royal blood, shall now shine far and wide by the splendor of the Amalian House [House of Amals, to which Theodoric belonged]. We send you an ornament for court and home, one that will enhance the whole tribe and bring the comfort of true counsel, that most gracious sweetness of marriage. She shall share the government with you and direct your people by her wise instructions. Happy Thuringia shall possess what Italy has brought forth, a maiden trained in the sciences, well-grounded in morality, enriched not only by her ancestry but also by her womanly dignity, that your country may become renowned no less by her excellent comportment than by its own triumphs.

The letter was written by Cassiodorus, who perhaps believed that the Gothic princess thus highly praised could occupy a place in the Thuringian kingdom similar to that which Galla Placidia, sister of the emperor Honorius, formerly held at Barcelona by the side of Ataulf, the Visigothic king. As the representative of a superior culture, Amalaberga was to gain the Thuringian ruler for Theodoric and his league of nations. The same aims likewise guided Theodoric when he disposed of his daughter Ariagne, or Ostrogotho, to the Burgundian crown prince Sigismund. He also took pleasure in parading before the eyes of the Burgundian king Gundibald, Sigismund's father, the cultural superiority of the kingdom over which he ruled, by sending him a sundial and a clepsydra, or water clock, which Gundibald had requested. The bearer of these gifts, as we have already seen, was Boethius, the greatest scholar of Italy.

With the gifts was sent a letter to the effect that Gundibald's people should abandon their barbaric customs. Strange in the mouth of Theodoric, but certainly reproducing the thoughts of Cassiodorus faithfully, are the words of this letter giving Boethius his commission, words haughty with pride of culture:[2]

---

1. Cassiodorus, *Variae*, IV, No. 1.
2. Ibid. I, 45, 46.

May all the foreign peoples realize, through you [i. e., Gundibald],
that we have such men as this, illustrious figures, who are read as authors. . . . And when they recover from their astonishment, they will
no longer dare to put themselves upon the same level with us, in whose
midst, as they now know, wise men have thought out such great things.

Theodoric also had Boethius procure for Clovis, the Frankish king,
whose sister was Theodoric's second wife, a zither-player, intended
to tame the savage hearts of the barbarians, like Orpheus, with
charming lays. Finally, he married another daughter to Alaric II,
the Visigothic king, and his sister to Thrasamund, king of the
Vandals.

As the suzerain of a league of nations, he took under his
protection the Alamanni, who had fled before King Clovis from the
regions of the Lower Main and the Neckar to the Swabian plateau
and the Alpine valleys. He likewise ordered Clovis to cease his
attacks against the Visigothic kingdom. And when the Franks and
Burgundians would not desist from the campaign in southern Gaul,
Theodoric marched against them (509), annexed Provence to his
kingdom, and guaranteed to the Visigoths Septimania, the important
link of communication between the two Gothic kingdoms. As
guardian of his grandson Amalric, the infant king of the Visigoths,
he protected his possession of the throne, himself governing the
Visigothic kingdom until Amalric attained his majority in 522.
During a famine in Gaul he forced Italian merchants to ship grain
thither, and when they suffered shipwreck reimbursed them for their
loss. In giving his sister Amalafrida in marriage to Thrasamund,
king of the Vandals, he bestowed on her as a dowry Lilybaeum,
the Sicilian bridgehead to Africa, and assigned her a retinue of
6,000 warriors who were to secure his influence in that country.

Thus it seemed as though the Western Roman Empire were to
be renewed under a Germanic king residing in the imperial city of
Ravenna. But Theodoric deceived himself. He commanded only
as far as his military resources extended, and they were much more
limited than his ambitions. For these he lacked the sound cultural
foundation which might have served as a unifying bond between the
diverse Germanic kingdoms. If he intended to seek this foundation in the old Roman culture, he overlooked the fact that there

existed profound, inherent differences between his Roman subjects and the Gothic warriors — differences of faith and of nationality. His plan and that of Cassiodorus to build a homogeneous kingdom on the basis of diversity, keeping the Goths and the Romans apart — the former ruling as proud warriors, the latter contenting themselves with the servant's role of culture-bearers — proved itself a dream, from which he was to be roughly awakened before the end.

Theodoric hardly merited the title of The Great for his political acumen. In this quality the Merovingian ruler, Clovis, far surpassed him. Clovis built his kingdom on the only sound basis: the fusion of the Franks and Romans through the common acceptance of the Catholic faith. Thereby he secured for the Frankish kingdom the ascendancy over the Germanic states. Had Theodoric followed this course, he would perhaps have fully deserved to be called "great." Had he and his Goths accepted the Catholic faith, the destinies of the West would have perhaps been different. He might then have realized his plans, for the Goths would have fused with the Romans. In view of their small number there existed for them no other alternative. Maintaining opposition to the Romans could only lead them to destruction. Had the Ostrogoths embraced the faith of the Romans, the Eastern Romans would scarcely have been able to reconquer Italy, nor would the Merovingian kings have attained a position so decisive that the political center of gravity was securely fixed in the north throughout the whole medieval period.

But neither did the Merovingians, in turn, accomplish to the full the solidifying of their power by means of a sound cultural foundation. For this, the reigning family showed itself far too weak morally. The whole ruling class, in fact, fell into a state of deep moral decay; nor did any remedy for this appear until the seed sprang up which the Roman Benedictines had sown in the kingdom of the Anglo-Saxons, and its ripened fruits were brought across the Channel by Saint Willibrord and Saint Boniface. These Anglo-Saxon missionaries, through their religious idealism and their moral strength, really created the cultural community of the West by entering into a close union with the head of the Church of Rome. On this basis Charlemagne could then erect an empire which was truly a cultural community. In it there were two separate centers of power. The political headship was vested at first in the Carolingians, then in their successors north of the Alps; the moral-religious headship was vested in the popes. In this form the cultural community of the West was to continue to develop during the Middle Ages.

This is the great historical frame within which was to be formed the cultural community of the West. It could not have come into being without the co-operation of the Church, which alone gave it a sound foundation and great intrinsic value. The development was not achieved without sharp struggles and mighty labors. We will try to become acquainted with its individual phases in the pages that follow.

CHAPTER ONE

GERMANIC ARIANISM AND ROMAN CATHOLICISM

THE first phase of the struggle for a cultural foundation in the West is seen in the conflict between Germanic Arianism and Roman Catholicism. It coincided with the conflict between the ruling Germans and the subjugated Romans, but also went beyond it. To the extent that it coincided, it became the question of whether the Germans would fuse with the Romans or not. Since the Romans were almost everywhere more numerous, fusion could only mean the final absorption of the rulers by the ruled. This process of absorption, retarded by the religious difference, began to be apparent soon after the difference had disappeared. But apart from the situation in Italy, the Germans residing in their native country and in England were also involved. They, too, were on the verge of being completely won over to Arianism. Had this happened, the Germans and Romans could never have been united into a cultural community, for such a community could be rooted only in religion. A Western civilization would then never have been formed. This shows us the importance of the struggle: its outcome determined the culture of the West.

The remarkable point is that at the start the religious conflict did not stem from the national; for the Germans had accepted Arianism, in the short time in which they were in contact with the Eastern Roman Empire, as the gift of Byzantine culture. The influence of the spirit of the ancient world upon the Germans at first had made itself felt from the East rather than from the West. The East-Germanic Gothic tribes, the first to move, had in the course of their migration from the Baltic to the Black Sea and the lower Danube reached the confines of the Eastern Roman Empire. Here, in 275, they forced the emperor Aurelian to relinquish to them the rich province of Dacia. These regions were so near the new center of Byzantine power and culture, the capital named for Constantine, that the religious influence from there was soon bound to be felt.

Christianity, however, was not first brought to the Goths by Byzantine missionaries, but by Christian prisoners whom they had captured, and by Gothic soldiers who had entered the Roman army serving on the frontier. As early as 325 there appeared at the Council of Nicaea a bishop from the country of the Goths.

A determining influence upon their choice of creed was exerted by the renowned Ulfilas. He was the son of a Christian family — his father was a Goth, his mother a Cappadocian — that had migrated from Asia Minor to the land of the Goths, and as their ambassador he himself came to Constantinople in 337. About four years later Eusebius of Constantinople consecrated him bishop of the Christians in the land of the Goths north of the Danube. A persecution of the Christians by Athanaric, the pagan king of the Visigoths, which produced such martyrs as Saints Sabbas and Nicetas, led Ulfilas to settle with his flock south of the Danube, in the province of Lower Moesia. Here Ulfilas enjoyed great esteem. He took part in several councils, and as spokesman for the Arians he had negotiations with the emperor Theodosius. Invited to a disputation at Constantinople, he died there in 383. Ulfilas invented a Gothic alphabet and translated the whole Bible into Gothic from the Greek text as it existed at the time. Thus he bequeathed to his people a work decisive for their faith, and which has remained for all time a highly valuable linguistic document. Many words in High German seem to prove that the Goths were the first among all the Germanic peoples to have phrased Christian concepts after Greek models. Such words are, for example, *Kirche* (church), *Bischof* (bishop), *Heide* (heathen), *Pfaffe* (cleric), *Samstag* (Saturday), *Pfingsten* (Pentecost), *Pfinztag,* that is, *Donnerstag* (Thursday according to the Greek πέμπτη — the fifth day), *Taufe* (baptism), and *Teufel* (devil).

In the meantime the Huns from the East had come upon the Goths; they had subjugated the Ostrogoths and forced a section of the Visigoths to seek refuge across the Danube in the Roman Empire, as Ulfilas had done earlier. In time these masses rebelled under the oppressions of Byzantine officials. The emperor Valens, who marched against them, was defeated at Adrianople in 378. Under Alaric they made their appearance in Italy, capturing Rome in 410:

the city's first fall. Alaric, who belonged to the second generation following the incorporation of the Goths into the Roman
Empire, had grown up as a Christian. This explains the restrictions
he placed upon the Goths in their three-day pillage of Rome, restrictions which Saint Augustine presents in the beginning of *The
City of God* as a particularly merciful dispensation — meanwhile
reproaching the pagan Romans because their ancestors had not
treated conquered cities with nearly as much mercy as the barbarians.
Actually it was a great blessing at this juncture, especially for the
Roman Church, that these warriors of Alaric were, if not Catholics,
at least Arians and not pagans. Reverence for the Princes of the
Apostles restrained them from laying hands on the basilicas of the
Apostles and other shrines of martyrs. Alaric had the two basilicas
of the Apostles declared an asylum, and how he was able to enforce
this command is described for us by the contemporary writer
Orosius in a scene which has often been retold.[1]

 While the rapacious warriors dispersed themselves throughout
the city to make as much use of the time allowed for plundering as
they could, one of the leading Goths came to a house situated near
Saint Peter's, where the ecclesiastical treasures of that basilica were
being guarded by a consecrated virgin. When the Goth beheld the
precious gold and silver plate, he was bewildered by the wealth
which they represented. The custodian called out to him: "These
are the sacred vessels of the Apostle Peter; desecrate them if you
have the audacity; settle that in your own mind; I am unable to
defend them." The Goth caused the incident to be reported to the
king, and Alaric commanded the treasure and its guardian to be
brought under safe-conduct to Saint Peter's. A strange procession
then wended its way amid the plunderers to the basilica, for many
Romans joined the armed escort to seek asylum. They sang hymns,
in which the barbarians also joined. "Thus resounded throughout
the falling city the trumpet of salvation." It was a memorable hour,
this, in which for the first time Romans and barbarians chanted in
unison the praises of God. Yet, though full of the promise of salvation, it was the sign of a future which seemed to recede the more

---

1. Orosius, *Hist.*, 7, c. 39.

the closer one approached it; and it was ultimately destined to show still more clearly the real depth of the cleavage created between the Goths and the Romans by difference of creed.

The first temporary *rapprochement* of the two races reached its climax soon after the death of Alaric, under his successor, King Ataulf. Ataulf marched on Gaul with the Visigoths, taking with him Galla Placidia — the sister of the emperor Honorius — who was made a prisoner when Rome was captured. It is to the Gothic chieftain's credit that he respected the dignity of this imperial princess during the several years she was his captive, and waited patiently until she freely declared herself willing to become his bride. At Narbonne in January, 414, the marriage, celebrated according to the Roman rite, took place in the home of a distinguished citizen. Adorned as empress in the Roman fashion, Placidia sat in the atrium of the mansion. Ataulf, in Roman dress, took his place at her left. It was at this time that Ataulf first formed the plan that Theodoric later tried to execute. Regarding this Orosius tells us some interesting things, related to him in Bethlehem by a citizen of Narbonne. According to this story, Ataulf apparently abandoned the old Gothic program in the city which had witnessed his nuptials, and adopted a new one in accord with the condition allegedly set up by Placidia for her consent to the marriage. Ataulf himself is supposed to have said that formerly he wanted to subjugate the whole Roman Empire with his Goths; when he had learned, however, through many experiences, that the Goths because of their unbridled savagery were unable to obey laws — without which no state can be a state — he aimed at securing for himself the glory of restoring and enhancing the Roman name with the help of the Gothic troops. Hence, as commander of the military forces, and under continuing Roman administration, Ataulf wanted only to provide for the safety and tranquillity of the Roman Empire.

The plan according to which Theodoric and Cassiodorus governed at a later time, had thus been devised earlier by Ataulf and Placidia. But it was doomed to be quickly frustrated. In Barcelona, where he had taken up residence with his wife, Ataulf suffered the loss of the son Placidia bore him. The birth of this child had been greeted with high hopes because he was to have been the guarantee for the reconciliation and fusion of the Romans and the Goths. In fact — and this is very significant — he was given a Roman name, that of his grandfather Theodosius, who unlike any other Spaniard, had acquired a brilliant reputation in the Roman Empire. In 415, soon after his son's death, the king himself was murdered by a servant, and forthwith there began a national reaction on the part of the Goths to gain control of the government. Placidia was compelled by King Sigeric, who had forcibly seized the reins of power, to walk more than two miles before him in the company of other captives; she must have been happy when, in recompense for a peace finally granted the Goths by Honorius, she was permitted to return to Ravenna. There, as the mother of Valentinian III, whom she bore in second marriage to the Roman general Constantius, she played the role of a Roman empress. It turned out to be a sorry one. Henceforth the Visigoths, especially under King Euric (466-485), pursued a national, anti-Roman policy which made itself felt by a strong insistence on Arianism as their national religion.

In the beginning the Goths had accepted the Arian creed without any particular investigation — which, indeed, it was hardly possible for them to make. But when they settled among the Romans in the West, they began to attach great importance to their confession in order to emphasize their own character as against that of the Catholic Romans and to mark the disparity between them. Arianism became their national religion. The Bible of Ulfilas was written in their language, and they also wanted to conduct their liturgy exclusively in that tongue. To the fundamental dogmatic opposition was thus added the difference in liturgical language, which many at that time felt to be even more important. Arianism, which had completely disappeared from Roman Christianity in the West from the time of Theodosius, took on a new lease of life as the Germanic creed. It spread with surprising rapidity from the Visigoths to the Gothic tribes under the suzerainty of the Huns, the Ostrogoths, the Gepids, the Heruls and the Vandals who had moved from Silesia to the Carpathian Mountains. Other German tribes who came to the middle Danube, also accepted Christianity in the form of Arianism. In Noricum, the Germanic tribes who came into contact with the Romans protected by Saint Severinus, were Arians also. And Arian Rugians accompanied Odoacer to Italy.

The importance of Arianism grew tremendously when the Vandals in Africa and the Visigoths in southern Gaul and Spain had established powerful national states; for these states, as a matter of policy, championed the cause of Arianism, regarded by them as their national creed. The Arian Church with its bishops and priests occupied in these realms the position of a state-church to which was assigned the task of serving the state's policy. This is noticeable among the Visigoths in the fifth century, who made vigorous propaganda for their religion. Through them Arianism, possibly present before in embryo, seems to have been strengthened among the Vandals when they came into contact with the Visigoths in Spain. The same thing happened among the Burgundians. Concerning the latter, we have reports that they had embraced Catholic Christianity after they settled on the middle Rhine, in the second decade of the fifth century. This seems questionable. In any case, if they really had adopted the Catholic religion at that time, it did not make a deep impression upon them, for soon after they were established in Sapaudia by Aëtius in 443, they appear very definitely as Arians.

A common campaign undertaken in 456 with the Burgundians against the Suevians in Portugal, afforded the Visigoths the opportunity either to gain the Suevians for Arianism or to confirm them in the Arianism already existing among them. These Suevians, to whom the emperor Honorius in 411 had assigned Gallaecia (Galicia), in the northwest of the Iberian Peninsula, as a place of settlement and whose capital became the city of Braga in Portugal, had a Catholic king as early as 450. But an alliance which their king, Remismund, concluded with the Visigoths in 464, led to their acceptance of Arianism. Ajax, an Arian bishop who had been sent to the Suevians with a Visigothic princess to effect a matrimonial alliance, actually introduced Arianism among them. We also hear of an Arian prince, Gibuld, among the Alamanni about 470, who certainly had been converted to Arianism through Visigothic influences.

Thus it came to pass that the Arian faith was called the Gothic faith, while the Catholic faith was called the Roman. The Catholics were designated as *Romani* or, also, as *Christiani*. The religious and national differences between Arians and Catholics, between Goths and Romans, coincided with and aggravated the opposition obtaining everywhere in the divisions of the former Roman Empire now governed by the Gothic tribes. This reached its climax at the end of the fifth century. As far as Christian rulers governed in the West at the time, Arianism held sway: in Italy through the Arian Ostrogoths, in southern Gaul through the Arian Burgundians and Visigoths, in Spain through the Visigoths and Suevians, and in Africa through the Vandals who developed their domination there under Genseric in 429.

A change was heralded at the beginning of the sixth century. Clovis, the Frankish king, received Catholic baptism, and after the battle of Vouillé in 507, took most of Southern Gaul from the Arian Visigothic king, Alaric II, son-in-law of Theodoric the Great. This reverse movement continued, spreading next to the Burgundians, whose king, Sigismund, before ascending the throne between 496 and 499, had been converted to the Catholic faith by the zealous Bishop Avitus of Vienne. Arianism lost its hold on the Burgundians completely when their kingdom was conquered by the Franks in 532. A little later, in 534, the Arian kingdom of the Vandals in Africa collapsed under the attack of Belisarius. The Ostrogothic kingdom also surrendered, in 553, to the generals of the Byzantine Catholic emperor, Justinian. Soon afterward, it is true, the half-pagan and half-Arian Lombards seized a foothold in Italy in place of the Ostrogoths. But though the conversion of the stubborn Lombards to Catholicism proceeded slowly in the seventh century, it proceeded irresistibly. The Spanish Visigoths, with King Reccared at their head, had, after a violent internal crisis, become Catholics as early as 586.

Thus the antagonism between Germanic Arianism and Roman Catholicism divided the West for almost two hundred years — that is to say, from the beginning of the fifth to the end of the sixth century.

This antagonism made itself felt in many directions. It dominated social relations as much as religion and politics. The Germans as the rulers were the representatives of the Arian creed, the Romans as the subjects were the representatives of the Catholic. The antithesis hindered the fusion of the two nationalities; and yet the actual establishment of governments in countries with a predominantly Roman population was possible only through such fusion. The Germanic rulers spent themselves in very diverse attempts to found secure and permanent states. In most of them the Germans lived scattered among the Romans, which should have resulted in the growth of social and economic relations between them. But Theodoric wanted to prevent this. He kept the Germans and Romans separated both religiously and socially, as was the case in the Burgundian and Visigothic kingdoms. By this policy, he only re-enforced the obstacle to that peaceful cohabitation which he so strongly desired. The obstacle became insurmountable when the Eastern Romans invaded Italy.

The scattered settling of the Germans among the Romans, which weakened the natural vigor inherent in their former tribal life, was bound up with the quartering law of ancient Rome. Odoacer had already made this law the basis of his demands for lands, and it was modified to such an extent that the Roman proprietor had to surrender to the Germanic warrior one-third of his house — not merely in usufruct but as the German's property — and, in addition, one-third of his land and slaves. When the Burgundians emigrated into Sapaudia, they demanded from the great Roman landowners one-half of their possessions; later they insisted on receiving two-thirds, a system which had been introduced by the Visigoths immediately upon their settlement in Aquitania.

Among the Vandals in Africa another system had been set up by Genseric, who wanted to preserve the tribal vigor which came from the union of the clans and their common life. The Romans were, for the most part, driven from the vicinity of Carthage in the plain country of proconsular Africa, or enslaved and distributed with the lands to the Vandals, who settled thereon in compact groups. Thus the antagonism took on an added provincial character here. Apart from this Vandalic district (the *sortes Vandalorum*, where the undivided estates had all been disposed of by lot to the Vandals), there stood the remaining three-fourths of the country where the Romans remained, governed by Vandal chieftains as counts and dukes. All this explains the peculiar bitterness of the antagonism in Africa, where the Vandals had already perpetrated unparalleled horrors at the very beginning of the conquest. Thousands of distinguished Romans had been reduced to slavery and this naturally aggravated the religious opposition. The final result was a persecution of the Catholics which nowhere else reached such extremes. The Vandals, moreover, were incited to these measures by the sect of Donatists, some remnants of whom still managed to survive. The hot climate of Africa may also have contributed its share, for the otherwise unbloody conflict between ancient paganism and Christianity had led to other shameful deeds of violence there, particularly in Egypt.

Alexandria, too, had been the scene of brutal religious struggles between the adherents of its local agitator, Arius, and the Catholics. The Vandal king, Hunneric (477-484), has left a particularly evil name behind him as a persecutor. Bishop Victor of Vita, writing contemporaneously, has described this persecution in powerful and graphic language. Martyrs and confessors were conspicuous here. Prominent among the bishops sent into the deserts or banished to Sardinia and Corsica, were Bishop Eugenius of Carthage, and the apologists Vigilius of Thapsus and Saint Fulgentius of Ruspe, the latter one of the greatest theologians at the beginning of the sixth century.

The persecuted Catholics received Belisarius, the Byzantine general, with open arms when he put an end to the Vandal kingdom. The opposition between the Catholic Romans and the Arian Vandals was thus not overcome internally, but decided against the latter by the power of the sword. This was also the case with the Ostrogoths.

The situation ended differently in the other Arian kingdoms — the Burgundian, the Visigothic, the Suevian, and finally, the Lombard. In these kingdoms the conflict was decided in favor of the oppressed by the superiority of the Roman Church and Roman culture. It was a long struggle, however, the fortunes fluctuating to and fro, especially in Spain and southern Gaul. In almost every

major city there were Gothic churches beside the Catholic ones and
Arian bishops beside the Catholic bishops. The centers of the Arian
churches were naturally the residential cities of the Arian rulers:
Ravenna, where there were six Arian episcopal churches during the
reign of Theodoric; Carthage, where a patriarch functioned as the
state's highpriest at the head of the Arian bishops; Barcelona,
where the Visigothic kings resided for a time; and Burgundian
Vienne. In Rome itself there were two Arian churches — Saint
Agatha's in Suburra on the Quirinal and another on the Esquiline —
which, however, are to be regarded only as military churches for
the Germanic soldiers like the Arian churches in Byzantium. Possession of the churches was often the subject of disputes. We
further hear of Catholic and Arian priests trying to gain admission
into families to work for the interests of their creeds. There were
mixed marriages also, which were additional subjects of dispute
between the priests of both faiths.

To what extent the difference of creeds penetrated into the
family is seen from an account found in the *Liber de gloria martyrum*
of Saint Gregory of Tours, a work rich in materials.[2]

A Catholic woman and an Arian man had entered into marriage. The wife wished to invite the Catholic priest to a banquet.
The husband consented, but invited the Arian priest also, whom he
placed to his right, the Catholic priest being at his left, and next to
the latter his wife. At the husband's invitation, the Arian priest
blessed the food with the sign of the cross. When he repeated this
act at the fourth course — this must have been, therefore, a pretty
good dinner — and thereafter ate, he burned himself so severely
with the over-hot food that he died on the spot. The Catholic
priest considered this a judgment of God and continued to eat with
pleasure. The Arian husband thereupon turned Catholic.

The narrative must have created a great impression, for Saint
Gregory relates it as a "celebrated case." One can well imagine
that the people of the period delighted in retelling the incident,
though its authenticity in every detail is open to doubt. It char-

---

2. Gregory, *Gloria martyrum*, c. 79.

acterizes well the social conditions existing in Southern Gaul in the second half of the fifth century and betrays the barbarous taste insinuating itself everywhere, even into religious conceptions; it marks at the same time that blending of the cultured and the barbarian that was taking place in Gaul as well as in the other countries. The Arian husband was certainly a high-ranking Gothic general or official, who had married a distinguished Roman lady and respected her finer training.

The point of the story lies in its exposing the powerlessness of the Arian priest and his blessing, for his sudden death while eating appears as a judgment of God. Judgments of God had a very great effect on the Germans. What moved the Germanic warriors most easily to forsake their cult, whether pagan or Arian, and profess the Catholic faith, was the conviction of God's *power*. This cannot surprise us in the case of those mighty yet naive men, who were impressed above all by external force and who submitted willingly when they believed the Supreme Power was manifesting itself in the ordeals. We encounter this frame of mind in many narratives. We find it in the account of Clovis' attitude in the battle with the Alamanni, when he vowed his conversion if the Christian God granted him victory; and again, in the tale of the felling of the oak of Thor at Geismar by Saint Boniface. It is remarkable, that the longing for judgments of God illustrated here, which fostered a boundless belief in miracles, penetrated also into Romance circles. It led, of necessity, to a barbarization of the Catholic faith which took centuries to overcome.

We see also from Saint Gregory's story how close the association between Arians and Catholics was at this time. There were even instances of Catholic ecclesiastics being invited to meals by Arian priests. This, however, was strictly forbidden at a national council held in Burgundy (at Epaon, near Vienne) in 517 — the first year of the reign of the Catholic king Sigismund. By its decree, a Catholic priest who partook of an Arian priest's meal was excommunicated for a year.[3]

---

3. Can. 15: *Mon. Germ. Concil.,* I, 22.

The principal centers of Catholicism in Gaul were Tours, where in the year 450 the magnificent basilica was erected over the tomb of Saint Martin, the Apostle of Gaul; and Poitiers, where Saint Hilary, the mightiest adversary of Arianism in the Roman West during the fourth century, was venerated. When, in 507, Clovis, the Catholic king of the Franks, marched against the Arian Visigothic king, Alaric II, and a decision between Arianism and Catholicism in Gaul was imminent, a messenger was dispatched to Tours to obtain for Clovis a sign of heaven's disposition. The messenger entered the basilica just as the celebrant intoned the antiphon: "Thou hast girded me, O Lord, with strength unto battle." Likewise, when Clovis came before Poitiers, he saw from his tent a column of fire shooting up from the basilica of Saint Hilary and inclining toward him.[4] These accounts show clearly that Clovis, in marching against Alaric, was regarded in Catholic circles as the ally of Saint Martin and Saint Hilary, and why the victory, which he gained at Vouillé, near Poitiers, was attributed to their intercession.

The marriages of rulers were regarded with particular suspense; the faith of the bride raised, on the one hand hopes, on the other misgivings. We see repeatedly how queens who differed from their husbands in faith, proselytized for their own — and sometimes even had to suffer for it. Religious disputations between representatives of the creeds were not rare, and at their conclusion an ordeal was proposed — doubtless because no other means seemed so decisive.

The religious differences naturally played a part in foreign politics. While the Eastern Roman emperor complained to the Vandals and Ostrogoths about the persecution of Catholics, Theodoric the Great and Hunneric the Vandal threatened reprisals to obtain religious freedom for the Arian Germans — doubtless soldiers in Constantinople. All this proceeded from that strained relationship which finally led to open war and the destruction of the Ostrogothic and Vandalic kingdoms. In Spain, the Frankish Merovingian power, which had already restricted the Visigoths to the strip of Septimania in Gaul, repeatedly intervened for the

---

4. Gregory, *Hist. Franc.*, Lib. II, c. 36 sq.

Catholics. The molestation of Catholic queens married to Visigothic rulers provided the principal occasion for intervention.
Clovis' daughter, the sister of the Frankish ruler Childebert, was
married to Amalric, the king of the Visigoths, who would not
tolerate his wife's attendance at Catholic services. He so far forgot
himself as to have the queen pelted with dung and other refuse
while she was on her way to church; finally he even beat her.
Clotilda, the chastised queen, appealed to her brother for help,
and sent him her bloodstained handkerchief as proof of the cruel
treatment accorded her. Inflamed with rage, Childebert advanced
in 531 with a Frankish army, defeated the Visigoths near Narbonne,
and took his sister under his own protection. King Amalric tried,
it was said, to reach the asylum of the Catholic church, but before
he could do so he was transfixed by a Frankish spear. According to
another version, however, he was murdered in Barcelona.

The Visigothic kings, in their capacity as Arian rulers, were
hemmed in even more when the Eastern Romans had regained
possession of northern Africa and were thus able to establish a
foothold in the maritime cities of the Visigothic kingdom. When
the Visigothic king Leovigild realized the danger, there arose within
him a terrible mistrust of the Roman Catholics — similar to that
which Theodoric experienced in his last days — and these were
made to suffer a severe persecution.

The king's suspicions did not even stop at his own son and
co-regent, Hermenegild. The latter was particularly hated by his
Arian stepmother Goisvintha, Leovigild's second wife and the
widow of his predecessor Athanagild. Hermenegild had married
a Catholic Frankish princess, Ingunthis (daughter of the ruler
Sigebert and Brunhilda): it was on this pair that the Catholics in the
Visigothic kingdom pinned their hopes for a brighter future. But
Ingunthis was actually Goisvintha's granddaughter, since Brunhilda
had been Goisvintha's daughter by the now dead Athanagild. And
the grandmother tried every means to compel Ingunthis to exchange
the Catholic faith for the Arian, finally having her rebaptized by
force. Hermenegild could not quietly accept this treatment of his
wife; and Leovigild, to prevent any future scandals, appointed him
a separate residence in Seville, whence he was to govern the southern

provinces of the realm. Here, with the help of Saint Leander, who was a monk, Ingunthis prevailed upon her husband to embrace the Catholic religion in 579. The father was highly indignant and wanted to exclude his son from the succession despite the fact that he had already been designated co-regent. To counter this design and procure protection and support, Hermenegild concluded a separate peace with the Byzantines, who were still at war with the Visigoths. He also sent Leander to Constantinople to solicit reinforcements from the emperor Tiberius. In the struggle that ensued between Hermenegild and his father, Leovigild was victorious; he took Seville and through a ruse had his son delivered up to him by the Greek commander of Cordova. Hermenegild, after refusing to receive Holy Communion from the hands of an Arian bishop, was beheaded in prison on Easter Day, 585. Catholics venerated him as a martyr.

Leovigild did not long survive the bloody end of his oldest son. He realized finally to what a pass he had brought his realm and that there was but one means whereby it could escape annihilation by the Franks and Eastern Romans — namely, acceptance of the Catholic faith. He had already attempted to bridge the fateful gap in his dominion by following a middle course: having a conciliatory creed set up by an Arian synod held at Toledo from 581 to 582, which did not demand the repetition of baptism but merely the imposition of hands. Despite the severity with which he characteristically tried to enforce acceptance of this creedal compromise, he had failed signally to do so.

Soon after his accession to the throne, Reccared established unity of faith in a different manner. In 586, for form's sake, he arranged a religious disputation, after which he publicly declared himself for the Catholic faith. Most of the Arian bishops followed his example. Only a very few in Lusitania and Septimania resisted, and their revolt was soon put down. The final chapter of the affair was a great council held at Toledo in 589 and attended by sixty-four Catholic bishops, in the early part of which the king made a personal profession of the Catholic faith. Eight Arian bishops and many clerics and Gothic nobles followed his example. Thus the Arian Church in Spain was undone, and the conversion of the Visigoths to Catholicism definitely begun. A short time before, Catholicism had also been introduced into the Suevian kingdom in the West when the king, Carriaric (550-559), embraced the Catholic faith. The winning of the Lombards — the only remaining adherents of Arianism — to the Catholic Church was only a question of time.

Let us now direct our attention to some of the Catholic leaders who were a determining factor in the overthrow of Germanic Arianism. Besides the Franks, whom we shall treat specifically later, these leaders were Saint Avitus of Vienne for Burgundy, Saint Martin of Braga for the Suevians, and Saint Leander of Seville for the Visigoths.

Saint Avitus came of a senatorial family in Auvergne, where Roman customs were adhered to with the greatest tenacity. At that time the Catholic episcopal sees were generally in the hands of those of senatorial birth, who were the best representatives of Roman culture and ecclesiastical interests. Thus, Saint Avitus' father and perhaps too his paternal grandfather and great-grandfather had been bishops of Vienne. Saint Avitus followed them in 490. He could appreciate fully the importance of Clovis' baptism, and wrote to him in his congratulatory letter: "Your faith is our victory."[5]

Avitus' motto, well illustrated by his activity, was: *"Speculator sum, tubam teneo, tacere mihi non licet."*[6] He enjoyed great esteem at the royal court in Burgundy and brought about the conversion of the crown prince Sigismund, who kept court first at Vienne and later at Geneva. He also approached King Gundibald, but the latter had not the far-sightedness which brought Clovis into the Church. Had Gundibald accepted the Catholic religion before Clovis, the Burgundians might possibly have taken over the leadership which instead passed to the Franks. He would have had an excellent adviser in Saint Avitus, one fully conversant with the importance of the Roman faith and of Rome itself. Avitus made it his concern to further the interests of the Church as well as those of culture, and proceeded to do so by entering into a close alliance with the Holy See. In one of his letters he wrote: "If the pope of Rome is doubted,

---

5. *Ep.* 36, ed. Peiper, p. 75.
6. *Ep.* 55, ibid., p. 84.

not only the individual bishop, but the whole episcopate begins
to totter."[7] To consolidate the Catholic Church in the kingdom of
Burgundy Saint Avitus held the synod of Epoan in 517. He died
in the year 526.

The authority by which Saint Avitus compelled respect from
the kings of his time rested not only on his ecclesiastical zeal, but
also on his culture and literary achievements, a statement applicable
to the other bishops of this dynasty as well. The considerations
with which he opposed Arianism he committed to writing in the
Conversations with King Gundibald, which date from the year 512
or 513. Besides this, there is a truly fascinating work, a comprehensive poetical composition which he himself entitled *Books Concerning the Events of Spiritual History,* though this hardly indicates
the contents. The first three books could better have been called
Paradise Lost. Milton, who won renown for his work bearing that
title, probably permitted himself to derive inspiration from the poem
of Saint Avitus, and possibly borrowed some points from it. Treating his subject freely and in a manner worthy of great commenda-
tion, Saint Avitus describes Paradise, the fall of man, and the ex-
pulsion from the Garden. The second part of the work, which deals
with the deluge and the passage through the Red Sea, is inferior to
the first. Of lesser grade still is another poem, dedicated to his
sister Fuscina, a nun who was familiar with the Bible and the Latin
poets. In this work he adopts a curious means to console his sister
and confirm her in her life of virginity, by depicting the sufferings
and miseries of married life!

On the other hand, the extremely active bishop appears again
in a highly estimable light in his numerous letters, which furnish
very valuable documentary sources for the cultural, no less than the
ecclesiastical and political, history of his time. We also have, in
the poem on Paradise already mentioned, an interesting contemporary picture; here he describes the calamities imposed upon the
earth through the fall of man: large cities will be converted into
deserts, masters will become servants, slaves will become masters,

---

7. *Ep.* 34, ibid., p. 65.

and the war-torn world will become depopulated. Thus realistically did a Roman of that period view his own age.

The decline of culture necessarily followed the decline of external institutions. The prose writings of Saint Avitus, in contrast to his poetry — this is still quite pure — demonstrate how the language of the educated was receding and how the language of the people, with its barbarisms, constituted a transition in the forming of the Romance tongues.

A position similar to that of Saint Avitus in the Burgundian realm of Sapaudia was occupied somewhat later in the Suevian kingdom by Bishop Martin of Braga. He differed from Avitus perhaps only in possessing a more profound missionary zeal and a more democratic spirit. Motivated by the former, he had come to Portugal from a great distance, for his home was in Pannonia. At first he undertook a pilgrimage to Palestine, where he became a monk and attained a degree of learning quite unusual for his period; he even acquired a knowledge of Greek. Reaching the Suevian kingdom by ship, he immediately founded a monastery at Dumio, near Braga, seat of the royal residence. He came at exactly the right time to reap a successful harvest, for the Catholic faith had finally begun to gain a footing among the Arian Suevians. Saint Martin completed the mission work, and rightly merits the honorary title of Apostle to the Suevians. He soon won the friendship of King Theodemir, who made him archbishop of his capital city, Braga, after he had been for a time bishop of Dumio. Under Theodemir's successor, King Miro, Saint Martin also enjoyed great esteem, zealously working among all classes, high and low, for the spread of the Catholic faith. His name was spoken with honor far and wide in the West. He died in 580.

In line with his apostolic activity, Saint Martin occupied himself in his writings mainly with ethics. To furnish the king, who was interested in the matter, with the arguments founded on reason for acting rightly, he composed a guide for a virtuous life, *Formula vitae honestae*. Therein he copied Seneca's method so completely that until the most recent times this work has been regarded as Seneca's own. It was intended primarily for lay people and is based on Seneca's *De officiis*. It naturally bears a general similarity also to Cicero's and Saint Ambrose's works of the same title. After the example of the Stoics, the duties are divided into middle and perfect duties, and the four cardinal virtues are treated successively. By way of appendix, Saint Martin speaks of the faults into which one may fall by an excess of the individual virtues, meritoriously following up this brief for moderation with a number of sound reflections. Saint Martin betrays his predilection for Seneca in yet another treatise compiled from that author — *On Anger,* which he dedicated to Bishop Witimir of Orense. While purely natural Stoic ethics are propounded in these writings, others by Saint Martin deal with ethics as broadened by Christianity; and their treatment of haughty presumption, pride and humility offers a valuable supplement to the Stoic doctrines.

From the standpoint of cultural history a sermon entitled *Concerning the Betterment of the Peasants,* which Martin wrote at the suggestion of Bishop Polemius of Astorga, has a much greater value. A synodal decision having ordered the bishops of the country to preach to the people on the occasion of their visitation of the churches, Polemius asked the saint to furnish him with a guide for these occasions. Martin begins with a history of superstition, which he follows up by a model sermon against it. Here we learn, with very great interest, the various types of superstition which then obtained. The simple, clear words with which Saint Martin addresses himself to country people express a pure missionary zeal, free from all literary vanity. These words certainly must have gained the bishop the confidence of his hearers.

In Spain Saint Leander, formerly a monk in Seville, was the outstanding personality connected with the Visigoths' conversion to Catholicism. We have already mentioned his part in Hermenegild's conversion and his journey to Constantinople to solicit auxiliary troops there for the prince. During this visit he became acquainted with the future Pope Gregory the Great, who was residing in Constantinople as the papal representative (*apocrisiarius*). Naturally Saint Leander was able to return to Spain only after Reccared's accession to the throne. Following the complete transformation of religious policy, he became, as the archbishop of Seville, the leading personality of the city. As such he stood out in bold relief, especially

at the Council of Toledo, held in 589, where he preached his sermon
on the victory for the Church involved in the conversion of the
Goths. This sermon is the only one of his writings preserved to us,
aside from a rule for nuns addressed to his sister Florentia; his
letters and two polemical works against the Arians have unfortunately been lost.

When Saint Leander died in 600 or 601, his youngest brother,
Isidore, succeeded him on the episcopal throne of Seville. Saint
Leander had directed Isidore's education and formed in him the
scholar who became the ornament of a now united nation.

Having followed the course of the struggle and its champions,
let us also try to present the reasons why Arianism was defeated.
In doing so, we must go back to the fundamental principle of that
creed.[8]

The essential point of the conflict was the dogma of the Trinity.
In contrast to the Catholic doctrine of the consubstantiality of the
three Persons in God, the doctrine of the Arian Germans came to
this: Christ is not God, but a creature. By this teaching, the most
precious jewel was removed from the diadem of Christian doctrinal
truths, and the most important foundation-stone for the building
of a Christian culture was cast aside. The task of culture is to make
man more and more perfect in the various aptitudes of his mind,
heart and soul, to bring these faculties into ever greater harmony, to
regulate the baser inclinations and subject them to the control of
the nobler. This cannot be done without religion, but it must be a
religion that can really hold man permanently. Without the ideal
of the God-man, religion will make in the long run no enduring
impression. Is there anything which can show man more clearly
God's love, God's benevolence, the gravity of sin and the mercy of
God, than the figure of the divine Redeemer? Belief in Him, and
that alone, is able to move man now and always to heroic sacrifice
and devotion. If Christ was only a man, even though a hero, the
principal motive of sacrifice vanishes and there remains to us at
best merely admiration — no devotion. More, the doctrine of the

---

8. For the following see Kurth, *Les origines de la civilisation moderne*, 6th ed., I,
324 sq.

Redeemer's death also collapses. Then the idea of God moves away from man and works only on the same level as Kant's categorical imperative, which will never inflame and capture men's hearts. In reality Arianism was not much more than a form of rationalism, making concessions to reason at the expense of faith; but, in doing so, as a matter of course, it shook Christian belief to its very foundations and paralyzed its civilizing force.

The example of the Arian tribes at the time of the migration of nations shows this clearly enough. When the Germanic peoples invaded the Roman Empire, the Catholic Romans by no means stood on the high moral plane worthy of the Christian religion. We have but to recall the gloomy picture which Salvian of Marseilles drew of Roman society in the middle of the fifth century. And we recall, too, that he contrasted the morally superior barbarians with the depraved Romans of his day, placing the heretics and even the pagans in a light superior to the Christians. In their cultural lack, the Germans of that period had this advantage: they were not yet affected by the excesses of the depraved culture into which the society of antiquity had fallen; and this advantage was, moreover, considerably enhanced by their natural purity of morals, which they had guarded in their clans and tribes.

The Catholic Christians among the Romans had been engulfed to a large extent in the moral decay of ancient society; and yet they possessed a means of moral regeneration which Arianism could not offer the Arian Germans once they began to degenerate. Their rapid moral decline after they began to live in the midst of the Roman Empire, was a result of their exposure, with no protection whatsoever, to the corruption of ancient society. The sole source of moral health which they possessed, their tribal bonds and tribal way of life, they gave up in settling separately among the Romans. They lost, at one and the same time, their clan traditions and their natural morality. Against this degeneration, Arianism offered them no remedy.

It was different with the Romans. Though the great majority had succumbed to moral depravity, belief in the divinity of Christ continued to live on in some. These had in no wise abandoned the ideals of the Christian teaching, but preserved and transmitted them in their purest light. On that day when the doomed Roman society, with its urban culture perverting both body and soul, had disappeared, moral regeneration could begin.

This is the secret of Christian culture: it possesses in the faith a remedy capable of healing all wounds, it has a fountain of youth whence humanity can again draw new, youthful vigor. In believing that Christ is the Son of God, humanity has not received the assurance that it will always maintain itself on a high moral plane, or that all the nations and states which have accepted the Christian faith will continue to exist. But it has received the means of lifting itself out of any moral depression; and when one nation dies, another springs from its ruins with new life, making use of the best forces of the one that has ceased to exist. We need not be surprised, therefore, if in medieval times we also see periods of decline, despite the fact that the Church exerted an external influence far and wide. These periods of decline prove nothing against the civilizing force of the Christian faith. Does the dying off of vegetation in winter disprove the fertility of the earth? But the regeneration following a decline speaks gloriously indeed for the moral force of the Christian faith, just as spring reveals over and over again the fertility of the earth in a manner gladdening to the heart of man. Do we observe even one instance when a moral regeneration was possible in paganism? Once the moral decline had set in, it marched on irresistibly, first among the Greeks, then among the Romans.

The case was similar with the Germans who had abandoned the foundation-stone of the Christian faith. Their Arian belief and their Arian priests were not only unable to raise the tribes to a higher morality; they could not even preserve the natural morality the Germans had possessed as pagans. Arianism was powerless against the dangers to which these primitive people were exposed when, cut off from the traditions handed down within the tribal union, they were placed in a world of enticing and intoxicating pleasures. When the Vandals arrived in Carthage, they put an end to the profligacies there — an action for which Salvian praises them. Their settlement in the metropolis, however, soon became for them in turn a distinct misfortune. A half century later the same immorality reigned among the Vandals as among the Romans. There was no difference between the two other than the fact that the Vandals combined the coarse barbaric sensual pleasures with the refined depravity of the supercultured Romans. Thus, when Belisarius came, the Vandalic race was found wanting in the stability conferred by a sound national strength, and collapsed miserably. We observe the same phenomena in the case of the other Arian races. The earlier generations are usually superior to the later; a regeneration never takes place. This proves clearly the impotence of Arianism, and its lack of moral force.

Where are their men who sound a call to regeneration and who, as idealists, attract and gather others about them to point the way to the heights of moral perfection? In vain do we look for saints among the Arians. The few martyrs who, in the first generation of the Christian Visigoths, laid down their lives for their faith during the persecution perpetrated by their pagan tribesmen, soon ceased to have any imitators. Among the priests of the Arian national church, no single one attracts our attention by his lofty moral stature.

On the other hand, the Catholic Church in that period was not lacking in saintly ascetics, pious monks, confessors courageous unto death, and moral mentors free from human fear but full of spiritual strength and ideal fervor. We need only to recall their names: Salvian, Saint Severinus, Saint Benedict with his monks, Saint Avitus of Vienne, Saint Martin of Braga, Saint Eugenius of Carthage, Saint Leander of Seville. To these we could add others: for example, Saint Epiphanius of Pavia, Saint Caesarius of Arles, Saint Fulgentius of Ruspe, together with the holy women and virgins, Saint Scholastica, Saint Caesaria and Ingunthis. It was just at this time that the monasteries in all parts of the Roman world took up the battle for the moral regeneration of Christendom. And that Germanic women, too, were able to comprehend with the light of the Catholic faith the high ideal of Christian virtue and the profound Christian conception of life, that a Germanic soul could be cultivated into a most beautiful blossom of ideal humanity, is shown us in the personality of the first German saint, the Thuringian princess, Radegunde. She founded a convent in Poitiers according to the Rule which Saint Caesarius of Arles had given the nuns directed by his sister, and during her lifetime it was a sanctuary of genuine piety, holy asceticism and intellectual activity. Among the Arians there was no asceticism, no monasticism and no consecrated virginity. The clergy, including the bishops, did not practice celibacy. Arianism also was far inferior to the Catholic Church in its entire ecclesiastical organization. The Church had an international, world-embracing character corresponding to her world-mission, an organization extending over all countries, with a firm ecclesiastical head in the successors of Saint Peter. The Arian churches, while indeed possessing bishops, lacked a hierarchical head and over-all leadership. The several churches developed as separate units and became national churches, which were at the same time state-churches, in which the tribal king had the final word. It was he who convoked the synods which administered justice; bishops were state officials, appointed and deposed by him at will. The Christian Church occupied here the position of the ancient pagan cult, the form of which was determined ultimately by the tribal chieftain; this explains the fact that his change of religion had a decisive effect upon the whole tribe. The bishops were the priests of the tribes; then came the priests of the inferior groups, the hundreds and the clans. The Arian clergy appears as an incorporated part of the army organization, and consequently, as a military clergy, is subject to the tribal king.[9] And as the bishops were dependent upon the king, so the lower-ranking clergy were largely dependent upon the great landowners. Since the latter, following the religious custom common to the Germans, erected private churches on their estates, they appointed their own priests, who were their dependents and essentially their clerical servants. Such a church could not lay claim to any moral authority; it was bound up with the fate of the state or tribe and must perish with it.

A final reason, which from the very beginning showed Arianism as the weaker party in the struggle with Catholicism, was its intellectual inferiority. Culture and intellectual activity were present only on the Roman or Catholic side. On the Arian, we cannot so

---

9. Cf. H. von Schubert, *Kirche im Frühmittelalter*, I, 26.

much as mention the name of one man prominent in the field of letters, with the exception of Ulfilas, who translated the Bible. The stimulus his work gave toward the creation of a literature in the Gothic language never met a response. Besides the Bible of Ulfilas, the only vestige of Gothic literature we have is the translation from the Latin of a commentary on Saint John, preserved in eight folios. Though the Gothic books in Spain were burned after the acceptance of the Catholic religion, we have no grounds for believing that they included anything but liturgical books and Bible manuscripts.

The inferior culture of the Germanic Arians was very largely due to the fact that the Arian liturgy was not in the classic languages of culture, but in Gothic, a tongue without a literature. They read the Sacred Scriptures in the Gothic tongue, and preached in it. The Gothic priests did not have to study the language of Rome, nor, with few exceptions, did they do so. The Arian Vandalic patriarch Cyrila declared at a religious disputation held at Carthage in 484: "I do not understand Latin."[10] Those who should have been the promoters of culture and the leaders of literary activity thus deprived themselves of the only opportunity to become acquainted with the treasures of ancient learning and hence the foundation for further development. Ulfilas appears, in this connection, more and more an exception. Trained as a theologian in the ecclesiastical circles of Eastern Rome, he had as a missionary used his knowledge of Gothic to make the Bible available to his father's countrymen. His example of going to school to the bearers of ancient culture was no longer followed because of the religious cleavage now existing as a result of the elimination of Arianism in the Eastern Roman Empire. This was the case soon after the time of Ulfilas.

The charge that the Gothic priests were uneducated will hardly be considered biased if one marshals against them the representatives of culture and literary activity in the Roman Catholic episcopate. These were particularly numerous during the period of the migration of nations, because learning hid itself in the Church and the monasteries. Any Roman who was outstanding by birth or culture and who wanted to live accordingly, either entered the

---

10. Victor of Vita, *Hist. persecutionis,* Lib. II, c. 18 (55).

service of the Church or gladly permitted himself to be drawn into it. There alone were to be found ideals which could never be overthrown.

Saint Sidonius Apollinaris is an example of the distinguished Roman who, entering the service of the Church, turned his attainments to account in it. Born at Lyons about 430, he was intimately associated with the last emperors of the Western Roman Empire. He composed a panegyric on Avitus, his father-in-law, who had allowed himself to be proclaimed emperor in 455, for which laudation Avitus gratefully erected a statue to him in the Forum of Trajan. This did not hinder Sidonius from composing a similar panegyric on Avitus' conqueror and successor, Majorian, in order to bespeak his favor also. Under Anthemius, Sidonius was appointed prefect of the city of Rome. But when the Church in Clermont-Ferrand desired him for its bishop, he willingly obeyed the call and renounced this type of composition, with its mythological allusions, as unworthy of his new office. Instead he wrote letters which are a good reflection of contemporary events. From them we may clearly gather how superior the cultured Romans of the time felt themselves to be to the German soldiery even though it protected them against worse foes. When, in 470, the Burgundians occupied Clermont, to protect it against Euric, the Visigothic king, Sidonius described the allies in a poem written on the occasion of the marriage of his friend Catullinus:

Am I to write poetry, surrounded by these long-haired hordes? I, who am condemned to put up with Germanic speech and to praise with serious mien the song the gluttonous Burgundian sings, who greases his hair with rancid butter? Shall I tell you what cuts my poetic compositions short? Since Thalia beholds our patrons, all of them seven-foot fellows, she avoids the six-foot meter, frightened away by the barbaric lute. You can call your eyes and ears lucky, lucky too your nose, which is not forced to inhale very early in the morning all of ten preparations of garlic and onions. Lucky you — whom, unlike the old grandfather and the nurse's man, giants do not visit before the dawn of day in such numbers and withal of such size, that the kitchen of Alcinous would hardly have been able to entertain them.[11]

---

11. *Carmen* XII: *M. G. A. a.*, VIII, 230 sq.

The satire, however, reaches its full height only in the fact that the Roman bishop allowed himself to be protected by these "patrons" against the Arian Euric, who was hostile to Catholics.

With few exceptions, among whom we list Boethius and Cassiodorus, all the writers of the sixth century were priests or monks of the Roman Church. How much emphasis was placed in ecclesiastical circles upon the cultivation of letters is shown by the mere catalogues of authors, the groundwork of which was laid by Saint Jerome in his work *De viris illustribus*. This work was continued by Gennadius, a priest of Marseilles (d. 492), and supplemented for the last time by Saint Isidore, bishop of Seville, and Saint Ildephonsus, archbishop of Toledo.

The series of ecclesiastical writers closes with Saint Isidore of Seville. Conscious, so to speak, of his position, he tried to collect all scientific knowledge then extant — a plan similar to that of Cassiodorus, whose example doubtless was before Isidore's mind. He owed it to the severe intellectual discipline of his older brother, the great Leander, that he acquired a comprehensive erudition. We have seen that he followed Leander on the archiepiscopal throne of Seville, which he adorned for almost forty years. He died in 636. Besides fulfilling his ecclesiastical obligations — we note him presiding at synods — he worked with the greatest zeal in the literary field. It is principally his great encyclopedias which have attracted posterity and which were a mine of information for the Middle Ages.

At the head of these encyclopedias stand, obviously, the twenty books of his *Etymologiae* or *Origines,* which were found in almost all the medieval libraries. We can understand this. The work was a dictionary of arts and sciences, in which Saint Isidore assembled the sum total of human knowledge as it existed in his day. He did this by making excerpts from the authors accessible to him, and for the Middle Ages this was a useful arrangement since it provided substitutes for writers whom they no longer possessed and no longer needed. This work establishes Saint Isidore as one of the greatest excerptors — perhaps actually the greatest. The work derived its title from the fact that, in compiling the diversified material, emphasis in each case was primarily laid on a definition, which generally goes no further than to give an eccentric explanation of the word. This method, at the time, was considered to be particularly scientific. The work begins with the seven liberal arts, and then treats of medicine, laws, the division of time (here the compiler inserts a short chronicle of the world's history), books and libraries, the hierarchy, the Church, language and nations (it is worth noting that the contemporary Latin is designated as *mixta* because of the accepted barbarisms), the human body, the animal kingdom, the forces of the heavens and the earth, geography, stones and metals, plants, military affairs, the theater, shipping, house-building, clothes, food, household utensils and farm implements — hence all possible topics.

Saint Isidore compiled several other encyclopedias; for example one of natural science, dedicated to the Visigothic king, Sisebut, which was highly esteemed and widely used in the Middle Ages. He likewise composed a work on the symbolism of numbers, and the catalogue of authors already mentioned. It is evident that none of these works have the value of originality; they are only compilations. But they answered a need of the age. Their purpose was to preserve what still existed until the time should come when men of leisure and judgment could go again to the authors themselves and imitate them. Thus every phase of medieval culture acquired the character of a renaissance movement, of a gradual rebirth of antiquity. The later promoters of this movement had no right to despise the earlier laborers, on whose shoulders they stood and who often proved themselves more original in their own thought than those who sought glory only in imitation. In the first place it was the Church alone who took the fragments of culture under her protection; and she thus acquired a special position at the beginning of the Middle Ages since she was exclusively the mediatrix of intellectual culture, the patroness of instruction, and the leader of education. This task was so exclusively hers that a grave crisis ensued at the end of the Middle Ages when her representatives had to be reminded that the primary mission of the Church did not lie in this direction.

The two historical works of Saint Isidore also have a special interest for us. One, a world chronicle, was at first produced separately; later he incorporated excerpts of it in his *Etymologiae* under the title *Concerning the Difference of the Times*. This chronicle follows the division, adopted from Saint Augustine, into six world eras, the sixth of which began with the Birth of Christ. Saint Isidore's second work in the field is a national history of the Visigoths, with appendices on the history of the Vandals and the Suevians. It exists in two recensions, one of which extends to 619, the second to 624. Although this work is in the main only a collection of excerpts, like Saint Isidore's other writings, it belongs nevertheless, in point of form and spirit, to a new type of historical works — national histories. We have already become acquainted with one such work, namely, Cassiodorus' Ostrogothic history.

This bishop, the scion of a Roman family, honors the Goths as his own people. Two centuries before, Orosius had intimated such sentiments as the spirit of a future age. In Saint Isidore we encounter that national spirit openly expressed; and we are brought to the realization that it was only necessary to remove the religious barrier in order to make of the Romans and the Germans a new nation. In his introduction, Isidore praises Spain with poetic fire as the most beautiful of all those countries which extend from the West to India; as the saintly and ever happy mother of princes and nations; as the ornament and decoration of the universe, richly endowed with valuable gifts of nature; as a land whose people, unlike any other nation, have by their bravery succeeded in resisting the Romans. The Spanish national feeling again finds expression in the conclusion, wherein the glorious reconquest of the maritime country of the Iberian peninsula from the Eastern Romans is attributed to the flourishing nation of the Goths, who knew not only how to rob Spain, but also how to love it, and under whom the country enjoys a blessed security.[12]

The various steps in the fusion of the Romans and the Germans, after religious unity had been established, can best be followed in the Visigothic kingdom by directing our attention to the juridical system. Besides the religious separation there existed in the Visigothic kingdom a sharp legal separation, which was imitated in

---

12. *Mon. Germ. A. a.*, XI, 267.

other Arian kingdoms. Two laws were in force — one for the Germans, another for the Romans. The first lawgiver for the Visigoths was the powerful King Euric (466-485), but only fragments of his decrees are extant. As the oldest written code, his book of laws for the Germans has had an influence, direct or indirect, on the Germanic legal codes which came into being thereafter: the Frankish *Lex Salica,* and the Burgundian, Bavarian and Lombardic codes.

When the son and successor of Euric, King Alaric II (485-507), was threatened with attack by the Franks, whose King Clovis had accepted the Catholic religion, he realized that the division between the Roman Catholics and the Germanic Arians, which was very sharp at that time, might become fatal to him. Hence he strove to effect a certain degree of reconciliation with the Romans. He wanted to give them the assurance that they could live according to their own law. To this end he had a collection made of the legal maxims in force for the Romans in his realm. Thus arose the *Lex Romana Visigothorum,* also named *Breviarium Alaricianum* after the king. A commission of Roman jurists appointed by the king compiled it by making extracts from the source-books of Roman law, an assembly of bishops and Romans from the province approved it, and Alaric gave it legal force by his sanction in 506.

The Church in the Visigothic kingdom, and later the Merovingians, regarded the collection as the legal code for the Roman population, and it was in this form that Roman law survived into the twelfth century in France, England and Germany. This compilation is worthy of notice in the history of Roman law for the reason that it is based on the codes in force in the Roman Empire prior to the *Codex Justinianus,* the codification made by the emperor Justinian I (527-565). In particular it depends on the *Codex Theodosianus,* compiled under the emperor Theodosius II (408-450). Among other prescriptions, even the one forbidding Arians to build churches was incorporated into this *Breviarium.* This prohibition naturally affected only the Roman Arians, not the Germanic. The Romans in the Visigothic kingdom were not to be permitted to form Arian parishes, so closely did the religious and national differences coincide at the time! Whoever was Roman must be Catholic and live according to this Roman law; whoever was a Goth belonged to the Arians and lived according to the Visigothic Germanic law.

The immediate purpose of the compilation, however, was not achieved. The acts of violence to which the Catholic bishops and churches found themselves exposed at the hands of the Arian Visigoths, prevented the healing of the breach in Alaric's kingdom. Hence, as we have seen, Clovis was welcomed south of the Loire by the Roman Catholics as their liberator from the hated Arian yoke.

Clovis naturally left this Roman code in force for the Roman population in the Frankish kingdom. It also acquired legal force in the kingdom of Burgundy, where King Gundibald had already had extracts from the source-books of Roman law compiled for the Roman population, known as the *Lex Romana Burgundionum* (erroneously called *Papianus*). As these extracts were very meagre, the more detailed *Breviarium Alaricianum* was drawn upon to complement them.

Gundibald had ordered the *Lex Romana Burgundionum* compiled as the companion piece to another lawbook of earlier composition in which, imitating the example of the Visigoths, he had the Burgundian tribal law recorded for his Germanic subjects. This is the *Lex Burgundionum,* called after him *Lex Gundobada* or *Lex Gombata,* though it exists only in a version published under King Sigismund at Lyons in 517. This collection of Burgundian decrees continued in force as a particular law after the incorporation of Burgundy into the Frankish kingdom, although the Church looked askance at it because it had been enacted by an Arian king for Arian Germans. In the Carolingian era, the *Guntbadingi* or *Gundibadi* — as the Franks who lived according to the Burgundian law were called — were actually very few but Archbishop Agobard of Lyons was unwilling to wait for the law to die a natural death and exhorted Louis the Pious to abolish it as the enactment of a heretical king. In this he could rightly point to the juridical ordeal as a barbaric remnant of the old Burgundian law; proof of how long the memory of the religious difference held sway there. The failure of the Burgundians, among whom Arianism disappeared earlier than among the Visigoths, to remove the difference in law is doubtless due entirely to the fact that the Burgundian kingdom was already conquered by the Franks in the sixth century, and that consequently a separate Romanic nation with a uniform law did not arise in the Rhone region.

Just as the Visigoths were more stubborn than the Burgundians in their adherence to Arianism, so, following its suppression, they were also more radical in removing the differences which still prolonged the separation. Fifty years after the acceptance of Catholicism King Reccesvinth (649-672) gave his people a uniform law, which was to apply identically to Goths and Romans. This was the *Lex Visigothorum Reccesvinthiana,* which was transformed, after several other revisions, into the *Lex Visigothorum Vulgata.* Though Reccesvinth's code consists essentially of Gothic law, still the influence of Roman legal concepts is clearly discernible. It was a combination of Gothic and Roman law.

The marriage impediment, which until then prohibited intermarriage between Goths and Romans, was abolished. Among the measures adopted from the Romans one must be noted especially: the use of torture, an unwholesome legacy, which Roman law left it to the discretion of the judge to prescribe. The Goths merely introduced a change in accord with their views, based on the ancient penal code of the tribe: the judge could order the use of torture only if the plaintiff demanded it and if the plaintiff and the accused were of the same class. Under such conditions the accused was not to be delivered over to the public torturer, as prescribed by Roman law, but to the plaintiff. The plaintiff then could apply torture as he wished for three days in order to extract a confession; the sole restriction being that if he let the accused die under the torture, he himself was delivered over to the tribe of the accused, which could do with him what it wished; it could even torture him to death in the same manner. Should the accused endure the torture, the plaintiff was in turn delivered over to him, to be treated as he pleased (short of killing) during his lifetime. It was further ordained that the plaintiff was not allowed to break any of the accused person's limbs in the course of the torture; and the torture was to be applied only in the presence of the judge and a number of honorable men of the community. The judge was to pledge his life and fortune that the torture would not exceed the point of endurance. We see from all this that the introduction of the use of torture was approved only with great reluctance. It was undoubtedly regarded in Gothic circles as applicable to serfs only.

While the Goths stood morally higher than the Romans in this point of their conviction of the value of the free man, the Church with her Roman culture prevented, at another point, the introduction of superstitious practices into the faith, by not allowing ordeals, which were not contained in the law originally. But in the course of time the Church yielded on this point, a sign that we can speak of the barbarization of the Church as well as of the language. In a law originating shortly before the end of the Visigothic kingdom, the ordeal called the kettle-test appears as a judicial means of producing evidence. The person condemned to furnish this proof was forced bare-armed to draw a ring or a stone from a kettle of boiling water; if his arm appeared uninjured after the lapse of a determined period, he was considered to have passed the test and established his case. This form of the ordeal was found in several parts of Spain. In addition, a particular form of the Visigothic ordeal reserved to the nobility was the juridical duel fought on horseback. This latter endured for centuries.

Thus we see Romans and Germans fusing into a mixed people, to which the former contributed something of their culture, and the latter something of their barbarity. But a healthy impulse of regeneration came with the collapse of the old, corrupt city-culture and the spread of rural life. The Church acted as supreme guide in this development, and formed an intimate union with the state. This union was not without danger to her, however. She became, in fact, almost a state Church, as in Byzantium, to which men of that epoch instinctively looked for models. And since the Spanish kingship was constantly being tossed to and fro in the struggles for the throne, the Church was likewise drawn into the party feuds. These civil wars weakened the kingdom to such an extent that it fell before the assault of Islam in 711. But though the kingdom fell, the new nation maintained itself, thanks to its faith. In struggles which dragged on throughout the whole medieval period and which completely submerged whatever still tended to keep the two races apart, the Spanish nation eventually regained its independence by force of arms. And it has remained permanently grateful to the Church, because she alone held it together.

Spanish nationality, sharply expressed in its harshness, its self-consciousness and its tenacious power of resistance, already shows us distinctly along what lines the new Romance nations will develop out of the shattered structure of the Roman Empire. Roman culture left a lasting mark upon all these nations by its legacy of the Latin language. But of all the Romance languages, the Spanish has most genuinely preserved the archaic form of Latin, by the retention of the final *s*. The vocabulary is also archaic, although not entirely Latin, showing as it does traces of the other racial elements assimilated there in the course of time. Of these, the earliest was the Iberian. This people, probably related to the Berbers, came over from Africa; the race is still to be found in its purity in the Basque country. Another section of it mixed with the Celts. The language of the Celtiberians, essentially Iberian, was the language spoken before the Romans took possession of the country, and many Iberian words survived when the people were Romanized. The language of the Visigoths, who represented the fourth element, has affected the Spanish language the least, because the Goths nowhere dwelt together and their language was not cultivated. What remained of it disappeared, along with the Arian liturgical language, when the Visigoths were won to Catholicism. Only in the numerous Germanic proper names has the Visigothic language left definite traces, and this is due to the fact that the reigning families bore these names, which consequently were readily adopted by their subjects. How eagerly the Visigothic kings acquired the Roman culture and language after their conversion to Catholicism is seen in the case of King Sisebut (612-620), who carried on an erudite correspondence with Saint Isidore and was highly praised for his mastery of language and learning. It was in Latin already tinged with a distinct Romance color, that Sisebut composed poems and wrote a life of Saint Desiderius of Vienne.

The influence of the Arabs, which was vigorous for many centuries and represented at that time a culture externally superior, was to be far greater on the Spanish language than that of the Visigoths. It is interesting, however, that the Arabian merely produced an enlargement of the vocabulary, especially in the number of juridical terms; it did not change the inflection and syntax of the Spanish language; these remained Romance in accord with the inherent qualities and spirit of the people.

If the Roman tongue — representative of the highest of the various cultural strata in Spain and the language of the Roman Church, which alone guaranteed unity — exerted a decisive influence on the language, such was not the case with regard to the character of the nation. This was determined in the main by the earliest element, the Iberian. This national temperament is most pronounced in the Castilians. In them we can still distinctly recognize the qualities of character which the Romans admired in the ancient Spaniards: contempt of death, heroic courage, akin to what the ancient Iberians manifested at the fall of Numantia, when they preferred voluntary death to slavery — and a strongly developed sense of individuality which expressed itself in an ineradicable particularism.

A parallel to the development of the Spanish language and nationality, identical in all essential features, is found in Portugal. The elements which represent the various racial groups and determine the development are the same. The Iberians, represented here especially by the Lusitanians, constituted the earliest element. Celts, who had come across the sea from Brittany and the mouth of the Loire, mixed with the Iberians. The Romans converted the conquered country into the province of Lusitania and Romanized it. In the age of the migration of nations the Suevians ruled and they quickly became Romanized after they had accepted the Catholic religion. The country was subject to the Arabs from the eighth century; then during the Crusade period there appeared yet another new element — the French-Burgundian knights who undertook the formation of the states: a topic we shall return to later.

We have still to observe the evolution of the Italian people, which was determined by the appearance of the Lombards. These had provoked the struggle between Arianism and the Church in Italy as a sequel to the great conflict of the fifth and sixth centuries. The conflict between Arianism and Catholicism, however, was less pronounced than were the political and cultural differences. It is a question of power, which is decided at first in favor of Arianism by the Lombards' ruthless use of force, but finally in favor of the Church by virtue of the fact that there in particular Roman culture asserts its superiority. In Italy, therefore, spiritual and ecclesiastical struggles are less prominent. Dramatic decisions, as in the case of the Visigoths, are lacking. Hence an account of the overcoming of the differences is not easy, especially since circumstances which we will be able to appreciate fully only later, enter into consideration. Nevertheless at this point, the triumph over Lombardic Arianism must be briefly sketched.

The Lombards, presumably an East Germanic tribe who had come from Scandinavia and the Elbe, were driven from Pannonia by the pressure of the Avars, who occupied the lands behind them. They appeared in Italy in 568 under Alboin — who, however, took up his residence in Pavia, and not in Ravenna, the ancient capital, where the Byzantine governor was still able to maintain himself. The Lombards conducted themselves in Italy in an entirely different manner than the Ostrogoths under Theodoric. They had no intention of forming a homogeneous state conjointly with the Romans, and they showed little consideration for Roman culture. Wherever they gained a footing, almost nothing of the Roman administrative system remained. They organized the conquered territories solely according to their own methods. Their holdings, in addition to northern Italy, were Tuscany and the duchies of Spoleto and Benevento. These two sections, in the north and south, were separated by the territories of Ravenna and Rome and the line of communication running through Perugia — territories which, like the whole south, remained Byzantine. In the Lombard holdings, the Roman landowners were banished or enslaved; they had to submit to the Lombardic law, which was codified only in 643 by edict of King Rothari. In the cities, however, the Lombards could not exterminate the Romans.

When the Lombards appeared in Italy, they were partly Arian, partly pagan; some few Catholics may also have been among them, but in general a deep religious interest was lacking. In the Catholic Church the Lombards saw only the religion of the Romans, for which they knew no mercy and felt no respect. Hence, the Church and the papacy were in great danger. The Catholic bishops (there were Arian bishops as well in most of the cities subject to the Lombards) were fortunate if they were permitted to exercise in any way at all even their most necessary offices. The Catholic churches had to pay taxes, their clergy, too, were subject to the jurisdiction of the Lombard king, their priests had to render military service. Thus they lost the privileged position which Justinian had granted them in 554. Rome itself was threatened more than once by the Lombards. Pope Gregory was so depressed over the disturbances of his time that he actually believed the end of the world was at hand and that a reawakening of culture was no longer possible. Raised to the chair of Peter in 590, he preached a sermon soon after his election in which with great emotion he depicted the misery of his age:

> Rome, once the mistress of the world, what has become of her? . . . Where is the senate, where the people? The senate is dissolved, the people annihilated; and still the suffering and the woeful cries grow every day among the wretched remnants of the population. Thus the empty city is now wasting away. What will become of the people when the buildings gradually deteriorate and collapse? . . . Where are they who once delighted in the splendor of this city? Where is their magnificence, their pride and their love of boundless pleasure? Once the sons of the world, in quest of their own advantage, gathered here, now desolation and sorrow reign in the deserted city; no one who seeks his own gain comes hither; none powerful in this world are left here. The city has been shorn of its eagle wings on which it was once accustomed to fly in search of prey. For all the mighty ones have been annihilated by the very means with which they once seized the possessions of others.[13]

But precisely in Gregory's time there began to take place a change noticeable in more directions than one.

King Authari, harassed by the Franks and also by powerful leaders of the Lombards whose ducal rule he had replaced, sought to strengthen his position by a family alliance with a neighboring power. Accordingly he married the Catholic Theodelinda, daughter of the duke of Bavaria. She it was who gave impetus to the con-

---

13. S. Greg., *Homiliarum in Ezechielem*, Lib. II, hom. 6.

version of the Lombards to Catholicism during the reign of Gregory the Great. After the early death of Authari, Theodelinda gave her hand to his successor, Agilulf, and thus became queen of the Lombards a second time. In 593, soon after he had purchased the lifting of the siege of Rome by Agilulf, Pope Gregory sent her his *Dialogues,* which concern the miracles of holy men, and entered into correspondence with her to thank her for her co-operation in the establishment of peace. Theodelinda had the son she bore Agilulf, as well as their previously born daughter, baptized as Catholics and she herself so informed the pope.

She also had a Catholic church built at Monza, in the form of a Latin cross. Here, in the treasury of this edifice, are still found precious souvenirs of Theodelinda and gifts from Gregory as proofs of her friendship with this great pope — for example, ampullae which contained oil from the lamps that burned before the tombs of the Roman martyrs. The Irish missionary, Saint Columbanus, also gained the friendship of the Catholic queen when, after his many wanderings, he finally went from Switzerland to Italy. Through her mediation he finally found a haven in Bobbio upon a tract of land donated by the king. There in 612 Saint Columbanus founded the monastery which became the home of monastic scholarship and at the same time a mission center for the conversion of the Arians. The saint himself composed a work against Arianism, but it has not been preserved. He died in 615, the same year which saw the death of Agilulf.

The latter was succeeded on the throne by Adaloald, the son of Theodelinda, who was empowered to serve as regent during his minority. Adaloald through his Catholic education had become susceptible to Roman culture. When he, therefore, entered into relations with the Byzantine governor at Ravenna, nationalist hostility was so aroused against him that he was deposed (625). Adaloald was not famed as a martyr, for actually he was religiously indifferent. But it is a fact not devoid of interest that a representative of the recently converted Visigothic royalty, Sisebut, Saint Isidore's disciple, should have sent King Adaloald a letter admonishing him to work for the conversion of the Lombardic people. To this end he held up to Theodelinda's son the brilliant example of his mother, whom he extolled as a most faithful servant of Christ, the friend of the Catholic flock, the constant enemy of the devil, and the fiercest foe of his earthly body, heresy.[14]

Theodelinda's influence did not end with the fall of her son, although he was followed by two Arian kings, Arioald and Rothari. They successively had as wife Theodelinda's daughter, the Catholic Gundiperga. Twice imprisoned, apparently, and liberated by Frankish intervention, Gundiperga was able, nevertheless, to work for the Catholic cause, for she founded a church at Pavia in honor of Saint John the Baptist. With Theodelinda's nephew Aribert (653-662), son of Duke Gundvaldus of Asti, who was brought up a Catholic, a Catholic dynasty took over the government. Interrupted only once — by Grimoald (662-671), who was hostile to the Romans — this dynasty remained in possession of the throne until 712.

At the end of the seventh century the victory of Catholicism in the Lombardic kingdom was assured. The last Arian bishop of Pavia entered the Catholic Church during King Aribert's reign. In 680 many Catholic bishops from the Lombardic kingdom took part in a Roman synod, proving thereby that ecclesiastical union had been accomplished. At this time Catholicism was also victorious in the duchy of Benevento through the efforts of Theoderata, who induced her husband, Duke Romuald, to extirpate the remnants of paganism there. Her adviser was Saint Barbatus, the bishop of Benevento. A strong political opposition undoubtedly still persisted, since the pope was the protector of those territories of central Italy which did not want to become absorbed in the Lombardic kingdom; but the Romanization of the Lombards could no longer be arrested.

The Lombards generally moved to the cities, which, like all things Roman, were in better condition here than anywhere else. The ambitious, free Lombard did not care to engage in agriculture, preferring to be supported by his Roman tenants, who delivered to him one-third of the produce; and the Lombardic nobility thus established itself principally as a patrician class — one which, later in the Middle Ages, was to distinguish itself in the movement

---

14. *Ep. Wisigot.,* 9; see *Mon. Germ. Hist. Epp.,* III, 673.

for independence initiated by the northern Italian cities. But Roman education and culture necessarily were more important in the cities than in the country; and yet, for a long time even after they were Romanized, the Lombards remained conscious of the differences between themselves and the Romans. The Germanic element was strengthened by the Franks, who conquered the kingdom of the Lombards in 774 — not to destroy it, however, but to annex it as an autonomous element to the Frankish kingdom.

The peculiar character of the Lombards continued to manifest itself distinctly in the struggle of the successors of Charlemagne for the possession of Italy and that of the Italian nobles for the imperial crown. Paul the Deacon — who while he was at the Lombard court of the duke of Benevento supplemented Eutropius' *Historia Romana,* and who later became a Benedictine monk — still felt himself to be wholly a Lombard. In praise of his people he wrote their history, while he was at Monte Cassino, after the fall of the royal dynasty of the Lombards. Still more remarkable is the case of Bishop Liutprand of Cremona, a tenth-century contemporary of Otto I. In common with the cultured Romans of his time, he delighted in reading the classics, and he knew how to write cleverly and to compose poetry; yet he considered it a great insult to be regarded as a Roman. He looked down upon the Romans as degenerates, despite the fact that his whole spiritual temperament was that peculiar to the Italians. It is true that this temperament was not identical with the stately character of the ancient Romans, but it corresponded closely to the national character, overlaid with an official veneer, as we find it in the epistles and satires of Horace.

The new Italian national language experienced greater difficulty in Italy than elsewhere in developing into a literary vehicle because the language of the schools, the *lingua grammatica,* had been conserved better here and the language of the people evolved directly from the Latin. The oldest Italian literary remains date as late as the time of Saint Francis of Assisi. On the other hand, foreign domination had contributed here to the strong, passionate spirit characterizing the development of national consciousness; which had also to assimilate the Greek, the Arabian and the Norman elements in Southern Italy. But everywhere this national feeling had for ally the common faith of the Catholic Church which it inherited from its ancestors.

We have wandered considerably from the period in which we desire to trace the birth of the new nations of the West during the conflict between Germanic Arianism and Catholicism. Hence we will return to those earlier times by directing our attention to the territory where, more than anywhere else, the victory of the Catholic Church determined the future.

The Frankish tribe, to which we now turn, was that Germanic tribe which immediately accepted the Catholic faith when it was confronted by the vital question of which Christian creed it should embrace in place of paganism. It soon realized the political advantage it gained thereby over the other Germanic tribes that had settled among the Roman population on Roman soil. It was spared the religious struggles and the internal differences which weakened and dissolved the other Germanic kingdoms, and gained instead in inward strength through the rapid fusion which took place there between the Romans and the Germans. The Franks utilized this advantageous situation to assert their superiority abroad. They became that tribe which propagandized everywhere for Catholicism and intervened in other nations in order to protect it. Thus the Franks supplanted the Visigoths, who had once propagandized for Arianism, and in so doing they embarked on a happier future.

It still remained an unsettled question, however, whether the union with Roman culture, doomed to destruction, might not also produce tribal disintegration. Arianism had offered no security against this: the Vandalic tribe was the typical example of Arianism's lack of moral strength. Was the Catholic religion, on the other hand, to succeed in making of the Frankish tribe, a typical example of its inherent power to produce an internal regeneration? Or was another tribe destined to manifest this?

CHAPTER TWO

THE CATHOLIC FRANKISH KINGDOM
IN THE SIXTH CENTURY

THE Franks, whose name appears for the first time in 258, were the tribe which embraced the West Germanic peoples along the middle and lower Rhine. Groups of them had early been planted in Gaul by Roman emperors as a reward for military services. Subsequently they crossed the Rhine in greater masses — at first in the vicinity of the delta. This swamplike region, belonging half to the sea, half to the land, had once enabled the Batavians to defy the Romans. The latter, for their part, avoided these territories as not worth colonizing; and in the middle of the fourth century we see the Franks moving thence into possession of the modern Campine, the land between the Schelde and the Meuse. Another advance of the Franks followed in the critical year of 406, when the Roman frontier on the Rhine was broken.

Through the invasion of the Vandals, Alans and Suevians — at the outset, the Franks as allies of the Romans had opposed them at Mayence — Roman life was to a great extent destroyed in the eastern frontier provinces of Gaul, in Upper as well as Lower Germany, and in the province of Belgica Secunda. The cities fell into ruins, amid which remnants of the population for the time being were able to earn but a bare existence. Heretofore the Franks had shown themselves in the course of their advances as half-way allies of the Romans; although they let the latter feel their ferocious strength now and then, they had nevertheless permitted the Roman population to live on undisturbed in the cities while they themselves occupied the surrounding plains. Now, however, the vacated land tempted them on their own part not to lag behind the other invaders. In the coastal regions Saxons, who had come by way of the sea, had been established since the middle of the fourth century. The Franks overran the entire tract along the middle Rhine; they occupied Cologne, conquered Treves, Tournai and Cambrai, and settled the whole territory between the left bank of the Leye (or Lys), the Canche and the sea. Around Tournai and Cambrai they still found a remnant of the Roman population, among whom they settled and intermingled — themselves becoming Romanized thereby, since their numbers were the fewer.

The manner of settlement was a decisive factor in the process of Romanization. Where the Franks settled in close groups, they preserved their Germanic characteristics; where they settled in scattered numbers among the Romans, they lost these characteristics. The Germanic place-names of the region prove this. In the vicinity of the Somme, these vanish completely. Where Germanic and Roman place-names are mixed, we can infer that Roman inhabitants maintained themselves side by side with the Frankish settlements. All Gaul, it is true, would be conquered in the course of time, but the conquerors as a whole no longer penetrated it. There were only individual warriors who with their retainers settled down among the Romans. And as a rule they rarely sought the cities (avoided indeed by most of the Germans). They did not feel themselves at home in narrow streets and lanes, but rather in the country where they could remain in close touch with nature. Large estates, which as governmental properties had become ownerless and were now being distributed by the Frankish king to his chief retainers, or plots of ground which had in one way or another lost their owners, attracted them. One will never be able to establish exactly the number of Franks who thus settled sporadically in Roman Gaul, but on the whole indications are that they were not many. Naturally, their number was greater in the north than in the south.

When the veil of obscurity covering early Frankish history lifts, we find a Frankish ruler, Childeric, of the Merovingian family as an ally of the Romans. The Roman leader in Northern Gaul then was Aegidius, the successor of Aëtius. After the death of Aegidius, Childeric occupied for a time the position of a protector of the Romans in Gaul against the Visigoths. In his manifold relations with the Romans he knew how to ingratiate himself with them. Though he was a pagan, he was not unfriendly toward Christianity, and the memory of this survived; for how else explain the story of Saint Genevieve, the saintly virgin, protectress of the

Roman population of Paris, who often obtained pardon from the pagan king for those condemned to death?

Thus Childeric prepared the way for his son Clovis, the "Constantine of the Franks," who acquired the Frankish sovereignty in 482. At his accession Saint Remigius of Rheims, the metropolitan of Belgica Secunda, greeted him sympathetically and exhorted him to rule justly and to respect the Church. Saint Remigius, as we see from this incident, knew how to accommodate himself to circumstances. Realizing, no doubt, that sooner or later the government in his country also would devolve upon the Franks, he had sufficient acumen and prudence to act in accord with the situation.

We can scarcely be surprised that the Roman general Syagrius, the son of Aegidius, meant no more to Saint Remigius than did Clovis, the son of Childeric, who equally with Aegidius had protected Romans and Christians. Syagrius governed on his own responsibility, with no better right than Clovis. He was not the incumbent of a Roman office, for since 476 there had been no Roman emperor who could have conferred offices in the Western Empire. His position rested solely on his actual power in those Roman cities which entrusted themselves voluntarily to his protection or his rule. Clovis laid claim to the same position. He already possessed it in part, but he wanted to possess it alone. The battle of Soissons, capital city of the territory of Syagrius, decided the question. The young Frankish king was victorious, and thereafter had no difficulty in making himself master of the country as far as the Loire. The bishops rendered the conquest easy for him by their friendly overtures; they imitated the example of Saint Remigius, if for no other reason than to avoid bloodshed.

Despite all the tribulations connected with the entry of the forces of wild pagan warriors, the Romans could, nevertheless, still consider themselves fortunate in view of the fate which the other Roman territories had to endure as a result of the Germanic invasions. Here, as a rule, the ancient inhabitants remained in complete possession of their lands; no division took place, as in the kingdoms of the Visigoths, the Burgundians and the Vandals. Neither were the inhabitants regarded as a vanquished people; instead the Romans were given civic status as subjects of the Frankish king and enjoyed the same rights as the Franks. Only one barrier remained to be removed — that of religion. When this had been effected, marriages between the two races soon began to take place, so that the fusion was accomplished after two generations and traces of differing lineage disappeared.

The Roman popular language, which had already supplanted the Celtic tongue of the Gauls — not without admitting many Celtic words — also became the language of the Franks who settled among the Romans and governed them. Naturally, German elements also were added to the Roman vernacular — a new contribution which bulked even larger than the Celtic, since it came from the ruling class. The Germanic terms relate to military and judicial affairs (which the Franks conducted in their own way), to hunting and navigation, to articles of clothing, to the manner of wearing one's hair and to colors of the hair. Many verbs and adjectives signifying intellectual qualities were also borrowed from the German.

Thus from the very genesis of the language it is seen that the Roman culture, far superior to the Celtic or the Germanic, determined the intellectual formation of the French and gave them the character of a Romance nation. The political organism and constitution of the Frankish kingdom were essentially Germanic, whereas education, ecclesiastical life, and also the manifestations of national life retained the Romance character in a preponderant degree.

The intrinsic character of the people, however, was determined, as in Spain and Italy, by the earliest element. This was the Celtic, for that culture had once had its home in Gaul. We still recognize this Celtic quality in the characteristics of the French people. Quick reaction to external impressions, sudden decisions, love of novelty, glowing enthusiasm, audacity, lack of patience and persistence, the gift of ready speech, telling gestures and quick perception, were from the first distinctly Celtic traits, whence the French inherited them. The ancient authors, Caesar, Dion Cassius, Diodorus, Ammianus Marcellinus, all ascribe such traits to the Celts. Julian, the future emperor, as governor of Gaul includes in a letter to the Athenians a picture of the life in Paris which reflects Parisian life of today in miniature. And Sulpicius Severus, the biographer of Saint Martin, has already furnished us an example of fluency and especially of the skillful narration of personal experience.

How was the religious barrier removed, making possible the rapid fusion into a new nation? As with the other Germanic tribes, the attitude of the ruler decided the issue. Clovis married the Catholic princess Clotilda, daughter of the Burgundian co-ruler Chilperic and the pious Caretene; they resided at Lyons, where Caretene had founded Saint Michael's church. Following the death of her father, Clotilda was reared at the court of her uncle in Geneva. Her older sister, Sädeleuba, founded Saint Victor's church in that city, afterward entering a convent as Sister Chrona. Clovis knew well the spirit that would come into his house with the daughter of such a family. From the beginning, the Catholic Frankish queen had the conversion of her husband at heart; but she did not achieve her purpose without difficulty. She found effective support for her efforts in Bishop Remigius.

The decisive factor was an incident which very closely parallels the conversion of Constantine. Upon their advance into Gaul, the Franks became neighbors of the Alamanni, who as early as the fourth century had seized the tithe lands (*Decumates Agri*) — that is, the pocket between the upper Rhine and the upper Danube, which had been colonized by the Romans. From there they had taken possession of Alsace and advanced still further across the Vosges and Eifel Mountains and along the Moselle. The inevitable question as to which of the two Germanic tribes was to rule Gaul, was decided in the Rhine valley in 497. The Alamanni were on the verge of victory when Clovis invoked the God worshiped by his faithful spouse, crying: "O Jesus Christ, of whom Clotilda says that Thou art the Son of the living God, do Thou support me. If Thou wilt grant me victory over the enemy, I will believe in Thee and be baptized." The fortunes of battle changed to the side of Clovis, the king of the Alamanni fell, and Clovis fulfilled the vow he had made by having himself baptized in Rheims by Saint Remigius on Christmas Day, 498 or 499.[1]

---

1. Cf. the article of L. Levillain in "Revue d'histoire de l'Eglise en France," 1935.

Though the baptism of Clovis was principally due to the influence of his wife, she must not be considered the sole cause. Like his father Childeric, Clovis had earlier adopted a favorable attitude toward Catholic Christianity — an attitude proved by two facts. The first fact is that Bishop Remigius could extend him a very friendly welcome; the second, that he himself took a Catholic princess as a wife, although of his two sisters, Lantechildis was Arian and Albofleda married the Arian Ostrogothic king, Theodoric. It is also quite probable that he promised his wife to have their children baptized Catholic. In any case it was a great concession on his part to permit such baptism for his first son; moreover, when the child died soon thereafter (and it would have been natural for a superstitious nature to ascribe the death to the baptism), he also allowed his second son to be baptized a Catholic. From the political angle, Clovis probably realized the great importance of the faith: he had seen proof of it in the position of esteem held by Catholic bishops, who had from the beginning offered themselves to him as allies. This political factor had to be considered when he faced the impending struggle with the Arian Visigoths for the possession of Southern Gaul. The latter were strongly opposed to Catholicism; the Roman population there was exclusively Catholic. Yet we must not regard Clovis' conversion to the Catholic faith exclusively as the result of political considerations. He convinced himself, as far as a man of his intelligence could, of the truth of the Christian religion and the Catholic faith, which his pious wife unflaggingly impressed on him.

The baptism of Clovis had very far-reaching consequences. In the first place, the conversion of the Frankish tribe to the Catholic faith was thereby decided. The king had himself baptized in the most solemn form by the foremost bishop of the country, and three thousand Franks, together with his bodyguard, his retainers, and his other sisters, were immediately baptized with him. The importance of the deed was actually recognized by his contemporaries. The Catholic bishops marked the significance of the event in their manner of greeting and congratulating Clovis. This was particularly true of Saint Avitus, bishop of the Burgundian capital city, Vienne, whose keen perception realized that the remaining German pagans would now be led to embrace the Catholic faith.

Christianity could look with hopeful expectation toward the dark forests east of the Rhine; a great and bloody conflict between Christianity and the lingering remains of paganism was hardly to be expected any longer. Clovis himself probably turned his eyes less in that direction than to the south, whither the path of Frankish conquest first summoned him. He could count on every Roman bishop in Gaul as a friend, and could rely on the Celtic-Roman population always to give preference to the new sons of the Catholic Church in the north when confronted with the choice between the semi-Arian Burgundians or completely Arian Visigoths, on one hand, and the Catholic Franks on the other. Alaric II, the Gothic king, was too late in his attempt to conciliate the Catholics by codifying the Roman law, and allowing a national synod to convene at Agde under the presidency of the archbishop of Arles. Clovis had them all on his side when he declared in his proclamation: "I cannot endure it any longer that these Arians occupy a part of Gaul; let us break camp with the help of God, and when the enemies are overcome, we will bring the country under our domination."[2] He even succeeded in drawing the Burgundians to his side. They were encouraged by Saint Avitus, who thus addressed the Burgundian auxiliaries then being sent to aid the Franks: "Engrave your faith upon your spears, obtain for yourselves the help of heaven by your petitions, arm your javelins with prayers."[3]

Southern Gaul was wrested from the Visigoths in 507 by the battle of Vouillé (Vouglé). Then, taking into account the political views which still animated his Roman subjects, Clovis had the incumbent emperor of the Roman Empire in the East, Anastasius, confer on him the title "Patricius"; and thus had his rule in Gaul recognized by the highest authority then existing.[4]

The Frankish kingdom — thanks to the unity of the Catholic faith which was all-embracing, and to the fusion of Romans and Germans — was the most homogeneous kingdom established on the soil of the ancient Western Roman Empire. It demonstrated its

2. Gregory, *Hist. Franc., Lib.* II, c. 37.
3. Avitus, *Ep.* 35. *M. G. Auct. a.,* VI, 74.
4. H. Günter in "Hist. Jahrb." (1934), 468 sq.

strength in the rapid expansion of its power, extending its domination particularly toward the east where many untried forces still lay dormant. The Thuringian kingdom was destroyed in 531, the Burgundian conquered in 532; and in 555 Bavaria also became dependent on the Frankish kingdom.

One observes that the Franks owed the great progress their power was able to achieve principally to their acceptance of Catholicism. In their naive boasting, they themselves acknowledged this. They extolled the Catholic faith as the source of their power, for that was the aspect under which they mainly appreciated it. They gave thanks to God for having brought them so much glory. They prided themselves on being Christ's particular protégés, who had especially merited this protection: the Lord of Lords had permitted dominion to fall to their lot instead of to the Romans because they had not defiled themselves with the slaughter of Christians, and because they had encased the bodies of the martyrs who had shed their blood under the Romans, in gold and adorned their repositories with costly jewels. Thus does the Salic Law of the sixth century, the period of their conversion to Christianity, praise the Franks for their religious creed. Christ is the King of their army.

> Long live Christ — thus reads the Law — who loves the Franks. May He guard their kingdom, fill their rulers with the light of His grace, protect their army, vouchsafe to them the pillars of faith; and may He, the Lord of Rulers, Jesus Christ, grant them peace, happiness and prosperous times.

The note struck here is a wholly new one and not at all what we heard in the age of Rome's decline. It is, certainly, very far removed from Saint Augustine's profound defense of the Christian faith and demonstration of its place in everyday life. A barbaric idea of power is associated with it. On the other hand, we must take the change of times into consideration. The era held in esteem only external power, and this was now allied with Christianity. The Christians were no longer despised and reviled; they were the rulers. With the delight in the power which they owed to Christ, there sprang up that joy of faith which dominates the Middle

Ages. It is not the old mentality of a dying period, cautious and careful to weigh all possible vicissitudes, that speaks to us, but the spirit of youth which, conscious of its strength, overestimates its vigor, and which is not overburdened by either culture or learning; it is the springtime of a new Western culture, which still has much to learn until it, too, acquires true wisdom by realizing the limitations of its strength.

There was much still wanting, even externally, in the Christianity of the Franks. Not all of them by any means had accepted Christianity at this time. In their ancient homes in the north, where they had settled in serried ranks, the Franks remained pagans for another century. For the time being, therefore, we do not include those parts when we speak of the status of the Church and culture in the Frankish kingdom during the sixth century. They did not enjoy any immediate importance. The essential fact is that Christianity was firmly established in the influential part of the tribe — so firmly that there never was a reaction toward paganism among the Franks as was the case with other Germanic tribes. The Frankish kings were Christians and so were the ruling classes. They lived in Roman Gaul and were the chief contributors to the formation of the new Romance French nation. True, their conversion was only external. A long time was to elapse before a deeper, internal Christian sentiment could penetrate the hearts of the Christian Franks, especially since the growing decline of education and culture and the triumph of external power with its attendant acts of violence constituted such great obstacles to the true and profound training of the heart and mind.

To begin with, the happiness in the Catholic circles of the Frankish kingdom over the outward change was as universal as it had been over the conversion of Constantine. The Church joyfully acknowledged the protection accorded by the Frankish kings, the respect they showed the saints, and the seriousness with which they combated heresy. The bishops could freely discharge their duties, and they made energetic use of this freedom to strengthen and expand the ecclesiastical organization and to influence the people according to the dictates of their pastoral office. At that time the bishops came almost exclusively from the Roman aristocracy, and the state willingly supported them in their activities, episcopal and intellectual, for these were universal in character. It was realized that here were the forces which could produce a superior culture, forces which safeguarded justice, practiced benevolence, and alone imparted learning. How thoroughly the power of the bishops in those times was protected can be ascertained from the fact that a bishop living according to Roman law was awarded nine times the wergild of the freeman, while the king's officials were to receive only three times that amount.

What gave the function of the bishops in the Catholic Frankish kingdom a particular force was their co-operation within the ancient hierarchical organization. The 125 bishops — this number can be authenticated for the end of the sixth century — under eleven metropolitans represented a power in comparison with which the impotence of the Arian church is at once wholly intelligible.

This power manifested itself especially in the many councils. Nor were these exclusively the limited synods of an ecclesiastical province. In fact, very little about the synods is known to us, though they must have been frequent, for the old regulation of the Council of Nicaea was revived, ordaining that provincial councils convene twice a year.[5] As a rule, they were held at least once a year, though the regulation had to be repeatedly stressed.[6] But they were completely overshadowed by the national councils, whose decrees are almost the only ones preserved to us. In the hundred years between 511 and 614 we know of more than thirty such national councils.

The first example of a national synod had been furnished by Archbishop Caesarius of Arles in the synod of Agde, which he convoked in 506 while the Visigothic king, Alaric II, still held the reins of government. The episcopal city of Arles came under Frankish rule in 536, and thus the example of Saint Caesarius, who had been created primate of Gaul by Pope Symmachus, was brought closely home to the Frankish bishops. His preaching activity likewise made him a special model, for during the forty years of his

5. II Synod of Tours (567), c. 1.
6. Aurel. II (533), c. 1; Arvern. (535), c. 1; Aurel. III (538), c. 1; IV (541), c. 37; V (549), c. 23; Elus. (551), c. 7.

episcopal career he preached at least once daily. It is now recognized that many sermons formerly ascribed to Saint Augustine should be accredited to Saint Caesarius. He also pointed the way to the visitation of churches, the erection of rural parishes, and the training of priests in ecclesiastical seminaries under the direction of the bishop. And it was he who gave the impulse to the first parochial schools by inducing the second synod of Vaison (529) to decree that priests, even those in the country, should take into their houses young people as pupils — this was customary in Italy — in order to instruct them and, if these so desired, to prepare them for the priesthood.[7]

That he composed a Rule for his sister Caesaria and her convent of nuns, as he had long before when abbot written one for his monks, has already been mentioned. It is probable that the *Statuta ecclesiae antiqua,* the oldest compilation of canon law in the West, also goes back to him.[8] The Frankish bishops could not find a more brilliant model than this archbishop of Arles, and though none of them attained his eminence, many, nevertheless, tried to follow his example.

The first Frankish national synod was held under Clovis in 511, the last year of his reign. It addressed itself to the Frankish king as follows:

> Because you, concerned for the Catholic faith, have commanded that the bishops assemble for the deliberation of urgent affairs, we, in response to your wish and having dealt with the matters proposed by you, have given our answer as to what we have resolved.[9]

Later also, as a rule, these national synods were convoked by the Frankish king; in almost all the protocols it is mentioned that the council convened at the king's command. All the bishops were entitled to take part. Now and then laymen also attended, but not as authorized members. Nor did the king himself take part in the

---

7. Conc. Vasense (529), c. 1.
8. Migne, *P. L.,* LVI, 879. Cf. Hefele, *Edition française de l'Histoire des Conciles,* II, 102 sq., 1374.
9. Conc. Aurel. I, *Conc. Merov.,* p. 2.

council's deliberations during the sixth century. Not until the seventh is there a change in this respect. Although the bishops appeared at the national diets as representatives of the spiritual aristocracy together with the lords temporal, the latter did not, conversely, attend the councils together with the bishops. We never find the name of a layman among the signatures.

A metropolitan always presided; he seems to have been elected each time from among the metropolitans present. General ecclesiastical affairs constituted the chief matter under deliberation, and these were decided according to the traditional regulations of the Church, which were either re-emphasized or taken as models for framing new decrees according to current needs. Abuses which had crept in were thus denounced and measures for their removal decreed. Concern for the religious and moral life of the people was shown on a comprehensive scale. More than once the wish to serve the public peace is specifically mentioned as the council's express purpose. Furthermore, the bishops often assembled to compose differences or to dispose of grave disciplinary cases which the ordinary courts of the metropolitans and bishops were not sufficiently competent to handle. Thus the council decided the case when a bishop was to be judged and the sentence of deposition passed on him. The king, too, assigned certain important state affairs to the bishops for their deliberation.

The bishops held the view that their decisions were to be effective without further recourse, although they welcomed the king's support in promoting enforcement. Sometimes the king even based civil laws on conciliar decisions. But unlike the Christian Roman emperors, the king did not make the validity of the decisions depend upon his sanction, nor did he regularly enforce their observance by civil means. In this the Frankish Church also differed from the Visigothic, where even the purely ecclesiastical decisions of the councils required the royal approval and the king always threatened punishments for violations of such decisions.

To particularize: among the cases dealt with, there recur often decisions concerning ecclesiastical administrations and the moral life of the bishops and priests, conditions in monasteries, the delimitation of ecclesiastical jurisdictions, abuses in sacred edifices, the

Church's right to extend asylum, the position of slaves, care for the poor, the attitude to be taken toward heretics, Jews and excommunicated persons. In the regulations concerning the religious life of the laity, stress is laid above all on the observance of the ancient ecclesiastical precepts regarding marriage, public penance and church attendance.

If we consider the value which such authoritative decisions of assemblies composed of the highest spiritual shepherds and the most cultured men of the country, had for civilization, we can hardly overestimate them — especially in view of the conditions of the time. There were at that period no moral factors capable of asserting themselves except the bishops. They were the first and only bearers of culture. We must also take into consideration the fact that after the fall of the Western Roman Empire and its disintegration into various new nations still only in the process of formation, the continued existence of any civilization in the West was not assured. It was far from certain that a new cultural center could really be created there. But concerning this fact, no doubt was possible: that the strongest civilizing force in existence resided in the Catholic Church, whose representatives were the best elements alike of the Roman population and of the surviving cultured class. A new civilization could not possibly have proceeded from the Franks alone. Hence it was of the highest importance that the chosen bearers of Christian culture convened often and mutually stimulated one another in carrying out the ancient religious and moral precepts. By surviving the Roman Empire these prescriptions had incontrovertibly proved their vitality. The councils functioned in this period as parliaments which seriously concerned themselves with the promotion of higher culture.

On the other hand, we are already able to note in the councils of this period the defects from which the Frankish Church was suffering — defects which became more glaring in the seventh century. The councils were national councils and the Church of the Frankish kingdom had a national character; more and more it was coming under the control of the kings. Though appointments to episcopal sees were to take place by canonical elections, after which the king signified his approval, his participation in the consecration was in the course of time given a fresh interpretation: to wit, that it was the king who invested the bishops with the insignia of their office or who simply conferred the office. The king, feeling himself the protector of the Church, made himself her master, and his power became the more dangerous the more arbitrarily it was used.

Autocratic rulers did not even shrink from doing violence to the shepherds of the Church. They wanted to subject the bishops as well as the rest of the clergy to the civil jurisdiction, to the king's or counts' courts, in criminal as well as in civil cases. Although the bishops opposed this, the most they obtained was that the national synod could first pass upon each case; and at times the kings even disregarded this. Bishops were cast into irons and tortured just as accused laymen were. However much the Church insisted that clerics be not summoned by laymen before the civil tribunal, in the end she had to be content if, at least in minor offenses and in civil suits, the judgment of the bishops' court of arbitration was accepted. Complaints concerning acts of violence to which the shepherds and ministers of the Church were exposed, multiplied in the councils of the seventh century; and these complaints even included acts perpetrated by bishops and priests themselves — a sign of the unworthy elements introduced into the Church by the kings.

As a result of the rich donations and gifts which the churches had received from kings and princes, they had grown wealthy in landed estates worked by slaves and serfs; further these properties enjoyed the privilege of immunity and were free from the jurisdiction of the counts and exempt from taxation. Because of the large number of dependents which the Church had created for herself by the liberation of slaves, by the leasing of lands for rent, and by the introduction of the tithes of all products of the soil after the example of the Old Testament, the episcopal sees became a source of power, wealth and influence which the kings began to regard with jealousy. King Chilperic complained: "Our state treasury has become poor, our wealth has passed over to the Church."[10] The kings strove to put these sources of power at their own disposal; at least they

---

10. Gregory, *Hist. Franc.*, VI, 46.

sought to bestow them upon supporters of royal power and upon royal favorites.

Side by side with dependence upon the king, which the Frankish Church as a national church incurred, there was a slackening of relations with the ecclesiastical center in Rome. The authority of the papacy was not denied, but there is no evidence that the Frankish bishops sought papal co-operation in the national councils. The primacy of the archbishop of Arles as papal vicar was waning. There existed not only the danger of the Frankish Church becoming involved in the decline of the Frankish State, as is distinctly noticeable in the seventh century, but the still greater danger that the ecclesiastical link with the rest of the Western world would be destroyed and the basis lost on which Western culture must be built.

The picture presented by the Church in the Frankish kingdom is rich therefore in contrasts, which in the course of time are not diminished but intensified. In the sixth century the bright colors still predominate. Regarding this period, we cannot deny that the bishops understood and fulfilled well the great task that had devolved upon them. They were in most instances zealously active, and that almost exclusively along those lines which were their immediate concern. Preaching, divine services, confirmation, the founding of parishes, the erection of churches and welfare work rounded out their activity.

One of the best bishops in the generation following Clovis was Saint Nicetius of Treves, who had been a monk before the direction of this diocese was entrusted to him. Treves was once the center of Christian Roman culture in the northeastern Celtic lands, but in the fifth century it had suffered great misfortunes and the city itself for the most part was a heap of ruins. Saint Nicetius ordered the devastated cathedral rebuilt by workmen from Italy. The Roman population had been very largely displaced by Franks; the bishop was confronted, therefore, by new and still partly pagan inhabitants in urgent need of religious instruction. Nicetius, by preaching daily, gave his clergy an excellent example; and the good effects of such an apostolic example are seen in his own successor, the saintly and efficient Bishop Magneric.

A bishop of this period had need of exceptional courage to oppose the arrogance and excesses of both the nobility and the king. In this, too, Saint Nicetius was a model. The occasion of his first appearance in his bishopric was immediately indicative of his lofty conception of his mission. Numerous prominent Franks had gone out to meet and escort him into his episcopal city. Having arrived in the vicinity of Treves in the evening he halted, because he intended to enter the city with solemnity the following morning. A camp of tents was pitched. It was springtime, the crops stood green around them; and when the horses were to be fed, the Frankish nobles inconsiderately turned the beasts into the fields as was their custom on military campaigns. Nicetius immediately rebuked them for the fields belonged, as he was told, to poor peasants of Treves. He threatened them with excommunication if they did not at once lead the horses out of the fields. Nor was he wont to rest on a threat, as we know from other instances. Thus, on one occasion, when his sovereign, Clovis' grandson, the Austrasian King Theodebert I, entered the church with a brilliant train, the bishop interrupted the Mass and in a loud voice commanded all those under the ban to leave the church. This affected not a few in the royal entourage who had incurred the bishop's excommunication.

Nicetius even excommunicated Theodebert and Clotaire because of their debaucheries, and for this he was exiled by the latter. After Clotaire's death, only a year later, the bishop was able to return to his church, where he died in 566, a spiritual shepherd after the model of Saint Ambrose. He gave clear expression to the fact that in the West a superior moral order was thenceforth to rule over the order determined by mere external might. For this, of course, there were needed courageous churchmen of his type. His motto was: "Joyfully I die for the right"; and by preference he sought to uphold his convictions before the mighty. Men had recourse to him to obtain the liberation of prisoners. He wrote to Clodosinda (daughter of the Frankish king, Clotaire I, and wife of the Arian Lombard ruler, Alboin of Pannonia) to confirm her in her Catholic faith and to urge upon her the salvation of her husband's soul. He protested to the emperor Justinian that the whole Western world was indignant at his support of the Nestorian heresy.

Of the same pattern was Nicetius' contemporary, Saint Germain, bishop of Paris (555-576). To prevent a fratricidal war between Kings Sigebert and Chilperic, he opposed Brunhilda. Like Nicetius, he exercised a lasting influence by his sermons. He is probably the author of certain directions for preaching, in which he exhorts the priests to explain the biblical texts properly and to use balance and moderation in the art of speaking, "lest a boorish manner give offense to the educated and a too highly ornate style become unintelligible to the peasants."[11]

Much care was devoted to the liturgy, for the people were not satisfied with the old hymns and desired new ones. Their wish, which shows us that the liturgy was felt as a very living thing, was, of course, granted; the second synod of Tours of the year 567 gave general permission for new hymns to be sung in addition to the Ambrosian songs. Thus we have two hymns from the sixth century which the Church still sings today. They were certainly composed by Saint Venantius Fortunatus, a poet who had acquired his fluency of style, not in Gaul — where the opportunity no longer existed — but in Italy.

Venantius Fortunatus occupies an anomalous position, worthy of note from a literary and ecclesiastical point of view. Born in northern Italy near Treviso, he received a comprehensive education at Ravenna and, to fulfill a vow, left Italy in 565, shortly before the Lombard invasion. Afflicted with a malady of the eyes, he had recourse to the intercession of Saint Martin and upon being cured, wished to make his thanksgiving at the saint's tomb in Tours. On the way he tarried for a long time with King Sigebert of Austrasia and with other princes, spiritual and temporal, delighting all with his occasional poems — banquet and thanksgiving, festive and laudatory poems — in which no one in the Frankish kingdom could excel him.

From Tours he went to Poitiers where intellectual converse with Saint Radegunde and her nuns detained him; and there he was made bishop in 600. He dedicated a biography to the daughter of the king of Thuringia, which is one of the most beautiful lives of the

---

11. Migne, *P. L.,* LXXII, 92.

saints written in that period. The events in the convent, great and small, as well as the narratives of Saint Radegunde, inspired him to many new and attractive compositions. Outstanding among these are a poem on the decline of Thuringia, in which he utilizes with profound feeling early reminiscences of Saint Radegunde, and the two Passion-hymns: *Vexilla regis prodeunt* and *Pange lingua gloriosi proelium certaminis*. The composition of the latter is also connected with an important event in the life of Saint Radegunde. In 569 she had dispatched a messenger to Constantinople with a letter of recommendation from the Frankish king, Sigebert, to the emperor Justin II and his spouse. The messenger was to petition them for a relic of the true Cross for the convent founded by her at Poitiers. He obtained his request, but the precious relic was brought to Poitiers only after many difficulties. Saint Venantius received it in the name of Saint Radegunde; it was as the relic, so anxiously awaited by her, was brought into the convent, that these triumphal hymns of the Cross were intoned for the first time.

The *Vexilla regis* is composed after the pattern of Ambrosian hymns. In *Pange lingua gloriosi proelium certaminis et super crucis tropaeo dic triumphum nobilem,* we hear the measured step of Roman soldiers, who liked to compose their songs for the march and triumphal processions in this heavy trochaic seven-foot meter. The deeply felt praise of the Tree, whence came the wood of the Cross: *Beata, cuius brachiis pretium pependit saeculi, Statera facta corporis tulitque praedam tartari,* not only reflects artistic credit on the poet, but also shows us a soul profoundly penetrated by Christian faith. The hymn to Mary, *Quem terra, pontus, aethera,* probably belongs also to Saint Venantius.

Although, as the last great Roman poet, he brought the ancient gift of words and art of versification with him from his mother country, he evidently responded to the deep piety of the clerical circles in the Frankish kingdom. This raised him above the externalism of those writers of occasional verse whose flattering and trifling manner we find echoed in many of his earlier poems. His growing spirituality is discernible also in his abandonment of pagan mythology, allegorical figures and rhetorical affectations of style. Art and feeling are brought into closer harmony. The poet is by no means so dependent upon ancient models as we perceive to be the case with other late Latin poets; and above all, he is more truthful. A sincere Christian spirit speaks from his poems, reflecting the pure ecclesiastical conception of the Middle Ages, freed from the trammels of the ancient conventional forms of society.

This trait of truthfulness is still more noticeable in a friend of Venantius — Saint Gregory of Tours, the historian of the Franks. Descended from a senatorial family of Clermont, he was made bishop at the tomb of Saint Martin in 573. He died there twenty-one years later. Closely associated with the ever-changing political scene, he wrote a national history of the Franks in ten books, which are the main source for the history of the Frankish kingdom in the sixth century. Both in form and content, this often-used source is a realistic picture of his epoch. He reports simply what he has seen and heard, and we are often surprised at his conscientious recording of the many deeds of violence and brutality of his age, which he does quite casually, as though these were matters to which one had become accustomed. His work places him in the ranks of those historians who clearly show us the rise of the new nations. He is thus associated with Cassiodorus, the historian of the Ostrogoths; with Paul the Deacon, the historian of the Lombards; with Saint Isidore, the historian of the Visigoths — to whom must be added Saint Bede, the Anglo-Saxon, and Widukind, the Saxon.

Saint Gregory labored under the influence of earlier opinions and still believed the end of the world to be near at hand. He also apologizes for his mistakes in grammar; and indeed his work shows that the feeling for inflectional endings has been completely lost. Yet his natural, simple and popular language is far more agreeable to us than the ridiculous attempts made by Virgilius Maro at the beginning of the seventh century, probably at Toulouse, to revive the *lingua grammatica* — attempts inspired by a vain desire for fame and pursued with the crudest ignorance.

We also have accounts of miracles and lives of saints by Saint Gregory of Tours. These are very important for a knowledge of the religious life of the period. Nothing was produced in the field of theology nor, for that matter, in the whole field of science. Attention was centered on the practical field where, in truth, much was to be done — and where, also, much was accomplished.

The first concern of the bishops was the building of churches. Saint Sidonius Apollinaris, bishop of Clermont, had complained in the second half of the fifth century that the old churches were barely being maintained and new ones were no longer being built. This situation took a new turn once the Catholic Franks had extended their rule over Gaul. Almost all the bishops of the sixth century in the Frankish realm were zealous in the erection of churches. No expense was spared in them: the pillars were marble and the walls inlaid with it; glass windows were installed; and numerous paintings were added.

In the face of economic changes, it was of the greatest importance to make provision for the pastoral care of souls in the rural districts. The Church had to take into account the decline of city culture which resulted from the back-to-the-land movement. In the Roman Empire the ecclesiastical organization had been a purely urban one, the diocese covering the same territory as the urban district. There was only one pastoral district, which coincided with this urban district. For this reason the diocese was also called *parochia,* parish. The bishop was ordinarily the pastor of his city and diocese, and the clergy who labored under him as his assistants had no independent position. In the diocese there were undoubtedly several churches in the city and some oratories here and there outside the city, but baptism could be administered only in the episcopal city — in most instances in a baptistry built near the cathedral church. Only from time to time did the bishop send a priest into the country to conduct divine services. This arrangement proved itself inadequate, especially in Gaul and Spain, where the cities were declining more and more and the population, following the custom of the Germans, was generally spreading to the country. Permanent pastors with independent churches were needed in the rural districts.

Slowly, retarded often by the unpropitious times, the development proceeded in this direction. The first rural churches were erected in the fourth century in the vicinity of Arles, Marseilles and Vienne; at the end of the same century we hear Saint Martin of Tours praised for establishing similar ones. These foundations became more frequent later, especially in the sixth century following the occupation of the country by the Franks, and the movement advanced from various centers. At first it was the bishops who built oratories, either on their own personal property or on the estates of the Church. Next came rich landlords who, imitating the bishops, had chapels erected on their *villae* (country estates) primarily for their private use. In the *vici* or *castra* there were, doubtless, groups of freemen who contributed jointly toward the building of public churches. Finally, hermits and monks who fled into the wilderness, and monasteries in lonely regions, also gave an impetus to the foundation of rural churches.

The site fixed upon was frequently the tomb of a martyr or a locality in some way connected with the memory of the saint — a practice that brought with it the custom of demanding relics for every altar. The status of the rural churches varied according to their origin. There were episcopal churches, monastic churches, free churches which had been founded by a group; and in contradistinction to these there were private churches that belonged to an ecclesiastical patron, since he or his ancestors had founded them.

Parishes were able to develop about the rural churches and these gradually detached themselves from the cathedral church. The earliest beginnings of rural parishes are found in the *vici,* in which the first detached parishes arose as *tituli maiores* (major parishes). At the head of such a major parish stood an archpriest, who had several priests and clerics under him to assist him in serving the smaller churches of the vicinity. These parish priests were in most instances sons of the same parish. The council of Vaison (529) ordained that rural pastors should have young students staying with them, as was customary in Italy, in order to train and educate them for the priesthood.[12] Every parish, therefore, was to train its own clergy. These came from the people among whom they had grown up and with whom they were in close touch.

Gradually the parish also acquired its own separate property. Every parish had to be endowed. At first the bishops claimed the right to dispose of parish property and income; then restricted this

---

12. Conc. Vasense (529), c. 1.

claim to only a part; and finally relinquished everything to the parish. The bishop merely reserved to himself a supervisory role, so that the pastor had to have the written authorization of the bishop to sell any of the parish properties.[13]

The creation of rural parish churches, which has continued through the whole medieval period into our own time, cannot be estimated too highly. This is true, in general, from both the ecclesiastical and the cultural point of view. Nothing could contribute more to the general elevation and culture of country folk than the fact of having among them a cultured person who would accompany them from birth to death with his exhortations and solicitude, and who would warmly urge on them the demands of Christian morality. Similarly beneficial was the feeling that in the church they possessed a place in which they were led to meditate on the problems of life and to rise in spirit above the stress and anxiety of their daily work. This was the first great social act of the Middle Ages. Necessarily it led also to the abolition of slavery and the amelioration of the condition of the serfs, with whom the priest now came into closer contact than ever before. Above all, these measures integrally comprised the regeneration that was to supersede the disappearing and decadent city culture. In them also we recognize that restorative force of rural life which the Greeks represented in the giant Antaeus struggling with Hercules: whenever Antaeus touched the earth in the course of the fight he received new strength.

This regeneration, however, besides giving rise to new and gave tasks for the Church, produced difficulties heretofore unknown. These latter were in the main connected with the private churches which existed not only among the Arian Germans but also in purely Roman regions of Italy. This institution was generally connected with the development of the rule of the great baronial lords. The need for rural churches induced such great landowners to erect oratories and chapels on their own estates. This they readily did, and also exerted themselves to procure priests for them. The Church was grateful for their diligence in this regard. But when these chapels became public churches and the barons claimed the right freely to

---

13. Conc. Aurel. (538), c. 5; 23; (541), c. 11; 33.

dispose of them and to appoint their priests, it was tantamount to the creation of a private church-government. The Church was compelled to reject and oppose this on principle. Yet the bishops had to be discreet in this struggle, since they depended in no small measure on the liberality of the barons for the erection and furnishing of the rural churches. Hence they contented themselves at first with demanding that patrons should not appoint strange priests to the oratories, that is, priests from outside the locality, without consulting the bishop of the place. Thus, ecclesiastical supervision and discipline, though obviously present in principle, were asserted only in a general way.[14]

The regulations obtaining for large countries and kingdoms proved to be necessary also on a smaller scale in the diocese. The purity of Christian doctrine and tradition demanded that the incipient decentralization in the diocese should not proceed too rapidly nor go too far and that the connection with the proper authority be preserved. This explains the regulation, recurring in the councils of the sixth century, to the effect that urban aristocrats might not permit the celebration of divine services in their rural chapels on high feastdays, particularly Christmas, Easter and Pentecost. On these days they were to go with their priests to the bishop and celebrate the feasts with him.[15] Again, all the priests of the diocese were to meet once a year with the bishop.

The bishop reserved to himself, in addition to those functions proper to him alone — for example the conferring of Holy Orders and Confirmation — the reconciliation of the penitents of the diocese on Maundy Thursday. Thus we learn that public penance was then still in force. Only grave public crimes, however, were punished with ecclesiastical penances, and this was determined by the bishop or the councils. Particular precaution was taken to insure the effect of this severest form of punishment, which was intended to serve as a deterrent. No other bishop than he who had imposed the ban of excommunication could lift it. Generally also, it was forbidden to

---

14. Conc. Aurel. IV (541), c. 7; 26.
15. Conc. Agath. (506), c. 21; Aurel. I (511), c. 25; Epaon. (517), c. 35; Arvern. (535), c. 15; Aurel. IV (541), c. 3.

have civic relations with those who had been excommunicated. Other disciplinary measures were necessary to protect churches against acts of violence which occurred only too often even within their walls. Churches in which a crime had taken place, were closed. So also were those in which insubordinate priests attempted to defy the bishop. In such cases, divine services were prohibited to guarantee the interdict's observance. All these disciplinary measures were based upon the fact that the population was genuinely church-minded, that it valued highly union with the Church and active participation in ecclesiastical life. It never failed to react when this participation was made impossible.

The source of this church-mindedness was true piety and sincere asceticism which was cultivated in monastic circles by monks and nuns and by hermits. This went so far at times that they did violence to their own persons. This evoked profound respect from the recently converted Catholic Franks. The silent sermon preached by example was understood even better than oral teaching, which at that particular time was inadequate. From these holy circles the leading bishops went forth. Saint Caesarius of Arles, Saint Nicetius of Treves and Saint Germain of Paris were monks before they became bishops. The Frankish kings, the bishops and the nobles or wealthy vied with one another in founding monasteries; and they preferred to turn to the south for their models, especially to Lérins. The diocese of Tours, the center of religious life in the Frankish kingdom, counted seventeen monasteries; the diocese of Clermont, twelve. An exceptionally large convent was that of Saint Radegunde in Poitiers, which numbered two hundred nuns at the death of its royal foundress.

Otherwise, however, the monasteries were usually small and poor, nor did they yet play an important role beyond their walls. They were not uniformly organized. The Benedictine Rule had not yet spread to Gaul and various rules were in force — for example, either those of Saint Basil and Saint Macarius or those of Saint Caesarius and Saint Aurelian of Arles in southern France. All the monasteries, it is true, were subject to the bishops, but their status was different according to the character of their founders. Monasteries founded by the laity were either royal or private, and, if they had not been granted the right to elect their abbot, the king or patron appointed the superior — a situation tending to bring upon the monasteries the fate of the private churches.

Anchoretism was restricted by the rise of monastic rules, which — as did the decrees of the councils — forbade monks to leave the monastery and live as hermits. Nevertheless, hermits appeared here and there dwelling in a wood and usually wandering on in search of a more solitary place as they became known and visited. A special class were the recluses, who, following a custom once prevalent in the East and in Italy, secluded themselves for life in a cell or a cave as captives of Christ. Localities counted themselves fortunate when a recluse of either sex came to live in their vicinity, believing they would receive a special blessing through such a person's prayers. In monasteries the most pious member was walled in, to spend the rest of his or her life in sacrifice and contemplation for the common weal; the scanty meals were handed in to them through a small aperture. These immured religious were sometimes called *incluses*. Saint Gregory of Tours describes the manner in which a nun in the convent of Saint Radegunde had herself immured. After a cell had been constructed according to her wish, the nuns escorted her thither with candles and the chanting of hymns. Saint Radegunde led her by the hand. At the cell door she took leave of all the Sisters, kissing each one. Then she entered the cell, in which she was shut up.

Still more interesting to us, however, is the activity of the Church in the social field. There she had no rival; indeed, she was practically alone in developing an activity which for this very reason deserves special recognition. Following the venerable Christian tradition, the Church regarded the care of the poor as both an obligation and an honor. The churches compiled lists of the poor, who in these entries were called *matricularii*. They were regularly given financial support and could solicit alms at the church doors. There existed also for the relief of the indigent pious foundations which were regularly remembered in wills. The first council of Orleans stated a very magnanimous principle: all those unable to work should receive, as far as possible, the necessities of food and clothing.[16] A synod of Tours in 567 decreed even more explicitly that every district should take care of its own so that the destitute might not wander from one locality to another;[17] that is, they intended to combat begging by giving relief to the poor. Finally, there were hospices (*xenodochia*) and hospitals, planned on Eastern models. In the founding of these houses, provision was often made for the smallest details. Thus in the seventh century we hear, in connection with the foundation of a hospital in Colombier, near Clermont — the work of Bishop Praejectus — that provision was made for twenty patients and that doctors and nurses were engaged.[18] In addition to these there were also leper homes, called lazar-houses; such were mentioned as existing in Châlon-sur-Saône, Verdun, Metz, Maastricht and Quincy.

The Church's most beautiful title to honor in the field of social action, however, lies in her contributions toward improving the lot of the slaves — the blackest stain in the escutcheon of famed antiquity. As regards the principle, indeed, no progress had been made since early Christian days. No one so much as thought of the abolition of slavery. Emphasis was laid only on the inner freedom of man; his external freedom had not yet received any special consideration; nor could one even entertain the idea, because the slave was regarded as a piece of property which, like any other, could not be taken from its owner. Hence, slavery continued to exist throughout nearly the whole medieval period, although latterly only vestiges of slavery, in the true sense, are found. During the sixth century the Church still had slaves everywhere on her estates. Similarly, she still recognized the reduction of an individual to slavery as a legitimate punishment. Thus in 511,[19] the council of Orleans decreed that an abductor of women, taking refuge in a church, shall indeed be spared the death penalty and grave corporal punishment, but must either become a slave or redeem himself by paying the wergild.

---

16. Conc. Aurel. I (511), c. 16.
17. Conc. Turon. II (567), c. 5.
18. *Mon. Germ. SS. rer. Mer.,* V. 235.
19. Conc. Aurel. I, c. 2.

However, the Church continued to work to her utmost in improving the condition of slaves. In this she was aided by the disappearance of urban culture and the dissolution of the Roman system of large landed estates. And it was, in sober truth, no small achievement that, as a result of the breakdown of the ancient and corrupt social order (a consequence of the transition from the financial to the natural system), the slave was now used by Germans, and then also by Romans, in a different manner than formerly.

First, the number of domestic slaves, who had been completely at the mercy of the master, declined greatly, for there were no longer many large households. Moreover, where they still existed — in royal palaces and the dwellings of great nobles — domestic slaves could often advance readily to a better, and at times to a very respectable, position, because now personal efficiency and military strength counted for more than before. The head servants of the Merovingian kings, the marshal (originally, equerry), the seneschal (chief steward), the chamberlain, the cupbearer, and the major domo, became the highest court officials, received estates as fiefs from the king, and were able to enter the first ranks of the nobility. Others, for example the servants of the nobles, were employed as troopers and were consequently highly regarded as *ministeriales* or *vassi* or *vassali;* they, too, were able to advance into a higher class. The workmen on the estates of the kings, who were valued for their skilled labor, formed a special class; still more appreciated were those serfs who, as *maiores* (mayors), administered the king's many properties. Most of the servants were employed in cultivating the land, which was done by a different system than that of Roman times. Since there were no longer any large landed estates and no capitalistic organizations which labored for foreign markets, the land was worked principally for immediate needs. The servant received for his own maintenance a hide of land on the master's estate or a section of a hide, whence he was called *servus casatus* or *mansuarius;* in return he had to pay rent in produce, for instance in pigs, bread, fowl, eggs, and the like. In addition, he was obliged to work in the master's fields about three days each week, rendering *corvée.*

This arrangement especially ameliorated the condition of the slaves, for the Roman landowners and the Church as a landed proprietor also subscribed to the new economic order. Using French terms, we speak of a transition from *esclavage* to *servage* — that is, the slave becomes a serf. Since he received a piece of land which he was permitted to manage independently, he became freer as regards the use of his time and labor; he was bound less to the person of his master. If he delivered his rent punctually and performed his *corvée* regularly, the master had no reason for complaint. Though inferior before the law, occupationally he was no differently situated than the peasant, who was of a higher class than he. In Roman times birth had decided profession; now a change began to set in, to the extent that profession affected the status of birth. By his occupation the former serf was brought closer to those who, though of a higher class, did the same kind of work. This improvement resulted from the higher evaluation of labor, which was no longer performed exclusively by serfs.

The Church took pride in the fact that her serfs were treated better than others; for this reason high-minded lords willed their slaves to the Church in order to assure good treatment for them. The council of Eauze ordained in 551 that the conditions stipulated in writing by the lords when bequeathing slaves, should be conscientiously observed, and added this beautiful statement: "The slaves of God's family ought really, out of compassion and justice, to be burdened with lighter work than those of private families. A fourth of their rent should be remitted to them as well as a part of their labor."[20]

The Church's serfs were also better situated legally: they were regarded as the property of the Church and enjoyed the greater protection which was accorded to her. Whoever killed a serf belonging to the Church had to pay a higher fine than was imposed for the killing of a serf belonging to a private individual. Once the churches acquired immunity, the Church's serfs were no longer judged by civil magistrates, but by Church officials. Yet the Church not only strove by her own example of humane treatment to practice

---

20. Conc. Aspasii episcopi Elúsani, c. 6.

the commandment of fraternal charity even toward slaves; she also approached the secular lords and directly urged them to adopt the same program. As she sought everywhere to oppose the violence of the age, so she also moved to protect slaves against every form of brutality and cruelty. The council of Epaon of 517 imposed an excommunication of two years upon any master who arbitrarily killed his slave.[21] Since it was believed impossible, once the legal title was admitted, to prevent the sale of slaves, an attempt was made at least to restrict it. There was a prohibition[22] on selling slaves out of Clovis' kingdom lest they fall into the hands of pagans; or, what would be still worse, into the hands of Jews who, it would seem, were regarded as slave-dealers.

Above all, the Church promoted the emancipation of slaves. Yet in this she proceeded cautiously, a course which finds its explanation in the very fact that the bishops felt themselves obliged to preserve intact the property of the Church as transmitted to them. No doubt, bishops actually often freed slaves belonging to the Church, but they could so act only when they took means to protect the Church against suffering any loss, by compensating her either out of their own fortune or by donations which they managed to procure.[23] In general it was forbidden to alienate slaves belonging to the Church by liberating them.[24] If laymen — presumably church-wardens were meant — liberated slaves belonging to the Church, they were bound by the *Lex Ribuaria* to compensate her by giving her others.[25]

While these decrees make clear that the trend of the times favored the liberation of slaves, they aimed at controlling it. Liberation was deemed a work of mercy and to the liberator accrued great spiritual merit. This was signified by the fact that under Roman Christian law the liberation took place in church in the presence of the bishop or a deputed priest and witnesses. A deed of emancipation was drawn up and signed by the bishop and the

21. Conc. Epaon., c. 34.
22. Conc. Cabillon. (639-654), c. 9.
23. Conc. Aurel. IV (541), c. 9. Cf. Dopsch, *Grundlagen*, II, 215.
24. Conc. Clippiac. (626), c. 15; Conc. Rem. (627-30), c. 13.
25. *Lex Rib.*, Tit. 58, c. 3, *Mon. Germ. Leg.* V, 243. Cf. Dopsch as above.

witnesses, whence those liberated were called *tabularii* or *ecclesiastici*. They continued, however, even thereafter to retain their connection with the Church just as did those who were liberated by testament and willed to the Church. This was a great advantage for them since their manumission was often contested. Attempts were made to reduce them to slavery again, especially by the heirs of the liberators, and it was against such moves that these former slaves needed protection.

With this class, liberation was not complete; the slave was still only half-free. According to Roman law, he could not appear in court personally, but had to be represented by a *defensor;* and he must still remain dependent upon his patron, although this dependence only affected him personally. In Frankish law, this dependent condition was extended also to the descendants of the liberated slave. He became a bondman, tied with his posterity to the piece of land he received at the time of his liberation. The Church then took the responsibility of guaranteeing the future of the liberated slave and his family. In this way the *tabularii* always became dependent upon the Church and subject to her protection; sometimes other freed slaves also entered into similar relations with the Church after their masters had allowed them to choose such a form of protection. The Church made it a point of honor to provide this protection; in return, she was to receive a periodic rent. She likewise designated her tribunals as courts for her wards, before which all claims against them were to be brought.[26] The civil law recognized this arrangement.[27]

The class of bondmen who rose from the condition of slavery and found protection through the Church, became fused with that of the Roman *coloni* who, though personally free, lived as tenants and paid rent. This betrays the gradual improvement of social conditions. The dependence already described had the advantage of affording the weak protection, the need for which was more urgent than the need for freedom. That the bondman could not leave the land on his own volition, but could be sold with it, was of less conse-

---

26. Conc. Aurel. V (549), c. 7; Matiscon. (585), c. 7; Paris. (614), c. 7.
27. Edict. Chlotarii. II (614). Cf. Dopsch, II, 216.

quence to many than the fact that they always remained bound to an estate which furnished them their livelihood. The permanent existence of a strong rural population under intelligent supervision was, without doubt, very important for the development of the art of cultivating the soil. Nor did the Church oppose a further improvement of the lower strata of the rural population; almost every member of this class had become a bondman at the height of the Middle Ages. The condition of the dependent peasants became serious only at the end of the Middle Ages when, with the rise of the cities, the economic system again became monetary. This turn of events induced the proprietors, who were becoming impoverished, to fix arbitrarily the *corvée* and the rents and to reduce the bondmen as well as the free peasants to serfdom.

The slavery question concerned the Church from yet another angle. What attitude was she to adopt when slaves desired to be admitted into the ranks of the clergy? In itself, the service of the Church was open to slaves as well as to everyone else: this was perhaps the most important contribution she made toward elevating the slave. Just as all men are equal before God, so the Christian slave was to be put on a par with other Christians. As a baptized Christian he could enjoy greater rights in the Church than his master if the latter was only a catechumen. Slaves were admitted into the service of the Church at an early date. There were even popes who had come from the ranks of slaves. Thus it is certain that Pope Callistus was once a slave; he had worked as a slave in the mines of Sardinia. Nor were there lacking slaves, both male and female, who were honored as martyrs.

Still, the fact could not be overlooked that masters asserted a right over their slaves. To say the least, admitting a slave into the service of the Church without the master's consent meant bringing a cleric into a precarious state of dependence upon a temporal lord, if it did not provoke a grave conflict of rights. Moreover, if slaves were admitted straightway, there was danger that many of them would enter the monasteries or the ranks of the clergy with no real vocation, merely for the purpose of escaping their masters and evading their onerous duties. In the fifth century, Roman law forbade the admission of slaves into the clergy; forbade it even when the master consented: he must liberate them if he wanted to make it possible for them to enter the service of the Church. Canon law had to take this ordinance into consideration.

The course of action to be followed in this particular situation was outlined in 443 by Pope Leo the Great, in a letter addressed to the bishops of Italy. He condemned the occasional practice of allowing slaves to enter the priesthood when they had not obtained freedom from their masters. We can understand the first reason given — the rights of the master may not be disregarded. The second reason — the sacred office would be defiled by the unworthiness of the candidate's condition — might seem strange, were it not clear from the context that the pope is thinking of slaves who had proved themselves unworthy of liberation. At the end of this decree appears the classic phrase: "He who wishes to be enrolled in the service of the Lord must be free from others, lest he be drawn from the Master's camp by some other obligations."[28]

The exhortation, however, does not seem to have been very effective, for Pope Gelasius (492-496) complained that everywhere slaves and *coloni* were running away from their masters in order to gain admission into the monasteries and among the clergy; Christian reputation as well as public order was suffering thereby, and the Church was open to blame for encroaching upon the rights of others.[29] To correct this abuse, the pope exacted the return of those who, contrary to the existing law, had fled from a dependent condition, or demanded proof of their liberation in the form of a document from their masters. When the slave was made dependent upon the Church or a monastery, the pope required the legal transfer executed by the master. It was, of course, difficult to force the return of those who had already obtained ecclesiastical positions and hence a distinction was made with regard to their rank. A priest could not be deprived of his sacerdotal dignity, but he lost his income (*peculium*). Clerics were to be returned to their masters in all instances; deacons, only when they could not supply their master with a substitute.

28. Migne, *P. L.*, LIV, 611.
29. XIV, Ep. 14. Thiel, *Epp. pontif.*, 370.

The priest, in such circumstances, probably entered the service of his master as a private chaplain — a position which naturally accorded in no wise with the Church's conception of the independence of her priests and makes it clear why the ecclesiastical authorities wanted to prevent these cases from arising. Thus a conflict of principles appeared: on the one hand was Christian idealism, which desired to open to slaves also the opportunity of entering the clerical state and the monastic life; on the other hand was respect for the existing law, and reluctance to transgress it. Finally, there was concern for ecclesiastical independence. We must keep these viewpoints, each of which has its own justification, well in mind if we would understand correctly the various regulations and remarks encountered in this period and not judge them unfairly. Considering the circumstances, we can see that it is certainly not the historian's business to blame the Church for not having abolished slavery. She could not do that. Only a biased idealist could pass such judgment.

The Frankish Church in particular observed the main points of these papal prescriptions,[30] but with this difference: that the deacon also, who had been ordained while a slave, was allowed to retain his dignity, while the bishop who knowingly conferred the priesthood or the diaconate upon a slave, had to pay the master double compensation,[31] or deliver the ordained slave to his master to serve the latter's private church.[32] This latter requirement, which appears to have been initially prohibited, was not unusual in the last phase of the Merovingian kingdom, when the system of private churches had become quite extensive and had led to those grave abuses against which Saint Boniface contended.

In formulating the regulations for admission into the ranks of the secular clergy, the Church thus adopted the legal point of view. The monasteries, however, advocated an idealistic attitude. They desired to leave their portals open alike to freemen and slaves without any discrimination; they also gladly liberated slaves who had been bequeathed to them. But the bishops, as we have seen,

---

30. Conc. Epaon. (517), c. 34.
31. Conc. Aurel. I (511), c. 8.
32. Conc. Aurel. V (549), c. 6.

did not emancipate their own slaves; and they were very reluctant to tolerate emancipation of the slaves of a monastery. The council of Epaon accordingly forbade the abbot to liberate slaves bequeathed to the monastery, arguing that it must be considered unjust that, while the monks labored daily in the fields, their slaves in virtue of their freedom could remain idle.[33] Fundamentally, without doubt, this prohibition derived from the legal viewpoint. We clearly note that it had to be forced upon the monasteries.

These had more latitude when it was a question of admitting slaves as monks. In such circumstances, they made little inquiry whether the master had assented, or even had liberated the slave. Pope Gelasius, like the Council of Chalcedon (451) before him, had no choice but to forbid the monasteries to admit slaves not previously liberated by their masters. Obviously it was especially difficult for the monasteries to investigate the antecedents of candidates at the time of admission. We find no mention of it in the Benedictine Rule. The Benedictines delighted in showing the slaves that worldly distinctions were no longer to have any value in the new official regulations for the militia of Christ. That is why Saint Benedict wrote these beautiful words in his Rule:

> Let not him who has entered as a slave be put after the free-born. . . . Whether bond or free, we are all one in Christ, and bear an equal burden in the army of one Lord: for "with God there is no respecting of persons."[34]

The Christian's consciousness of being a slave of God made it easy for him to put himself on the same plane with him who had been a veritable slave; just as this same conviction made it easy for many slaves in Christian antiquity to continue to live in the world as slaves. It was in regard to this latter sense that Saint Augustine had once written, in a chapter of *The City of God,* a passage which sounds like a sermon:

> The good man is free, even when he serves as a slave. The bad man, on the other hand, is a slave, even when he rules, and indeed he is

33. Conc. Epaon. (517), c. 8.
34. *Regula,* C. 2. Cf. Delatte-McCann, pp. 42-43.

the slave not only of one man but, what is worse, of as many masters as there are vices in him. With regard to these vices Holy Writ says: "By whom a man is overcome, of the same also he is the slave."[35]

When we imagine that there then existed in peoples completely imbued with Christian sentiments a great longing for worldly freedom, we are introducing modern ideas into an age of different concepts. There was, rather, a contest among them in the service of the Highest Master.

Whatever idealism might desire, even the monasteries could not overlook the injunctions of the Church and the dictates of prudence. By admitting slaves without the consent of their masters, they exposed themselves to great dangers, including the serious encroachment upon their independence of powerful laymen, if not a threat to their entire existence. Hence we are not surprised that Saint Aurelian, archbishop of Arles (546-551), in his monastic rule ordained:

> Let no slave be admitted; regarding a liberated slave, however, if he is an adult and comes with letters from his patron, it shall rest with the abbot whether he ought to be admitted.[36]

Such concern with the master, even when admitting emancipated slaves, finds its explanation in the fact that Saint Aurelian feared that this might give rise to difficulties for the monastery, since the liberated slave remained in a way dependent upon his patron.

We may be at a loss whether to designate these prescriptions of Saint Aurelian as wise or narrow-minded; but it certainly was a sign of narrow caste-feeling when, in the later Middle Ages, such ideas were extended to bar all but sons of the nobility from many monasteries. This was justly characterized as a very scandalous practice by the Dominican writer, Cardinal John of Turrecremata (Torquemada), in his commentary on the Rule of Saint Benedict.[37] At the beginning of the Middle Ages it had become the rule for

---

35. *De civ. Dei*, IV, c. 3.
36. C. 18: Migne, *P. L.*, LXVIII, 390.
37. Joh. de Turre Cremata et Smaragdi, *Reg. S. Benedicti cum commentariis* (Cologne, 1575), p. 62.

monasteries to demand of slaves before admitting them, the written endorsement of their liberation on the part of their masters. No one could condemn this practice, in view of the danger to which monastic independence was continuously exposed at the time. It always remained a credit to these institutions that they never esteemed a member less because he had once been a slave. The monasteries were the first to carry out fully the ideals of social liberation.

The stand which we see the Church taking for the protection of freed slaves was paralleled by her attitude toward women in want of assistance. In the Church woman's dignity, needs and freedom in the choice of a state of life found their best protection. No one having even a slight acquaintance with the measures which the Church took in this direction can be deceived by the gross misinterpretation occasioned by a remark of Saint Gregory of Tours concerning the council held at Mâcon in 585.[38] But since this error has given rise in our own time to slogans eagerly accepted, there has been difficulty in eradicating it. The council in question is called "the misogynous council" because it is supposed to have denied woman a soul. The error was occasioned by Saint Gregory's report to the effect that a bishop arose in the council and said: *"Mulierem hominem non posse vocitari."* This was mistakenly translated: "A woman cannot be called a human being." The correct rendering, of course, is: "A woman cannot be called *homo.*" In Latin, *homo* rarely denoted a woman, and in popular Latin the word transformed itself into the French concept *homme* (a man) while retaining the universal concept "human being." The bishop merely intended, therefore, to make a philological observation: a woman (let us continue in French, in which the misunderstanding immediately becomes evident) *ne pouvait pas être appelée homme* — could not be called a man. Saint Gregory concludes: "But after the bishop had been given an explanation by his confreres, he held his peace." The incident then was speedily closed and the misunderstanding also should now be laid to rest.

---

38. Gregory, *Hist. Franc.*, lib. VIII, c. 20. Cf. Kurth, "Le concile de Mâcon et les femmes," *Rev. d. quest. hist.*, 51 (1892).

It was precisely this council of Mâcon of 585 which guaranteed widowed women the assistance of the Church in the courts of law. It demanded that a judge, before taking measures against widows and orphans, should make known his intention to the bishop under whose jurisdiction they were living. The proceedings were to be conducted only in the presence of the bishop, the archdeacon or a priest. If the judge did not fulfill this demand, or committed any injustices against widows and orphans, he was threatened with excommunication.[39]

The Church championed especially those widows who, not intending to remarry but wishing, like pious virgins, to live in the world as consecrated women, found themselves beset by covetous and powerful suitors. The king had undertaken to protect them, but this protection was probably often inadequate. Hence the Church used her influence on their behalf and specifically forbade the commission of any violence against them.[40]

The Church similarly proceeded against the repudiation of wives by their husbands — a not infrequent practice among the Germans. To this end the council of Orleans in 533 forbade the breaking up of a marriage because of the illness of one of the parties.[41]

Unfortunate mothers who disowned their children yet desired to secure protection and support for them, resorted to the Church. Usually such children were deposited at a church door, for the mothers knew that this insured their being taken care of in one way or another. The emperors Honorius and Theodosius II had decreed that whoever found and gave shelter to such a child was allowed to keep it, with the Church exercising control over it. Therefore, anyone finding an exposed child had to report the fact to the Church. The clergy thereupon publicly exhorted the parents to present themselves. If after ten days no one acknowledged the child, it was assigned to the finder, but only after witnesses had vouched for the fact that no one had presented himself, and the bishop had endorsed

---

39. Conc. Matiscon. II, c. 12.
40. Conc. Paris. (556-573), c. 6.
41. Conc. Aurel. (533), c. 11.

the document drawn up to that effect. If no one was found to care for the child, the Church assumed the responsibility.[42]

The care of prisoners goes back as far as a Roman law of the year 409. The council of Orleans of 549 decreed that prisoners should be visited on Sunday by the archdeacon, who should console them and ascertain their needs. The bishop was to appoint a specially qualified person for this duty — one faithful and conscientious, who should make it his business to provide for the support of the prisoners out of church funds.[43] Following an ancient custom, the bishops sought to redeem prisoners of war. In those times of violence, when so many captives were carried off from battle, when unjust condemnation and cruel treatment of the imprisoned were so frequent, these works of mercy aroused special thankfulness. In the lives of many saints we have proof of such gratitude for what they achieved through their intercession for the welfare of prisoners and for men condemned to death, through the paying of ransoms or the working of miracles to effect their liberation. In the eyes of contemporaries, such works of mercy characterized the saint.

The Church magnanimously used her influence in behalf of those who had fallen into economic distress. In the first place, she espoused the cause of small landowners and peasants oppressed or dispossessed by the great proprietors. The second council of Mâcon, which we have mentioned repeatedly, threatened with excommunication those who by violence or fraud robbed the poor of their land.[44] Next, the Church helped needy peasants and strangers by leasing to them smaller estates in usufruct according to the Roman form of *precaria*. This was also the form in which many conveyed their estates to the Church in order to secure to themselves a life interest. Aged persons, incapable of working, established a type of insurance for themselves by conveying to the Church their landed property in return for which she guaranteed them a life-annuity.

---

42. *Formulae Turonenses* 11 (ed. Zeumer). *Mon. Germ. Form.*, p. 141. Cf. Dopsch, *Grundlagen*, II, p. 221.
43. Conc. Aurel. (549), c. 20.
44. Conc. Matiscon. II, c. 14.

The Church proved herself a beneficent creditor in various other exigencies by giving persons in need of money — for example, those desiring to undertake a pilgrimage — a certain sum in exchange for a form of leasehold on their estates; meanwhile granting them the option of redeeming the conveyed estates at a prearranged price. Persons entirely without means could obtain loans from the Church by giving her their freedom as a pledge. Those who had forfeited their freedom could regain it if she paid their ransom. Those condemned to death through failure to pay a fine, could escape the death penalty by pledging themselves and then being ransomed by the Church. The sentiment which led the Church to grant easy credit to the needy, brought her at this early date to practice what would be her immemorial policy of combating usury, always hateful to her. In the third council of Orleans (538) she forbade all deacons and higher clerics to lend money out at interest or to seek gain in commercial enterprises.[45] Another decree, emanating from a council held in the beginning of the seventh century, at a place which cannot now be determined, opposes a usurious exploitation associated with the *corvée,* whereby a man gave himself and his freedom as pledge for a loan and assumed the obligation of rendering services on fixed days of the week.[46]

The fields of instruction and education were not the only ones in which the Church revealed herself to the new nations as the transmitter of the great experiences of former times. This was true in the usage of legal forms, as well. In virtue of her great social importance, she was able to secure the application of what she transmitted. Her statutes showed posterity the way, for ecclesiastical legislation blazed the trail for civil legislation. This, however, did not prevent the Church from coming into conflict occasionally with the norms of Germanic law.

Above all, the Church wished to exercise a determining influence in the field of marriage legislation, for here she must protect the basis of human society. Just as she always laid weight upon regulations restraining sexual desire, so she preferred to

---

45. Conc. Aurel. III, c. 33. Cf. Conc. Clippiac. (626), c. 1, and also Dopsch, *Grundlagen,* II, pp. 226, 510.
46. Conc. incerti loci post 614, c. 14. *Mon. Germ. Conc.,* I, 195.

go too far rather than not far enough in her antipathy to sexual unions between blood relatives. This antipathy, we may remark, had been particularly characteristic of the pagan Romans, whose mores, in many respects, had from early times prepared the way for Christianity. We will particularly appreciate this if we recall that marriages between relatives, even between brothers and sisters, were not unusual among the non-Indo-Germanic peoples of Asia, in Egypt, among the Picts, and perhaps also among the pre-Roman Italians. This custom seems to go back to matriarchal concepts,[47] and many Semitic and Indo-Germanic peoples had also allowed themselves to be contaminated by it. We find marriages between brothers and sisters frequent in the Persian dynasties, in the Hellenistic dynasties of Asia Minor (such as the Seleucidae), and among the Ptolemies in Egypt. An attempt made by the emperor Caius (Caligula) to introduce it into the imperial family of Rome had, however, to be abandoned because of the opposition it encountered. Christianity was able to build further on this naturally healthy sentiment of the Romans, who specifically designated such marriages as impure (in-cesta).

In line with Saint Augustine's teachings, social motives also entered into consideration here: through marriage contracts, new bonds of love were to be constantly forged between families not already related and thus relationships between men multiplied.[48] It was then principally a question of determining how remote consanguinity must be. At first the Church followed the Mosaic and Roman marriage prohibitions, which confined themselves to the nearest relatives. The emperor Theodosius, already under the influence of Christian ideas, had, it is true, forbidden marriage between first cousins, but later emperors abrogated this. The Church pursued an independent course when the Burgundian national council of Epaon (517) forbade marriages between first and second cousins[49] — a ruling endorsed by later Frankish national synods. Though the civil law was ready to follow the Church's lead, there

---

47. Cf. Kornemann, "Die Geschwisterehe im Altertum," *Mitteilungen der Schlesischen Gesellschaft für Volkskunde,* XXV (Breslau, 1923), 17 sqq.
48. *De civ. Dei,* XV, 16.
49. Conc. Epaonense, c. 30.

nevertheless arose difficulties with regard to the marriage prohibition concerning second cousins. These difficulties multiplied when
marriage between blood relations was universally forbidden, for
blood relationship was variously limited, besides being computed
differently by the Germans than by the Romans. In the Carolingian
period, when the Germans entered the Church in greater numbers,
these difficulties became even more acute.

In view of the great importance, cultural and social, of the
Frankish Church, her rigid organization, and her intimate relation
with the king and the Frankish nobles, it was inevitable that the
scattered remnants of Frankish pagans living among the Catholic
Romans should soon be absorbed. Thereupon paganism itself,
which had spread along the fringe of the Roman population as a
result of the Germans' advance, was doomed to recede. Here the
progress of Christianity was simply a reconquest on the part of
Christian culture — merely a question of permitting old traditions,
half-extinct Christian organizations, and abandoned bishoprics to
revive.

Among the Salian Franks the diocese of Arras, which had
ceased to exist with the Frankish conquest, had been re-erected under
Clovis. The hermit Saint Vedastus came as a missionary bishop
into the city, which lay completely in ruins. There were neither
Christians nor churches to be found; hence he created a new Christian community out of the Frankish population. A similar situation
obtained in the Rhine country among the Ripuarian Franks. The
metropolitan provinces of Treves and Cologne took on a new life:
in the former, where the populace had weathered the times fairly
well, Metz, Toul and Verdun again appeared; in the latter, where
a scant remnant of the Roman population maintained itself, there
emerged the bishopric of Maastricht. It is probable that this see was
established under Clovis himself in place of the ancient bishopric
of Tongres. Mainz, together with the bishoprics of the upper Rhine
region — Worms, Speyer and Strassburg (Argentoratum) — rose
again from their ashes. During the sixth century paganism still
completely dominated the right bank of the Rhine.

In Switzerland, the bishop of Vindonissa (Windisch), who still
held this title in the first half of the sixth century, transferred his

see first to Avenches and then at the century's end to Lausanne. During this transition period we meet Marius, a native of Autun, as bishop in Avenches. He wrote a brief world-chronicle whose chronology reveals the author's traditional, legitimistic point of view. He designates the years from the first consul to the last (Basil, in 541); then for a time he continues to count the years from this last consulate; and finally he computes them to the terminal year, 581, by the Byzantine emperors. Hence for him the Roman Empire still existed, at least as a cultural unity superior to the Frankish kingdom.

Toward the end of the sixth century the episcopal see for the canton of Valais, then exposed to Lombardic invasions, was similarly transferred from Octodurum (Martigny), which lay along the old mountain pass leading over the Great Saint Bernard, to Sion. In Rhaetia, where the Romans continued to remain after the Franks forced the Ostrogoths to cede it to them in 534, the episcopal see had probably existed at Chur without interruption; the first mention of its being there, and of one Bishop Asinio, occurs in the year 451. On the other hand, in the diocese of Augsburg, founded, like Chur, by the Church of Northern Italy, Christianity had barely been able to survive. At the end of the sixth century Augsburg was separated from Aquileia and joined to the Frankish Church. But an active ecclesiastical life in the territories occupied by the Alamanni manifested itself only in the seventh century. In the sixth, a reawakening is more noticeable along the middle and lower Rhine than in the Alpine regions and among the Alamanni.

There is a certain amount of concrete evidence showing to what extent the Frankish power supported the Church. King Theodoric I (511-533) had many clerics sent from Clermont to Treves to assist the bishop of that city in his missionary activity, for many pagans and also many idols remained in the vicinity. In Cologne, the pagan cult existed side by side with Catholic worship; and when a zealous young missionary named Gall set fire to a pagan shrine, he was protected against the fury of the pagan population by Theodoric's intervention. A similar episode is related in the life of Saint Radegunde, during the period in which that Thuringian princess still dwelt at the side of Clotaire I as his spouse — probably in the forties of the sixth century. It is supposed to have occurred in the vicinity of Athies on the Somme. The queen, accompanied by a royal train and traveling on horseback, was on her way to keep an engagement with a certain matron named Ansifrida. Hearing of a pagan sanctuary in the neighborhood, she forthwith rode thither, had it set afire and, defying the armed multitude which had gathered, remained until the fire had accomplished its task.[50] Paganism certainly could no longer have been a serious adversary if members of the royal family themselves thus set about destroying places of pagan worship.

Synodal decisions of the sixth century forbidding pagan customs and proceeding against them are numerous. Participation in pagan sacrificial banquets as well as the pronouncement of pagan oaths and formulas over the head of an animal or a drinking-horn were prohibited. In this the civil authority actively supported the Church. An order of King Childebert (d. 558), who resided in Paris, forbade landed proprietors to resist Christian priests engaged in removing idols set up on their estates; it also prohibited pagan feasts, songs and dances.[51] This order was probably directed against those vestiges of Gallo-Roman paganism to which the canon of a synod of Tours of the year 567 refers: it vigorously opposed the worship secretly accorded trees, stones and fountains as well as the adaptation of pagan customs to Christian feastdays. This canon mentions that the ancient sacrifices to the Manes were still being offered on the feast of the Chair of Saint Peter (February 22) and that nocturnal carousals and dances were being held in the churches on Martinmas (November 11), a time when the pagan harvest feasts had been celebrated.[52] In the north, Germanic paganism had taken even deeper root among the Franks.

However, there were really many Germanic Franks who had sincerely accepted the Christian religion. We possess an important clue to this in the Germanic names which we meet among the clergy. Of course, we must not assume that such names always indicate Frankish descent: following the example of the Frankish nobles,

---

50. *Vita S. Radegundis*, Lib. II, c. 2.
51. *Mon. Germ. Capit.*, I, p. 2.
52. Conc. Tur. II (567), c. 23.

German or Frankish names were also adopted by the Roman population, especially by those of the higher classes who had relations
with the Frankish court. But in some cases Frankish descent is
directly proved or doubt of it is indirectly excluded. At all events,
from the increasing frequency of Germanic names among the
Frankish bishops and priests one can draw the general conclusion
that the Church was attracting the Frankish tribe and its members
in a growing measure. While in the fifth century the bishops were
almost without exception of Roman nationality, in the course of
the sixth the number of bishops and priests bearing Germanic names
is on the increase: three Germanic occurring to a round twenty
Roman-Greek names.

In this regard a distinction is to be made between the various
sections of the country, in accordance with what we note in other
respects concerning the fusion of the population. In the south,
where the population was practically all Roman, the episcopate is
still recruited exclusively from the Roman circles of distinguished
provincials. In Central and Northern Gaul, however, we discover
several bearers of Germanic names, and these become more numerous in the ecclesiastical provinces of Rheims and Treves; in the
Rhine regions they occur at least as often as the bearers of Roman
names. In Southern Gaul we do not find any bishops with Germanic
names until the eighth century, whereas at the end of the seventh
they have almost exclusive possession of the episcopal sees of the
rest of Gaul. At the synod of Paris of 614 we find among seventy-
nine bishops thirty-seven with Germanic names.

Now, the increase of these latter precisely at this time is not
in itself, of course, proof of the genuine spread of Christianity
among the Franks. There was so much honor and such a wealth
of power attaching to the office of bishop in the Frankish kingdom
that it is possible the extrinsic advantages induced many a Frankish
noble to enter the clerical state; or that royalty particularly inclined
to confer episcopal sees upon persons who had enjoyed a position
of special trust at court. But an incontestable proof of the deeper
grasp of Christianity on the part of the Franks is the large number of
Frankish saints from the upper as well as the lower classes. Of the
Frankish royal family we may mention Clovis' grandson, Saint

Clodoald, founder of the monastery which was named "Saint Cloud" after him; from the common ranks we single out the saintly hunter Brachio, who during a boar hunt in Auvergne encountered the holy hermit Emilianus and was led by his example to embrace a hermit's life. At this point, we need only recall Saints Clotilda and Radegunde, who have been frequently mentioned.

Let us now proceed to the most important question: What were the total results achieved for religious and moral life by the Church's activity?

Externally, the Christian faith rapidly conquered the paganism which had flourished here and there in Roman-Frankish Gaul; and the Franks felt proud of being members and defenders of the Catholic Church. In like manner they were willing to fulfill outwardly the duties of the faith. The divine services on Sundays were well attended. When the bell rang for Matins, the people rose and came to church in goodly numbers for its recitation. At Mass the churches were densely crowded. King Guntram, fearing that an assassin might get too close to him in the crowd that filled the church, always surrounded himself with many retainers when he entered. The crowds of people thronging the churches were naturally larger on the great feasts and the feastdays of those saints who were especially venerated. On these occasions many people also came from afar; and, if they found no night's lodging elsewhere, they accommodated themselves in the church itself. (The synod of Auxerre, however, moved against this practice in 585.) Large crowds also participated in the processions held on the three Rogation Days — the three days immediately preceding the feast of the Ascension — the introduction of which is attributed to Saint Mamertus, bishop of Vienne (d. 475).

Those who assisted at Mass on Sundays generally received Holy Communion also. The laity was obliged to go to Holy Communion at least on the three principal feasts: Christmas, Easter and Pentecost. Since the frequent reception of the Holy Eucharist accorded with the practice of Christian antiquity, the early manner of receiving was also adopted. Standing, the communicants received the Body of the Lord in their right hand, which was supported crosswise by the left hand. Women were not allowed to receive the Eucharistic Bread bare-handed but must cover the hand with a cloth. (Their heads also had to be covered.) The form of the Eucharistic Bread was that of a large wreath (*corona*); from this pieces were broken off and distributed among the communicants. Large dishes (*patenae*), generally of silver, were used for this distribution — so large, indeed, that they could be sacrilegiously misused for bathing the feet. The present manner of administering Holy Communion — the placing of the consecrated host on the communicant's tongue — probably dates from the eighth or ninth century, when the form of the host was also changed. After the reception of the Eucharistic Bread the deacon presented the chalice, holding it to the lips of the faithful. When many communicated, this was an especially large vessel, with several handles; it might be made of glass, wood, copper, tin or precious metal.

But outside of church people also prayed in connection with many of their daily acts, and especially at their meals. They did not drink a glass of water without making the sign of the cross over it. The dead body of a Christian was accompanied to its last resting place by priests, amid the chanting of psalms. Suicides were not to be buried near the graves of Christians.

There was certainly no lack of faith, of religious conviction, in the Frankish kingdom. Even those who most despised Christian morals did not scoff at Christian belief, but shared it in common with other men. Actually, a particular abuse arose partly in connection with this very fact: for, since faith culminated mainly in the thought of God's power and manifested itself to a marked degree in the fear of God, people were prone to demand direct proofs of God's power in the form of supernatural occurrences and so were extremely credulous with regard to miracles.

Several beginnings at reasonable criticism were indeed made, but these were unable to check the excess. Thus the people easily became the victims of impostors. For instance, a man from Bourges who deceived not only the peasants but also some of the priests, declared himself to be Christ, while a woman who wandered about with him asserted she was his sister; he directed that she be called Mary. When he approached a place, he sent ahead to announce his arrival persons who danced about unclothed. The lack of judgment which could accept such fantastic phenomena was naturally bound up with the retrogression of education. The declining culture of the Romans became mixed with the barbarism and superstition of the Germans.

Great was the veneration of saints. The age of the martyrs was, we remember, not very far removed from that period. To the list of martyrs of the Roman persecutions, new martyrs were added in the fifth century; these had died for their faith during the migration of nations. Real and deep as the veneration of the saints certainly was, historical knowledge of their activity was meager. Written tradition was at a low ebb, and those who still judiciously watched over it were only few in number. Most of the legends concerning Merovingian saints were set down as late as the eighth century, and are often based merely on attenuated and doubtful tradition, if not entirely on fiction.

Every city considered itself fortunate in possessing some relics of martyrs or saints. The national patron of the Franks, Saint Martin, was especially venerated. The Merovingian kings carried his mantle (*capa*) about with them as a precious relic. The repository of the relic was called the *capella,* and the priest guarding it the *capellanus,* whence are derived our designations of chapel and chaplain. The tomb of the saint in Tours was the Franks' principal place of pilgrimage. In front of the basilica was an atrium, a large quadrangular court, surrounded by colonnades and buildings of the most varied types, in particular by cells in which pilgrims could spend the night. Here one also saw stone crosses, miniature houses containing relics, and small monuments erected in memory of miraculous cures.

This court acquired a particular importance because it enjoyed the privilege of immunity: as an aslyum it was the best place of refuge in the Frankish kingdom. No state official was allowed to violate its immunity or perform in it any function whatsoever; a magistrate could not exercise his office nor could any taxes be collected there. Here was respected the important right of asylum, which the Christian churches had inherited from the pagan temples and which was an extraordinary boon for all classes high and low, in that age of violence. Those who violated the right of asylum incurred excommunication.

The haven protected everyone persecuted, regardless of his position, whether master or slave; but it often gave rise to problems by no means easy to solve. The Church was unwilling to deliver up the person who had fled to her unless he became an *excusatus*. In that case she had exacted the promise under oath that capital or even corporal punishment would not be inflicted upon him. If this promise was not given, the Church could let the malefactor escape and demand that the priests involved be exempt from liability for it. The case of slaves was difficult, since the Church laid herself open to the suspicion that she wanted to withhold them from their masters. Hence it was agreed that the slave, too, was to be delivered up only as an *excusatus,* the master having promised not to punish him in life or limb; but the priest must not allow a slave to escape, otherwise he would have to reimburse the master for his loss. But what if the slave refused to leave the asylum? In such an instance, according to a decision of the council of Orleans in 542, the Church was to accord the master the right to seize the slave. Freemen condemned to death, who had fled to the asylum, obtained the commutation of their sentence to exile or slavery.

In all cases the Church had the noble opportunity of acting as the mediator in behalf of the unfortunate, and gladly did she make use of it. Thus it happened that the asylum of Saint Martin was visited by many such persons. Here they remained for weeks and even months, because they were not sure of their lives elsewhere. In addition to those fleeing from justice, many of the faithful frequented the shrine from far and near. So did crowds of curiosity-seekers, traders who took advantage of the concourse of people to offer their wares, storytellers and jugglers who made their profit by entertaining. The result was the development here of that movement to provide the people with all sorts of amusements as an adjunct to the pilgrimages, which may be observed at many other shrines as well.

The tomb of the much-honored martyrs of the Theban Legion — Saint Maurice and his companions — at Agaunum, and of

the later Saint Maurice in the canton of Valais, also enjoyed particular veneration. Sigismund, the young Catholic king of Burgundy,
had instituted in Agaunum a *Laus perennis* — a perpetual chanting
of psalms by alternating choirs of monks — in atonement for his
crime, the murder of his own son. Following this example, peren-
nial chanting was also instituted in other churches — for example in
Châlon-sur-Saône and at Saint Denis.

The growth of the veneration of relics, evidenced in very many
writings of the period, is closely associated with the homage paid
to the saints. By relics were understood the bodies of the saints or
any part of these, and also (though of lesser importance) all objects
which had come in contact with the saints or their dead bodies.
Relics were honored as the remains of a saint and regarded as
remedies through contact with which men hoped for efficacious help,
especially in times of sickness. At this time in the West, men
still shrank from directly touching the bodies of the saints, and
consequently the people of the Frankish kingdom did not employ
as remedies the actual remains, but rather the material enclos-
ing the sacred bones — that is, the reliquary. Even the dust that
settled in the crevices of saints' tombs was thus used and preserved as a treasure. Capsules containing small pieces of cloth,
which had been placed upon the tombs of saints, were regarded as
relics (called *brandea*) and often held to possess miraculous power;
in like manner, soil taken from the graves of the saints was venerated. Such souvenirs from the tombs of saints were the types of
relics men of that age in the West sought as a rule to obtain and to
distribute. Other relics were: particles of the saints' clothing, leaves
that lay in the tombs, wax from the candles that burned at the
tombs, oil from the lighted lamps suspended from the ceiling of
the tombs; likewise, water from a spring dedicated to a saint,
splinters from the door of a church dedicated to a saint, flowers
which had touched the reliquary or stood on the altar, and earth
from a church, and particularly from the Sacred Places in Jerusalem.

The Greeks, who at that time already dismembered the bodies
of the saints so that they could distribute parts of them, belittled
the Latin Church for the alleged impotence of her relics, since these
consisted only of such objects as had been in contact with the saint

during his life and, particularly, his martyrdom — clothing he had worn, objects he had touched, and the like. In the West, however, public sentiment was entirely opposed to the dismemberment of the bodies of the saints; this sentiment even shrank from moving the bodies without special reason.

Thus, removal seldom occurred in the West during the early Middle Ages save for the purpose of providing a worthier resting place. The earliest instances were the translation of the remains of Saints Gervasius and Protasius, which Saint Ambrose had discovered outside the city and had transported in 386 to the new basilica erected by him in Milan (the present Sant'Ambrogio Maggiore); and that of the bodies of Saints Vitalis and Agricola in Bologna in 392. But Saint Gregory the Great still declared the touching of a saint's body sacrilegious, and no removals took place in Rome until the eighth century. The change was brought about when the saints of the catacombs were reburied in the city because of the frequent devastation of its environs by the Lombards. From the eighth century on the Church began to give the bodies of saints away as presents — at first the whole body, later only some part of it; these went chiefly to the Frankish kingdom, where there was a great demand for them. Thus the fear entertained formerly, of profaning the original resting place of the saints, had vanished because the necessities of the times had forced the removal of many saints' bodies from their burial place.

Considering the great demand for relics and the almost unlimited confidence in their miraculous power, one cannot be astonished at the fact that some persons did not scruple to obtain possession of them unlawfully. Records proving the theft of relics (certain priests, even, incurred such guilt) are not lacking. The moral outlook became more and more lax in this regard, so that in the eighth century we find the stealing of relics common throughout the whole of Christendom; it was a transgression readily condoned by the general mind, which saw only the praiseworthiness of the desire for these holy mementoes. We can find a parallel today in the common laxness regarding the return of borrowed books. What public library does not have constant grounds for complaint on this score? By the end of the Middle Ages, vainglory, overcredulousness and misunderstanding had led to the amassing of collections of relics in holy places — a fact over which one cannot feel unmixed joy. Herein was manifest a form of religious externalism which, unfortunately, was widely characteristic of the Middle Ages, along with their many beautiful qualities. As we see, it began as early as the sixth century.

But we will arrive at a more profound judgment of this epoch if we ask ourselves what, in general, was the status in the Frankish kingdom of morality, the touchstone of religious life? Unfortunately the impressions in this field are bad rather than good. We observe conditions similar to those in the other Germanic states founded on Roman soil, where the population rapidly sank morally. In the Frankish kingdom this is noticeable to a marked degree in the royal family itself. For the present, we will not take into account what is told of the bloody deeds of Clovis, for there is good reason to believe that these tales are borrowed from popular legends current among the pagan Franks. Their storytellers delighted in scenes of cunning cruelty, readily inventing details and skillfully attributing them to those known for their power and prudence. Under Clovis' successors, however, we meet authentic acts of atrocious cruelty and brutality which cannot be explained away and which constitute a lasting blot upon the Merovingian dynasty. Such deeds were occasioned in most instances by the unfortunate Germanic conception that a kingdom, like a private inheritance, must upon the death of a ruler be equally divided among all the sons.

Of the sons of Clovis, Clodomir was the first to die — in 524, at the battle of Véséronce, in which Franks fought against Burgundians. He was survived by three male children whom their grandmother, Saint Clotilda, took under her protection. Their uncles wanted to do away with them so that they could divide Clodomir's kingdom among themselves. By a ruse they kidnaped the youths, then sent a messenger with a pair of scissors and a naked sword to the grandmother: she was to decide whether her grandsons were to be the victims of the scissors — that is, to lose their hair and be sent into a monastery — or of the sword. Saint Clotilda, who wished to safeguard their rights of succession, exclaimed: "I would rather see them dead than robbed of their locks." Receiving this answer, Clotaire seized the elder of his nephews by the arm, threw him down, and thrust a knife into his shoulder. As the boy shrieked, his brother fell at the feet of the other uncle, Childebert, and implored his mercy. Childebert was moved, and begged Clotaire to spare the boy's life. But Clotaire turned upon Childebert and charged him with having instigated the whole affair. Thereupon Childebert pushed the lad away, and Clotaire stabbed him to death along with his brother. The murdered princes were ten and seven years old. The third son, Clodoald, who had been successfully concealed by loyal protectors, cut his own hair, and became a priest and a saint, and the founder of the monastery bearing his name: Saint Cloud.

The really shocking thing to be noted is that such acts of violence soon ceased to arouse public horror. They were repeated in so many forms that the people became accustomed to them. Moreover, their repulsiveness increased by being associated with unbridled sensuality. Very few of these rulers respected the sanctity of marriage. The most notorious incidents are those connected with the name of Fredegund, who was the mistress of Chilperic, son of the Clotaire just mentioned. For a short period following the death of his brother Childebert, Clotaire had united the kingdom under his rule (558-561). After his death it was again divided, this time among his sons, Charibert, Sigebert, Guntram and Chilperic. Chilperic regarded with envy the court of his brother Sigebert, the ruler of Austrasia, who had married Brunhilda, the Visigothic princess. Brunhilda, by her illustrious descent, her excellent training and her education, shed a brilliancy upon Sigebert's court in sharp contrast to Chilperic's, which was dominated by his paramour, Fredegund. Chilperic accordingly resolved to rise to the level of his brother by marrying Brunhilda's sister, Galswintha. Her father gave his consent only after Chilperic had promised under oath to accord to her alone the position of queen. But the king's oath was quickly violated and Fredegund regained her ascendancy. Galswintha begged to be sent back to her father; instead, Chilperic had her strangled and took Fredegund to wife. This woman was a monster, whose rule in Neustria was marked by a series of murders: she did away with the only surviving son of Chilperic, borne to him by another woman; this son's mother and sister, as well as King Sigebert of Austrasia, the bishop of Rouen, and many others suffered the same fate. More than once she hired assassins in an effort to do away with the hated Brunhilda.

But we need not go through the entire list of crimes which disgraced the Merovingian throne. A prophecy which was recorded in the seventh century best characterizes the decline of that dynasty. The mother of Clovis is supposed to have beheld in a vision the fate of her progeny in a succession of various animals. First she saw a lion, the symbol of her son Clovis, then leopards and unicorns, thirdly ravenous bears and wolves, finally dogs which tore each other to pieces while the peoples about them were in full strife.

It is true that the reigning dynasty far surpassed their subjects in licentiousness and immorality; but actually the general moral level was low — among the Romans as well as the Franks, for here, as elsewhere, there had gradually ceased to be any distinction separating the two racial elements. The officials usually regarded their office merely as an opportunity to enrich themselves, and their subordinates followed their example. Judicial punishment was carried out with such cruelty and disregard of all established forms that it appeared rather as an act of revenge than as a penalty imposed by law. The Church herself was only too often helpless in the face of this brutality. An instance will point this out. Albinus, the governor of Provence (who later became a bishop, and was not one of the worst of men) wished to arrest the archdeacon Vigilius of Marseilles because he had upheld the governor's thievish servants. It was the feast of Christmas, the bishop had entered the church, the Mass was about to begin, and the archdeacon advanced to conduct the bishop to the altar as was the custom. At this moment the governor sprang from his seat, pounced upon the archdeacon, maltreated him with blows and kicks, and had him cast into prison regardless of the solemnity of the place and occasion or the entreaties of the bishop and the people.[53]

But the people themselves could be just as brutal, where occasion arose for them to give vent to their passions. In Austrasia

---

53. Gregory, *Hist. Franc.*, IV, c. 43.

during the reign of Theodebert I, the official Parthenius was profoundly hated because of the tax burdens he imposed upon the people. He had blackened his soul with many acts of violence; in addition he was notorious as a debauchee. Upon the death of the king (548), he fled into the church of Treves, where the priests concealed him in a trunk and covered him with liturgical vestments to save him from the general fury. The mob pushed into the church, examined every corner, forced the custodians to surrender the keys to the trunk, and discovering the hated official, dragged him out with all manner of abuse, bound him to a column, and stoned him to death.[54] The Church's right of asylum, in fact, was disregarded even more by the populace than by the rulers.

Saint Praetextatus, archbishop of Rouen, was stabbed to death at the altar of his cathedral on Easter Sunday (586) at the instigation of Fredegund, because he had upbraided her for her shameful deeds.[55] During King Chilperic's reign a man desired to take the oath of purgation in the church of Saint Denis for his daughter, who was accused of adultery. When he had sworn, the opposite party accused him of perjury. The two families came into open conflict, drew their swords, and fought in the very church itself.[56] If the sanctity of the church was so little regarded as this episode shows, we cannot be surprised at the fact that discipline and order were no longer upheld anywhere; especially since savagery and cruelty were fed anew by the many domestic conflicts. Men robbed, pillaged, desecrated and murdered in their own country just as they did in a foreign land. Saint Gregory of Tours, the veracious historian of the Franks, concludes the account of the sufferings of the churches during the struggles between the brothers Sigebert and Chilperic with the words: "There were in those days greater lamentations in the churches than in the days of Diocletian's persecution."[57]

Side by side with this brutality there existed a wild indulgence in gross pleasure. All classes were addicted to drunkenness. The sanctity of marriage was only too often trampled upon, and the

---

54. Ibid., III, c. 36.
55. Ibid., VIII, c. 31.
56. Ibid., V, c. 32.
57. Ibid., IV, c. 47.

praise that Salvian once bestowed upon the chastity of the Germans was no longer merited. Ruthlessly men strove for pleasure, honor, power and money, regarding the sacredness of human life as little as they respected the precepts of Christian morality or the obligations of fidelity or the sanctity of an oath. A priest of Tours — one of ill repute, of course — was wont to say that one could not overcome a prudent man except by perjury.[58]

Women, and even bishops and priests as well, were drawn into this moral decadence. Austrechildis, the sick wife of King Guntram, clinging passionately to life, was so enraged at her physicians when she felt her end to be near that she made Guntram swear he would have these men put to death for shortening her days with medicine. And the king, who was surnamed the Good and even venerated as a saint because of his generosity in building churches, fulfilled his promise! Saint Gregory of Tours cautiously appended these words to his account of this episode: "That this was not done without sin is the opinion of many prudent people."[59]

A frightful couple were Bishop Badegisel, who declared he would not allow his priestly status to restrain him from exacting revenge, and his wife, whose atrocious cruelties were of so extreme a nature that they cannot be repeated.[60] Cautinus, the bishop of Clermont, was cursed by everyone because of his way of living. He drank to such an extent that four men could hardly carry him home from a drinking bout. When a priest named Anastasius refused to surrender his possessions to him, the bishop, intending to bury him alive, had him put into a sarcophagus together with a corpse and enclosed in a crypt. Saint Gregory of Tours describes for us the manner in which the priest succeeded in escaping this frightful death. Concerning Cautinus he adds this remark:

> In him was nothing holy, nothing worthy of respect. Of books he possessed none whatever, neither those spiritual nor profane. To the Jews, however, he was very dear and devoted, not because he was concerned about the salvation of their souls as would have befitted a shep-

---

58. Ibid., V, c. 49.
59. Ibid., c. 35.
60. Ibid., VIII, c. 39.

herd, but because they sold him wares, in most cases at a price higher than they were worth.[61]

On the other hand, there were cases of bishops being not only insulted and mistreated but even murdered by their clerics. And the assassins whom Fredegund once sent, disguised as beggars and armed with daggers, against Brunhilda's son Childebert, were priests.[62]

These examples may suffice to discharge the historian's duty of disclosing all sides of the picture. Horrified, we ask ourselves: how was it possible at all for such persons to insinuate themselves into the service of the Church, which, in spite of everything, still gave so many proofs of her beneficent activity? The reason is to be traced, if not exclusively at least in great measure, to the fact that the Church had been put under the king's control. In gratitude for the exalted position which she owed to the Merovingians, she delivered herself almost entirely to them. Thus arose the same situation that we observe under Constantine and his sons, except that the influence of the Merovingians, corresponding to the barbarism of the royal house, became especially disastrous in matters of morality. Along with the dynasty, the episcopate also deteriorated; while, in the sixth and at the beginning of the seventh century, despite all adverse circumstances, it still, on the whole, fulfilled its mission properly, thereafter it dropped appreciably below that level. Ecclesiastical discipline fell into decline. The bonds of the metropolitan organization were severed. Councils were held more and more infrequently and finally ceased altogether. The missionary activity of the Frankish Church came to a standstill. The bishoprics were regarded as private estates, and men contended for them with all the means at their disposal, both fair and foul. In the seventh century, the number of ignorant, superstitious and depraved priests noticeably increased.

We may inquire further: where, then, is the difference between the Arian and Catholic Germanic kingdoms? Where is the civilizing

---

61. Ibid., IV, c. 12.
62. Ibid., VIII, c. 29.

force of Catholicism manifesting its superiority? It did manifest itself precisely in this grave period. The Frankish Church had not been completely shackled by nationalist forces and hence was not doomed to complete destruction. Thanks to her Catholic character, thanks to her universality, the Church could be succored from without. This help came first from Ireland, then from the Anglo-Saxons — in both instances from countries which had not been contaminated with the corruption of Rome's superculture. The struggles for reform will constitute the subject matter of the following chapters.

CHAPTER THREE

THE ACTIVITY OF THE IRISH MISSIONARIES —
DECLINE OF THE FRANKISH CHURCH

THE coming of the Irish missionaries marks the first significant attempt on the part of the representatives of pure Celtic stock to participate in the development of Christian culture on the continent. The race had, however, greatly influenced prehistoric culture there. The Celts had been widely dispersed over Western Europe, occupying almost the entire territory of the Alps, Southern Germany, Western Germany from the Rhine eastward to the watershed between the Rhine and the Weser, the whole of Gaul and the British Isles. In historic times we see them advancing from these lands in three great migrations. One went to Spain, where the Celts occupied the southwestern half of Aragon and the whole northern and eastern sections of Old and New Castile, constituting the second basic element in the formation of the Spanish nation. Others, coming by ship from the mouth of the Loire and from Brittany, settled in the northwest of the Iberian Peninsula among the Iberian tribe of the Lusitanians. Later, in the fourth century before Christ, a branch of the Celts occupied the Po valley in Northern Italy, which was named *Gallia* after them. In the following century, some Celts of the tribe called Galatian moved still further eastward into the Balkan Peninsula, sacked Greece, and settled in Central Asia Minor, where the Roman province Galatia, whose capital was Angora, perpetuated their name. Saint Paul's Epistle to the Galatians still reminds us of them.

Standing higher in culture than the neighboring Germans, the Celts were their first teachers. They transmitted the bronze and subsequently the iron culture to the Germans; they also taught them the rudiments of political organization, for the words *Reich* and *Amt* are derived from Celtic speech. In time, almost all the Celts were subdued by the Romans, but Roman culture did not everywhere influence them to the same extent: the further they were removed

287

from the Roman fatherland, the weaker was its effect. All the Celts, however, accepted Christianity at the hands of Rome.

Their race had kept itself relatively pure in the lands farthest west — French Brittany, Wales, the Isle of Man, Scotland and Ireland. Scotland was conquered only to a limited extent by the Romans, Ireland not at all, whence it really remained the home of the Celtic race. During the first centuries of the Middle Ages the Irish were called Scots; they transmitted their name to Scotland where, as early as the fifth Christian century, they had dislodged the ancient Picts. The name of Ireland was originally Erin — in British, *Iwerdon,* which the Romans, following the Greeks, converted into *Hibernia.* But until late in the Middle Ages Ireland is still called *Scotia,* being designated in contradistinction to Scotland, as *Scotia major* or *Scotia hibernica.* Hence in the Middle Ages the "Scottish monks" and "Scottish monasteries" denote the Irish as well.

Characteristic of the Celtic race was its enthusiasm in embracing Christianity — an enthusiasm manifested with unique intensity in Ireland itself. It is seen also in the many missionaries who went forth from Ireland; it still continued to exist in the French who, influenced by their essentially Celtic temperament, persevered in carrying on the Crusade movement, which originated in France. With this temperament, however, is associated a certain lack of stability and organizing power — a lack we can already observe in the Irish missionaries of the seventh century.

Christianity was organized in Britain also while it was still a Roman province, and the episcopal sees of York, London and Lincoln were represented at the council of Arles in 314. In a tradition of Verulam, near London, we can still recognize traces of the story of Saint Alban's martyrdom at the time of Diocletian's persecution.

Pelagius, born in Roman Britain, probably of Irish parents, caused much disturbance in the beginning of the fifth century by spreading in Rome, Africa and in the Orient the heresy bearing his name. He had not preached it in Britain, however, and only later did it gain a footing there. Twice thereafter did Saint Germanus, bishop of Auxerre, go to Britain (429-431 and 447), by order of a Gallic synod, to exterminate Pelagianism there.

Soon after the Roman legions evacuated Britain (407 A. D.), the Anglo-Saxons appeared. Some landed as early as 428, and they came after this in ever-increasing numbers, pushing the Britons westward. As a result of this pressure one section of the Britons forsook their ancient home and emigrated to the peninsula of Armorica, which lay opposite them. They made this peninsula Celtic, and today it is known as Brittany or *Britannia minor*. Some settled in Galicia, on the Iberian Peninsula. Those who remained in Britain tenaciously defended Christianity against the encroaching pagan barbarians with the help of the culture transmitted to them by the Romans.

The material and spiritual tribulations of the Britons were described by Saint Gildas, founder of the monastery Gildas-de-Rhuys in Brittany. Himself a rigid ascetic, he views his epoch in a manner similar to that of Salvian of Marseilles. The conditions among the Britons of his locality were not much different from those surrounding Salvian in southern Gaul in the fifth century. In his work, *Concerning the Fall and Lamentation of Britain,* which was written about 540, he records how the Romans had first dominated and then deserted Britain, and next describes how God punished the Britons because of their sins (he mentions particularly immorality and lying) by abandoning them to their enemies, the Picts, Scots and Anglo-Saxons. He complains that a victory, which Divine Providence once again granted them near Bath (c. 500) under the leadership of the brave and truthful Ambrose Aurelian has contributed but little to their improvement. Then he addresses himself in a severe exhortation to his contemporaries, especially to the ruling classes — the kings and priests. Speaking to the former, he describes certain wicked personalities; for the benefit of the latter he scourges the vices of the priestly group in general, particularly simony. Thus we witness here also the unfortunate legacy which the Romans everywhere bequeathed in the form of social corruption. From this some few, indeed, were able to save themselves; but for the whole nation this was impossible at a time when the monasteries were the only places of refuge for those striving after Christian ideals.

Saint Gildas' style distinctly reveals the Celtic propensity for metaphorical and poetic language, and for modes of expression overloaded with imagery which yet clothe a sincere and profound devotion to the Christian ideals of virtue.

About the same time a strange work entitled *Hisperica famina* was produced in a monastic school in southwestern Britain. Written in what seems like a cryptic language, it is a collection of school compositions on diverse topics — for instance, the daily occupations of the monastic pupils, the heavens, the sea, fire, light, the earth, wind, and all manner of other themes. The compositions, of which several versions have been found, were written with the aid of a glossary which contained very rare and distorted word-formations. In Britain there must naturally have been even more than the usual difficulty in imparting knowledge of the language of the schools, and this literature shows to what desperate lengths teachers resorted in their efforts to do so. And here, too, where Roman domination had long since been a thing of the past, it is more clearly evident than anywhere else that it was the Church alone who preserved and transmitted the residue of a superior culture.

The Church it was, also, which brought Ireland, never subdued by the Romans, into contact with Western culture. It was her first expansion beyond the confines of the Roman Empire. Saint Patrick, venerated as the Apostle of Ireland, was born in the north of Britain, brought to Ireland by Irish pirates, and employed there as a shepherd. Thus he became conversant with the language of the people. Making his escape from Ireland, he prepared himself in Gaul for an apostolic career. He became acquainted with monastic life at Lérins, spent a goodly time at Auxerre, and returned to Ireland as a missionary in 432. He was also active as a writer, supplementing missionary work in which he labored until his death, with his literary productions. His authenticated writings consist of a species of autobiography entitled *Confessio,* a letter to the Christian subjects of the British ruler Coroticus, and some verses in the Celtic tongue under the title "Lorica" (armor of faith). The great number of legends based on his life testify to the profound impression he made on the Irish by his battle against paganism and to his solicitude for the salvation of souls.

The organization of the Church was adapted to local conditions as they existed in Britain and Ireland. They were based on the clan system, a division into tribes each governed by a chieftain. Since cities did not exist at all in Ireland, and those in Roman Britain had fallen into decay, the dioceses coincided with the tribes of the several chieftains. As Christianity spread in Ireland, the tribal chieftain generally donated a plot of ground for the church and a monastery; and the monastery assumed for the most part the pastoral care of the tribe. These special features could develop undisturbed in the Irish Church, since it was thrown almost entirely on itself and had also the good fortune to be spared the successive national migrations. For the first time we are able to observe how much more favorable the soil was for the germination of the Christian seeds when the corrupt society of antiquity did not form the substratum — a condition which everywhere on the continent, even in the Church itself, had brought about confusion and decadence.

If on the continent it was mainly the monasteries that effected the moral renovation of Christians, this was even truer in Ireland. Nowhere were there so many monasteries as there, nowhere at the time were religious idealism and enthusiasm so great. And we also find among the monks an extraordinary seriousness in pursuing Christian perfection. The cradle of this flourishing religious life was the monastery of Clonard in Meath, on the east coast. Founded in 520 by Saint Finnian, the disciple of Saint David and the British bishop of Menevia, it is reputed to have numbered three thousand monks. Many branch monasteries were established by Clonard — Bangor, near Belfast in the northeast, became the most famous of them. We possess a liturgical document of Bangor in an antiphonary of Bobbio composed between 680 and 691. It preserves the hymns chanted at Bangor during divine services, and commemorates especially the founder of the monastery, Saint Comgall or Comgill.

In these monasteries there prevailed a considerable degree of culture. The monks knew how to compose Latin verses after ancient models, to treat astronomical questions, and to make chronological calculations. They were also engrossed in the study of the Greek language, which was introduced from monasteries in the East, and in the ninth century some of them attained an extraordinary proficiency in Greek. At the same time these monks, far more than those on the continent, cultivated their native tongue; we find them using it for their prayers, their religious poems, their sermons, and their theological tracts. The Gaelic language even found its way into liturgical books, and was employed also in composing their annals and the lives of saints.

Among the studies, Sacred Scripture naturally occupied the first place, and the monks' knowledge of it, in addition to their advanced asceticism, attracted many foreign priests and monks to the Irish monasteries from the seventh century on. Manuscripts and scriptural commentaries spread the results of the Irish monks' literary activity in the form of biblical glosses far and wide on the continent. In addition, apocryphal literature, especially in its treatment of the angels, attracted the Irish. Here their imagination found satisfaction; it led to visions and dreams — and also, to be sure, to many a superstition. The inclination for the strange and the mysterious and the predilection for the symbolic, which were early characteristic of their Druids, impress us most vividly in their manuscripts, to the execution of which careful attention was given in the monasteries.

The scribes enjoyed a special measure of respect in the monasteries, and in society at large. Their wergild was as high as that of an abbot or bishop. Several assistants worked in the writing room under the supervision of the well-experienced scribe. The scribes have left us in chance remarks many an original expression indicative not only of the pains they had to take, but also of their piety and their delight in their work. Thus we read in one instance: "I shall remember, Christ, that I have written this for Thee, for I feel very tired today, Sunday evening." In another: "O my hand, thou that hast written on white parchment! Thou hast made the parchment famous, but what will become of thee? The withered extremity of a heap of bones...."[1] A few verses taken from a codex of Saint Gall show us a monk who, allured by the gentle May breeze, set up his writing table in the open, and in his work provided an excellent demonstration of his delight in nature:

---

1. Gougaud, *Les Chrétientés celtiques*, 332.

Enclosed as I am in the depth of a forest grove, the blackbird's song comes traveling to my ear; while I busy myself with my many-lined parchment, there sounds about me the trilling song of the birds. From treetops the cuckoo, in gray mantle, calls to me with a clear voice. Forsooth — the Lord protect me — it is beautiful to write under the canopy of the forest.[2]

The Gospel books and Psalters especially were embellished with great care in the Irish monasteries. The symbols of the Evangelists were represented on one page, which was divided into four fields by a cross and framed by an artistic interlaced border; or the Evangelists might be depicted separately at the beginning of each Gospel. Sometimes the Saviour, or the Last Judgment, formed the subject of ornamentation. In the Psalters, David was represented with a harp, which instrument became a part of the escutcheon of Ireland, characterizing aptly the pensive imagination of the people. Rich ornamentation appeared especially in initial letters and in the first lines of the manuscripts; even today the colors — cinnabar, green and yellow were used — retain a remarkable luster. In the representation of figures, we are struck by the lack of a sense of perspective, proportion and expression as well as by the clumsiness in the depiction of garments, which makes the figures appear rather as though they were wrapped in rolls of ribbon, in some cases actually with the effect of a caricature. But though the Irish illuminators possess little talent for exactly perceiving and reproducing natural objects, they become really skillful and inventive as soon as their powers of imagination are brought into play. In the endless interlaced lines, they display an extraordinary gracefulness and precision, as well as great artistic originality; qualities which attain complete development in the eighth and ninth centuries. Artistic convolutions are characteristic of Celtic art: all kinds of birds, swans, peacocks and storks are interwoven in the manifold mesh of spirals; but, curiously enough, there are no motifs from the plant world.

In this ornamentation we perceive the Celtic penchant for enigmatic convolutions, for the unusual and sometimes bizarre,

---

2. Kuno Meyer in *Kultur der Gegenwart,* Abt. XI, 1, p. 81.

which so often manifests itself in their literature as well as in the nature of certain individuals and in their asceticism. It would be unjust, in speaking of the asceticism of the Irish monks, to overlook what they accomplished daily in cultivating the soil, working as they did without the assistance of animals; or their devout application to prayer. Yet at the same time, one may be permitted to recall that, deprived of the opportunity of martyrdom, they tried to outdo one another in their attitudes at prayer. They would pray with arms outstretched in the form of a cross, now standing, now kneeling or prone — a posture which constituted, in virtue of the long period they persevered in it, a particular form of mortification. The story is told, doubtless with poetic exaggeration, that some ascetics remained in such a posture for years, permitting the birds to build nests on their head and in their hands. Another peculiar form of mortification consisted in their lowering themselves into the cold water of rivers or ponds while reciting psalms. Those for whom the austerities of monastic life did not suffice withdrew as hermits to abandoned island reefs, where the expanse of the sea and the roaring of the waves would remind them perpetually of the power of the Creator. Here, solitude and privation were theirs in fullest measure.

The Irish monasteries had no uniform rule; every community of considerable size possessed its own. Naturally, however, the main features were the same, obedience, poverty and chastity forming the basis of the common life. In appearance a monastic community resembled a colony of huts. In each hut (generally built of wood) dwelt a few monks, or only one. The abbot's residence stood on somewhat higher ground, overlooking the other cells. In the monastic city there were special, but always very modest, places for the kitchen, the refectory, the guest quarters and the workshops. Since the monasteries were tribal foundations, and through the payment of tithes and all the first fruits of land and beasts were supported by the tribe to which the founder belonged, the chieftain of the tribe generally appointed a member of his own family as abbot. He was thus the actual religious head of the tribe; often he was also a bishop, or at least had associated with him a monk who had been consecrated a bishop. Attempts have been made by modern historians to set this organization in sharp contrast with the continental Church and her hierarchical order; but in point of fact there was no fundamental difference. The subordination of the monk-bishop to the abbot, who was only a priest, had reference only to jurisdiction, not to rank in Holy Orders; as an ecclesiastic, the bishop had precedence over the abbot. Secular priests and the various grades of the clergy are likewise clearly recognizable in the Irish Church. And when we hear of the wives of priests or deacons or even of bishops, we must not conclude from this that the obligation of celibacy had been abolished. Such references also occur in Rome at this time and are to be explained as follows: one who had married as a layman or as a minor cleric, and perhaps had had children, transmitted his higher title also to his wife, although he no longer had marital relations with her. This peculiar custom, associated with the marked prominence of the monasteries, is explained by the clan system and the important role the monasteries played in evangelizing the country. Similar conditions might well exist even today in mission lands, where monasteries are the centers of a mission district.

Other differences also have been exaggerated in the attempt to represent the Irish-British Church as one independent of Rome. In view of the isolated position of the Irish Church, it was natural that not every development which spread rapidly on the continent, should have found imitation in Ireland. The same may be said regarding any innovation emanating from Rome. For example the new Alexandrian reckoning of Easter, introduced in Rome by Dionysius Exiguus, was not adopted by the Irish. This external difference later became very prominent, it is true, but it certainly was not fundamental. The authority of Rome was fully acknowledged in Ireland, even though the Irish were not inclined to follow Rome indiscriminately in their customs. No difference whatever in ecclesiastical teaching existed between the Irish Church and that of the continent. The external differences which did obtain were merely the result of the individualistic Celtic character, and their growth was favored by the isolated position of Ireland and the wholly different social conditions found there.

Peculiar to the Irish, too, was the roving spirit, which received an ascetical turn from Irish monks, who regarded the severance of one's connections not only with one's native land but also with one's native monastery, as a sacrifice made to the Lord. The most curious among the wanderers were the legendary pilgrims who, following the example of Saint Brendan, entered a barque and abandoned themselves on the vast sea to the will of God. How much of this is to be accounted true it is difficult to say. But the Celtic imagination liked to occupy itself with the narration of such voyages, which provided an opportunity to depict fabulous countries visited by the hermits of the sea.

The roving spirit soon became a missionary spirit, for which the Irish can never be praised enough. They were accustomed through their monasteries to concern themselves with the salvation of the tribe to which they belonged. And the same apostolic solicitude accompanied them to foreign lands, whither they generally went in groups to give it expression. Such an idea was until then alien to the monasteries of the continent, which had tended rather in the opposite direction; a tendency, indeed, that had brought them into existence. They strove to withdraw from the turbulent and worldly society of the time, and influenced the outer world only through certain individuals like Saint Severinus and Saint Martin of Braga, who followed a special call or were directed as bishops to leave the monastery and become shepherds of souls. Apostolic times aside, missionary activity had until then restricted itself to the Roman Empire. Even that of the Franks, properly speaking, was limited to spreading the Church among the pagans in the Frankish kingdom or the tribes conquered by Frankish arms.

The idea of carrying the Gospel beyond the confines of one's own kingdom was hardly conceived. If, notwithstanding, the Christian teaching did spread beyond the frontiers, this happened almost exclusively because Catholic princesses married pagan princes and secured the exercise of their religion, and better protection, by having a Catholic priest or bishop accompany them. Thus did Theodelinda go to the Lombards and Saint Clotilda to the pagan Frankish king, Clovis; and we will become acquainted with yet another example when we treat of the Anglo-Saxons. But if particularly favorable circumstances were lacking, such as were found in the case of the Franks and Lombards, where Catholic queens could extend a helping hand to the bishops of subjected Romans, it was impossible for the seeds of faith to develop. To the Irish belongs the credit of being the first to send apostolic workers across national boundaries. This was of the greatest importance for the planting of Christian culture in the West. No longer did the sword effect a contact which in most instances was only of doubtful value for Christianity; instead, the force of internal conviction moved missionaries to approach others in the spirit of helpfulness, seeking a voluntary union. This at last was in full accord with the Saviour's command: "Go and teach all nations."

The missionary activity of the Irish began under Saint Columban the Elder (commonly known as Saint Columba or Columcille), disciple of the monastery of Clonard and founder of the monasteries of Darrow, in Meath, and Londonderry, in North Ireland. He became the Apostle of Scotland when he left Ireland (563 or 565) with twelve monks and erected a mission station on the little island of Hy or Iona, to the west of Scotland. An attractive impression of his cheerful personality is conveyed by his biographer, Saint Adamnan, who says of him: "In the midst of all his cares he showed himself courteous and friendly to all; he carried the joy of the Holy Ghost in the secret folds of his heart."[3] He began in northern Scotland the conversion of the Picts, who were still pagan, by establishing various monasteries which remained under the control of the parent monastery at Iona. There Saint Columba died on June 9, 597. And by the seventh and eighth centuries Christianity had spread from there, by way of the Orkney, Shetland and Faroe Islands — the *ultima Thule* of the ancients — to Iceland.

The activity of Saint Columban the Younger (better known as Saint Columbanus) was to extend in another direction. A native of Leinster, the southeastern portion of Ireland, he was induced by a recluse to become a monk. When his mother attempted to prevent his departure by throwing herself directly across the threshold of their home, he jumped over her prostrate body and called to her

---

3. Adamnan, *Vita Col.*, Praef. II, ed. of Fowler, p. 6.

to rejoice since he would never see her again in this life but was going where the way of salvation would open up for him. This sternness of will remained with him as long as he lived. In the monastery of Bangor he submitted himself to the abbot, Saint Comgall, to be trained in strict monastic discipline, and to imbibe in rich measure whatever the Irish monastery could offer in the way of learning. For those times, this was not insignificant. In his extant letters and verses, written in his later life, we can admire his skillful handling of Latin to present his opinions and express his feelings and emotions.

Having overcome the opposition of his abbot, he betook himself with twelve companions to foreign parts, stopping first in Brittany. But feeling himself still too much at home there among the Britons, he continued his journey into the Frankish kingdom, presumably about the year 590. These Celtic visitors were bound to create a sensation by their very appearance. While the monks of the West cut off their hair in the form of the so-called Petrine tonsure — a short crown of hair being left to grow around the head — the Irish let the hair of the back of the head grow so that it reached to the shoulders; the front hair, however, was shaved off, except for a short half crown. In their hand they held long sticks; from straps slung over the shoulder depended water-flasks and leather sacks in which they kept the liturgical books; about their necks they also carried receptacles for relics and vessels for preserving consecrated Hosts.

We are acquainted with the heavy shadows which, at the end of the sixth century, cast a pall of gloom over religious life in the Frankish kingdom, and so are able to understand the situation when the saint's biographer, Jonas of Bobbio, explains:

> Because of the frequent incursions of external foes or the carelessness of the shepherds, the forces of religion had all but come to grief there. Only the Christian faith remained; the remedies of penance and love of self-denial were scarcely found anywhere, or only in a few places.[4]

---

4. Jonas, *Vita Columbani*, I, c. 5.

The last sentence had, moreover, a particular meaning because of the rigorous penitential discipline which Saint Columbanus brought from Ireland and with his companions introduced on the continent.

In Europe proper, public penance, imposed since Christian antiquity for sins that were unequivocally mortal in character, was essentially the only practice followed in dealing with the laity. It was bound up with the custom of conferring baptism on adults alone and after a prolonged catechumenate, during which the candidate strove by means of the so-called baptismal penance to cleanse himself internally from sin. Those thus received into the Church as full-fledged members, free from all guilt of sin, were regarded as confirmed Christians. A violation of their baptismal vow was not expected of them. When subsequently guilty of grave sins (which had to be confessed, it is true, if they were not manifest), they were punished by the Church with official excommunication and public penance. After this penance was performed, forgiveness of the sins and readmission into the Church was accorded only once more by the *reconciliatio,* administered by the bishop. Venial sins were expiated by prayer, fasting and good works; only here and there were they expiated also by private confession, after which one petitioned the priest for some admonition and, doubtless, also for the imposition of a private penance. This last measure, however, was regarded merely as an act of voluntary piety.

In this connection, however, we must not overlook the fact that the Church, leaning on the Saviour's words, has from the beginning claimed and exercised the right to forgive sins. The *reconciliatio* was not only a restoration of full communion with the Church, but also a remission of sin. The custom of confessing in secret all sins, even venial sins and sins of thought, that they might be atoned for by means of prayers in common, was first adopted in the monasteries of the East. Thus did Saint Basil speak of confession in his Rule. Cassian recommended to his monks that they confess even the most hidden thoughts to their senior. Saint Benedict similarly spoke of the practice in his Rule: the monk should confess his secret sins to the abbot or to the spiritual seniors, "who know how to heal their own sins and those of others, but not to disclose and publish them."[5]

In the Irish monasteries the monks were required to confess twice a day to their superior. The rule for nuns (compiled from the Rules of Saints Columbanus, Benedict and Caesarius of Arles by Saint Donatus, bishop of Besançon, who had been reared at Luxeuil) ordained that they confess three times a day to their superioress — the practice followed in the convent of Faremoûtier, where the superioress also imposed the penance.[6]

A further step in Ireland was the introduction of the monastic practice among the people. This was due to the influence which the monasteries exerted on the laity through their pastoral ministrations, and can probably also be explained by the fact that public penance with its accompanying reconciliation had not been introduced there. To provide pastors with a guide, penance-books or collections of penance-regulations called penitentials, were compiled, which specified for the various sins appropriate punishments, to be imposed by the monk to whom the layman confessed.

Such a penitential was composed early in the sixth century by one Vinnianus whom some identify with Saint Finnian the Elder, abbot of Clonard (d. 548), others with Saint Finnian the Younger, abbot and bishop of Maghbile (Moville; d. 589). At any rate Saint Columbanus was acquainted with this book. He himself was probably the composer of a penitential written in the same spirit, during his labors in Gaul. It is a strange work, adapted to the circumstances he encountered there. The sins for which it prescribes punishments were those so seriously debasing moral life in the Frankish kingdom: the brutalities of clerics and laymen, impurity, immoderate eating and drinking, perjury and sins against the Seventh Commandment, and participation in pagan sacrificial repasts. Periods of penance of varying length were imposed, together with fasting and almsgiving, banishment from home, entrance into a monastery. The most important point to be noted is that Saint Columbanus insisted upon

---

5. *Benedicti Regula*, C. 46, trans. Delatte-McCann, *The Rule of Saint Benedict: A Commentary*, p. 300. For the above expositions in general, see also Rauschen, *Eucharistie und Bussakrament*, 2. Aufl. (Freiburg i. B., 1910).

6. *Regula Donati ad virgines*: Migne, *P. L.*, LXXXVII, 19, 23. Jonas, *Vita Columbani*, II, c. 19.

the confession of sins, sharpening men's consciences thereby. The concept of mortal sin, heretofore understood rather in an external sense, began to acquire a deeper and more detailed meaning, and in consequence obligatory confession became more frequent. Moreover, confessing one's sins regularly before communion was introduced as a pious custom.

A more intensive pastoral ministry could now progress. Public penance had fallen into decline because, while on the one hand fervent souls who perhaps did not need penance, were eager to perform it as an ascetical exercise, those who deserved it performed it only when forced to do so. Now a more individual treatment of sinners could be introduced, and as auricular confession unburdened the heart, so prompt absolution strengthened the weak man for a new struggle. Old Irish had a special name for the father confessor, showing us the extent to which he was esteemed. He was called *aumchara,* a term equivalent to "friend of the soul." To Saint Comgall of Bangor, the teacher of Saint Columbanus, is attributed the saying: "A man without an *aumchara* is a body without a head."[7]

Of course, whatever took place in private confession for the moral betterment of individuals, remains, for the greatest part, hidden from the historian. Only in a general sense can we trace the great achievement of Saint Columbanus and his disciples. It is to be rated all the higher since the severity and harshness of Saint Columbanus, coupled with his narrow-minded adherence to certain of the external practices which he brought with him from his native land, caused him many difficulties. Men were displeased especially by his mode of reckoning Easter and by the Irish tonsure. In consequence he created for himself an opposition which could rightfully demand that he yield to the traditional customs of the country, particularly in such a clear-cut external question as the computation of the date of Easter. On the other hand, however, it was precisely the seriousness of the preacher of penance which drew people to Saint Columbanus. The Frankish kingdom had need of such a man at that time: and for more than half a century he dominated it to a

---

7. Gougaud, 278.

large extent with his spirit and produced a considerable, even though temporary, renewal of religious life.

Soon after he had founded a monastery at Annegray in the Vosges Mountains, signs of general approval began to be manifest, showing that the germs of religious life in the Frankish kingdom had not died out, but were merely awaiting resuscitation. The people of the surrounding country helped him in the actual building of the monastery. The number of monks increased so rapidly that Saint Columbanus was able to establish a second monastery at Luxeuil, and then a third at Fontaines. Luxeuil became the center of the religious revival, reaching the height of its development under his successor in the abbacy, Saint Eustasius (d. 629). Three other monasteries were founded by Luxeuil, including Grandis Vallis (Grandivalle) in Münsterthal, diocese of Basel. To these must be added many other monasteries which indirectly owed their origin to Saint Columbanus, since they were founded by persons who had received their inspiration from Luxeuil, as monks or laymen; for numerous illustrious families sent their sons to Luxeuil to be educated. The origin of not a few monastic foundations of the succeeding epoch can be traced, conclusively if indirectly, to Saint Columbanus. Some of these had been founded by persons upon whom the stern, prophetlike figure of the saint had made a profound impression during the receptive period of their youth. Several flourishing monasteries in the district of Brie, east of Paris, owed their origin to the children of families in which Saint Columbanus had once enjoyed a brief hospitality during his journey from Nantes to Austrasia.

In the house of Count Chagneric, an intimate friend of the king, he had blessed the count's little daughter, Burgundofara, who later, on the paternal estate near Meaux, built and directed the convent of Faremoûtier which greatly attracted the daughters of the Frankish and Anglo-Saxon nobility. Saint Burgundofara's brother, Saint Chagnoald, joined Saint Columbanus, becoming a monk at Luxeuil, and subsequently bishop of Laon; Saint Faro, another brother, was made bishop of Meaux. Both bishops showed favors in many ways to the monasteries following the rule of Saint Columbanus.

The stimulus provided by Saint Columbanus' visit with the nearby family of the Frankish nobleman Autharius had a similar effect. The eldest son of this household, Saint Ado, founded the convent for nuns at Jouarre on the Marne, whence came the first abbess of Chelles, a foundation of the saintly Queen Bathildis. The second son, Saint Audoenus or Dado, who had been the king's chancellor, as bishop of Rouen founded the monastery of Rebais, together with his brothers. Saint Filbert, who was trained at Rebais, in turn established the monasteries of Jumièges, near Rouen, and Noirmoutier, at the mouth of the Loire. The monastery of Reuil, on the Marne, was established by Rado, a third son of Autharius, who had occupied the position of treasurer at the king's court.

The impulses emanating from these monasteries continued to multiply rapidly. Older monasteries were reformed after the model of Luxeuil. More than fifty monasteries can be counted which came under the Irish influence brought to the continent by Saint Columbanus. One can go further and say: Whoever in this period distinguished himself in the cultivation of the religious life, can be presumed in most cases to have been inspired by Luxeuil or by the disciples of Saint Columbanus.

Nor was it the religious life alone that was fostered in these monasteries; for many, founded in the forests or in the wilderness after the land had been cleared by the manual labor of the monks, merited the distinction of being the first cultural pioneers in the economic and intellectual fields. A large portion of the still uncultivated land in Gaul was prepared for tillage by the monks — especially in the Vosges Mountains, in the Ardennes and Flanders, in the still uninhabited regions of the lower Seine, and in the province of Champagne.[8]

This cultural activity of the monasteries, which constituted the beginnings of so many settlements and cities, continued to spread with only a few interruptions, particularly on the right bank of the Rhine. It received its main impulse from the disciples of Saint Columbanus, whose hands were as apt to perform hard agricultural labor as they were to write delicately upon parchment — and whose

8. Imbart de la Tour, "Les paroisses rurales," Revue hist., 61 (1896), 35.

most important concern remained the directing of souls by their profound words of exhortation. The saint's disciples were the first monks on the continent to engage in parochial work.

Conscious of their individual character, these monasteries strove to obtain a position in the Frankish kingdom similar to that occupied by the Irish monasteries in their native country. This, however, ran counter to the hitherto prevailing custom on the continent; that monasteries were to be subject to diocesan bishops had been inculcated by the first council of the Frankish kingdom, held at Orleans in 511. Despite this regulation, the new monasteries strove for an independence so complete that the diocesan bishop would have no authority over them, even to perform ordinations. They sought to reinforce this anomalous position by means of royal and episcopal privileges, whereby there would be secured by charter not only the free election of the abbot and the inviolability of their possessions but also their exemption from the jurisdiction of the diocesan bishop and their right to have Holy Orders conferred by any bishop of their choice.

This was the form in which the monastery of Rebais, organized "after the manner of Luxeuil," obtained these privileges in 637 or 638. The abbot either was himself a bishop, or had the episcopal consecration conferred upon one of his monks, or approached itinerant bishops, who through the influence of the Irish were beginning to make their appearance, for the conferring of Holy Orders. That a dissolution of the continental diocesan organization might be thus inaugurated, was not perceived by many at the time. The feeling was one of rejoicing that the spirit of Luxeuil could be kept so pure. Nor, in all truth, could the inspiration of Luxeuil be denied in the growth of monasteries and the invigoration of religious life.

We can clearly perceive the spirit emanating from Luxeuil in the rule written by Saint Columbanus for his monks. It falls into two parts. In the first, positive precepts are given, in the second, the punishments to be imposed for violations are enumerated. The rule is characterized by extraordinary strictness and severity. Obedience toward the abbot and the practice of self-denial were strongly impressed upon the monks. The punishments were unusually rigorous. Even minor infractions of monastic observance were punished with lashes of the scourge, whose number ranged from six to two hundred, to which was added confinement. He who did not await the abbot's blessing at table, or answer *Amen,* he who lifted his spoon without making the sign of the cross over it, he who spoke unnecessarily and loudly during meals received six lashes; he who cut into the table with his knife received ten; he who coughed at the beginning of the Office in choir, or chanted falsely, six; he who did not ask the abbot's blessing upon leaving the house to labor in the field or go on a journey, twelve. Herein we find revealed the harsh personality of the Irish abbot, who, as some have remarked, can be placed alongside the figures of the Old Testament prophets.

Columbanus brought this Old Testament severity and intolerance with him from his native land. We recognize them again in the great importance accorded the Mosaic laws in the eighth-century compilation of canonical precepts, the *Collectio Hibernensis* — for instance, in the regulations concerning the jubilee year and the dietary laws with their distinction between clean and unclean foods. But the sternness manifested by Saint Columbanus was probably necessary to instill respect into the Franks, men of brute strength that they were.

Columbanus refused to defer to the weakness of human nature, and even declined to conform to others in external and unessential matters. In this we note a certain narrowness, which could not be maintained for any length of time in any sound movement. Hence we comprehend why his monastic rule was soon surpassed by others.

The rule of Saint Columbanus lacked regulations concerning the constitution and administration of the monastery. He reserved all these activities to himself: he appointed the superiors in the monasteries, he established and designated his successor in Luxeuil. Those desiring to found a monastery after the pattern he had given them lacked theoretical rules once the image of the founder had faded. Provision for this contingency was made in the Rule of Saint Benedict, which became known in the Frankish kingdom soon after Saint Columbanus had departed from it. The Benedictine Rule showed wisdom in methods of government that had been acquired in Rome, prudent moderation that had immemorially been taught by the ancient philosophers, and organizing ability — all of which were more or less wanting in Saint Columbanus. The Rule of Saint Benedict was both more valuable because of the directions it bequeathed to the abbot, and wiser because of its organization of a monastic council and the fixing of the abbot's election; it was juridically clearer because of its regulations concerning the admission of members; but above all it was more elastic and practical because of the moderate spirit which sought to attain the attainable instead of the highest ideal conceivable. This explains the fact that the Rule, coming from Rome, to which on the continent men were always accustomed to turn first in matters ecclesiastical, was soon adopted also in Columbanian monasteries — at first combined with the statutes of Saint Columbanus, later as the sole prevailing order.

The Benedictines were able to adjust themselves to the manifold conditions then taking shape in the West where divers nations dwelt side by side; but not so Saint Columbanus. He always remained an Irishman, claiming the privileges of a foreigner; although these were not accorded him without further ado when they were in opposition to the ecclesiastical order of the country. Thus he had a conflict with the Frankish bishops, which began with the difference over the computation of the date of Easter. The Frankish bishops had reached an agreement at the fourth synod of Orleans (542) to accept the computation set up by Victorius of Aquitaine in 457. Saint Columbanus attacked this method and tried to have it supplanted by the Irish mode of reckoning. When, in the year 600, he failed to celebrate Easter on the same day as the Frankish Church, the bishops summoned him to appear before a synod and explain his conduct. He did not obey, but since he desisted from his efforts to make his computation binding upon all, the bishops also yielded in part: they allowed him and his monasteries to retain the Irish computation for the time being.

Saint Columbanus, however, was to experience the consequences of his separate position in another direction, for when he became involved in a conflict with the king's court, he received no support from the bishops. Luxeuil belonged to the so-called Burgundian section of the kingdom, which was subject at the time to the young Merovingian Theodoric II, the grandson of Brunhilda. As an adviser, Brunhilda had an influential voice in the government. Theodoric's brother, Theodebert II, ruled in Austrasia, and true to their Merovingian traditions, the two brothers, who were anything but estimable characters, soon began to quarrel. Greedy for lands and immoral from early youth, they dug their graves with their own hands. At the age of fifteen Theodebert was already a father; at the age of twenty he had four sons, none of them legitimate. When he finally decided to marry a Spanish princess, he tired of her after a year's marriage and sent her home. Saint Columbanus was the last man to remain passive in the face of such a scandalous situation. Theodoric, who in the beginning had shown the abbot a certain amount of respect, had to listen repeatedly to sharp reprimands from him.

On one occasion the saint came to the royal villa of Vitry, near Arras, where Brunhilda was staying with her great-grandsons, the illegitimate sons of Theodoric. Following the custom of the times, Brunhilda sent the children to meet the abbot so that he might bless them. Saint Columbanus believed it imperative even in this instance to enforce his stern principles. He refused to impart his blessing to the children, and informed them that none of them would wield the royal scepter for they were the fruits of a sinful union. Soon thereafter Saint Columbanus arrived at the villa where the king was sojourning and had his presence announced. It was evening. The king wished to accord the man of God the honor due him and ordered that food and drink be set before him. Columbanus refused the food — it was the gift of an impious man— and smashed the goblet. By this action he undoubtedly meant to express the fact that he regarded the king as excommunicate and could not share his table. The following day the king, together with his grandmother, called on Saint Columbanus, and both tried to induce him to take a milder attitude. Theodoric promised to amend his ways; but when the change for the better did not set in, Saint Columbanus threatened the king by letter with open excommunication. Brunhilda, realizing that this might have unfortunate political consequences for her grandson, now decided to take some countermeasures. In the *Vita Columbani*, written by the abbot Jonas, Brunhilda is described as a she-devil in her attitude toward the saint, and this judgment has been universally repeated until Kurth advocated another view.[9] Saint Columbanus certainly had every reason to reproach King Theodoric with his life; whether he employed the right method to lead the king into better ways is another question. But we must not fail to recognize the fact that in this situation Brunhilda acted only from motives of state; and that, on the other hand, in her attitude toward the saint when she executed her plan to get this troublesome mentor out of the country, she imposed upon herself a form of moderation which compares favorably with the violent deeds of her day. She took advantage of the tension existing between the bishops and Saint Columbanus to make her action seem justified.

The young king ordered Saint Columbanus, in the name of the saint's adversaries, the bishops, to give up his peculiarities; in particular, to forego his strict prohibition against laymen entering the monastery. Theodoric himself came to Luxeuil. Saint Columbanus resolutely refused to admit the king into the monastery building proper and addressed some harsh words to him. The king answered these remarks with an irony that ill became him, but which, nevertheless, reveals his moderation: "Thou dost hope, no doubt, that I will give to thee the martyr's crown; know thou that I am not such a fool as to commit so great a crime."[10] He then added that he gave Columbanus the choice of conforming to the customs of the country or of returning to his native Ireland.

At first the saint was banished to Besançon. There, however, he was not particularly guarded, and one day he returned to his monastery. At once Brunhilda and Theodoric dispatched soldiers who, without harming him in any way, brought him to Nantes, on the boundary of the kingdom, where he was to be put on board a ship bound for Ireland. In Nantes, however, Saint Columbanus escaped, very few precautions having been taken to prevent this. He fled to Fredegund's son, Clotaire II, who was ruling over Neustria. From there he proposed to go to Italy, but changed his plan and decided to devote himself to mission work among the Alamanni, who were subject to the Austrasian king.

---

9. Kurth, "La reine Brunehaut," *Revue des questions historiques,* juillet, 1891.
10. Jonas, *Vita Columbani,* I, c. 19.

The fact that it was not a Frank but an Irishman who approached the Alamanni as a missionary, gives us an insight into the degree to which the vitality of the Frankish Church was exhausted. But before we take up the missionary journey of Saint Columbanus, let us first inform ourselves briefly about the Alamanni.

The Alamanni, or Swabians as they called themselves — here we have a vestige of the tribal name Suevi — had advanced from the region of the Havel and the Spree westward to the middle Rhine and then spread along the rampart which the Romans had erected between the upper Rhine and the upper Danube. Here they began at an early date to undermine the boundaries of the Roman Empire. In the second half of the third century they swarmed over the rampart and sought to spread out over the *Agri Decumates* lying beyond. In the fourth century the Romans counted themselves fortunate to be still capable of defending the Rhine frontier against them. After the Rhine boundary had been broken by the Vandals, the Alamanni took possession of Alsace, pushing forward in the south at the same time across the Lake of Constance into what is Switzerland today and into Vindelicia up to the Alps. Clovis in 496 repulsed their advance in the north, and as a result they were driven back from the middle Rhine and the Main to the Swabian plateau and the Alps. When Theodoric the Ostrogoth admitted them into Rhaetia, their tribal home became fixed, comprising the southern portion of modern Würtemberg and Baden, Alsace, that part of Bavaria west of the Lech, Vorarlberg and German Switzerland.

Since Ostrogothic Alamannia had been relinquished to the Franks in the year 536, the whole tribe acknowledged their suzerainty. The Franks thus had a political interest in introducing Christianity among the Alamanni; it was a means of securing their own rule. They took some measures to this end on the banks of the upper Rhine. At the end of the sixth or the beginning of the seventh century the bishopric of Strassburg was erected on the site of the ancient Argentoratum. About the same time a new episcopal see was created at Constance to replace the bishopric of Windisch, which had been transferred to Avenches; the bishopric which had been established in Roman times at Augusta Rauracorum, or Basel, was also restored in the latter place. However, the information concerning the beginning of these last two bishoprics is very uncertain. Only after the appearance of the Irish missionaries do we obtain surer data concerning the origins of Christianity in these regions. But Frankish domination must have already prepared the way for the spread of Christianity; the king had some possessions in the land of the Alamanni, and the administration of these scattered royal estates had been entrusted to Franks, who certainly were Christians. The Alamannic ducal family, which maintained relations with the Frankish royal court, was Christian at the beginning of the seventh century. It was Theodebert II, king of Austrasia, to whom Saint Columbanus went from the court of Clotaire II, who inspired the banished Irish missionary to go to the pagan Alamanni. With several monks who had come to him from Luxeuil, he journeyed to the Rhine and then up the river into the Alamannic territories of Switzerland, halting at Bregenz on the Lake of Constance. There he encountered Christians and pagans participating in a libation of beer in honor of Wotan. In the vicinity there still existed a small, dilapidated church dedicated to Saint Aurelia and dating from Roman times, in which the pagans had set up statues of their gods. It was because of this church that the Christian priest laboring in Arbon, not far distant, had directed Saint Columbanus thither.

All the conditions for a fruitful activity seemed to be present. Yet after only a few years Saint Columbanus found it advisable again to terminate his sojourn, since the political conditions in the Austrasian portion of the Frankish kingdom, on which Alamannia depended, had changed. Theodebert, its ruler, the protector of Columbanus, had been overcome by his brother Theodoric, the same as had formerly banished the saint. Columbanus could no longer hope for anything good for himself from the occupation of Austrasia by Theodoric. Hence he looked about for another field of activity. For a time he considered carrying his apostolate to the Slavs, but at length he reverted to his earlier plan of going to Italy.

Here he established his last monastery, that of Bobbio, which has already attracted our attention by its importance in the struggle against Lombardic Arianism. In addition, Bobbio became the scene of brilliant literary developments initiated by its cultured founder.

Notable for centuries because of this activity, Bobbio was able to unfold its unique character for the reason that it was the first monastery outside the Roman ecclesiastical province to be exempted from the jurisdiction of the diocesan bishop and placed under the immediate authority of the pope. This was effected by Pope Honorius I in the year 628.

At Bobbio the Irish monk whose whole life had been given to noble purposes, passed away on November 23, 615, and there at his tomb he has always been remembered and venerated. There, too, the Italian, Jonas of Susa, was trained, who, sojourning in the Frankish kingdom some thirty years later, described the activity of Saint Columbanus and his disciples.

Saint Columbanus was a powerful man, physically and intellectually. In him we can clearly perceive for the first time the fresh blood, bubbling over with energy, which the new peoples gave to the Western Church. When he was seventy years old he helped the monks to carry down steep inclines the heavy tree trunks which had been felled for the building of the monastery at Bobbio. His followers delighted to relate how the saint, endowed with all the qualities to subdue and tranquillize both men and animals, calmed the wild bears in the wooded regions about Bregenz. Had his nature developed without restraint, he would have lived for the pleasure of defiance; actually, much of that spirit remained in him. He approached not merely popes, but the very saints in heaven, in a commanding manner. Passing through Tours on the way to Nantes, he spent the night in prayer at the tomb of Saint Martin, as was undoubtedly customary at that time. Meanwhile, the baggage which he and his companions had left in the ship on the Loire was stolen. Saint Columbanus immediately returned to the church and reproached Saint Martin for having allowed the theft to occur, declaring he had not prayed the whole night at the saint's tomb in order to suffer such a loss thereby. Soon after Saint Columbanus had thus given vent to his pious ill humor and left the church, the thieves brought back the stolen articles!

Better known is the story concerning the frankness with which he wrote to Pope Boniface IV, after having allowed some schismatic bishops of northern Italy to talk him into believing that the pope had once favored heresy in the Three Chapters Controversy. The letter is characteristic of Saint Columbanus in many respects. While gravely reproaching the pope, he unequivocally recognizes the papal authority; while humbly ridiculing his own person, he proudly boasts of the perfect orthodoxy of the Irish; while venerating the place of the Apostles' tombs, he expresses contempt for the worldly power of the Rome which had not subjugated Ireland. He introduces himself as a bald-headed person whom one might be tempted to regard as an insolent babbler, since he speaks without invitation; yet he begs to be taken seriously because he is driven to speak out of love for the Church, whose faith he supposes to be in danger. Then he appeals to his status of Irishman as entitling him to a voice in the matter:

> All we Irish (who live at the earth's extremity) are the disciples of Saints Peter and Paul and the disciples of all who have, with the help of the Holy Ghost, written the Holy Rule of Faith. We have accepted nothing except the doctrine of the Evangelists and Apostles. Among us there have been no heretics, no Jews, no schismatics, but the Catholic faith is steadfastly adhered to in the form in which it was first transmitted by you the successors of the holy Apostles.[11]

In the course of this long letter he reverts once more to the relations of his native land with the Holy See, using elevated and strangely compounded words — words which reflect the Irish imagination, and sometimes also suggest Virgil, Ovid and Horace:

> We, as I have said before, are closely bound to the see of Saint Peter. Though Rome is great and renowned, to us it is mighty and glorious only because of this see. The name of the ancient capital of the world with its Ausonian splendor is indeed something wholly august, elevated above the lower ethereal regions, carried by the too great acclaim of almost all peoples far and wide over the face of the whole world unto the setting of the sun, to the places lying on the boundary of the other world, where the triumphant whirlpools of the ocean rush up by leaps and bounds without let or hindrance, as it were from every quarter. But to us thou art great and renowned only since the time in which God has deigned to become man and has stirred up the waters and multiplied by thousands the war-chariots of innumerable peoples, by riding through the

---

11. *Mon. Germ. Epp.*, III, 171.

sea of peoples together with those two most fiery chargers of God's Spirit, the Apostles Peter and Paul, whose precious remains have made thee blessed. Ever since the supreme charioteer, who is Christ, has come unto us across the currents of the sea, across the backs of dolphins and the surging billows — only since that time has Rome itself become more illustrious and renowned for us.

And if one may call this pair of Apostles heavenly, according to the utterance of the Holy Ghost, who calls those heavenly that proclaim God's glory, of whom it is said that their fame will be published over the whole earth and their words unto the ends of the whole world, then thou, too, art almost heavenly, and Rome is the head of all the churches of the world — always reserving to the place of the Lord's resurrection the special dignity due to it. But as thy honor is great in consequence of the dignity of the see which thou dost occupy, so must thou take especial care that thou lose not thy dignity because of any perversity whatsoever. Thy power will remain with thee as long as correct understanding is maintained, for he is the proper doorkeeper of heaven who by means of true knowledge opens the door to the worthy and closes it to the unworthy. If he acts otherwise, he will be able neither to open nor to close. . . .[12]

Conscious of the boldness of this address, Columbanus immediately begs pardon for his frank and rude manner of speech. It was a corollary of his natural strength of will, which led him to reproach others and prescribe for them with unrestrained severity; but only after it had learned self-mastery during his youth, subordinating itself to what had been recognized as the law and the rule of conduct. Having such a temperament, he well knew how difficult (and also how necessary) it was to curb one's will. Therefore did he inculcate in his rule and in his letters, above all, subordination, renunciation of one's own will, respect and humility, and the scourging of pride:

Before all the other vices, sell pride first and purchase in exchange, for your good fortune, humility, in order that you may thereby become like unto Christ, who says: "Learn of Me, for I am meek and humble of heart."[13]

Saint Columbanus also knew how to provide an example of meekness, and it was this trait in the strong-willed man that particu-

12. Ibid., 174.
13. *Zeitschr. f. Kirchengesch.*, XIV, 79.

larly attracted others. On the one hand, he knew how to speak stirringly of the world's impending end and of self-communion for the purpose of repentance; on the other, he was able to play with the birds in the forest and to attract children to himself. This union of sharply contrasted qualities, which were placed in the service of the Lord, undoubtedly explains the deep impression this man of God made upon all whom he encountered. It was precisely his unique individuality which influenced those who saw and knew him. When these had died, the charm he had exerted, ceased to exist; and it then became evident that he had not created that strong organization which, unlike this purely personal impression, would have given his labors permanence. That is the chief reason why those labors did not continue to survive in the form he would have desired, even though the impulse that emanated from him still achieved rich blessings in many directions through the efforts of his disciples.

Thus, in particular, his brief sojourn among the Alamanni gave stimulus to a missionary activity with broad ramifications among the German tribes. There he had left, although reluctantly, Saint Gall, who had emigrated from Ireland with him. Over the tomb of Saint Gall was built the monastery which, bearing his name, was to become the center for the spread of Christianity and culture in German Switzerland. Two factors combined to make Saint Gall's labors especially successful: he had full command of the German language, and he did not share the instability of his countrymen. He remained loyal to the region of the Steinach where Divine Providence had placed him.

Whether Saint Fridolin, the founder of the monastery of Säckingen, was an Irishman is uncertain; in any case, he worked independently of Saint Columbanus. He came to Säckingen from Poitiers, bringing with him relics of Saint Hilary, who thus became the patron saint of the monastery. The missionary activity of Säckingen is recognizable in the numerous churches dedicated to Saint Fridolin which are found in southwestern Germany and northern Switzerland, and also in the name Glarus, named for Saint Hilary because it belonged to Säckingen.

The progress which Christian belief and culture made among the Alamanni is more clearly revealed in the revision of the Alamannic law, undertaken between 717 and 719. This new code was ratified by an assembly of Alamannic tribes under Duke Lantfrid. In it the nation is treated as a Christian organism, and the rights of the Church and her protection are recognized in full measure. Servile work on Sunday is prohibited and ecclesiastical penance inculcated. The oath is no longer to be taken in the pagan manner, by placing the right hand on one's weapons, as had been demanded by the older Alamannic law, but in the Christian manner, by placing the hand on the altar. The judges are to be God-fearing men, hence Christians. Particular stress is laid upon instilling in the people respect for their bishops. The episcopal seal is given force equal to that of the duke, and the same punishment is inflicted upon the murderer of a bishop as upon the murderer of a duke.

For the killing of a pastor the threefold wergild is exacted, for the killing of a deacon or a monk, the double wergild. The punishment affixed for the violation of the right of asylum is justified by its purpose; namely, that others (there were still some pagans at this period) might gather therefrom what the fear of God meant for Christians, and the churches might be accorded a measure of honor.[14] Anyone was to enjoy the right of asylum who took refuge, not only in the interior of the church, but also (for the edifice was no doubt frequently locked) under the roof over the entrance. This sheltered spot before the church took the place of the vestibule, which was accorded the right of asylum in the large basilicas of Gaul. No obstacles to the practice of their religion were to be put in the path of those who had embraced Christianity, nor were impediments to be set up against those who desired to give their goods to the Church.

We see, therefore, that the latter had still to contend with certain difficulties, for these protective decrees against deeds of violence may fairly lead us to suppose that ecclesiastical edifices were broken into on occasion and robbed, that the dwellings of priests were attacked, and that priests and also bishops were insulted,

---

14. "Leges Alamannorum," *Mon. Germ. LL.,* t. V, pt. I, p. 70.

beaten and even murdered. Priests were the more exposed because there were no large settlements where several lived together — the earliest cities were scarcely in the process of formation.

The zeal of Luxeuil for Christian teaching had also made its influence felt on the Bavarian tribe that dwelt east of the Alamanni up to the Enns river. The land occupied by the Bavarians had been inhabited before them by Celts and Rhaeti, who had accepted Roman culture and Christianity. The Christian influence exerted here during the period of Roman domination was stronger than on the Rhine, since Italy bordered directly on these territories. That Christians were already to be found in Augsburg at the time of Diocletian's persecution may be concluded from the martyrdom of Saint Afra; Regensburg also had produced martyrs for the faith. In Noricum there persisted a tradition concerning a Roman official named Florian, a Christian, who had been thrown into the Enns at Lauriacum (Lorch) with a stone tied around his neck; similarly, the veneration of a saint named Maximilian survived in the Salzburg Alps. Of the bishoprics, the previously mentioned Lorch (situated at the confluence of the Enns and the Danube where the Roman fleet of the Danube once had its base) and Tiburnia (on the upper course of the Drave, in modern Carinthia) had disappeared. The sees of Saben (Sabiona), near Brixen, and Augsburg, however, were still in existence. When the Roman regime collapsed in the fifth century — the *Vita* of Saint Severinus has already shown us that it was beginning to totter in that region — Christianity had continued to live on in some remnants of the Roman population. Just as the Alamanni, south of the Lake of Constance, came into contact with such remnants, so were they also to be found in the Alps further east. The Bavarians had not exterminated these but absorbed them.

The name of the Bavarians (*Baiuarii*), occurring for the first time in the year 520, denotes that they were among the most recent German tribes. It signifies "inhabitants of the land of Baju," that is, the land of the Celtic Bojer, Bohemia. Bavaria and Bohemia, therefore, are two names having the same root. In Bohemia the Bavarians had derived principally from the ancient Marcomanni, and hence were West Germans and closely related to the Alamanni.

Though some Arian influences were present, which must have come from the Goths, the Bavarian tribe was for the most part pagan when it immigrated at the beginning of the sixth century to the new land to which it gave its name. From the Roman people whom they encountered, the Bavarians acquired the knowledge of Alpine farming and probably also something of Christianity. The influence of the latter increased when the country came under the domination of the Franks. A Frankish ruling family was set up over the Bavarians, and from this family descended the Catholic ducal dynasty of the Agilolfings. We have already met Theodelinda, daughter of the Bavarian duke, who as queen of the Lombards labored for the spread of Catholicism among her husband's tribesmen.

Our first positive information concerning Christian missionary activity among the Bavarians is derived from the circle of Saint Columbanus' disciples. Saint Eustasius, the abbot of Luxeuil, had worked for a time among the Bavarians as a missionary. He was probably directed to them by the Varasci, an Alamannic tribe, partly pagan and partly Arian, who had come from the upper Palatinate region to the country bordering on the Doubs, in the vicinity of Luxeuil. Saint Eustasius worked with great solicitude for their conversion, and through them probably hit upon the design of going to the Bavarians. Disciples of Saint Eustasius continued to labor among the Bavarians, who were also visited by itinerant bishops.

These latter remind us of Irish customs. The most renowned among them was Saint Rupert, the real Apostle of Bavaria, who went thither to labor as a missionary bishop under Duke Theodo at the end of the seventh and the beginning of the eighth century. Near the ruins of the ancient city of Juvavum, in Salzburg, below the duke's castle, he erected a church dedicated to Saint Peter, and a monastery. Somewhat later a convent for nuns was also built. Saint Rupert's memory endured among the people of the surrounding territory, as is evidenced by the many churches and chapels bearing his name. Other itinerant bishops who appeared about the same time are Saint Haimramm (Heim-Rabe), or Emmerammus, and Saint Corbinianus. The former, whose name like Saint Rupert's reveals German descent, suffered a violent death

318 CHURCH AND CULTURE IN THE MIDDLE AGES

after he had founded at Regensburg the monastery which developed into the cathedral chapter; the latter, for whose Irish origin more positive information is available, labored in Freising as its first bishop.

Duke Theodo took great interest in ecclesiastical problems. In the year 716 he went to Rome — the first Bavarian to do so — and while there received directions from Pope Gregory II for the organization and strengthening of the Church in Bavaria. That these directions were not carried out was probably due to Theodo's death, for in his country all such matters depended upon the representatives of the state's supreme power. This explains also why the three bishops, Saints Rupert, Emmerammus and Corbinianus, developed their activities in the residential cities of the dukes. In this period, the episcopal sees had not yet been locally fixed, the dioceses not yet delimited, the ordination of priests was often doubtful and their education very deficient. Saint Boniface was the first to give the Bavarian Church a firm organization. But even in his time we still find an Irishman in Bavaria: Saint Virgilius, who was appointed bishop of Salzburg by Duke Odilo. It was either he or another Irishman of the same name who took over, probably from the encyclopedia of Martianus Capella, the doctrine of the antipodes — an idea related to that of the spherical form of the earth — which shocked the ecclesiastical writers of his age as well as those of previous times, because they believed it to be a contradiction of the doctrine of the unity of the human race.

Irish missionaries, finally, also worked among the Thuringians, whose tribe extended at the beginning of the sixth century from the Harz Mountains to the Danube. Christianity had some adherents in this region even prior to its conquest by the Franks; the ancient dynasty to which Saint Radegunde belonged, was Christian — partly Arian, partly Catholic. Following the imposition of Frankish rule, Franks established their settlements as far as the regions of the upper Main; thus these regions became peopled with Christian inhabitants. About the year 630 the Frankish king, Dagobert, again gave Thuringia its own duke in the person of Radulph, a Christian. In Würzburg, the duke's residence, another Irishman labored: Saint Kilian, who was later assassinated by a noble, which betokens that the status of Christianity was still rather precarious here in the seventh century.

The reception of Christianity by all these German tribes on the right bank of the Rhine who were subject to the Franks — the Alamanni, the Bavarians and the Thuringians — was weak, almost reluctant. It is true that little open resistance was offered to Christian missionaries (nor would such resistance have remained unpunished). When individual conflicts did arise, they were occasioned in general by the moral demands which the missionaries made upon the nobles. Moreover, many of the converts may have turned to Christianity willingly, because of the higher culture associated with it, to which no intelligent person could refuse his respect. But just as there was no sign of great and systematic opposition, so also there was no manifestation of any particular enthusiasm. The contrast becomes sharply evident to us when we consider the ardor with which the Irish flocked into the monasteries. Such monasteries as were founded in the seventh century in the Frankish kingdom on the right bank of the Rhine were few in number, and led but a miserable existence. Only on the part of the Bavarian dynasty of the Agilolfings, with Theodelinda and Duke Theodo, do we perceive a more active interest in ecclesiastical affairs.

The reason for this lukewarm reception of Christianity lay in the first instance in the political circumstances. If the Irish, and later the Anglo-Saxons, so joyfully opened their hearts to Christianity, it was because their conversion was effected as a free tribal affair with their native chiefs taking the lead. On the continent, only the baptism of Clovis constitutes anything similar to their conversion. With the German tribes on the right bank of the Rhine, the acceptance of Christianity was not consequent upon the free decision either of a ruler or of a council of his nobles; instead, it was the result of their incorporation into the Frankish kingdom. This had been bound to take place sooner or later, but that it was borne very unwillingly their incessant rebellions show. The fact principally explains why that enthusiasm and self-sacrificing spirit were lacking which are wont to animate a group following a course freely chosen.

That weight was given to free decision is discernible from the provision of the Alamannic code at the beginning of the eighth century, already mentioned: "It shall be permitted a Christian man to serve God voluntarily." According to the context, this provision means that a freeman can offer himself or his goods and chattels to the Church and that he may not be hindered by anyone if such is his free will. It is significant that such a provision was decreed by an assembly of Alamannic nobles under one of their own dukes, Lantfrid, and placed at the head of the national code. Something of the wish to embrace Christianity as a free concern of man, not simply at the command of foreign masters, was still alive here. Though the dukes of the Alamanni were native-born, they had to follow the Frankish direction in all political matters, nor had they been able freely to decide for themselves on the acceptance of Christianity. Thus, especially in the beginning, there were no natural centers for a national movement, no centers whence the impulse to a free and joyous decision could have come.

Clovis' baptism had been decisive for the Franks — but, precisely, only for the Franks who had followed Clovis to Gaul. It meant nothing to the other Franks, and still less to the tribes on the right bank of the Rhine who had passed through an independent evolution side by side with the Franks and acknowledged the Frankish supremacy only by compulsion. The dukes of the Bavarians and Thuringians, appointed by the Franks, did not constitute stirring examples of the manner in which members of the oldest and best families of the tribe broke with the traditions of their ancestors and passed from paganism to Christianity. They brought Christianity with them, along with the orders of the Frankish ruler. Only gradually did they become full-fledged sons of the tribe, and that is why Christianity spread only slowly under their protection.

The Celtic missionaries were perhaps more welcome to the Germans than the Frankish missionaries, because with the Celts every political consideration was excluded. They needed only the protection of the political power. For the rest, like Saint Columbanus, their leader, they seized every opportunity to demand, even from the mighty of this world, the observance of the laws of Christian morality. They certainly did not fail, moreover, to stress the fact that they themselves were not Franks and that they did not follow any directions from higher up. Of course, it was just here that their weakness also lay. They were lacking in superior direction, in a systematic distribution of their forces, and in organization. Their activity was not properly co-ordinated, nor was there any provision for the recruiting of permanent missionary forces. The Church of the Merovingian kingdom was unable to do this because her own organization at the end of the seventh century was dangerously loosening. The Irish missionaries were pronounced individualists, each man or group of men acting separately. But all this does not diminish the debt of gratitude the Germans owe their first missionaries.

In spite of everything, some real progress had been achieved by their activity, principally, if not exclusively, during the seventh century. By the beginning of the eighth, the three tribes on the right bank of the Rhine, Alamanni, Bavarians and Thuringians — hence southern and central Germany — had been gained externally for the Church, and the soil prepared for Christian culture. The need now was for organization, and that capable men should enter the service of the Church as priests. There had not yet been found the means to make that difficult transition, of decisive importance for the future of every missionary country: the training in significant numbers of a capable native clergy. The Celts appear to have given little thought to the problem; at all events, not much was achieved by them in this direction. Was it, perhaps, because they were monks? On the other hand, it was precisely because they were monks that they had undertaken this missionary work; as monks, they had renewed religious life in the Frankish kingdom on the left bank of the Rhine.

A few things yet remain to be said. The stimulation of ecclesiastical and religious life in the Frankish Church was indubitably effected through the influences emanating from Luxeuil from the first decade of the seventh century. The example of the austere monks, the preachers of penance, who went forth from Luxeuil, had everywhere evoked a new spirit, which manifested itself on episcopal thrones and in newly erected monasteries. Royalty, as represented by Clotaire II, and his son Dagobert, also fostered this spirit for a time. Clotaire II, the son of Chilperic and Fredegund, took a friendly attitude toward the monks of Luxeuil, if for no other reason than that he felt himself one with them in their common enmity toward Brunhilda and her descendants. In fact, it was with him that Saint Columbanus had taken refuge when he was ordered out of Burgundy. In the year 613 Clotaire had, in union with the Austrasian and Burgundian nobles, finally brought about Brunhilda's downfall. The son of Fredegund had taken revenge on the aged queen in a frightful manner. After she had fallen into his hands at Orbe, in the Pagus Ultraioranus, he had her tortured for three days and then led about on a camel through his camp to be ridiculed. She was finally bound to the tail of a wild horse by the hair, one foot and one arm, and torn to pieces. Next, Clotaire extirpated her whole family. Thus he became sole ruler, and the Frankish kingdom enjoyed under him and his son Dagobert twenty-six years of peace.

This period benefited the Church, especially since her internal, spiritual forces had been strengthened. To win over the bishops, Clotaire offered to work out with them an understanding regarding the appointments to episcopal sees. At the national assembly in 614 he admitted that the canonical regulations on elections must be observed: the clergy and people should elect the bishop, the metropolitan together with the bishops of the province should consecrate the bishop-elect, and the king should approve the election before the consecration. To be sure, he still expressly reserved to himself the right to determine that the choice be not limited to the diocesan clergy of the vacant see; stipulating that an official of the court could be elected, who if he was worthy was also to be consecrated. Clotaire further moved to settle the disputes over jurisdiction. For a time we hear of no complaints from the Church concerning the interference of the temporal power in episcopal appointments.

The power of these two kings, Clotaire II and Dagobert, energetically supported the missionary activity among the pagan Franks and Frisians (in whom, naturally, the Frankish government also had an immediate political interest). And here, too, the disciples of Saint Columbanus were the first to help. Saint Audomare, who bequeathed his name to Saint Omer and was the first bishop of Boulogne and Therouanne, was a disciple of Saint Eustasius, the successor of Saint Columbanus at Luxeuil. In this period also we meet a missionary-monk, Saint Amandus, who, though actually still associated with the disciples of Saint Columbanus, nevertheless occupies a singular position, indicative of a new epoch.

Amandus was reputed to have come from Aquitaine. It is uncertain whether he made a pilgrimage to Rome, as his biographer — who is known to be unreliable — reports of him. At all events, we note that he lays particular stress on union with Rome. This is apparent in the fact that wherever he established churches and monasteries he dedicated them to the Princes of the Apostles, Saints Peter and Paul; and even more distinctly in the fact that he sought the pope's advice and begged him for relics and books. With regard to the latter petition Pope Martin (649) was forced to tell him that the supply of books in the library was exhausted and that new ones could not be copied before the messenger was due to depart. While both his relationship with Rome and his reliance on the rulers of the Frankish kingdom show Saint Amandus to be the forerunner of the Anglo-Saxon mission period, he stands, by reason of his restlessness, even closer to the Celtic missionaries of his own time.

His memory is principally associated with the monastery he founded at the confluence of the Elnon and Scarpe rivers in Flanders, which was later named for him. The Italian, Jonas of Bobbio, biographer of Saint Columbanus, spent several years there at his side. The monastery lay on an important borderline between two countries and two nations. The clanlike settlements of the Franks extended from the north southward to this borderline, which thus became the boundary between the German and Romance languages; during the Middle Ages the French and German kingdoms touched each other here. The place where Saint Amandus had preached to the still pagan Franks also became an important clearing house for German and Romance literature. In manuscripts of Saint Amand we have before us items that belong to the oldest monuments of French and German literature: the French sequence of Saint Eulalia and the German *Ludwigslied*.

From his monastery the zealous missionary abbot-bishop was able to penetrate still farther into pagan territory by sailing from the Scarpe into the Schelde, from which he could reach the sea and the Frisian border. By this route he traveled to the stronghold of Antwerp, where he built a church dedicated to Saints Peter and Paul; and into the region of Maastricht, of which, according to his biographer, he became bishop. This, however, is to be doubted, as are his reported missionary journeys to the Slavs and the Basques. Amandus died at his monastery about the year 676; the Anglo-Saxons, who later followed in his footsteps in the Frisian mission, commemorated the day of his death on the sixth of February.

Saint Eligius of Limoges spent himself in the same field of labor as Saint Amandus. He was the ornament of the royal court in Paris during the reign of Dagobert by virtue of his artistic skill as a goldsmith, as well as for his rectitude, charity and piety. For a time he was master of the mint at Marseilles, where he gave all he had to ransom prisoners, offered there for sale by all nations. Prominent among the many monasteries he established from his own means was the richly appointed foundation of Solignac, in his native district, near Limoges. The monks were to live according to the rules of Saint Benedict and Saint Columbanus; in important matters, however, they were to be subject to the supervision of the abbot of Luxeuil. They were exempt from episcopal authority.

In 639, after Dagobert's death, Saint Eligius left the royal court, entered the service of the Church, and became bishop of Noyon; this diocese was merged with that of Vermandois and Tournai and comprised the whole northern coastal region. Like Saint Amandus, Eligius dedicated himself to the conversion of the still pagan Franks. He died on December 1, 660, and was venerated far and wide as a saint. He became the patron saint of smiths and goldsmiths, and peasants also particularly sought his intercession when their horses were sick. A beautiful testimony of his pastoral zeal is found in some fragments of sermons in which, following Saint Caesarius of Arles as his model, he admonishes the faithful in simple and dignified speech to prepare themselves for the Judgment and the imminent end of the world; he exhorts them, in particular, to charitable works and brotherly love, and at the same time, because of certain pagan customs he has observed, warns them against superstitious practices.

After the middle of the seventh century, the decline of the Frankish Church visibly began. The brief revival which the spirit of Luxeuil had brought about, vanished since the chaotic political conditions again prevailing affected the Church. The Merovingian kingship had become the apple of discord among the nobles, who, relying on the particularism of the several divisions of the kingdom — Austrasia, Neustria and Burgundy — arrogated the power to themselves. By developing the feudal system or state of vassalage, the nobles at the head of the movement forged the means to their desired end. In ever greater measure they made the persons who received land from them in usufruct as a *feudum* or *beneficium,* also personally dependent; thereby these persons commended themselves to their lord, the seignior, as servants or vassals. The need for such real and personal dependence grew with the domestic disorder, for it alone conferred even passable protection; but it dissolved the state.

In addition, there was an extension of the privileges of immunity which had been associated with conditions of the later Roman era. Thereby the governmental official was forbidden to visit the territories of the privileged class; the lord enjoying immunity had the rents and taxes collected by his own officials and exercised jurisdiction in the first instance through a special representative, the bailiff (*advocatus*). The state no longer ruled directly over its subjects. The seignior led his dependents, his vassals, to the king's army.

Land was everywhere the basis of feudal dependence. Since the counts, the instruments of royal administration, were also invested with landed property, their interests were identified with those of the provincial nobility. In 614 Clotaire II had been forced to promise to designate counts exclusively from the landowners of the district. The dependence of the counts upon the king was thus destroyed; and they strove to make their office hereditary in their families. The military retinues which the landowners built up for themselves and sought to use solely for their own interests, would

have inevitably led to complete anarchy, had not a force gone forth
from the nobility itself which restrained and controlled it in turn.

This force was represented by the *Hausmeier* (Mayors of the
Palace), formerly the leaders of the king's retainers. During periods
of regency they exercised the supreme authority at the court and
arrogated to themselves the management of the affairs of government. The increasing weakness of the Merovingian kings and their
quarrels facilitated these designs of the *Hausmeier*. At first the
kings used them to curb the rebellious nobility, but after the seventh
century the *Hausmeier* put themselves at the head of the nobility
in opposition to the king by presenting to the monarchy the demands
of the aristocracy. They forced the ruler to entrust his minor son
to them so that they could rule the youth's portion of the kingdom
in his name. After a long struggle they overcame Brunhilda, who
was unwilling to surrender the exercise of strong monarchical
power. In this manner, finally, arose the Carolingian dynasty, which
put an end to the Merovingian kingship. The new dynasty possessed the power which the Merovingians lacked — the power not
only to consolidate the Frankish kingdom once more, but also to
unite the whole West.

Nor is this political achievement the only factor of progress
visible in the chaotic welter of the Frankish kingdom at the end of
the seventh and in the first half of the eighth century. If we keep
the general cultural development of the West in mind, there is
another point meriting perhaps even greater attention. The very
limitation of that royal authority which always tends toward absolute
power, had a decidedly good side in the matter of internal development. The growth of an absolute royal authority would not have
been a blessing for the new Western culture; it would have led to
conditions like those obtaining in Byzantium, whither men were
ever directing their gaze. To offer a small but significant illustration of this attitude: in the German language the word for
physician (*Arzt*) had been borrowed from Byzantium. It was derived from the Latinized *archiater* (pronounced *arziater*), the title
of the chief physician. The new culture of the West was to be
distinguished chiefly by variety and liberty in contrast to the centralized imperialism and Asiatic despotism of Byzantium. The

developing feudality of the nobles certainly contributed to the founding of this liberty, which was threatened by any royal authority inclining to absolutism.

The power of the nobles was brought about, of course, by reducing the number of freemen, since those who acknowledged themselves as their dependents were no longer free. But this was counterbalanced by the fact that feudalism entailed the elevation of the lower classes. This twofold development took place as follows.

The freemen who lived on a nobleman's estate as tenants or as peasants paying tithes or as joint-peasants, or who became under-tenants (as they were generally called), gradually formed one class with the bondmen who, like them, had received land from the lord and were represented by him in the courts of law. The free under-tenants gladly left the performance of their military service to the manorial servants; the rise of immunity also abetted this practice, since many freemen acknowledged the lord enjoying immunity as their lord and were counted among his officials. When the free under-tenant thus surrendered his political rights and duties to his lord, he became a freeman of a lower order; he became absorbed in the class of bondmen and was accorded a smaller wergild than the man who was wholly free. This infiltration of free elements, however, resulted in raising the status of the bondmen and also that of the slaves, to which many freemen had been reduced in virtue of their occupation as farmers.

From the political standpoint, the immediate consequence of the extension of baronial rule and of districts enjoying immunity was naturally the disintegration of the Merovingian state into little, individual principalities.

The Church at first gained much externally from this economic-social development; but in time she exposed herself to serious spiritual danger. Her landed property had continuously increased through donations and bequests; through freemen who conveyed their property to the Church in order to receive it back from her as dependents upon her protection or in order to receive it back as a fief, since they were without property; through the increase of freemen who sought her protection; and through bondmen who were given to her together with the landed properties. The Church sought and usually obtained the privileges of immunity, which resulted in her exemption to a great extent from public burdens. Since she also knew how to provide good care for those dependent upon her, men generally desired to come under her protection. Nor was she un-interested in keeping her property intact; she did not dissipate it as many secular proprietors were doing. The bishops enhanced their position by virtue of their authority as ecclesiastical leaders.

But the vast property and the influence which they enjoyed threatened to affect their character. There was danger that their priestly vocation would be overshadowed by their economic im-portance as powerful landowners and by their political position as influential lords. The bishops set themselves up as a spiritual aristoc-racy alongside the temporal aristocracy. They made common cause with the latter in the prosecution of their aristocratic interests; but they also shared the latter's disadvantages, by becoming involved in the mutual struggles of the nobles and in the conflict with the king, who treated them merely as powerful factors in the economic and political field. The phenomenon was not found only in this epoch; it endured throughout the whole medieval period and, especially in Germany, led to the abuses from which the Church suffered there at the end of the Middle Ages. If men considered the higher ecclesi-astical positions from the viewpoint of income, power, authority, it was inevitable that some unworthy persons should strive by the most questionable means to occupy those positions, and that mitered dynasties should spring up as a result of a bishop's efforts to be-queath his diocese to his son or nephew. The usual road to this end was the favor of those in power, who on their part did not fail to use this power for rewarding their adherents or gaining new ones.

Let us examine a few examples which, confirming these general remarks, characterize the period. To what extent the Church be-came involved in strife among the nobles is pointedly demonstrated in the person of Saint Leodegar (Léger), bishop of Autun, and adversary of the Neustrian major-domo, Ebroin. History first places him in Poitiers as the nephew of Bishop Didon, by whom he was made archdeacon and given a monastery in Poitiers. Through the mediation of Queen Bathildis (who had come from England as a slave and later was venerated as a saint), he obtained the bishopric of Autun, for which two aspirants had contended with arms for two years, one of them finally being slain. As bishop, Leodegar soon showed himself to be an energetic man; he restored churches, rebuilt the city's walls, and inspired much ecclesiastical ornamentation. The aristocracy elected him as their leader when Ebroin, instead of allowing himself to be led by the nobles, attempted to impose restrictions on them. Ebroin had had Bishop Sigbrand executed for opposing him, and induced Queen Bathildis, the regent, to retire to the convent of Chelles, on the Marne, where she died in 680.

When in 673 the nominal Merovingian king, Clotaire III, the son of Saint Bathildis, died — young in years, like most of these rulers — Ebroin immediately had Theodoric, the younger of the dead king's brothers, proclaimed his successor in Neustria and Burgundy. The aristocracy were unwilling that Ebroin should decide the succession to the throne; they wanted an assembly of nobles to speak the decisive word in the matter. Ebroin denied the nobles access to the court. Thereupon the nobility proclaimed the Austrasian king, Childeric II, the elder brother, king. Ebroin was forced to acknowledge himself defeated and then to enter the monastery of Luxeuil; his candidate for the throne was shorn of his hair and brought to the monastery of Saint Denis.

Thereafter Saint Leodegar, the leader of the victorious nobility, was the most powerful man at the court. But he retained for only a short time the favor of the vacillating king, who was also offended by the saint's reproaches on the matter of the king's marriage with his niece. Two years later, Saint Leodegar was deposed and sent to Luxeuil. But soon another change occurred: Childeric II and his queen were murdered while hunting, and Theodoric III became king a second time. Ebroin was able to leave Luxeuil, along with Saint Leodegar, and to begin the game all over by setting up another Merovingian against Theodoric. The latter, now the legitimate king, was supported by Saint Leodegar. Besides Ebroin's candidate, still a third king was proclaimed in Austrasia. The people believed that the advent of the Antichrist was at hand, and a comet which was then observed threw them into a panic of fear. Saint Leodegar was besieged in Autun by the partisans of Ebroin, by Duke Waimer of Champagne, and by Bishop Desideratus of Châlon. He rejected the demand to forsake his king; but being unwilling to expose his city to the fury of his adversaries, he delivered himself up to them. The captive was blinded; later his lips and tongue were also mutilated. Finally, at the instigation of Ebroin, he was condemned by a synod in 679 on the slanderous charge of having been a party to Childeric's murder, and was thereupon beheaded. He deserves to be venerated as a martyr.

To what greatness of soul the once martial bishop rose in his sufferings can be seen from a letter which, blinded and maimed, he wrote to his mother, Sigrada — already mourning the violent death of her other son, Saint Gairinus, who had been stoned. Sigrada had retired to a convent at Soissons. There, writes Saint Leodegar, she is to seek consolation and peace; and may she also forgive their enemies:

> Since God calls to battle His warriors, for whom He holds in preparation the crowns to be conferred after victory, so also has He given them weapons such as the enemy hath not: the shield of faith, the breastplate of justice, the helmet of hope and the sword of the spirit, that is, of the Word of God. . . . Our King does not desire to find His warriors with ancient weapons and armor, but that, being spiritually renewed, they be tested in battle. Anything still remaining over from old habits, even though it appears slight, produces, nevertheless, very great harm. This is particularly the case if any hatred against one's enemies has remained in the heart. May God keep it far from the Christian faithful!

What the monasteries could still offer at that time — the letter was written about the year 675 — can be measured by the words he directs to his mother in praise of the peace which she can find in her convent (this was probably a dual foundation, a monastery for men and a convent for women):

> Hear and see how the Lord has already rewarded you in the present life. In exchange for the household of servants He gave you all the holy brethren who pray for you daily; for the service of the maids He gave you the holy sisters whose company you enjoy; for the restlessness of worldly life, repose in the monastic community; for the loss of fortune, Sacred Scripture, holy meditation and earnest prayer. For the loss of parents you have the venerable and saintly lady abbess, Astheria; she is to you a mother, a sister, a daughter. . . . I trust, therefore, that you have received all this, because I have received these gifts from Christ, not on

account of my merits, but solely through the mercy of Christ, through your prayers and your holiness.[15]

Such words of peace and forgiveness in those wild times of civil conflict show us how alive Christian ideals still were in the hearts of men. But the danger ever increased that these ideals would finally be extinguished, since those who could teach them were becoming fewer and fewer. What the fate of Saint Leodegar reveals of his epoch is borne out by many other examples.

When the bishoprics themselves became the objects of the nobles' struggles for power, the might of the protectors or the money of the aspirant decided the issue. Canonical appointments became rare, and simony spread far and wide. Bishops as well as temporal princes sought to get possession of rich monasteries, and thus the disorders penetrated into the monastic field, and no less generally into the ranks of the clergy. It was not uncommon for bishops and priests to lay aside their priestly garb and appear instead in military dress with lance and sword. War and the chase constituted their activity. The synods, which had done so much formerly for the maintenance of ecclesiastical discipline, ceased to meet; what appears to have been the last Frankish synod before the age of Saint Boniface was held in 695 — a diocesan synod of Auxerre, which ordained that the priests of the diocesan churches and monasteries should take turns in conducting the divine services in the cathedral church, since it no longer had any priests of its own. The national synods had already been discontinued before this, the last ones having been nothing but assemblies in which the king forced his will upon the bishops — in particular, to push through sentences of punishment against his adversaries. The bonds of the metropolitan organization were severed. (An added factor in accelerating the dissolution of the diocesan bonds of union, it is evident, had been the Columbanian monasteries, exempt according to Irish custom from episcopal authority, together with their monastic and itinerant bishops.)

Conditions reached their worst stage under Charles Martel, who did not shrink from employing any means whatever to gain

---

15. *Mon. Germ. Epp.*, III, 465 sqq.

complete control of the kingdom. The distress of the times likewise forced upon him a policy of ruthlessness: for he had to crush the Arab attempt to trample underfoot the seeds of Christian culture in the West.

Since there were no more crownlands available, Charles Martel sought (after the example of certain former kings) to bind his vassals to himself by compelling many churches to surrender their property. With this, in the form of fiefs, he then invested the laymen. Thus the tendency, already well established, of substituting a system of fiefs for a system of dependence, a tendency which led to the development of the feudal state, was accelerated; the nobles and the officials all became dependent upon the ruler as his vassals. It is true that the laymen thus endowed with church property were to hold it in usufruct only and not as their own possession; but one does not speak of the Church's secularization by Charles Martel without good reason. Earlier the bishops had correctly characterized the situation when they declared at the third synod of Paris (556-573) that they were in such cases only the custodians of the deeds of donation, no longer the custodians of the donated lands.[16]

To Charles it was immaterial who occupied an ecclesiastical office or whether it was occupied at all. Bishoprics not infrequently remained vacant for long periods. The bishops and abbots whom he installed generally lacked the ecclesiastical spirit. Occasionally they were even laymen, for the king's political and military interests alone decided the appointments; nor did he mind conferring several bishoprics and abbeys on the same person. One of his nephews, Saint Hugo, received the archbishopric of Rouen, the bishoprics of Paris and Bayeux, and the rich abbeys of Saint Wandrille and Jumièges. Milo, whom Charles esteemed as a warrior, obtained the bishopric of Rheims in addition to that of Treves. (This bishop met his death in a boar hunt.) It is said that several of the bishops and abbots installed by Charles were unable to read.

He also deposed bishops without hesitation if their loyalty came into question in any degree. Keeping church property in good

---

16. Conc. Paris., III, c. 1 (conclusion).

order had naturally also become a thing of the past. Much church property was squandered. The churches became impoverished: in Rheims they could no longer even support their priests.

The manorial lords governed their private churches in the same way as the rulers, managing them without any reference to the bishop. They gave churches away or bequeathed them, sometimes together with the serflike priest who was stationed there. Thus the Frankish Church, once so flourishing, had fallen into complete decay.

The literary activity deteriorated with the moral life. Virgilius Maro, an eccentric writer who lived in Toulouse probably at the beginning of the seventh century, evidences this decadence. He proposed to restore the effete speech of the schools, ventured the most bizarre word formations, and contrived an obscure language far cruder than the vernacular into which he continually lapsed despite all his efforts. Better known than the treatises and letters of this grammarian is a historical work which appeared in the seventh century. This chronicle was published as the result of a misunderstanding under the fictitious signature of "Fredegarius Scholasticus." It begins with a compilation of material from various historical works, in particular those of Saint Jerome, Saint Isidore and Saint Gregory of Tours, to which are appended original continuations, with some information that is important in parts. The Latin is barbaric beyond measure. In the vocalization and the combinations of consonants we already clearly recognize the Romance folk-tongue out of which the French language developed. The authors, however, for several co-operated in its production, were trying to write in the language of the schools: they have still retained the inflectional endings, but they apply them in a thoroughly arbitrary manner, as they also do the gender of nouns. Nevertheless, it is difficult to reproach them for this in view of the prologue, whose author apologizes for his rustic language, referring thus disarmingly to his predecessors:

> I, too, would have wished that such a gift of speech had been meted out to me, so that something even remotely similar would have been the result; but one draws water sparingly when it does not run continually from the spring. The world has grown old, and the keenness of our

intellect has therefore become dull; none of our contemporaries are able or even try to equal the orators who have gone before.[17]

This feeling of senility affected precisely the literary circles which still applied the standards of bygone days and did not surmise that a new linguistic life was endeavoring to evolve from the ancient Latin. These circles, with their antiquated knowledge and far-fetched interpretations, stand in sharp contrast to the exuberant consciousness of power of the young nations whose wild nature was scarcely to be restrained. How ridiculous is the attempt of an interpolator in the chronicle we are considering, to prove by a series of absurd misinterpretations the descent of the Franks from the Trojans, thus putting into circulation a fiction which became firmly established! Nor was this a harmless academic discussion; it was the result of a sharp political tendency. The purpose in tracing the descent of the Merovingian kings back to Priam, the ancient ruler of Troy, was to present the dynasty as particularly venerable and stigmatize, even by literary means, any rebellion against it. The tendency appears all the more striking because the authors otherwise represent an opposite position. They write in the service of the major-domos who desire to wrest the power from the kings. At the end there is inserted a continuation which almost becomes an official family chronicle of the mayoral dynasty that eventually succeeds in completely supplanting the Merovingians — the Carolingian.

They were destined to renew the kingdom and the Church. For this task the Anglo-Saxon Benedictines put new spiritual forces at their disposal.

Before we turn to these pioneers of culture, let us look back once more on the Irish missionaries, whom we have lost sight of in these last pages. It remains their merit to have given the impulse in several countries for a successful religious development. They established the Christian culture in Scotland and exercised a salutary influence upon the Anglo-Saxons, who had advanced to their very borders, with results we shall later examine. In southern Germany and far into central Germany they appear as the first messengers of Christianity and the purveyors of a higher culture; and in the

---

17. *Chronicarum q. d. Fredegarii*, IV, Praef. ed. Krusch, p. 123.

Frankish Church they reveal themselves as renewers of the religious and moral life.

But only rarely did a lasting effect follow their activity. True, their work did not suddenly end with the period so far treated, for in the literary field their influence upon the Frankish kingdom reaches its height only in the ninth century. But in general the broad cultural effect they had produced, began to flag as early as the seventh century. In the second half of that century their influence on the religious life of the Frankish kingdom also began to wane. We must note that this was only in small measure their fault and that of their disciples; the chief cause was the external changes which took place in the political, the economic, and the social fields and which were most unfavorable for spiritual life and aspirations.

Once again the situation was such that the Frankish kingdom was unable to produce the forces necessary to lift itself out of its religious and moral degeneracy, which had lowered the whole cultural level. Again the impulse had to come from without. On this occasion, however, an even more intensive force was necessary to right the troubled conditions, for the decline had progressed much further than at the time when Saint Columbanus appeared with his twelve companions. We have already said that the superiority of Catholicism over Arianism consisted in this, that Catholicism was of a more universal nature and possessed an inherent and strong hierarchical organization. The universal character of Catholicism made it possible in the seventh century for the Irish missionaries to bring new warmth to the frozen Frankish Church. The other advantage of the Catholic Church — her hierarchical organization and her organizing power — had not yet made itself felt. It was to be realized when Rome cast her glance for the first time toward the Germanic pagans and sent out monks who, in connection with their labors, cultivated the most intimate relation with Rome, the center of the Church and of culture.

CHAPTER FOUR

GREGORY THE GREAT —
THE ROMAN BENEDICTINE MISSIONARIES IN ENGLAND

WHEN Saint Columbanus, the representative of the remote West, went to the continent at the end of the sixth century, the papacy, at a turning point in its history, found itself in an extremely difficult position. But just at this time of greatest need there had ascended the papal throne a man able to recognize the necessities of the hour, and to meet them with the decisiveness of the born ruler. This man was Gregory the Great.

With the destruction of the Ostrogothic kingdom by the Eastern Romans and their reconquest of Italy, the pope had become the subject of the Byzantine emperor, who made him feel this relationship very pointedly. When the popes were not selected outright, like Vigilius and Pelagius, they had to be approved in Byzantium, and for this, moreover, were compelled to pay a considerable sum. In Italy itself the Lombard invaders had appeared and were penetrating so steadily that more than once the days of Rome seemed to be numbered. Schism was added to the material danger when, in the Three Chapters Controversy provoked by Justinian's demand that three persons charged with Nestorianism be condemned, the bishops of northern Italy separated from Rome. Even after 571, when the archbishop of Milan submitted, the archbishop of Aquileia, protected by the Lombards, continued in schism.

The papal authority stood in urgent need of some security and support lest it be delivered up to the caesaropapism of Constantinople or sacrificed to Lombardic oppression and the aspirations of the metropolitans for autonomy. Where was the papacy to find such help? Completely imbued, up till now, with the ideas of the Roman *imperium*, it had looked only to the East — to the emperor in Constantinople who, hardly able to provide adequate protection against the open attacks of the Lombards, was attempting to prescribe rules of faith for the Church! Not yet had the popes dared to turn their eyes toward that other quarter, where barbarians or heretics were entrenched.

The situation changed under Gregory the Great. No one sensed the distress of the time so keenly, or came so near to being crushed by its weight, as this pope. Yet it was his very knowledge of the prevailing misery that sharpened his vision. Gregory united in himself everything that was most needed for the guidance of the Church. Born of an illustrious family in the city of Rome, he had first embraced the career of a public servant, exercising the office of city prefect in the years 572 and 573. But realizing ever more clearly that Rome's future now lay in another course, he turned away from all worldly ambitions. The huge fortune he inherited upon his father's death he used to found six monasteries in Sicily. Further, he established in the family palace on the Coelian Hill a Benedictine monastery dedicated to Saint Andrew, which he himself entered in 575.

The Church, however, needed him outside the monastery. Pope Pelagius II appointed him to the most important ecclesiastical mission of the time by sending him as *apocrisiarius* (papal representative) to Constantinople. There he acquired a knowledge of world affairs (for example, his contact with Saint Leander of Seville enabled him to acquaint himself with the critical conditions prevailing in the Visigothic kingdom), and learned to deal prudently with men. He understood how to acquire at the imperial court the confidential and trusted standing necessary for the discharge of his office. Among other things, we learn that he became godfather to the son of the emperor Maurice.

Returning to Rome in 585, he served as secretary to Pope Pelagius II while that pontiff was engaged in ending the Aquileian schism. It was to Gregory that the eyes of all inevitably turned when it became necessary, in 590, to provide a successor to the deceased Pelagius.

His many letters (they number close to 860) inform us of his great activity as pope, and his numerous sermons, which have come down to us, evince the spirit of these labors. Gregory's detailed exposition of the Book of Job, commonly called the *Moralia,* and in particular his *Regula pastoralis* — a program of priest-

ly activity which enjoyed wide circulation in the Middle Ages —
serve the same purpose. This latter work contains the pope's answer
to Archbishop John of Ravenna justifying his own reluctance to
accept the papal dignity. In the exposition of the pastoral duties
we hear the echo of the admonitions for an abbot which Saint
Benedict presented in his Rule. Gregory had also borne witness in
his *Dialogues* (colloquies on the pious men of Italy) to his veneration for the monastic founder by giving a minute character sketch
of him. Now he paints the ideal of a good shepherd of souls in
the same manner as Saint Benedict depicted his ideal abbot:

> Let him be pure in thought, exemplary in deeds, prudent in silence,
> helpful in speech, compassionate with each individual as his neighbor,
> above all devoted to meditation, a humble companion with the just,
> superior to the vices of the delinquent by his zeal for justice; let him
> neither grow less concerned for the interior life because of his occupation
> with external affairs, nor omit care for external necessities through zeal
> for the interior life.[1]

This is the moderation and the being all things to all men
which Saint Benedict had urged upon his abbots. In Gregory's
ability to combine spirituality and external activity, he reminds us
indeed of Saint Ambrose, whom he further resembles through the
circumstances of exalted birth, initial worldly career, and application of the old Roman wisdom in government. Like Saint Ambrose,
Gregory attached no importance to a florid and affected style, but
contented himself with the simple speech that goes to the hearts
of men. The practical interest which, again like Saint Ambrose,
he took in the development of divine services is manifested by
his many-sided solicitude for the liturgy, his alteration of certain
texts of the Mass, and his regulation of ecclesiastical chant — an
activity in which a votary of Saint Benedict could not but have a
particular interest.

Gregory won the hearts of the Romans at the very beginning
of his pontificate by his profound compassion for their heavy trials;
for, in addition to the Lombardic danger, a serious plague had

---

1. S. Gregorius PP., *Reg. pastor.*, Pars II, c. 1.: Migne, *P. L.*, LXXVII, 26 sqq.

visited Rome. The people knew that this monk, the most superior man among them, had assumed the burden of caring for them, and that there was no other willing or able to do so.

It was during this period that the Roman Senate disappeared; it is mentioned for the last time in 603. The office of the city prefect, who was governor, judge, police director and mayor, also lost its prestige and importance. This was the office which Saint Gregory himself had filled before he entered the monastery, and he knew only too well how thankless and difficult a task it was in those days.[2] We recall his earlier civic labors when we perceive with what stirring emotion he describes Rome's demise, in his eighteenth homily,[3] preached in the face of the Lombardic approach (593); a sermon which Gregorovius designated as the funeral oration at the grave of ancient Rome.[4]

In truth, ancient Rome did die; but in its place arose the Rome of the popes, destined to become the one rallying point around which the nations of the West would gather to form a new cultural community. Saint Gregory did not guess to what an extent his own age was being prepared for this change. Like Saint Columbanus, his contemporary, and many earlier Romans, he believed that the end of the world was at hand.[5] It is all the more fascinating, therefore, to observe the new germs of life which came into being in his era, whose growth was fostered by no one so much as Gregory himself. If the external tribulations may be viewed under the figure of fructifying showers, he belonged pre-eminently among those who represented the warming rays of the sun. The solicitude which the papacy manifested under him for the social welfare of Rome, of Italy and of the lands beyond, contributed not a little to direct the eyes of men everywhere to the pope and turn their hearts toward him. In Rome it was principally he who provided for the feeding of the city as well as for its liberation from the Lombardic danger. The Byzantine officers were undoubtedly jealous of this

---

2. K. Heldmann, *Das Kaisertum Karls des Grossen* (Weimar, 1928), 191, 204 sqq. and 221 sqq.

3. See quotation above, p. 225.

4. Gregorovius, *Gesch. der Stadt Rom*, II[4], 45.

5. *Dial.*, lib. III, c. 38: Migne, *P. L.*, LXXVII, 317. Cf. Columba, *Ep. ad Bonifatium* IV: *Mon. Germ. Hist.: Epp.*, III, 171, 176.

position of Gregory, but they themselves could not win the respect and love of the Roman populace since their claims were not reinforced by appropriate deeds.

The necessity of organizing resistance against the Lombards with the weak military forces available had led the Byzantine emperor to set up in Italy an arrangement which we would call a state of war or siege. This system, established first on the Roman frontiers for their defense, was extended to all the harassed regions of Italy. Civil as well as military powers were concentrated in the hands of the higher Byzantine officers. The zones of the military commanders, who were formerly known as *duces* and *tribuni,* supplanted the old administrative divisions. Thus the territory of Rome now became the duchy of Rome, under the command of the Byzantine *dux.* We shall see later, however, that his authority gradually passed over to the pope, and that Byzantium, which had fettered the pontiffs, brought about by its own measures the breaking of those bonds.

In any case the commander of Roman territory was dependent upon the pope in the matter of levying troops since the papacy was by far the greatest landowner in Italy. Indeed, the practical measures for the social weal which Saint Gregory was able to adopt, were rendered possible by these great possessions, the *Patrimonium Petri.* The former public functionary made it his special business as pontiff to cultivate this patrimony and administer it prudently. It had accrued out of the land grants with which first the emperors and then the Roman nobility had endowed the Church. Many ancient names of famous Roman families continued to survive in the titles of the estates they had once given the Holy See, though the families themselves had long since become extinct. The distress of the times, too, induced the sons of numerous wealthy clans to enter the service of the Church — the only place where men's energies could still find a field of labor and the faithful be assured of consolation and rest; in most instances they then gave, either during their lifetime or on their deathbed, their temporal possessions to the Church. These land grants reached their peak toward the end of the sixth century, after which there were few such gifts: since the emperors had less to distribute and wealthy families with large landed estates were not numerous. The Lombards, however, again stripped the Church of many of her possessions.

The estates of the Church were naturally most numerous about Rome, but the holdings were spread over all of Italy; there were especially valuable ones in Campania, in southern Italy and in Sicily, the granary of Rome. Some also lay outside of Italy — in Gaul near Marseilles, in Africa and Dalmatia, in Sardinia and Corsica. The extent of these possessions made the pope, as we have said, the greatest landowner in Italy, and this alone gave him an extraordinary social and political influence, which everyone had to reckon with. However, it was not an alien or external thing, but bound up in a most intimate way with the destinies of Italy. The revenue from the estates (which were worked by slaves or *coloni*) was employed, first of all, for the needs of the Church — the support of the clergy, the maintenance of buildings, the endowment of monasteries, the erection of new churches; then, chiefly, for the relief of the poor. The duty of furnishing the needy and unemployed with sustenance, formerly discharged by the civil authorities, had now passed into the hands of the Church: this was the first sovereign function which the popes exercised in Rome in the emperor's stead. In addition, almshouses, hospitals, orphanages and hostelries for pilgrims were also supported. Everyone in want and distress, no matter what part of Italy he lived in, turned to the pope. The biographer of Gregory the Great calls the Church of this period a granary open to all men; and the pope himself he calls the father of Christ's family.[6]

The pontiff's expenditures were further augmented by his efforts to preserve the city from the Lombards; sometimes he even paid them to depart. He summarized his achievements in this direction in a letter written in 595 to the empress Constantia:

> For twenty-seven years we have been living in this city under the Lombards' swords. What sums are given them daily by the Church in order that we may be able to exist among them, I will not enumerate. . . . I will say only this: just as the emperor has in Ravenna a paymaster

---

6. Joannes Diaconus, *S. Gregorii papae vita*, lib. II, 26 and 51: Migne, *P. L.*, LXXV, 97 and 109.

sergeant attached to the first army of Italy, who defrays the daily expenses for current needs, so am I in like manner his paymaster for this city. . . .[7]

The many efforts of the papacy to turn away foreign foes, together with its general concern for the destitute of all classes, made the popes of that epoch extraordinarily beloved by the Italian people. It can assuredly be said that the papacy has never again been so popular in Italy as during the period of the barbarian invasions between the fifth century and the eighth: from the pontificate of Leo I, who pleaded with Attila and Genseric to spare Rome, to the day when Stephen II, accompanied by the weeping populace, set out to seek protection from the Frankish king, Pippin, against the Lombards. The pope gradually became the representative of the political interests of the peninsula against all foreigners — those who came from the north as well as those who sent their orders to Italy from the East. This development was certainly furthered by many remoter circumstances, some of them to be studied later, others already known to us: the fall of the Western Roman Empire and the conquest of Italy by the Ostrogoths no less than the danger from the Lombards and the pressure of the Byzantine government — a pressure shared equally by the pope and the inhabitants of Italy.

Saint Gregory was naturally aware that material and political affairs ought not to preoccupy him, and he unhesitatingly accorded first place to ecclesiastical activities. If we can assume a certain preference among his churchly concerns, it would be for the monasteries of the Benedictine Rule. It had become known in Rome after the destruction of Monte Cassino, when the sons of Saint Benedict established themselves on the Lateran, and was introduced by Gregory into the monasteries of his own foundation.

It was the pope's wish that the monastic units preserve their distinctive character. To this end he forbade the combining of monastic offices with ecclesiastical duties beyond the monastery enclosure, and even the holding of public services in monastic churches. Moreover, he guaranteed the monks the free election of their abbots. Thus he secured the monasteries against pressure

---

7. *Mon. Germ. Epp.*, I, 328.

from without. On the other hand, he had no intention of exempting them from the general discipline of the Church; they were subjected to the supervision and jurisdiction of the bishops, who were accorded the right of ordaining the abbots. The monasteries, finally, were always allowed to call upon the pope in any exigency.

That Gregory made it his business to safeguard his position as metropolitan in Italy and primate of the whole Church, need not be emphasized in view of his character. We may, however, point out the difficulties he encountered and sought to overcome in achieving this.

Particularly noteworthy is the fact already adverted to: that, unlike his immediate predecessors, he took great pains to effect a closer bond between the Church and the neglected West. It was perhaps natural, in view of his earlier association with Saint Leander in Constantinople, that he should direct his attention first to Spain. Hopeful prospects had opened out in that land shortly before he ascended the papal throne, when King Reccared entered the Church (589). Saint Gregory welcomed with great joy the reports of that event which Saint Leander and the monarch directed to him. He sent the king a key containing some iron from Saint Peter's chains, and a piece of wood from the cross of Christ, admonishing him to rule temperately and to resist overweening ambition and anger:

> The government of subjects must be conducted with great moderation. Lust for power must not be allowed to creep in. A kingdom is governed well when inordinate ambition does not dominate the ruler's mind. Care must also be taken that anger does not assert itself. . . . If anger has once taken possession of the mind, a cruel undertaking will be regarded as just.[8]

It is evident that he knew these Germanic kings well, in whom moderation was only too often lacking.

The letters which Gregory sent to Leander were particularly affectionate. It was to this friend that he dedicated his commentary on the Book of Job. He also conferred the pallium upon him as

---

8. Ibid., II, 224.

the metropolitan of Spain. Gregory's answer to one of the several questions put to him by Leander signally attests his own prudent moderation. The Spanish saint had inquired whether the Catholics of his country might continue to administer baptism by a single immersion, or whether they must employ triple immersion (at that time the usage in Rome). Since Arians also had the practice of triple immersion, the pope clearly realized how difficult it would be for Spanish Catholics to effect this change in the rite without its being hailed as an Arian victory. He therefore told Saint Leander that they might continue to baptize in their traditional manner in order to demonstrate their difference from the heretics: granted unity in faith, a difference in customs is not detrimental to the Church.

Despite all Gregory's efforts, a close union between the papacy and the Catholic Church in the Visigothic kingdom was not achieved, for that Church, in virtue of its intimate connection with the state, was a national establishment.

This was largely true also of the Frankish Church; only with southeastern Gaul, where the archbishops of Arles had been appointed papal vicars since 514, had the papacy a close bond. The Frankish rulers, even after Provence had been ceded to the Franks by the Ostrogoths in 536, did not concern themselves much about these papal vicars. It is true that King Childebert I repeatedly used his influence to have the title of papal vicar conferred on the incumbent archbishop of Arles; but this was undoubtedly done only as a matter of form, to assert the prerogative of the Frankish State in the affair, since Pope Vigilius had once declared (after the death of Saint Caesarius of Arles) that before he could bestow the pallium upon the archbishop of Arles he must have the authorization of the Eastern Roman emperor.

The archbishops of Arles, however, could not attain a real exercise of the rights proper to a representative of the pope. Great stress was indeed laid in the Frankish Church at large upon unity of faith with Rome; but it became customary to regulate the practical affairs of that Church without reference to the pope, and the pontiffs in the sixth century seemingly accepted this state of things. They probably hoped that the Frankish domination would be only transient, and that the Eastern Roman emperor would once more gain a foothold in southern Gaul; for Bishop Marius of Avenches (574-594) counted the years at that time according to the era of the Eastern Roman emperors, and in 545 Pope Vigilius had exhorted Archbishop Auxanius of Arles to pray for the Eastern imperial couple and to be solicitous for good relations between Constantinople and the Frankish king.

Pope Gregory I was evidently of a different opinion. He knew only too well, from personal experience in Italy, the weakness of Byzantine power; and being a realist in politics, he took the Germanic kingdoms of the West into account. That is why he labored indefatigably for a closer union between the Frankish Church and Rome. He admonished Archbishop Vigilius of Arles, whom he reappointed as papal representative, to remove the abuses in the Frankish kingdom: Vigilius was to make remonstrances to King Childebert II regarding, in particular, simony and the appointment of laymen as bishops. Pope Gregory tried himself to get in touch with Brunhilda, as well as her son and grandsons, in the hope of bringing about a synod to restore ecclesiastical organization in the realm and extirpate simony. But such a synod was never convened, hard as the pope worked for it. He did not succeed, either, in having a special papal legate admitted into the Frankish kingdom for the purpose of reforming ecclesiastical conditions there. The time was not yet ripe. Only considerably later, and by a roundabout road, was the Holy See to reach the goal for which Saint Gregory strove. But to him belongs the credit for having indicated that road.

The way to the Frankish kingdom lay through the Anglo-Saxons. The conversion of this people was a decisive factor in the forming of the West into a cultural community, and one in close union with Rome. Gregory I hardly foresaw this, but he unquestionably has the personal merit of having sent the Roman Benedictines as missionaries to England, and of having given the impetus to this fruitful mission. He was led to take the step by the knowledge that the Frankish Church, on which it would in the first place have devolved, was incapable of accomplishing it. As early as 595 he commissioned his agent Candidus, who was charged with managing the patrimony of the Church on the lower Rhone, to purchase young Anglo-Saxon slaves in Gaul so that they could be educated to the clerical state in Roman monasteries. That he had this thought even before he became pope, on beholding some fair Anglo-Saxon youths in the slave-market in Rome, and that he himself set out to England as a missionary but was brought back by the Romans, may be doubted. It is a tradition encountered only later. For all that, we can gather from the commission given Candidus that the idea of the mission came first from contact with Anglo-Saxon slaves. As early as 596 the plan was put into execution by this pope of rapid decisions. From his own foundation, the monastery of Saint Andrew, which most faithfully exemplified his spirit, Saint Gregory sent the prior, Saint Augustine, with forty monks to England.

Nothing less than the vision and force of will possessed by this pope could have brought the Romans to the point of dispatching for the first time missionaries to the barbarians, so intensely were the barbarians feared in Rome. This fear is noticeable in Saint Augustine himself. He had proceeded no further than the Rhone, in Gaul, when he became so terrified by the dire things related there of the Anglo-Saxons that he turned back and made his misgivings known to the pope. Saint Gregory held fast to his purpose. However, he now amply provided the monks with letters of recommendation designed to secure them the support of the Frankish bishops and rulers; especially were Brunhilda and her grandsons urged to lend their assistance. They did so; and Bishop Syagrius of Autun likewise acceded to the pope's request, being rewarded with the pallium. Clotaire II, who controlled the coastal regions in Neustria, was also won over to the project. Accompanied by Frankish priests as interpreters, Saint Augustine (who had probably received episcopal consecration while passing through Gaul) was able to land in Kent at the end of the year 596.

Augustine's fear of the Anglo-Saxons, though exaggerated, was not unreasonable, for they occupied a unique position among the Germanic tribes which had settled on Roman soil. In the interval since the middle of the fifth century, when they had first come from the German coasts of the North Sea in Schleswig-Holstein and settled in Britain, the Saxons and Jutes, together with the Angles, had almost completely exterminated the Romanized Britons whom they found in their new home. They proceeded even more ruthlessly than did the Vandals in Africa, who ejected only the Romans in the vicinity of Carthage, whereas the Britons disappeared from the greater portion of the country which had been theirs. However, this took place only after a struggle lasting for two centuries. The resistance of the Romanized Britons could not endure as long as that of the Romans on the continent, for they were relatively few in number, while the invaders continually received fresh reinforcements from their home across the sea. The kingdoms founded by the Anglo-Saxons evidenced a pure Germanic character, such as was manifested by neither Franks nor Burgundians, Goths, Vandals, Suevi or Lombards. In them, practically every vestige of Roman administration, society, literature and culture vanished. Only a few Latin and Celtic words passed into the Anglo-Saxon vocabulary. And like the Roman language, the Christian religion, too, was abolished. The religion of Wotan and the spirit of barbarism triumphed over Christianity and culture.

These were the only Germanic invaders who completely rejected the religion of the kingdom which they overthrew, and the racial and religious gap that arose between them and such Christian Britons as were still able to maintain themselves in the west and the south, was the widest that existed anywhere during the period of the migration of nations. The Britons who were driven out and settled as refugees in that part of western Europe which was named after them, Brittany, transmitted this hatred and fear of the hostile pagans to the nearby Frankish kingdom.

The Anglo-Saxons had brought with them to their new home not only their religion, but also their ancient legal customs, with the old penal law, the judicial gatherings of the freemen, and the traditional order of classes. Their exalted regard for their national customs would of itself inevitably have produced in them strong opposition to Christianity. But in the long run not even the Anglo-Saxons were able to escape the superior culture which Christianity offered. This culture came to them from two quarters: Scotland in the north, through Irish missionaries; and the continent, through the missionaries sent out directly from Rome. And this latter circumstance, in particular — that missionaries from the seat of ancient culture and the heart of the Church made their appearance in England — was destined to be of primary importance.

The country was organized into seven or eight small kingdoms. Saint Augustine went to the one directly opposite the Frankish coast — Kent, where a favorable point of contact presented itself. Bertha, the wife of King Ethelbert, was a Frankish princess, daughter of King Charibert, who once reigned in Paris, and great-grand-daughter of Clovis. Her hand had been given to the pagan king only after he had promised to grant her the free exercise of her religion and to allow her to retain as her permanent chaplain the bishop who would accompany her to Kent. Thus had Bertha come to England in the company of Bishop Liuthard. An old forsaken chapel surviving from Roman times was given her for divine services; she had it dedicated to Saint Martin, the patron of the Franks. And so it came about that here also, as was so often the case in Germanic kingdoms, a king's wife opened the door to Christianity. When Saint Augustine landed on the Isle of Thanet, Bishop Liuthard had already died. Queen Bertha's joy at the news of the arrival of papal missionaries must have been all the greater, therefore, and she could hope that her husband would not bluntly repel these strangers for whom she evinced so much sympathy.

Ethelbert, at the first meeting, did not modify that unbending gravity of demeanor with which the Germans were accustomed to arm themselves against ideas from abroad, and which was characteristic of the attitude they adopted in general during their first contacts with Christianity. Surrounded by his warriors, he received the monks under the open sky as they approached him in solemn liturgical procession, at the head of which was borne a silver crucifix and a picture of the Saviour. When Saint Augustine had finished his sermon on the life, death and resurrection of Christ, and on His teachings and promises, and the address had been translated by the Frankish interpreters, the king said:

> Your words and promises are indeed beautiful, but they are new and uncertain; I cannot, therefore, assent to them without further ado and give up for them everything which I and the whole English

people have observed for so long a period. But since you have come from afar, we will not molest you, but will receive you hospitably; neither will we hinder you from gaining for your faith those who are ready to embrace it.[9]

Thus, without any prejudgment, the Germanic king permitted the missionaries to enter his country. He desired to investigate their teaching with a calm mind. For such a type the even-tempered Roman Benedictines, who proceeded with moderation and who can hardly be said to have favored the heart over the intellect, were the best missionaries.

The monks built a monastery near the outer walls of Canterbury, and, cherishing Roman traditions, dedicated its church to Saints Peter and Paul. On Christmas of that year, 597, their patient waiting was rewarded. King Ethelbert was baptized and gave up his palace to Bishop Augustine. Here the latter erected an episcopal basilica and dedicated it to the Redeemer in memory of the Church of the Redeemer on the Lateran. The monks attached to this church, which later became famous under the title of Christ Church, formed the episcopal cathedral chapter. The institution thus created became typical of England, most episcopal chapters thereafter being composed of monks under a bishop who was at the same time their abbot.

Just as the Roman monks on foreign soil remembered the sacred places of Rome, so at the center of Christendom the progress of the missionaries was followed with the liveliest interest. Saint Gregory was not sparing of letters and gifts to encourage them and promote their work. Particularly memorable are the instructions he sent Augustine. These show, among other things, how inexperienced the Benedictines were, lacking as they did any training in parish and especially in missionary work; how anxiously they sought Rome's decision in matters great and small; how, true to the purpose of their mission, they labored only in accordance with Rome's instructions; and, in particular, how far-seeing the pope was in his judgment of this field of activity. We see him, imbued with the spirit of the Benedictine Rule to which he had pledged

---

9. Bede, *Hist. eccles. Anglorum,* lib. I, c. 25.

himself in the monastery of Saint Andrew more than twenty years before, counseling moderation and mildness and constantly inculcating consideration for those weak ones from whom as much cannot be expected as from the strong. With this spirit he combined, as an old Roman legacy from those born to guide and rule, that sureness of decision which he had had no opportunity of revealing fully while he was prefect of the city.

He first ordered the destruction of the pagan temples in Britain, but speedily changed his mind as to the advisability of this, informing Saint Augustine as soon as he could, through the new group of missionaries being sent out from Rome. The later directions ran as follows:

> Tell Augustine that I have decided, after long considering the matter of the Angles, that their pagan temples need not be destroyed; only the idols set up in them should be demolished. The temples should be sprinkled with holy water; then altars should be erected and relics placed in them; for if those temples are well built, it is fitting that they be employed for the worship of the true God instead of for the cult of demons. If the people see that their temples are not destroyed, they will all the more readily banish error from their hearts and in the knowledge and worship of the true God confidently assemble in the places where they were wont until now to come together. And since they are accustomed to slay many steers as a sacrifice to the demons, they should also be permitted some festivity of this kind, but in another form. On the feast of the dedication of the church or of the saintly martyrs whose relics are there deposited, they might construct tents out of tree branches around the pagan temples now converted into churches and organize in good fellowship a great public banquet; they should not offer the animals to the devil, but they should consume them for the glory of God and then give thanks to the Giver of all gifts; to the end that, if they be permitted some external joys, they will more easily enter into interior joys. For it is, without doubt, impossible to take everything away from hard hearts with one blow. He who desires to climb a high mountain reaches the top only by slow steps, not by leaps.[10]

When the pope had occasion, soon after this, to answer Saint Augustine on certain specific problems, he manifested in all his responses the same prudent and pedagogical broadmindedness.[11]

---

10. *Mon. Germ. Epp.,* II, 331.
11. Ibid., 334 sqq.

Saint Augustine had inquired among other things how he was to act with regard to the difference of rites, Gallican and Roman. He naturally gave preference to the Roman usages in which he had been reared. The pope could not but approve this, but continued:

> I wish you, however, to select carefully that which may please Almighty God the most, regardless of whether you find it in the Roman, the Gallican, or any other Church, and then transmit this to the English Church, which is still young in the faith; for we ought not to love things because of their location, but rather a locality because of its good things.

In answer to Saint Augustine's question of how a church thief was to be punished, Saint Gregory argued the principle that charity must not be forgotten while meting out punishment: "We must punish the faithful just as good fathers punish their own sons, whom they chastise, it is true, but to whom they also bequeath everything they possess." The question whether a woman who is with child may be baptized impressed the pope as somewhat strange. Saint Augustine could have answered it himself and, doubtless, merely wanted papal approval for his own opinion. "Why should it be impossible for such a woman to be baptized? Fecundity is certainly no fault in the eyes of Almighty God. How can that which was given human nature as a gift of Almighty God be a hindrance to the grace of holy Baptism?"

Not only are the responses of Saint Gregory worthy of note for this period, and as bearing on the conversion of the Anglo-Saxons; they became the program according to which later missionaries, laboring with Saint Boniface in Germany, would act. The many ancient popular customs still surrounding the Christian feasts in England and Germany very likely find their explanation in the consideration shown, by Saint Gregory's instructions, to the national folkways. Hence, too, Saint Bede is undoubtedly correct in asserting that the name *Easter* (replacing the *paska* found in the Gothic as well as the Hebrew and the Romance languages) was taken over from that of an Anglo-Saxon goddess of spring, *Eóstre,* whose feast formerly occurred during this period.[12]

---

12. Bede, *De temporum ratione*, c. 15: Migne, *P. L.*, XC, 357.

It was certainly also in accordance with Saint Gregory's instructions that the missionaries, who alone in England knew how to write, put themselves at the disposal of King Ethelbert to record in the Anglo-Saxon language the old traditional law. At its beginning was now placed one single provision concerning the protection of the Christian Church. Thereafter, all Anglo-Saxon legal codes were written in that language, in contrast to the codes of the other Germanic tribes on the continent which at this time were transmitted only in Latin.

The moderate policy of Rome soon produced positive results. By no other Germanic tribe was the Christian religion regarded as a freely accepted creed in the same measure as it was by the Anglo-Saxons. Behind the Roman emissaries stood no foreign political power, posing as their protector and aiming to establish its own domination. The people understood the unselfishness of the missionaries, and their just claim to gratitude: they had brought to England a superior creed, a superior code of morals, and a superior culture, and were moreover anything but obstructive to the development of the national character. Many a time, no doubt, the need of patient, deliberate slowness taxed the zeal of the missionaries to the utmost, but it had this result: that those who had become uncertain in their pagan beliefs finally pushed toward a decision themselves, and the new teaching was much more firmly professed by the converts from the very beginning because they had freely accepted it.

We have a striking example of this in the account of the evangelization of Northumbria: an account which reveals, incidentally, what type of argument impressed the pagans most. For one thing, it was the consideration of the impotence of their own gods, which they demanded should be tested by an ordeal; next, it was their own reflections upon the great mystery of life, upon the purpose of man's existence and the possibility of a life hereafter. Here is excellent testimony to the seriousness of these barbarians and the quality of their intelligence, and proof that not all of them, by any means, were absorbed in the pleasures of this life.

The king appearing as the central figure in the account is Edwin, who had gained the throne of Northumbria in 617, and, proceeding from York, had brought all the other Anglo-Saxon kingdoms save Kent under his rule. With a view to establishing connections with Kent also, he sought the hand of Ethelbert's daughter, Ethelburga, now destined to assume a role similar to her mother's. Like Bertha, she accepted her royal suitor only after he promised to let her live according to her faith; he was, moreover, to allow Paulinus, one of the Roman monks, now consecrated a bishop, to reside near her in York.

Paulinus labored for a long while to convert the king. Finally Edwin convoked a *witenagemot* and asked the attendant nobles for their opinion, beginning with the pagan high priest Coïfi. With unprecedented frankness the fiery Coïfi renounced the ancient gods: "If the gods had any power, they would have better supported me, who have served them with extraordinary zeal. If that which is now preached to us is better and proves itself more powerful upon being tested, we will accept it without hesitation." Next, one of the *ealdormen* gave his opinion:

> When thou, O king, art seated at table about the hearth in a comfortably heated hall in winter time with thy earls and thanes, when the storms howl without and the snow and rain come lashing, it may possibly happen that a sparrow flies rapidly through the hall; it comes in through one door and goes out by another. For the short time that it is in the room the harsh weather does not touch it, but when it disappears from thy gaze, it soon returns to the dark winter. This seems to me to be the case with the life of man. We know not what has gone before it nor what will follow it. If the new teaching furnishes us with something certain about that, it deserves to be followed.

Upon Paulinus' then expounding his doctrine, Coïfi openly declared himself for it. The king followed him.

In addition, however, Coïfi wanted to prove conclusively to all present the powerlessness of the pagan gods. Since a pagan priest was forbidden to touch arms and might ride only a mare, Coïfi besought the king that weapons and a stallion should be brought to him. When the dismayed multitude beheld the priest riding toward them thus armed and mounted in deliberate defiance of the ancient gods, they believed he had suddenly gone mad. But Coïfi galloped straight up to the pagan temple, and before the eyes of all hurled his lance against it without suffering any injury. No one then prevented the temple from being fired and destroyed.[13]

We already know that the Germans were extremely susceptible to demonstrations like this, which had the effect of ordeals. At the same time their instinct was to resist any teaching combined with foreign customs, or imposed by force. The Roman missionaries acted with prudence, therefore, in respecting the Anglo-Saxon national character. How far this attitude was carried is seen in the fact that the Anglo-Saxons whom we meet in the days of these Roman missionaries manifest exactly the same traits as the Englishmen of today, their good qualities as well as their weaknesses—their tastes and amusements, their pride, their evenness of temper, their energy and love of self-government, their very parliamentary system, are identical. The missionaries also showed great regard for the Anglo-Saxon language. While it is true that Latin became the medium of the liturgy and of intellectual culture, it is significant that King Ethelbert of Kent, the first ruler to be converted by Saint Augustine, began the recording of Anglo-Saxon laws in the native tongue. Still more noteworthy is it that these codes are purely German in legal content, untouched by the influence of Roman law.

Just as a growing youth is attached to an understanding teacher who aims not at suppressing his pupil's individual traits, but merely at supervising and regulating them, so did the Anglo-Saxons show themselves grateful to Rome. This became particularly evident during the period of trial which the Anglo-Saxon mission, like every other, had to undergo.

Ancient paganism tried more than once to fight back. The very political differences between the various kingdoms led some to adhere to paganism because others adopted Christianity. In Kent, paganism experienced a revival under Ethelbert's son, which in turn was offset in Northumbria where the seed sown by Paulinus of York sprang up most promisingly under Ethelbert's son-in-law, King Edwin. But when Edwin was defeated and killed in 633 by the pagan king of Mercia, paganism reigned once more in the north also. When the time came that the generation of the Roman

---

13. Bede, *Hist. eccles. Angl.*, lib. II, c. 13.

missionaries was dying out with the kings they had baptized, Christianity was still essentially restricted to Kent.

At this juncture, Irish missionaries entered the breach. They came from the colony of monks established by Saint Columba on the island of Iona, where Edwin's nephew Oswald had been reared in exile. When Oswald reconquered Northumbria in 635, he immediately called in the Irish missionaries, prominent among whom were saints possessed of rare and deep piety. As a mission center for Northumbria, a second Iona arose on the lonely island of Lindisfarne in the North Sea. Because the Irish missionaries leaned less on the kings than did the Roman, they gained the masses more easily. They were more popular and sympathetic, devoting themselves especially to the poor and the oppressed. Saint Aidan, for example, the founder of Lindisfarne, never gave the nobles presents, and when he himself accepted such, immediately distributed them among the needy or used them for the ransom of captives.

But those Anglo-Saxons who critically compared the method of the Irish missionaries with that of the Roman emissaries could not remain in doubt as to which side should be given preference.

The Celts — the dislodged Britons in the west even more than the Irish — were at this time the national enemies of the Anglo-Saxons, and this enmity was mutual. The Christian priests of the Britons refused to have any communion with Saint Augustine. In the first place, they found it insuperably hard to acquiesce in the salvation of the ruthless barbarian peoples who had driven them from their homes and murdered so many Christians; secondly, they feared further national extinction and political oppression. The Anglo-Saxons, on the other hand, could not easily be induced to submit themselves to Celtic leaders even in purely spiritual matters. In fact, if the Celts alone had dominated the mission field, the Anglo-Saxons would have become Celtic in part, just as on the continent there ensued a Romanization of the Germans who lived side by side with the Romans and were converted by them. The Celts also were much less disposed than the Roman Benedictines, guided by Saint Gregory's instructions, to accommodate themselves to the national character of the Anglo-Saxons. Even more narrowmindedly than on the continent they adhered to their own external peculiarities — their tonsure, their mode of computing Easter, and their monastic organization. They showed little of the consideration whereby the Romans attracted converts — instead repelling the greater number by their inconsiderate severity. Finally, comparing the British-Irish Church and its saints, deserving though these certainly were of all honor, with the tradition of the Roman Church and its martyrs, headed by Saint Peter, the Prince of the Apostles, there could be no doubt as to where the pre-eminence of authority, of tradition and of history lay.

Decisive in fixing the Anglo-Saxon's choice upon the Romans was Saint Wilfrid, prototype of the Englishman who goes his own way and perseveres in it in the face of all opposition. He early entered the monastery of Lindisfarne; but as the Irish practices did not suit him, he left when a youth of eighteen (about 652) and went to Canterbury. There the young man formed the unusual resolution of traveling to Rome in order to become acquainted with the customs of that Church which attracted him as the center of Christendom. Arriving in Rome, he first visited Saint Andrew's, the monastery whence Saint Augustine had come. On his return journey Saint Wilfrid received the Petrine tonsure at Lyons, thus setting himself early, at least in one important external detail, in opposition to the Celtic missionaries. On his return to England, he introduced the Roman practices, and some time later also the Benedictine Rule, into the monastery of Ripon.

In 664 King Oswy of Northumbria, Oswald's brother and successor, organized a synod in the monastery of Streaneshalch (now Whitby), at which the Irish and the Roman parties were to discuss their differences, and particularly the Easter question. Saint Wilfrid was the spokesman for the Roman group, Saint Colman, abbot-bishop of Lindisfarne, for the Irish. Saint Wilfrid finally swung the decision in his favor when he retorted to the Irish representative:

> Even if your fathers were saints, can a small community in a corner of an outlying island be preferred to the Universal Church of Christ, which is spread over the whole world? And if your Columba, who is also ours insofar as he belonged to Christ, was a saint and mighty by his virtues, can he for any reason be accorded precedence

over the most holy Prince of the Apostles, to whom the Lord said: "Thou art Peter and upon this rock I will build My Church and the gates of hell shall not prevail against it: and I will give to thee the keys of the kingdom of heaven"?

The king then closed the debate with the words:

> Since this Peter is the gatekeeper of heaven, I will not contradict him, but will obey his orders in all things to the best of my knowledge and ability, so that, when I arrive at the portals of the kingdom, the one who can open them will not fail me. This would certainly happen if he who has the key of heaven turned away from me.[14]

The nobles assented to their king's decision. Saint Colman departed with his brethren from Northumbria. Saint Wilfrid, however, could not possess in peace the episcopal see of York, to which he was soon afterward elected. Twice he went to Rome to vindicate his rights, the last time in 703; upon his return he had to content himself with the small and recently established bishopric of Hexham and the monastery of Ripon.

Everywhere, in the course of his many journeys, he zealously advocated the acceptance of the Roman customs. He founded several monasteries in which he introduced the Benedictine Rule, and delighted to imitate in his monastic churches the splendor and magnificence observed in the basilicas of Rome and Gaul. The culture which he had witnessed in Rome, preserved and transmitted by the Church, he wanted to give to his native England as well. But in this design he always remained the monk, holding monasticism to be, as it actually was, the support of civilization. He died on October 12, 709, leaving a testament which clearly reflects his ideas. His gold and silver was divided into four portions; Rome was to receive one portion, the second was to go to the poor, the third was to be given to the abbots of Ripon and Hexham, and the fourth was to be distributed among those who had accompanied him on all his voyages.

Saint Wilfrid did not in fact accomplish the organization of the Anglo-Saxon Church. For such a task his impetuous nature

---

14. Ibid., lib. III, c. 25.

lacked the requisite calm. He had, however, blazed the trail for a new intervention on the part of Rome, and through this intervention the Anglo-Saxon Church was finally organized.

Not long after the decisive synod of Whitby, the kings of Northumbria and Kent petitioned the pope by embassy to send them a new archbishop. Pope Vitalian selected the seventy-year-old monk Theodore, then residing in Rome, for this difficult post. Born in Cilician Tarsus, the native city of Saint Paul, and educated in Athens, Theodore possessed extraordinary learning. He came to Canterbury in 669 and rewarded the Anglo-Saxons for their adherence to Rome with all that the ancient culture and the Roman talent for organization could offer them. After visiting the churches throughout the kingdoms, Theodore held the first general synod for the Anglo-Saxon Church at Hertford in 672 or 673. Among the resolutions there formulated, the first dealt with the celebration of Easter, which was to be observed in accordance with the Roman calculation. Gradually the Britons and Irish were won over to this, which in turn brought about a more friendly attitude toward them, so that a mutual interplay of good qualities became possible. Roman experience, traditional classic learning, Celtic asceticism, and wholesome Anglo-Saxon vigor were reconciled, and in consequence the Anglo-Saxon Church and Christian culture soon after Theodore's arrival entered a period of unique flowering.

That such a development was impossible on the continent can be explained only by the fact that the influence of corrupt ancient society produced a general decline of morality there. This influence did not operate in England to disturb the natural course of events. Once again we see confirmed the opinion so often advanced in this book: that the Roman Empire had to be destroyed in order to allow a new Christian culture to unfold itself in the West.

The new forces matured quickly. Anglo-Saxons began to enter the service of the Church in great numbers. The spirit of the Church permeated the entire population, and expressed itself spontaneously and freely. Institutions of learning rose on all sides and unparalleled literary activity manifested itself. The English cultural advance was soon recognized by the Frankish kingdom, which now sought its own teachers in England. This was a circumstance of no little significance. It should have been the task and duty of the Franks to evangelize and educate the Anglo-Saxons and serve as the link between them, on the one hand, and Rome and the countries inheriting the ancient culture, on the other. Their king, Clovis, had been baptized a hundred years before Ethelbert, the first Christian king of the Anglo-Saxons; in his period the Frankish Church still possessed intact the organization that dated from Roman times, whereas that of the Anglo-Saxon Church was not acquired until some two hundred years later. Geographically the Franks were much closer to the bearers of Rome's cultural tradition than were the Anglo-Saxons. Yet it was the latter who first earned the distinction of bringing to the countries north of the Alps the renaissance that marked the Middle Ages. To enter into relations with Rome was regarded by the Anglo-Saxon nobility as the highest honor. This accounts for the desire on the part of many Anglo-Saxon kings to make pilgrimages to Rome; the nobles, and especially the women, followed.

The synod of Hertford in 672/3 laid the foundation for all this by replacing the fluctuating status of a mission church with a firm external and internal organization. It ordained that no bishop might interfere in the diocese of another, nor encroach upon the liberty and possessions of the monasteries; that the monks might not wander about from place to place; that clerics should remain faithful to their dioceses; and that a general synod should be held once a year on the first of August at Clovesho. To the old bishoprics were added new ones, so that finally there were sixteen under the jurisdiction of the primate, the archbishop of Canterbury. The organization of parishes was more difficult, since few local centers were in existence. Hence the priests betook themselves to the estates of the nobles, where they erected crosses around which the people gathered for divine services. These visible signs of the triumph of Christianity — symbols as well of the victory of civilization over barbarism — made a particularly deep impression, which was manifested especially in sculpture and poetry. Tall stone crosses were made, often adorned with a wreath that encircled the arms, and with inscriptions and images.

The monasteries also helped out in the rural districts, and their position grew in importance because of the fact that an episcopal see was almost always connected with a monastery. Thus the English Church was very largely the result of the activity of the monks. This corresponded to the initial stages of the mission that emanated from the Roman Benedictines and made the English Church similar to the ancient Irish Church. The abbots of the monasteries, freely elected, enjoyed great esteem and actually were often members of the royal family. The kings vied with one another in their grants to monasteries and churches.

In caring for the souls of the laity, penitential books were employed — one of these is traceable to Theodore, who as a monk could not but approve the introduction of monastic confession among the laity. Confession was required before Holy Communion, but as a rule the laity received only on Christmas, Epiphany and Easter. Apparently they were not urged to more frequent reception, for Saint Bede laments that even the most pious laymen dared not communicate often. "There are countless persons," he declares, "who could without any scruples communicate every Sunday and holyday, as you yourselves have witnessed in the holy, apostolic Roman Church."[15] We learn from this that the ancient practice of receiving Holy Communion every Sunday was gradually abandoned. On the other hand, special attention was directed to preaching, since here, of course, the language of the liturgy was not the language of the people. The instruction of the laity in the vernacular was expressly prescribed. First of all, the monks and priests must explain the Ten Commandments, the Our Father, and the Creed, but they were also to translate for the laity the principal parts of the Mass and the words pronounced at baptism. Besides this, they were required on Sundays to read and preach upon the Epistle and Gospel in the popular tongue. Numerous Anglo-Saxon homilies and translations from Sacred Scripture are preserved to us as proofs of this instruction.

Sunday rest was strictly observed. The penitential book ascribed to Theodore enumerates quite minutely which forms of

---

15. Bede, *Ep. ad Egbertum*: Migne, *P. L.*, XCIV, 666.

work were forbidden on the Lord's Day. In this connection the several occupations for women are reviewed — knitting, sewing, spinning, laundering, wool-picking and sheep-shearing. Everyone had to attend church on Sundays. The divine service, which was conducted according to the Roman liturgy, acquired a particular charm through the solemn Roman chant and the music of the organ. This instrument, mentioned in a document of the year 680,[16] had probably been introduced by Theodore from Greece; we hear of it in Rome for the first time under Pope Vitalian, who had sent Theodore to England.

The achievements of the Benedictines in cultivating the arts and humanities stand out with particular brilliance. Archbishop Theodore and the African Hadrian, who accompanied him from Rome, established a famous school at Canterbury, in which they themselves delighted to teach exegesis, ecclesiastical arithmetic, that is, chronology (computation of the Church calendar), prosody, astronomy and music, but especially Latin and Greek. Theodore possessed a copy of Homer, in which he often read. The knowledge of Greek gave the Anglo-Saxon monastery schools a special pre-eminence. Many of the monks had such a command of the classical languages that they could use them as fluently as their mother tongue. And following the example of Canterbury, men and women in general sought to educate themselves in monasteries and convents respectively. In view of the general cultural needs, particular stress was laid upon creating libraries, and efforts were also made to procure books from Italy, in addition to relics and images.

The monastery schools did not limit themselves to training future monks; the sons of the nobility were also sent there to be educated. The sound pedagogical principles embodied in their Rule undoubtedly qualified the Benedictines in a special way to nurture young minds with wisdom. The impression we gain of their educational activity in England is indeed an excellent one, and the paternal interest the teachers had in their pupils was an outstanding characteristic. We will cite briefly two examples out of many.

---

16. *Mon. Germ. Auct. ant.*, XV, 510; cf. ibid., p. 356, v. 71.

Saint John of Beverley, a monk under Princess Hilda, abbess of the twin monastery at Whitby, was later bishop of Hexham and then of York; it was he who conferred the priesthood upon Saint Bede. This distinguished prelate devoted himself patiently to giving a poor deaf-mute training in speech; incidentally, a very important piece of information for the history of the education of these unfortunates. Another time we see the same bishop going on one of his visitations, followed by his pupils on horseback. The pupils proposed to take advantage of an inviting meadow to arrange a race — we know how old this sport is in England. Only reluctantly did the bishop give his permission, because he had forebodings of an accident; and one actually did befall, as he had feared.

Let us observe more closely some of the monastery schools and monastic scholars. One of the pupils of Theodore and Hadrian was Saint Aldhelm, a member of the West Saxon royal family, who became the celebrated abbot of Malmesbury, in Wessex, and later bishop of Sherborne. Here he died in 709. The monastery, founded by an Irishman, was converted by Aldhelm into a school for Anglo-Saxon and Irish pupils, who lived peaceably there with one another. What importance he attached to relations with Rome can be gauged from the fact that he himself undertook the journey thither. His knowledge of Latin poetry was very remarkable, covering the works of Virgil, Prudentius, Venantius Fortunatus and Sedulius (whose *Paschal Ode,* written in Achaia in the fifth century, contains the oldest example in a Latin hymn of a direct invocation to the Blessed Virgin Mary: *Salve, sancta parens*). In addition to studying these poets Saint Aldhelm likewise imitated them, albeit in a very artificial manner. Prone to indulge in word-play, and with a fondness for acrostics and logogriphs, he had also a persistent penchant for alliteration and rhyme. His Germanic predilection for riddles appears in his letter on metrics to King Aldfrith of Northumbria, to which he appended a hundred riddles in rhyme, doubtless patterned on the riddle poems of the fourth-century writer Symphosius. In a work intended for nuns which blends prose and verse, Aldhelm combines a treatment of the excellence of virginity with a poem on the eight principal vices, composed after the manner of Prudentius' *Psychomachia.* One of his extant letters, addressed to King

Geraint of Wales at the request of an ecclesiastical synod, remonstrates with western Britons for adhering to the old Celtic computation of Easter and form of tonsure.

A similar and even more important influence was that of Saint Benedict Biscop, founder of the two closely connected monasteries of Wearmouth and Jarrow, near York, in Northumbria. He, too, was of noble descent. He was repeatedly in Rome — on the first occasion, with Saint Wilfrid — and sojourned at Lérins for two years to imbibe the monastic spirit there. He was one of the monks commissioned by Pope Vitalian to conduct Theodore to England when the latter was appointed archbishop of Canterbury. Whatever Benedict was able to acquire in Italy in the way of works of art and books, he stored in his monasteries; thus he initiated in them that tradition of absorbing and transmitting ancient culture which his successor, Ceolfrid, fostered to an even greater degree.

The name of Saint Ceolfrid is connected with a famous codex of the Bible: he had three copies made of Saint Jerome's translation of the Scriptures. One of these was intended for the pope, and although Ceolfrid himself died on his way to Rome to make the presentation (716), his companions carried out his intention. This codex wandered from Rome to the Cistercian abbey of Monte Amiata, near Siena, in consequence of which it came to bear the name of *Codex Amiatinus;* today it is the ornament of the Laurentian Library in Florence, renowned as representing the oldest text of the Vulgate. It was because of these copies which Saint Ceolfrid caused to be made that the excellent Vulgate texts spread from Northumbria to Italy and the Frankish kingdom. Thus early was England able to pay her debt of gratitude to Italy, which had sent her so many scholars and books.

Saint Benedict Biscop and Saint Ceolfrid were especially instrumental in preparing the ground for a literary burgeoning of extraordinary richness. This is, in more than one respect, of universal interest for the history of civilization. It makes plain to us that impulses proceeding from different national groups work with peculiar effectiveness in co-operation with each other. Not wisely nor truly may it be assumed as a matter of course that a pronouncedly one-sided, nationalistic education is the best foundation for cultural development. On the contrary, not a few outstanding centers of culture lie on the frontiers of national groups. Parallels to Jarrow are found later in the regions of northern France and northern Italy, where Germanic and Roman elements intermingled, and in Prague, Berlin and Vienna, where Slavic and German elements came in contact with one another.

The monasteries of Saint Benedict Biscop brought their influence to bear upon Celts as well as Anglo-Saxons. This is apparent even in the hagiography produced in this circle. Eddius wrote the biography of Saint Wilfrid, severe opponent of the Irish — the oldest known Latin work by an Anglo-Saxon. Another subject of literary treatment in this epoch was Saint Aidan's admirer, the holy Saint Cuthbert, who was first a shepherd and then a monk. Cuthbert was very active in missionary work in rural districts, and also in monastic offices; later he lived as a hermit on the barren, rock-bound island of Farne, whence Theodore summoned him in 685 to consecrate him bishop of nearby Lindisfarne. His tomb here was highly venerated throughout the Middle Ages. At this time, too, a biography of the Irish monk Saint Fursey was written in the Frankish kingdom. He had preached among the East Angles and then gone to France (about 641), where he founded the abbey of Lagny near Paris. An Irish colony grew up around his grave in Péronne, which became the continental mart for the literature of the British Isles during the Carolingian period.

In the life-story of this Irish missionary (a work which made a considerable stir), we can observe how the Irish character and the Roman Benedictine spirit were reconciled and fused — the end for which the Northumbrian monks, and especially Saint Ceolfrid, had been working. The visions described in this writing present for the first time material to which believing minds turned often in the Middle Ages until it received its most perfect expression in the immortal work of Dante. Saint Fursey during a severe illness sees himself in vision as transported to the kingdom of the heavenly spirits. Even while he enjoys their blissful companionship, he senses the punishments of the reprobate. At the same time he is instructed as to how the actions of men on earth are judged in heaven; and here the Irish imagination, excited by the thought of the imminent end of the world, is tempered notably by the moderation and wise discretion characteristic of the Roman Benedictines. The seer undoubtedly must accuse himself of having sometimes wrongfully engaged in worldly affairs, but he hears the teaching of Saint Beoan (Benedict) announced in the principle: "Do not always hold yourself aloof from the world, nor always show yourself in public."[17] He does not regard corporal mortification as the highest ideal, but reflects that meat and drink are created by God and that God has permitted men to use created things. Pride he must abhor, however, as the root of all sin. The combination we find here of Irish religious ardor and moderating Benedictine wisdom was one that bore the finest fruits.

Just as the Irish finally came to appreciate the calm and quiet activity of the Benedictines, so the latter admired and imitated the Irish passion for producing artistic manuscripts. And Saint Bede, one of the most eminent of the Anglo-Saxon Benedictines, well knew how to do justice to Irish sanctity.

Bede shone as a brilliant star among the writers of this group, and was later given the well-merited title of "Venerable." Externally, his life reveals little variety. It is the quiet life of the scholar, who spends himself in studying and teaching; at the same time it is also the life of a sincere and kindly man, venerated by the few who know him. Born in the monastic domain of Wearmouth in 672 or 673, he was entrusted to the monastery at the age of seven and ordained a priest at the age of thirty. He spent his whole life in the twin monasteries of Wearmouth and Jarrow and died a peaceful death in 735. He used the many valuable library treasures of his monastery to the best of his rare scholarly ability. In addition he procured, through friends who gladly aided him, other materials, especially for his historical works. He composed grammatical and metrical treatises designed to serve as textbooks, exegetical writings, works on mathematics and the natural sciences, and finally, the historical narratives which have earned for him his greatest fame.

---

17. *Acta SS.*, Jan. II, 40.

Among his works in the field of mathematics and the natural sciences were two written only for the classroom: *De temporibus,* a short chronological treatise based entirely upon Saint Isidore; and *De natura rerum,* upon Saint Isidore and the ancient naturalist Pliny. Later Bede wrote a more extensive work on chronology, *De temporum ratione,* to which end he studied the ancient and Christian chronologists and chronographers. This work, which remained fundamental throughout the whole medieval period, influenced thought particularly in the fact that it introduced to the West the Dionysian computation of years according to the birth of Christ. From Isidore, Bede borrowed the division of world history into six eras analagous to the six days of creation. Finally, he appended to each chronological work a historical summary, which would appear often later as the basis for the first part of medieval chronicles. The summary incorporated in the *De temporum ratione* must be appraised at a considerably higher value than the short abstract in the *De temporibus,* for in the former Bede went beyond Isidore's model, adding a seventh and eighth period to the six world eras, and treating the history of the Britons and the Anglo-Saxons more extensively.

Saint Bede also wrote a history of the abbots of the twin monasteries of Wearmouth and Jarrow, dwelling in particular on the labors of the founder, Saint Benedict Biscop; this is the first history of English monasticism. He likewise dealt, in both prose and poetry, with the life of Saint Cuthbert, the pious bishop of Lindisfarne.

His most important work is the *Ecclesiastical History of the English People,* which he completed in 731. He strove most conscientiously to procure reliable sources for this work and even had papal documents sent him from Rome. In critical exactitude, sound chronology and in form of presentation, Saint Bede's history far excels the work of Saint Gregory of Tours and the other national histories dating from these times. It constitutes the finest illustration of the heights to which the young Christian culture of the Anglo-Saxons had rapidly attained. Bede's calm, deliberate manner of judgment and his pure patriotic sentiments gave his work great value.

If we review the writings of Saint Bede and their effect on the minds of men, we must call him one of the foremost and best teachers of the medieval period. In his own native country, the fruits of his quiet activity were soon perceptible. They manifested themselves first in his pupil Egbert, a son of the royal family. He was elevated to the see of York, and in 735 he received the pallium together with the long withheld rights of a metropolitan of that see. In a prudent epistle to which we shall return later, Saint Bede outlined for his former pupil a program of wise episcopal activity.

Most helpful to the practical success of Egbert's efforts was his close agreement with his brother, King Eadbert of Northumbria. The harmony between the two found expression in the coins of the period, which carried legends of both the king and the archbishop. Through the latter's exertions, the cathedral school of York became a center of ecclesiastical learning which soon eclipsed Jarrow: it may be regarded as having been for the next half-century the intellectual center of the West. In particular, Egbert must be credited with early discovering among his pupils the one who would be foremost in raising the learning and repute of York to the heights of honor — Alcuin, whom he sent to the continent to collect manuscripts. In 766, Alcuin himself became the director of the cathedral school. The activity in which this renowned teacher engaged on the continent, when Charlemagne called him to his side, will be treated later.

The convents, which show an extraordinary growth during this period, had their own part in the literary awakening. Indeed, the enthusiasm and the ideal aspirations evinced in them were hardly paralleled anywhere in any age. One tends to recall the era of Saint Ambrose and Saint Jerome, when Roman matrons exhibited so beautiful a conception of the position to which woman had been raised by Christianity. But that earlier movement, bound up almost entirely as it was with the personal activity of the great churchmen, endured only for a short time. In England the movement proceeded in much greater measure from the women themselves, and therefore lasted much longer. It can be traced in full vigor for at least a hundred years; only at the middle of the eighth century does it begin to flag. Its external manifestations here are also much more striking and peculiar.

Understandably, there has been a great deal of speculation on the causes of this enthusiasm of Anglo-Saxon women for the ideals of the Christian religion. An answer quickly suggests itself in the fact that it was the women of the chief Anglo-Saxon families, above all those of the blood royal, who were the leaders of the movement. They were the first to submit to a more intensive cultivation of the heart and mind by embracing the Christian teaching; and they were particularly responsive to the opportunity of raising the honor and dignity of womanhood which the idealizing of virginity made possible. They felt themselves called to play a new role as bearers of culture. Considered from this point of view, the flourishing state of the Anglo-Saxon convents is bound up with the service performed by the queens of the Germans, and in particular of the Anglo-Saxons, in introducing Christianity; among others who might be recalled, we mention only Bertha of Kent and Ethelburga of Northumbria.

But there are other factors which must be taken into consideration. Count Montalembert, in *The Monks of the West,* writes a very sympathetic chapter, still valuable today, on the Anglo-Saxon nuns,[18] pointing out that their approach to Christianity derived from the lofty position of Germanic women in pagan times as the custodians of spiritual culture. He adds that it was also an effect of that high regard for chastity which Tacitus lauded among the Germans.[19] We should like to amplify this. We find a similar situation obtaining among the Irish. It is the natural morality of peoples who are primitive and barbaric, but uncorrupted. In contrast to that decadent Roman society which could be transformed only by Christianity — this was accomplished on the Continent only after the collapse of the Roman Empire — the natural morality we have been considering prepared a favorable foundation for Christianity, especially in the women.

The Irish, finally, have a special share in the credit for the enthusiastic reception of Christianity by Anglo-Saxon women. Dur-

18. *Les moines d'Occident,* V, 5.
19. *Germania,* c. 8, 17, 19.

ing the Christian beginnings in England, the daughters of numerous illustrious Anglo-Saxon families were sent to Gaul to be educated in convents erected in those centers under the influence of Saint Columbanus. For examples, we meet very many of these women in Faremoûtier.

Soon convents were being established in England itself, and the number of nuns in one foundation often ran into the hundreds. These convents, endowed with royal liberality, formed kingdoms with many subjects; they were generally directed by abbesses of royal blood. In the convent of Ely three queens — one from Northumbria, one from Kent and one from Mercia — served successively as abbesses. These women occupied a high place in secular society in virtue of their birth. They also appeared at councils, if one may so name those assemblies in which both clergy and laity took part. Saint Hilda, the foundress of the great convent of Whitby, in Yorkshire, on the black rocks facing the North Sea, attended the council held there in 664. She was approached by the kings for advice as though she were the sovereign princess of the country. The monastery connected with her convent Saint Hilda converted into a seminary for bishops and missionaries; here also lived Caedmon, the poet-herdsman, whom she took from obscure servitude and educated. Her successor, Saint Elfleda, defended Saint Wilfrid at the council on the Nidd river in 705, which was presided over by Archbishop Brihtwald of Canterbury. The acts of the council of Beccanceld, held in 694, bore among others the signatures of five abbesses. Most remarkable of all was the post many abbesses occupied as directresses of twin monasteries: which situation arose when a monastery of monks had been joined to a convent of nuns, both houses being then subject to the abbess.

In these joint monasteries the literary occupations of the monks were soon imitated by the nuns, and thus we see the cultural level in Anglo-Saxon convents rising to a degree extraordinary for that time. The nuns wrote Latin with ease, and took the greatest pains to make their mark even in the artificial accomplishment of versifying in that tongue. They also copied books. On the other hand, they did not neglect needlework; indeed, they gained renown for their proficiency in this art, particularly in the making of ecclesiastical vestments. Costly embroidery was for a long time designated as *opus anglicum* (English work). Sometimes, it is true, they also used their skill to make fancy articles of clothing for themselves; and for this they were severely reprimanded.

Two convents were outstanding for their studies. One, which both the sister and the wife of King Ine had entered, was at Barking, on the Thames. It was to the nuns of this convent that Saint Aldhelm addressed several letters, as well as his somewhat pedantic poem in praise of virginity. From Barking, the cultivation of learning was transplanted to the convent of Wimborne, in the vicinity of the royal residence of Wessex. Here there were five hundred nuns. And here Saint Lioba, that amiable nun who followed Saint Boniface into his mission field in Germany, was educated. The letters written by the Anglo-Saxon nuns to the Apostle of Germany are our chief witnesses alike to the high degree of culture of these nuns and their profound spirituality. The legends entwined about the memories of many of them enable us to understand the impression which saintly women aspiring to the highest ideals of the human mind and heart made upon contemporary society.

The joy they so clearly found in uniting themselves in pious communities to strive for a common aim, has been looked upon by some in our own time as the first sign of the emancipation of Englishwomen. The position which so many former queens and daughters and sisters of kings occupied as the heads of joint monasteries certainly reveals something of that satisfaction connected with independent action and that spirit of personal initiative which are perhaps more characteristic of Englishwomen than of any others. Similarly, the many pilgrimages of English nuns to Rome — Saint Boniface later painted in somber colors the disadvantages these involved — remind us of the passion for traveling so evident in modern Englishwomen. Yet we must not allow ourselves to forget that the efforts of the great majority of nuns were directed simply and unselfishly toward the Christian ideal, which they sought to attain by submitting to the Church's authority and to monastic obedience. The development considered above was for the most part only an effect of their joyful longing to experience how woman is appreciated by Christianity *as* woman, with her tender feeling and devotion, her spirit of sacrifice and patience. A new era had dawned. Man's energy and strength were no longer the only themes of praise, but woman's endurance and renunciation as well. Now, not only the man could give his existence a higher value by refusing to marry in order to be free for his bold deeds as a feudal retainer, but the woman also, who renounced marriage to consecrate her whole life to the service of the Highest Master.

The changes which took place in the Anglo-Saxon soul in connection with its conversion to Christianity are observed likewise in the poetry of the period. This deserves attention as the first example of the use of their language by a Germanic people to express the sentiments implanted in their hearts by the teachers of the Catholic Church. It seemed a miracle to the men of that day when Caedmon, a stableman at the monastery of Whitby who had never been able to sing secular songs, spontaneously composed a hymn in honor of the Creator, the Good Guardian of Heaven, the Father of Glory and Leader of the Hosts from all eternity. Saint Hilda, the abbess, made it her concern to foster this talent which had been discovered within her territorial domains. She had the poet received into the monastery as a lay brother and instructed in spiritual things, with the result that he put into verse much additional Scriptural matter as it was related to him. Soon, other poets followed in the path marked out by Caedmon.

This early development of vernacular religious poetry, which took place between 657 and 680, while the abbess Hilda presided over the monastery, accorded with the pastoral tradition of Lindisfarne. Whitby always manifested a greater interest in popular Anglo-Saxon customs than was shown in the south of England; there, when Saint Aldhelm wrote poetry and even personally recited popular poems, it was in the learned Latin tongue. Just as the form of Caedmon's *Hymn* corresponded in rhythm and alliteration to the ancient national song of praise, so too the images, and even the sentiments, were borrowed from what was most deeply rooted in the race. The naive yet stirring manner in which the power of God was celebrated illustrates this. In their ancient lays the Anglo-Saxon pagan warriors praised above all the man of strength, the intrepid leader who excelled all others, and the loyalty of those who followed him as comrades. The warlike deeds of such a hero were sung with awe and admiration and embellished with wild, barbaric imagination.

But new tones, springing from Christian sentiments, also found their way into this poetry. In *Beowulf,* the only ancient Anglo-Saxon poem of secular content preserved in its entirety, the pagan folklore originating in the Danish kingdom and in Gothland is shot through with Christian ideas and feelings. It was a Christian poet at the royal court of Mercia who, working from oral traditions, and seemingly with Virgil in some measure as his model, gave this epic its fixed form at the end of the seventh or the beginning of the eighth century. Not content with merely praising the strength of Beowulf, he also describes his hero as a moral paragon who modestly and unselfishly spends his strength to free his people from monsters. Beowulf is the "mildest of men," who has already acquired something of the new virtues of Christianity about which the men at the king's court first learned from the missionaries.

The poem *Exodus,* the first of several epics to take their material from Sacred Scripture, presents the new ideal of virtue in an even bolder manner. Composed by a cleric who imitated Caedmon, it deals with the departure of the Israelites from Egypt. It is based on the most important composition treating Biblical themes which Latin poetry has to offer: a work of Saint Avitus including a section on the passage through the Red Sea. The central figure in this Anglo-Saxon poem is Moses; but the native notions are preserved by making the great Jewish lawgiver into a sort of liege lord and protector of the people, such as the newly converted kings were still considered to be.

The Saviour Himself appears thus in the famous hymn of the Cross, which was not of Caedmon's authorship, as has been claimed, but composed by a countryman of his some decades later. The composition was occasioned perhaps by the spread of the feast of the Exaltation of the Cross, for which Pope Sergius I (687-701), a native of Syria, labored zealously. The poetic theme is similar to that of Venantius Fortunatus in the *Pange, lingua, gloriosi proelium certaminis,* which he wrote in praise of the relic of the True Cross sent from Constantinople to Poitiers for Saint Radegunde. In the

Anglo-Saxon poem, however, we encounter Germanic conceptions interwoven with the main idea. Christ is the hero, lamented over by His nobles who have pledged Him their fidelity. The cross itself is personified and represented as a retainer of the Saviour. The deeply sensitive poet mourns for his fellow-warriors whom death has taken from him. He hopes to find them again, however, with the King of the heavenly army; and the cross has been sent him by God as a companion to help him realize this hope. The hymn reminds us of the special veneration which the Anglo-Saxons, no less than the Irish, accorded to the crosses set up in the rural districts; hence it is not surprising to find a portion of this hymn of the Cross carved in runic characters on one of the most renowned of these, the High Cross of Ruthwell.

In the course of time these Germanic concepts receded. None are found in the Biblical epic *Genesis,* which in unmistakable imitation of Caedmon recounts the creation. In the epic *Daniel,* an Old Testament hero is again the central figure, but one whom the poet praises as a sage and prophet, not as a warrior. No longer is the physically strong man the ideal. He has been supplanted by the wise and experienced man of God, who knows how to control himself, how to suffer, and how to seek his peace in God. Such was the hero of another Anglo-Saxon poem, the holy hermit Guthlac who departed this life in 714. It was over the relics of Saint Guthlac that the abbey of Crowland in Lincolnshire was built, and there, probably, that his legend was turned into verse. To teach confidence in God is also the purpose of the poem *Andreas,* which presents legendary material possibly borrowed from the Latin revision of a Greek original. Here we still find something of the old interest in sea voyages and combats with monsters. Very close to the author of this poem stands another poet, Cynewulf — the first to whom we can with certainty ascribe several works. Actually, however, he belongs to the second half of the eighth century. A priest who had once lived a worldly life, he turned his knowledge of liturgy and hagiography, as well as his former experiences, to the poetic treatment of a variety of religious topics. In depicting scenes of combat, Cynewulf often imitates *Beowulf.* His extant works include a poem on the Ascension, one on the miracle of

Pentecost, the legends of Saints Helena and Juliana, and a short composition on the fates of the Apostles.[20]

In considering the recasting of Germanic notions into Christian concepts, we must allow for the fact that the ancient poems, when they came to be written down, were written down by priests, for only priests knew how to write. (On the other hand, it is also priests, and they alone, whom we have to thank that remnants of the poetry of pagan times have survived.) The new materials which the ecclesiastical poets shaped and the new evaluations which they suggested naturally affected the readers or hearers, and especially those susceptible to spiritual suggestions. We can thus observe in these poems not only the persistence of many native popular ideas, but also the education of the Anglo-Saxons to Christianity; we can behold the barbarous man of might, who strives after military glory, transformed into a champion of the Christian faith who seeks not himself but only the glory of God. Further: just as the human virtues were purified and completed in this process, so too a rich store of new material was now added in the intellectual field as a result of acquaintance with the Bible and the culture of antiquity.

As the number of monks and priests multiplied and their culture grew more profound, their influence upon the minds and hearts of the people necessarily increased. This influence was reinforced on the external side by the beauty and the solemn services of the monasteries, which became more and more imposing. Instead of the wooden churches that were almost exclusively the rule in the beginning, edifices of stone were built according to the example of Rome. Saint Wilfrid was one of the first to erect magnificent churches in his abbeys at Ripon and Hexham. Glaziers were imported from the continent to make the windows. Ornaments were wrought of gold after Frankish and Celtic models, and gold-embroidered vestments and tapestries were fashioned by skilled Germanic craftsmen engaged for this purpose.

The new spirit that emanated from the excellently trained and educated bishops and abbots in the period following Arch-

---

20. Cf. especially Alois Brandl in H. Paul's *Grundriss d. germ. Philol.*, II², 1050 sqq. and preceding.

bishop Theodore was bound to manifest itself also in social and even political ways. As in the good days of the Frankish Church, we see churchmen espousing the cause of the lower classes, protecting the needy and helpless against acts of violence on the part of the nobles, who here, too, provoked most of the complaints. The religious leaders labored to restrain and reform by means of the penitential works they imposed and by inciting men to benevolent undertakings and pious foundations. Social works were often directly assigned as a penance: for example, the liberation of slaves, the improvement of bridges and highways, the support of peasants reduced to starvation by the domestic wars, the rebuilding of homes that had been destroyed or burned. The monks were always ready to befriend the slaves, among whom were very many made captive in the wars with the Britons and in the constant strife among the several kingdoms. It was due to the monks that the number of those enslaved declined and their lot gradually improved: we are told, for example, that Saint Wilfrid freed two hundred and fifty slaves whom he had acquired with an estate donated for a monastery. The Church also favored such liberation and recommended it to others; at the very least, she sought to protect the slaves' Christian rights. One law ordained that the slave who was forced to work on Sunday must be given his freedom;[21] another, that the master who let his hired servant work on Sunday must pay a fine of eighty *solidi*.[22] Liberations by testament were numerous — a fact traceable to the influence of the monks: religious motives are almost always indicated in the documents of emancipation. Further, the formal observances connected with the conferring of freedom were customarily held in the church, where the instrument of liberation was registered on the flyleaves of the Gospel books or in other ecclesiastical books.

The social influence of the Church was so powerful because of the lofty position of bishops and priests, deriving alike from old Germanic traditions and new cultural factors. With the pagan Germans, religion was a public affair and the priestly office was

---

21. Laws of Ine (688-95), 3: Liebermann, I, 91.
22. Laws of Wihtred (695-696), 9: ibid., I, 13.

highly respected. The priests were present at the great national assemblies; in the *witenagemot* they shared the deliberations of the wise men, and often had the determining voice. We recall the priest Coïfi, whose words in the *witenagemot* of King Edwin were decisive for the adoption of Christianity. This position had now been inherited by the Christian bishops and priests. The dioceses coincided as a rule with the several kingdoms, while the parishes were partitioned off along the lines of the hundreds or villages. The bishops took their place at the *witenagemot* among the nobles, occupying the first seats next to the high nobility, the *ealdormen,* descendants of the ancient "folkland" kings. Since this body treated spiritual matters as well as temporal, the prelates exerted an influence on civil legislation as well as on religious matters.

The State intervened with its power for the observance of ecclesiastical discipline and the commandments of the Church; it demanded by statute that priests observe the canons, that baptism be received in due time, that the ecclesiastical taxes be paid, and that Sunday rest and the marriage laws be kept; it punished the violation of ecclesiastical peace.

The bishops belonged to the highest officials of the state and to the highest nobility, and hence there was an intimate bond between Christianity and the aristocracy. In England, moreover, even more than elsewhere, Christianity was synonymous with that higher culture of the mind and heart which was desired especially by the upper classes. Let us never forget that during the Middle Ages the Christian faith nowhere appeared as a sign of intellectual inferiority, as it did in its primitive days and does in part today; it was everywhere identified with intellectual superiority. Missionaries from the heart of the ancient world had brought Christianity to England and with Christianity the traditions of the great culture and learning of antiquity. In the council of the wise men the lords spiritual certainly showed themselves in most cases as intellectually surpassing the other members. It is not astonishing, then, that in England great numbers of the nobility should have thronged to the priesthood and the monastic state.

What has already been noticed in Ireland repeated itself here, with the aristocracy participating on a scale perhaps even greater.

From the seventh to the eleventh century we count in England thirty-three kings or queens of the various Anglo-Saxon dynasties who ended their days in monastic retirement, and twenty-three kings and sixty queens, princes or princesses who became saints. The figures clearly demonstrate how great was the enthusiasm in the upper classes for Christianity. The prince or noble who entered the priesthood or the monastic life would naturally soon obtain a bishopric or abbey, the princess would become an abbess; and by their birth they increased still more the reverence which men were accustomed to accord these offices: the dignity of the bishop and the abbot was further enhanced. It was taken for granted that the Church should enjoy a high degree of legal protection; but in fact the bishop's commands acquired a legal force similar to the king's. The bishop was not required, any more than the king was, to confirm his word with an oath; it was indisputable. Moreover, the abbot, the priest, even the deacon, had to do no more than solemnly give his word before the altar, for it to have full legal force.[23]

The bond of unity existing between the royal and the episcopal dignity in England was moreover strengthened by the fact that the bishop blessed and anointed the king upon his accession to the throne. This was an old Oriental custom, found among the ancient Hindus and the Egyptians and passed from the latter to the Israelites. The Jewish practice was revived by the Christian nations of the West. The Visigothic kings from the seventh century onward were anointed in their capital city. The first certain record of this ceremony dates from 672 and refers to King Wamba. But much earlier (about 547), Saint Gildas wrote of the anointing of the kings among the Britons.[24] We know, further, that the abbot Columban the Elder (Saint Columba), anointed the Irish king Aidan in 574. Irish monks from Iona helped the Anglo-Saxon Oswald in 634 to gain the royal throne in Northumbria, and it is possible that the blessing and anointing of the king was introduced among the Anglo-Saxons at the time he ascended the throne.

---

23. Laws of Wihtred, 16-18: Liebermann, I, 13.
24. Gildas, *De excidio Britanniae: Mon. Germ. A. a.,* XIII, 37.

The pontifical of Bishop Egbert of York (732-766) describes the anointing ceremony. From a horn the bishop poured blessed oil upon the king's head pronouncing at the same time certain prayers which referred to the anointings in the Old Testament. This was followed by the presentation of the scepter and the staff, the imposition of the helmet, and the enthronement. The kings attached great importance to the Church's blessing and unction, especially at the inauguration of a new dynasty or when the throne had been contested, because it was regarded as divine confirmation of the royal dignity. The king was declared, as clearly as was possible, ruler by the grace of God, but he was also reminded of the duties of a Christian ruler. In the prayer that accompanied the unction, the consecrator, referring to the dove with the olive branch that had announced the end of the deluge, implored the Almighty in these terms:

> May God aid the new king, His servant, that he, like the dove, may vouchsafe to the people placed under his care the peace of simplicity; that he may zealously imitate Aaron in the service of God, may always preserve the dignity of his office in wise counsel and just judgment, and always show to his people a joyful countenance.

At the presentation of the scepter the king was again reminded of the ideal of a ruler pleasing to God, by a prayer directed to the King of kings:

> May he always be subject to Thee in reverence, may he fight for Thee, may he together with his kingdom and his nobles be protected in peace under Thy shield, and may he without battle be everywhere victorious.

At the end of the Mass which followed the blessing, these three decrees were read as the first message of the king to his Christian subjects: (1) that the Church of God and all Christian people preserve true peace always; (2) that all forms of brigandage and all injustices be forbidden all classes; (3) that justice and mercy reign in all the courts.[25] This ceremony notably expressed the high cultural mission of Christianity in guiding the nations. As it di-

---

25. Cabrol, *L'Angleterre chrét.*, Append., pp. 311 sq.

rected the mind of the king heavenward and strengthened his authority, so also it allowed to shine forth in their true brightness the bishop's duty to direct the ruler to heaven, and his authority as God's representative.

The entire Anglo-Saxon episcopate was further able to develop a special authority which extended over the several kingdoms. As long as these remained separate, the episcopate represented to a certain degree a higher national unity. The primate of England in Canterbury was, as such, of greater importance than any of the individual kings. For a long time the Anglo-Saxon kingdoms had no political procedure to match the plenary synods of the Anglo-Saxon bishops, which in a sense were a sort of national parliament in embryonic form.

Dissension between Church and State was not yet to be feared, for in this epoch they worked side by side in rare, almost ideal harmony. Nowhere else was the union so intimate. Far from looking upon the national welfare as endangered by the Church, men knew it was promoted by her. The representatives of ecclesiastical Rome had completely put aside the narrowness of outlook which had once clung to the idea of the *Imperium Romanum* — in effect, the idea of imperialism. They fully appreciated the natural morality of the Germans, and richly rewarded the complete confidence reposed in them by these people. The extinction of Germanic nationality never even occurred to the churchmen, nor were they in any wise interested in Romanizing the people. They recognized without reservation the right of national self-determination.

What their efforts tended to was a higher spiritual union among all the Western peoples and nations. This was a concept bound to arise spontaneously as various nations sprang up and attached themselves to the Church; but no national group in the course of the eighth century contributed as much as the Anglo-Saxons to the idea of organizing the West into a cultural community under the leadership of the Church of Rome. Thus did they show their gratitude to that Church for the freedom in which they had been educated. For the Roman missionaries had not treated them as barbarians lacking all good traits, whose native customs must be replaced by foreign ones. Instead they had sought to ennoble the

Germanic characteristics, to develop the good tendencies and regulate the bad.

In this manner, and here more than anywhere else up to this time, did the Church as an international society practice her new mission of putting national characteristics to good account. And having found the method, she has systematically adhered to it ever since. She is in no wise the enemy of national feeling, but she must ever oppose the pagan principle of exclusivism that manifested itself in the attitude of the Romans toward the barbarians. She must also oppose that chauvinism and that national conceit which distinguishes between nations destined to rule and nations condemned to be ruled. She opposed and opposes this principle because it denies the fundamental truth that all men are brothers.

However, to affirm again what has been affirmed more than once in these pages, the emergence of the new order of things in the West was made possible only by the destruction of the Roman Empire; the ancient power had to perish in order to make room for that Christian culture which was destined to become a world culture. Not one kingdom nor one language was to reign; but there would be various nations and various tongues, and above them all a unity of faith and of Christian culture.

But just as it is given to few persons to abide always in the company of ideal thoughts, so too it has not been possible for the several nations to remain during any lengthy period on the loftiest heights. Even in the bright picture of co-operation presented by the Anglo-Saxon nation and the Church, certain dark spots could be noted, which were soon to stand out in bold relief. Not separation of Church and State, but union between them, is certainly the ideal in the Church's mind — but an ideal always as difficult to realize as it is to achieve a harmonious marriage. The whole medieval period exhibits to us not only the effort to attain this ideal but also the obstacles hampering the effort. The fact that Church and State were intimately united and even appeared as a single unit; that the higher ecclesiastics were in a certain sense also officials of the State; that the bishops appeared at the *witenagemot* and the kings and temporal lords took part in the assemblies of the bishops and abbots of their kingdom; furthermore, that the bishops required the king's approval for their appointment; finally, the fact that royal monasteries, which were often handed down as an inheritance, dotted the country — all this inevitably gave rise to abuses and to reciprocal encroachments.

No less conducive to these were the excessive riches and power which had accrued to the Church. The grants were, in large part, carved out of the "folkland" by the king with the consent of the *witan*. The tenants on these estates given to the Church were freed from military service as well as from the usual assessments. Only for three purposes — the *trinoda necessitas* — were they compelled to pay taxes: the maintenance of bridges and the highways, the national defenses, and needs in time of war. The many grants made especially to monasteries were bound to result in a reduction of the country's military power. The number of proprietors who were obliged to render personal military service grew smaller, partly because many estates fell to the monasteries, whose servants were exempt from military service, partly because many men liable to army service entered monastic life. The prudent Bede already felt some concern about this situation when he wrote for the year 731:

> In peaceful times many men in Northumbria, nobles and freemen with their children, strive to put aside their arms; they have their hair cut and prefer to assume monastic vows rather than render military service. Whither this will lead, the future will show.[26]

In the letter to the archbishop of York already noted, he expresses himself even more clearly, saying that the national defense is being endangered by the many grants.

There were, of course, other particular abuses which had their beginnings in this period. An example will suffice. Because so many privileges attached to the monastery estates, some nobles obtained large grants of land on the pretext of erecting a monastic foundation. They founded something in certain respects similar, it is true, but in reality not a religious society at all. They surrounded themselves with their vassals and certain monks who had

---

26. *Hist. eccles.*, lib. V, c. 23.

flocked to them, and called themselves abbots; but they lived just as they had before with their wives and children and servitors. There were even instances where these foundations bore no resemblance whatever to a monastery. Saint Bede earnestly demanded that an end be put to such grants based on fraudulent representation.

But we are still in a period when such abuses have hardly become noticeable. We have yet to consider the finest expression which the English Church gave of her vigor: namely, the sending forth of her sons to the continent. There they made the conversion of Germany certain, reformed the Frankish Church, transplanted their art and learning to the Frankish kingdom, and brought the northern countries into close relations with the papacy. The result was a union that dominated the whole medieval period.

CHAPTER FIVE

SAINT BONIFACE AND THE PAPACY

AN ATTEMPT to organize the German missionary Church was made as early as the beginning of the eighth century by the Bavarian Duke Theodo. While in Rome he petitioned Pope Gregory II for a legate, and a plan of missionary action was arranged in some detail. It was not carried out, however: the ducal family possessed too little independence for such a task. Had they and the Thuringian and Alamannian dukes been able to exercise a free initiative — that is to say, had the weakening of the Frankish central power progressed any further — these dynasties would perhaps have taken the establishment of the Church in hand. Frisia and Saxony also would probably have been converted without the sacrifices which in actuality had to be made to achieve this end, for if they had been able to embrace Christianity without the Frankish domination, they would hardly have resisted long.

But it is doubtful whether the result in the end would have been satisfying. The increase in strength of the tribes would have led to a wider separation from one another, to heightened friction, and to bitter struggles for hegemony such as the Anglo-Saxons carried on throughout the seventh and eighth centuries until the kingdom of Wessex finally succeeded in imposing unification. It is also certain that the general development of Western culture would have been, not quickened, but retarded. It was to their own interest that the various kingdoms and nations which took shape following the chaos of the great migrations, should be brought closer together, united by a common bond, and induced to a mutual interchange of ideas. Those German tribes especially which lagged behind the others in development, could only gain by close contact with nations on a higher level.

It was no misfortune, therefore, that the reins of the Frankish government, which had slipped from the hands of the Merovingian dynasty, passed to the Carolingians, natives of the Ardennes. By overcoming the Neustrian Mayor of the Palace at Tertry in 687, Pippin II (often called Pippin of Heristal) extended the sway of this family over the whole kingdom. He reigned henceforth over Austrasia, Neustria and Burgundy as "duke and prince of the Franks." As soon as he had secured this controlling power he endeavored to consolidate the Frankish kingdom at a point which was potentially of great danger to his own private possessions in the Ardennes. He directed his energies against the Frisians, who controlled the mouth of the Rhine and who until now had stubbornly resisted the Franks and Christianity. Saint Amandus, who labored among the pagan Franks, Saint Eligius, the bishop of Noyon, and Saint Cunibert, the bishop of Cologne, had attempted without success to convert these people. The one small church which had been erected, in Utrecht, soon disappeared again.

Such was the situation when the Anglo-Saxon missionaries came to Germany. As a forerunner of these, Saint Wilfrid had appeared in Frisia, which lay close to England, in 678, in the course of a journey to Rome. He tarried there until the spring of 679, and was actually permitted to preach, but he was unable to do more than explore the missionary field. It was Anglo-Saxon missionaries living in Irish surroundings who first seriously heeded the vocation to the continental missions. When the antagonism between the Anglo-Saxon and Celtic monastic groups began to subside, many Anglo-Saxon monks visited Ireland to acquaint themselves with its stricter monastic life and study under its famous masters. From this circumstance, a particular ascetic tendency, which we have already noted among the Irish, played a part in the Anglo-Saxon missionary movement: the desire to renounce native country in the hope of meriting more surely by this sacrifice admission into the heavenly fatherland.

One of these Anglo-Saxons, Saint Egbert, abbot-bishop of the Irish monastery of Rathmelsigi (Mellifont), vowed during a plague never to return to England, but to go to the pagans in Germany, whence his people had emigrated. The missionary program carried out long ago by the Irish was thus revived by Saint Egbert and given the character of a national cause, as manifested in his solicitude for the spiritual welfare of his racial kindred. He was about to embark when a storm intervened, confirming the warnings of a companion, who believed himself commanded by God in a vision to prevent Saint Egbert's departure. Thereupon the abbot-bishop sent out his disciple and countryman, Wigbert (about 686).

This monk was less fortunate even than Saint Wilfrid had been. The new Frisian ruler, Ratbod, did not want to hear anything about the religion of the Franks, his enemies; and after two years Wigbert was constrained to return to his master in Ireland without having achieved anything. Saint Egbert, however, did not give up; he repeated the attempt, but this time on a larger scale. Just as Saint Columbanus had once done, he collected a group of twelve apostles; at their head he placed the priest Saint Willibrord, who had been a pupil of Saint Wilfrid in the monastery of Ripon.

The group were soon able to show results, since they took advantage of a new political star. A year earlier (689), Pippin II had defeated the Frisian chieftain Ratbod at Wyk-te-Duerstede, the coastal town where the ships coming from London usually docked. Saint Willibrord and his companions approached the victor, who assigned them the conquered territory of southwestern Frisia as their mission field. Here they were protected by the power of the Franks, the importance of which may be judged by the fate that somewhat later befell two English priests who lacked it. They were brothers bearing the surname Ewald who also came from Ireland, where they had learned about the labors of Saint Willibrord and resolved to emulate them in pagan Saxony. Shortly after arriving there they fell victims to pagan fanaticism and were martyred.

In accord with the traditions of the Anglo-Saxon Benedictines, Saint Willibrord went from Frisia to Rome to solicit a papal commission for his undertaking. Pope Sergius I joyfully gave him what he desired — faculties, relics, and his blessing. It seems to have been in line with the pope's intentions that the missionaries in Frankish Frisia, following Saint Willibrord's return, elected one of their group a bishop. Their choice fell upon the mild Suitbert, who was probably the oldest among them. Since the archiepiscopal see of Canterbury was vacant at this time following the death of Saint Theodore, Saint Suitbert was consecrated by Saint Wilfrid in England in 692 or 693. Pippin took umbrage at this procedure. That a bishop should have been created without recourse to him, in a territory on whose destiny he was keeping a particularly vigilant eye, was something he would not pass over lightly. He refused to recognize Saint Suitbert's authority or office. The latter sought another sphere of action among the Bructeri on the Lippe and Ruhr rivers. But after the Saxons destroyed his mission work in that region, he had no choice but to place himself under the protection of Pippin. The ruler's wife, Plectrude, procured him Pippin's favor once more, and the island of Werth in the Rhine was given to him. Here he founded the monastery of Kaiserswerth.

This is another demonstration of the fact that missionaries were able to accomplish very little here without Pippin's support, much less against his will. The English Benedictines, however, accustomed to act in agreement with the civil authorities, were ready to accommodate themselves to the situation as long as it did not involve the sacrifice of their ecclesiastical authority. Hence a compromise was easily reached in Frisia.

Having effected an agreement with the monks, Pippin sent Saint Willibrord, who always remained in his confidence, to Rome with the petition that the pope would consecrate him an archbishop to organize the Church among the Frisians. The saint received episcopal consecration on November 22, 695, and Pippin immediately assigned him a site for a cathedral in Utrecht. Thereafter, the results of Willibrord's Frisian mission multiplied. He was less successful in his attempt to preach to the Danes. He went by ship to visit their king, Ongendus, probably at Ribe, in Jutland, but could not influence the pagan ruler. Returning home with thirty Danish youths, Willibrord was driven onto the island of Helgoland, where he was taken prisoner while baptizing at the ancient sacred spring there. He was brought before the Frisian King Ratbod and could but be thankful that the latter again released him to Pippin. Thenceforth he restricted himself to consolidating the Frisian Church and to creating a missionary center which was to become a school for the training of a native clergy and at the same time a haven of refuge for missionaries laboring in regions exposed to danger. For this purpose he acquired Echternach on the Sauer river, where he established a monastery. The foundation shortly obtained land endowments in Thuringia, opening up very promising prospects for those regions.

These were the bases on which that missionary built who was destined to crown the work of the Anglo-Saxons in Germany: Winfrid, now known to all the world as Saint Boniface. Winfrid was born in 675, the son of a Saxon nobleman residing in the kingdom of Wessex in southwestern England, which through long-drawn-out struggles with the Britons had widened its boundaries toward the west, and now extended from the upper Thames to the Severn river. Christianity had been introduced here little more than forty years before Winfrid's birth by Saint Birinus, a Benedictine sent thither by Pope Honorius from Saint Andrew's monastery in Rome. Birinus (who had been consecrated a bishop in Genoa) baptized the king in 633 — the first of the ancient dynasty of Cerdic to become a Christian. In spite of the severe struggles with pagan barbarism which ensued, the new doctrine soon took a profound hold on the people. King Centwine abdicated in 685 and entered one of the monasteries he had founded. Caedwalla, his successor, who at first had rejected Christianity, was won to belief by Saint Wilfrid. Hardly thirty years of age, the ruler decided to atone for his earlier brutalities by making a pilgrimage to the center of Christendom. He appeared there in 688 — the first Anglo-Saxon to visit Rome. Caedwalla was baptized by Pope Sergius I, and dying soon thereafter, was buried in Saint Peter's. He was succeeded by Ine (688-725), who was both a successful warrior and a friend of abbots and bishops. Ine is renowned also for his legal code, which shows express regard for Christian views and customs. Like his predecessor, he finally abdicated his throne in order to make a pilgrimage to Rome and end his days as a poor pilgrim at the tomb of Saint Peter. Among the representatives of the Church in Wessex at that time, Saint Aldhelm, the learned abbot of Malmesbury, who is already known to us, enjoyed the highest esteem. He was closely connected with the king both as a relative and as a friend, and was highly venerated by all for his versatile scholarship and his religious leadership. He, too, made the journey to Rome, in order to place his monastery under the protection of Pope Sergius.

These were the determining events, and these the men representative of intellectual and religious life in Wessex, in the days when Winfrid was growing into manhood. His youth beheld important victories, which left lasting impressions on the mind: that of Christianity over pagan barbarism, of the Benedictine Rule over Celtic monastic practices, of Roman traditions over insular peculiarities. He saw kings and prelates making pilgrimages to Rome. He had before him in Saint Aldhelm the example of the most learned man of his time proclaiming the authority of Rome and the merits of the Benedictine Rule. These youthful impressions determined the course the future Boniface was to adopt.

His father allowed the boy Winfrid to enter the Benedictine monastery of Exeter as an oblate. He was further educated in the monastery of Nutshalling (modern Nursling), between Winchester and Southampton. He would have been made a monastic teacher, and doubtless would have distinguished himself as one, but his heart's desire was for the foreign missions. His abbot did not hold him back, for these Benedictines were true disciples of those Roman monks to whose renunciation of their native land all England owed the knowledge of salvation. It must be added that if any worldly enjoyment was still rooted in the hearts of Anglo-Saxon monks, it was enjoyment of travel; which fact was further conducive to their missionary inclination.

In the spring of 716 Winfrid landed on the coast of Frisia. He could not suspect how unfavorable the prospects for the preaching of the Gospel there had become a short time before. In 714, upon the death of Pippin II, the Frisians had taken up arms in the resolve of regaining that part of their country which had been ceded to the Franks. It was only when Winfrid came ashore at Wyk-te-Duerstede that he learned the Franks had been defeated and evicted from the territory they formerly held as conquerors. It is true that, since he had no connection with the Franks, he was not personally molested. But his preaching was such a complete failure that even before the approach of winter he returned to England. However, he did not abandon his missionary plans; his only desire now was to have the pope assign him a mission field, since he did not know where to go.

He would put himself at the disposal of the successor of that great Gregory who had sent Saint Augustine and the Roman Benedictines to England. In the winter of 718-719, therefore, he appeared before Pope Gregory II, accompanied by a group of English pilgrims. Gregory, a native Roman, at first received the English monk with reserve. He was undoubtedly surprised to see at the head of a train of pilgrims a member of an order on which permanence of abode had been imposed as a special monastic obligation. But since Winfrid was able to produce a letter of recommendation from his bishop, and to give entirely satisfactory answers to all questions, the pope authorized him to go as a missionary to Germany. Before Winfrid departed, his name was changed to Boniface, the name of a martyr honored in Rome. The Romans could not reconcile themselves to the harsh-sounding names of the Anglo-Saxons. Pope Sergius I had given King Caedwalla the name Peter in 689, when that ruler presented himself for baptism at the tomb of the Prince of the Apostles, and the monk Willibrord the name Clement in 695, when he was consecrated archbishop of the Frisians.

It was only orally that Thuringia was assigned to Boniface as his special mission field. In his written faculties no country was named. The apostolic missionary was merely enjoined always to administer the sacrament of baptism according to the Roman rite, and in all other matters to get instructions from Rome.

The commission Boniface obtained from Rome was the first link in a momentous chain. What Pope Gregory I had begun by sending the Roman Benedictine, Saint Augustine, to England, the second Gregory now continued by sending the Anglo-Saxon Benedictine, Saint Boniface, to Germany. The Anglo-Saxon Church gave back to Rome what she had received from Rome; and there set in from the remote northwest corner of Europe a movement of return which, passing through the Frankish kingdom, was soon to make itself felt as far as Rome, and eventually also in Constantinople. For the nascent cultural world being formed in the West by the Romance and Germanic peoples, union with the papacy and the

Roman Church was becoming a definite thing. How decisive was the turn of events precisely in Saint Boniface's day is best demonstrated by the fact that within his lifetime the last journey ever undertaken by a pontiff to an Eastern Roman emperor was made (by Pope Constantine in 710); and that forty-three years later, Pope Stephen III* crossed the Alps to meet Pippin III — the first pope to come seeking help from a Germanic king. Saint Boniface himself was to become one of the most valuable agents in promoting the cultural unification of the West.

The fact that the pope did not assign him a definite mission territory was, no doubt, due mainly to the troubled conditions in the Frankish kingdom at this time. The pope, who wished to direct Boniface in concert with the ruler of the Franks, simply did not know who might safely be considered such. Pippin II's son, Charles Martel, who was now Mayor of the Palace, had not yet brought to a conclusion the struggle to regain the power his father had wielded. Not until the end of year 719, when he had conquered the hostile Neustrian nobles and Duke Eudo, was he to be regarded as the undisputed ruler of the whole Frankish kingdom. Saint Boniface had plainly intended from the beginning to labor among the Frisians and the Saxons, north German tribes related to his own people and speaking a language he knew. But the Saxons absolutely refused to admit the bearers of the religion of the hated Franks; and useful missionary activity could be hoped for among the Frisians only when their relations with their former conquerors had improved again. This explains, to repeat, why Boniface received from the pope only oral instructions to strengthen Christianity on the southern frontier of the Saxons, among the Thuringians and Hessians, until a bridge could gradually be thrown from these points to the Saxons. No doubt it was left to the saint's discretion to change this plan if better prospects opened out elsewhere.

In reality, Boniface did not stay long among the Thuringians. He came into conflict with the delinquent priests whom he found there, and could not prevail against their opposition because he had

---

*Translator's note: Throughout the translation, this pope is reckoned as the third Stephen, in accordance with the listing in the *Annuario Pontificio*. Professor Schnürer calls him Stephen II, following certain early listings which omitted the original Stephen II because he died without consecration, three days after election.

not a bishop's jurisdiction. Learning that the Franks had regained the ascendancy in Frisia, he went thither. The Frisian chieftain Ratbod had died in 719, and his successor, Aldgild the Younger, no longer resisted Christianity, which now enjoyed Charles Martel's protection. Seemingly, the time had come for a sure harvest in Frisia. Boniface labored there for the next three years under his countryman, Archbishop Willibrord, reaping much valuable experience. When, however, the aged Willibrord proposed to have him named as his successor, Boniface, mindful of his commission from Rome, declined the offer in order to remain a free lance at the disposal of the pope. The missionary apostolate was now safely going forward in the diocese of Utrecht, recently organized by Saint Willibrord. It would certainly be more in line with Rome's intentions for Boniface to spend his efforts where the missions were suffering the greatest need.

He decided to return, for an interval, to southern Saxony, the scene of his former labors. In the course of this journey he stopped at the convent of Pfalzel on the Mosel, whose abbess was a daughter of the Merovingian king, Dagobert II. During the meal the reading was entrusted to the abbess' grandson Gregory, a boy of fourteen who had just come from court and undoubtedly possessed a certain amount of education. When the lad had finished the Latin reading, Boniface asked him if he understood what he had read. Gregory answered in the affirmative and began to repeat the Latin text. But the saint was not satisfied with this, and asked the Frankish lad to give the sense of the Latin in the German language. This Gregory was unable to do, so Boniface himself explained the passage in German, to the great joy of all at table. He was rewarded by winning the heart of young Gregory, who went on with him when he resumed his journey, and became one of his most faithful companions. Later Gregory labored with much success, according to his master's plan, as head of the school of Utrecht.

What especially delights us in this story, which is told by Saint Ludger, the first bishop of Münster in Westphalia, is Saint Boniface's reproof for the rotelike repetition of poorly understood Latin texts and the importance he attached to the rendering of their sense in the vernacular. This approach was of the greatest consequence now for the apostolate in Germany, just as it had been formerly among the Anglo-Saxons. Moreover, by keeping his companions and disciples to it, Boniface also inspired the writing down of the ecclesiastical monuments of German literature.

It was in the year 722 that Boniface arrived among the Hessians. Though they were in great part still pagan, their territory belonged to the Frankish kingdom, and they had suffered much from the Saxon invasions. Among them the holy missionary found an extremely favorable field for his activity; he established at Amöneburg, on the great basalt rock beside the Ohm, his first monastic settlement. When he reported this to the pope, he was invited to come to Rome for a personal interview, and on the feast of Saint Andrew (722) he received the episcopal consecration from Pope Gregory II. At the same time Saint Boniface took the oath of fealty to the pope, as the bishops in the vicinity of Rome were wont to do; promising to adhere with sincere faith to Catholic doctrine, to guard the unity of the Church, to support the pope at all times, and in particular to abstain from communion with such bishops as desired to deviate from the ancient customs of the Fathers.

In one point the oath taken by Saint Boniface shows a remarkable departure from the customary formula specifying an obligation of loyalty to the *res publica* (that is, the Roman Empire) and the "most pious prince" (that is, the Byzantine emperor). There could be no question of requiring this in the case of Saint Boniface; indeed, the formula had already been changed for the bishops of the Lombardic kingdom, who were obliged merely to promise that they would concern themselves at all times with maintaining peace between the *res publica* and the Lombard people. We see from this that the men in Rome had had to adjust themselves at last to the fact that the idea of the Roman Empire and of dependence upon an emperor residing in Constantinople was no longer universally held, and that provision must be made for exceptions (which were soon to become the rule). The new community, for which Rome would become the ecclesiastical center, was made up of the northern countries; and the pilgrims who came to Rome from those regions with ever greater frequency showed how eagerly a close union with Rome was desired there.

That Boniface might have a norm for his practical ministry, he was given a copy of the collection of canon law then in use in Rome, which was probably that of Dionysius Exiguus. In addition, Pope Gregory gave him a letter of recommendation to "Duke Charles Martel." The saint presented this in person, and received in exchange a letter of safe-conduct in the usual form recommending him to all the dignitaries and officials in the kingdom. Consecrated a bishop by the pope, and protected by the supreme power of the Frankish State, Saint Boniface was now able to act with greater authority among the Hessians, the first to whom he returned.

The Anglo-Saxon homeland followed the missionary bishop with the liveliest interest, and helped him in many ways; fellow-workers came to join him, gifts, especially of books, and many letters were sent. One letter, from his old friend Bishop Daniel of Winchester, is of particular importance, revealing as it does the writer's desire to transplant to the continent the spirit that had developed in the Anglo-Saxon Benedictine monasteries out of their experiences in converting their own country. Bishop Daniel explains in detail the method by which, in his discourses, Saint Boniface should lead the pagans to the great question concerning the origin of the world and direct them, in the face of the impotence of their own gods, to the omnipotent Creator existing from all eternity:

> This you should hold up to them — not in a scolding manner, which is apt to provoke them, but in a calm tone and with great moderation. In between, you will have to contrast the truths of our Christian faith with their superstitions, in such a way that you stir their feelings at the same time; the pagans, confounded rather than embittered, will then blush over their foolish superstitions; and moreover, they will see that we are really aware of their shameful practices and myths. This point should also be touched upon: If the gods are all-powerful, benevolent and just, they must not only reward those who adore them, but also punish those who despise them.... Why, then, do they spare the Christians, who are drawing almost the whole world away from their cult and destroying the idols? And why do the Christians possess fertile countries, rich in oil and wine and teeming in other treasures, while to the pagans who still worship those false rulers, the gods banished everywhere else, are left the countries always benumbed with cold? The prestige of the Christian world should also be held up to them frequently: by way of contrast, they constitute only a very small minority still persevering in the ancient folly. And lest they boast of the

rule of the gods over their own peoples as traditional from the very beginning of time, and on this account legitimate, they should be made to understand that the whole world worshiped false gods until, by the grace of Christ, it was reborn, reconciled to God and enlightened through the knowledge of the One True God, the Omnipotent Creator and Ruler of the universe. If Christian baptism is a matter of daily occurrence, is not its purpose to cleanse individuals from the taint and guilt of paganism, with which the whole world was once infected?[1]

It is the general superiority of Christian culture that is put into words here by the Anglo-Saxon bishop. For the rest, the arguments he suggests are substantially those which were once decisive in the conversion of the Anglo-Saxons. In the first place, an appeal is made to reason. It is also urgently necessary, however, to prove the powerlessness of their own gods and the power of the Christian God to these primitive peoples to whom power and external force mean so much.

New converts, in particular, regarded such proofs as very important in their attempts to gain their hesitating countrymen for Christianity. What they desired, characteristically, was to have the impotence of the pagan deities concretely demonstrated through the performance of some act which, according to pagan conceptions, would provoke the gods to retaliate; when they did not, the faith of the pagans would be proportionately shaken. Thus, we recall, had Coïfi, the high priest of King Edwin of Northumbria, discredited the ancient gods by attacking their temple.

Something similar now came to pass in Hesse. Following the successful activity of the missionaries, a Christian party had formed among the Hessians in opposition to the pagan party. The latter tenaciously adhered to the heathen sacrifices which had been offered, some secretly, some publicly, at certain traditionally sacred places, trees and springs. They were unwilling to relinquish their belief in the efficacy of these sacrifices, and clung to the hopes and fears associated with prophecies, exorcisms and enchantments. The Christians, with the design of destroying this superstitious faith, advised the bishop to produce a conclusive argument by striking at the

---

1. Translator's note: This and the following citations from *The Letters of Saint Boniface and Lullus* are quoted by Schnürer from the German edition of Tangl (pp. 40 sq. for the above).

gigantic sacred tree immemorially venerated at Geismar, near Fritzlar. The people assembled as for an ordeal. The bishop with his priests and the Christians stood on one side, a multitude of pagans on the other. Saint Boniface himself undertook to swing the axe to the roots of the tree. When the mighty trunk crashed down, the people who formerly cursed the preaching missionaries were convinced. Out of the wood of this tree Saint Boniface built a chapel in Fritzlar in honor of Saint Peter, remembering Rome even in this northern forest.

We shall misunderstand the action of Saint Boniface in felling the oak if we impute it to anger on his part; we must rather view it as a courageous act of faith in answer to a challenge — an act providing a form of proof demanded by his followers and convincing to his enemies. Such demonstrations were not unknown at that time, nor were they fundamentally in conflict with Bishop Daniel's instructions; for if anyone agreed with the bishop's admonition about teaching and discussing the truth calmly and moderately and not berating and provoking one's hearers, it was Saint Boniface. This manner of procedure was in accord with the Rule of his Order, which had been deeply engraved upon his mind, and no less with his own personal inclination. His, indeed, is a character so strongly governed by reason, so schooled in co-operating with its dictates, so unshakable in spiritual poise, that one is almost tempted to wish there had been occasions capable of disturbing the well-nigh monotonous perfection of that restraint.

However, it would be a mistake to think of Boniface as destitute of feeling. That he had an emotional side is revealed in his correspondence with his native land — if only indirectly, since in this case we possess nothing but the answers to letters that he had written. From the letters of English nuns confiding to him their cares, great and small, it is clearly evident that a sympathetic heart beat beneath his monastic habit. This heart did not indeed bare itself to strangers, but it was very far from being insensible to the human anxieties connected with its owner's work; and his exile from his native land was offered to God as a sacrifice continuously felt. But a will well-tested for a long period in self-control had full mastery over his emotions.

The sequel to the episode of the felling of the sacred tree shows that this was not regarded by the pagans as an act designed to offend them. Nowhere have we any indication that Saint Boniface was personally unsympathetic to the pagan Germans. On the contrary, everything points to the fact that when they were moved to listen to Christian teachings and to talk with Christian missionaries, they preferred to do so with Saint Boniface above all. This was not only because, to him, an Anglo-Saxon, no political ambitions could be attributed, but especially because his calm and reasonable manner, together with a profound but hidden inner life, corresponded to the best in the German nature. Apart from his immediate surroundings, this was known only to the poor and distressed.

Saint Boniface undoubtedly had powerful personal enemies. These came from what should have been the least likely quarter. Certain of the Frankish clergy, as we have already seen, were accustomed to regard any ecclesiastical position as merely a source of power and income, without giving a thought to the conscientious fulfilment of the obligations attached to it. They only wanted to reap the benefits which the unselfish labors of Saint Boniface could bring them, and hence they sought to supplant the foreign missionary bishop. Least of all men could Saint Boniface be expected to judge such opponents leniently, for in them he was combating the enemies of true spiritual life. It was they who were to blame for the long duration of paganism in Germany. He remained in conflict with them all his life.

Profoundly conscientious as he was, he could not but be acutely mindful in this situation of the oath which he had sworn to the pope, binding himself to break off communion with other bishops whose lives did not accord with right ecclesiastical standards. In Thuringia, whither he had gone from Hesse, the contact with this sort of depraved representatives of the Church was particularly painful to him. Accustomed, like Saint Augustine of Canterbury in earlier days, to seek the pope's advice in all questions, large and small, he now inquired how he was to conduct himself with regard to priests and bishops who were slaves of vice and whose personal life was a disgrace to the priesthood; whether, for example, he might converse and eat with them as long as they were not heretics.

Gregory II replied with the mildness and prudence Gregory I had shown in his own day:

> You might on the strength of Apostolic authority reprimand them, admonish them, and lead them back to the purity of ecclesiastical discipline. If they listen then, they will save their souls, and you yourself will have gained for yourself a reward. Refuse not, however, to speak with them and to sit at table together with them. Many, if they are punished, will hesitate to hold themselves to the standard of truth, but by the incessant mild admonition of their companions they are generally brought back to the right path.[2]

Saint Boniface never regretted his compliance with these words.

The pope seldom followed a severer view in his responses than the inquirer. An exception appears to have concerned the partaking of horseflesh. When Pope Gregory III heard of this practice, he was deeply shocked. "We beseech you, O most holy brother," he wrote, "do not permit this in the future under any circumstances, but suppress it with the help of Christ by all the means at your disposal, and impose on them a fitting penance, for it is unclean and detestable."[3]

Saint Boniface found hardly any earnest support from the clergy scattered throughout the territories on the right bank of the Rhine. These men lived in close association with pagans and made many undue concessions to paganism. So much the more welcome to him, therefore, were the added missionary forces which joined him from England in the third decade of the century. Priests, monks and nuns, all distinguished for the profound culture, moral purity and idealism which were cultivated in the Anglo-Saxon monasteries, answered his plea for helpers. Particularly attractive among the nuns is the delightful figure of Saint Lioba, or Leobgytha, a relative of Boniface, who once in a simple naïve letter had petitioned him, according to the custom of the time, to become her spiritual brother. In the convent she had learned the highly esteemed art of versification and transmitted to Boniface a little example of her work. Tetta, the strict and prudent abbess of the

---

2. Ibid., p. 47.
3. Ibid., p. 50.

double monastery of Wimborne, had trained her excellently and given her a good education without suppressing that amiable nature which made Lioba the favorite of all. Boniface held her in added esteem on this account, that she was pre-eminently fitted to be a teacher and a superior. By nature she possessed that inner balance and prudent moderation to which Saint Benedict had attached particular importance in his admonitions.

Within the Frankish territory about the Main river, in sheltered places remote from the dangerous Saxon frontier, Saint Boniface established several convents for the nuns. Saint Lioba he placed at the head of the convent of Bischofsheim. How prudently she applied the principle of moderation in directing her convent is well characterized by one of her rulings which corresponds to an instruction of Saint Benedict's. Knowing that a fresh mind is necessary for prayer and intellectual work, both of which she emphasized as most important, she insisted that the hours of sleep be not reduced for the nuns. In summer all in the community were to take a short midday rest. If the period of sleep is shortened, she said, the power of understanding is also reduced, especially in reading. She herself, however, as a rule, had someone read to her during her rest period. The direction of the convents of Kitzingen and Ochsenfurt was entrusted to a saintly relative of Saint Lioba named Thecla. These convents soon attracted girl pupils from far and near, who in turn would be qualified to spread more widely the culture transmitted by their eminent teachers. Illustrious families gladly entrusted the education of their daughters to the convents; and widows also retired to them. How highly the services of these Englishwomen should be rated — these nuns, outstanding in culture of heart and mind, who labored for the development of Germany — can be judged from the fact that they are absolutely the first cultured women we encounter in that country.

In the meantime, Rome had enlarged Saint Boniface's field of labors. Pope Gregory III, who ascended the papal throne in 731, named him archbishop, and delegated him to appoint bishops and in general to define the limits of dioceses in the Frankish kingdom on the right bank of the Rhine. Saint Boniface hesitated. The move seemed to him somewhat premature, and he doubtless realized, besides, that the Frankish ruler did not wish to be ignored in the matter. He himself was moved not at all toward such an expansion of his personal power; his one desire was, and remained, to penetrate to the Saxons and Frisians, his nearest kinsfolk. Hence Pope Gregory III summoned him to Rome for a personal interview. On this, his third visit, which lasted a year (737-38) he found in the papal city a number of new and distinguished collaborators.

Since King Ine of Wessex had spent the last part of his life in Rome as a pilgrim, the number of pious Anglo-Saxons who tarried there for longer or shorter periods had continually increased. They now accorded their countryman, the missionary invested with archiepiscopal dignity, the greatest veneration: he could not appear often enough in their midst to delight them with his addresses. It was undoubtedly due to Boniface's spirit of organization that the Anglo-Saxon pilgrims banded together and took up residence near Saint Peter's in a group of small wooden houses called (after the year 799, when these pilgrims obtained their own church) the *Schola Saxonum,* or *Burgus.*[4]

At this time the Bavarians, following the precedent set by their Duke Theodo, as well as the Franks, who were influenced by the example of the English pilgrims passing through their country in ever-increasing throngs, were strongly represented in Rome; and they, too, honored the archbishop as one of their own. Boniface was, in truth, the inspiration of the groups streaming to the Eternal City from the north. They saw in him the herald of a new age, whose battle cry was: Rally round the papacy!

Under such circumstances it was not difficult for Saint Boniface to inspire young men to enlist under him for the missionary work which, as enlarged by the pope, so vitally needed new recruits. Probably at this time Saint Lullus joined him, who was later to become the leader of his disciples, and to transmit his memory to posterity. It was Lullus who built up that valuable collection which contains the letters of Boniface and his circle of friends and the important writings of the popes to him. It was Lullus who, together

---

4. Cf. Wilfrid Moore, *The Saxon Pilgrims to Rome and the "Schola Saxonum,"* a dissertation (Fribourg, Switzerland).

with Bishop Megingoz of Würzburg, induced the priest Willibald of Mainz to write the first biography of the saint. Like Boniface, Lullus was a native of Wessex, and though thirty years his junior, he had received his education in the same circles. The spirit of Saint Aldhelm still dominated those circles, and its influence upon the younger man was even more direct than upon the elder, since Lullus was educated in the monastery of Malmesbury itself, which Saint Aldhelm had once directed.

Saint Burchard, the future bishop of Würzburg, also joined Saint Boniface at this time. From among Boniface's own relatives came Saint Winnibald; and ten years later, at the pope's command, Winnibald's younger brother, Saint Willibald, once a rover, who had become a monk in Monte Cassino after a pilgrimage to Jerusalem. Saint Walburga, the sister of these brothers, also came to Germany, where she was first attached to Saint Lioba's convent.

Pope Gregory III did not wish Saint Boniface to restrict himself to the pagan mission in the territories bordering on Saxony. Rather, it was his desire that the archbishop organize all the territories of Germany subject to the Franks on the right bank of the Rhine, into an ecclesiastical province. By special document, therefore, Boniface was made papal legate for Bavaria and Alamannia, a position similar to that accorded the archbishop of Canterbury. Complying with this mandate, and with the support of Duke Odilo, the saint finally gave the Bavarian Church a formal organization by defining the four dioceses of Passau, Salzburg, Freising and Regensburg. He now also held the first Bavarian national synod.

He did not, however, reach Alamannia — apparently because opposition arose at the court of Charles Martel, to whom Alamannia was then immediately subject. Also, independent ecclesiastical forces at work in Alamannia perhaps viewed the proposed entry of the English missionary with disfavor. For years Saint Pirmin, a contemporary of Saint Boniface, labored there under the protection of Charles Martel. Saint Pirmin, who had fled from the Visigothic kingdom, appears to have remained under Irish and Frankish influences. He had founded the Benedictine monastery of Reichenau on the Lake of Constance; then, driven out by Duke Theudebald, had gone to Alsace, where he established the monastery of Murbach and several other foundations. His last foundation was Hornbach in the Palatinate, where he died in 753. There remains from his writings a work of popular instruction entitled *Dicta Pirminii,* which was manifestly influenced by the sermons of the saintly Archbishop Caesarius of Arles and Saint Martin of Braga's sermon for peasants.

Instead of proceeding to Alamannia, where after all the dioceses of Strassburg, Basel and Constance already existed, Saint Boniface went to Thuringia, where he established three new bishoprics: Würzburg, with its seat at the ancient residence of the duke; Buraburg, near Fritzlar; and Erfurt. (The last two sees could not be maintained; but in their stead may be counted the flourishing diocese of Eichstätt, established by Boniface at that time in the northern district of Bavaria, which then had to be ceded to the Franks by the duke of Bavaria.) The Thuringian mission, conducted exclusively by Anglo-Saxons, continued for a time unsettled. It lacked a strong bond of union with the Frankish Church and was not an object of interest to the Frankish clergy, whose motive was not as purely religious as that of the Anglo-Saxons. The situation would be changed only when Saint Boniface was given the opportunity of imparting his spirit also to the Frankish Church along the Rhine and to the left of it. The hour for this struck in 741, with the death of Charles Martel.

Charles Martel had granted protection to Saint Boniface, but he had no essential interest in the labors of the Anglo-Saxons. Enough for him that he had not yielded to the worldly-minded bishops of his court, a group anything but favorably disposed toward the foreigners or willing to promote the success of men whom they regarded as troublesome monitors. This group had to be defeated if any progress was to be made in clearing the way for the growth of Christian thought and life in Germany and the Frankish kingdom. Only then would it be possible for the precious cultural seeds brought over by the Anglo-Saxons to attain their full development. Fortunately Charles Martel's sons, Carloman and Pippin the Short, showed some appreciation of this problem. Their father divided his kingdom so that Carloman, the elder, received the eastern countries — Austrasia, Swabia and Thuringia — and Pippin the western — Neustria, Burgundy and Provence. It was

Carloman, therefore, whom Saint Boniface had to consider first as the bearer of that authority which would determine the missionary's mode of action.

The two princes had received an education in the monastery of Saint Denis which had made them very responsive to the general interests of the Church. Carloman, after ruling for six years, went to Rome, to be received into the priesthood by the pope and then to do penance in monastic retirement for his deeds of violence. Pippin, the younger brother, through the medium of his friendship with Pope Stephen III would later, as the first Carolingian king, establish the pact which became the model for the amicable relations between empire and papacy in the Middle Ages. The foregoing will more than suffice to show the friendly disposition of both brothers toward the Church — a disposition of which, indeed, they were to give Saint Boniface proofs even before the pact was made.

Soon after he had taken over the reins of government, Carloman sent for the archbishop and disclosed that he intended to bring order into the confused ecclesiastical situation in his part of the kingdom through the instrumentality of a council. Boniface was requested to take the matter of this convocation in hand. Since the suggestion proceeded solely from the temporal ruler (without whom, of course, nothing could be achieved), the saint, accustomed to acting at all times in accord with the pope, wrote to the new pontiff, Pope Zachary: "If I am to take this affair in hand, at your word and at the request of the prince, I desire to have the approval and the direction of the Apostolic See, supported by the canons of the Church."[5] Boniface went on to show the necessity of the intended reform, painting an extremely dark, but true, picture of the condition of the Frankish Church. The Franks, he pointed out, had not held a synod for more than eighty years; they had no archbishop; the canonical regulations were everywhere ignored. Further, the episcopal sees had been conferred for the most part upon laymen who considered them merely as title-deeds; while those incumbents who had come into possession of dioceses as priests were in the main immoral and desirous of using the diocesan revenues for pro-

---

5. *Letters of Saint Boniface*, edition of Tangl, p. 82.

fane purposes. Many had prepared themselves for the priesthood by evil lives, and continued after ordination as before, without being hindered thereby from rising even higher. Other bishops, who could not be charged with immorality, were addicted to drink; or they completely neglected their spiritual office for hunting or warfare, scrupling not in the latter case to kill both pagans and Christians with their own hands.

Pope Zachary was long in answering. A Greek from southern Italy, he had learned his politics in a different school than his predecessor, Gregory III, who had called upon Charles Martel for help against the Lombards. Pope Zachary, on the contrary, had come to an understanding with the Lombards, and by sending a legate to the Bavarian duke, Odilo, had lent him moral support in his rebellion against the Frankish princes. Probably Zachary (who was to be the last Greek upon the papal throne) did not wish to be associated with the plan toward which Gregory II and Gregory III had directed their efforts — namely, for a political union with the northern countries which presupposed an alliance against the East. But even though Zachary's policy temporarily rendered co-operation in the ecclesiastical sphere between the pope and the archbishop more difficult, it did not hinder this completely, for Saint Boniface always held himself aloof from politics and would have been the last to defend the sacrifice of religious principles to political ends. There is no doubt that Pope Zachary subsequently approved Saint Boniface's having initiated the reform of the Frankish Church.

In the meantime, two councils had taken place. The first one — the first synod of German bishops ever to be held — had been convoked by Carloman on April 21, 742; at what place is not known. The decrees were immediately proclaimed by the ruler as ordinances which he had formulated with the advice of the spiritual and temporal nobles (for the latter were also present). Church and State thereby entered into a very close union, as in the Anglo-Saxon kingdoms. At the head of the protocol stands the announcement that bishops have been appointed for the larger cities and that Boniface, the ambassador of Saint Peter, has been placed over them as archbishop. This was not only in recognition of the prelates newly installed by Boniface in Hesse and Thuringia, but also in reference to the projected filling of several vacant sees. Metz, Verdun, Speyer and Liége received new incumbents at that time or soon afterward. Still more important was that part of the statement describing the creation of a metropolitan organization for the Church in Carloman's kingdom and the conferring of the position of metropolitan upon Boniface. Until then, neither the bishops nor the civil authority had acknowledged him as such. Thus Carloman secured to him the position which Rome had already in part accorded and in part intended to accord, and made it possible for him to carry out the needed reform of the Church in Carloman's domain.

The other decrees either aimed at full correction of the conditions pointed out by Boniface in his complaints to the pope, or were a part of the program outlined for him by Rome. In the future a synod was to be held every year. Impostor-priests and immoral clerics were declared to have forfeited their post and income, and were to be compelled to perform the penance imposed by the Church. The servants of God were forbidden to go to war, to fight, to bear arms or to hunt. Solely for the exercise of their ministry in the army, one or two bishops were permitted to accompany the prince into the field; an individual general might have only one priest. All priests were to be subject to their diocesan bishop according to the regulations of the canons, and were to give an account of their work. Bishops and priests who were unknown were to be admitted to an ecclesiastical office only after a synod had examined their ordination and found it in order.

Acting together with the count, who was described as "the defender of the Church,"[6] the bishop was to suppress all pagan and superstitious practices; thus did the State now put its power at the Church's disposal. Crimes of immorality on the part of clerics, monks, priests and nuns were to be punished with bodily chastisement and imprisonment on bread and water for periods of varying length. No priest or deacon should tolerate a woman in his house. Ecclesiastical dress must be worn. Monks and nuns were to live according to the norms of the Benedictine Rule. The intricate question of restoring the sequestered possessions of the Church was

6. Ibid., p. 100.

discussed in full accord with the desires of Saint Boniface. "We have restored the stolen ecclesiastical revenues to the churches," Carloman declared.[7] (In the sequel, however, the arrangement thus proclaimed proved to be rather theoretical than capable of thoroughgoing practical application.)

In conjunction with the usual spring assembly of the temporal lords, held on March 1, 743, a second synod was convened, at Estinnes (Lessines), a royal villa in Hainault. Again the decrees were approved by both bishops and secular princes, and proclaimed by Carloman. The decisions of the first synod were confirmed. Moreover, in accord with the concerted judgment of the bishops, a plan of procedure against forbidden marriages was adopted, and the sale of Christian slaves to pagans was prohibited.

Finally, the decree concerning the restitution of church property was modified on the strength of certain understandable arguments. Carloman was engaged in active warfare against the Alamanni and the Bavarians, and was besides confronted by events which were soon to make a campaign against the Saxons necessary. He had to retain the good will of his vassals for these military operations, and hence could not abruptly deprive them of the church lands earlier granted them by Charles Martel. Hence a compromise was struck whereby the legal principle was at least safeguarded. The Church's ownership of the alienated properties was not denied, but the properties were to remain as fiefs (*precariae*) in the hands of the present holders until their death. In return the holders were obliged to pay to the respective church or monastery one *solidus* for every household within the property. If the sovereign deemed it necessary, the estate might be leased again after the death of the holder, provided that in every case sufficient was left the church concerned to prevent its suffering want; if it was very poor, all its alienated property was to be returned to it.

Had a strict discharge of the former decree of restitution been demanded, probably the whole reform enterprise would have come to nought. The secular princes, all of whom undoubtedly held some church lands from the time of Charles Martel, would have

---

7. Ibid., p. 99.

opposed execution of the decree, and allied themselves against it with the still numerous ecclesiastical opponents of the reform and of Saint Boniface himself. Carloman could not have withstood the coalition; he would have had either to yield to it or to witness the dissolution of his empire. In either case, a further advance along the adopted path of ecclesiastical reform, which was at the same time the path of cultural progress, would have been impossible.

It was after this second synod that the answer of Pope Zachary arrived, approving the holding of councils. The pontiff also addressed a special letter to Carloman, encouraging him to proceed hand in hand with Saint Boniface. The aged saint now manifested an astonishing vigor in his efforts to complete the reform already begun, and to bring the Frankish Church to the flourishing state of the Church in his own native land. He insisted that henceforth, in accordance with ecclesiastical precepts, councils be held every year. In these, the bishops of the Frankish kingdom assembled round him now in ever greater numbers. Nor did he henceforth lack the support of the princes. In the spring of 744 a third synod took place in the Austrasian kingdom of Carloman, although we learn of it only through certain allusions in the letters of the pope.

Greater importance attached to another, held simultaneously (March 2, 744) at Soissons, in the western Frankish kingdom of Pippin, because it inaugurated the reform movement in Neustria. Saint Boniface, it is true, is not mentioned as presiding, but he appears, nevertheless, to have conducted the synod, for it conformed entirely to his views. In addition to twenty-three Neustrian bishops, a number of secular nobles were present. Following his brother's example, Pippin convoked the assembly and proclaimed its decrees, which repeated for the most part those of the two Austrasian synods. In particular they provided for the re-establishment of the metropolitan organization in the Church of Neustria; and Saint Boniface conferred the episcopal consecration upon those selected to be the metropolitans of Rheims, Rouen and Sens.

A plenary synod of all the bishops of the Frankish kingdom pointed to further progress. Following special arrangements between the pope and the two Frankish rulers, it was held under the presidency of Saint Boniface at some place we cannot now identify,

in the spring of 745. Its purpose was to insure the practical realization of the ecclesiastical reform movement in the case of certain
persons who had given public scandal. One of these was a religious
fanatic named Adalbert, a man of lowly extraction who had a great
following among the common people. He claimed to have received a special mission from heaven at the hands of an angel, who
had brought him from the farthest ends of the earth relics endowed
with miraculous power. With these he pretended to be able to
attain whatever he asked of God. Not only did the rural population
cling to him, but some illiterate bishops were also won over and
through them he obtained the episcopal consecration. Thenceforth
he considered himself the equal of the Apostles, regarded pilgrimages to their tombs as superfluous, and disdained to dedicate churches
in their honor or that of the martyrs; instead, he dedicated prayer
houses to which he gave his own name. He would erect crosses or
chapels in the field, at springs, or wherever else pleased him, where
he conducted divine services which attracted the multitudes to such
a degree that they left the churches. He distributed his hair-clippings
and nail-parings as relics. Those who wished to go to confession he
restrained, saying he knew their sins and would forgive them without confession. Besides the alleged messages from heaven (of a
type which originated in the Orient, and have been eagerly received
by the ignorant and superstitious from the first centuries to the
present), he distributed another curious piece of literature of his
own composition: a prayer to the "Father of the Holy Angels," in
which occurred the names of angels never heard before.

A different type of heretic was Clement the Irishman, an intellectual who had compounded his own religion. He rejected the
laws of the Church and refused to accept some of the writings
of the Fathers. Though he called himself a bishop, he did not
wish to submit to the law of celibacy; he held, too, that marriage
with the widow of one's deceased brother was permissible. He had
his own doctrine on Christ's descent into hell; according to him the
Saviour, on that occasion, freed all the damned. Clement also
taught predestination.

The sentence which the council passed on both these men, of
imprisonment in a monastery, was not executed for they succeeded

in making their escape. They must have had influential protectors. The Neustrians were unwilling to give Adalbert up despite the fact that their ruler, Pippin, had ordered the field crosses set up by him to be burned. Both Adalbert and Clement soon appeared in public once more. Only after a Roman synod had also condemned them, were they stripped of all their priestly offices. Adalbert was sentenced to imprisonment in a monastery, while Clement was excommunicated.

A third troublemaker against whom the Frankish plenary synod of 745 proceeded, was the typical opponent of the reform movement and at the same time an old personal antagonist of Saint Boniface. This was Bishop Gewilieb of Mainz. He and his father Gerold, who occupied the see before him, belonged to that class of bishops whose immoral and unecclesiastical lives were the subject of complaint. Against them in particular were directed the synodal decrees which prohibited bishops from hunting, bearing arms and engaging in battle. They had been supported by Charles Martel, with whom they stood in high favor. Gerold is supposed to have fallen in battle at the head of his troops in one of Charles' campaigns against the Saxons. Gewilieb, on the other hand, is said to have invited the Saxon who killed his father in battle to an interview in another campaign and treacherously slain him. This was probably the reason for proceeding against him now, for Saint Boniface designates him as a murderer. The synod deposed him.

A synod convened by Saint Boniface in the spring of 747, representing the ideal which he desired to achieve in the Frankish kingdom, constituted the climax of the reform activities. At the head of the decrees, which were joyfully accepted by the pope, stood the profession of the Catholic faith, accompanied by a declaration of the assembled bishops promising willing subjection to the successor of Saint Peter at all times and obedience to his direction in all things. The metropolitans were to procure the pallium, external symbol of their duties and their greater right of supervision, from the Roman See. The prescriptions of canon law and the Benedictine Rule were to be read and inculcated anew at the annual synods. The metropolitan was to admonish and supervise his suffragan bishops. The bishop was to keep a watchful eye on his diocesan clergy. Every priest was to give his bishop an account, in Lent, of his faith, his baptisms, and the whole performance of his public duties. The bishop was to visit his diocese each year; he was to confirm and teach, take measures against pagan practices and superstition, and strive to lead an exemplary life; in particular, the chase, luxurious dress and military attire were forbidden him. The ideal bishop of Saint Boniface must not show himself in outward appearance as a ruler parading splendor, or as a fighting vassal, but as the servant of God which he ought in reality to be.

The directions of the council must be communicated to each diocese at a diocesan synod to be conducted soon thereafter by the bishop and participated in by priests and abbots. Abuses which the bishop was unable to correct in his diocese must be reported to the metropolitan previous to the synod of the ecclesiastical province, just as the metropolitan was obliged to inform the Roman Church of those matters which he himself could not amend; in this way each was able to divide responsibility for the souls entrusted to him.

But this program, which looked toward a most intimate union between the Frankish Church and Rome, met with difficulties in its execution. The fact that only thirteen bishops from both parts of the kingdom attended the synod which adopted the program, and that there is no mention of the rulers, makes it clear that Saint Boniface was here surrounded only by his most loyal supporters. The Frankish rulers were perfectly willing that the Church be reformed; but they were not willing to sacrifice anything of the ancient suzerainty of the Merovingians over the national ecclesiastical body. They wanted to execute reform without letting the Church get out of their hands as a result of it.

Particularly concerned over this matter was Pippin, who had brought the whole kingdom under his control in 747, when his brother Carloman retired from the government to go to Rome and enter the priesthood there. Pippin now obstructed the plan of organization outlined by Saint Boniface, which was to give the metropolitans much more power than formerly and bring them closer to the position the archbishop of Canterbury had attained in the Church in the English missions. Undoubtedly Pippin feared the Frankish Church would thereby be withdrawn from his domination. He paid no heed to the decrees which the last synod had formulated. He likewise feared a strengthening of particularistic tendencies as a result of the projected metropolitan system; and being above all apprehensive of such an eventuality in Austrasia, refused to appoint Saint Boniface metropolitan there.

It cannot be questioned that Saint Boniface validly possessed the status of archbishop and papal legate by appointment from Rome; but he had no episcopal see, to serve as the seat of a metropolitan. His adherents had at first considered Cologne for his see, but that project did not materialize. They then fixed on Mainz, to which Saint Boniface no doubt gave his assent because the mission field nearest his heart, that of Thuringia and Hesse, depended upon Mainz. The pope was certainly in accord with this; but not so Pippin. Saint Boniface had to content himself with becoming merely bishop of Mainz and petitioning Pippin to acknowledge Saint Lullus, his faithful disciple, as his coadjutor with the right of succession.

The letter in which Saint Boniface solicited this favor from Pippin, who had in the meantime been raised to the kingship, discloses the deeper reason for his misgivings in regard to a successor. At the same time it is valuable as a proof of the loyalty with which he clung to his old missionary colleagues and pupils, and also of the difficulties with which these poor, unambitious Anglo-Saxon missionaries wrestled. Pointing to his infirmities and his no longer distant end, the saint beseeches the king to relieve his anxiety concerning the welfare of his disciples:

> They are, so to speak, almost all strangers. Some are appointed as priests to serve the Church and the nations in many localities; others dwell as monks in our cells or as children who are being instructed; there are also old men among them who have labored with me and supported me for a long time. For all these am I weighed down with anxiety. I earnestly pray that they may not fare badly after my death, but rather may receive reward and protection from Your Highness, that they be not dispersed as sheep who lack a shepherd, and that the nations of pagan frontier-lands destroy not the Law of Christ. Therefore I urgently beseech your Benevolent Highness in God's name to install my beloved son and chorepiscopus Lullus, if God so wills and it please Your Benevolence, as the servant of the nations and the churches and to appoint him the preacher and teacher of the priests and peoples. And I hope, if

God so ordains, that the priests will have in him a master, the monks a teacher in conformity with the Rule, and the Christian nations a faithful preacher and shepherd. But the reason why I am begging this favor is principally because my priests are eking out a very poor livelihood on the confines of the pagan lands. They are doubtless still able to find the bread required for their sustenance; but, as I have maintained them until now, they cannot procure clothing unless they have an adviser and helper elsewhere who will assist them to survive in those parts and to persevere in the service of the people.[8]

By this humble address, allowing the king the decisive word in the appointment of bishops and completely setting aside the plan for metropolitan organization, Boniface prevailed with Pippin. The king agreed that the succession to the see of Mainz be accorded the saint's candidate Lullus, but only as bishop. Thirty years later, however, after the saint's death, his patient waiting finally bore the desired fruit: Lullus was able to obtain the pallium, and Mainz actually became the metropolitan see and the seat of the primate of Germany.

The relations of Boniface with the Frankish rulers were thorny, but not because these men were unsympathetic to his aims. His activity as a missionary among the Hessians and Thuringians had been possible only through the protection vouchsafed him by Charles Martel. His reform of the Frankish Church could never have succeeded to such an extent — could never have been undertaken — had not Carloman and Pippin proffered a helping hand. He himself openly acknowledged this. We find it most loyally spoken in a letter to his old friend, Bishop Daniel of Winchester, to whom he often bared his soul:

Without the protection of the Frankish ruler I could neither govern the people of the Church nor defend the priests and clerics, monks and handmaids of God; neither would I be able to suppress the pagan practices and the idolatry in Germany except for his command and the people's fear of him.[9]

But despite the real and important co-operation accorded especially by Carloman and Pippin, the saint's relations with them

---

8. Ibid., pp. 213 sqq.
9. Ibid., p. 130.

never became intimate or personal. His long sojourn in the Frankish
kingdom could not make Boniface feel anything but an Anglo-Saxon.
He thus preserved, on the one hand, a sense of independence, which
only confirmed him in his efforts in favor of an independent organization of the Church; and on the other, remained aloof from the
rulers' political aims (of which indeed his purely religious bent
allowed him but little understanding). He always found attendance
at court difficult because he met there those bishops whose unecclesiastical lives repelled him; they, however, were well liked there
as veteran supporters and friends of the Carolingian house.

Had Saint Boniface been other than he was, had he possessed
even a moderate hankering to play a political part, he certainly
could have achieved a prominent one. The powerful role of mediator between king and pope would have fallen to his lot in 751,
when Pippin was raised to the kingship. As it was, the famous
decision of Pope Zachary concerning Pippin's election to the kingship was not procured through Saint Boniface at all, but through
Fulrad, the abbot of Saint Denis, and Burchard, the bishop of
Würzburg. Saint Boniface asserted himself so little while anointing
Pippin — a ceremony undoubtedly performed at the pope's direction
according to the Anglo-Saxon custom — that his collaboration is not
mentioned by most historic sources.

Totally different was his position with regard to the papacy.
Here he always felt like a son who remains closely united with his
father by a bond of reverence while he enjoys at the same time a
freedom enheartening him to express himself on everything, great
or small, that worries or oppresses him. In the questions which he
directed to Rome, there was evident a candor that is perhaps best
explained by the spirit of the Rule of his Order — its author began
it with the words: "Hearken, O my son, to the precept of your
master, and incline the ear of your heart: willingly receive . . . the
admonition of your loving father."[10] Thus also may be explained
his openly voicing his opinion when some report reached him about
happenings or conditions in Rome which he regarded as mistakes or

---

10. *Benedicti Regula,* Prologus, trans. Delatte-McCann, *The Rule of Saint Benedict:
A Commentary,* p. 1.

abuses. And a blessing rested upon this candid relationship. It was only through the mutual co-operation of missionary and pope that the great result was brought about with which Saint Boniface's name is connected in history. He had need of his prudent adviser and paternal leader. Had he not been directed by a more authoritative hand and a broader vision from Rome, where one surveying the West from a high lookout discerned what was possible at the time and what was necessary in the first place, he would probably have pursued only his immediate aim and fallen an early victim to the plots of the Frisians or Saxons. History might have reported hardly more about him than it did about the Ewald brothers, who were slain by the Saxons.

Saint Boniface's success in establishing Christianity firmly in central Germany and in reforming the Frankish Church is in large part also the success of the contemporary popes. Boniface was the first to recognize this. He might at times address remonstrances and requests to Rome which caused astonishment there, but he always remained mindful of the obligations he had voluntarily assumed to the papacy. In one of his last letters, written in 751, he undertook an examination of his conscience on the manner in which he had kept the oath he had sworn to Gregory II. He concluded that he had certainly always supported good bishops and priests, but those unfaithful and wicked he had not always avoided. It was an old reproach, which he could never fully silence, that visits to the court had frequently brought him into association with such clerics and he had not refused social relations, even though he had refrained from all ecclesiastical communion with them. He further asked himself the question whether in accordance with the prescription of Gregory II, he had always informed the Apostolic See of the behavior of the peoples he had taught. He believed he could answer in the affirmative. But it still weighed on his mind that he had yielded too much to Pippin's shifting policy in the affair of the metropolitan appointment, and he begged the pope in due form to forgive him on this score.

In the face of such dispositions toward the Holy See, there could be no real estrangement. It was precisely during Boniface's final labors for the reform of the whole Frankish Church that the union between him and Zachary became especially close. The applications of the saint for papal directives increased, as did the pope's answers and heartening words. In support of his legate Zachary dispatched letters to the most varied recipients. He wrote to the Frankish rulers encouraging them to collaborate with the reform endeavors. He addressed a letter to all the clerics and the laymen in the Frankish kingdom admonishing them to obey Boniface and to avoid the condemned bishops and priests who opposed him; and the clergy he exhorted, moreover, to live as servants of God and not to disgrace their office. In answer to the complaints which Boniface sent to Rome regarding grave abuses connected with the churches and monasteries erected on private estates, Pope Zachary sent a letter to certain powerful laymen involved, laying down the accepted ecclesiastical principles: No priest might be appointed to a church unless ordained by the diocesan bishop or received into his diocese on the strength of reliable recommendation. Abbots and abbesses (often arbitrarily installed by the owners of monasteries) were to be blessed by the diocesan bishop after their election by the community and after an examination regarding their competence and training. The ecclesiastical tithes were to be left to the churches. No one was to be ordained unless his position and mode of life were clearly known. And (since landowners sometimes had their bondmen ordained, by whoever would do it, for appointment to the churches on their estates) the pope added that no bondman could be raised to the priesthood or assigned a church.

Saint Boniface received particular proof of papal confidence when he undertook to establish in Germany a model monastery conforming to the original traditions of the Benedictine rule, which he had had repeatedly proclaimed in the reform councils as the only true monastic standard. He selected with great care a site on the Fulda river, and sent his disciple, the Bavarian Sturm, to Rome to familiarize himself with the institutions of the Benedictine monasteries. Sturm repaired to Monte Cassino, which, after lying desolate for a long time, had risen anew under Pope Gregory II and entered upon a second period of flowering. In accord with fundamental Benedictine principles, the new monastic community in Fulda sought to provide independently for its own support.

Saint Benedict desired this in order that his brethren might be kept as remote as possible from contact with the world. It was with this idea in mind that he and his disciple had searched in the forest of Buchonia with such care for a foundation site far away from human settlements. The location finally chosen forced the brethren as a matter of necessity to follow Saint Benedict's prescription of manual labor, for they had to erect the necessary buildings and clear the surrounding region for tillage. The aged archbishop himself did not hesitate to lend a helping hand occasionally, for the purpose of demonstrating how highly he esteemed the regulation of the Order's founder and the value of bodily toil.

Besides agriculture, the productive crafts and the arts flourished in Fulda; it became for central Germany what Saint Gall was for Switzerland: an economic center which exerted by its example a beneficial influence far and wide. Moreover, the humanities soon found a home there as well, for the high culture of the Anglo-Saxon monasteries was transplanted to Germany. (Saint Boniface himself, we recall, had once been a teacher in England, and, besides his letters, there remain a grammar, some fragments on metrics, and some riddle-poems composed after the models of Saint Aldhelm, to bear witness to his literary activity.) Within a few decades of its foundation, Fulda had become a center of learned activities.

In order to secure this favorite foundation — he had chosen it as his burial place — against the sort of encroachment from outside influences which might extinguish its new life, Saint Boniface had recourse to a special precaution. Many a monastery had been imperiled at the height of its prosperity by an abbot who was forced upon it. From this eventuality he wanted to save Fulda, which, like the church of the Lateran, had been dedicated to the Saviour. Accordingly, he proposed to place it directly under the protection of Rome; under that authority with whose aid he had repeatedly given worthy shepherds to so many dioceses. He presented this petition to Pope Zachary as a personal request. The pontiff acquiesced gladly and gave the monastery the privilege of exemption whereby every ecclesiastical authority was restrained from exercising any jurisdiction whatsoever over it (751). However, as papal exemption was a completely new idea in the Frankish kingdom, Saint Boniface was not able to obtain its ratification by Pippin.

Saint Boniface served yet a fourth pope: Stephen III. In his congratulatory letter, dated 752, the aged archbishop begged the new pontiff to accord him the honor of continuing to serve the Holy See under him as faithfully and devotedly as he had served it under his three predecessors, the two Gregorys and Zachary, who by their letters had always strengthened him with their encouragement and supported him with their authority:

> I beg Your Excellency to deign to do the same, that I may be the better able to fulfill Your paternal commands completely; for if I have done anything useful for the Church in the course of the commission which I received from Rome and in which I have been engaged now for thirty-six years, I would yet finish it and amplify it. If it is found, however, that I have acted without experience or done or said anything wrong, I willingly and humbly promise that I will amend my ways according to the judgment of the Church of Rome.[11]

We perceive that the man advanced in years was still young in purpose, with fresh plans for the future. These led him, whose life and labors reveal a rare constancy, back to his starting point. He could not be reconciled to his almost complete failure to convert the Frisians and Saxons, the kinsfolk of his own people. The undertaking had once aroused his youthful enthusiasm. Now, though success among the Saxons was completely out of the question, he wished to make the attempt once more among the Frisians, since he had provided for his brethren and arranged his burial place.

He had a presentiment of what was in store, for he caused a shroud to be put in the chest of books which he took with him. In a farewell visit with the abbess Lioba, who journeyed to Fulda for the purpose at his request, he begged her not to leave this alien country to which she had come for his sake, but rather to persevere in her fruitful labors here to the end. He gave her, moreover, a special proof of his brotherly love. Recalling Saint Benedict's parting from Saint Scholastica, he arranged that after Lioba's death her body should be interred in the same tomb as his own at Fulda;

---

11. *Letters of Saint Boniface,* edition of Tangl, p. 234.

that their earthly remains might await together the day of resurrection, whose dedicated lives had served Christ in the same endeavors and with the same ardent devotion. Although the authors of that period were not skilled in describing human emotion, it is clear from what is set down how difficult the parting was for these two, whose love for each other was fused in their common longing for their native land; and how highly is to be rated the sacrifice, which they made by remaining in exile for the sake of God.

Some of his countrymen accompanied the aged archbishop on his last missionary journey. On June 5, 754, pagan Frisians fell upon the camp on the Borne river in the vicinity of the present city of Dokkum, where Saint Boniface was waiting to baptize many newly instructed converts. Admonishing his companions to stand firm, the saint, now almost eighty years old, awaited the attack. One by one the missionaries succumbed to the savage blows. When Boniface's turn came, he tried to shield his head from the deathstroke with a book he held in his hand. This codex survives in Fulda today; it contains various treatises of dogma and proves by the plainly recognizable imprints of the blows how steadfastly Boniface adhered in death to the faith of the Church of Rome, which during his whole lifetime had been his guide and consolation. Fifty-two companions died with their shepherd for that faith.

If any doubt existed regarding the idealism which animated Saint Boniface and his companions, it was dissipated by their manner of death. Saint Boniface's martyrdom in particular had a powerful effect on the age. There was an urgent need to present both priests and people with just this ideal of the spiritual shepherd in all its purity and to wean them from the notion that the episcopal office was merely an aggregate of authority, worldly power and material possessions.

And while the concept of the true priest was thus being spiritualized, the culture of the whole nation was rising. The period of barbarism introduced by the Germans when they overthrew the Western Roman Empire, had lasted its term and was now approaching an end. Out of the ruins of the age of the migration of nations sprang the germs of a new culture, destined to integrate the treasures of the ancient civilization, now gradually reappearing, with what the

Germans had to offer in the way of healthy naturalness, fresh and youthful vigor. The fine fruits of Anglo-Saxon achievement in the religious, moral and literary fields were brought over to the continent. Hence it was that the period of Charlemagne could follow hard upon the period of Boniface. The latter had been the pioneer for what we may call the Carolingian renaissance. The seed he planted in the Frankish kingdom sprang up majestically and brought forth the splendid harvest which Charlemagne was able to reap.

But his importance transcends his epoch. Through Saint Boniface a living and intimate union was established between the several centers of religious life in Western Christendom. The churches in the Anglo-Saxon and Frankish kingdoms entered into a warm reciprocal relationship with each other and with Italy, which removed them from the danger of internal stagnation and paralysis. Active union with the head of the Church, the successor of Saint Peter, brought with it a regulated religious life, the refreshing of the continuity of tradition, and the reassertion of the teaching authority. Men learned to view religious problems with the large vision which transcends national boundaries. Finally, ecclesiastical unity was followed by general intellectual and cultural unity. And, to repeat, it was principally Saint Boniface who brought the popes closer to the Frankish kingdom, and the German lands, then beginning to absorb Christian civilization, closer to the Romance countries, especially Italy.

The cultural community of the West had come into being. This was evident also from the action of the papacy in severing at this time the political union which had bound it for centuries to the East. The action had been preceded by a long series of events, which we must further consider if we are to gain a full insight into the final outcome. Simultaneously, the West was forced into a closer internal union by the attack of Islam, which wrested the Iberian Peninsula from it. Thus was accelerated the birth of the cultural community of the West, and thus was conditioned the formation of its first league of nations.

Chapter Six

SEPARATION OF ROME FROM CONSTANTINOPLE —
THE ATTACK OF ISLAM

THE beginnings of the Middle Ages are characterized by the formation of two new cultural communities in place of the one which had embraced the whole Mediterranean shore, with Rome for its center. In the West, as we have seen, the Roman Empire had fallen apart, and upon the ruins there arose a congeries of culturally united nations. In the East the Byzantine Empire was in the process of consolidation, developing meanwhile a more and more specialized character.

The separation of the Eastern half of the Roman Empire from the Western was inevitable from the beginning because the fundamental strata of society in the two were different. The Western had a Roman or Romance population; the Eastern was Greek or Hellenized. This difference first became more sharply pronounced as a result of the political separation effected by the emperor Diocletian, who transferred his residence to Nicomedia in the East and divided the imperial administration not only among different persons but also according to geographical districts. His purpose was not at all a division of empire, but merely a uniform and energetic assertion of the administrative authority in the various imperial territories; indeed, he took special precautions to give external prominence to the unity of the empire. For example, the Augustus (emperor) of the West was to be subordinated to the Augustus of the East, who was Diocletian himself. Moreover, all edicts, laws, inscriptions and public documents, even when they emanated from only one Augustus, carried the names of both. But since the military and civil authority in each part was completely separated from that in the other part, and this division under two emperors coincided with national differences, it was inevitable that the empire should finally resolve itself into two independent halves.

Frequent attempts were made to halt or reverse this development, the most important by Constantine, who immediately upon coming into power reunited the empire. But in point of fact he only increased the divergencies by giving to the East a fixed and magnificent center through his conversion of the ancient Greek commercial town of Byzantium into a residential city, Constantinople. Situated on the confines of two continents, the new imperial residence had a far more auspicious location than ancient Rome, which it was soon able to rival in splendor and importance. The division of the empire can be regarded as permanent from the year 364, when Valentinian I shared the imperial lands and the armies with his brother Valens. It was only temporarily that Theodosius united them once more in the last year of his life. The division which he planned and which became effective after his death in 395 was all the more decisive when his sons Arcadius and Honorius took over the East and West respectively.

The final boundary line between the Eastern and the Western empires was also fixed. While Valentinian I had drawn the whole of Illyria to the West, its eastern portion was now added to the Byzantine empire. This, then, comprised two large districts. One of these was subject to the *praefectus praetorio per Illyricum,* who resided in Sirmium near Mitrowitza — a most dangerous spot — and governed Dacia, Macedonia and southern Greece. The other part was subject to the *praefectus praetorio per Orientem,* who had residence in Antioch and ruled over the Asiatic provinces, besides Egypt, Marmarica (Libya) and Cyrene (Cyrenaica or Barca) in Africa, and Thrace in Europe.

The unity of the empire now survived only in the appointment of the two consuls, after whom the years were still named, one being appointed by each emperor.

In the first onslaughts of the migrating nations it seemed as though the Eastern empire would succumb even before the Western. But the founding of Constantinople, the military center of the empire, not far from the lower Danube, which was the line exposed to danger, had considerably increased the Eastern power of resistance. And fortune favored the East as well. In the beginning, it is true, it had borne the brunt of the attack but soon the pressure of the races shifted westward. The Visigoths moved toward Italy; the Huns, too, finally poured into the Western empire; the great masses of Western Germans advanced over the Rhine frontier into Gaul.

While the West was thus falling a prey to the barbarian, we observe the Eastern empire striving to strengthen itself internally. This is particularly evident in the codification of the imperial constitutions by means of which the legal records of former centuries were given a lucid exposition. The emperor Theodosius II first ordered a collection published in 438 as an official code. This was acknowledged in the West as well as the East, which thereby became the custodian of the ancient traditions of the Roman Empire, a fact explaining the sentiments of the Roman population of Italy in the fifth and sixth centuries.

It was only natural, therefore, that the Eastern Roman emperors should have conceived the plan of reasserting Roman domination in the West and driving the barbarians out. This plan, which was not devoid of a certain grandeur, was inaugurated by the emperor Leo I (457-474), whom the Greeks called "the Great." In 468 he undertook an expedition to wrest the province of Africa from the Vandals. Though he did not succeed, the general policy was not abandoned on that account, and we note in the East from this emperor's time onward a reaction against the separation of the two parts of the Roman Empire. This is easily understood: the Eastern empire felt itself the stronger part, the one upon which devolved the preservation and continuance of the ancient imperial traditions.

This active attitude, however, was confined almost solely to the East; in contrast, the West was passive toward the prospect of division. It became increasingly evident, indeed, that the historical development of the West pointed, not to reunion, but to definitive separation. The Eastern Roman emperors failed to realize that just as important as driving the Germans out of the occupied countries — Africa, Italy and Spain — was inspiring the Romans in the West to support this project and not allowing anything to arise which would estrange them from the East. From the very first they adopted a religious policy fatal to the design of union — a policy which strengthened those opposing religious currents that were the outgrowth of profounder differences between the Oriental and the Occidental mind.

The Roman emperors, even after they had become Christian, had been unwilling to renounce the function they had exercised in pagan times of pronouncing final and decisive judgment in religious matters. After Constantine had proclaimed Christianity as the state religion, his successor concluded that, because it was their duty to safeguard the unity and purity of the faith, it was their right to have a voice in religious controversies. In a word, the imperial power always carried within itself the tendency to develop into caesaropapism. Had the imperial power continued in existence in the West, that tendency would hardly have failed to declare itself there, and the unhampered ecclesiastical development of the West would not have been possible. There were other circumstances, too, which intensified the growth of caesaropapism in the East. In vast tracts of the Eastern empire, Christianity had been forced upon the people. Paganism, which had strong roots here as a result of the Neo-Platonic philosophy and the prestige of Hellenistic schooling, had in no small measure been overcome through the forceful intervention of the imperial power, frequently to the accompaniment of bloodshed. While there now remained among the Romans of the West hardly any distinct traces of paganism, the emperor Justinian was still fighting it in the East. One of his measures was to command the immediate baptism of all who were still pagan, and there proved to be many of these, especially among the educated classes in Constantinople. Not until the year 529 were the pagan schools in Athens closed.

In the West, by way of contrast, the victory over paganism had been more internal than external, and had been achieved without bloody struggles. Curiously enough, the invading Germans had indirectly fostered the triumph of Christianity. The Roman officials fled, while the bishops remained — we recall that it was the highest types from among the aristocratic and educated classes who devoted themselves to the service of the Church. Those circles from which paganism had principally drawn its leaders turned away from it in the distress of the times. Everything that was Roman, high and low, became one at heart again in the Catholic Church to oppose the barbarians. It was by the same process that the still Celtic rural population of Gaul was Romanized when it was visited by the barbarians in the fifth century. All those who felt themselves hard pressed, namely, the *Romani* or *Christiani,* combined to form a united front against Arianism, the religion of the Germanic rulers.

The struggle of paganism and Christianity in the West found a parallel in the struggle between Arianism and Catholicism in the East. Arianism was widespread in that region, and for a brief time in the fourth century was actually the official religion; the Germans borrowed it from there. It was exterminated principally as the result of the drastic measures of the emperor Theodosius I. The situation was different in the West, where Constantius had been able to introduce Arianism only by fraud and for a time.

These circumstances help us to understand why the Church in the East always retained the marks of a state church. The emperors did not wish to tolerate ecclesiastical autonomy side by side with their own. Those who resisted this tendency sought and in most cases found protection from the papacy in Rome (as instanced earlier in the case of Saint John Chrysostom, who was banished from the imperial court). It was not that the Eastern rulers denied the ecclesiastical authority of the successor of Saint Peter; but they sought to restrict it. The emperor Marcian had indeed adopted a thoroughly correct attitude at the Council of Chalcedon in 451 which acknowledged as a rule of faith the now famous dogmatic epistle of Pope Leo I against the teaching of Eutyches. In the last session, however, after the papal legates had left the Council, it was decreed that the bishop of New Rome should have the same honorary privileges as the bishop of Old Rome!

The patriarchs of Constantinople, mere puppets in the hand of the emperors, showed only too clearly what might have become of the papacy had the emperors continued to maintain their residence in Rome alongside the pope's. The principle recognized by Marcian, that ecclesiastical authorities shall independently decide ecclesiastical matters, was soon abandoned. With the design of clearing the atmosphere in the controversies concerning the nature of Christ, the emperors proceeded to prescribe formulas of faith by legislation —

thereby, of course, only provoking fresh dissensions. A whole series of such religious laws came into being. The popes combated them on principle, struggling as much for the independence of their own position as for the freedom of the whole Church. Italian circles came gradually to understand this, and to realize that in the Roman pontiff they had the only dignitary whose importance went beyond the confines of Italy. But their aversion to the emperor in Constantinople also increased in the same proportion as their understanding grew of the importance of independence for the papacy.

Thus, as we have said, the religious policy of the Eastern Roman emperors counteracted their political policy, which aimed at regaining the West. This is above all patent in the Acacian schism which formed a sequel to the religious edict of the emperor Zeno. Intent upon putting an end to the persistent Monophysitic controversies, this ruler issued a religious law in 482 promulgating for general acceptance, in a formula called the *Henotikon,* the elements common to the religious beliefs of the various dissident factions. The adherents of the Council of Chalcedon (451) necessarily took exception to this action, which treated the Council's authority as an open question. One of the chief collaborators of the *Henotikon,* Bishop Acacius of Constantinople, was excommunicated by Pope Felix III for his heterodox views; and the accompanying controversy, though it revolved about the name of Acacius, was in reality a contest between the emperor and the pope over which was to be the authority in matters of faith. The Acacian schism divided the East and the West for the thirty-five years from 484 to 519, actually forming the prelude to the later schism. Its background is interesting as showing how religious and political circumstances played upon each other.

This was the time when Theodoric the Ostrogoth, after conquering Odoacer, had taken possession of Italy. At the very beginning of the period of foreign domination, the Roman senators were seriously concerned about preserving relations with Constantinople. The schism being extremely inconvenient to this endeavor, they were anxious to do away with it even at the cost of the Roman pontiff's authority in matters of faith. Out of the conflict between this Byzantine party and the purely papal party, if we may use the phrase, there arose a division in the Church itself, called the Laurentian schism from Lawrence, the papal candidate supported by the Byzantine party. Against this group Pope Symmachus was able to maintain himself only with the help of Theodoric. It was during the conflict that the so-called "Symmachian Forgeries" appeared — spurious letters, acts of councils, decrees and historical reports, all composed by papal partisans with the design of proving that no power on earth had competence to judge the pope. However, the need of citing a historical basis for papal authority produced at the same time that valuable collection of biographies of the popes, the *Liber Pontificalis*. Continued at various intervals over the following centuries, these constitute precisely our best source of information on the trials of the papacy in the long struggle with the Eastern Roman Empire.

It is during this initial conflict between the empire and the papacy that we hear for the first time theoretical observations concerning the relations of these powers. Pope Gelasius writes to the emperor Anastasius in 494 as follows:

> There are two forces whereby the world is principally ruled: the sacred authority of the priests and the royal power. Of the two the importance of the priests is so much the greater, in that they must also render an account before the judgment of God for the kings of men.[1]

The papacy received expressions of enthusiastic sympathy from the West — from Italy, Africa and Burgundy. But the forces of the contestants were very unequal since, notwithstanding the conflict, the emperor in Constantinople was the recognized successor of the Roman emperors. The same Pope Gelasius, despite the fact that he was at variance with the emperor, had clearly expressed how the common bond still united Old and New Rome:

> As a born Roman I love the Roman emperor and honor him and acknowledge him, and as a Christian I wish to possess, in accordance with our knowledge of truth, the same zeal which he has for the glory of God.[2]

---

1. Thiel, *Epp. Rom. Pont.*, I, 350.
2. Ibid., 349.

If the consciousness of a common cause was still so strong in times of religious dissension, we can gauge something of the attraction still existing between Eastern and Western Rome.

When the Acacian schism was eventually suppressed in 519 by Justin, successor of the emperor Anastasius, the situation between the papacy and the Romans, on the one hand, and Theodoric, on the other, immediately altered. As long as the ecclesiastical opposition between Constantinople and Rome lasted, the political opposition between Theodoric and Rome did not assert itself. Now, ecclesiastical unity strengthened once more the consciousness of political homogeneity between the Romans of Italy and those of the East, and intensified in the same degree the differences between the Italians and the Goths, who were barbarians and Arians.

This was the period which witnessed the condemnation of Boethius and Symmachus, already recounted, as well as Theodoric's conflict with Pope John. In order to show that the pontiff was subject to him and under his control, the Gothic ruler sent John to Constantinople in 525 to obtain from the emperor cessation of the official persecution being directed against the Arian Goths in the East. The pontiff had no choice but to undertake the painful journey — the first made by any pope to the Greek capital. He had no reason, however, to be dissatisfied with his reception. The emperor Justin, who had received the crown very soon after his accession from the patriarch of Constantinople, as was customary since the time of Pulcheria (450), now had himself crowned by the pope instead of by the patriarch, according to the traditional ceremonial during the solemn services on Easter. John's stay in Constantinople thus lasted until after the feast of Easter in 526. Immediately upon his return he was incarcerated in Ravenna by Theodoric, who was displeased with the answer which he brought back. The imprisonment was soon terminated by death, and the ensuing papal elections were dominated by Theodoric's influence. The popes sought to escape this situation by a desperate attempt to vest in the pontiff the right to appoint his successor.

But the power of the Ostrogothic kings declined very rapidly. It was terminated by the outstanding Eastern Roman emperor Justinian I, who systematically prosecuted a plan for uniting East and West under his scepter, and in large measure succeeded in making this a reality. In the years 533-534 his general, Belisarius, conquered the kingdom of the Vandals in Africa, and soon afterward began the reconquest of Italy and Rome. However, the papacy was unfavorably affected by the military regime of Belisarius, who ordered the deposition of Pope Silverius in favor of Vigilius.

The year 535 is the last in which a Western consul is appointed. During their reign in Italy the Goths had named the Western consul and the emperor at Constantinople apparently recognized him. When the war between the Ostrogoths and the Eastern Romans broke out, the joint naming of consuls ceased. In the East also, after 541, consuls disappear. Thus vanished a bond, external it is true, but very important nevertheless, between the East and the West.

With the destruction of the Ostrogothic kingdom, Italy became, as Africa had already become, a province of the Eastern Roman Empire. Questions now arose: were the other countries of the West to follow Italy? or was Italy to be torn from the West and belong to the East? or would she separate from the East altogether and enter into a new union with the West? For the present, the Eastern Roman campaign was still progressing along the lines so energetically laid down by Justinian, its latest activity being the occupation of a number of the coastal cities of Spain. The luster which this policy of reconquest has given to Justinian's reign is second only to that imparted by his legal monument the *Corpus iuris,* which is still held in honor today. This compilation had been entrusted, at his command, to a commission of jurisconsults headed by Tribonian.

Justinian took the most diversified measures to attach Italy, and especially the Church of Italy, firmly to the Eastern Roman Empire. By means of the pragmatic sanction decreed in 554 at the request of Pope Vigilius, the emperor's civil code was introduced into Italy; and those decrees of the last Ostrogothic ruler which had been in any way adverse to the Romans were now abolished. The Roman administration was completely restored, and the Church was accorded a vast amount of consideration and a position of trust. Protective laws helped her secure herself against wanton or forced alienation of church property: any prescription of her rights was to be effective only after a hundred years. Further, the Church was able to strengthen her privileged position as a court of justice: not only was her jurisdiction over clerics recognized in all spiritual matters, but the ecclesiastical tribunal now became obligatory for clerics — it had originally been only optional — as the first instance in civil suits as well. In a criminal case against a cleric the civil judge had to transmit the records of the suit to the bishop, who then either deposed the cleric and delivered him over to the civil judge or appealed to the decision of the emperor. Since, moreover, the emperor needed the bishops in the government of the country (for the public officials did not inspire sufficient confidence), the bishops had a share not only in the free-will jurisdiction, but also in the naming of guardians and trustees and the supervision of prisons and of the right of asylum. They were authorized to intervene wherever in their opinion an official gave cause for complaint or offense. They were considered as a board of supervisors, who could always appeal to the emperor and who had a voice particularly in the financial management of the cities, the control of their food supplies, and the requirements of communication.

But in granting the bishops these powers the Eastern Roman Empire merely furnished Italy with the means of going her separate way should she regard union with the East as against her own interests. That time was not long in coming. The splendor of the Byzantine rule very soon proved itself to be a mere external show rather than the manifestation of real power. This became obvious within a few years of the annihilation of the Goths, when the Lombards burst into Italy. The forces which the Eastern ruler was able to muster were too small to provide any effective resistance against the invaders, and it became customary to deal with them by means rather of diplomacy than of arms. This, of course, did not particularly increase the Romans' respect for Constantinople. Moreover, the Byzantine officers not infrequently made themselves hated by their avarice and injustice. Hence it was that Gregory the Great could write these bitter words:

The malice of the exarch inflicts greater harm upon us than the Lombards' sword, so that the enemies who kill us seem to us more tenderhearted than the imperial commanders who, by their malice, their system of robbery and their duplicity, rend our hearts asunder.[3]

If protection against the injustice of the Greek officers was to be found anywhere at all, it was solely with the pope. After the disappearance of the Roman Senate (which is mentioned for the last time, as we have seen, in 603), the papacy became the sole glory and pride of the Roman populace. If the Greeks of the East had the Roman Empire, the Latins of Italy had the custodian of the faith, who was also their advocate in affliction. To protect his freedom and independence and to enhance his position was now among the first concerns of the inhabitants of central Italy. They were able to do this effectively once they themselves had taken up arms again because of the insufficiency of the imperial troops to hold the Lombards in check. The Roman militia — fighting units organized from among the native population — is mentioned for the first time about the middle of the seventh century. It came to acquire, in Rome and outside it, considerable political influence. At papal elections, as well as at episcopal elections in many Italian cities, it constituted a separate electoral body whose vote was often of great consequence.

In the course of time these soldiers felt themselves called upon to protect the independence of the papacy — and indeed, only too often did it stand in need of such protection. After Italy's incorporation into the Eastern Roman Empire in 555, every papal election had to be ratified in Constantinople, nor was consecration permitted until this approval (for which a fixed tax must be paid) had reached Italy. In consequence the papal throne remained vacant for months after the death of each pope, a state of things particularly hard to bear in those troubled times. Finally, to obviate this inconvenience, the emperor went so far as to cede the exercise of the right of approval to his representative, the exarch in Ravenna. This right of approval, be it remarked, was no mere empty form. Often the attempt was made through its agency to compel the pope's acquiescence in the emperor's views on dogmatic disputes. Conflicts were frequent, and the papacy had more than once to submit to force

3. *M. G. Epp.*, I, 330.

until, protected by the Latins of Italy, it was able to extricate itself from the imperial power.

When Pope Martin I refused to acknowledge the *Typus*, the heretical religious edict of the emperor Constans II, he was taken prisoner and — like the unfortunate Silverius who had been pope at the time of the Gothic wars — was sent to Constantinople and there ignominiously condemned. Forty years later, however, in 692, when the emperor Justinian II planned to inflict the same treatment on Pope Sergius, the Italian milita intervened. This time the question concerned the decrees of the second council *in Trullo*, convoked by the emperor, to which the pope refused his approval. Zachary, captain of the emperor's bodyguard, proceeding from Ravenna to Rome to arrest Sergius and bring him to Constantinople, was followed by the militia of Ravenna and the Pentapolis intent on defending the pontiff. With drums beating they marched into Rome, and the officer who had been sent to abduct the pope was forced instead to seek the pope's protection: he actually crawled under the pontiff's bed to escape the excited multitude, which however did not disperse until it knew that the emperor's envoy had quitted Rome.

Similar episodes are recorded from time to time. In none is the devoted loyalty of the populace to the papacy more evident than in the dispute of Gregory II with the emperor Leo III, the Isaurian. In the beginning it was purely a question of financial demands which the pope resisted; religious matters were not involved. Various attempts to remove the pontiff were frustrated by the Roman populace, including an effort by armed troops dispatched to Rome by the exarch. Then, in 727, the emperor's edict against the veneration of images entered into and aggravated the conflict. The militia of the duchies of the Pentapolis and Venice refused to participate in any measure of force against the pope. They even went further. They renounced their obedience to the imperial officers and chose their own leaders — an example which found imitators throughout Italy. Several Byzantine commanders were killed, including the exarch of Ravenna; and the Romans vowed never to permit any act of violence against the pope, the protector of the Christian faith and the defender of ecclesiastical liberty.

It would have been, even at that time, an easy task for the popes to overthrow the Greek domination in central Italy. But they did not do so; on the contrary, they sought to explain to their defenders the difference between the legitimate power of the imperial government and an individual unjust decree of a heretical emperor. It was naturally to their interest to sustain the shaky structure of imperial government until some other support should present itself, for had the Byzantine domination been thrown off without the pope's having an alternative power to rely on, central Italy would certainly have fallen to the Lombards. We understand, therefore, why the popes began, from the middle of the eighth century, to look northward where their legate Saint Boniface was developing his successful reform program. They had already at this time approached the Franks as well. Politically, the final issue of these efforts was to be the foundation of the Papal States and the reestablishment of the Western empire under Charlemagne. As far as their sympathies were concerned, the detachment of the Latin population of central Italy from Greek rule had been effected as early as the first half of the eighth century.

A mere review of the names of the pontiffs is interesting as indicating the separation of Rome from Constantinople. Up into the eighth century, popes of Greek or Eastern origin are not rare. Of the seven immediate predecessors of the Roman Gregory II, some were Syrian, some Greek. Gregory II was followed by one more Syrian, Gregory III (731-741), and one Greek, Zachary (741-752). From the latter's death until the present time, there has been no addition to the series of Greeks among the successors of Saint Peter. The last pontiff to go to Constantinople was Pope Constantine, in 710, and he was accompanied by the young deacon who later succeeded him as Pope Gregory II — and who even thus early gained great esteem by his prudent and courageous speeches in the course of the negotiations. It was Gregory II who received Saint Boniface in Rome in 719 and sent him across the Alps, first as an apostolic missionary, then as a suburbicarian bishop. The papacy had already begun to visualize the great change which was to unite it with the countries to the north. Pope Stephen III (752-757), the successor of the last Greek pope, carried the plan to completion by founding the Papal States and thus initiating the political rupture between the papacy and Constantinople. Only in southern Italy, which had an essentially Greek population, did the Byzantines succeed in maintaining themselves; they stayed until the Normans came, and even today the Greek liturgy is still used in the churches.

As early as the beginning of the seventh century, the Byzantine emperor had lost the territory he controlled on the Spanish coast; and in the course of that century the Saracens conquered the whole north coast of Africa. Thus the threads which had been spun from the West to the East were becoming fewer and fewer. Traffic on the Mediterranean Sea was being disturbed, rendered more difficult from decade to decade by the Mohammedan Arabs, who were experienced seamen.

The growing ecclesiastical and political estrangement was strengthened by national differences which could no longer be concealed. The old particularism of the East had clearly reasserted itself in a Hellenizing movement which was pushing upward from below and reaching outward to an ever-widening periphery. Old Byzantium not only became a new geographical and political center, but also a new literary center; whence we cease speaking of an Eastern Roman Empire and instead designate it as Byzantine. The culture of the East manifests a new character which we call Byzantine also, distinguishing it from the old Roman culture.

For a considerable period the emperors sought to counteract the rise of this particularism, since it was not in accord with their political plans. They wanted to appear as the legitimate representatives of the ancient Roman Empire, and called themselves and their subjects Ῥωμαῖοι. (The term has survived far and wide in the East even to the present day.) Latin was retained for a long time as the official language of the courts and of the administration of government, despite the fact that it was becoming less and less the native tongue. In Justinian's code Latin was still used; but most of Justinian's *Novels* were written in Greek, as were the laws of his successors. From the time of the emperor Maurice (582-602), Greek was the commercial language also. It is particularly interesting to follow the gradual introduction of Greek on the coins. As the language of the lower classes, it appeared first on copper coins, later on silver, and eventually on the aristocratic gold. Greek inscriptions are first found under the emperor Heraclius (610-641), who replaced the motto *In hoc vince* on copper coins with its Greek equivalent, 'Εν τούτῳ νίκα. In the eighth century the Latin title *Augustus* is replaced by the Greek Βασιλεύς or Δεσπότης.

Paralleling this progression is the slow but definite change observable in the nationality of the rulers. The Latin family of Theodosius became extinct with his granddaughter Pulcheria in 453. She was followed, until the time of Justinian, by a motley group of Romanized barbarians whom the army, itself composed of diverse elements, brought to the throne in succession. After the extinction of the Justinian dynasty, the first Greek emperor appears — Tiberius (578-582). (A later chronicler, Michael the Syrian, calls Justin II, who preceded Tiberius, the last Roman emperor.) Afterward, it is true, other non-Greek emperors reigned, men of Romance-Asiatic and Greek-Slavic origin, and only the last dynasties from the eleventh century on — the Comneni, the Ducases, the Angeli, the Palaeologi and Cantacuzenes — were purely Greek. Nevertheless we continue to note a growing use of the Greek language from the end of the sixth century: it can be seen in the inscriptions on coins and in the language of administration. After the seventh century we also recognize a new type of imperial heads on the coins, with low, broad foreheads, heavy moustaches, and sideburns.

In the field of letters we encounter for a time a last flowering of ancient literature, identified especially with the historians Procopius, Agathias, Theophanes of Byzantium and Theophylactus. It forms a parallel to the literary activity of Boethius, Cassiodorus and Saint Isidore, whom we have met as the last compilers of ancient learning in the West. Here also it survives into the seventh century, to be followed by a sterile period; and though this latter is marked by a less profound decline than in the West, new activity does not show itself in the East until the commencement of the ninth century. The situation is no different in the field of art, especially as regards architecture, which continued for the time being along the early Christian Hellenistic and Roman lines, although Eastern influences were very pronounced. This style reached its climax in the pompous domes of Hagia Sophia, the edifice which

Justinian erected in his capital — ten thousand laborers working on it for five years — to proclaim to the world what degree of splendor he had conferred upon the Church. Soon afterward, in the seventh century, a decline of the old stylistic tendencies set in, to continue until a new growth of independent character asserted itself in the ninth century. This new style is in bold contrast with that of the West: the domical structure with its central arrangement of the church, or the structure in the form of a Greek cross, is cultivated, while in the West the Roman basilica construction determines the ground plan, and the domical type appears only in isolated cases.

Finally, the history of law also betrays a decline in the seventh century, which is followed by a distinctively Byzantine development. Thus, in all the fields of culture until the end of the sixth century, we observe tendencies which were still associated with the West; then, after a period of stagnation more or less prolonged, the clearly defined appearance of a unique form which we are accustomed to designate as Byzantine.

In most instances when we hear the word Byzantine, we think only of a bureaucratic and narrow-minded State, ceremonious manners, classes of functionaries and their precedence at court, servile court lackeys, court intrigues, arbitrary and despotic action. These things indeed did characterize court life at Constantinople since imperial absolutism, reinforced by the examples of Asiatic despotism near at hand, was able to unfold itself there. These things, however, were really to be met with wherever absolutism held sway; they were found at the Spanish court of Philip II and at the French court of Louis XIV and Louis XV. In the Eastern empire these adjuncts of absolutism appeared immediately after the administrative reforms of Diocletian and Constantine changed the old Roman military monarchy into a great bureaucratic organism. From time to time the army intervened with a brutal hand — not, however, with the intention of destroying the system, but merely to set up one of its own generals as the central figure, around whom everything revolved mechanically as before, while the autocrat, cleverly kept at a distance from the people, exercised an arbitrary rule of the worst type by means of a subtly contrived ceremonial system.

The above by no means constitutes the sole characteristic of the new system noticeable in the East from the seventh century onward in contrast to the system in the West. But it is what was chiefly felt by the West as a difference for several reasons: first, because the West had broken with the ancient bureaucratic tradition of the Romans as a result of the influence of the Germans; next, because no ruler was able to develop his own power to an absolute degree; and finally, because the rulers of the separate kingdoms were limited in their authority by the nobles, who held the balance of power against them and sometimes even outweighed them.

However, something does strike us as essentially new in the East of the seventh century: the fact that it was being Hellenized. This was bound to happen, of course, once the domain ruled by the emperor of Constantinople became restricted to the sections inhabited by a Greek or Hellenized population — Greece and Asia Minor as far south as the Taurus. In contrast, Syria, Egypt and Africa were inhabited by Semites or Berbers who, having once been subject to the Romans, were dominated by the idea of the classic Roman Empire and Hellenized only superficially, if at all. This lack of a strong bond with the East explains why they had succumbed so rapidly to the assaults of the Arabs, who always encountered stronger opposition in the territory north of the Taurus. Since the Byzantine Empire became thus confined to the ancient Greek or completely Hellenized countries, and Justinian's policy of again incorporating the Roman Empire of the West had suffered shipwreck, the Greek element in Constantinople was bound to have increasing importance.

This development forms a clear parallel to that in the West, for in both sections the classic Latin receded in favor of the popular idiom. Everywhere the official Roman veneer was wiped off and the lower strata came to the surface; and this fact manifested itself linguistically in the local peculiarities of the popular tongues. Though the lower classes in the West were far more standardized in speech than was the case with the Greeks in the East, their racial vigor reasserted itself in the shaping of the various national characters out of the ancient racial traits. For example, the principal strain in the French character is the Celtic, that of the Spanish is the Iberian.

An important difference between the East and West lies in this, therefore, that the lower classes in the East enjoyed a higher and more unified culture — one which was strong enough to assert itself again with great force when the old form of the State was destroyed. It was rooted in the ancient Greek culture that existed before the Roman. This cultural superiority of the Byzantine East over the West made itself felt for several centuries.

As a final difference between the East and the West, we have the added fact that in the West the German strain was added to the old strata, in the East the Slavic strain. Each part of the former Roman Empire thus constituted a separate cultural community. The West formed, by the fusion of Roman and Germanic elements, the group of Romance-Germanic nations; the Byzantine Empire became a cultural center for a succession of new peoples from the East, principally the Eastern and the Southern Slavs. Thus each half of the former vast imperial whole received a separate mission which directed it into new paths. Had their dangers, tribulations and enemies remained the same, there would have appeared, as in earlier ages, a number of points of contact. Certainly, a temporary *rapprochement* was brought about at the time of the Crusades by common opposition to the Saracens; but the estrangement, especially in the ecclesiastical field, had already gone too far by then to render a lasting union possible. In the early Middle Ages such a union might have been feasible; but just at this period new peoples moved into the area where East and West might have made contact, interposing their alien presence and thereby interrupting direct communication.

After the departure of the Ostrogoths from Pannonia, the Gepids were the only Germanic tribe remaining on the lower Danube — nor did they remain long. New peoples appeared on the Danube, following in the wake of the Huns and, like them, members of the Turanian race. First came the Bulgarians, dreaded for their ferocity and hardy enough to have survived to the present day. The advance guards of the Slavic family of nations followed (in some cases preceded) the Bulgarians into the northern part of the Balkan Peninsula. The third national group to appear were the Avars, related to the Huns; it was they who allied themselves with the Lombards to crush the Gepids in 567 and take possession of their land. They extended their domination over the Slavs and the Bulgarians, and were for a time the leaders of the assaults directed from the north against the Byzantine Empire. Perhaps the emperors would have acted more wisely had they set their plans of conquest in that direction instead of against the Ostrogoths and Lombards. They would then have permanently conquered the threat from the Danube, and at the same time would have established connections with the West instead of provoking hostility there. As it was, they acted only defensively against the pressure from the north, and hence were never able to close the doors on the Danube once and for all.

Among the new nations occupying the northern portion of the Balkan Peninsula, the Slavs became the most powerful. They ravaged the whole Peninsula, absorbed for the most part the Roman population still located in the northwestern section (here it was the tribes of the Croats and Serbs who were the particular aggressors), and even succeeded in imposing their nationality upon the Bulgarians. These Slavs were to play a similar role in the Byzantine Empire to that formerly played by the Germans in the Western Roman Empire. Just as the Germans are linked with the traditions and the vestiges of the Roman cultural world in a union from which our Western culture proceeds, so eventually did the Slavs form with the Greeks the culture of Eastern Europe. The progress and conquests of this influence among them are evidenced in the spread of the Greek Church — just as we have followed the growth of Western culture in the spread of the Roman Church. Not all Slavic peoples, be it remarked, were drawn into the orbit of Greek culture, but, in general, only the Eastern Slavs and those from the south. The missionary work of the Greek Church had begun among them as early as the seventh century, though it was not to reach its zenith until the ninth.

As a result of the separation of the two Churches, Europe was divided into two cultural communities. The division was based on national, political, and cultural as well as ecclesiastical differences. Yet the former were not so great that they could not, at some future time, have been overcome.

Graver by far than the breach which opened up between East and West in the seventh century was that caused by Islam between the countries north and south of the Mediterranean Sea. After Mohammed, the prophet of Islam, had died in 632, his followers rapidly propagated their religion with the sword. Omar, the second successor, conquered Syria, Palestine, Persia, Egypt as far as Cyrene, and even Tripoli. Then, when the Ommiad caliphs under Mo'awiya took up their residence in Damascus in 661, the campaign against Constantinople began. In 672 the city was besieged by land and sea, and this investment lasted for seven years. Finally the Arabs were forced to abandon hope of taking the capital so excellently protected and so wisely defended. In the West, however, Carthage fell into their hands and was leveled to the ground in 698. As early as 700 the troops of Musa, a high Moslem official, were able to push their domination to the shores of the Atlantic. Here the Arab forces were joined by the Berbers, a mongrel race who had accepted Islamism and who, under the name of Moors, were soon to become a terror to the West. The strait which separated Europe and Africa was stamped with the Arab character in 711 by Berber troops, who named its northern height Gibraltar, "Mountain of Tarik," after their leader. Their advance into the interior of Spain was promoted by internal dissensions there, since the relatives of King Witiza, the deposed Visigothic ruler, hoped to regain their power through Tarik's invasion. Roderick, the new king, met the Berbers in July of the year 711 near the Guadalete river, not far from Jerez de la Frontera; but since he controlled only part of a nation internally divided into several factions, he was defeated. Musa then came from Africa and completed in person the conquest of Spain as far as the Basque provinces in the north.

Thenceforth the attacks of the Arabs upon Europe increased year after year, now in the East, now in the West. In the East their assault upon Constantinople, persisting for a whole year, was again repulsed in 717. In the West, however, even the Pyrenees were no barrier against them. The land of Eudo, the duke of Aquitaine, was conquered; about 731 Abdar-Rahman, the Moslem leader, stood on the Loire. But in October of the following year Charles Martel, in command of the full forces of the Frankish kingdom — fortunate-

ly for the West, they had been united by the Carolingian rulers —
was finally able to defeat him at Tours, near Poitiers. By this
victory the West was saved and the tide of Mohammedan advance
for the time being halted.

But the Arab threat still remained, grave and imminent, by
reason of their conquest of the Visigothic kingdom and the control
they exercised over the Mediterranean Sea. Inevitably, this danger
acted as a serious warning to the West to unite its forces and bend
all its efforts toward saving itself. Thus everything urged the
Carolingians to consolidate the continental West under their rule,
as the need of the times demanded. But even later, when the
Carolingian empire had collapsed, the common danger from the
Arabs held the West together. This danger was not only military;
it was a religious and cultural matter of the first order.

Islam had become, subsequent to the collapse of the ancient cultural empire, the third aspirant to the leadership of the world's culture, rivaling in this the Byzantine Empire and the West. Perhaps an even greater portion of the ancient cultural inheritance
had fallen to the lot of the countries conquered by Islam — embracing as these did the culturally oldest territories — than to the West.
The intellectual and artistic legacy of the past, especially as diffused
by the highly intelligent Syrians, enabled the Arabs to evolve, in
Cordova, Bagdad, Damascus and Cairo, a brilliant culture — one
indeed far superior to that of the West. In addition, the Arabs at
that time controlled the world's commerce, which was largely a
system of bartering carried on over the Mediterranean Sea between
Europe, Asia and Africa, although we can also trace the land-routes
of their merchants — for example through the heart of Russia to
the Baltic Sea. The physical strength and military prowess of their
warriors were at least equal to anything exhibited by the West in
the eighth century. Even their repulse by the combined forces of
the Frankish kingdom under Charles Martel constituted a check
only at that point. They continued during the ninth century to advance, slowly and by short stages; they conquered Sicily, plundered
the coasts of Italy, and established themselves firmly at the mouth
of the Rhone. Their offensive force was still unbroken. Up to the
period of the Crusades, their ships controlled the Mediterranean

Sea. Their warriors advanced as far as Turkestan and India in Asia, as far as the Great Saint Bernard Pass in Europe, and deep into the interior of Africa, where they were not pushed back until our own time.

And yet the Arabs — so far advanced in civilization, so powerful in arms that in the ninth and tenth centuries East and West alike could barely survive against them — did not after all attain the leadership of the world's culture. The reason was intrinsic. Lacking Christianity, they lacked the determinant civilizing force. Islamism, by its principle of spreading belief with the sword, certainly strengthened the military power of the Arabs, whose caliphs were at one and the same time their generals and the successors of their prophet, the leaders of their faith and of their armies. But even though Islam was able to overthrow States by powerful offensive movements, its strength slackened after each conquest and was quickened again only by the absorption into its sphere of action of fresh, primitive peoples such as the Berbers, the Seljuks and the Ottomans.

Islamism lacked the calm and organizing force possessed by Christianity, which is bent on developing the intellect and disciplining the will. "Go and make disciples of all nations," was the command of the Risen Saviour. As teachers, not as warriors, as men who had nothing and wanted nothing, the Apostles were to gain the minds and hearts of universal mankind for Christian truth. In this teaching there was no difference between master and servant; woman enjoyed human dignity side by side with man; not war but peace was the password by which the Christian proponents made themselves known. Such a doctrine laid the foundation for the development of the individual no less than of the nation; it gave a most powerful impulse to a social order based on the command of brotherly love; it furnished the best principles for the regulation of the conscience of the private man as well as of the public State. Islamism, devoid of these elements, could only form States with despotic governments; whereas the future belonged to those nations which knew how to combine national strength with the greatest possible freedom of the individual consonant with peace and order. The organizing force inherent in Christianity by virtue of its mission of peace and its appeal to religious truth, was employed by the Church first of all to develop her own form of government after ancient models. Subsequently, through the spiritual advisers of the various rulers, the magnificent example offered by the constitution of the Church helped the Western States notably in the course of their own development.

But why, then, did not the Byzantine Empire retain the leadership of the world's culture, which it had so plainly acquired in the sixth century, during the reign of Justinian? The ancient traditions, never wholly interrupted, were certainly stronger there than anywhere else. The East was the cradle of Christianity, and the Christian religion had produced there a much more ardent devotion to the service of God than in the West; monasticism was first developed there, its Western forms being only improvements on models borrowed from the East.

From what has previously been said, we know that it was caesaropapism and the unbroken tradition of ancient absolutism which strangled independent ecclesiastical and political life in the East. In contrast to this, it was tremendously significant that the spiritual and temporal authority were separated in the West and that the Church had in the successor of Saint Peter an independent ruler who affirmed himself to be exempt from the authority of any man. The freedom which the Church managed to preserve for herself here through her proper and universally acknowledged head was further enhanced by the special role which had fallen to her as the transmitter of the ancient traditions, the guardian of the spiritual treasures, and the leader of the intellectual development of the West. In the Byzantine Empire, where the ancient traditions were not destroyed, this mission was not accorded the Church in anything like the same measure. In the West, the ancient State and the ancient society perished; the new nations were educated by the Church, who thus occupied toward them the place of a gratefully venerated teacher.

Between the spiritual and temporal powers, between the Church and the State, between the empire and the papacy, friction and conflict were certainly not lacking in the West. We may deplore them, but we must not close our eyes to the fact that they were a great advantage in cultural development, since they preserved that balance of power so necessary between the two jurisdictions and secured the independence of both. At times, undoubtedly, men on both sides went too far: on one side, trying to make the Church a state body; on the other, advancing the theory that the temporal power received its authority from God solely through the good offices of the ecclesiastical power. Neither a State-Church government nor a hierocratic system would have been advantageous to the development of Western culture.

In still another field a happy distribution of forces may be noted in the West in contrast to the Byzantine Empire, which shows an unhealthy, abnormal concentration of forces at this point. We refer to the virtually unlimited authority of the emperor, whose powers — and especially the mode of their transmission — were, in comparison with the otherwise very detailed regulations, almost undefined. Usurpations and struggles for the throne were the inevitable result, and any intellectual effort directed to the adjustment of differences between the crown and its subjects was impossible. It has been calculated that of the 107 persons who bore the imperial title from the accession of Arcadius in 395 to the taking of Constantinople by the Turks in 1453, only 34 retained the title for the term of their natural lives. The others were forced to abdicate, died in prison of either starvation or maltreatment, were killed in battle, or were murdered: in the last category alone were 20 emperors. A continuing struggle for the throne fluctuated with varying fortunes between the party of the capital's officials and the army — a type of struggle characteristic of decadent cultures.

The Byzantine Empire lacked, for the regulation of its domestic affairs, the equalizing influence of the spiritual power represented by the Church and also the fresh contribution of the Germanic love of liberty, which had not only broken the ancient bureaucratic traditions of the Romans in the West but had long made it impossible for Western rulers to develop their authority to the point of absolutism. Here the nobility adopted toward the wearers of the crown an entirely different attitude from that found in the East. On the medieval Byzantine miniatures we see the nobles depicted as prostrate on the floor before the emperor; on those of the West, they are in a reverential attitude, it is true, but standing beside the ruler. Only during his investiture did a noble kneel, and then merely on one knee. The medieval knight felt himself bound to his liege lord by a personal bond of moral loyalty, voluntarily assumed. Later we shall have occasion to show how real a cultural achievement the feudal world transmitted to us in the development of the beautiful ideal of the *homo legalis,* the loyal man, who measures and performs his duties toward both his lord and his own vassals by the moral standards of fidelity and honor.

There was, furthermore, no lack of decentralizing forces here to keep a rigid imperialism down; the West favored, instead, an organization of manifold, equally balanced parts with ample opportunities for growth. The secret of the new culture of the West lay in this counterbalance of opposite forces, the universal and concentrating against the national and decentralizing, the feudal against the sovereign; it lay in the equilibrium maintained alike by the empire and the papacy, and by the several nations among themselves. There resulted a certain freedom of action which, constantly renewing itself, gave the West a preponderance over Islam as well as over the East and finally awarded it the leadership of the world's culture.

The first step toward the formation of this cultural community was the solid rallying of the West around the papacy, which bound together the various parts — Romans, Celts and Germans — by means of the common ecclesiastical tie. At the same time there took place the papacy's separation from the East, and the Frankish kingdom's repulse of the Arabs which gave security to the new cultural community. Henceforth the Western nations could undertake — though always with a sword in hand — to develop those cultural gifts with which a kind Providence had endowed them. The establishment of a unified State on the continent, the Carolingian empire, effecting as it did an intimate relationship between the spiritual and temporal powers, began this cultural development. But the future of the West was not to be bound to the life of any centralized State: that would have been merely to settle into the Byzantine groove. The Carolingian empire soon fell apart, and the dissolution temporarily paralyzed the forces of the Church, which espoused the cause of the central State with all her energy. But out of the collapse was to emerge an organization of individual States, an organization which could not but be advantageous to culture, for it threw into bolder relief the spiritual factors forming the cohesive element of the union. These are the great trends which determine the development in the Carolingian kingdom.

CHAPTER SEVEN

THE UNION OF PAPACY AND EMPIRE

THE cultural community formed in Western Europe was based, as is evident beyond dispute, on that common faith and that intimate union with the pope in Rome which it had been the principal aim of the Anglo-Saxon Benedictines to promote. The reform of the Frankish Church carried out by Saint Boniface culminated in the close union with Rome. But Rome was also the center of literary traditions, a foremost effect of whose revival would be to raise the general cultural level. The pilgrims appearing in Rome from the beginning of the eighth century demonstrated to the popes and to the Romans at large how many forces were ready to work for unity.

If the cultural community was to have any kind of organic form, the pope could not in any case be excluded from it. But neither could the political power to the north be left out of consideration. It had demonstrated its importance clearly enough by the victory of Charles Martel at Tours and by the assistance which his sons rendered Saint Boniface. It was, therefore, only natural that this cultural community should find expression in the union of this political power with the papacy. A further impulse in the same direction was given by the desperate plight of the papacy and the Romans in central Italy, unwilling to become subject to the Lombards and yet abandoned by the Byzantine emperor. Who was there to help them against the Lombards? No one but the Frankish rulers. As much as a century and a half earlier one of the popes had with prophetic view seen in the Franks the protectors of Rome: Pope Pelagius II, who in 580 wrote to Saint Aunarius, bishop of Auxerre, that the orthodox Frankish kings were destined by Divine Providence as neighbors of Rome and of the whole of Italy to become their saviours.[1] Now the time had arrived when the Franks were to translate these prophetic words into reality.

---

1. *M. G. Epp.*, III, 449.

In 739, when Liutprand, king of the Lombards, pressing Rome hard once more, laid waste the duchy of Rome and took possession of the important frontier fortresses on the Tiber, and when all help from Ravenna was cut off, Pope Gregory III sent the first embassy to Charles Martel, the powerful Mayor of the Palace of the Frankish kingdom, appealing to him to protect the tomb of the Apostles. To symbolize the petition, the embassy carried precious gifts — highly revered relics, and keys to the tomb of Saint Peter containing a small portion of the chains of the Prince of the Apostles. Without doubt, the importance of this mission was sensed by all. The letters of Gregory III urging his appeal form the beginning of that valuable collection of documents addressed by the popes to Charles Martel, Pippin and Charlemagne, which is known among scholars as the *Codex Carolinus.*

The pope's repeated call for help, however, did not have the desired result. Charles Martel was on terms of intimate association with the king of the Lombards, which circumstances forbade him to relinquish. In 738, when forced to proceed against the Saxons, he had called upon Liutprand for aid against the Saracens, who had again invaded southern France. Charles Martel evidently did not realize the importance of the pope's spiritual authority to himself and his house. His sons were much more alive to it. Carloman, the elder, having abdicated in 747, went to Rome to be received into the clerical state by Pope Zachary and to seek a place of monastic retirement in the vicinity of Rome, at first on Mount Soracte, then in Monte Cassino. Shortly afterward an even more famous royal head received the tonsure — that of the Lombard ruler Rachis, Liutprand's successor, who had been so affected by Pope Zachary's appeal to his conscience after he had broken the peace, that he went to Rome with his wife and daughter and followed Carloman's example.

Pippin, the sober and calculating brother of Carloman, who was now sole actual ruler of the Frankish kingdom, designed to use the pope's rapidly increasing spiritual authority to further his plan of acquiring the royal title to that kingdom. Many approved this plan, wishing to put an end to the impossible situation whereby the government remained nominally in the hands of the weak

Merovingians although for almost a hundred years it had been essentially and substantially in the hands of the Carolingian Mayors of the Palace. It was well known that this grave incongruity contravened an old principle of Germanic law demanding that the king be not merely royally born but also personally fitted for kingship. Yet there were some who hesitated to give Pippin their support, and it was vital to him to secure his throne against all objections regarding legitimacy. Who possessed the authority of judgment to which all would yield? There was little delay in replying to that question. Only the pope, the head of the Church, could give such a decision. Burchard, the bishop of Würzburg, and Fulrad, the abbot of Saint Denis, were sent to Rome to place the matter before the pope. The question was, whether it were not better that he be called king who had the power to rule, rather than he who lacked it. Pope Zachary answered in the affirmative, whereupon Pippin was elected king. Following the custom introduced among the Anglo-Saxons by the Irish, Pippin's kingship received the permanent blessing of the Church with the anointing by the bishops, among them Saint Boniface.

It is one of the most remarkable coincidences in history that the power of the Carolingians was definitively established just at the time when they were called to intervene in the most memorable manner in the destinies of the papacy and to determine the form in which the cultural community of the West was to be cast. In the same year, 751, in which Pippin was made king of the Franks, the Byzantine power in central Italy collapsed. Ravenna, the residence of the exarch, was taken by the Lombards under Aistulf, Rachis' successor; and thereby was settled the fate, long in suspense, of the exarchate, the Pentapolis, and the territories around Ravenna and Ancona. The central section of the Adriatic coast also fell to the Lombards. Only the duchy of Rome had not yet come under their power. How was this small territory to withstand the Lombard might? Aistulf was not the type of man on whom the spiritual authority of the successor of the Prince of the Apostles would make the lasting impression it had made upon Liutprand and Rachis. Nothing more was to be obtained from him by the pleas of the pope. The fulfillment of the Lombardic design — the conquest of the whole peninsula — would now have been rapidly realized had not a foreign power superior to the Lombards entered the picture.

Pope Stephen III, a Roman, did not hesitate to throw his whole spiritual and personal authority into an effort to induce the new Frankish king to intervene at this juncture. Accompanied by bishops and priests, the highest officials of his chancery, he crossed the Alps to appeal to the monarch. The popes had journeyed often to Constantinople; but never before had one of them traversed the Alps on such a mission. That Stephen now bent his steps northward instead of to the East clearly shows the new direction in which the papacy was tending. The route lay over the Great Saint Bernard Pass, and through Saint Maurice and western Switzerland — the ancient cultural highroad where east Frankish and Italian influence met. Pippin, awaiting his guest in Ponthion, near Bar-le-Duc, went an hour's distance to meet him and greeted him with profound respect. He dismounted, knelt, and then for a time proceeded on foot leading the pope's horse by the bridle — a form of deference which King Liutprand had previously shown toward Pope Zachary. From it arose the ceremonial observed later by emperors at like meetings, which Frederick I arrogantly attempted to disregard.

This first memorable meeting occurred on January 6, 754; it was soon followed by the conclusion, at Saint Denis, of the alliance which inaugurated the union between the papacy and the empire in the Middle Ages. The pope and the king of the Franks solemnly pledged mutual love and friendship. Pippin with his two sons, Charles (Charlemagne) and Carloman, promised to defend the Church and the pope at all times. In return, the pope conferred upon the king and each of his sons the title of *Patricius,* or Patrician, of the Romans. In so doing, Stephen must certainly have had in mind that the exarchs of Ravenna, the highest Byzantine officials in Italy, had borne this title as a token of their solemn obligation to protect the Holy See and Rome. Pippin would presumably attach more importance to the fact that the pope, by anointing and blessing him and his sons as kings and *Patricii,* was legitimizing a second time, as it were, the Frankish kingship of the Carolingians. In requital of this confirmation of the dynasty in the presence of the nobles of the kingdom, the pope could expect effective counter-services in Italy.

To insure liberty for the pope, as well as for the Romans recently subjugated by the Lombards, for whom the pope appeared as spokesman, and to secure them against the Lombard threat, Pippin drew up the documents establishing the Papal States. To carry these commitments out, however, he was twice forced to march against the Lombards — in 754 and again in 756.

Originally the new Papal States were the domain of those who wished to remain Roman and not to become subject to the Lombards; in a certain sense, this polity was the last vestige of the Roman Empire. But it maintained itself only because it was now used as an endowment for the pope, who, on entering the cultural community of the West, was given the assurance that no one would infringe upon his independence and that he could exercise the spiritual leadership of the West in complete freedom.

It is perhaps unnecessary to say that the reality frequently did not quite correspond to this ideal. As the capital of the Papal States, Rome showed less unity than before. With the accession of a considerable amount of temporal power to the Holy See, there soon ensued disgraceful party strife for its control. In 767, after the death of Paul I, brother and successor of Stephen III, Duke Toto of Nepi enforced the ordination and enthronement of his brother Constantine. Conditions became so disordered that Desiderius, the Lombard king, was called in to free the Church from this interloper. Thereupon the Lombard party, in turn, tried to substitute their own papal candidate, the priest Philip. Only after this second pretender had been removed could a regular election take place in the ancient Forum, where finally the clergy, the Roman army with its leaders, and all the citizens elected Stephen IV, the confidant of Paul I. The mob then took a terrible revenge on the antipopes and their adherents, going so far as to blind Constantine and tear out the eyes and tongues of several of his partisans. Very understandably, a synod attended by Frankish bishops and held in the Lateran in 769, after solemnly condemning Constantine, forbade all future participation of the laity in papal elections (a prohibition which, however, could not as yet be enforced). Shortly afterward, the rabid leaders of the Frankish party, who were responsible for the above-described mutilations, were overtaken by the vengeance of their adversaries, and the chancellor Christopher and his son Sergius had their eyes gouged out. Another incident even more prejudicial to the Church's position was precipitated by Archbishop Leo of Ravenna, who attempted to establish a pontifical state of his own in the exarchate.

Amid these disorders, the very existence of the young Papal States was seriously endangered. That the danger was countered must be credited in the main to the prudent Pope Adrian, son of an illustrious Roman family, who may be considered the second founder of the Papal States. Against Desiderius, the Lombard king, whose attitude was hostile, he called upon the Frankish ruler for aid. This ruler was Charlemagne — Charles the Great — who, as the mightiest of his line, must now occupy for a time the central place of our narrative.

Following the death of his father in 768, Charlemagne at first shared the Frankish kingdom with his brother Carloman; after the latter's death in 771, he ruled alone. In answer to the pope's request he appeared in Italy with troops in 773. The Lombard king, after enduring a long siege in his capital city of Pavia, was forced to surrender, and Charlemagne proclaimed himself ruler of the Lombards. He already bore the title of Patrician, which Pope Stephen III had once conferred upon him together with his father and brother at Saint Denis, so that the full title of his dignities ran: "King of the Franks and of the Lombards and Patrician of the Romans."

In the year 774, during the long-drawn-out siege of Pavia, Charlemagne had gone to Rome to celebrate the feast of Easter. The first northern protector to enter the Eternal City, he was accorded an official reception similar to that given the former exarchs. As far away as Lake Bracciano, thirty miles from Rome, the Roman authorities appeared bearing the banner of the city, to greet him in the name of the pope. The troops of Rome had taken up their position at the foot of Monte Mario, on the city's outskirts; near them were grouped the school children carrying palms and olive branches. Charlemagne was welcomed with an outburst of cheers. When he saw the representatives of the Church approaching with crosses and flags, he dismounted and walked the remaining distance to the basilica of Saint Peter.

There in the vestibule Pope Adrian awaited the distinguished visitor. Following a pious custom, Charlemagne kissed every step as he mounted upward. Pope and king met with an embrace; then hand in hand they entered the interior of the basilica, while clergy and congregation intoned the *Blessed be he who cometh in the Name of the Lord*. After Charlemagne and his retinue had made their first adoration, Adrian descended with them into the crypt of Saint Peter, and there, in the most hallowed spot in Rome, the pope and the king swore to each other mutual allegiance. Next they proceeded to the Lateran basilica, where Charlemagne attended the baptismal ceremonies of Eastertide, now performed on the afternoon of Holy Saturday instead of, as formerly, in the night. For the solemn services on Easter Sunday, the king was escorted from his residence to Saint Mary Major's by the Roman authorities and troops at the pope's command. On Easter Monday he assisted at the pontifical Mass in Saint Peter's and on Easter Tuesday in Saint Paul's.

Having thus worshiped in the most renowned churches and at the most famous tombs, Charlemagne began in Saint Peter's, on the Wednesday after Easter, important political negotiations. These closed with his declaring his readiness to have an undertaking drawn up in favor of the pope, repeating the promises made by Pippin to Pope Stephen III in a document drafted at Quierzy in 754 prior to his Italian campaign. The new instrument was placed by Charlemagne and his nobles on the altar, then on the confession of Saint Peter, the customary way of asking the saint to accept a document of this kind; actually, it was made out to Saint Peter and his successors and the Prince of the Apostles was directly addressed in it. Only after this ceremony, and after they had repeated the solemn oath to fulfill all the promises therein, did they hand it to the pope.

That the relations thus assumed were not restricted to the question of the possession of the Papal States is evident from the fact that Charlemagne took with him, as a gift from the pope, a collection of the canons prepared by Dionysius Exiguus to which had been added several papal decretals. The ruler thus undertook to perform his part in diffusing the knowledge of the official legal code of the Church as the norm and likewise the authoritative record of Christian law. This *Collectio Dionysio-Hadriana,* or simply *Hadriana,* replaced the earlier collections of canon law in use in the Frankish kingdom; at the council of Aix-la-Chapelle in 802, it was declared the *Codex Canonum,* the universal canon-law book of the Frankish Church.

To carry out the agreement which Charlemagne had so solemnly drawn up and handed over, proved very difficult, however. The original basis of the papal claim to the promised donation had been rapidly obscured by the events which followed the making of the promise. Pope Stephen III had implored Pippin's help for the benefit of the Latin population who did not wish to become subject to the Lombards; he had been given this help as the representative of Saint Peter and the primate of the Church. The thought of the pope's actually having crossed the Alps for the preservation of national interests had soon receded into the background. It was only for Saint Peter's honor and for the liberty and power of the Church that Pippin had drawn his sword; the fact that the Romans were appealing to him for help undoubtedly moved him as little as the petition of the Greek envoy that he hand over any territory taken from the Lombards to the Byzantine emperor, who had not even been able to fulfill the duties inherent in his sovereignty. Hence the popes were constrained to speak less of the juridical basis of their claims than of the honor and prestige of Saint Peter, which were certainly preserved and secured in the best way by the foundation of the Papal States. Thus the means by which the restoration of the Lombardic conquests had been obtained from Pippin, became the end. The enhancement and expansion of the Church was almost exclusively the subject of the negotiations, while the Romans who were to be succored against the barbarian Lombards were mentioned less and less. The temporal sovereignty of the pope, first conceived only as a device for securing that protection against the Lombards, and then openly declared to be the prime object, became an independent legal claim.

Charlemagne had indeed recognized this title in the new contract. But when he became king of the Lombards, he began to view the situation from a different angle and to re-examine the development through which the pope's claim had come into being. A Lombardic power hostile to the papacy no longer existed; the end which Stephen III had had in view on his journey, had disappeared. Hence the question arose in the circle surrounding Charlemagne whether the means to that end, the temporal power of the pope, should continue to be recognized as in the past. Actually, it was only through the mighty arm of Charlemagne that the pope exercised protection over central Italy; was it not appropriate, therefore, that Charlemagne should also have the sovereign rights in that territory? Could he not claim these on the strength of the same legal theory by which the popes had acquired the temporal power?

Moreover, just as Charlemagne had replaced Desiderius as king of the Lombards, so he also wished, in virtue of the title of Patrician of the Romans, which he only now began to use, to assume the right to dispose of the lands until recently subject to the former Patrician, the exarch of Ravenna. He read into the title a significance beyond the conception which his father, and he himself until now, had had — and certainly also beyond the conception which the popes had in conferring it. They claimed the right of self-determination for themselves and the Romans, and inclined to regard the Frankish kings merely as the protectors of that right. This is why Charlemagne now hesitated to recognize the pope as a temporal sovereign along with himself; at best, he was willing to allow the pope temporal power under his suzerainty, with the reservation to himself of authority to pass on certain disputed claims regarding parts of the Papal States — for example, the legal claims of the archbishop of Ravenna, whose death in 777 certainly relieved the situation for the pope.

Adrian had perforce to pursue the course desired by Charlemagne. He attempted, meanwhile, to prove his legal rights in detail to the king; but as no other titles existed save the donations which created the patrimony, the pope had recourse to reminding Charle-

magne, in 778, of the times of Constantine the Great, in suggestive
terms which have been much discussed:

> Just as in the times of the saintly Roman pontiff Sylvester, God's
> holy, catholic and apostolic Roman Church was lifted up and exalted
> through the generosity of the pious Constantine, the great emperor of
> blessed memory, and just as he deigned to give her power in these
> parts of the West, so, in the present age, under your glorious reign, . . .
> may God's holy Church, the Church of the blessed Apostle Peter, more
> and more thrive and rejoice and be exalted in perpetuity; that all nations
> which learn thereof may be able to say: Lord, preserve the king and hear
> us when we cry to Thee! for behold, another most Christian and pious
> emperor, a new Constantine, has arisen in this our day, and through him
> has God deigned to give His Church, the Church of Saint Peter, the Prince
> of the Apostles, all things.[2]

Some have connected Adrian's words with the celebrated
forgery known as the *Donation of Constantine,* which would seem
to be exactly calculated to deliver in documentary form the difficult
proof demanded by Charlemagne concerning the juridical foundation of the papal claims. In our estimation, it is possible to perceive
in the pope's letter no more than the legendary background against
which a later unscrupulous but very learned forger was able to
elaborate his fabrication. Again in our opinion, those go too far
who believe that the quoted passage necessarily leads to the inference
of a previously existing forgery. It is safer to see in Adrian's intent
the first stirrings of a plan to designate Charlemagne, the protector
of the new commonwealth of nations in the West, as the successor
of Constantine and the emperor of the West.

The king and the pope finally arrived at a compromise. Charlemagne had too high a regard for the spiritual authority of the
Holy See to entertain the possibility of a rupture between himself
and Adrian. Nor could he afford to do so; he needed the papal
authority too much for his great plan of organizing his constantly
growing domain internally as a cultural empire, of which the spiritual center would be the pope. In addition, he must really have
meant to fulfill the obligations in part assumed by himself at Saint
Denis, in part inherited from his father, for he acknowledged them

---

2. Ibid., 587.

as binding. Adrian, also, fully realizing his situation, was too prudent to oppose a fair adjustment. The agreement was reached in 781, when Charlemagne again visited Rome. The pope gave up the idea of basing his demands on the promises of Quierzy; he no longer claimed sovereignty over Spoleto and Tuscany and was satisfied on the whole with the exarchate, the Pentapolis, and the duchy of Rome.

In compensation, his personal relations with his Patrician were greatly strengthened. The pope anointed and crowned as kings the two sons accompanying Charlemagne, Pippin and Louis. Four-year-old Pippin, the pope's godchild, was destined, as king of Italy under regents appointed by Charlemagne, to form an independent government for the kingdom of the Lombards; while Louis was to rule as king of Aquitaine. Charlemagne recognized the pope as the sovereign of the Papal States and reserved to himself in his capacity of Patrician only the right of receiving appeals in criminal cases. He also undertook to guarantee that the papal elections should be held in orderly fashion by the Romans alone. In 781 Adrian began to date his documents according to the years of his reign and no longer according to the years of the emperors. As sovereign of Rome, he also had his own coins struck.

At that period an understanding was reached as well with Constantinople, where the empress Irene, regent for her young son since the death in 780 of her husband, Leo IV, desired to reintroduce the veneration of images, and likewise to attain closer accord with the pope and Charlemagne. In 785 the empress and her son, Constantine VI, invited the pope to attend in person the Council of Nicaea, which was to settle the Iconoclastic controversy. Had not the situation in Italy been at least tacitly recognized by Constantinople, Adrian could not in his reply have set up Charlemagne — "his son and great friend, the king of the Franks and the Lombards and the Patrician of the Romans" — as an example for the Byzantine rulers. Adrian's words concerning Charlemagne are interesting in more ways than one:

> Obeying our admonitions and fulfilling our will in all things, he has brought all the barbarian peoples of the West under his foot....

That is why he, in his great love, has also given God's Apostolic Church several gifts, results of his arduous struggles, as a permanent possession, provinces as well as cities, fortresses and other territories. . . .[3]

The pope was justified in praising the progressive development of Charlemagne's power as a cultural achievement for the West. He had advanced his arms far into Saxony, still clinging tenaciously to its paganism, and carried on there the struggle which, after thirty hard years, would result in domination by the Franks, and by Christianity. All the German tribes obeyed Charlemagne. When he had put an end to the duchy of Bavaria by condemning its ruler Tassilo and firmly linked that land to his empire, the Frankish Church opened the mission among the Slavs in the territory east of the Alps. This mission was made secure on its eastern frontier by the subjugation of the Avars.

Even more appreciated in Rome was Charlemagne's progress in the southwest. In 778 he ventured an advance across the Pyrenees, which did not succeed in its purpose but redounded in a particular way to his glory and that of his followers, for they were celebrated in the *Song of Roland* as crusading heroes. The ancient duchy of Aquitaine, which had been brought again into the Frankish kingdom by Pippin, was now chosen by Charlemagne as the point from which to wage the offensive against Islam. He also provided it with a special government, installing his three-year-old son Louis as viceroy there in 781 and appointing a regency to aid him. A portion of the ancient Visigothic kingdom of Septimania, the country between the Pyrenees and the lower Rhone, was assigned to Aquitaine. In 795, two years after the Saracens staged near Carcassonne what proved to be their last raid north of the Pyrenees, Charlemagne laid the foundation for the Spanish March by erecting frontier fortresses in the southern Pyrenees. Thereby he increased the prospect that the domination of the Moors over the Iberian Peninsula would eventually be shattered.

Charlemagne's rule now extended from the Ebro to the Eider in Schleswig and from the Frisian coast to Dalmatia and southern Italy. Since the fall of the Roman Empire, no such power had

---

3. Mansi, *Concil.*, XII, 1075 sq.

been concentrated in the West. Even rulers who were not subject to him sought his friendship as though he were their suzerain. King Alfonso of Asturias and Galicia, who particularly esteemed the friendship of this ally against the Arabs, used to send Charlemagne a share of his spoils after successful campaigns. Scottish and Irish chieftains designated themselves his subjects and servants. A king of Northumbria was installed with his assistance. Charlemagne could in all truth be regarded as the master of the West. His power acquired a unique moral importance through its union with the Church. His warriors fought for the spread of Christianity alike on the banks of the Elbe and the Danube and the slopes of the Pyrenees.

Adrian died in 795, to be revered by Charlemagne in memory as he had been revered in life. His successor, Leo III, also a Roman, perceived the necessity of immediately renewing with the ruler both the formal agreement and the friendly alliance. At the time of announcing his election to Charlemagne and vowing him loyalty, he had the keys to Saint Peter's confession transmitted to him, together with a flag of the city of Rome, and petitioned that a Frankish noble be sent to administer to the inhabitants of the Papal States the oath of fealty toward the pope. Probably not long thereafter, Leo concluded with Charlemagne an agreement identical with the one Adrian had made with him in 781, save that the donation of the Sabine country and some Beneventan and Tuscan cities was more explicitly indicated. More precise regulations respecting the sovereign rights of the *Patricius* also seem to have been added. We note that the papal chancery now began to date the years according to Charlemagne's reign.

A rebellion against Leo, led by Adrian's relatives, urged him on to even closer union with the Frankish ruler. On April 25, 799, while the pope was leading the Saint Mark's procession on horseback according to ancient custom, he was attacked and thrown to the ground, his pontifical robes were snatched away, and he was for a time in danger of having his eyes and tongue torn out according to the Byzantine custom of dealing with an enemy. Imprisoned in the monastery of Saint Erasmus, he escaped by means of a rope, and succeeded with the help of faithful friends in getting to Saint

Peter's. But he did not feel himself safe — against the Romans themselves he needed the protection which only Charlemagne could give him.

For the second time a pope crossed the Alps to implore help. Leo met Charlemagne at Paderborn in July of 799 — the first pontiff to set foot on German soil. Pope and king embraced in tears. Then royal emissaries led Leo back to Rome and sat in judgment upon his enemies. But this did not suffice; Charlemagne himself had to come to Rome. When the adversaries renewed their reproaches, Leo swore an oath of purgation from the pulpit of Saint Peter's.

This was on December 23 in the year 800. On the same day a party of monks arrived from Jerusalem who, as envoys of the patriarch, presented the Frankish ruler with the keys of the Holy Sepulcher and of Mount Calvary, and in addition the keys of the city of Jerusalem and a flag. Thereby the patriarch symbolically paid his homage to the king of the Franks as his suzerain and entrusted the Holy Places to his protection. Nothing could more clearly proclaim Charlemagne as a world-ruler and the protector of Christendom. Obviously the title "King of Franks and Lombards and Patrician of Romans" was no longer adequate. Men wanted to see him designated as the head of a Christian league of nations, not as the ruler of individual kingdoms. His empire was to form one great international unit.

Nor could there be any room for doubt as to what title Rome would choose to signify all this. The memory of the Roman Empire and the belief in its continued existence to the end of time had not died out even now. It was, in fact, given an element of new support by the revival, just at this time, of the pursuit of classical studies. Rome's faith, Rome's culture, Rome's great traditions, constituted the spiritual tie that embraced all the subjects of Charlemagne's empire: whence was that empire to get its name if not from Rome, that city which as none other could be called the imperial city, and which contained the greatest shrine of the West, the tomb of the Prince of the Apostles?

Only with an emperor at its head could the West meet the East on equal terms. And only an emperor of the West was of sufficient dignity to negotiate effectively regarding the Holy Places with the supreme head of Islam, the caliph of Bagdad, who controlled the conditions affecting Christians in Jerusalem. Charlemagne had the power of an emperor, as was evident to all. The same principle that had prompted the elevation of Pippin to the Frankish kingship applied now to his son. Should not he who had the power receive the title and office? Should not the protector of Rome be proclaimed Roman emperor?

Rome was well aware that since the time of Pulcheria (450) the emperor of Constantinople had received the crown from the hands of the patriarch. Indeed, the *Liber Pontificalis*[4] recorded that, instead of a patriarch, one of the popes, John I, had actually crowned an emperor there, on Easter Day of 526. Was it not fitting that in the West the pope should now confer upon his protector this same distinction and perform the act of consecration which the patriarchs had long performed in the East? Did not a pope have a far greater right to do so since one of his predecessors had helped the Carolingian dynasty to obtain the royal dignity among the Franks?

During the pontifical Mass on Christmas Day in the year 800 — the beginning, according to the chronology in vogue at the time, of a new year and a new century — Pope Leo III placed a crown upon Charlemagne's head as he was about to rise from his prayers before the tomb of the Prince of the Apostles. Thereupon the assembled congregation shouted: "Life and victory to Charles, the pious Augustus crowned by God, the great and peace-providing emperor!" Thus was the new emperor solemnly acclaimed by the people; the pope meanwhile offering homage on bended knee, according to the Byzantine ceremonial. Then the pontiff anointed Charlemagne's eldest son, who bore his father's name and was supposed to succeed him (d. 811).

Charlemagne's biographer, Einhard, tells us that the ruler was taken unawares by this coronation,[5] and we have no right to contest

---

4. Edition of Duchesne, I, 275 — *Vita Iohannis I.*
5. *Vita Caroli*, c. 28. Although Himmelreich, *Die Kaiserkrönung Karls* (Kerkrade, 1920), and Halphen, *Revue hist.*, 134 (1920), 58 sqq., wish to set Einhard's statement aside or give it a fresh interpretation, the present writer firmly adheres to it in its natural and literal meaning. In his opinion, the tendency is to seek the explanation of Einhard's words rather in later conceptions than in those prevailing at the time.

the statement. Though the underlying idea of imperial office was not foreign to Charlemagne, the form in which it was expressed had been agreed upon by Roman circles together with the pope, without the Frankish ruler's having given his explicit assent. In truth, Charlemagne did not attach much value to such archaic forms: they seemed strange to him. Just as he preferred Frankish dress to Roman, so he felt out of place amid Roman conventions, and received no gratification from the idea of making a fine display in Rome as emperor.

He accepted the coronation, therefore, as a special act of consecration and homage performed in the sacred place of Rome, without attaching any particular importance to it for the present, and without assuming any particular obligations as a result of it. He did not intend to accord the pope the right to recognize his successors as the legitimate rulers of his empire, nor the right to crown them. This is evident from the fact that he himself, in 813, solemnly placed the crown upon the head of his son Louis in Aix-la-Chapelle, while those present exclaimed: "Long live the emperor Louis!" Not until three years later did Pope Stephen V repeat that coronation at Rheims. The same thing happened in the case of Lothar, Louis' son, who was first crowned in Aix-la-Chapelle by his father in 817, then by Pope Pascal I when he visited Rome in 823. Rome did not become Charlemagne's residence. He never appeared there again after his coronation, preferring Aix-la-Chapelle to the old imperial city. Louis, the second of the new emperors, never went to Rome as emperor.

Pope Leo III had acted on his own initiative on that Christmas Day of the year 800, even though the Romans wanted to have a voice in the matter. It is expressly emphasized that the Romans acclaimed Charlemagne as "Augustus" on this occasion, but the pope, nevertheless, was the sole agent of the coronation. In placing the crown on the ruler's head as he knelt before the tomb of the Apostle during the Mass, and afterward anointing King Charles, his eldest son and heir to the imperial dignity, the pontiff acted as the representative of the Romans and the ruler of the Papal States, the last remnant of the old Roman Empire; further, he acted not merely after the manner of the court bishops of Constantinople, but as the sole high priest and Vicar of God on earth. The precedent of the Old Testament which shows the high priests anointing the kings — a practice unknown among the Greeks, but followed in the West by the Visigoths, the Irish, the Anglo-Saxons, and finally the Franks — took on here a weight of added symbolism, becoming one with Roman tradition and determining the action of the successor of the Prince of the Apostles. Just as the Jews were the chosen people of God, so the new cultural community of the West was to be solemnly consecrated as God's community through its head, who was being crowned by the pope. The anointing of the emperor's son presented him as destined by God to succeed his father.

This act was not simply a renewal of the Roman Empire in the West. The close union with the Church, of which the crowned emperor was to be the protector, brought into being a new thing. The old emperors traced their authority back to Augustus. The new empire was to be in a very special sense a government by the grace of God and in accord with His will. The emperor was to rule his empire, a chosen group of nations, in such a way that the laws of God and the Christian order were to be everywhere the determining principle; the kingdom of God was to be established on earth, to triumph over all other kingdoms and spread throughout the world. Just as there was only one Vicar of Christ in Rome, so he who was so visibly marked and consecrated the temporal protector of the Church was to be the only emperor, without any peer; and after him his descendants were to stand forth as the chosen heirs of the imperial succession.

All this embodied an extraordinarily high idealism, but the symbolic act designed to express it was understood readily and in ever widening circles. However often, or however sharply, the facts might contradict the symbol, it always came to life again; it dominated the Middle Ages. Need this surprise us, who see how profound an impression has been made in our day by the concept of a league or union of nations? When all is said and done, can the idea of the peaceful co-operation of all peoples for the cultivation of a nobler humanity ever become totally extinct? At the time of which we write, that idea had a more assured foundation than ever before or since, for it rested upon a firm common faith, an acknowledged ecclesiastical unity, and cultural traditions which everyone desired to follow.

Joyously men gave themselves to the hope that a new era had dawned, one which would promote men's happiness beyond all preceding ages, and guide them to their eternal goal. These were fantastic hopes, few of which were to materialize. But that men were able so to hope was, nevertheless, a blessing for them as it has been for many who came after them. Gone was the gloomy notion that humanity faced its own old age and impending extinction. Men felt themselves young; full of creative energy and constructive ardor, they were ready to assume the leadership of the world. No longer was barbarism contrasted with antiquity, but instead there was a realization that the merging of uncivilized but healthy natural energies with the good elements preserved from ancient tradition had produced a new and better community and society. Nor in this did men deceive themselves. The Western commonwealth of nations became the leader of the world's culture. This period of history, defamed by the belittling designation of "Middle Ages," witnessed the birth and early growth of the Western nations — their cities, their literature, their universities; it saw the ejection of Islam from the Iberian Peninsula; it laid the foundations for an ever wider conquest of the world's seas and for the spread of Christianity over the whole earth.

That the Romans were the first to comprehend this lofty idea does them special credit, but it should not strike us as unexpected. Recent events had shown them their own urgent need of a defender who should be able to protect them against internecine strife and maintain peace and order among them. But the designation of this defender as "Patrician of the Romans" could hardly satisfy them. In the first place, as compared to the title combined with it, "King of the Franks and Lombards," it looked very insignificant, making Rome appear only an accessory to the other powers named. But there was also a deeper objection. Recalling the sad times when Rome was a neglected province of the Byzantine Empire, ruled from Ravenna by another Patrician, the hated governor of the foreign emperor of Constantinople, Roman citizens did not wish to be freed from the Byzantine domination in order to be protected (and thus incidentally supervised) by a mere Frankish sovereign who was in addition the successor of the Lombard kings of unhappy memory. Franks and Lombards were barbaric tribes, and the words which designated their ruler rang unpleasantly in Roman ears. By way of contrast, the title borne by the emperor in Constantinople was of an entirely different order; he was the successor of the glorious line which had begun in Rome.

We recall that Rome had changed the barbaric names Willibrord and Winfrid to the Roman names Clement and Boniface. Now it was found desirable to replace the sovereign's barbaric title, to which was joined that of a Byzantine official, with a purely Roman title — the highest Rome was ever able to bestow. In the course of the rebellions which had frequently broken out in Rome against the Frankish party and the popes who adhered to it, the reproach was probably often voiced that it was disgraceful for the Romans to be subject to barbarians. Non-Frankish pilgrims who came to Rome to visit the martyrs' tombs and to admire the city's ancient traditions undoubtedly expressed their regret to the Romans that the latter were no longer capable of establishing a suzerainty of their own. All this helps to make clear what the Romans of that day wanted to express by choosing their protector themselves, as it were, and designating him, not as a foreigner and a barbarian, but as one of their own; one who would carry on among them again the splendid imperial line, and who, as emperor of the Romans, would be alien to none in the West but the common sovereign of all. Henceforth Romans need not feel humiliated at the spectacle of Constantinople, for Rome had its own emperor as well — and one much closer to God, since the Vicar of Christ had given him the crown and assigned to him a particularly Christian and religious mission in virtue of which Church and State were to dwell side by side as under one roof.

The imperial coronation by the pope excluded caesaropapism and threw the distinction between the two powers into bold relief: the one as closer to God and spiritual, the other as stronger in secular authority. The spiritual leaders personally bound the bearer of the highest civil power in the West to their cause even more firmly than before; at the same time, they ennobled and broadened his sphere of action in a spiritual sense. The memory of Rome was to accompany the emperor everywhere; not only was it to remind him of his duty as Patrician to protect the Papal States, but it was to keep before him the ideal mission of spreading everywhere the faith and the institutions of Rome. In the Frankish kingdom, laws and practices were to be renewed according to the Roman pattern, and the arts and sciences were to be cultivated. Rome had brought the Anglo-Saxon kingdoms to a high degree of culture; Anglo-Saxon missionaries, who had revived the Frankish Church by order of Rome and in accord with the instructions of the popes, demonstrated what seeds could be spread by Rome. To guard these seeds was to be the emperor's task, the emperor's honor. He was, moreover, to be the sword of the Church; for especially against the enemies of the Christian faith, against the pagans and the Saracens, did the Church have need of a powerful protector.

Though Charlemagne at first may possibly have regarded with some suspicion the new dignity which had been conferred upon him without his suggestion, his natural idealism quickly led him to perceive the lofty concept embodied therein. He showed plainly that he was now basing his calling as a ruler upon this concept. In the spring of 802 he issued an edict ordaining that all in his wide empire, both clergy and laity, who had formerly vowed fealty to him as king should take a new oath of loyalty to him as emperor; and that all who had now reached the age of twelve should also be required to take the oath. An additional particular aim of the edict was to insure that everyone would consecrate himself to the sacred service of God according to his own powers and understanding, since the emperor could not bestow on each separate individual the care and discipline necessary to bring this about. Let no one henceforth, by a false oath or any other deception, withhold from the emperor serfs or land or any other thing due. Let no one in any wise incur the guilt of robbery, fraud or outrage against God's holy Church, or against widows, orphans or strangers, of whom — after God and the saints — the emperor is the protector. Other admonitions follow: fulfill civic duties faithfully, render military service loyally, obey the emperor's commands, pay debts and rents, preserve and practice justice in the courts.

All the clergy were to pray for the welfare of the emperor and his family. The ecclesiastical regulations contained in conciliar decisions and papal decrees were to be the rule of conduct for the Church, while the Rule of Saint Benedict became the norm for monasteries. The old tribal laws were to be revised. Unity of faith was to bind all the subjects of the empire together with a spiritual tie, and the service of God was to be the source of men's duties to the State and the emperor.

We see from all this how intent Charlemagne was on establishing a new moral order — albeit he conceived that order as being very closely related to his own person. His moral zeal may explain why, as is reputed, he enjoyed having Saint Augustine's *City of God* read to him.

Charlemagne was also desirous of giving expression to his new dignity before the eyes of Constantinople, deeming it important to acquire the equality of status which at first was denied him there. After long negotiations a settlement was at last reached in 812-813, whereby Charlemagne was accorded the imperial title by the Byzantine ambassadors, and in return gave up his claims to Venice, Dalmatia and southern Italy. Venice thus acquired an intermediate position between East and West which enabled it to enjoy an independent development of great importance.

How Rome understood Charlemagne's position is shown in one of the mosaics adorning a triclinium in the papal palace of the Lateran. In the center we see the Saviour standing on a hill, from which flow the four rivers of Paradise. He is surrounded by His disciples, whom He is instructing, and holds an open book on which one can read the words *"Pax vobis."* Below is the inscription: "Go, therefore, and make disciples of all nations." To the right and left are panels showing how the Saviour's doctrine of peace has been realized in the harmony of the highest powers. One depicts Christ with Pope Sylvester and Constantine at His feet, to whom He is holding out the keys and the imperial standard, respectively. In the other, Pope Leo III and Charlemagne kneel before the Prince of the Apostles. To the pope Peter gives the pallium, the symbol of the highest priestly dignity; to the protector of the Church he commits the banner under which he is to fight and conquer for

CHURCH AND CULTURE IN THE MIDDLE AGES

Christ's kingdom (as Leo, at the beginning of his pontificate, had
sent Charlemagne the standard of Rome). In the inscription —
"May Saint Peter grant Pope Leo life and King Charles victory" —
the word "king" indicates that the imperial coronation had not yet
taken place when the panel was executed. Its symbolism acquired
even more justification after the year 800. Since it was not possible
to extend the frame sufficiently to fit an added interpretation, the
inscription was put over the arch of triumph which encloses this
representation of God's kingdom on earth. There one reads the text
which is the canticle of canticles of Christian culture: "Glory to God
in the highest, and on earth peace among men of good will."

Artists and poets can indulge in the delineation of such an
ideal conception. The historian too will know how to appreciate
it, for the very fact that ideals are set up and recognized at all
certainly ennobles an age. But history has the task as well of explaining the manner in which the ideals have been realized and the
extent to which men have lagged behind them. The functioning side
by side of emperor and pope, who were to be closely united with
each other — each of them, indeed, was to remain in his own sphere
of action and take care lest he infringe upon the rights of the
other — invited, from the very outset, the stronger party to encroach upon the weaker. The stronger party at that time was not
the pope. Leo III, banished from Rome, had been returned to the
papal throne by Charlemagne, and maintained himself there only
through the protection which Charlemagne's power afforded him.
As late as the year 808 Leo, writing to Charlemagne, said incidentally of himself and the bishops: "We all look to your protection for safety."[6]

In the Christian community of the West at that time,
Charlemagne's word counted for more than the pope's. He did not
allow himself to be misled by the glamour of the new imperial title
into foolishly exhibiting great splendor and displaying in Rome an
imperial power which did not correspond to the reality, as Otto III
later attempted to do. He was too prudent for that and knew the
real foundations of his power too well.

---

6. "Nos omnes in vestro servitio salvi existere cupimus" (M. G. Epp., V, 91).

He never went to Rome again. However, Pope Leo III visited him once more in the capital he had selected for himself north of the Alps, the county palatine of Aix-la-Chapelle, near the home of the Carolingian dynasty. Charlemagne chose it because of the warm baths in the locality and spent most of his time there during the last years of his life. He had the royal palace and the cathedral built side by side. The latter, which was intended, like the Hagia Sophia of Justinian, to be the church of the court and of the State, was erected on the same plan, a central structure topped by a mighty dome; the nearest model for this design was the Church of San Vitale in Ravenna, the city of Theodoric. Laborers were imported from all parts of the empire. Rome, Ravenna and the ruins of Treves were requisitioned to supply columns and marble ornamentation.

It was here, on his native soil, that Charlemagne wished his tomb to be. Despite his supernational power and his title of Roman emperor, he felt himself a German. He had the German epics then being sung, committed to writing; he gave the months German names; he undertook, as his biographer Einhard relates, to compose a so-called grammar of his mother tongue. He could speak Latin as well as his native language, but he never could master writing despite the great pains he took to learn. That he was deeply attached to the simple manners of his people is evident from another statement of his biographer: that he appeared as a rule in Frankish dress and actually donned the Roman costume — long tunic, chlamys and sandals — only twice, at the request of Popes Adrian and Leo.

In external points, indeed, Charlemagne was not easily tempted to go too far. But his extraordinarily energetic nature prompted him to assert his great organizing ability everywhere, and there was no ecclesiastical question in which, once it was brought to his attention, he did not wish to intervene with decisiveness. He was also urged on in this by his court theologians (in particular Alcuin), who desired to demonstrate to Roman circles — certainly their superiors in point of the cautious weighing of problems — that their theological learning was of a higher type. These theologians praised him as a priest, as the preacher of Christ, the chosen man of God, the son of God, the soldier of Christ;[7] as not only the *defensor ecclesiae* who protected the Church against unbelievers and heretics, but also the *rector ecclesiae* who built up, directed and disciplined the Church. In comparison, the pope seemed virtually no more than the praying priest who, like Moses with arms upraised, implored the blessing of God upon the emperor's deeds.[8]

Thus it came about that Charlemagne, exactly as Justinian had done, began to render decisions in matters of faith. He had theological discussions conducted in his presence, and would always uphold the opinion of his own doctors. During a religious debate held in Rome in 810, Pope Leo III warned the Frankish theologians to take heed lest they come to regard themselves as being on the same level as the Fathers.[9] This was on the occasion of the controversy concerning the insertion of *filioque* into the Nicene-Constantinopolitan Creed. The Franks urgently demanded the adoption of the hotly contested word in opposition to the Greeks. Their purpose was to bring out in the clearest manner the truth that the Holy Ghost proceeds not only from the Father but also from the Son. As we now know, the term *filioque* was used in the pre-Ephesian formula of faith of the year 400; but the pope hesitated to take sides with the Franks in this purely liturgical question.[10] He did not wish to create a new and wider religious chasm between the East and the West.

Another controversy concerned the Adoptionist heresy, widespread in Spain and especially flagrant in the Spanish March, which taught that Christ as man was merely the adopted son of God. Here, Charlemagne acted in agreement with the popes, but the manner in which he intervened in the controversy was, to say the least, striking. He convened a Frankish national synod at Regensburg in 792, and had it condemn the heresy; later (in June, 800), he had Alcuin debate the question in his presence at Aix-la-Chapelle with the heresiarch Bishop Felix of Urgel.

---

7. Alcuin, *Epistolae: M. G. Epp.*, IV, 294, 241.
8. *Ep. Caroli Leoni III P.: M. G. Epp.*, IV, 137; cf. ibid., 209, 224.
9. *M. G. Concil.*, II, 1, p. 241, lines 27 sq.
10. W. Peitz, *Das vorephesinische Symbol der Papstkanzlei* (Rome, 1939): *Miscellanea historiae pontificiae*, I, 49 sqq.

His attitude in the matter of the veneration of images was even more remarkable. To settle the Iconoclastic controversy, the empress Irene had convened in 787 the Second Council of Nicaea, which condemned the Iconoclasts in the presence of two papal representatives. When the acts of the Council (poorly translated into Latin) were sent to Charlemagne from Rome, they gave great offense in the circles about him — first of all because of the subject matter. The Franks objected to the external forms of veneration practiced in the East. Just as they were scandalized at the acts of prostration by which the emperors and their pictures or statues were honored in Constantinople, so also they regarded this mode of venerating the images of the saints as unlawful.

But political motives also played a part in the Frankish reaction. They were unwilling to regard a Byzantine council as ecumenical, and were jealous of the role the empress Irene had played in the affair. A short time before, Charlemagne had clashed with Constantinople in the duchy of Benevento and in consequence had broken off his daughter's engagement with Irene's son. He wished now to show that he too could speak his mind in matters of faith, and his theologians gladly seized upon the occasion to prove that they were wiser than the Greeks. He submitted the acts of the Council to them for scrutiny — he even solicited opinions on the matter in England — and had them prepare a refutation, the *Libri Carolini,* in which the theologians presented their point of view as his own. Essentially, their judgment on the root of the question was correct: they did not reject images as a means of church decoration. However, they declared themselves against that *adoratio* of images which they conceived to be idolatry, whereas it was in fact only the customary form of veneration practiced in Constantinople, the *Proskynesis.* Charlemagne wanted the pope to repudiate the Second Council of Nicaea. When Adrian, on the contrary, with due reserve, defended the Council, Charlemagne convoked in opposition to it a Western synod at Frankfort on the Main in 794. He presided over this gathering, addressed it repeatedly, and conducted the discussions according to his own will. The Adoptionist heresy and the veneration of images were condemned, and the Second Council of Nicaea was denied ecumenical status.

Only the prudence of Adrian prevented a break with Charlemagne over this question, which though important in practice had no essential bearing on principle. At all events, Charlemagne was now on the surest road to emulating the course of the Byzantine emperors and setting himself up as an authority in matters of faith. The only reason why no conflict ensued for the time being was that pope and emperor considered themselves intimately bound together, each feeling he had need of the other. Thus Charlemagne did not neglect, even in purely political acts concerning the future of his dynasty, to make sure of the pope's assent. When he issued a law at the Diet of Diedenhofen, in 806, regarding the division of the empire after his death, he sent Einhard to Pope Leo with the document that its execution might be guaranteed by the pontiff's signature.

This confusion of the spiritual and temporal powers could endure without disruptive friction as long as the advantages accruing to both parties from their close union were evident. It was certainly a blessing for the West that such an intimate association obtained at least long enough to secure the unity of the Western cultural community. But once this gain had been firmly established, it was inevitable that the conflicts resulting from the very closeness of the bond should increase, each side complaining of infringements by the other. Charlemagne's grandson Lothar transformed the papacy's union with the empire into a state of dependence on the empire to which Rome could not long submit. Pope Gregory IV and the Frankish Church allowed themselves to be drawn into the struggle between Louis the Pious and his sons in such a manner that the authority of the papacy and the Church suffered. Both declined with the decline of the Carolingian empire; and thereafter the Church had to begin all over again laboriously to build up her discipline and inculcate in her servants the ideal conception of their vocation. The kingdom of God, a spiritual society, could not be regulated as though it were a secular power.

These points will help us to recognize the limits which we may not transcend in praising Charlemagne and his times. Within these limits, nevertheless, there is still room to depict him and his period — though it endured but briefly — in glorious terms. The deeper reasons for this glory lay in the eventual florescence of the slowly maturing seeds of the Western cultural community. Charlemagne contributed his share, as a prudent and tirelessly active gardener, in bringing these seeds to maturity, diffusing them, and protecting them against the influences of destruction.

CHAPTER EIGHT

FIRST RENAISSANCE OF THE WEST —
THE GOVERNMENT OF CHARLEMAGNE

CHARLEMAGNE'S broad vision as an organizer reveals itself in the manner whereby, in an empire that embraced the most diverse peoples, he retained existing customs and institutions while working to achieve the needed unity of the whole. He allowed the several peoples their ancestral laws, and the old principle that everyone was to live and be judged according to his own law, was repeatedly enunciated anew. This was, indeed, to become fundamental in the development of liberty in the West. It was without doubt also an essential factor in bringing about the ready acceptance of Charlemagne's rule by the subjected countries, and in permitting the feeling that they belonged together to grow strong among these peoples with little opposition. Even the Lombards and the Saxons retained their ancient law, though they had been subjugated by the sword.

After Charlemagne became emperor, he had the various legal codes read to him and examined, and then delivered to each tribe its own proper code. The tribal law of the Saxons and the Frisians was committed to writing for the first time during his reign. Thus, there was one law for the Salic Franks and another for the Ripuarian Franks; there were separate codes for the Burgundians, who lived according to the ancient law of Gundobad, for the Alamanni, the Bavarians, the Saxons and Frisians, for the Goths in the Spanish March, for the Lombards, for the Romans in the Papal States, or Romania, as these States were sometimes called. A characteristic of the law was that it guarded the rights of the individual — a sign of how much the person of the free man was respected. In Rome, everyone was permitted to declare whether he chose to live according to the Roman or the Frankish law.

The unity of the empire found expression in the great national assembly which by former Frankish custom had taken place early in spring, but now was held later, usually in May. This was the

"Marchfield," the old gathering of the free Franks constituting the regular fighting troops of the nation. The spiritual and temporal lords and the soldiers of the regular army summoned for the occasion attended this meeting; in addition, the free men living in the vicinity might also be present if they desired.

This gathering was a vestige of the ancient Germanic popular assembly. Those who attended were accounted legally as the representatives of the whole nation with a decisive vote in all major questions. This type of assembly still reveals something of the spirit of liberty which the Germanic nations injected into Western institutions in contrast to the principle of absolutism set up by the Roman law: *Quod principi placuit legis habet vigorem.* According to the Germanic conception, which was now accepted in the West, nothing of importance was to be decided by the prince alone; he was to be bound by public opinion or its representatives. This was often clearly brought home to the successors of Charlemagne; thus, for example, in 864 at the Diet of Pîtres on the Seine, Charles the Bald was addressed with these words: "The law is made by the assent of the people and the decree of the king."[1]

The national assemblies decided on war and peace, on changes of the laws, and on the most diverse affairs, of great import and small. The deliberations, in which the nobles conducted the discussion and the ruler was occasionally able, according to the force of his personality, to bring his will to bear upon them, had no fixed procedure. Both spiritual and temporal matters might be discussed, in which case both the spiritual and the temporal lords attended. Sometimes, however, they deliberated separately, the synod and the diet usually taking place in the same locality and at the same time. Thus, the national synod which condemned Adoptionism and declared itself against the Byzantine form of venerating images was held at Frankfort on June 1, 794, simultaneously with a diet. But this synod also had before it a temporal matter, since it was there that Tassilo, the deposed duke of Bavaria, declared his acceptance of the sentence previously passed on him.

---

1. *M. G. Cap.,* II, 313.

Charlemagne convoked the national synods — we can count sixteen of them under him — as well as the imperial diets, often presided over and addressed them, directed the resolutions according to his own will or accepted them as expert opinions, and carried them out after he had had them sanctioned at a diet. The resolutions, known as "recesses," of the imperial diets were recorded as capitularies.

Just as the imperial diets and the synods overlapped each other, so too the laws contained both spiritual and civil prescriptions. The spiritual ordinances acquired validity through the State, which furnished the public force to secure their execution — namely, the king's ban. Here was the veritable condition of a state church, calculated to fill men with uneasiness, especially since Charlemagne also gave orders in ecclesiastical matters even independently of any synod. Had several such monarchs ruled successively, there might have developed a state of caesaropapism similar to that prevailing in the East: certain predilections toward imperialistic absolutism were not lacking in the ruler we are considering. However, the nobles were subsequently to oppose such a development, although the temporal lords among them were not the elected but only the accepted, or born, representatives of the people. This action can afford some consolation to those who are inclined to lament the decline of Carolingian power.

The temporal lords were those who excelled in riches or in number of vassals. Almost all of them held offices and fiefs from the king; they were his crown vassals and officials. The spiritual lords were the bishops and abbots. They were increasingly regarded as spiritual officials, although this tendency was less evident under Charlemagne than before or after him, since he prudently attached great importance to the co-operation of the clergy in the education of the people. On account of their exalted dignity, he accorded them, in a certain measure, a position of the highest rank and was always seriously concerned that they fulfill their ecclesiastical duties.

The importance of the clergy was particularly great at the time because they were almost the sole representatives of culture; only they could write, and solely through them, therefore, was it possible to draw up official documents in Latin, the language of decrees and laws. Hence it was that the clergy played an important role at the court. Those who were in permanent attendance were members of the royal chapel. In the royal or palatine chapel they had charge of the divine services and were employed in the most diversified diplomatic and political affairs. They were attached to the sovereign by a particular bond of fidelity, for they had to accredit or bind themselves personally to him by placing their hand in his. Their superior was the head chaplain, who was customarily consulted by the sovereign in matters ecclesiastical. It was he who examined petitions pertaining to churches and monasteries, and his post was one of such influence that the pope usually conferred on him the pallium with the title of archbishop. Since the chapel served as the archives, the head chaplain was likewise in charge of the chancery, which at that time was exclusively staffed by clerics. Later this office of chancellor attained particular importance, and the head chaplains who filled it were the highest ecclesiastical dignitaries. These court ecclesiastics constituted the emperor's cabinet, so to speak. We read that after Charlemagne's death an ecclesiastical reform party on one occasion organized itself in opposition to the government as carried on by this cabinet.

To the ecclesiastical members of the royal chapel and the chancery were added councilors, who resided at court for a longer or shorter period at the sovereign's request and enjoyed his special confidence. Prominent among these was the Frank, Angilbert. At first attached to the royal chapel, he received in 790 the abbey of Saint Riquier, which he enriched with costly edifices and valuable manuscripts, although even as an abbot he usually lived at court. He maintained an illicit relationship with Charlemagne's daughter Bertha, by whom he had two sons — a situation which Charlemagne did not resent. Angilbert was employed on many political missions and occupied a position in Charlemagne's circle which we would designate as that of cabinet secretary. He was also very highly esteemed for his poems, which earned for him the sobriquet of "Homer." Later he was, with little justification, accredited a saint in a biography which praises him for his solicitude concerning his abbey. Worthier personalities were the brothers Saint Adelhard and Wala, Charlemagne's cousins. Adelhard, though brought up at the court, withdrew from it and entered, first the monastery of Corbie, and later Monte Cassino. Charlemagne gave him the abbey of Corbie, and appointed him to a high position of trust in the government of Italy at the side of the young Pippin. Wala succeeded his brother as abbot of Corbie, and subsequently accompanied Pippin's son Bernard to Italy when the latter was made king. The brothers later fell into temporary disgrace with Charlemagne's son, the emperor Louis the Pious. Saint Adelhard's treatise on the organization of Charlemagne's court, which was to serve as a model to posterity, exists unfortunately only in a later redaction.

Charlemagne's real governmental officials were, as in the Merovingian period, the governors of the counties (*Gaugrafen*), who must be chosen from the landed proprietors of the county, and consequently were fairly independent. In order to have administrators who would be completely under his control, the emperor created — and this was something new, revealing his keen vision as an organizer and his administrative talents — the office of the *missi dominici* or the *missi regis:* the king's messengers (also called *Waltboten*). Two such *missi* were regularly sent each spring into certain large districts of the empire to supervise in the king's stead the entire administration. At first they acted rather in the character of personal confidants of Charlemagne; but two years after he became emperor he invested the office itself with greater importance by commissioning a high ecclesiastical dignitary and a great nobleman as his deputies to investigate whether all the officials in a particular section of the empire were discharging their duties properly.

The ecclesiastical deputies were bishops or archbishops, through whom the clergy were given a large share in the education of the people as well as in the supervision of the government — also, inevitably, becoming deeply involved in the secret game of politics. On the other hand, since the *missi,* who were in fact the king's representatives, had to see to it that all was in order in the churches, church administration and discipline also came under the supreme direction of the sovereign. The whole institution recalls the position which the Church acquired in the Byzantine Empire during the reign of Justinian, when the bishops together with the *praefecti praetorio* controlled the civil government.

The confounding of ecclesiastical with civil matters at this time is seen particularly in the penal code. Infractions of the commandments and the ordinances of the Church were visited with civil punishments, and conversely, civil offenses with ecclesiastical punishments. Thus, civil penalties were decreed for the refusal to pay ecclesiastical tithes and for participation by the clergy in the chase.[2] Violations of ecclesiastical discipline and customs among the Saxons, converted by the sword, met with severe punishments consonant, no doubt, with their ancient tribal law.[3] But there were cases in which the Church was forced to follow the State in exercising her right to punish. Those guilty of incest or murder, besides suffering the secular punishment, had also to perform an ecclesiastical penance.[4] The counterpart of this is to be found in the fact that the bishops in particular were subject to the civil courts in all secular matters, whether of a criminal or a civil nature.

The collaboration of Church and State under Charlemagne was due chiefly to the fact that Charlemagne, acting in the spirit of the Church, imposed upon his empire a cultural mission which he conceived in a serious and ideal sense. Next to the gigantic task of political unification, it is here that his great merit lies. Not that he was the first to have conceived this mission in all its phases. The reform synods held under Saint Boniface already functioned toward the same end — this is true, in fact, of all the labors of Saint Boniface and his Anglo-Saxon companions, both monks and nuns.

But a comparison with the program prosecuted by Saint Boniface permits us to see still another aspect of Charlemagne's attitude toward the Church — an aspect which has been more distinctly recognized in recent times.[5] Although Charlemagne built on the foundation which Saint Boniface had prepared, the latter's reform program was nevertheless essentially altered by him in some features, if not completely annulled. The Church was used by him

---

2. *M. G. Cap.*, I, 94 sq., cap. 33, c. 15, 19.
3. Cf. below, p. 527.
4. *M. G. Cap.*, I, 97, cap. 33, c. 32, 33.
5. For the latest treatment cf. Lesne, *Histoire de la propriété ecclésiastique en France*, II.

in the first place for his own political ends, and was obliged to serve those ends in such a manner that at the close of his reign there existed many of the identical conditions which Saint Boniface believed his reform synods to have removed forever. Charlemagne, indeed, merely continued on the course which his father Pippin had already adopted.

One of the most important ordinances of the reform synods was that the church property which had been secularized, principally by Charles Martel, was to be restored. A decree to that effect was issued by Carloman, brother of Pippin the Short, in accord with the decisions of the first reform synod of 742. However, it proved impossible to put the decree into effect, and as we have already seen, a compromise was reached in the synod of Estinnes (Lessines) the following year. Most of the alienated properties were to remain for the time being with the present holders as fiefs, but the Church's ownership of them was to be legally recognized by the payment of a quit-rent of one *solidus* by every homestead; while poor churches and monasteries were to receive back at least as much as was necessary for their maintenance.[6] It was intended, therefore, to right as far as possible what was acknowledged to be a wrong; and however doubtful it might seem that all the properties could ever be restored to the Church again, further secularization was looked upon as forbidden. This view of the matter was adopted at first also by Pippin the Short. However, Saint Boniface hesitated to approve the compromise by accepting the quit-rent, until Pope Zachary expressly authorized him to do so, writing him in 751 as follows: "As regards the ecclesiastical rents — that is, the *solidus* which is to be paid by every household — just accept it and do not hesitate any further."[7]

This occurred after Carloman's retirement, when Pippin had long been ruling alone. Soon afterward, however, he struck out into new paths. He began to secularize church property once more, and Charlemagne continued the practice in a way which showed that he felt himself entirely free to dispose of ecclesiastical and

---

6. See above, p. 405.
7. *Letters of Saint Boniface,* edition of Tangl, p. 199.

monastic possessions. The work of the reform synods in this respect
was completely destroyed, the rulers merely borrowing from the
synodal decisions formulas whereby secularization was perpetrated anew and developing them further in a very different sense
indeed. What had been proposed earlier in order to render an old
wrong bearable for a time until it could be removed entirely, was
now employed as a formula to make a new wrong appear right.

The formulas already used by Pippin in this connection are
very clearly perceptible in the capitulary which Charlemagne proclaimed at Heristal in 779.[8] He who had received or was still
receiving church property from the sovereign was supposed to pay
the church a tenth and a ninth or a double tithe — that is, a fifth
of all the revenues accruing therefrom — besides which, a quit-rent
was also to be paid by the homesteads. However, this latter was
much smaller than the one previously proposed, being only one
solidus for fifty households, half of a *solidus* for thirty, a third of a
solidus for twenty. The holder of church property was, of course,
expressly to acknowledge himself a usufructuary by having the
church make out to him a bill of enfeoffment testifying that he had
received the property as a lease on the authority of the king
(*precaria verbo regis*). In order to guarantee the churches their
maintenance universally, it was decreed at this time — but probably
also earlier by Pippin — that the tithe demanded heretofore only
by the Church (for example, by the second council of Mâcon in
585) be paid to the bishops by all the inhabitants of the diocese
who did not pay the double tithe. This represented an innovation, and one of no little consequence: that the payment of the tithe
was now exacted and enforced by the State.[9]

Although the general material condition of the Church was
not impaired — perhaps rather improved — by this arrangement, the
secularization policy of Pippin and Charlemagne proved in the issue
to be seriously damaging to ecclesiastical life. It was disastrous
for the Church that the sovereign should put church property in
the same category as royal property and dispose of it entirely at

8. Cap. 20, c. 7, 13: *M. G. Cap.*, I, 48 (cf. 42), 50.
9. Cap. Harist., c. 7.: *M. G. Cap.*, I, 48.

will and at the instance of the nobles. Apart from the bad example he gave thereby, Charlemagne's procedure brought about a radical change in that conception of ecclesiastical office which Saint Boniface held and inculcated as the ideal. Charlemagne disposed of episcopal offices and abbacies as arbitrarily as he did the properties connected with them. After the death of a prelate he took advantage of the vacancies, often purposely prolonged, to reap profits for the State, for the crown claimed the revenues of a vacant bishopric or monastery. Eventually Charlemagne appointed the new incumbents according to his own good pleasure. If now and then a bishop was still elected, this happened only by virtue of a special privilege from the sovereign.

The monasteries found themselves in a desperate situation. It is true that their importance continued to make itself felt in the German mission field, and had led to many new foundations, especially in Bavaria under Odilo and Tassilo, the last dukes of the Agilolfingian dynasty. But Saint Boniface had striven to make the monasteries as independent as possible — the exemption procured for Fulda shows this. After the saint's death, Pippin tried to place the monasteries under the jurisdiction of the bishops, which led to some bitter conflicts, such as we encounter, for example, between Constance and Saint Gall and between Mainz and Fulda. Finally it was the king who gained control of the monasteries since he was unwilling that the bestowal of the rich lands connected with them should slip from his hands. In conferring the abbatial dignity, Charlemagne considered in most cases only the income attached to it. Once again, abbots who were monks were rare; secular priests were frequently at the head of monasteries as *abbates canonici;* and monasteries were even conferred on laymen — monasteries of men no less than of women. At the end of Charlemagne's reign, conditions had in many respects sunk to the level of Charles Martel's day.

This manifested itself most significantly in the obligations which Charlemagne imposed upon his prelates in connection with his system of conferring bishoprics and monasteries. Regarding church property as crown lands, Charlemagne imposed the same obligations upon the prelates as upon the laymen enfeoffed of crown lands: in particular, that of furnishing military forces. The churches now began, generally by leasing their benefices, to train warriors who were at the disposal of the bishop or abbot as vassals of the church or monastery, and were sent by him to the king when the latter issued a call for them. Thus we again behold the bishops and abbots taking the field at the head of their armed forces as they had during the Merovingian period — a practice which Saint Boniface had with great difficulty suppressed. The sole difference was this: that what was formerly felt to be an abuse was now demanded as a duty. Under the banner of the patron saint of the bishopric or monastery its vassals took the field. The nature of the burdens imposed upon a prelate in connection with this military service is apparent from a summons sent by Charlemagne to Fulrad, the abbot of Saint Quentin. The abbot was to present himself with his vassals by a fixed date at a national assembly in Starasfurt on the Bode River, from which point a campaign was to be launched against the Saxons.

> You must come with your vassals to the designated place, equipped thus, that you may be able to take the field from there whithersoever our command ordains: with arms, appliances and tools, and with food and clothing, so that every horseman has his shield as well as a lance, a sword, a dagger, and a bow and a quiver of arrows; and your wagons, too, must be fitted out with complete gear, namely: hatchets, sledge hammers, battering-rams, axes, gardener's shovels, spades, and everything that is necessary for a campaign.[10]

In the beginning not all vassals were enfeoffed with church property by the bishopric or the monastery; hence many of them were maintained in common. As a result instances undoubtedly arose in which large monasteries were forced to establish barracks. From the rent-rolls of Saint Riquier, the monastery so magnificently appointed by the abbot Angilbert, for the year 831 we learn of the existence near the monastery of soldiers' quarters (*Vicus militum*) housing one hundred and ten men, each with a horse and weapons of every sort at his disposal.[11]

---

10. *M. G. Cap.*, I, 168.
11. Hariulf, *Chronique de Saint-Riquier,* edited by F. Lot ("Collection de textes," volume 17, Paris, 1894), Append., p. 306. Cf. Werminghoff in *Hist. Aufsätze* presented to K. Zeumer (Weimar, 1910), 35 sq.

Inevitably, the militarization of the monasteries did not leave the abbots themselves unaffected. The prohibitions against the clergy's bearing arms so often issued by Saint Boniface were undoubtedly still upheld in theory; but in practice they were only too frequently violated after Charlemagne demanded the personal participation of the bishop or abbot in military expeditions. The mission of peace of the servants of the Church was thus seriously menaced. Pope Adrian realized this and it is to his credit that he remonstrated with Charlemagne against the bearing of arms by bishops and priests:

> He [the sovereign] should not permit this on any condition; the bishops and priests whom he desires to accompany him everywhere should zealously devote themselves to prayer; they should preach to all that which is necessary for the salvation of their souls and for eternal life, and should hear confessions; the other bishops and priests, however, should remain in their churches, and each one should strive to direct the people entrusted to him by God under the powerful protection of the king and according to the prescriptions of the Church.[12]

The zealous patriarch Paulinus of Aquileia urgently prayed for the king:

> Mayest thou do battle for us against the visible foes of Christ out of love for Christ and with God's help. We will implore the power of the Lord for thee against the invisible enemies and fight for thee with spiritual weapons. May the priests of the Lord be permitted to serve the Lord in simplicity according to the Gospel and the precepts of the Apostles and to render military service only in the camp of the Lord; because no man can serve two masters.[13]

Charlemagne would have sacrificed nothing of his political greatness had he departed from his chosen path in these matters.

Just as the bishops were obliged to render military service, so they had to attend at court continuously and assist the ruler as his most prominent councilors, precisely as though they were state officials — one in this capacity, another in that. Saint Boniface knew well why he should scrupulously absent himself from court;

---

12. *M. G. Epp.*, III, 625.
13. Ibid., IV, 525.

but only a few bishops under Charlemagne imitated his example. To these personal services were added still other onerous material obligations. Gifts, formerly presented to the sovereign voluntarily by the bishops and abbots, were made an obligatory tax by Charlemagne. He writes to Fulrad of Saint Quentin as follows:

> Send us your gifts, which you are to bring to us at the national assembly in the middle of May, wherever we shall be. If you can bring them yourself, that will be still more agreeable to us. But see to it that you be not guilty of any negligence if you desire to retain our favor.[14]

Finally, the hospitality claimed by the king was a very heavy burden upon the bishops and abbots. Not only the ruler with his retinue, but also the members of the royal court, the king's messengers, and in general all who could produce a written order from him, had a right to shelter. This included lodging and sustenance, and in addition being furnished with the necessary means of transportation. These obligations were collectively conceived as "the service of the king." In return, the episcopal and abbatial offices conferred by him were regarded as royal honors, *honores regni.*

The natural result of such a conception was that churchmen became worldly-minded. The prelates constantly employed by the king on secular affairs became absorbed in such matters. They sought only the favor of the sovereign; just as they were to strive above all to increase his power, so their efforts tended also, and too greatly, to increase their own power through his favor; as dignitaries, they desired to rival the temporal lords in worldly splendor.

The monasteries fared the worst under these misdirected tendencies. Since they now frequently passed for imperial or royal institutions, their income was for the most part claimed, if not by the king, then by the secular-minded royal abbots, with the result that not only was spiritual leadership lacking but the community soon became materially destitute as well. In a distressed letter which should be dated before 800, the monks of one such monastery implored the king to come to their aid, reminding him that they prayed day and night for him, for his family and his kingdom:

---

14. *M. G. Cap.,* I, 168.

For from the day on which thou didst give us in fief and we were
removed from thy protection, we have had no clothing, no shoes, neither
oil nor soap nor food, as we formerly had. Lift us out of our want,
most pious king; do not thou, who callest the pagans to join the Christian world, let us who are Christians perish.[15]

Nor were other general complaints lacking in regard to these
conditions. Archbishop Arno of Salzburg had complained bitterly
to his friend Alcuin, the confidant of Charlemagne, about the many
temporal affairs he was forced to engage in, and directed the blame
against the emperor himself. Alcuin sought to console him, but
at the same time warned him against speaking loudly lest the
emperor hear and withdraw his favor. Arno says in another letter:

Of the lord emperor's good will I am positive. He certainly endeavors to regulate everything in the kingdom entrusted to him by God
according to a just standard, but he has fewer helpers about him than
frustraters of justice and fewer preachers than despoilers [*nec tantos
praedicatores, quantos praedatores*], and there are more who seek their
own ends instead of God's.[16]

He distinctly refers to the cause of the Church's growing worldliness
in these words:

Temporal cares torment the pastors. They who are to be ever ready
for God in heaven are forced to travel much about here on earth. The
soldiers of Christ are made to serve the world, and with any kind of an
excuse they conceal the sword of the Word of God in the enclosure of
the mouth. On the day of battle they show themselves as hired mercenaries, not as free warriors.[17]

From this exchange of opinions, we see how only in trusted
circles could men express themselves on the destructive consequences
brought about by the inordinate political claims made upon the
Church. If louder complaints were not voiced, it was because men
understood to a certain extent the reasons motivating Charlemagne's
procedure. His first aim in controlling the property of the Church
and in enlisting the spiritual lords for his service was to collect

---

15. *Formulae salicae*, edition of Merkel, 61. *M. G. Form.*, 262.
16. *M. G. Epp.*, IV, 422 sq., 411.
17. Ibid., 409.

forces wherewith to strengthen and extend his empire, in whose unity and greatness the Church herself had a particularly vital stake. With the secularized church property, he endowed the temporal lords who helped him conduct his almost unceasing wars; thus he secured and maintained the military forces he needed so badly. That is why, soon after Charlemagne's death, his successor, Louis the Pious, declared that the secularizations put in effect by his father had been occasioned by the force of circumstances (*necessitate compellente*).[18] The same reason that motivated Charlemagne in enfeoffing his vassals with church lands made him influence bishops and abbots to invest their vassals in the same way. The "feudalization of society" is the general formula characterizing this situation. Church property was used by Charlemagne especially for endowing his counts — the chosen props of his political and military power — with lands to fortify their positions.

In the final analysis, it was Charlemagne's military policy based on a doctrine of might which led him to make his far-reaching claims on church property, and brought about the conception of bishoprics and abbeys as imperial properties, fiefs of the crown, with their prelates as its vassals. The question inevitably rises whether the unfavorable results which can be seen flowing from this policy after Charlemagne died, were really counterbalanced by its temporary gains. The unified empire could not be maintained for long, nor was the weakness of Charlemagne's successors alone to blame for this. The entanglement of Church and State and the worldly character of the ecclesiastical leaders were sooner or later bound to provoke a counter-movement returning the bishops to their spiritual and pastoral duties. The longer this readjustment was protracted, moreover, the graver would be the conflicts necessarily involved in it. In the last analysis, it was not even the state that won out, but the individual temporal lords. They had been kept amenable by means of revenues in the form of lands of which only the income should have gone to them. But having thus acquired, as it were, the capital along with the interest, they strove to keep the capital itself within their families — that is, to make the fiefs

---

18. *M. G. Cap.*, I, 279.

hereditary and alienate them forever from their owner, whether State or Church.

All these eventualities, of course, could not be foreseen at that time; whereas everyone could see the great power of the unified empire of the West, which was capable of opposing Islam and Constantinople — and which at first was beneficial to the Church and unquestionably did serve her aims. If the Carolingian kingship had a sacred character after Pippin's consecration, which Pope Stephen had repeated at Saint Denis in 754, this was enhanced when Charlemagne received the imperial crown from the sovereign pontiff. Thereafter the clergy of the West saw in Charlemagne the temporal head of Western Christendom, the collaborator with the spiritual head in an alliance sealed by official agreement.

The Carolingians had rendered undeniable services in Germany, endowing so many bishoprics there that they had to be regarded in some degree as their founders. Daily it could be perceived anew that Charlemagne willingly allowed himself to be guided by the ideals of Christian culture. More — he made himself responsible for the protection and the welfare of the Church, provided the interests of his own power were not thereby directly affected; just as he guaranteed order in the Church, the enforcement of her discipline, and the spread of her doctrine.

He tried his utmost to prevent the abuses connected with the private churches by allowing those who possessed minor churches as their personal property to deal with them as such and sell or give them away. However, these proprietors were not permitted to divert an ecclesiastical edifice belonging to them from its original purpose or to diminish its endowment. To this end they were obliged to permit the bishop to supervise the church and its priests, and had to reach an understanding with him regarding the appointment and dismissal of priests. Finally, they were forbidden to employ the clergy attached to their private churches in a manner unworthy of the sacred calling — for example, as overseers or farmers.[19]

---

19. Conc. Francof., c. 54: *M. G. Conc.*, II, 171; *Missat. generale* (802), c. 15: *M. G. Cap.*, I, 94; *Cap. eccl.* (810-813), c. 2, 13, pp. 178 sq. Cf. *Conc. Vern.* (755), c. 16, p. 36.

Who can fail to recognize that Charlemagne made excellent provisions for protecting church property from loss and for increasing it through good administration? In peace times such property enjoyed the special protection of the sovereign or his governmental messengers (*missi*). Almost all of it now participated in the privilege of immunity — that is, it was exempt, like the crown lands, from taxes and from the jurisdiction of the civil courts. In order to exercise their subordinate jurisdiction — only later was the superior jurisdiction also added — all bishops, abbots and abbesses were to have bailiffs (*advocati*) appointed either by Charlemagne himself or by his *missi*, except when his counts were allowed to appoint them. By having his *missi* also supervise the activities of the bailiffs, he showed how much he was concerned about the good administration of their office.

With respect to one matter which Saint Boniface had had very much at heart, Charlemagne fulfilled to a certain degree the wishes of the reform synods. After he had learned from Dionysius Exiguus' collection of canons which Adrian I sent him in 774, that the metropolitan organization was ordained by old ecclesiastical law, he did not, like his father, oppose the appointment of metropolitans. The according of their historical rights to the ancient metropolitan sees in Gaul and the creation of new metropolitans through the conferring of the pallium by Rome on the archbishops of Salzburg and Mainz — that is to say, the restoration of the rank superior to that of simple bishops — constituted an innovation, something indeed unknown throughout the Merovingian period. It corresponded, at least in part, to the program which Saint Boniface had brought with him from his Anglo-Saxon home. Just as Charlemagne appointed the bishops, so he selected the archbishops; but the pope assigned them to their office by conferring on them the pallium. Generally speaking, there is henceforth no archbishop without it. The friendly accord between Charlemagne and Adrian has thus achieved what Saint Boniface failed to accomplish because of Pippin's reluctance. The metropolitan archbishop belongs to a more exalted rank and exercises a real and personal authority over his subordinate bishops, who are designated suffragans, a term coined at this time.[20]

Saint Boniface's aim in this matter had been the hierarchical organization of ecclesiastical pastors under Rome. Charlemagne regarded it rather as a system facilitating the control he liked to apply everywhere, but in particular to the Church, as was instanced in his appointment of the ecclesiastical *missi*. Only in this sense did he wish to use the archbishops; in no way did he relinquish the supervision which he reserved to himself even over the Church. Thus, the archbishops had no voice in the election of bishops; national synods took precedence over provincial synods; the supreme direction of the Church in the Frankish kingdom was not so much exercised by the pope through the metropolitans as by Charlemagne, and the metropolitans had to look to him rather than to Rome. On the other hand, he firmly established the diocese as the fixed district of ecclesiastical administration; bishops and priests were not permitted to function outside diocesan limits without proper credentials, and all monasteries within the diocese were made subject to the bishop.

Charlemagne further deserves high recognition for his solicitude in the social field. During the Roman and Merovingian periods the care of the poor was assigned chiefly, if not exclusively, to the Church and the bishops. Charlemagne, as supreme secular head, considered himself the person on whom primarily devolved that protection of the weak and needy which was in keeping with the duties of a cultured Christian State. He forbade anyone to deny shelter and hospitality to travelers (in those days, hostelries could not be counted on), and decreed punishment for such as refused to come to the aid of a ship in distress. Thus did the emperor convert into actuality the beautiful saying found in one of his capitularies, that after God and His saints, the ruler had been set up as the protector and supporter of the destitute.[21]

The Church's role in the care of the poor, organized in accord with the conditions obtaining in Roman cities, was bound to decline

---

20. Cf. Lesne, *La hiérarchie episcopale*, 57 sq.
21. *M. G. Cap.*, I, 93.

with the change in the economic situation whereby urban bishoprics lost their former importance and large new dioceses were coming into being which extended over wide stretches of open country, and, in Germany, were only partly urban even at their centers. However, the Church still continued — and that with the emperor's approval and encouragement, and often on a vast scale — to befriend the poor. This was seen not only in the survival of her old hospices and inns for pilgrims in the Italian cities, and no doubt also in the episcopal cities in the western part of the Frankish kingdom, but above all in her new methods of service which corresponded to the customary practice in country places. There the care of the poor was no longer in the hands of an official organization with its headquarters in the episcopal church, but was entrusted to the individual ecclesiastical institutions and monasteries and carried on as well as the means of each one permitted. In some measure all these institutions distributed alms, some more, some less. Extraordinary charity was practiced by the monastery of Saint Riquier, where, besides a hundred and fifty widows, three hundred poor also received alms daily. In most instances the large monasteries had an inn for strangers, sometimes also a hospital. Separate homes for lepers, which were necessary because of the danger of contagion, were found here and there; one was erected, for example, in the monastery of Saint Gall. The growing number of travelers further emphasized the need for hostelries along difficult mountain routes, such as the church of Chur maintained on the Septimer Pass. There developed between the various monasteries and institutions, to which new associations were later added, a rivalry in charitable activities that constitutes one of the finest phases of medieval culture.

Charlemagne early stressed the fact that prudent judgment should govern men in carrying out all such charitable works.

A broad social view is manifested in an ordinance commanding everyone to provide for his dependents and serfs, that they may not be reduced to poverty nor wander about as beggars.[22] In general, the Church certainly took the principle to heart. But what she was

---

22. Cap. 46, c. 9. (806): *M. G. Cap.*, I, 132.

prepared to do in this regard seems to have been obscured here and there by the ambition of some of her members to enrich themselves with goods and lands. Charges of that nature are specifically intimated in capitulary number 72, which enumerates several points submitted by the emperor to the bishops. In one, the question is asked whether certain ecclesiastics have not been guilty of social injustices in their anxiety to increase their own possessions:

> Has he renounced the world who ceases not, day after day, in every way and by every artifice, to increase his possessions, while now promising the happiness of heaven, now threatening the eternal punishments of hell? Has he renounced the world who in the name of God or some saint robs both the rich and the simple of their goods; who deprives legitimate heirs of their inheritance, inducing many men thereby to commit crimes and misdeeds because of the poverty to which they have been reduced? — for they are in a certain measure forced to steal and rob, since their personal inheritance has been taken away by another.[23]

These were undoubtedly only isolated cases, to which reference is made as a deterrent measure, nor should we overestimate the need that actually existed for such distrustful warnings, which flowed probably from an ecclesiastical pen: they correspond to the Carolingian administration's universal and stringent system of supervision. We shall arrive at a more comprehensive judgment by following those who try to sketch a complete picture of the whole economic development of the period from its many individual documents.[24] Thereby we perceive that the entire system of administering the goods of the Church really led to great social progress for the broad masses of the laity.

Free gifts to the Church in absolute ownership were becoming less and less the rule. In most instances, gifts were made only conditionally: the donor reserved a life interest in the donated property, or it was released to him — sometimes also to his children — at a fixed quit-rent, or the right of repurchase was reserved. It also frequently happened that, when the donated property was

---

23. *M. G. Cap.*, I, 163.
24. Cf. especially Dopsch, *Die wirtschaftliche Entwicklung der Karolingerzeit*, § 4 and §8, whom I here follow.

conveyed in usufruct, some of the old ecclesiastical alodium was added in the form of *precaria remunerativa*. Hence no one was found at the council of Tours in 813 to substantiate the charge alleged in the above-quoted imperial *admonitio* (cap. 72) that people were being robbed of their inheritance by the conveyance of the properties to the Church; and the council replied to the question submitted there[25] with the statement: "There is hardly anyone who conveys his property to the Church without receiving from the Church's property as much as he has given, or twice or thrice as much in usufruct."[26]

This practice of the *precaria remunerativa* may not always have been harmless. It awakened the passion for gain, whence might flow unethical business dealings; or, on the other hand, the squandering of the Church's property might be the result. By and large, however, these measures had a wholesome effect, socially and politically. The *precaria* contracts resembled our life annuities, the usufructuary lending his piece of property in place of capital and receiving as rent the usufruct of the properties granted him in *precaria*. Such grants of property were also made as a means of providing for one's surviving dependents. The making of agreements of this nature by those beginning a pilgrimage or departing for war, or those afflicted with sickness or a lingering malady, reminds us of modern old-age or accident insurance.[27]

Further, the distribution of the ground-rents generally avoided the disadvantages arising from the accumulation of large estates in a few hands. The institution of the *precaria* as practiced by the churches and monasteries also afforded a livelihood to many poor landless freemen, whose labor, in turn, not infrequently stimulated the improvement of the property and the clearance of the land. In this way, seemingly, the Bavarian bishoprics and monasteries, in particular, were able to make arable the fertile valley bottoms in the Alps, and the Church in Würzburg to effect the colonization

25. See previous page.
26. *M. G. Conc.* II, 1, p. 293, c. 51.
27. Cf. above, p. 268.

of the Slavic territories between the Main and the Rednitz. The documents of the monastery of Saint Gall show that it bestowed great care especially upon the clearance of lands in the Black Forest.

The advance in the economic field was thus associated with the improvement of the condition of the great social masses. The belief that one is in duty bound to complain about the growth of mortmain can lead one only too frequently to overlook what in reality was done by the Church at that time — as before, and long after — for the betterment of the middle and lower classes, through her diversified system of leasing lands. She enabled many freemen to assert themselves economically and thus to escape becoming socagers — that is, workers absorbed by the estates of the nobility. Furthermore, as members of the Church's *familia,* her tenant farmers enjoyed the advantages of her territorial rule and her immunity. They were given the opportunity also to form parish co-operative unions — groups in which it was possible for new social forces to germinate and, to a certain degree, develop. Modern scholars have amassed much significant evidence to refute the opinion that a general oppression of freemen, in which the Church notably participated, was characteristic of the Carolingian period.

Closer investigation has proved that instances of voluntary surrender of services by freemen with the intention of transferring their property to the Church were rare. If it was not (as it often was) an instance of a childless donor giving himself over to the *mundiburdium,* that is, protection of the monastery, because he desired to enter religion, it was as likely to be a freeman whose purpose was to have a life income settled on him by the monastery; frequently, too, it was a case of men without property wanting to obtain support and clothing. (Clerics, however, who gave themselves to a church with their property do not come into question here, since they did not as members of the Church renounce state or rank like monks.) Finally, the placing of oneself under the protection of the Church did not necessarily mean the renunciation of one's freedom; it is possible that only the obligation to pay interest was meant — as, for example, the payment of interest in wax, a transaction in which the freedom of the individual was sometimes expressly reserved.

Social betterment was further promoted in a very special way by the many manumissions which, as in earlier times, were the fruit of pious sentiment. The Church frequently played a role here, particularly when she assumed the obligation of protecting the freed man.[28] The number of serfs increased constantly as a result of the many emancipations from the servile class, and thus was obtained the manpower used in the various forms of *corvée* for the improvement of the manorial estates.

In the course of these economic and social developments many things arose, it is true, independently of the Church's activities and sometimes even contrary to her aims and her economic interests. The same thing is seen in the rise of the cities, the first beginnings of which are apparent in this epoch. The popes had contributed to this new development in Germany by advising Saint Boniface to choose a populous area for the episcopal see when erecting a new bishopric, that the prestige of the bishop might be enhanced.[29] At Charlemagne's death there were about thirty episcopal sees in Germany which were to typify more or less the new social, economic, intellectual and political life in its embryonic stage. Within these localities, Church and State alike allowed those offices to spring up which were to be especially decisive factors in the new organization. There, as in other populous places, the first centers of trade and industry arose; and although these were not destined to become outstandingly important until later, they manifested from the first a more detailed development than scholars have hitherto supposed. Here Italy and France naturally had the advantage over Germany because of the remnants of city life which they had salvaged from the past.

Associated with this new economic expansion we find certain limitations affecting the clergy, which were dictated by their spiritual duties. Numerous ordinances, both contemporary and future, established beyond question that these restrictions were heeded.

---

28. See pp. 258 sqq. above.
29. *Letters of Saint Boniface,* ed. of Tangl, no. 28, p. 50; no. 51, p. 87.

Regarding the administration of ecclesiastical property in general, the Church was merely restating the best principles of earlier times when she ordained in 813, at the council of Châlon, that priests should not appropriate the surplus produce of the estate in order to sell it at a high price and amass a fortune, but should use it when necessary to aid the poor.[30]

Consciousness of social distress went hand in hand with the attitude taken against the exploitation of men by the practice of usury. The general prohibitions against interest-taking were repeated, but they refer principally to the clergy.[31] Charlemagne thus followed the example of the Church. His views are shown above all in the *Capitulare missorum* of Nimwegen of 806.[32] This order, or better, instruction, to the *missi* particularly aims to prevent the buying up of grain and wine for resale at an illicit profit, and tries to establish on the basis of ancient ecclesiastical principles the difference between fair commercial enterprises and those aiming at sordid gain. In order to protect the poor against exploitation during a period of shortage, food prices were fixed, as they had been in 794; in 808 the prices of clothing were also fixed.[33] We are not justified in seeing in these regulations a tendency hostile to trade. On the contrary, they are measures friendly to trade, as they favor the consumers and are directed against the tendency to monopolize articles indispensable to life.

High praise should be accorded the objectives which Charlemagne was endeavoring to realize in all such ordinances. He took a very broad view of the function of Christian solidarity. And when we turn our attention to the intellectual developments in his age, a still brighter picture confronts us. Here above all we are justified in speaking of a first renaissance, which reveals an extraordinarily fruitful exchange of ideas between the various sections of the West.

Charlemagne personally had a considerable share in bringing this about, since his powerful arm achieved political union and his

30. *M. G. Conc.,* II, 276, c. 8.
31. *M. G. Cap.,* I, p. 244, c. 14, 16; p. 54, c. 5, 39; p. 103, c. 18. Cf. p. 268 above.
32. Ibid., 132, c. 10 sq.
33. Ibid., 74, c. 5; 140, c. 5.

great interest in cultural matters made the most of that union for intellectual purposes. But, as we have already seen, political union presupposed in turn an earlier intellectual *rapprochement*. Charlemagne's thirst for knowledge, his creative aspirations, his delight in making contacts in all directions, and his suggestions and encouragements, quickly brought that which before him was in an embryonic and formative condition to a state of advanced development and florescence. The Frankish kingdom, inferior to the other sections of the West — Spain, Italy and England — as regards culture in general, and religious learning in particular, was now stimulated to fresh energy by these countries.

At the very outset, Charlemagne's keen eye had taken in the situation. This is evidenced in his first capitulary of the year 769, ordaining that illiterate priests be suspended until they had acquired the necessary learning, and that those unwilling to acquire it be deprived of office; since he who did not understand the law of God could not preach it to others.[34] At the same time, Charlemagne realized that he had not the men in the Frankish kingdom who could promote learning — here it was almost exclusively a question of ecclesiastical learning, for there was no other. Therefore he procured such men from abroad. Let us now study some of these exponents of culture whom he invited to his realm.

They were first and foremost Anglo-Saxons — evidence once more that the wave which had carried Saint Boniface still continued to move forward. Beyond all question the most outstanding was Alcuin (or Alchoin), one of the disciples of Archbishop Egbert of York. He was born in York about 730, and educated at the cathedral school there. While still very young he accompanied Egbert's successor, Ethelbert, to the continent, and on to Rome, for the purpose of procuring treasures for their library, in accordance with the practice long prevalent in Anglo-Saxon scholastic circles. In 781, in the course of another journey to Rome, he met Charlemagne at Parma. The ruler immediately became interested in Alcuin, who was then in his full maturity and had become director of the school of York. Communication was opened between them which resulted

---

34. Ibid., 19, c. 15, 16, p. 46.

in Alcuin's settling permanently in the Frankish kingdom in 793 or 794. Charlemagne entrusted to him three of its famous abbeys — Ferrières and Saint Loup in Troyes, and later on the renowned and very wealthy abbey of Saint Martin in Tours, where Alcuin died in 804.

Through Alcuin, all the scholarship and culture of the Anglo-Saxon monasteries was transplanted to the Frankish kingdom. His life was devoted solely to learning and teaching. He was a bookworm, but also a good and beloved schoolmaster — to a certain extent, indeed, sharing in the schoolmaster's weaknesses of pedantry and dogmatism. But any weaknesses he possessed were wholly eclipsed by his merits. These are noticeable first of all in his writings, which are concerned primarily with purely theological matters. His principal work is a dogmatic treatise on the Trinity in three volumes, which he dedicated to the emperor. Regarded as the earliest theological work of the Middle Ages, it stimulated the very able German translation of Saint Isidore of Seville's treatise *De fide catholica contra Iudaeos,* made in Murbach apparently during this period. Great attention was also aroused by Alcuin's theological treatises against the Adoptionist Bishop Felix of Urgel, whom he opposed under the protection of the emperor.

Alcuin was never exclusively absorbed in learning for its own sake, but cultivated it in an ideal sense and always with an ardent interest in teaching and educating others. This is borne out by the great number of his didactic writings and letters. Man's moral advancement was of higher importance to him than man's intellectual culture (a standard he imparted to his royal pupils as well), and he did not like to see Virgil preferred to Sacred Scripture. A devotional book which he wrote for a layman, Count Guido of Brittany, bears witness to his simple piety. It treats of the virtues and vices, and exhorts the reader to place all his trust in God, and to beg Him for forgiveness of sins in a contrite confession. Alcuin's interest in the religious life of the laity is likewise shown by a prayer manual of the canonical hours which he composed for them at the request of Charles, the imperial prince. A number of psalms were chosen for each day, and to them were added some short prayers; the work was thus, in a certain sense, a layman's equivalent of the monks' psalter, about which Alcuin composed a separate treatise.

Several disciples followed Alcuin from England. Others he trained in the Frankish kingdom, and these were soon to surpass him in style and achievements. His most distinguished disciple was undoubtedly Rabanus Maurus, a native of Mainz, who made Fulda the most renowned school of Germany.

From Italy Charlemagne invited the deacon, Peter of Pisa, who was addicted to sarcasm, and who has left us a grammar in addition to several poems; and Saint Paulinus, a native of Friuli, who in 787 received from Charlemagne the patriarchate of Aquileia. Saint Paulinus was to serve Charlemagne also as a teacher of grammar, and at his request was to take up his pen repeatedly against the Adoptionists. Besides theological works he composed poetry, and one of his poems in particular, written in honor of the margrave Eric of Friuli, conqueror of the Avars, shows a singular warmth of feeling. To this same Eric, Paulinus likewise dedicated a devotional book, a sort of *Fürstenspiegel* composed of extracts from a fifth-century work by Pomerius, the countryman and disciple of Saint Augustine.

Prominent among the scholars whom Charlemagne drew to his court from Italy was Paul the Deacon, a man of high scholarship and refined feeling, whom we already know as the historian of his people, the Lombards. At the court of King Rachis, in Pavia, he had received in youth an education from the grammarian Flavianus thorough enough to include Greek. Paul's learning later profited the daughter of Desiderius, the last Lombard king: it was for this lady, who was the wife of Duke Arichis of Benevento, that he wrote a continuation of Eutropius' *Breviarium historiae Romanae* to the time of the emperor Justinian. The misfortunes of the Lombard dynasty affected him very closely, and he returned to the cloister — at first probably to the monastery at Civate on Lake Como, where he wrote the earliest explanation of the Benedictine Rule; after the catastrophe of 774 we find him in Monte Cassino.

When his brother suffered the confiscation of his fortune for having been implicated in a Lombardic uprising, Paul journeyed to the Frankish kingdom (782) to solicit the remission of this punishment. He was cordially received at Charlemagne's court, and was soon employed there as a teacher, poet and writer. At the request of Bishop Angilram he wrote a history of the bishops of Metz, among whom was the brilliant and saintly Arnulf, ancestor of the Carolingian rulers. This episcopal chronicle was the first example of a class of writings which were to appear very frequently later on. For Charlemagne himself, the learned Lombard wrote an epitome of the archeological collections of Pompeius Festus (who lived presumably in the third century) to enable the emperor to inform himself regarding his city of Rome. In addition, Paul composed a commentary on Donatus' school grammar, and many sepulchral inscriptions in verse for Charlemagne. However, when hostilities broke out between the latter and Duke Arichis of Benevento, Paul returned to Monte Cassino. Here he wrote homilies, a biography of Gregory the Great, and his principal work, the *History of the Lombards.*

The Goth Theodulf, a refugee from Spain, brought to the Frankish kingdom the classical learning still obtaining in that country. He, too, stood high in the estimation of Charlemagne, who gave him the bishopric of Orleans. Later, Pope Leo III conferred the pallium upon him. By Charlemagne's command he wrote a treatise on the procession of the Holy Ghost, *De Spiritu Sancto,* which manifests the influence of his countryman Prudentius. This influence is even more marked in Theodulf's verse, which nevertheless reveals him as an original poet, capable of vivid impressions and richly endowed with esthetic sensibility. Some of his extant poems are serious, others satirical and ironic, still others full of complaints and denunciations — for Theodulf was not an optimist in outlook. The fate of his native country, subjugated by the Arabs, possibly engendered this attitude, which inclined him to see the seamy side of life in both Church and State. In consequence, he was unable to banish from his mind the belief that the end of the world was imminent. He criticized the German penal code severely, and also turned his irony upon the court poets, whom he compared to cackling and croaking birds. He even described Charlemagne with a touch of satire, depicting him seated at table and dealing out large portions of food.

Theodulf, however, knew how to treat religious topics fittingly, and his thorough appreciation of the ecclesiastical reform movement is evidenced by his diocesan regulations. He showed no less appreciation for art. In Germigny-des-Près, near Fleury, he erected a church which has been much admired, after the model of the cathedral of Aix-la-Chapelle. He stimulated the artistic crafts by placing orders for the execution of handsome manuscripts of the Bible and for a table service of great beauty.

By Charlemagne's wish, these foreign intellectuals served as teachers — first of all at court, where he attended the instructions in person, with his sons and daughters. For instructing adults a method was employed which had been brought over from England by Alcuin, consisting in social conversation, a form that is especially profitable in the branches of logic and philosophy. The members of the group also liked to instruct one another by propounding enigmatic questions. There was reading at table — a poem or perhaps a historical work, or again, the writing of a Church Father. Theological questions were the subject of earnest discussion, but this did not prevent clever jokes and witticisms from being welcomed. Besides the private instruction given to the royal family, classes were conducted in the old Palace School, in which emphasis was laid upon rhetoric to impart competence in the art of drawing up official acts or documents. Alcuin, who was especially prominent in the Palace School, composed an introduction to the study of rhetoric for Charlemagne based on Cicero's *De inventione,* and the ruler followed the course of instruction with great interest. The Palace School operated under only one disadvantage: it had no fixed location, but went about in the train of Charlemagne, whose activities made him frequently change his place of residence.

The pride of the Palace School was Einhard, who apparently succeeded Alcuin as its director. He was a Frank, born in the valley of the Main, and as an educated layman constituted an exception in the court circle. Einhard was an accomplished artist, and had distinguished himself in the decoration of the cathedral at Aix-la-Chapelle, for which reason the court academy gave him the name of

Beseleel, after the builder of the Tabernacle in the Old Testament. He had supervision of the royal buildings, and Charlemagne also entrusted him with political missions. Einhard is best known as the author of Charlemagne's biography — a work which, despite its excessive stylistic dependence upon Suetonius, throws the personality of its subject into excellent relief. Its success was rapid and widespread.

This biography typifies in the clearest manner the renaissance character of the budding culture of the time, which sought as its highest goal the formal imitation of ancient authors; thereby overrating form and underrating real values. Einhard borrowed the whole plan of his presentation from Suetonius, but he leaned on other Roman historians as well: Caesar, Livy, Florus, Tacitus, Justin, Orosius. He also utilized the valuable imperial records formerly called the *Annals of Lorsch* (he was not their original author, as was once supposed). Notwithstanding his being a layman, and married, Charlemagne conferred several abbeys upon him in reward for his services; and Einhard, for his part, showed a real ecclesiastical spirit by founding the abbey of Seligenstadt at Mühlheim on the Main over the remains of the martyrs Marcellinus and Peter which he had transferred thither. Further manifestations of this spirit appear in works glorifying the martyrdom of these two saints and describing the translation of their relics, and in his writing on the veneration of the True Cross.

The renaissance touch just noted in Einhard's biography of Charlemagne is also reflected in an epic poem of different authorship on the meeting of Charlemagne and Leo III at Paderborn in 799. Coming down to us only as a fragment of a larger epic, this describes in vivid colors and with strong imaginative effect the external events attending that memorable meeting. However, the poet paints the splendor of the royal residence according to Virgil's description of Carthage, going so far in imitation of his great model as to create for Aix-la-Chapelle an imaginary harbor with buildings appropriate to a port! The poet's identity is not known; the assumption that it was Angilbert is disputed.

The happiness of the court in the possession of ancient and ecclesiastical learning, the delight with which that learning was shared, can be seen in the nicknames which Charlemagne gave himself and his learned favorites, the members of the court academy. He designated himself as David, after the poet-king of the Old Testament; Alcuin was Horatius Flaccus, Angilbert was Homer, and Einhard, as has already been said, was Beseleel. But to Charlemagne's mind learning did not exist only to furnish entertaining conversation; its representatives were to serve him as guides for the ushering in of a higher intellectual culture and an ecclesiastical regeneration in his kingdom.

The court was not the sole place of instruction. In a famous circular letter,[35] Charlemagne decreed that the episcopal sees and monasteries "entrusted to our direction by the grace of Christ," besides observing their regular routine of life and maintaining their pious activities, were to occupy themselves also in the cultivation of learning; moreover, they were, each according to its ability, to provide instruction for those who by the grace of God were capable of responding to it. In other words, teaching was to be systematically carried on at the cathedrals and in the monasteries. Both the secular and the regular clergy were thus explicitly assigned the task which the general historical evolution had already accorded them, of caring for the intellectual advancement of the people; for while the education of the secular clergy and of the monks was primarily sought, the legislator by no means intended to exclude the laity from its benefits.

The parish priests also conducted schools in their churches — principally, however, to impart the sort of catechism instruction which we call Christian doctrine today. A regulation of the synod of Mainz in 813 mentions that pastors are to teach the Creed and the Our Father, in Latin — or at the very least in the native tongue— since knowledge of these was made a minimum requirement for all adults.[36] That all children should be given a general elementary schooling — this was demanded in an appendix of undetermined origin attached to a questionnaire issued in Bavaria — was and remained only a beautiful wish, like so many ordinances of this

35. Ibid., 29, I, 59.
36. *M. G. Conc.*, II, 271.

period.[37] Bishop Theodulf of Orleans decreed that priests of his diocese attached to rural parishes or private churches were to conduct schools, were not to send away untaught any child whom the parents were willing to entrust to them, and were not to demand any payment for their instruction.[38] This undoubtedly led to the rural pastor's teaching studious and alert youths to read the psalter and preparing them first for their choir chant and then for the ecclesiastical state; they would thus be able in his absence to recite the Office in choir and take his place in the school.[39] No doubt, many of the pupils never became priests, but for centuries to come it was still exceptional for laymen to be able to read and write. Charlemagne himself, as his biographer remarks,[40] could not acquire the difficult art of writing, despite the fact that he often placed the writing tablet under his pillow upon retiring in order to practice if he were wakeful.

Instruction in the ancient branches of the trivium and the quadrivium was diligently imparted in the monastery and cathedral schools, to be followed eventually by lectures in theology. Among the cathedral schools, Metz excelled in music. The most outstanding monastic school was that of Saint Martin in Tours, which was newly organized by Alcuin and functioned principally as a training center for teachers. Next in importance was the monastery school of Saint Riquier, which according to Angilbert's regulation was always to have a hundred students under instruction. The school of Saint Gall came to the fore later. At this time, the ancient account of its founder's life was being revised by the famed Wettin because of barbarities in the original composition. Subsequently, Alcuin's disciple Grimald was abbot there. The school of Fulda also acquired a great reputation. Here at the tomb of the restorer of the Frankish Church, Baugulf was called upon to take over after the death of the first abbot, Sturm. Besides carrying out an active building program, Baugulf bestowed great attention upon the school

37. *M. G. Cap.*, I, 235.
38. Migne, *P. L.*, CV, 196, 20.
39. Cf. *M. G. Cap.*, I, 238. Alcuin, *Epistulae: M. G. Epp.*, III, 278. Council of Nantes (9 cent.) in Regino's *De eccles. discipl.*, I, 207: Migne, *P. L.*, CXXXII, 229.
40. Einhard, *Vita Car.*, c. 25.

and upon intellectual life in general. Here Einhard received his first instruction, and it was Baugulf who later sent him to the Palace School for his higher education. Alcuin visited the school of Fulda, and thereafter Baugulf's successor, Ratgar, sent to him at Tours his most gifted monks, Rabanus and Hatto.

The German monasteries deserve great credit for their determined efforts to utilize the German language for both pedagogical and literary purposes. This was first attempted in the glosses by adding German translations to the Latin words — sometimes in the form of an interlinear rendering above the Latin text, sometimes in separate glossaries alongside the individual Latin words arranged in alphabetical or topical order. With the aid of these glosses the German monks, following the example of their Anglo-Saxon brethren, made the acquisition of Latin easier for themselves in the first place and then continued, not without pain, to increase their vocabulary. Thus equipped, they were able to attempt fluent translations and independent compositions in German prose. The glosses enable us to perceive how foreign ideas, Roman and Christian, were communicated to the Germans and how the intellectual inheritance of the past was prepared for transmission to them.

It was, of course, the purpose of religious instruction and ecclesiastical learning that first prompted this procedure and determined its method. Of all texts, the Bible was the most frequently glossed; next came the canons; then the works of Gregory the Great, which were important for the care of souls; then the poems of Prudentius, which appealed to the Germans because of their battle scenes; lastly the classic poets, especially Virgil. A codex of Fulda has a conversation manual composed in Bavaria about the year 800, which contains the most important German expressions for the benefit of Romance travelers in those parts. This work of translation flourished especially in Saint Gall, Reichenau, Murbach in Alsace, the Bavarian monasteries of Saint Emmeram in Regensburg, Tegernsee, Benediktbeuren, the cathedral school of Freising, and the monastery of Werden on the Ruhr.

Besides compilation of the German vocabularies there was the translation of those liturgical passages which it was essential to teach the people during their religious instruction, or to use for missionary purposes. This meant, first of all, the colloquy and the abjurations employed in baptism.[41] Then, the Creed and the Our Father had to be taught the people in their mother tongue — the earliest German form is extant in a clumsy translation which was made at Saint Gall about 790. To these two prayers was added the catechism of Weissenburg (named after the monastery in the diocese of Speyer), which contained an explanation of the Our Father, an enumeration of the capital sins, the Athanasian Creed, and the translation of the *Gloria in excelsis*. Besides this, the exercise of the ministry demanded the translation of the formulas for confession; and here we must distinguish between the common confession of public faults, which the priest read after the sermon on Sunday, and the private confession containing accusation of sins, form for contrition, the promise to perform the penance assigned and the petition for intercession. The oldest known German formula of confession, which seems to belong to Charlemagne's period, is in the Bavarian dialect, but points to an earlier Frankish model. Most such formulas are extant only in later texts, which is to be explained by the need which was felt of revising the older ones.

A product of Saint Boniface's missionary activities is the so-called *Prayer of Wessobrunn*, also in the Bavarian dialect, which is preserved in a codex of the monastery of Wessobrunn in upper Bavaria. Its first part, written in poetic form, corresponds to the instructions Saint Boniface had received from his old friend, Bishop Daniel of Winchester.[42] It should be made clear to the pagans, the bishop explained in detail, that the world is not eternal and must consequently have had a beginning, therefore a Creator. The *Prayer of Wessobrunn* enters into this subject, explaining the idea that the material universe did not always exist; then it praises the Creator; finally there is appended a short prose prayer. Here, then, for the first time the German language is used to glorify the God of Christendom in verse and prose:

---

41. See below, p. 513.
42. See above, p. 393.

> This did I learn among men as the greatest piece of knowledge,
> That neither the earth nor the firmament were,
> That neither tree . . . nor mountain existed,
> Nor a single star; that neither did the sun shine
> Nor the moon shed its light; nor did the majestic sea exist.
> When there were no extremities and limits,
> There existed the One Almighty God,
> And the Mildest of Men. There were also with Him
> Many glorious spirits, and the holy God. . . .

Here the poetic portion breaks off, and there follows the prayer:

> Almighty God, Thou who hast made heaven and earth and hast given men so many good things, grant me the proper faith in Thy grace, good will, wisdom, prudence and strength to resist the devils, to avoid evil, and to do Thy will.[43]

The *Prayer of Wessobrunn* has great value not only as one of the oldest literary monuments, but also as a cultural record, a witness to the manner in which the German intellect took hold of Christian teachings.

Men also gradually ventured, under Charlemagne, to translate more difficult works: the Benedictine Rule and the hymns of Saint Ambrose in Reichenau; there too, or in Saint Gall, the psalms. In Murbach, or in Hornbach (the Palatinate), the difficult treatise of Saint Isidore of Seville, *De fide catholica contra Iudaeos,* was rendered into German. The monastery of Monsee in the diocese of Passau (conferred by Charlemagne upon his head chaplain, Archbishop Hildebold of Cologne) produced a manuscript which contained not only this same translation of Saint Isidore's work but also a translation of Saint Matthew's Gospel, a sermon of Saint Augustine, and some other fragments. These productions, which may be considered the beginnings of systematic theology in the German language, seem to have been connected in some way with the mission to the Avars.

The German monks, however, were not interested only in works connected with ecclesiastical tradition; they also delighted in re-

---

43. Translator's note: Here Schnürer quotes the translation of Ehrismann, from *Geschichte der deutschen Literatur,* I, 133, 137. The latest edition of the original text is by E. Steinmeyer, *Sprachdenkmäler,* 16.

cording for the ages something of the poetical inheritance of their own race. About the year 800 the *Song of Hildebrand* was written down in the monastery of Fulda — the only vestige of epic poetry which has come down to us in Old High German. The conflict between father and son portrayed in this poem conveys to us the fatalistic sentiment prevalent in the days when the ties of vassalage were close.

The active intellectual intercourse between the several monasteries and schools attested by the manuscripts in which these oldest remains are transmitted, is also borne out by the many letters and poems exchanged among the individual scholars themselves. The desire for books played a prominent part in such intellectual intercourse, and we hear much about collections of these. Books were intimately connected with the schools by their very production, since they were the work of copyists. Charlemagne encouraged the diligent and careful copying of manuscripts, and many an ancient text is preserved to us only through transcripts from the Carolingian age. Most of the originals came from England or Italy. We still have the library catalogue of the monastery of Reichenau for the years 820 to 842, to tell us there were four hundred and fifty manuscripts there at that time: the works of Latin and Greek ecclesiastical writers, and in addition many biographies of saints, compositions of grammarians, monastic rules, the Theodosian Code, the national codes of the Germanic peoples, and the works of Virgil and some Christian poets.

Somewhat different from the picture north of the Alps, however, was that offered by Italy. There the monasteries and churches were not so exclusively the educational centers. In northern Italy especially, the cities had managed to maintain themselves in part, and their schools of rhetoric had been continued under the direction of laymen. It was in these schools that the laity still acquired their formal education. Here illustrious Lombards, like Paul the Deacon, still accepted teaching positions; and here, too, a small group of educated laymen — notaries, physicians and artists — survived, who no longer produced literary works, but yet were able to serve Charlemagne as teachers.

These were the channels through which the new culture flowed, and since the churches and monasteries played a leading role in its spread, this culture naturally also stimulated the religious life. Let us turn our attention to this latter, which furnished the guarantee for the firm establishment of the fresh-springing culture of the West.

We have already said that the unfortunate results deriving from Charlemagne's treatment of the Church as a state church became glaring and unmistakable only later. During his reign we notice rather the advantages produced by his great interest in the Church's mission, by the devotion of his administrative ability to the promotion of that mission, and by the influence in its behalf of his commanding personality. He was greatly concerned that the bishops should fulfill their pastoral duties zealously and conscientiously. He required them to live regularly in their dioceses, allowing them no more than three weeks' residence on their private estates. They were to be diligent in making visitations and in holding diocesan synods. Yet when we think of the manner in which Charlemagne appointed bishops to the various sees, and had recourse to them for political purposes, we cannot avoid the conviction that he himself notably hampered the carrying out of his own excellent regulations.

He was certainly directly responsible for the vacancies which over long periods deprived many dioceses of legitimate and fully responsible shepherds. Possibly he justified himself in his own eyes by the fact that in such cases the bishops' functions could be performed by *chorepiscopi*. These were a characteristic phenomenon of the period, their appearance undoubtedly having some connection with the Irish itinerant bishops, though, unlike the latter, they were attached to fixed sees. As vigorous assistants to aging bishops or to those overburdened with missionary work — the example of Saint Lullus and Saint Boniface comes to mind — their appointment was warranted, especially if they were eventually to succeed to the see. But when they appeared as substitutes for non-existent bishops or for such as were occupied with political and military affairs, a division of responsibility was bound to result which was an abuse, and was felt to be such soon after Charlemagne's death.

On the other hand we can demonstrate again and again that Charlemagne's purposeful exhortations were successful, inspiring excellent bishops to their best. Thus the Bavarian Archbishop Leidrad of Lyons, who had been previously employed as a royal *missus*, tells us how he reformed his diocese in accord with Charlemagne's admonitions; how he had been inspired with solicitude for the training of a worthy body of clergy; how he reorganized divine services, founded schools, furnished places of worship with vestments, and restored churches and monasteries.

Such knowledge as we have concerning episcopal visitations, which were very frequent during Charlemagne's reign, is interesting. When a bishop came to a locality, the priests and monks, together with the laity, assembled in the church. The bishop first informed himself concerning the knowledge of the priests and the administration of their office; examining them on the Creed, the Our Father, the laws of the Church, and the requirements for penance, then questioning them about their performance of divine services, the celebration of Mass, the administration of baptism, and preaching. Next the monks and canons were questioned about their rule and their routine of daily life. Finally it was the turn of the laity, who were examined and exhorted regarding the faith. Out of this practice of exhorting and reprimanding the laity there soon evolved the circuit courts (*Sendgerichte*), to which sworn lay representatives were summoned to report on the faith and moral conduct of the parishioners. The latter point of procedure was similar to that followed by the king's messengers during the reign of Charlemagne.

In the larger churches to which several clerics were attached, Charlemagne desired the introduction of the canonical rule of life as it had been established by that excellent bishop of Metz, Saint Chrodegang. This representative of a noble family of Hasbangau, near Liége, had served previously as *referendarius* in the chancery of Charles Martel. He became bishop of Metz in the year 742, when the reform synods of Saint Boniface were beginning to be held. Chrodegang too, in his own way, worked for the reform and for intimate union with Rome. As Pippin's ambassador he escorted Pope Stephen III to the Frankish kingdom, and it was this same pontiff who, after Saint Boniface's death in 754, raised Chrodegang to the rank of archbishop by conferring on him the pallium. Thereafter, he occupied a position in the Frankish kingdom similiar to Boniface's own: he continued the reform of the Church and remained the confidant of the pope, the *missus sancti Petri*. He transformed the liturgy after the Roman pattern, introduced plain chant, and founded a Benedictine monastery at Gorze which was long a model, serving in particular as the norm for the monastery of Lorsch, the object of Charlemagne's particular favor. Then, following ancient traditions which had not yet been completely forgotten, Chrodegang organized the communal life for the priests attached to the cathedral of Metz.

To this end he compiled a rule, based partly on the Benedictine, and partly on that followed by the canons of the Lateran, with which he had become acquainted in Rome. The clerics lived in one house, the residence of the canons, ate together, and slept in a common dormitory. But it was not intended by any means that all distinctions be done away with; those created alike by hierarchical rank and by difference of fortune remained. Priests and deacons ate at separate tables, the former receiving three glasses of wine, the latter only two. In addressing one another, clerics were required to use the correct individual titles. Archbishop Chrodegang was not only devoted to both the king and the pope, but a believer in the propriety of external forms in other respects. For example, he forbade clerics to enter a church with a walking stick. They were to live respectably, always conscious that as servants of the Church they must be a credit to her. Their property they were to regard as dedicated to her. He who entered the community was to renounce his property in favor of the Church, to the extent of designating her as his heir, although he would enjoy the usufruct thereof during his lifetime like any vassal. He was not, therefore, permitted to bequeath it to anyone else, or to dispose of it in any other way.

All members of the community were obliged to appear in choir for the recitation of the Office. Every Sunday and feastday they received Holy Communion, and they were required to go to confession at least twice a year. They were to assemble daily in chapter, where a passage from Sacred Scripture, or from some devotional book, or from Chrodegang's Rule, was read aloud. On these occasions, particular ordinances were also announced and reprimands given. On Sunday, all the clergy of the city were to take part in the chapter gatherings. The community embraced, therefore, in the first place, those who lived in common with the bishop as his family — that is, the residents of the episcopal palace — and, in addition, those boys and young men who were being trained for the clerical state. It was, consequently, also a clerical seminary. The whole institution set up an ideal for the common life of the secular clergy which was soon justly appreciated and imitated; it was introduced in cathedral and collegiate churches.

It was greatly to the credit of Charlemagne's ecclesiastical spirit that he fostered such an institution. We should not be justified, however, in concluding from this marked encouragement given by him to the introduction of monastic manners among the secular clergy, that his ecclesiastical legislation particularly favored the monasteries. Such was not the case. Rather, we perceive a certain distrust, manifesting itself clearly in the inconsiderate way he disposed of monastic property and his arbitrary giving away of abbeys. Still, in Charlemagne's general regulations for monasteries there recurs also the idea of unity and order — an idea, indeed, that runs like a thread through all of Charlemagne's centralizing legislation. Thus he had a copy of the order of divine services sent him from Rome. In like manner he secured, in 787, an authentic text of the Benedictine Rule from the mother monastery of Monte Cassino, which made possible the readoption of the pristine ordinance in these northern lands, where it had fallen into almost complete oblivion. A demand for the rigid enforcement of the Rule was made by the synod of Aix-la-Chapelle of 802; the monks were to learn the Rule by heart, if possible.

Charlemagne bestowed a great deal of attention on the activities of secular priests. He considered preaching as their principal work — and preaching was indeed becoming more and more important in his realm, where the language of the Church was not the vernacular. He often repeated his admonition to them to preach zealously — of course in the mother tongue. Sermons were to be delivered every Sunday and holyday. The bishops were to set a good example; nor did they fail on their part to admonish their clergy in this direction. Some sermons have been preserved to us in Latin, which must not lead us to conclude that they were delivered in that language; rather, they are outlines which merely give us the general sequence of the preacher's thought. They are chiefly exhortations to a life of virtue. In order to make preaching easier, standard homilies were written, and those which are extant belong among the oldest examples of German literature. Charlemagne commissioned Paul the Deacon to compile a collection of these homilies. Favorite sources of sermon material were the works of Augustine, Caesarius of Arles, Cassian, Gregory the Great and Bede. Gregory's *Cura pastoralis* and the *Liber de officiis ecclesiasticis* of Isidore of Seville furnished the rule of conduct for the pastoral ministry.

The application of the Church's penitential discipline presented greater difficulties than preaching, from the fact that the old public penance had fallen into disuse.[44] Such penance, being demanded at this time only for public sins and having application only to the punished criminal, appeared, in consequence, as an addition to the civil penalty. It had this further thing in common with civil punishment, that it was enforced by the State through the episcopal visitations developed by Charlemagne; and since the reconciliation took place before the completion of the penance, the latter no longer had the old significance of excommunication. The public penance consisted in fasting and making difficult pilgrimages, in addition to prayer and almsgiving.

Private penance and auricular confession had, on the other hand, experienced a very lively diffusion, especially through that manner of exercising the pastoral office transplanted to the continent by the Irish and Anglo-Saxon monks. Thereafter, confession was demanded at regular intervals; and especially were pastors to exhort the faithful to go to confession on Ash Wednesday. Curiously enough, the inhabitants of the southern part of the empire refused for a time to confess to priests, probably because they still held to the ancient ecclesiastical practice of public penance. This opposition, however, must have been overcome shortly, for the people undoubtedly came to realize that only confession at regular intervals

---

44. See above, pp. 298 sq.

made the individual and thorough care of souls possible. Alcuin, too, must certainly have made an impression upon the inhabitants of Septimania, who were opposed to private confession, when he wrote to them: "If, according to Solomon, war is to be waged under superior direction, with what audacity shall we presume that we can fight against the devil without the counsel of the ecclesiastical leaders!"[45] The many Latin and German formulas of confession which have come down to us show that the people of the Carolingian empire, in general, readily responded to the exhortation that they go regularly to confession. Every priest was supposed to possess a penitential — a manual in which were listed the various penances to be imposed for individual sins. The fact that the several penitentials did not agree in their penalties was acknowledged as being less than ideal; but it was difficult to achieve uniformity because a Roman standard was lacking.

Uniformity was more easily arrived at in the field of liturgy. Besides the Roman liturgy of the Mass, there were employed in Gaul various uses which had been developed after Byzantine models. A special form of the Gallican liturgy found in the Spanish kingdom of the Visigoths was called, following the Arabian conquests, the Mozarabic rite. Charlemagne had procured from Pope Adrian a copy of the so-called Gregorian Sacramentary, which contained the liturgy of the Mass then in use in Rome, and according to this form Mass was thereafter generally celebrated in the Frankish kingdom.

All this betokens how much men there were occupied with liturgical questions. Gregorian chant was introduced along with the Gregorian liturgy. Great influence was exerted throughout the Middle Ages by the liturgical writings of Alcuin's pupil Amalarius of Metz, which contributed measurably to the spread of the Roman rite.

Holy Communion, received three times a year as a rule by adults, was still administered in most instances under both species. Baptism was administered as formerly, by either triple or single immersion, and generally at Easter and Pentecost; the baptistries were traditionally set aside for this service. The liturgy of baptism

---

45. Alcuin, *Epistulae*, 138: *M. G. Epp.*, IV, 218.

assumed an added importance at this time for the reason that many
pagans were still being received into the Church. With the experiences of the missionaries in mind, Alcuin composed a form
for the baptismal service which Charlemagne decreed should be
used; and later the ruler required the archbishops to report to him
how their suffragans instructed the clergy and the faithful in the
liturgy of the sacrament. The colloquy concerning the faith, and
the abjurations (*abrenuntiationes*), were translated, as we have
already said, for the benefit of the laity; these are among the oldest
German translations. From the foregoing we can see that Charlemagne placed particular value upon the instruction which was to
be associated with baptism. The imparting of that instruction was
also emphatically presented to the sponsors as constituting their
obligation toward their godchildren.

Charlemagne's interest in divine services inevitably led him
to encourage the building of churches; and equally, it must be
supposed, his position as a ruler with a world empire at his feet
caused him to take delight in having his power and wishes reflected
symbolically in artistic works. The signs of new life which his
epoch shows, in contrast to the preceding period of accelerating
decline, are hardly less distinct in the field of art than in the domain
of letters and education. This new life looked for stimulus to that
country whence both the inspiration and the models for intellectual
activity and ecclesiastical conduct ordinarily came. The alliance
with the papacy had drawn the Carolingians closer to Rome; the
annexation of the Lombard kingdom had firmly established political
union with Italy; thereafter it was from Rome and Italy pre-
eminently that artistic inspiration came to the Franks.

First of all, the materials there were much choicer than any to
be found north of the Alps, where building was limited to either
wooden structures (the wooden churches of the Irish monks were
said to be built *more Scotico*), or rough, irregular stones bound
together with mortar, *more Gallico*. Not much could be accomplished with these materials. In Italy, the Frankish rulers as well
as the spiritual and temporal lords in their train were able, like the
Anglo-Saxon pilgrims before them, to admire the freestone edifices
constructed *more Romano*, out of cut stone.

It was this monumental type of construction which Charlemagne had in mind when he set about building a palace chapel for himself in Aix-la-Chapelle. The immediate model chosen for the magnificent edifice was the church at Ravenna, which had been begun while Theodoric was still alive, and mingled Roman, Germanic and Byzantine elements in a composite whole. From Ravenna also he took the bronze equestrian monument of Theodoric to set it up in the court of his palace. The much admired central form of structure in the cathedral of Aix-la-Chapelle reveals the grand ideal of its builder, who would establish the kingdom of God on earth, just as the church of Hagia Sophia in Constantinople had symbolized the ideals of that Eastern ruler whom Charlemagne so much resembled: Justinian. But in spite of his manifold lofty plans and his valuable services to religion, he was even less able than Justinian to regulate the interior life of the Church in a permanent way.

Nor did his palace church in Aix-la-Chapelle, insofar as its central form of structure was concerned, become the decisive style for the churches of the West. Rather, their style was determined during the following centuries by the monastery type of church (a development of the basilica form), in line with the great influence the monasteries exerted on religious life in northern countries. The transformation of the antique basilica into the Romanesque was effected through the introduction of the form of a cross in the ground plan by inserting a transept. The basic impulse for this development came directly from Rome, when in 754 Pope Stephen III, sojourning at the monastery of Saint Denis, concluded with Pippin the pact which for centuries impressed upon the Western commonwealth of nations the character of the Middle Ages.

The church of Saint Denis was itself pure basilica in type, with three naves, a transverse section and a projecting apse after the Roman model. It was a church worthy to serve as the burial place of the first Carolingian king, who owed his throne to Rome, who had greeted the first pope to travel north of the Alps, and had created the Papal States. The same pattern is found again principally in those churches whose construction was in some way connected with the court — for example, the palatinate chapel at Ingelheim, Einhard's church at Steinbach in the Odenwald, which is still extant, as well as his other church in Seligenstadt, and Angilbert's monastery church at Saint Riquier. Other monastery churches, such as those of Fulda, Saint Wandrille, Moyenmoutier and Saint Gall, represent a transition to the Romanesque style. The extant ruin of the monastery of Lorsch, consisting of a one-story hall with columns and three portals, reminds us of other Roman models; it is probably a free imitation of one of the gates of the city of Rome.

Men were so zealous in building churches that eventually Charlemagne had to warn them against overdoing it. He pointed out that "the ornament and the pre-eminence which good morals give a parish are to be esteemed above a beautiful church."[46] Nevertheless, he found pleasure in the many beautiful churches in his empire; and it was certainly in accord with his intentions that the author of the *Libri Carolini,* scornfully reproaching the Greeks for their dilapidated churches, put this characteristic boast into his mouth:

> In the empire entrusted to us by God, the basilicas abound in gold and silver, precious stones, jewels and the most lovely ornaments; and though we decline to burn lights before images or to incense them, we certainly adorn the places consecrated to the divine services with the most precious objects.[47]

Many new developments are visible during this period which were the result of the zeal for church ornamentation — for example, the mosaic decorations of the cathedral of Aix-la-Chapelle in which Christ is depicted between the Evangelists — and especially of the care bestowed on liturgical books. Plastic artists working in ivory produced precious book covers, and Gospel books were adorned with exquisite miniatures, which were in most cases imitations of ancient models. Among the several outstanding Gospel books are: that of Vienna, on which the emperors were wont henceforth to take the oath at Aix-la-Chapelle; the Gospel book illuminated by Godescalcus, which is preserved in Paris; and the Ada Manuscript in Treves, named for the emperor's supposed sister, who had it executed. These testify in what esteem Charlemagne and his court

---

46. *M. G. Cap.,* I, 164 (Cap. 72, 11).
47. *Libri Carolini,* IV, c. 3: Migne, *P. L.,* LXXXXVIII, 1188.

held the Word of God, which they continued unceasingly to prescribe to all as the rule of Christian life.

Let us revert here to Charlemagne's decrees for the laity. As he attached importance to the proper training of priests, he must naturally have had the religious instruction of the laity at heart as well. He demanded, as we have seen, that every adult in his empire be able to say the Creed and the Our Father. To secure the co-operation of the laity and encourage them in spreading the Faith, he recommended the careful choice of baptismal sponsors. Only those should be permitted to serve as godparents who knew the minimum of Christian doctrine already described. Exhortations to attend divine services on Sunday are very frequent. (Archbishop Theodulf of Orleans further insisted especially on this point: that the faithful remain in church until the end of divine services.) A capitulary ordained that the congregation sing the *Gloria Patri* and the *Sanctus* with the priest.[48] When the clerics attached to the collegiate churches and the monks in the monasteries assembled in choir for the recitation of the Office, the bells were rung so that those who could not come to church would nevertheless be reminded to pray. Sunday rest, on which great stress was laid, began on Saturday evening; all public works, business transactions, sports of the chase and theatrical performances were forbidden on Sunday, and markets could be held only where this was a custom of long standing. There were naturally, even at that time, provincial differences in the public celebration of feasts, but the following holydays were listed for universal observance: Christmas and its octave, the feasts of Saint Stephen, Saint John the Evangelist, the Holy Innocents, the Epiphany and its octave, the Purification, all of Easter week, the Rogation Days, Ascension, Pentecost, the feasts of Saint John the Baptist, Saints Peter and Paul, the Assumption, Saint Martin and Saint Andrew. The feast of All Saints was an ecclesiastical holyday, but not a public holiday. The observance of the ecclesiastical fast days was also strictly enjoined. In times of public distress, famine, war, or of scarcity of provisions, Charle-

---

48. *Admonitio gen.*, c. 70: *M. G. Cap.*, I, 59.

magne ordered public prayers to be said, just as he ordained days of thanksgiving for victory and peace.

The Church's matrimonial legislation continued to encounter difficulties. First of all, there was the matter of prohibited degrees of relationship. Since Pope Gregory the Great had declared to the Anglo-Saxons that marriages between the grandchildren of brothers and sisters were licit,[49] Saint Boniface was astonished when Pope Gregory II informed him that marriages between the great-grandchildren of brothers and sisters (relatives of the fourth degree according to canonical calculation) were still prohibited; that only marriages between the great-great-grandchildren of brothers and sisters (relatives of the fifth degree according to canon law), could be regarded as valid; and that even this was merely a special concession made to the barbaric Germans.[50] Pope Gregory III pushed the prohibited relationship back further, namely, to the seventh generation; and in 747, Pope Zachary addressed the Frankish clergy to the same effect, writing that, "according to the custom and law of the Christian world and the religion of the Romans," marriages are not valid as long as relationship can be traced — that is, up to the seventh degree.[51]

In determining these limits the Church was decisively guided by Roman law, which fixed the bounds of relationship at the seventh degree when the right of succession was involved. (German law in certain cases did likewise.) The application of this method of computing to matrimony caused some confusion, however. For one thing, degrees of kinship were determined in one way by Roman law, in another by German law, and in still a third by canon law. Then, the Germans actually had no fixed norms concerning marriage impediments on the grounds of relationship — at most they barred cousins from marrying. In view of their undeveloped means of communication and the fact that they lived together in clans, it must be admitted that they often had difficulty in finding wives free from all relationship. This explains why the prescriptions of the popes could not be carried out in Germany.

---

49. *M. G. Epp.*, II, 335.
50. *Letters of Saint Boniface*, edition of Tangl, 26, p. 45; 33, p. 57.
51. *M. G. Epp.*, III, 485.

In 756, the council of Verberie commanded that marriages of the third degree by German computation (fourth canonical degree) were to be declared null, while those of the fourth German degree (fifth canonical degree) could be accepted. The council therefore took the position of Gregory II.[52] The synod of Compiègne issued a similar decree in 757. Bishop Haito of Basel did the same, doubtless in Charlemagne's lifetime.[53] But the synod held in Mainz under Charlemagne in 813 adopted a somewhat stricter course by requiring that marriages in the fourth generation — hence of the fifth canonical degree — be dissolved.[54] And Rome tried for a long time to maintain the radical position — that is to say, to extend the forbidden relationship to the seventh degree. Innocent III was the first to relinquish this position (in the Fourth Lateran Council) by fixing the fourth canonical degree (great-grandchildren of brothers and sisters) as the prohibitory limit.[55]

Consideration of the symbolism of numbers had also at times played a part in this matter. Seven appeared in many respects to be a sacred number, and in determining the seven degrees, Pope Leo III cited the fact that God had rested on the seventh day in the work of creation. Pope Innocent III, on the other hand, spoke of four fluids which, like the four elements, were to be found in the human body.[56]

The question concerning the extension of affinity had a similar history. Roman law prohibited marriage with one's mother-in-law, daughter-in-law, stepmother or stepdaughter. Canon law took an independent course by forbidding also marriage with a brother- or sister-in-law, basing its position in part on Jewish law. The synod of Orleans of 511[57] forbade marriage with the widow of one's brother or the sister of one's deceased wife, while the council of Epaon of 517[58] forbade, in addition, marriage with the wife of

---

52. *M. G. Cap.*, I, 40, c. 1. Cf. *Conc.*, II, 55. For the computation, cf. Freisen, *Gesch. des kan. Eherechts²*, 385, 412.
53. *M. G. Cap.*, I, 37, c. 1-3 (*Conc.*, II, 59); 365, c. 21.
54. *M. G. Conc.*, II, 273, c. 54.
55. Mansi. *Conc.*, XXII, 1038.
56. Jaffé. *Reg.*, 2503. Freisen, 386.
57. *M. G. Conc.*, I, p. 6, c. 18.
58. Ibid., p. 26, c. 30.

one's uncle. The other synods of the Merovingian period, as well as its civil legislation, repeated these regulations with few variations. In computing the forbidden degrees of affinity, the idea was established that, since husband and wife are to be regarded as one flesh, the same limits must be defined for affinity as for consanguinity. Marriage with a person related by marriage was therefore subject to prohibition in the same degrees as marriage with a blood relative. Here, too, the computation was by degrees, but the same difficulties were encountered. In Rome, the Church wanted to carry the prohibition out to the seventh degree of affinity,[59] while in Germany, the restriction was not favored beyond the third degree.[60] Eventually Innocent III fixed the impediment of affinity at the fourth degree. The council of Compiègne shows us that the marriage impediment of affinity arising from illicit relations was also recognized. Canon law pursued an entirely independent course in this question.[61]

The marriage impediment induced by spiritual relationship is first encountered in the West during the Carolingian epoch. It had already been recognized in the East as early as 530 by Justinian, who had forbidden marriage between the sponsor and the person baptized. In 692 the council *in Trullo* likewise recognized this impediment, and forbade marriage between the sponsor and the mother of the person baptized. The council of Rome held in 721 renewed this decree.[62] In 747, Pope Zachary informed Pippin of these prohibitions, adding that their violation was so great a crime that neither the holy Fathers, nor the councils, nor the Church of Rome had dared to pronounce judgment on it, but had left its punishment to God.[63] In this matter no difficulties were encountered. The spiritual relationship arising as in the case of baptism was applied by deduction to confirmation also.[64]

Still more important was the Church's struggle on behalf of the indissolubility of marriage. Though the position adopted by

---

59. Roman synod of 721: Mansi, *Conc.*, XII, 263, c. 9.
60. Synod of Compiègne (757), c. 4: *M. G. Cap.*, I, 38.
61. Cf. Freisen, 453 sqq.
62. C. 4; Synod of 743, c. 5: *M. G. Conc.*, II, 14.
63. *M. G. Epp.*, III, 485.
64. Synod of Mainz (813), c. 55: *M. G. Conc.*, II, 273.

the Christian Roman empire, especially in the East, gave only slight consideration to the rigorous concept of marriage held by the primitive Christians, and though ecclesiastical writers often vacillated in their opinions, the popes have always adhered tenaciously to the strict doctrine.

The difficulties were not lessened when the Church undertook to educate the Germans. In their tribes, the matrimonial relationship was established by means of a contract whereby the wife passed into the protective power of the husband in return for a monetary compensation. The relationship could be dissolved by divorce, and at first the Church seems to have been powerless to carry through any decisive measures against this practice. Save for one canon of the second synod of Orleans (533),[65] which punished with excommunication the dissolution of marriage because of sickness, we do not find the question of divorce treated in the numerous Frankish councils of the Merovingian epoch. Only in England and in the Visigothic kingdom, where the Church had acquired greater influence, was the strict position upheld by the synods of Hertford (673) and Toledo (681) respectively and the remarriage of divorced persons interdicted. For the rest, at least this much was achieved by the influence of Christianity: that the husband's arbitrary power to divorce his wife was restricted, and the wife was able to obtain equality with the husband insofar as she also was conceded the power, by certain laws, to divorce her husband if she so willed. In this connection one might regard divorce by mutual agreement as a step in the progress of culture, since the sexes were placed on an equal footing — which is, indeed, the basis for the principle of the absolute indissolubility of marriage.

It appears likewise that the bishops occasionally exerted some influence on the civil courts, which decided the question of guilt before a married person divorced his or her partner. In a canon of the synod of Agde, in 506, those planning to submit divorce cases to these courts are exhorted to present them first to the bishops of their province.[66]

---

65. C. 11: *M. G. Conc.*, I, 63.
66. C. 25: ibid.

Not until the time of Saint Boniface, however, did the Church have the opportunity of intervening efficaciously. A response given in 726 by Gregory II to an inquiry of Saint Boniface is certainly misunderstood if one gathers from it that the pope had allowed a man to leave his wife when she became ill and to marry another.[67] This response is undoubtedly to be understood of a marriage which, though validly contracted, was not yet consummated; for the same pope had, in 716, issued an instruction for Bavaria in which he reminded the people that a husband may not dare to enter into another union while his wife is living.[68] Pippin issued a similar decree at Soissons in 744:[69] one party to a marriage was not to contract another marriage during the lifetime of the second party; nor could a man dismiss his wife unless she had been apprehended in adultery. This was an evident departure from the civil law, which permitted divorce and remarriage in so many other cases. The decree in question also indicated a new tendency toward the Church's strict traditions, even though it can be assumed that the man in the given case, who divorced his wife because of adultery, was not forbidden to remarry.

In a letter the following year (745), Pope Zachary strongly reminded Pippin of the ancient prohibition against the remarriage of divorced persons, which allowed no exceptions whatsoever.[70] But as in other matters, this rigorous principle could not be enforced all at once in the Frankish kingdom. The councils of Verberie (756) and Compiègne (757) show us a return to laxer conceptions. The former[71] decreed in its fifth canon:

> If a woman conspires with other men to murder her husband, he — even though he has killed another while defending himself — may dismiss the wife and, if he so wills, marry again.

Canon nine reads:

> If one is obliged in a case of urgent need to flee into another duchy or province, or has followed his liege lord, to whom he cannot refuse his

---

67. *Letters of Saint Boniface,* edition of Tangl, p. 45.
68. *M. G. LL.* (fol.), III, 451.
69. C. 9: *M. G. Cap.,* I, 30.
70. *M. G. Epp.,* III, 482, c. 7 and 12.
71. *M. G. Cap.,* I, 40 sqq.

loyalty, and his wife, out of affection for her parents or her property, refuses to go with him despite the fact that she may and can, she must always remain unmarried as long as her husband, with whom she has refused to go, is living. But her husband, who has been forced to flee to another place, can, if he is unable to remain continent, take another wife after having performed a penance.

In canon seventeen we read:

> If a woman maintains that her husband has never cohabited with her, she may go to the cross [in order to submit herself to the ordeal of the cross], and if it be proved true, they may be separated, and she may do what she wills [i. e., may marry again].

The synod of Compiègne likewise permitted divorce and remarriage in various cases, chief among which were the following: a leper might give his or her spouse permission to contract a new marriage (canon nineteen) ; a married person who had permitted the other party to enter religious life might marry again (canon sixteen); and in still other cases the marriage was to be dissolved because of incest and the innocent party allowed to remarry.[72]

The above synodal decisions continued to affect practice in the Frankish kingdom for a long time — the more especially since they accorded in effect with the lax enforcement of the penitentials. Charlemagne, it is true, was ready to recognize the principles of Rome; it was his sincere desire to conform in all matters to the *Dionysio-Hadriana* — the formulation of the canons sanctioned by Rome. Thus we find that in his *admonitio generalis* of 789 he repeats the canon of the synod of Carthage of 407, which is contained in the *Dionysio-Hadriana:* namely, that neither wife nor husband may enter a new union during the lifetime of a divorced partner.[73] But even though this strict point of view would find later staunch proponents as well, in practice it still took a considerable period to overcome the opposite trend. Many a custom and belief continued to linger on in this way, often with the passive connivance of the civil authority: for example, the belief in a

---

72. Ibid., 38 sq.
73. Ibid., I, 56, c. 43; cf. 103, c. 22.

husband's right to kill his adulterous wife (which indeed was not questioned even by the councils).[74]

If we ask ourselves what was the general moral picture, there is, when all qualifications are made, just one answer possible. Externally, the ecclesiastical prescriptions were certainly observed faithfully, any lapses being due rather to weakness than to obstinacy. Spiritually, the authority of the Church was perhaps greater at this time than it had ever been. It must also be accepted as beyond question that the insistence upon auricular confession and the practice of penance in general produced good results for the interior life of individuals. If we wish to draw any conclusions from the sins listed most prominently in the penitentials, we find that it was immorality against which the Church had to fight hardest, then as always. This was also dealt with very often in the councils and the capitularies. But we cannot conclude, from the exceptionally large number of ordinances regarding immorality which have come down to us, that the situation was worse in that regard than in former ages. The most seriously unfavorable circumstance was that the court, to which the eyes of all were directed as rarely before or afterward, did not give a particularly good example in the moral field. It might also be said that the sensational manner in which ordinance after ordinance was issued leaves the impression that too much energy was spent in combating vice externally, by means of decrees and paragraphs; and that one would rather behold instead more shining examples of saintly pastors and holy men and women among the laity.

At this time there began also a certain beclouding of the Church's real mission. Because she was regarded, with truth, as a cultural institution, she became engrossed in the needed promotion of learning, art and economic progress to the degree that her purely religious mission was pushed into the background. This, indeed, becomes characteristic henceforth of the whole cultural development of the Middle Ages, though manifesting itself flagrantly only in the last years of that period, when ecclesiastical leaders saw them-

---

74. Synod of Tribur (895), c. 46: *M. G. Cap.*, II, 240.

selves rather as promoters and beneficiaries of intellectual and economic culture than as spiritual pastors and guides of the religious life. Under Charlemagne, we perceive rather the disadvantage, produced by his universal initiative in the Church's behalf, that she became accustomed to rely too much on the arm of the State and to expect from it the impulses for her own activity. Hence we behold in the brilliant picture which this first renaissance of Western culture offers us, notwithstanding the abundance of light, some shadows, which were to grow darker in the course of time.

A glance at the Church's missionary activity leaves us with the same impression. In the general effect there is much of grandeur, for the Church and Christian culture made tremendous progress during Charlemagne's lifetime. But the quality of the missionary work is no longer on such an ideal plane everywhere as it had been in the days of Saint Boniface. Then foreign monks worked in the pagan missions, and while they allowed the State to protect them, it was not their intent to labor for the State. They sought nothing but to preach the Gospel; it was in this spirit of sacrifice that they had left their native country to toil abroad. Now the State took charge of the missionary work: where the Franks reigned, there, too, the Christian religion was to reign. The resistance to the Frankish rule was broken by force, and whoever opposed Christianity was likewise subdued by force. The king commanded acceptance of the Christian faith together with the Frankish supremacy, and his warriors and officials attended to the execution of the command.

When Charlemagne ascended the throne, there were still pagans in the Frankish kingdom. A large number were to be found among the Slavs, who from the seventh century had been gradually penetrating the territories of the upper Saale and Main: Thuringia, Hesse and Franconia. Most of these Slavs were serfs: the name of the race had in fact at this time become the class name of unfree serfs ("slaves"), since the serfs who had been captured in war were almost all Slavs. The use of the term in this sense appears for the first time in the Alpine regions, where the Bavarians and Slavs had come into collision with each other. Previously the Germans had had another designation for Slavs — Wends or Winds, a term frequently met with in the composite place-names of central Germany.

Even today it clings to the Slavic group which remains on the upper Spree. The Slavs on the upper Main had been the advance guard in this region of the gradual Slavic movement westward from the Vistula to the land called Mauringa, which had become vacated through the advance of the West Germans and the migration of the East Germans. The Slavs had proceeded in this way across the Elbe and as far as the Saale and the Fichtel mountain chain, and even beyond. Saint Boniface had encountered Slavs in the vicinity of Fulda. At that time there was as yet no design for their conversion. Now, however, the formal Christianization of the Slavs, especially those on the upper Main, who still in the eighth century dwelt together in tribal masses, became an urgent necessity.

Slavs isolated among Franks as serfs were gradually won over to Christianity without any special measures; they became Christians by the very fact that they were Germanized. The situation was different with these Slavs on the upper Main, who now became Christians "at one blow," because Charlemagne demanded their conversion. The bishops of Würzburg built churches for them perforce; but pagan superstition and pagan customs continued to survive in those regions for centuries.

Among the Germanic tribes of the Saxons and Frisians, paganism offered a much more stubborn resistance. The martyrdom of Saint Boniface and his companions by the Frisians had demonstrated what powerful pagan fanaticism remained there. Pippin had not even dared to punish the murderers. But the Christian Frisians gradually made headway among their own people. The center of this evangelizing movement was Saint Martin's monastery in Utrecht, presided over by Saint Boniface's eminent disciple Saint Gregory, whom both Pippin and Pope Stephen II had commissioned to preach among the Frisians. This was a missionary after the heart of Saint Boniface. Though he was at the head of the diocese, he wished the episcopal dignity to be conferred, not upon himself, but upon one of his companions. Of a different type, his successor, Blessed Alberic, discharged both the abbatial and the episcopal office; supported by Charlemagne's power, he sent his monks out to destroy the pagan idols and sanctuaries. Still more was accomplished, however, by Saint Ludger, a native Frisian. After a journey to Italy which included visits to Rome and Monte Cassino in 785, he completed (by Charlemagne's order) the conversion of his people.

The Frisian code, composed at this time, informs us of the condition of Christianity among the Frisians at the end of the eighth century. How much Christian teaching and practice needed public protection is shown by the severe penalties under which the damaging of churches was forbidden and the observance of Christian precepts inculcated. A ninefold punishment was inflicted upon him who violated the peace of the Church. On the other hand, not only he who as a refugee sought asylum with her, enjoyed the Church's protection, but also he who was on his way to a church.

It is worthy of note that in this code the pagan ordeal of lots was incorporated, in Christian garb. When a person was slain in a public disturbance and his murderer was not known, the dead man's clan, to which the wergild was due, had the right to accuse seven of the rioters. Each of the accused must then, with the help of twelve compurgators, try to clear himself of guilt by swearing the so-called oath of compurgation. Next they were led to a church where the casting of lots was to decide the question finally. Two rods wrapped in wool, one of them being marked with a cross, were placed on the altar. Those present implored God to make known whether the seven had taken a just oath. A priest, or if no priest was present, an innocent boy, then chose one of the rods. If it showed the cross when unwrapped, the seven were held to be innocent. If not, the ordeal was continued by requiring each of the seven to hand in a rod marked with his family symbol and wrapped in wool; six of these rods having then been removed by the priest, the seventh designated him whom, according to the import of the law, the Christian God recognized as guilty, just as the pagan god had formerly done. The sign of the cross had merely replaced the old runic sign.

The Saxon tribe defended its paganism and its political independence against the Christian Franks with the greatest resoluteness. The most conservative of all the German peoples, the Saxons adhered to their ancient tribal law and customs as tenaciously as they clung to their old gods. Within the tribe they therefore preserved a certain barbaric morality, although of course this did not govern their relations with outsiders: no pledge given to an alien was binding. The Saxons were thus the neighbors especially feared by the Franks. Conflicts between the two had begun early in the sixth century, and a tribute imposed on the Saxons after defeat only increased the animosity. Under Charlemagne, the final, complete conquest of the tribe was to put an end to this situation; but first there were extremely bitter struggles, in which the Saxon nobility usually took sides with Charlemagne against the lower classes. Repeatedly the Frankish officials placed by Charlemagne over the Saxons were expelled, together with the Christian missionaries, and members of the tribe who had received baptism were killed or forced to return to paganism. Charlemagne horribly avenged one uprising of this nature that occurred in the year 782 by having four thousand of the culprits (delivered up to him by the Saxon nobility) slaughtered in one day at Verden on the Aller. Finally, Widukind, the leader of the pagan opposition, submitted and was baptized at Attigny in 785. At Charlemagne's request the pope ordained a feast of thanksgiving for the whole Christian West, which was celebrated on June 23, 26 and 28, 786.

Charlemagne immediately had his first Saxon code promulgated; it shows that even now he was able to secure Christianity only with the sword.[75] Pagan practices and pagan superstitions — in particular cremation, the killing of alleged witches, and the eating of human flesh — were punishable by death. Those also incurred this penalty who refused to be baptized or who ate meat during Lent without a grave cause. Within a half-year all Saxon children were to be baptized. Every community was to allot an estate for the endowment of a church and also as much land as was contained in two peasant farms; while every hundred and twenty inhabitants must furnish a serf and a maidservant to till the land given to the Church. Besides this, all men had to pay tithes to the Church. Charlemagne had Saint Willehad, a native of Northumbria and a friend of Alcuin, consecrated the first bishop of the Saxons, with residence in Bremen. The bishoprics of Verden and Minden were undoubtedly established at this time also.

---

75. Cap. 26: *M. G. Cap.*, I, 68 sqq.

But in 792 another insurrection broke out, in protest against the collection of the ecclesiastical tithes. Four years later Alcuin wrote:

> If the sweet yoke and the light burden of Christ were preached to the stubborn Saxon race with the same perseverance as the payment of tithes and the performance of severe penances for the smallest faults are demanded, many indeed would not detest baptism. Would that the teachers of the faith would from time to time model themselves after the example of the Apostles! Would that they were *praedicatores* and not *praedatores!*[76]

We must not, however, on the strength of this statement, pass a judgment admitting of no exception. There were also many among the Saxons who in the new outburst of violence adhered so strongly to the faith they had embraced with their whole heart, that they preferred to die as martyrs for Christianity rather than to re-embrace paganism. Still, it required ten years for the insurrection (which had its roots in the general masses in the north) to be put down. In fact the task was not accomplished until Charlemagne, employing a new means, had transplanted the Saxons by the thousands in Frankish regions.

This done, he continued the organization of the Church. To Bremen, Verden and Minden were added the new bishoprics of Paderborn and Münster, the latter being conferred on Saint Ludger, the well-deserving missionary of the Frisians. Besides the bishoprics there arose many monasteries, and all these new ecclesiastical institutions did excellent work. The doctrine, once so hated, now struck deep roots in the Saxon tribe and was accepted so fervently that the Church could point with particular joy to this new conquest.

Of the difficult and silent labor of the missionaries who brought this result about, we have less distinct traces than of Charlemagne's fierce wars. In the wording of the table of contents (*indiculus*) which survives from one work, the corresponding chapters unfortunately being missing, we are reminded of the paganism which Christian preachers continued to combat in the form of lingering super-

---

76. *M. G. Epp.*, IV, 161.

stitions.[77] Besides this fragment, we possess a sermon on superstition which was undoubtedly used at that period.[78] From these sources we are able to gather that for a time sacrifices were still offered to Wotan and Thor and that the people still venerated the sacred groves and the places of sacrifice near springs and on cliffs. Images of the gods adorned in appropriate robes still existed. Cakes shaped to represent them were still made on their festivals. In Westphalia to this day the bread baked for Shrovetide is called *Heidenweck,* which means "pagan roll"; and other instances of survival of such pagan customs in Christian form are the variously shaped cakes still baked for Saint Martin's Day, Christmas and Easter. The chasing out of winter in February (a popular custom which has lived on into the present) is also mentioned in these sources as a pagan superstition; but it was a very harmless one. In contrast, the belief in unlucky and lucky days was understandably opposed, since only on lucky days were the people willing to drive the herds to pasture or begin plowing. (We still have many vestiges of the belief in luck: for instance, sneezing or getting out of bed on the left side are supposed to invite misfortune.) It was considered an omen of evil to meet a priest or a monk early in the morning. "Wise men" and "wise women" read the many different signs. There were fortunetellers, too, who threw rods into the air and divined the future from the position in which they fell. Something similar lingers among us today in the belief that if a girl throws an apple-peeling over her shoulder it will fall to form the initials of her future husband. There were numerous incantations against witchcraft, for the healing of wounds, for health in times of illness. Many superstitious practices were connected with fire, which was produced by rubbing pieces of wood together. Jumping over these flames, for example, was thought to preserve people from harm. Such fires were later connected with Christian feasts, especially with Easter and the feast of Saint John, near the summer solstice.

77. *M. G. Cap.,* I, 223.
78. Caspari, *Eine Augustin fälschlich beigelegte Homilia Christ.,* 1886.

The manuscript we are considering, which originated in Mainz, passed thence first to Heidelberg and next to Rome, contains besides this list of superstitious practices, three Latin sermons showing how priests tried to strengthen faith in the hearts of the new Christians. In one, which was preached before the reception of Communion, love of the Saviour is aroused by these beautiful words:

> Behold, dearly beloved, the message we bring cometh not from a man who can be won by gifts, but from Him to whom you are bound, since He hath shed His blood for you. . . . Let no one who is tainted through illicit relations approach to receive the body of such a Master before he hath properly fulfilled his duty of repentance; he would not be healed, but wounded. . . . My dear brethren, though we are men covered with dirt, yet we do not wish to be touched by one unclean. Can we believe that the Incarnate Son of God will permit His body to be defiled by our sins? My brethren, our King, who hath judged us worthy of this office, seeks us without ceasing: let us prepare for Him a pure dwelling place if we desire Him to dwell in our bodies.[79]

The second sermon takes up the reproach we have already seen leveled against Christianity in the days of Eusebius: Why was the truth made known so late? Why did Christ permit so many people to be lost before His coming? The objection was refuted by adroit questions, for example: "Why dost thou, O man, complain against the Sun of Justice, that it has risen too late, thou who art still walking in darkness after its rising?"

We can see from this literature that Christian priests had no easy task. But they spared no pains, nor were they wanting in good will, and hence their efforts were rewarded.

Besides Saxony, Frisia and the territory along the Main, we must mention a fourth district where great things were accomplished under Charlemagne, namely, the eastern Alpine countries. The missionary activities here were undertaken principally by the Church in Bavaria which, organized by Saint Boniface, soon produced a gratifying florescence manifest on all sides. Numerous parish churches were established, and many monasteries as well, and the bishops were zealous in holding synods. When Duke Tassilo was

---

79. Mansi, XII, 377. Cf. Hauck, *KG.*, II[4], 410, n. 2; Müllenhoff-Scherer, *Denkmäler*, II[3], 25; Steinmeyer, *Sprachdenkmäler*, 20.

deposed in 788 and Bavaria was incorporated, like Alamannia, into the Frankish kingdom, Charlemagne still allowed the Church of Bavaria to retain its independence by uniting the Bavarian bishoprics into an ecclesiastical province under the metropolitan of Salzburg. This was done in 798, with the pope's assent.

Salzburg acquired prominence at this time, and two of its bishops in particular were excellently qualified for their office. The first was Saint Virgilius, a Germanized Celt, whom we have already mentioned[80] as having been involved in a controversy with Saint Boniface over the concept of the antipodes. Saint Virgilius must receive credit for being the first to promote missionary activity among the Slavic tribes. Upon his death in 784 he was succeeded by Arno, a Bavarian, who had been educated in the monastery of Saint Amand in Hainault. Having become abbot there, he established relations with the court and with Alcuin; the latter's devoted friendship for him was of great importance to the Church in Bavaria inasmuch as Alcuin's influence, exercised through Arno, transplanted to this frontier country the culture that flourished in Alcuin's circle. Learning was eagerly cultivated in Salzburg. Arno created a library for which he had more than a hundred and fifty volumes copied, and Alcuin sent his pupil Witto (Wizo) to Salzburg as a teacher.

The new forces which were developing here, were also a major benefit to the Slavic missions. We have seen that in the seventh century the Slavs had pushed after the Germans into the Alpine countries, just as they did on the Main. In so doing, they had destroyed the last remnants of Roman Christianity in the Eastern Alps. They had advanced as far as the Brenner Pass, but when they were being hard pressed by the Avars, the forward movement came to a stop (eighth century) and they were forced to seek an alliance with the Franks. It thus became possible for Christian missionaries to find a favorable reception among them. Borut, the Duke of the Slavs and a contemporary of Saint Virgilius, surrendered his son and his nephew to the Germans as hostages and allowed them to be brought up as Christians in the monastery of Chiemsee.

---

80. See above, p. 318.

When Cheitmar, the nephew, took over the reins of government, he visited Salzburg every year and the first missionaries were able to work under his protection. Modestus, appointed a separate regional bishop by Saint Virgilius, established the first Christian churches in the territory of the Slovenian Carantanes — the modern Carinthia. Besides Salzburg, several other agencies took part in this missionary work: the monastery of Innichen, which had been founded by Duke Tassilo in 769 on the pass between the Puster and Drave valleys — the frontier of the German and Slavic territories; then the diocese of Passau; and lastly the monastery of Kremsmünster, situated in the district of Traun, which Tassilo had also founded.

This mission, too, experienced some reverses — the first after Cheitmar's death in 772. The pagan party, gaining the ascendancy, began a war with Tassilo; but the Bavarian duke was victorious, Waltung, a new duke and apparently a German, assumed leadership of the Slavs, and the mission was able to make further headway. Even the fall of Tassilo did not interrupt its progress. The subjugation of the Avars constituted another great advance since, on their recognition of the Frankish domination in 796, they promised to embrace Christianity. Thus a wide field east of the Enns was opened to the Christian missions. After the Lombardic troops of Duke Eric of Friuli, the friend of Aquileia's patriarch Saint Paulinus, had assisted in subduing the Avars, Aquileia also took a hand in the missionary work. Arno and Saint Paulinus labored together in the field, encouraged by their friend Alcuin. The mission program was facilitated further by the settlement of a group of Germans on the Danube.

There remains to us the protocol of a conference between Charlemagne's son Pippin and several bishops concerning this mission: it took place in 796 during the campaign against the Avars and was recorded by Saint Paulinus the patriarch. The question was how the subjugated Avars, who were disposed to receive baptism, were to be brought over to Christianity. Since they were a people devoid of all education and culture, it was decided to forego mass baptisms and to have the people instructed first. As it was impossible in the circumstances to limit the conferring of the sacrament to the regular baptismal times, Easter and Pentecost, the deliberators contented themselves with restricting its administration to Saturdays. The instruction before baptism was not to last less than seven nor more than forty days. Eternal life and eternal punishments, not the punishment of the sword, were to be taught the candidates. Baptism was not to be forced upon anyone.

The extensive mission territory was divided between Salzburg, Aquileia and Passau. Alcuin followed the progress of Christianity in these regions with the greatest interest, and his letters gave warm encouragement and valuable counsel to his friends Arno and Saint Paulinus. In 796 he wrote to Archbishop Arno as follows:

> Be a preacher of piety, and not a collector of tithes, because the young soul is to be nourished with the milk of piety until it has grown up and become robust and strong enough to assimilate solid foods. The tithes have, it is said, destroyed the faith of the Saxons. How can we impose upon the necks of the uneducated a yoke which neither we nor our brethren were able to bear?

Next he insisted upon the training of capable and pious missionaries. Above all, he warned against the use of force:

> How can a man be forced to believe what he does not believe? He can, indeed, be forced to submit to baptism, but not to believe. . . . He who is capable of understanding reasonable instruction is to be instructed, therefore, and attracted by sermons as well, that he may realize the truth of our holy faith. But besides this, we must especially implore the mercy of Almighty God for him.

Finally, he desired that the weakness of the new converts be given some consideration, and was averse to the immediate imposition of ecclesiastical penances:

> One should also be particularly mindful of how the young plant is to be cared for so that the first blossoms of faith shall be able to form fruit and not wither away under the frost of severe treatment. . . . The good shepherd should not be always reprimanding the erring sheep with harsh rebukes, but instead should often try to correct them by means of comforting exhortations.[81]

---

81. Alcuin, *Epistulae*, 107, 114: *M. G. Epp.*, IV, 154, 164 sqq.

Alcuin properly appeals at this point to Pope Gregory the Great, whose instructions, given long ago to the Anglo-Saxon missionaries, he now passes on.

It is worthy of note that Christianity led to the awakening of the national culture in this region. Just as the oldest monuments of German literature proceeded from the instructions of the missionaries, so did those of the Slavs. The oldest survivals in the Slovenian language, the so-called monuments of Freising, are two formulas for confession and a sermon on confession. The latter, in recalling the Roman Christians who once lived in these parts, speaks a noble language — one that goes to the heart:

> Now we kneel in their churches, we invoke them, we drink to their honor, we offer sacrifices for the welfare of our bodies and our souls. We can become like unto them if we perform the same works they performed. They fed the hungry, gave drink to the thirsty, and clothed the naked. Through such works have they drawn close to God; we, too, must implore the Almighty Father in the same manner until He grants us a dwelling place in His kingdom.[82]

Nothing lasting was to be accomplished among the Avars, however. This people no longer possessed any racial consistency, which fact soon led to their being absorbed by the Slavs. The substantial results obtained, by contrast, among the Slavs in the Alpine countries, can be appreciated justly only when we take a general survey of the effects consequent upon the Christian missions.

The period between the fall of the Western Empire and the eighth century was the severest crisis the Church had to weather. She had successfully resisted the great danger of being drawn into the ruin of the Roman Empire. She had done even more. By the mere fact of her continued existence, she had saved the most valuable elements of antiquity — the treasures of classical learning — and transmitted them to the new culture in process of formation in the West.

We can appraise the external progress made by Christianity if we compare its boundaries in the year 400 with its boundaries

---

82. Hauck, *KG.*, II⁴, 480.

four centuries later. About the year 400 the Danube and the Rhine were the approximate northern frontier of the Christian religion in Europe. In the year 800 the old frontier had not, it is true, been regained on the lower Danube, for the Bulgarians residing to the southward were still pagan; but on the middle Danube there was at least the certainty of advancing Christianity to its ancient limits; while on the upper Danube and the Rhine it had gone far beyond them, having gained all the German tribes as far as the Elbe, the Saale and the Böhmerwald, and standing now upon the boundaries of the Slavs. The gain may not seem to be particularly great for four hundred years, but we must remember that during that same period large territories which had been lost were also regained. The pagan Germans had all but annihilated Christianity in eastern and northern Gaul as far as the Vosges mountains and the Somme; the Anglo-Saxons had to a very great extent destroyed the Roman-British Church; in the Alps, Christianity had been so reduced, partly by the Germans, partly by the Slavs, that only a few insignificant remnants were to be found. All these regions had been reconquered for the faith.

But great dangers still threatened. Though the oldest sites of Christianity were not annihilated, they were so submerged by the Mohammedan flood that it was all but meaningless henceforth to speak of religious life in those sections. The whole of north Africa and Egypt had succumbed to Islam, and Spain had fallen under its domination. And even so the offensive force of the Arabs had not slackened. They controlled the Mediterranean Sea. From north Africa and Spain they strove to invade Italy and southern France. Asia Minor was exposed to their attacks. At the same time an onslaught from two other directions menaced Christianity: from the pagan Normans who controlled the northern seas, and from the Hungarian horsemen who were advancing from the Theiss Plains.

It was of the greatest importance that, prior to the gathering of the storm clouds, Western society, composed then of Romance and Germanic peoples, had succeeded in forming both a political union under the rule of Charlemagne and an even more permanent spiritual union under the Holy See. Had this not been achieved, Western Europe would have perished in the ninth century together with the germs of culture inherent in it. The new forces which the first renaissance of the West had produced, were to preserve it from this fate.

INDEX

BIBLIOGRAPHY

As explained in the Translator's Preface (page V of this book), the asterisk * marks titles added by the translator. No asterisk has been put beside titles of later editions, or English translations, of works already listed by Professor Schnürer.

The Bibliography is arranged under general heads corresponding to the divisions of the book. However, there is necessarily much overlapping of references, and titles bearing mainly on one division will often pertain to several others.

Chief Works Cited Throughout in Abbreviated Form

Acta SS.	Acta Sanctorum
C. S. E. L.	Corpus Scriptorum Ecclesiasticorum Latinorum
Migne, *P. G.*	Patrologiae Cursus Completus, Series Graeca
Migne, *P. L.*	Patrologiae Cursus Completus, Series Latina
Mon. Germ. Hist.:	Monumenta Germaniae Historica:

under which general title various sections are cited, thus:

Auct. ant.	Auctores antiquissimi
Cap.	Capitularia
Conc.	Concilia
Epp.	Epistolae
SS. rer. merov., etc.	Scriptores rerum merovingicarum, etc.

AUTHOR'S FOREWORD

*Baunard, L., *Ozanam in His Correspondence,* trans. by a Vincentian. New York, 1925.

Borinski, K., *Die Weltwiedergeburtsidee in den neueren Zeiten: I, Der Streit um die Renaissance und die Entstehungsgeschichte der historischen Begriffe Renaissance und Mittelalter* (Sitz.-Ber. der Münch. Akad., Phil.-hist. Kl., 1919). Munich, 1919.

*Emerton, E., "The Periodization of History" (Massachusetts Historical Society Proceedings, Oct.-Dec., 1918).

Febvre, L., Tonnelat, E., Mauss, H., Niceforo, A., Weber, L., *La civilisation, le mot et l'idée* (Publications du centre internat. de synthèse). Paris, 1930.

Göller, E., *Die Periodisierung der Kirchengeschichte und die epochale Stellung des Mittelalters* (inaugural address). Freiburg i/B., 1919.

Goyau, G., *Frédéric Ozanam.* Paris, 1925.

Kurth, G., *The Church at the Turning Points of History,* Eng. trans. by V. Day. Helena, Mont., 1918.

———, *Les origines de la civilisation moderne.* 2 vols., 7th ed., Brussels, 1923.

———, *What Are the Middle Ages?* Eng. trans. by V. Day. Privately printed, 1924.

547

Lehmann, P., "Vom Mittelalter und von der latein. Philologie des Mittelalters" (Quellen und Untersuchungen zur lateinischen Philologie des Mittelalters, V). Munich, 1914. *For a brief summary cf. Burr, G. L., "How the Middle Ages Got Their Name" (American Historical Review, XX [1915], 813-814).

*Michels, T., Das Heilswerk der Kirche. 1935.

Moras, J., Ursprung und Entwicklung des Begriffes der Zivilisation in Frankreich. Hamburg, 1930.

Ozanam, A. F., Oeuvres complètes. 11 vols., 9th ed., Paris, 1925.

*———, History of Civilization in the Fifth Century, Eng. trans. by A. C. Glyn. 2 vols., London, 1868.

Schmalenbach, H., Das Mittelalter: Sein Begriff und Wesen (Wissenschaft und Bildung, No. 226). Leipzig, 1926.

*Schütz, A., Gott in der Geschichte. 1936.

Sorrento, L., "Medio evo, il termine e il concetto" (Annuario della Università cattol. del Sacro Cuore. Anno Accadem., 1931). Milan, 1931.

Varga, L., Das Schlagwort vom finsteren Mittelalter (Veröffentlichungen des Seminars für Wirtschafts- und Kulturgeschichte an der Univ. Wien, No. 8). Baden, 1932.

*Zeiller, J., "Der Kirchenbegriff in den ersten vier Jahrhunderten" (Revue d'Histoire Ecclésiastique [1933], 571 sqq., 827 sqq.).

INTRODUCTION

Bardenhewer, O., Patrology, Eng. trans. by T. J. Shahan. Freiburg i/B.-St. Louis, 1908.

———, Geschichte der altkirchlichen Literatur, I-III. 2nd ed., Freiburg i/B., 1913-23.

Baudrillart, A., Moeurs paiennes, moeurs chrétiennes: I, La famille dans l'antiquité et aux premiers siècles du christianisme. Paris, 1929.

Bihlmeyer, K., and Tüchle, H., Kirchengeschichte, I-II. 12th and 13th ed., Paderborn, 1951-52.

*Burns, C. D., The First Europe: A Study of the Establishment of Medieval Christendom, A. D. 400-800. London, 1947.

Cavallera, F., St. Jérôme, sa vie et son oeuvre. 2 vols., Louvain-Paris, 1922.

De Broglie, A., L'église et l'empire romain au IVe siècle. 6 vols., 7th to 3rd ed., Paris, 1869-77.

*Dill, S., Roman Society from Nero to Marcus Aurelius. London, 1925.

Duchesne, L., Early History of the Christian Church from Its Foundation to the End of the Fifth Century, trans. from 4th French ed., 3 vols., London-New York, 1909-24; vols. 1-2, rev. ed., 1912-13.

———, L'église au VIe siècle. Paris, 1925.

Dufourcq, A., Le christianisme et l'empire. 9th ed., Paris, 1931.

Ehrhard, A., Urkirche und Frühkatholizismus. Bonn, 1935.

Eusebius of Caesarea, Opera (Die griechischen christlichen Schriftsteller der ersten drei Jahrhunderte). 7 vols., Leipzig, 1902-26.

*Fletcher, C. R., The Making of Western Europe: 300-1190 A. D. 2 vols., London, 1912-14.

*Freeman, E. A., *Western Europe in the Eighth Century and Onward.* London-New York, 1904.

Geffcken, A., *Der Ausgang des griechisch-römischen Heidentums.* 2nd ed., Heidelberg, 1929.

Grützmacher, G., *Hieronymus: Eine biographische Studie zur alten Kirchengeschichte* (Studien zur Geschichte der Theologie und Kirche, VI and X, 1-2). 3 vols., Leipzig-Berlin, 1901-08.

Grupp, G., *Kulturgeschichte der römischen Kaiserzeit: I, Untergang der heidnischen Kultur; II, Anfänge der christlichen Kultur.* 2 vols., Munich, 1903-04; vol. I, 3rd ed., Regensburg, 1921.

Harnack, A. von, *Geschichte der altchristlichen Literatur bis Eusebius.* 2 vols., Leipzig, 1893-1904.

————, *Mission and Expansion of Christianity in the First Three Centuries,* Eng. trans. by J. Moffatt (Theological Translation Library). 2 vols., 2nd ed., London, 1908.

Hartmann, L. M., *Der Untergang der antiken Welt* (Hartmann, *Weltgeschichte,* I, 3). 2nd ed., Gotha, 1921.

*Hayes, C. J. H., *Christianity and Western Civilization.* Stanford, 1954.

*Hughes, P., *A History of the Church,* I-II. New York, 1934-35.

Jerome, Saint, *Opera.* Ed. by Vallarsi, 11 vols., Venice, 1766-72; Migne, *P. L.,* XXII-XXX; *C. S. E. L.,* LIV-LVI and LIX.

Jordan, H., *Geschichte der altchristlichen Literatur.* Leipzig, 1911.

Kirsch, J. P., *Die Kirche in der antiken griechisch-römischen Kulturwelt* (Kirchengeschichte, I). Freiburg i/B., 1930.

*Lebreton, J., and Zeiller, J., *L'église primitive* and *De la fin du deuxième siècle à la paix constantinienne,* Paris, 1934 and 1935 (*Histoire de l'église,* I-II, Fliche, A., and Martin, V., eds.). Eng. trans. by E. C. Messenger: *The History of the Primitive Church,* 2 vols., New York, 1949.

*Lot, F., *End of the Ancient World and the Beginnings of the Middle Ages.* London, 1931; reprint, 1953.

*Palanque, J.-R., Bardy, G., and Labriolle, P. de, *De la paix constantinienne à la mort de Théodose,* Paris, 1936; *Histoire de l'église,* ut supra, III). *Eng. trans. by E. C. Messenger: *The Church in the Christian Roman Empire,* New York, 1953.

Rivière, J., *Expansion of Christianity in the First Three Centuries, according to the Conclusions of Harnack,* trans. from the French. St. Louis, 1916.

Romeyer, B., *La philosophie chrétienne.* 2 vols., Paris, 1934-36.

Schultze, V., *Geschichte des Untergangs des griechisch-römischen Heidentums.* 2 vols., Jena, 1887-92.

Seeck, O., *Geschichte des Untergangs der antiken Welt: I-IV,* 3rd ed., Stuttgart, 1910; VI, 1920.

Stein, E., *Geschichte des spätrömischen Reiches: I, Vom römischen zum byzantinischen Staate,* Vienna, 1928;* II, *Histoire du Bas-Empire: De la disparition de l'empire d'occident à la mort de Justinien* (476-565), ed. by J. Stein and J.-R. Palanque, Bruges, 1949.

Wendland, P., "Die hellenistisch-römische Kultur in ihrer Beziehung zu Judentum und Christentum" (Handbuch zum Neuen Testament, 3rd ed.), Tübingen, 1912.

BOOK ONE

THE ROMAN EMPIRE AND THE CHURCH:
PILLARS OF WESTERN CIVILIZATION

Bardenhewer, O., *Geschichte der altkirchlichen Literatur:* III (2nd ed.)-V. Freiburg i/B., 1923-32.

Baumgartner, A., *Geschichte der Weltliteratur,* IV. Freiburg i/B., 1900.

*Cochrane, C. N., *Christianity and Classical Culture: A Study of Thought and Action from Augustus to Augustine.* New York, 1940.

*Curtius, E., *European Literature and the Latin Middle Ages,* Eng. trans. by W. R. Trask. New York, 1953.

Ebert, A., *Allgemeine Geschichte der Literatur des Mittelalters im Abendlande bis zum Beginn des elften Jahrhunderts.* 3 vols., Leipzig, 1874-87; I in 2nd ed., 1889.

*Hoare, F. R., *The Western Fathers* (The Makers of Christendom, No. 1). London-New York, 1954.

*Kuhnmuench, O. J., *Early Christian Latin Poets* (4th-6th cent.). Chicago, 1929.

Labriolle, P. de, *Histoire de la littérature latine chrétienne,* 3rd ed., rev. by G. Bardy, Paris, 1947. *An inadequate Eng. trans. is available: *History and Literature of Christianity from Tertullian to Boethius,* by H. Wilson, New York, 1925.

*Laistner, M. L. W., *Christianity and Pagan Culture in the Later Roman Empire.* Ithaca, 1951.

———, *Thought and Letters in Western Europe, A. D. 500-900.* New York, 1931.

Manitius, M., *Geschichte der christlichen lateinischen Poesie.* Stuttgart, 1891.

*Raby, F. J. E., *History of Christian-Latin Poetry from Its Beginnings to the Close of the Middle Ages.* 2nd ed., Oxford, 1953.

*Rand, E. K., *Founders of the Middle Ages.* Cambridge, Mass., 1928.

*Rose, H. J., *A Handbook of Latin Literature to the Death of St. Augustine.* 3rd ed., London, 1954.

Schanz, M., *Geschichte der römischen Literatur:* IV, 1, *Die Literatur des vierten Jahrhunderts,* 2nd ed.; IV, 2, *Die Literatur des fünften und sechsten Jahrhunderts,* by M. Schanz, K. Hosius, and G. Krüger (Handbuch der Altertumswissenschaft, VIII). Munich, 1914-20.

Smith, W., and Wace, H., *A Dictionary of Christian Biography, Literature, Sects and Doctrines.* 4 vols., London, 1877-87.

Teuffel, W. S., *History of Roman Literature,* Eng. trans. by G. C. W. Warr. 2 vols., London, 1900.

*Wace, H., and Piercy, W. C., *A Dictionary of Christian Biography and Literature to the End of the Sixth Century A. D.* Boston, 1911.

*Wright, F. A., and Sinclair, T. A., *A History of the Later Latin Literature (c. 350-700).* London, 1935.

CHAPTER ONE

SAINT AMBROSE AND HIS SCHOOL

Ambrose, Saint, *Opera.* Ed. by J. de Frische and N. Le Nourry, 2 vols., Paris, 1686-90; Migne, *P. L.,* XIV-XVII; *C. S. E. L.,* XXXII, LXII, LXIV.

Baudrillart, A., *St. Paulin, évêque de Nole* (Les Saints). Paris, 1905.

Baunard, L., *Histoire de St. Ambroise.* 3rd ed., Paris, 1899.

Bernays, J., *Über die Chronik des Sulpicius Severus.* Berlin, 1861.

Brockhaus, C., *Aurelius Prudentius Clemens in seiner Bedeutung für die Kirche seiner Zeit.* Leipzig, 1872.

Broglie, A. de., *St. Ambroise* (Les Saints). 5th ed., Paris, 1901.

Delehaye, H., *St. Martin et Sulpice Sévère* (Analecta Bollandiana, No. 38). Brussels, 1920.

Dreves, G. M., *Ambrosius, der Vater des Kirchengesanges* (Ergänzungsheft der Stimmen aus Maria-Laach, No. 58). Freiburg i/B., 1893.

Dudden, F. H., *The Life and Times of St. Ambrose.* 2 vols., Oxford, 1935.

Labriolle, P. de, *The Life and Times of St. Ambrose,* Eng. trans. by H. Wilson. St. Louis, 1928.

Lagrange, F., *Histoire de St. Paulin de Nole.* 2 vols., 2nd ed., Paris, 1884.

Lavertujon, A., *La Chronique de Sulpice Sévère,* 2 vols., Paris, 1896-99.

Palanque, J.-R., *St. Ambroise et l'empire romain.* Paris, 1934.

Paulinus of Nola, Saint, *Opera. C. S. E. L.,* XXIX-XXX.

Prudentius, *Opera.* Migne, P. L., LIX-LX; *C. S. E. L.,* LXI.

———, *Carmina,* ed. by F. Arevalo. 2 vols., Rome, 1788-89.

Puech, A., *Prudence.* Paris, 1888.

*Rand, E. K., *Prudentius and Christian Humanism.* Cleveland, 1920.

Sulpicius Severus, *Opera. C. S. E. L.,* I.

Thamin, R., *St. Ambroise et la morale chrétienne au 4e siècle: Etude comparée des devoirs de Cicéron et St. Ambroise.* Paris, 1895.

Wirtz, R., *Der hl. Ambrosius und seine Zeit.* Treves, 1924.

CHAPTER TWO

THE CULTURAL ETHICS OF ST. AUGUSTINE

Augustine, Saint, *Opera.* Ed. by the Benedictines of St. Maur, 11 vols., Paris, 1679-1700; Migne, *P. L.,* XXXII-XLVII; *C. S. E. L.,* 18 vols. to date: 1887-1923.

———, *Confessiones.* Best ed. by M. Skutella, Leipzig, 1934; text with commentary by J. Gibb and W. Montgomery, 2nd ed., Cambridge, 1927.

*Eng. trans.: T. Matthew, ed. by R. Hudleston, London, 1954, Chicago, 1955; by E. B. Pusey (Everyman's Library), New York, 1907, and often reprinted; by F. J. Sheed (Books I-X), New York, 1942.

————, *De Civitate Dei.* Best ed. by B. Dombart and A. Kalb, 2 vols., 4th ed., Leipzig, 1928-29. *Eng. trans. by M. Dods, 2 vols., Edinburgh, 1871 and later reprints.

————, *Sermones post Maurinos reperti.* Ed. by G. Morin (Miscellanea Agostiniana, I), Rome, 1930. *Selections trans. by T. C. Lawler (Ancient Christian Writers, No. 15), Westminster-London, 1952.

*Bardy, G., *Augustin.* 6th ed., Paris, 1946.

*Batiffol, P., *Le catholicisme de S. Augustin.* 2 vols., 5th ed., Paris, 1929.

Bernheim, E., *Mittelalterliche Zeitanschauungen in ihrem Einfluss auf Politik und Geschichtsschreibung,* I. Tübingen, 1918.

Bertrand, L., *Augustin.* 34th ed., Paris, 1913.

*Bourke, V., *Augustine's Quest of Wisdom: Life and Philosophy of the Bishop of Hippo* (Science and Culture Series). Milwaukee, 1944.

*Boyer, C., *Augustin.* Paris, 1932.

————, *Christianisme et Néoplatonisme dans la formation de S. Augustin.* Paris, 1920.

Combès, G., *La doctrine politique de S. Augustin* (dissertation). Paris, 1927.

————, *S. Augustin et la culture classique.* Paris, 1928.

*D'Arcy, C., Blondel, M., et al., *A Monument to St. Augustine.* London, 1930.

Feuerlein, E., "Die Stellung Augustins in der Kirchen- und Kulturgeschichte" (Historische Zeitschrift, XXII [1869]).

Fuchs, H., *Augustinus und der antike Friedensgedanke.* Berlin, 1926.

Gerosa, P., *S. Agostino e la decadenza dell' impero romano.* Turin, 1916.

Gilson, E., *Introduction à l'étude de Saint Augustin.* 3rd ed., Paris, 1949.

*Henry, P., *La vision d'Ostie.* Paris, 1938.

Hertling, G. von, *Augustin* (Weltgeschichte in Charakterbildern). 2nd ed., Munich, 1904.

Holl, K., *Augustins innere Entwicklung.* Berlin, 1923.

Jolivet, R., *S. Augustin et le Néoplatonisme chrétien.* Paris, 1933.

Lesaar, H., *Der hl. Augustin.* Kempten, 1930.

*Marrou, H. I., *S. Augustin et la fin de la culture antique.* 2 vols., Paris, 1938-49.

Mausbach, J., *Die Ethik des hl. Augustin.* 2 vols., 2nd ed., Freiburg i/B., 1929.

*Pontet, M., *L'exégèse de S. Augustin, predicateur.* Paris, 1946.

*Pope, H., *St. Augustine.* London, 1937.

Portalié, E., "S. Augustin," *Dictionnaire de théologie catholique,* I, coll. 2268-2472.

Salin, E., *Civitas Dei.* Tübingen, 1926.

Schilling, O., *Die Staats- und Soziallehre des hl. Augustinus.* Freiburg i/B., 1910.

Seyrich, G. J., *Die Geschichtsphilosophie Augustins.* Leipzig, 1891.

Stegemann, V., *Augustins Gottesstaat* (Heidelberger Abhandlungen, No. 15). Tübingen, 1928.

*Switalski, B., *Neoplatonism and the Ethics of St. Augustine: I, Plotinus and the Ethics of St. Augustine* (Polish Institute of Arts and Sciences Series, No. 8). New York, 1946.

Troeltsch, E., *Augustin: Die christliche Antike und das Mittelalter im Anschluss an die Schrift "De civitate Dei."* Munich-Berlin, 1915.

*Willis, G. G., *St. Augustine and the Donatist Controversy.* London, 1950.

CHAPTER THREE

THE PAPACY UNDER LEO THE GREAT —
FALL OF THE WESTERN ROMAN EMPIRE

Collectio Avellana (imperial and papal letters, 357-553), ed. by O. Guenther. *C. S. E. L.*, XXXV, 1-2, Vienna, 1895-98.

Epistolae Romanorum pontificum, I (to 440). Ed. by D. Coustant, Paris, 1721; re-edited by Schoenemann, Göttingen, 1796.

Epistolae Romanorum pontificum genuinae et quae ad eos scriptae sunt, 461-523, ed. by A. Thiel. Braunsberg, 1868.

Batiffol, P., *Le siège apostolique (359-450).* Paris, 1924.

Baudrillart, A., *St. Sévérin.* Paris, 1908.

Caspar, E., *Geschichte des Papsttums*, I. Tübingen, 1930.

*Dill, S., *Roman Society in the Last Century of the Western Empire.* 2nd ed., London, 1899; often reprinted.

Eugippius, *Vita Severini.* Ed. by H. Sauppe (*Mon. Germ. hist. Auct. ant.,* I, 2), 1877; ed. by T. Mommsen (*Script. rer. Germ.*), Berlin, 1898; ed. by P. Knöll (*C. S. E. L.*, IX, 2), Leipzig, 1883.

Getzeny, H., *Stil und Form der ältesten Papstbriefe* (dissertation). Tübingen, 1922.

Grisar, H., *Geschichte Roms und der Päpste im Mittelalter*, I, Freiburg i/B., 1901. *Eng. trans. by L. Cappadelta: *History of Rome and the Popes in the Middle Ages,* 3 vols., London, 1911-12.

Harnack, A. von, "Über die Herkunft der achtundvierzig ersten Päpste" (Sitz.-Berichte der Berliner Akademie, 1904).

Jaffé, P., *Regesta pontificum Romanorum.* 2nd ed. by S. Loewenfeld, F. Kaltenbrunner, and P. Ewald. 2 vols., Leipzig, 1885-88.

*Jalland, T., *The Life and Times of St. Leo the Great.* London-New York, 1941.

Kehr, P., *Regesta pontificum Romanorum: Italia Pontificia,* I sqq. Berlin, 1906 sqq.

Leo I, Saint, *Opera.* Ed. by P. and H. Ballerini, 3 vols., Venice, 1753 sqq.; Migne, *P. L.*, LIV-LVI.

Lietzmann, H., *Petrus und Paulus in Rom.* 2nd ed., Leipzig, 1927.

Méjean, E., *Orose et son apologétique* (dissertation). Strasbourg, 1862.

Orosius, P., *Libri VII historiarum adversus paganos.* Ed. by E. K. Zangemeister (*C. S. E. L.*, V), Leipzig, 1882; editio minor, Leipzig, 1889.

*Eng. trans. by I. W. Raymond (Records of Civilization: Sources and Studies, No. 26), New York, 1936.

Salvian, *Libri VIII de gubernatione Dei.* Ed. by C. Halm (*Mon. Germ. hist. Auct. ant.,* I, 1) 1877; ed. by F. Pauly (*C. S. E. L.,* VIII), Leipzig, 1883. *Eng. trans. by E. M. Sanford, New York, 1930.

*Schäfer, A., *Römer und Germanen bei Salvian.* Breslau, 1930.

Seeck, O., *Regesten der Kaiser und Päpste, 311-476.* Stuttgart, 1919.

Seppelt, F. X., *Geschichte des Papsttums,* I. 2nd ed., Leipzig, 1939.

Sommerlad, T., *Die Lebensbeschreibung Severins als kulturgeschichtliche Quelle.* Leipzig, 1903.

Steinberg, F., "Das Christentum des fünften Jahrhunderts im Spiegel der Schriften des Salvianus von Massilia" (Theologische Studien und Kritiken, 82, 1909).

Wurm, H., *Die Papstwahl* (Vereinsschrift der Görres-Gesellschaft). Cologne, 1922.

Zschimmer, W. A., *Salvianus, der Presbyter von Massilia und seine Schriften.* Halle, 1875.

CHAPTER FOUR

SAINT BENEDICT AND HIS AGE

Arnold, C., *Cäsarius von Arelate und die gallische Kirche seiner Zeit.* Leipzig, 1894.

*Barrett, H. M., *Boethius.* Cambridge, 1940.

Benedict, Saint, *Regula monachorum.* Ed. by C. Butler, 3rd ed., Freiburg i/B., 1935; ed. by B. Linderbauer, with philological commentary in German (Florilegium patristicum, No. 17), Bonn, 1928.

Berlière, U., *L'ordre monastique des origines au 12e siècle.* 3rd ed., Paris, 1924.

Besse, J. M., *Les moines d'Orient antérieurs au concile de Chalcedoine (451).* Paris, 1900.

———, *Les moines de l'ancienne France: periode gallo-romaine et mérovingienne.* Paris, 1906.

Boethius, *Opera.* Migne, *P. L.,* LXIII-LXIV; *C. S. E. L.,* XLVIII and LXVII, Leipzig, 1906, 1934.

———, *De consolatione philosophiae,* ed. by A. Fortescue, London, 1925. Eng. trans. by "I. T." (1609), rev. by H. F. Stewart (Loeb Library), London, 1918; also trans. by W. V. Cooper (Temple Classics), London, 1902.

———, *The Theological Tractates,* with Eng. trans. by H. F. Stewart and E. K. Rand. London, 1918-26.

*Brechter, H. S., ed., *Benedictus, der Vater des Abendlandes.* Munich, 1947.

Butler, C., *Benedictine Monachism.* 2nd ed., London, 1924.

Cabrol, F., *St. Benoît* (Les Saints). 2nd ed., Paris, 1933.

Caesarius of Arles, *Opera,* ed. by G. Morin. 2 vols., Maredsous, 1937-42.

————, *Regula sanctarum virginum,* ed. by G. Morin (Florilegium patristicum, No. 34). Bonn, 1933.

Cassian, John, *De institutis coenobiorum et de octo principalium vitiorum remediis libri XII* and *Collationes XXIV,* ed. by M. Petschenig (*C. S. E. L.,* XVII and XIII). Leipzig, 1886-88.

Cassiodorus, *Opera.* Ed. by J. Garetius, Venice, 1729; Migne, *P. L.,* LXIX-LXX.

————, *Variae,* ed. by T. Mommsen (*Mon. Germ. hist. Auct. ant., XII*). 1894.

*Chadwick, O., *John Cassian: A Study in Primitive Monasticism.* Cambridge, 1951.

Chapman, J., *St. Benedict and the Sixth Century.* London, 1929.

*Cooper, L., *A Concordance of Boethius.* Cambridge, Mass., 1928.

*Cooper-Marsden, A. C., *The History of the Island of Lerins: Monastery, Saints and Theologians of St. Honorat.* Cambridge, 1913.

*Delatte, P., *The Rule of St. Benedict: A Commentary,* Eng. trans. by J. McCann. London, 1921.

Franz, A., *Magnus Aurelius Cassiodorus Senator.* Breslau, 1872.

Godet, P., "Boèce," *Dictionnaire de théologie catholique,* II, coll. 918-922.

Gregory the Great, Saint, *Vita Sancti Benedicti in dialogis.* Ed. by U. Moricca (Fonti per la storia d'Italia, No. 57), Rome, 1924. *Eng. translations: by E. G. Gardner, *The Dialogues of St. Gregory,* London, 1911; by J. McCann, *The Second Book of the Dialogues,* Worcester, England, 1941.

*Hannah, I. C., *Christian Monasticism.* New York, 1925.

*Heimbucher, M., *Die Orden und Kongregationen der katholischen Kirche.* 2 vols., 3rd ed., Paderborn, 1932-34.

Herwegen, I., *Der hl. Benedikt.* 3rd ed., Düsseldorf, 1926.

Hilpisch, S., *Geschichte des benediktinischen Mönchtums.* Freiburg i/B., 1929.

*Hodgkin, T., *Theodoric the Goth.* New York, 1891; new ed., London, 1923.

Hörle, G. H., *Frühmittelalterliche Mönchs- und Klerikerbildung in Italien.* Freiburg i/B., 1914.

*Lechner, P. P., *St. Benedict and His Times.* London, 1900.

McLaughlin, T. P., *Le très ancien droit monastique de l'Occident de S. Benoît de Nursie à S. Benoît d'Aniane* (dissertation). (Archives de la France monastique, No. 38). Paris, 1935.

Malnory, A., *St. Césaire, évêque d'Arles, 503-543* (Bibliothèque de l'École pratique des hautes études de Paris, CIII). Paris, 1894.

Montalembert, C. F. R. de, *Les moines d'Occident,* 7 vols., 6th ed., Paris, 1878-82. *Eng. trans.: *The Monks of the West,* 7 vols., Edinburgh, 1861-79; ed. with introd. by F. A. Gasquet, 6 vols., London, 1896.

Morin, G., "Problèmes relatifs à la règle de S. Césaire" (Revue Bénédictine, 44 [1932]).

*Moris, H., *L'abbaye de Lérins.* Paris, 1909.

*Patch, H. R., *The Tradition of Boethius: A Study of His Importance in Medieval Culture.* Oxford, 1936.

Pfeilschifter, G., *Der Ostgotenkönig Theoderich der Grosse und die katholische Kirche.* Münster, 1896.

Spreitzenhofer, E., *Die Entwicklung des alten Mönchtums in Italien bis St. Benedikt.* Vienna, 1894.

Thiele, H., "Cassiodor, seine Klostergründung Vivarium und sein Nachwirken," *Studien u. Mitteilungen zur Geschichte des Benediktinerordens,* 50 (1932).

Thorbecke, H., *Cassiodorus Senator.* Heidelberg, 1867.

Tosti, L., *Saint Benedict,* Eng. trans. by W. R. Woods. London, 1896.

*Ueding, L., *Geschichte der Klostergründungen der frühen Merowingerzeit* (Historische Studien, No. 261). Berlin, 1935.

*Vidmar, C. J., *St. Benedikts Leben und die kulturelle Tätigkeit seines Ordens.* 1933.

BOOK TWO

FORMATION OF THE CULTURAL COMMUNITY OF THE WEST BY THE CHURCH

Bühler, I., *Deutsche Geschichte,* I. Berlin, 1934.

*Dawson, C., *The Making of Europe.* New York, 1932.

————, *Religion and the Rise of Western Culture.* New York, 1950.

*Dopsch, A., *The Economic and Social Foundations of European Civilization,* Eng. trans. by M. G. Beard and N. Marshall, and condensed by E. Patzelt, from the 2nd ed. of the 2-volume German original. London, 1937.

Dufourcq, A., *Le christianisme et les barbares.* 7th ed., Paris, 1932.

Fliche, A., *La chrétienté médiévale, 395-1254* (Histoire du monde, VII, 2). Paris, 1929.

Goetz, W., *Das Mittelalter bis zum Ausgang der Staufer* (Propyläen-Weltgeschichte, III). Berlin, 1932.

Grupp, G., *Kulturgeschichte des Mittelalters,* I. 3rd ed., Paderborn, 1921.

Günter, H., *Deutsche Kultur.* Munich, 1932.

Gutsche, G., and Schultze, W., *Deutsche Geschichte von der Vorzeit bis zu den Karolingern* (Bibliothek der deutschen Geschichte). 2 vols., Stuttgart, 1894-96.

Halphen, L., *Les barbares* (Peuples et civilisations, V). 2nd ed., Paris, 1930.

Hefele, C. J. von, *Konziliengeschichte,* 7 vols. 2nd ed. in 6 vols., Freiburg i/B., 1873-90; cont. by J. A. C. Hergenröther, vols. 8-9, 1887-90. *Eng. trans. by W. R. Clark: *History of the Christian Councils,* I-V (to 787), Edinburgh, 1871-96. Trans. into French, augmented and revised by H. Leclerq: *Histoire des conciles,* Paris, 1908 sqq.

*Labriolle, P. de, Bardy, G., Plinval, G. de, and Bréhier, L., *De la mort de Théodose à l'élection de Grégoire le Grand* (Fliche-Martin: *Histoire de l'église,* IV). Paris, 1937.

*Latourette, K. S., *A History of the Expansion of Christianity,* I-II. New York, 1937-38.

Lot, F., Pfister, C., Ganshof, L., *Les destinées de l'empire en Occident de 395 à 898* (Glotz, G.: Histoire générale, moyen âge, I). Paris, 1928.
Manitius, M., *Geschichte der lateinischen Literatur des Mittelalters:* I, *Von Justinian bis zur Mitte des dreizehnten Jahrhunderts.* Munich, 1911.
Schnürer, G., *Die Anfänge der abendländischen Völkergemeinschaft* (Geschichte der führenden Völker, No. 11). Freiburg i/B., 1932.
Schubert, H. von, *Geschichte der christlichen Kirche im Frühmittelalter.* Tübingen, 1921.
Steinbüchel, T., *Christliches Mittelalter.* 1935.
Wattenbach, W., *Deutschlands Geschichtsquellen im Mittelalter,* I, ed. by R. Holtzmann. Stuttgart, 1938-43.

CHAPTER ONE

GERMANIC ARIANISM AND ROMAN CATHOLICISM

Leges Burgundionum, ed. by Salis (*Mon. Germ. Leges,* I, 2). 1892.
Leges Langobardorum: Edictus Theoderici, ed. by F. Bluhme (*Mon. Germ. Leges,* fol. IV and V). 1869-75.
Leges Visigothorum, ed. by K. Zeumer (*Mon. Germ. Leges,* I, 1). 1902.
Lex Romana Visigothorum, ed. by G. Haenel. Leipzig, 1847.

Apollinaris Sidonius, *Epistolae et carmina,* ed. by C. Luetjohann (*Mon. Germ. hist. Auct. ant.,* VIII).
Avitus, Bishop of Vienne, *Opera.* Ed. by R. Peiper (*Mon. Germ. hist. Auct. ant.,* VI, 2); ed. by U. Chevalier (Oeuvres complètes). Lyon, 1890.
Binding, C., *Geschichte des burgundischen Königreiches.* Leipzig, 1874.
Blasel, C., "Übertritt der Langobarden zum Christentum" (Archiv für katholisches Kirchenrecht, 83 [1903]).
———, "Die kirchlichen Zustände Italiens zur Zeit Gregors des Grossen" (ibid., 84 [1904]).
Brunner, H., *Deutsche Rechtsgeschichte,* I. 2nd ed., Munich, 1906; II, rev. by C. von Schwerin. 2nd ed., 1927.
*Bury, J. B., *The Invasion of Europe by the Barbarians,* ed. by F. J. C. Hearnshaw. London, 1928.
Dahn, F., *Die Könige der Germanen.* 13 vols. in different editions, Leipzig, 1870-1911.
Duchesne, L., "Les évêchés d'Italie et l'invasion lombarde" (Melanges d'archéologie et d'histoire, XXIII [1903], XXV [1905]).
*Ensslin, W., *Theoderich der Grosse.* Munich, 1947.
Fulgentius, Bishop of Ruspe, *Contra Arianos ad Thrasamundum regem Vandalorum* (Migne, *P. L.,* LXV).
Gabotto, F., *Storia della Italia occidentale nel medio evo,* I. Pinerolo, 1911.
García Villada, Z., *Historia ecclesiastica de España,* II. Madrid, 1932.
Görres, F., "Kirche und Staat im Vandalenreiche" (Deutsche Zeitschrift für Geschichtswissenschaft, 10 [1893]).

————, "Kirche und Staat im Westgotenreich bis auf Leovigild" (Theologische Studien und Kritiken, 66 [1893]).

Gregory the Great, Saint, *Opera* (Migne, *P. L.*, LXXV-LXXIX).

————, *Epistolae,* ed. by P. Ewald and L. M. Hartmann (*Mon. Germ. Epp.,* I).

Halban, A. von, *Das römische Recht in den germanischen Volksstaaten.* 3 vols., Breslau, 1899-1907.

Hartmann, L. M., *Geschichte Italiens im Mittelalter,* II, 1-2. Gotha, 1900-02.

Helfferich, A., *Der westgotische Arianismus und die spanische Ketzergeschichte.* Berlin, 1860.

Hodgkin, T., *Italy and Her Invaders.* 8 vols. in 9, Oxford, 1880-99; I-VI in 2nd ed., 1892-1916.

Hydatius de Lamego, *Chronicon,* ed. by T. Mommsen (*Mon. Germ. hist. Auct. ant.,* XI).

Isidore, Saint, *Opera.* Ed. by F. Arevalo. 7 vols., Rome, 1797-1803; Migne, *P. L.,* LXXXI-LXXXIV.

————, *Historia de regibus Gothorum, Vandalorum, et Suevorum* and *Chronicon,* ed. by T. Mommsen (*Mon. Germ. hist. Auct. ant.,* XI).

Jahn, A., *Geschichte der Burgundionen und Burgundiens.* 2 vols., Halle, 1874.

John of Biclaro, Bishop of Gerona, *Chronicon,* ed. by T. Mommsen (*Mon. Germ. hist. Auct. ant.,* XI).

Leclercq, H., *L'Afrique chrétienne.* 2 vols., 2nd ed., Paris, 1904.

————, *L'Espagne chrétienne.* 2nd ed., Paris, 1906.

*McKenna, S., *Paganism and Pagan Survivals in Spain up to the Fall of the Visigothic Kingdom.* Washington, 1938.

Magnin, E., *L'église visigothique au VIIe siècle.* Paris, 1912.

Mansi, J. D., et al., *Sacrorum conciliorum nova et amplissima collectio,* XI-XII.

Mansion, J., "Les origines du christianisme chez les Goths" (Analecta Bollandiana, 33 [1914]).

Martin, Saint, Bishop of Braga, *Opera,* ed. by C. W. Barlow. New Haven-London, 1950.

————, *De correctione rusticorum,* ed. by C. P. Caspari. Christiania, 1883.

Martroye, F., *L'occident à l'époque byzantine: Goths et Vandales.* Paris, 1904.

Paulus Diaconus, *Historia gentis Langobardorum,* ed. by G. Waitz (*Mon. Germ. Hist. SS. rer. langobard.*). *Eng. trans. by W. D. Foulke: *History of the Langobards by Paul the Deacon,* Philadelphia, 1907.

Pfeilschifter, G., *Theoderich der Grosse und die katholische Kirche.* Münster, 1896.

————, *Theoderich der Grosse.* Mainz, 1910.

Schmidt, L., *Allgemeine Geschichte der germanischen Völker bis zur Mitte des sechsten Jahrhunderts* (Handbuch der mittelalterlichen und neueren Geschichte). Munich, 1909.

————, *Die germanischen Reiche der Völkerwanderung* (Wissenschaft und Bildung). 2nd ed., Leipzig, 1918.

————, *Geschichte der deutschen Stämme bis zum Ausgang der Völkerwanderung: Die Ostgermanen.* 2nd ed., Münster, 1934; rev. reprint, 1941; *Die Westgermanen,* I., 2nd ed., and II, 1938-40.

————, *Geschichte der Wandalen.* 2nd ed., Leipzig, 1942.

Schröder, R., *Lehrbuch der deutschen Rechtsgeschichte.* 6th ed., Berlin-Leipzig, 1922.

Schubert, H. von, *Das älteste germanische Christentum und der sogenannte Arianismus der Germanen.* Tübingen, 1909.

————, "Die Anfänge des Christentums bei den Burgundern" (Sitz.-Berichte der Heidelberger Akademie, 1911).

————, *Staat und Kirche in den arianischen Königreichen und im Reiche Chlodwigs* (Historische Bibliothek, No. 26). Munich-Berlin, 1912.

Secrétan, E., *Le premier royaume de Bourgogne.* Lausanne, 1868.

Streitberg, W., *Die gotische Bibel.* 2 vols., Heidelberg, 1908-10.

Victor, Bishop of Vita, *Historia persecutionis Africae provinciae,* ed. by C. Halm (*Mon. Germ. hist. Auct. ant.,* III, 1); ed. by M. Petschenig (*C. S. E. L.,* VII), Leipzig, 1881.

Vigilius, Bishop of Thapsus, *Contra Arianos, Sabellianos et Photinianos.* Migne, *P. L.,* LXII.

Wietersheim, E. von, and Dahn, F., *Geschichte der Völkerwanderung.* 2 vols., 2nd ed., Leipzig, 1880-81.

Zeiller, J., "Les églises ariennes de Rome à l'époque de la domination gothique" (Mélanges d'archéologie et d'histoire, XXIV [1904]).

————, "Étude sur l'arianisme en Italie à l'époque osthrogothique et à l'époque lombarde" (ibid., XXV [1905]).

Ziegler, A. K., *Church and State in Visigothic Spain* (dissertation). Washington, 1930.

CHAPTER TWO

THE CATHOLIC FRANKISH KINGDOM IN THE SIXTH CENTURY

Concilia aevi Merovingici, ed. by F. Maassen (*Mon. Germ. Leges,* Sect. III). 1893.

Epistolae Merovingici et Karolini aevi, I (*Mon. Germ. Epp.,* III). 1892.

Formulae Merovingici et Karolini aevi, ed. by K. Zeumer (*Mon. Germ.*). 1886.

Lex Salica, ed. by H. Geffcken. Leipzig, 1898.

Scriptores rerum Merovingicarum, I-VII (*Mon. Germ.*). 1885-1920.

Arnold, C., *Cäsarius von Arelate und die gallische Kirche seiner Zeit.* Leipzig, 1894.

Auriac, J. d', *La nationalité française.* Paris, 1913.

*Beck, H. G. J., *The Pastoral Care of Souls in Southeast France during the Sixth Century* (Analecta Gregoriana, No. 51). Rome, 1950.

Bernoulli, C. A., *Die Heiligen der Merowinger.* Tübingen, 1900.

*Brogan, O., *Roman Gaul.* Cambridge, Mass., 1953.

Caesarius of Arles, *Opera.* Migne, *P. L.,* XXXIX and LXVII.

Dahn, F., *Die Könige der Germanen:* VII, 1-3, *Die Franken unter den Merowingern.* Leipzig, 1894-95.

*Dill, S., *Roman Society in Gaul in the Merovingian Age.* London, 1926.

Duchesne, L., *Fastes épiscopaux de l'ancienne Gaule.* 3 vols., Paris, 1894-1915.

Fustel de Coulanges, N. D., *Histoire des institutions politiques de l'ancienne France:* II, *L'invasion germanique et la fin de l'empire;* III, *La monarchie franque.* 3rd ed., Paris, 1911-12.

Gregory of Tours, Saint, *Opera,* ed. by W. Arndt, M. Bonnet, and B. Krusch (*Mon. Germ. SS. rer. merov.,* I). 1884-85.

*————, *Historiae Francorum libri X,* Eng. trans. by O. M. Dalton: *The History of the Franks by Gregory of Tours.* 2 vols., Oxford, 1927.

*Haarhoff, T., *Schools of Gaul: A Study of Pagan and Christian Education in the Last Century of the Western Empire.* Oxford, 1920.

Hauck, A., *Bischofswahlen unter den Merowingern.* Erlangen, 1888.

————, *Kirchengeschichte Deutschlands,* I. 6th ed., Leipzig, 1922.

*Holmes, T. S., *The Origin and Development of the Christian Church in Gaul during the First Six Centuries of the Christian Era.* London, 1911.

Imbart de la Tour, P., "Les paroisses rurales dans l'ancienne France" (Revue historique, 60-61 [1896]).

Koebner, R., *Venantius Fortunatus, seine Persönlichkeit und seine Stellung in der geistigen Kultur des Merowingerreiches.* Leipzig, 1915.

Kurth, G., *Saint Clotilda,* Eng. trans. by V. M. Crawford. London, 1906.

————, *Clovis,* 2 vols., 3rd ed. Brussels, 1923.

    (Concerning the baptism of Clovis, see the following: B. Krusch: *Neues Archiv,* 49 [1932]; L. Saltet: *Bulletin de littérature ecclésiastique,* 33 (1932); W. von den Steinen: *Historisches Jahrbuch,* 53 (1932), and *Mitteilungen des österreichischen Instituts, Ergänzungsband* 12 (1933); L. Levillain: *Revue d'histoire de l'église de France,* 21 [1935].)

Lavisse, E., *Histoire de France,* II, 1. Paris, 1903.

Lesne, E., *Histoire de la propriété ecclésiastique en France:* I, *Époques romaine et mérovingienne* (Mémoires et travaux preparés par des professeurs de Lille, Fasc. VI). Lille, 1910.

Loebell, J. W., *Gregor von Tours und seine Zeit.* 2nd ed., Leipzig, 1869.

Löning, E., *Geschichte des deutschen Kirchenrechts:* II, *Das Kirchenrecht im Reiche der Merowinger.* Strassburg, 1878.

Malnory, A., *St. Césaire, évêque d'Arles, 503-543.* Paris, 1894.

Marignan, A., *Études sur la civilisation française:* I, *La société mérovingienne;* II, *Le culte des saints sous les Mérovingiens.* 2 vols., Paris, 1899.

Meyer aus Speyer, W., "Der Gelegenheitsdichter Venantius Fortunatus" (Abhandlungen der Gesellschaft der Wissenschaft zu Göttingen: Phil.-hist. Klasse, N. F. IV). 1901.

Molinier, A., *Les sources de l'histoire de France.* 6 vols., Paris, 1901-06.

Pirenne, H., "De l'état de l'instruction des laïques à l'époque mérovingienne" (Revue bénédictine, 46 [1934]).

Schaub, F., *Studien zur Geschichte der Sklaverei im frühen Mittelalter.* Berlin, 1913.

Stutz, U., *Geschichte des kirchlichen Benefizialwesens* I. Berlin, 1895.

Ueding, L., *Geschichte der Klostergründungen der frühen Merowinger-zeit* (Historische Studien, No. 261). Berlin, 1935.

Vacandard, E., "Les élections épiscopales sous les Mérovingiens" (Revue des questions historiques, 63 [1898]).

———, "L'idolâtrie en Gaule au VIe et au VIIe siècle" (ibid., 65 [1899]).

Venantius Fortunatus, *Opera,* ed. by F. Leo and B. Krusch (*Mon. Germ. Auct. ant.,* IV, 1). 1881.

Waitz, G., *Deutsche Verfassungsgeschichte,* II. 3rd ed., Berlin, 1882.

Weyl, R., *Das fränkische Staatskirchenrecht zur Zeit der Merowinger* (Untersuchungen zur deutschen Staats- und Rechtsgeschichte, vol. 27). Breslau, 1888; reprinted, 1935.

Wieruszowski, W., "Die Zusammensetzung des gallischen und fränkischen Episkopates bis zum Vertrag von Verdun" (Bonner Jahrbücher, 127 [1922]).

CHAPTER THREE

THE ACTIVITY OF THE IRISH MISSIONARIES — DECLINE OF THE FRANKISH CHURCH

Hisperica famina, ed. by F. J. H. Jenkinson. Cambridge, 1908.

The Tripartite Life of Patrick, with Other Documents, ed. and trans. by W. Stokes, 2 vols. (Rolls Series), London, 1887. *More recent ed. by K. Mulchrone (Royal Irish Academy), Dublin, 1939.

Vitae S. Galli, Fridolini, Hrodberti, Haimrhammi et Corbiniani, Kiliani, Andomari, Amandi, Eligii (*Mon. Germ. SS. rer. merov.,* III-VI).

Adamnan, Saint, *Vita Sancti Columbae.* Best ed. by J. T. Fowler; 2nd ed., Oxford, 1921. *Eng. translations: by W. Reeves: *The Life of Saint Columba by Adamnan,* Edinburgh, 1874; by W. Huyshe (New Universal Library), London, 1906.

Bauerreiss, R., "Irische Frühmissionäre in Südbayern" (Wissenschaftliche Festgabe zum 1200 jährigen Jubiläum des hl. Korbinian, ed. by J. Schlecht). Munich, 1924.

Bellesheim, A., *Geschichte der katholischen Kirche in Irland,* I, Mainz, 1890.

———, *History of the Catholic Church in Scotland,* trans. by O. Hunter-Blair. Edinburgh-London, 1887.

*Bieler, L., *The Life and Legend of Saint Patrick.* Dublin, 1949.

Bigelmair, A., "Die Anfänge des Christentums in Bayern" (Festgabe für A. Knöpfler). Munich, 1907.

Brunner, H., *Deutsche Rechtsgeschichte:* I, 2nd ed., Munich, 1906; II, rev. by C. von Schwerin, 2nd ed., 1927.

Bury, J. B., *The Life of St. Patrick and His Place in History.* London, 1905.

Camerlinck, O. P., *Saint Léger, évêque d'Autun, 616-678* (Les Saints). Paris, 1910.

Columban, Saint, *Regula monachorum S. Columbani abbatis; Regula coeno-bialis S. Columbani aut Ordo S. Columbani de vita et actione mona-chorum; Poenitentiale Columbani;* all three ed. by O. Seebass (Zeitschrift für Kirchengeschichte, XIV [1894], XV [1895], XVII [1897]).

——, *Epistolae,* ed. by W. Gundlach (*Mon. Germ. Epp.,* III).

Du Moulin-Eckart, R., *Leudegar, Bischof von Autun* (dissertation). Bres-lau, 1890.

Finsterwalder, P. W., "Die Wege und Ziele der irischen und angelsäch-sischen Mission im fränkischen Reich" (Zeitschrift für Kirchenge-schichte, XLVIII [1928]).

Fournier, P., "Étude sur les pénitentiels" (Revue d'histoire et de littérature religieuse, VI-IX [1901-04]).

——, "De l'influence de la collection canonique irlandaise sur la forma-tion des collections canoniques" (Nouvelle revue historique du droit français et étranger, XXIII [1899]).

——, "Le liber ex lege Moysi et les tendances bibliques du droit canoni-que irlandais" (Revue celtique, XXX [1909]).

Frank, H., *Die Klosterbischöfe des Frankenreiches.* Münster, 1932.

Fredegarius, *Libri chronicarum quae dicuntur Fredegarii Scholastici,* ed. by B. Krusch (*Mon. Germ. SS. rer. merov.,* II).

*Fuhrmann, J. P., *Irish Medieval Monasteries on the Continent* (disserta-tion). Washington, 1927.

Funk, F. X., "Zur Geschichte der altbritischen Kirche" (Historisches Jahr-buch, IV [1883]).

Fustel de Coulanges, N. D., *Histoire des institutions politiques de l'an-cienne France:* V, *Les origines du système féodal — le bénéfice et le patronat pendant l'époque mérovingienne,* rev. and re-edited by C. Jullian. 4th ed., Paris, 1914.

Gildas, *De excidio et conquestu Britanniae,* ed. by T. Mommsen (*Mon. Germ. Auct. ant.,* XIII).

Gougaud, L., *Les chrétientés celtiques,* 2nd ed., Paris, 1911. *Eng. trans. by M. Joynt: *Christianity in Celtic Lands,* London, 1932.

*——, *Gaelic Pioneers of Christianity: The Work and Influence of Irish Monks and Saints in Continental Europe* (VI-XII century), Eng. trans. by V. Collins. Dublin, 1923.

——, "L'oeuvre des Scotti dans l'Europe continentale," (Revue d'histoire ecclésiastique, IX [1908]).

——, "Les scribes monastiques d'Irlande au travail" (ibid., XXVII [1931]).

*Graham, H., *The Early Irish Monastic Schools.* Dublin, 1923.

Hauck, A., *Kirchengeschichte Deutschlands,* I. 6th ed., Leipzig, 1922.

*Healy, J., *Ireland's Ancient Schools and Scholars.* 5th ed., Dublin, 1908.

*Henry, F., *Irish Art in the Early Christian Period.* London, 1940.

Inama-Sternegg, K. T. von, *Deutsche Wirtschaftsgeschichte,* I. 2nd ed., Leipzig, 1909.

Jonas of Bobbio, *Vita S. Columbani.* Ed. by B. Krusch (*Scriptores rerum germanicarum in usum scholarum*), 1905. *Eng. trans.: *The Life of St.*

Columban (Translations and Reprints from Original Sources in European History, Dept. of History, University of Pennsylvania, Vol. II, No. 7), Philadelphia, 1895.

Jungmann, J. A., *Die lateinischen Bussriten in ihrer geschichtlichen Entwicklung*. Innsbruck, 1933.

Kenney, J. F., *The Sources for the Early History of Ireland*, I. New York, 1929.

Laux, J. J., *Der hl. Columban*. Freiburg i/B., 1919.

Lesne, E., *Histoire de la propriété ecclésiastique en France:* II, *La propriété ecclésiastique et les droits régaliens à l'époque carolingienne;* Fasc. I: *Les étapes de la sécularisation des biens de l'église du VIIIe au Xe siècle* (Mémoires et travaux preparés par des professeurs de Lille, Fasc. XIX). Lille, 1922.

Levison, W., "Die Iren und die fränkische Kirche" (Historische Zeitschrift, 109 [1912]).

Löning, E., *Geschichte des deutschen Kirchenrechts:* II, *Das Kirchenrecht im Reiche der Merowinger*. Strassburg, 1878.

*Macgregor, M. B., *The Sources and Literature of Scottish Church History*. Glasgow, 1934.

*McNeill, J. T., *The Celtic Penitentials and Their Influence on Continental Christianity*. Paris, 1923.

*McNeill, J. T., and Gamer, H. M., *Medieval Handbooks of Penance*. New York, 1938.

*Mahr, A., and Raftery, J., *Christian Art in Ancient Ireland*. 2 vols., Dublin, 1932-41.

Malnory, A., *Quid Luxovienses monachi ad regulam monasteriorum et ad communem ecclesiam profectum contulerint*. Paris, 1894.

Martin, E., *St. Columban* (Les Saints). Paris, 1905.

Meyer, K., "Bruchstücke der älteren Lyrik Irlands" (Abhandlungen der Berliner Akademie, Phil.-hist. Klasse, 1919).

———, *Die Irisch-gälische Literatur* (Die Kultur der Gegenwart).

*———, *Learning in Ireland in the Fifth Century, and the Transmission of Letters* (lecture). Dublin, 1913.

Mühlbacher, E., *Deutsche Geschichte unter den Karolingern*. Stuttgart, 1896.

Patrick, Saint, *Libri Sancti Patricii: The Latin Writings of Saint Patrick*. Ed. and trans. by N. J. D. White (Proceedings of the Royal Irish Academy: 25, sect. C, No. 7), Dublin, 1905; *more recent ed. by L. Bieler (Classica et Mediaevalia, XI and XII), 1950-51.

*———, *The Works of Saint Patrick. St. Secundinus' Hymn on St. Patrick*, trans. by L. Bieler (Ancient Christian Writers, No. 17). Westminster (Md.)-London, 1953.

Pfister, K., *Irische Buchmalerei*. Potsdam, 1930.

*Pochin-Mould, D. D. C., *Ireland of the Saints*. London, 1954.

Porter, A. K., *The Crosses and Culture of Ireland*. New Haven, 1931.

Ribbeck, K., *Die sogenannte Divisio des fränkischen Kirchengutes* (University of Leipzig dissertation). Berlin, 1883.

Robert, B., *Étude critique sur la vie et l'oeuvre de St. Patrick* (dissertation). Paris, 1883.

*Robinson, S., *Celtic Illuminated Art*. Dublin, 1908.

Roger, M., *L'enseignement des lettres classiques d'Ausone à Alcuin*. Paris, 1905.

Roth, P., *Geschichte des Beneficialwesens*. Erlangen, 1850.

————, "Die Säkularisation des Kirchengutes" (Münchener Historisches Jahrbuch, I [1865]).

Ryan, J., *Irish Monasticism: Origins and Early Development*. Dublin-Cork, 1931.

Sauer, E., "Die Anfänge des Christentums und der Kirche in Baden" (Neujahrsblätter der Bad. hist. Kommission). Heidelberg, 1911.

Schröder, R., *Lehrbuch der deutschen Rechtsgeschichte*. 6th ed., Berlin-Leipzig, 1922.

Schultze, W., "Die Bedeutung der iro-schottischen Mönche für die Erhaltung und Fortpflanzung der mittelalterlichen Wissenschaft" (Zentralblatt für Bibliothekswesen, VI [1889]).

*Simpson, W. D., *The Celtic Church in Scotland*. Aberdeen, 1935.

*————, *The Historical Saint Columba*. 2nd ed., Aberdeen, 1927.

*————, *St. Ninian and the Origins of the Christian Church in Scotland*. Edinburgh, 1940.

Stangl, T., *Virgiliana*. Munich, 1891.

*Stokes, G. T., *Ireland and the Celtic Church* (to 1172). 7th ed., London, 1928.

*Stokes, M., *Early Christian Art in Ireland*. 4th ed., Dublin, 1933.

*Sullivan, E., *The Book of Kells*. 5th ed., London-New York, 1952.

Virgilius Maro, *Opera*, ed. by J. Huemer. Leipzig, 1886.

Waitz, G., *Verfassungsgeschichte*, II, 3rd ed.; III, 2nd ed. Berlin, 1882-83.

Wasserschleben, H., *Die Bussordnungen der abendländischen Kirche*. Halle, 1851.

————, *Die irische Kanonensammlung*. 2nd ed., Leipzig, 1851.

*Watkins, O. D., *A History of Penance to A. D. 1215*. 2 vols., London, 1920.

Zettinger, J., "Das Poenitentiale Cummeani" (Archiv für katholisches Kirchenrecht, 82 [1902]).

Zimmer, H., "Galliens Anteil an Irlands Christianisierung im vierten und fünften Jahrhundert und altirischer Bildung" (Sitz.-Berichte der Berliner Akademie, 1909).

————, "Keltische Kirche" (Realenzyklopädie für protestantische Theologie und Kirche, X, 3rd ed., Leipzig, 1901). *Eng. trans. by A. Meyer: *The Celtic Church in Britain and Ireland*, London, 1912.

————, "Sprache und Literatur der Kelten" (Die Kultur der Gegenwart, I, Abt. XI, 1). Berlin, 1909.

————, "Über die Bedeutung des irischen Elementes für die mittelalterliche Kultur" (Preuss. Jahrbücher, 59 [1887]). *Eng. trans. by J. L. Edmonds: *The Irish Element in Medieval Culture*, New York, 1891; reprint, London, 1913.

Chapter Four

GREGORY THE GREAT —
THE ROMAN BENEDICTINE MISSIONARIES IN ENGLAND

Aldhelm, *Opera,* ed. by R. Ehwald (*Mon. Germ. Auct. ant.,* XV). 1913.

Batiffol, P., *St. Grégoire le Grand* (Les Saints). 2nd ed., Paris, 1928.

Bede, The Venerable, *Opera.* Migne, *P. L.,* XC-XCV.

————, *Complete Works,* ed. with trans. by J. A. Giles. 12 vols., London, 1843-44.

————, *Chronica,* ed. by T. Mommsen (*Mon. Germ. Auct. ant.,* XIII). Berlin, 1898.

————, *Historia ecclesiastica.* Best ed. by C. Plummer, 2 vols., Oxford, 1896. *Best Eng. trans. by A. M. Sellar, London, 1912.

Brandl, A., *Geschichte der altenglischen Literatur:* I, *Pauls Grundriss.* 2nd ed., Strassburg, 1908.

*Bréhier, L., and Aigrain, R., *Grégoire le Grand: Les états barbares et la conquête arabe* (590-757) (Fliche-Martin: *Histoire de l'église,* V). Paris, 1938.

Brou, A., *St. Augustin de Cantorbéry et ses compagnons* (Les Saints). 5th ed., Paris, 1900.

Brown, B., *The Arts in Early England:* I, *Ecclesiastical Architecture in England from the Conversion of the Saxons to the Norman Conquest;* II, *The Life of Saxon England in its Relation to the Arts.* London, 1903.

*Browne, G. F., *Augustine and His Companions.* 2nd ed., London, 1897.

————, *The Conversion of the Heptarchy.* 2nd ed., London, 1906.

Byrne, Sister Mary of the Incarnation, *The Tradition of the Nun in Medieval England.* Washington, 1932.

Cabrol, F., *L'Angleterre chrétienne avant les Normands.* 2nd ed., Paris, 1909.

Caspar, E., *Geschichte des Papsttums,* II. Tübingen, 1933.

*Duckett, E. S., *Anglo-Saxon Saints and Scholars.* London, 1947.

Dudden, F. H., *Gregory the Great: His Place in History and Thought.* 2 vols., London, 1905.

Eddius Stephanus, *Vita S. Wilfridi,* ed. by W. Levison (*Mon. Germ. SS. rer. merov.,* VI). *Ed. with Eng. trans. by B. Colgrave: *The Life of Bishop Wilfrid by Eddius Stephanus,* London-Cambridge, 1927.

Finsterwalder, W., *Die Canones Theodori Cantuariensis.* Weimar, 1929.

*Gasquet, A., *The Mission of St. Augustine.* London, 1924.

Gregory the Great, Saint, *Opera omnia studio monachorum O. S. B. e Congregatione S. Mauri.* 4 vols., Paris, 1705; Migne, *P. L.,* LXXV-LXXIX.

————, *Dialogi: Libri IV,* ed. by U. Moricca (Fonti per la storia d'Italia, LVII). Rome, 1924.

————, *Registrum epistolarum,* ed. by P. Ewald and L. M. Hartmann (*Mon. Germ. Epp.,* I-II). Berlin, 1891-99.

Grein, M., and Wülker, R. P., *Bibliothek der angelsächsischen Poesie.* 3 vols., Kassel, 1881-98.

Grisar, H., "Die Gregor-Biographie des Paulus Diaconus in ihrer ursprüng-
lichen Gestalt" (Zeitschrift für kath. Theologie, XI [1887]).

――――, "Il pontificato di Gregorio Magno" (Civiltà cattolica, V [1890]).

Gross, C., *The Sources and Literature of English History from the Earliest
Times to about 1485.* 2nd ed., New York-London, 1915.

Haddan, A. W., and Stubbs, W., *Councils and Ecclesiastical Documents
Relating to Great Britain and Ireland.* 3 vols., Oxford, 1869-78.

Hodgkin, R. H., *A History of the Anglo-Saxons.* 2 vols., Oxford, 1935.

Hörmann, W. von, "Bussbücherstudien" (Zeitschrift der Savigny-Stiftung
für Rechtsgeschichte: Kanonische Abteilung, 32-34 [1911-13]).

*Howorth, H. H., *The Golden Days of the Early English Church from the
Arrival of Theodore to the Death of Bede.* 3 vols., London, 1917.

――――, *St. Augustine of Canterbury* (Birth of the English Church, II).
London, 1913.

――――, *St. Gregory the Great.* London, 1912.

Hunt, W., *The English Church from Its Foundation to the Norman Conquest.* 2nd ed., London, 1907.

*Jeudwine, J. W., *First Twelve Centuries of British Story: Social and
Political Conditions in the British Islands from 56 B. C. to 1154 A. D.*
London-New York, 1912.

Joannes Diaconus, *Vita S. Gregorii* (Gregorii Opera, IV). Migne, *P. L.,*
LXXV.

Krusch, B., "Die Einführung des griechischen Paschalritus im Abendlande"
(Neues Archiv der Gesellschaft für ältere deutsche Geschichte, IX
[1883]).

Liebermann, F., *Die Gesetze der Angelsachsen.* 3 vols., Halle, 1903-16.

*Lietzmann, H., *Das Sacramentarium Gregorianum nach dem Aachener
Urexemplar.* Münster, 1921.

Montalembert, C. F. R. de, *Les moines d'Occident,* 7 vols., 6th ed., Paris,
1878-82. *Eng. trans.: *The Monks of the West,* 7 vols., Edinburgh,
1861-79; ed. with introd. by F. A. Gasquet, 6 vols., London, 1896.

*Norberg, D., *In Registrum Gregorii Magni studia critica.* 2 vols., Uppsala,
1937-39.

Oakley, T. P., *English Penitential Discipline and Anglo-Saxon Law.* New
York, 1923.

Obser, K., *Wilfrid der Aeltere.* Karlsruhe, 1884.

*Oman, C., *England before the Norman Conquest.* London, 1910.

*Peitz, W. M., *Das Register Gregors I.* Freiburg i/B., 1917.

*Reed, T. D., *The Rise of Wessex.* London, 1947.

Schmid, J., *Die Osterfestberechnung auf den britischen Inseln* (University
of Königsberg dissertation). Regensburg, 1904.

――――, *Die Osterberechnung in der abendländischen Kirche vom Konzil
von Nicäa bis zum Ende des achten Jahrhunderts* (Strassburger Theol.
Studien, IX, No. 1). Freiburg i/B., 1907.

Seppelt, F. X., *Geschichte des Papsttums,* II. Leipzig, 1934.

*Snow, A., *St. Gregory the Great, His Work and His Spirit.* 2nd ed.,
London-New York, 1924.

*Spearing, E., *The Patrimony of the Roman Church in the Time of Gregory the Great.* Cambridge, 1918.

*Stenton, F. M., *Anglo-Saxon England.* Oxford, 1943.

Stuhlfath, W., "Gregor der Grosse: sein Leben bis zu seiner Wahl zum Papste" (Heidelberger Abhandlungen, 39 [1913]). Heidelberg, 1914.

Thompson, A. H., *Bede, His Life, Times and Writings.* London, 1935.

Wasserschleben, H., *Die Bussordnungen der abendländischen Kirche.* Halle, 1851.

Werner, K., *Beda der Ehrwürdige und seine Zeit.* 2nd ed., Vienna, 1881.

*Wilson, H. A., *The Gregorian Sacramentary.* London, 1915.

Winkelmann, E., *Geschichte der Angelsachsen.* Berlin, 1883.

Wolfsgruber, C., *Gregor der Grosse.* 2nd ed., Regensburg, 1897.

Würdinger, H., "Einwirkung des Christentums auf das angelsächsische Recht" (Zeitschrift der Savigny-Stiftung für Rechtsgeschichte: Germ. Abteilung, 55 [1935]).

CHAPTER FIVE

SAINT BONIFACE AND THE PAPACY

Concilia aevi Carolini, ed. by A. Werminghoff (*Mon. Germ. Conc.,* II, 1). 1906.

Vita Stae. Leobae, ed. by G. Waitz. *Mon. Germ. SS.,* XV, 1.

Vita Sti. Sturmi, composed by Eigil. Ibid., II.

Vita Willibaldi et Wynnebaldi, composed by a nun of Heidenheim, ed. by O. Holder-Egger. Ibid., XV, 1.

Vita Willibrordi, composed by Alcuin. Ed. by A. Poncelet (*Acta SS.,* Nov. III), 1910; *Liber I,* ed. by W. Levison (*Mon. Germ. SS. rer. merov.,* VII), 1919; *Liber II metricus,* ed. by E. Dümmler (*Mon. Germ. Poetae Carolini,* I), 1881.

Vitae Sti. Bonifatii. Ed. by W. Levison (*Mon. Germ. SS. rer. germanicarum*), Hanover, 1905; trans. into German by M. Tangl, 3rd ed., 1920. *Eng. trans. by G. W. Robinson: *The Life of St. Boniface by Willibald* (Harvard Translations), Cambridge, 1916.

Boehmer, J. F., and Mühlbacher, E., *Regesten des Kaiserreiches unter den Karolingern.* 2nd ed., Innsbruck, 1908.

Boniface, Saint, *Opera.* Ed. by J. A. Giles, 2 vols., London, 1844; Migne, *P. L.,* XCIX.

Boniface, Saint, and Lullus, *Epistolae,* ed. by M. Tangl (Epistolae selectae in usum scholarum), Berlin, 1916. *Eng. trans. by E. Emerton: *The Letters of Saint Boniface* (Records of Civilization, Sources and Studies, No. 31), New York, 1940; *see also *The English Letters of St. Boniface,* ed. by E. Kylie (King's Classics), London, 1911.

Breysig, T., *Jahrbücher des fränkischen Reiches unter Karl Martell (714-41).* Leipzig, 1869.

*Browne, G. F., *Boniface of Crediton.* London, 1910.

Caspar, E., *Geschichte des Papsttums*, II. Tübingen, 1933.

*Crawford, S., *Anglo-Saxon Influence of Western Christendom* (600-800). Oxford, 1933.

*Grieve, A., *Willibrord*. London, 1923.

Hahn, H., *Bonifaz und Lul: ihre angelsächsischen Korrespondenten*. Leipzig, 1883.

——, *Jahrbücher des fränkischen Reiches (741-52)*. Berlin, 1863.

Hauck, A., *Kirchengeschichte Deutschlands*, I. 6th ed., Leipzig, 1922.

Jecker, G., *Die Heimat des hl. Pirmin, des Apostels der Alamannen* (with new ed. of the "Scarapsus"). Münster, 1927.

*Koch, H., *Die Stellung des heiligen Bonifatius zur Bildung und Wissenschaft*. Braunsberg, 1905.

Kurth, G., *Saint Boniface* (Les Saints). 4th ed., Paris, 1913.

*Lampen, W., *Saint Willibrord*. Utrecht, 1916.

Laux, J. J., *Der heilige Bonifatius, Apostel der Deutschen*. Freiburg i/B., 1922.

Levison, W., "Willibrordiana" (Neues Archiv der Gesellschaft für ältere deutsche Geschichte, 33 [1908]).

*——, *England and the Continent in the Eighth Century*. Oxford, 1946.

*Moore, W. J., *The Saxon Pilgrims to Rome and the Schola Saxonum* (dissertation). Fribourg, 1937.

Mühlbacher, E., *Deutsche Geschichte unter den Karolingern*. Stuttgart, 1896.

Nottarp, H., "Die Bistumserrichtung in Deutschland im achten Jahrhundert" (Kirchenrechtliche Abhandlungen). Stuttgart, 1920.

Oelsner, L., *Jahrbücher des fränkischen Reiches unter König Pippin*. Leipzig, 1871.

Schnürer, G., *Bonifatius: die Bekehrung der Deutschen zum Christentum* (Weltgeschichte in Charakterbildern). Mainz, 1909.

Schubert, H. von, *Geschichte der christlichen Kirche im Frühmittelalter*. Tübingen, 1921.

*Talbot, C. H., *The Anglo-Saxon Missionaries in Germany* (The Makers of Christendom, No. 2). London-New York, 1954.

Wattenbach, W., *Deutschlands Geschichtsquellen im Mittelalter*, I, new ed. by R. Holtzmann. Stuttgart, 1938-43.

CHAPTER SIX

SEPARATION OF ROME FROM CONSTANTINOPLE — THE ATTACK OF ISLAM

Codex Theodosianus. Ed. by T. Mommsen and P. M. Meyer, Berlin, 1905; ed. by P. Krüger, Berlin, 1923. *Eng. trans. by C. Pharr, in collaboration with T. S. Davidson and M. B. Pharr, Princeton, 1951.

Collectio Avellana (imperial and papal letters, 357-553), ed. by O. Guenther (*C. S. E. L.*, XXXV, 1-2). Vienna, 1895-98.

Corpus iuris civilis. Ed. by P. Krüger, T. Mommsen, J. Schoell, and G. Kroll: I, 15th ed., Berlin, 1928; II. 9th ed., Berlin, 1915; III (*Novel-*

lae), 5th ed., Berlin, 1928. *Eng. translations: by J. B. Mayle, *The Institutes of Justinian*, 5th ed., Oxford, 1913; by C. H. Monro, *The Digest of Justinian*, 2 vols., Cambridge, 1904-09.

Epistolae Romanorum pontificum genuinae et quae ad eos scriptae sunt, 461-523, ed. by A. Thiel. 2 parts, Braunsberg, 1868.

Liber pontificalis, I. Ed. by L. Duchesne, Paris, 1886; ed. by T. Mommsen (*Mon. Germ. Gesta Pontificum Romanorum*, I), 1898. *Eng. trans. by L. R. Loomis: *The Book of the Popes*, to the pontificate of Gregory I (Records of Civilization, No. 3), New York, 1916.

Alivisatos, H. S., *Die kirchliche Gesetzgebung des Kaisers Justinian I.* Berlin, 1913.

Batiffol, P., "L'empereur Justinien et le siège apostolique" (Recherches de science religieuse, VI [1926]).

Baumstark, A., *Geschichte der syrischen Literatur*. Bonn, 1922.

*Baynes, N. H., and Moss, H. S. L. B., edd., *Byzantium*. Oxford, 1949.

Becker, C. H., *Christentum und Islam*, Tübingen, 1907. *Eng. trans. by H. J. Chaytor: *Christianity and Islam*, New York, 1919.

———, *Islam-Studien: vom Werden und Wesen der islamischen Welt.* 2 vols., Leipzig, 1924-32.

Brockelmann, C., *Geschichte der arabischen Literatur*. 2 vols., Weimar, 1898-1902.

———, *Geschichte der arabischen Literatur* (Die Literaturen des Ostens, VI, 2). 2nd ed., Leipzig, 1919.

*———, *History of the Islamic People*, trans. by J. Carmichael and M. Perlmann. New York, 1947.

Bury, J. B., *History of the Later Roman Empire from Arcadius to Irene (395-800)*. 2 vols., London, 1889.

———, *History of the Later Roman Empire from the Death of Theodosius I to the Death of Justinian (395-565)*. 2 vols., London, 1923.

Caspar, E., *Geschichte des Papsttums*, II. Tübingen, 1933.

Diehl, C., *Byzance, grandeur et décadence*. Paris, 1919.

———, *Figures byzantines*, 2 vols.: I, 4th ed.; II, 3rd ed. Paris, 1909. *Eng. trans. by H. Bell: *Byzantine Portraits*, New York, 1927.

———, *Histoire de l'empire byzantin*. 12th ed., Paris, 1934.

———, *Justinien et la civilisation byzantine au VIe siècle*. Paris, 1901.

———, *Manuel d'art byzantin*. 2nd ed., 2 vols., Paris, 1925-26.

Diez, E., and Quitt, J., *Ursprung und Sieg der altbyzantinischen Kunst* (J. Strzygowski: Byzantinische Kunstdenkmäler, III). Vienna, 1903.

Duchesne, L., *L'église au VIe siècle*. Paris, 1925.

———, "Vigile et Pélage" (Revue des questions historiques, XXXV [1884]).

Gelzer, H., *Byzantinische Kulturgeschichte*. Tübingen, 1909.

———, "Das Verhältnis von Kirche und Staat in Byzanz" (Historische Zeitschrift, 86 [1900]).

*Gibb, H. A. R., *Arabic Literature: An Introduction*. London-Oxford, 1926.

Goldziher, J., *Die Religion des Islam* (Kultur der Gegenwart, I, Sec. III, 1). 2nd ed., Berlin, 1906.

Gregorovius, F., *Geschichte der Stadt Rom im Mittelalter*, 8 vols., 5th ed., Stuttgart, 1903. *Eng. trans. by A. Hamilton: *History of the City of Rome in the Middle Ages*, 8 vols. in 13, London, 1894-1902.

Grisar, H., *Geschichte Roms und der Päpste im Mittelalter*, Freiburg i/B., 1901. *Eng. trans. by L. Cappedelta: *History of Rome and the Popes in the Middle Ages*, 3 vols., St. Louis, 1911-13.

*Grunebaum, G. von, *Medieval Islam: A Study in Cultural Orientation.* Chicago, 1946.

Hartmann, L. M., *Geschichte Italiens im Mittelalter*, II. Gotha, 1903.

Hell, J., *Die Kultur der Araber* (Wissenschaft und Bildung, No. 64), 2nd ed., Leipzig, 1919. *Eng. trans. by S. Khuda Bukhsh, Cambridge, 1926.

Hertzberger, G. F., *Geschichte der Byzantiner und des osmanischen Reiches bis gegen Ende des sechszehnten Jahrhunderts.* Berlin, 1883.

Hildebrand, P., "Die Absetzung des Papstes Silverius" (Historisches Jahrbuch, XLII [1922]).

*Hitti, P. K., *History of the Arabs.* 5th ed., New York, 1952.

*Holmes, W. G., *The Age of Justinian and Theodora.* 2 vols., 2nd ed. London, 1912.

Huart, C., *Histoire des Arabes.* 3 vols., Paris, 1912-13.

———, *Littérature arabe*, 2nd ed., Paris, 1912. *Eng. trans. by M. Loyd: *History of Arabic Literature* (Short Histories of the Literature of the World), New York, 1903.

Jaffé, P., *Regesta pontificum Romanorum*, 2nd ed. by S. Loewenfeld, F. Kaltenbrunner, and P. Ewald. 2 vols., Leipzig, 1885-88.

Kehr, P., *Regesta pontificum Romanorum: Italia Pontificia*, I sqq. Berlin, 1906 sqq.

Kissling, F., *Das Verhältnis zwischen Sacerdotium und Imperium von Leo dem Grossen bis Gelasius I.* Paderborn, 1921.

Knecht, A., *Die Religionspolitik Kaiser Justinians I* (dissertation). Würzburg, 1896.

Kremer, A. von, *Geschichte der herrschenden Ideen des Islams.* Leipzig, 1868.

———, *Kulturgeschichte des Orients unter den Chalifen*, 2 vols., Vienna, 1875-77. *Partial Eng. trans. by S. Khuda Bukhsh: *The Orient under the Caliphs*, Calcutta, 1920.

Krumbacher, K., *Geschichte der byzantinischen Literatur*, 2nd ed. by A. Ehrhard and H. Gelzer. Munich, 1897.

Martroye, F., *L'occident à l'époque byzantine: Goths et Vandales.* Paris, 1904.

Müller, A., *Der Islam im Morgen- und Abendland.* 2 vols., Berlin, 1885-87.

Pargoire, J., *L'église byzantine de 527 à 847.* Paris, 1905.

Procopius of Caesarea, *Opera omnia*, ed. by J. Haury. 3 vols., Leipzig, 1905-13.

*———, *De aedificiis*, Eng. trans. by A. Stewart et al.: *Of the Buildings of Justinian* (Palestine Pilgrims Text Society). London, 1896.

*————, *De bellis*, Eng. trans. by H. B. Dewing: *Procopius, History of the Wars*, Books I-IV, 4 vols. (Loeb Library). London-New York, 1914-28.

*————, *Historia arcana*, Eng. translations: by the Athenian Society, Athens, 1906; by R. Atwater: *Secret History of Procopius*, Chicago, 1927.

Schubert, H. von, *Geschichte der christlichen Kirche im Frühmittelalter*. Tübingen, 1921.

Seppelt, F. X., *Geschichte des Papsttums*, II. Leipzig, 1934.

*Vasiliev, A. A., *History of the Byzantine Empire*. 2nd ed., Madison, 1952.

*Young, T. C., ed., *Near Eastern Culture and Society*. Princeton, 1951.

CHAPTER SEVEN

THE UNION OF PAPACY AND EMPIRE

Annales Laureshamenses, ed. by G. Pertz (*Mon. Germ. SS.*, I). Hanover, 1826.

Annales regni Francorum, ed. by F. Kurze (*Scriptores rer. germanicarum*). Hanover, 1895.

Capitularia regum Francorum, I, 1, ed. by A. Boretius (*Mon. Germ. Cap.*, I, 1). Hanover, 1881.

Codex Carolinus, ed. by F. Gundlach (*Mon. Germ. Epp.*, III). Berlin, 1892.

Concilia aevi Carolini, I, 1, ed. by A. Werminghoff (*Mon. Germ. Conc.*, II, 1). Hanover, 1906.

Epistolae: Adrian I — Leo III, ed. by K. Hampe (*Mon. Germ. Epp.*, V). Berlin, 1899.

Liber pontificalis. See preceding chapter.

Libri Carolini, ed. by H. Bastgen (*Mon. Germ. Conc.*, II, *Supplementum*). Hanover, 1924.

Abel, S., and Simson, B. von, *Jahrbücher des fränkischen Reiches unter Karl dem Grossen*. 2 vols.: I, 2nd ed., Leipzig, 1888; II, 1883.

Alcuin, *Epistolae*, ed. by E. Dümmler (*Mon. Germ. Epp.*, IV). Berlin, 1895.

Boehmer, J. F., and Mühlbacher, E., *Regesten des Kaiserreichs unter den Karolingern*. 2nd ed., Innsbruck, 1908.

Brackmann, A., "Die Erneuerung der Kaiserwürde im Jahre 800" (Geschichtliche Studien A. Hauck zum siebzigsten Geburtstag dargebracht). Leipzig, 1916.

Caspar, E., "Das Papsttum unter fränkischer Herrschaft" (Zeitschrift für Kirchengeschichte, 54 [1935]).

————, *Pippin und die römische Kirche*. Berlin, 1914.

*Duchesne, L., *The Beginnings of the Temporal Sovereignty of the Popes, 754-1073*, Eng. trans. by A. H. Mathew. London, 1908.

Eichmann, E., "Die Kaiserproklamation (800)" (Theologie und Glaube, 24 [1932]).

Einhard, *Vita Caroli Magni*, ed. by G. Waitz (*Scriptores rerum germanicarum*). 6th ed., Hanover, 1911.

Fredegar Scholasticus, *Chronica* and *Continuationes*, ed. by B. Krusch (*Mon. Germ. SS. rer. merov.,* II). Hanover, 1888.

Fustel de Coulanges, N. D., *Histoire des institutions politiques de l'ancienne France: VI, Les transformations de la royauté pendant l'époque carolingienne.* 3rd ed., Paris, 1914.

Halphen, L., *Études critiques sur Charlemagne.* Paris, 1921.

Hartmann, L. M., *Geschichte Italiens im Mittelalter,* II, 2. Gotha, 1903.

Hauck, A., *Kirchengeschichte Deutschlands,* II. 3rd and 4th ed., Leipzig, 1912.

Heldmann, K., *Das Kaisertum Karls des Grossen.* Weimar, 1929.

Kampers, F., *Karl der Grosse* (Weltgeschichte in Charakterbildern). Munich, 1910.

Ketterer, J. A., *Karl der Grosse und die Kirche.* Munich, 1889.

Kleinclausz, A., *Charlemagne.* Paris, 1934.

——, *L'empire carolingien: ses origines et ses transformations.* Paris, 1902.

Lamprecht, K., *Die römische Frage von Pippin bis Ludwig dem Frommen.* Leipzig, 1889.

Levillain, L., "Le couronnement impérial de Charlemagne" (Revue d'histoire de l'église de France, 18 [1932]).

Lilienfein, H., "Die Anschauungen von Staat und Kirche im Reiche der Karolinger" (Heidelberger Abhandlungen, I [1902]).

Molinier, A., *Les sources de l'histoire de France.* 6 vols., Paris, 1901-06.

Mühlbacher, E., *Deutsche Geschichte unter den Karolingern.* Stuttgart, 1896.

Oelsner, L., *Jahrbücher des fränkischen Reiches unter König Pippin.* Leipzig, 1871.

Ohr, W., *Die Kaiserkrönung Karls.* Tübingen, 1904.

*Russell, C. E., *Charlemagne.* London, 1931.

Schnürer, G., "Die Entstehung des Kirchenstaates" (Vereinsschrift der Görres-Gesellschaft). Cologne, 1884.

Schubert, H. von, *Geschichte der christlichen Kirche im Frühmittelalter.* Tübingen, 1921.

Sickel, W., "Das byzantinische Krönungsrecht bis zum zehnten Jahrhundert" (Byzantinische Zeitschrift, VII [1898]).

——, "Die Kaiserwahl Karls des Grossen" (Mitteilungen des Instituts für österreich. Geschichtsforschung, 20 [1899]).

Waitz, F., *Deutsche Verfassungsgeschichte,* III. 2nd ed., Berlin, 1882.

Wattenbach, W., *Deutschlands Geschichtsquellen im Mittelalter,* I, ed. by R. Holtzmann. Stuttgart, 1938-43.

*Woodruff, D., *Charlemagne.* London, 1934.

CHAPTER EIGHT

FIRST RENAISSANCE OF THE WEST —
THE GOVERNMENT OF CHARLEMAGNE

Leges Saxonum et Lex Thuringorum, ed. by C. von Schwerin (*Fontes iuris germ. ant.*). Hanover, 1918.

Lex Frisionum, ed. by K. von Richthofen (*Mon. Germ. Leges*, III). Hanover, 1863.

Libri Carolini. See preceding chapter.

Monumenta Germaniae Historica. Capitularia, I. Berlin, 1893.

Monumenta Germaniae Historica. Concilia, II, 1. Berlin, 1906.

Monumenta Germaniae Historica. Diplomata Carolina, I. Berlin, 1906.

Monumenta Germaniae Historica. Epistolae, IV-V. Berlin, 1895-99.

Monumenta Germaniae Historica. Poetae latini medii aevi, I. Berlin, 1881.

Vita Sti. Liudgeri (*Mon. Germ. SS.*, II), ed. by W. Diekamp (Geschichtsquellen des Bistums Münster. IV). Münster, 1881.

Abel, S., and Simson, B. von. See preceding chapter.

*Amann, E., *L'époque carolingienne* (Fliche-Martin: *Histoire de l'église*, VI). Paris, 1937.

*Browne, G. F., *Alcuin of York*. London, 1908.

Chrodegang, Bishop of Metz, *Regula canonicorum*. Ed. by W. Schmitz, Hanover, 1889; Migne, *P. L.*, LXXXIX.

Dehio, G., *Geschichte der deutschen Kunst*, I. 4th ed., Berlin, 1930.

Dopsch, A., *Die Wirtschaftsentwicklung der Karolingerzeit vornehmlich in Deutschland*. 2 vols., 2nd ed., Weimar, 1921-22.

*Duckett, E. S., *Alcuin, Friend of Charlemagne: His World and His Work*. New York, 1951.

Ehrismann, G., *Geschichte der deutschen Literatur: I, Die althochdeutsche Literatur*. Munich, 1918.

Einhard. See preceding chapter.

Enlart, E., *Manuel d'archéologie française: I, Architecture religieuse*. Pt. I, 2nd ed., Paris, 1919.

Fahrner, F. J., *Geschichte des Unauflöslichkeitsprinzips und der vollkommenen Scheidung der Ehe*. Freiburg i/B., 1903.

Fastlinger, M., "Die wirtschaftliche Bedeutung der bayrischen Klöster in der Zeit der Agilolfinger" (Studien und Darstellungen aus dem Gebiete der Geschichte, II). Freiburg i/B., 1903.

Freisen, J., *Geschichte des Kanonischen Eherechtes*. 2nd ed., Paderborn, 1893.

*Gaskoin, C. J. B., *Alcuin, His Life and His Work*. London, 1904.

Goldschmidt, A., *Die Elfenbeinskulptur aus der Zeit der karolingischen und sächsischen Kaiser*, I. Berlin, 1914.

Hauck, A., *Kirchengeschichte Deutschlands*, II. 3rd and 4th ed., Leipzig, 1912.

Heer, J. M., *Ein karolingischer Missionskatechismus*. Freiburg i/B., 1912.

Kampers, F. See preceding chapter.

Ketterer, J. A. See preceding chapter.

Klauser, T., "Die liturgischen Austauschbeziehungen zwischen der römischen und fränkisch-deutschen Kirche vom achten bis elften Jahrhundert" (Historisches Jahrbuch, 53 [1933]).

*Kleinclausz, A., *Alcuin* (Collection Annales de l'université de Lyon, Fasc. 15). Paris, 1948. See also preceding chapter s. v. Alcuin.

Konen, W., *Die Heidenpredigt in der Germanenbekehrung* (University of Bonn dissertation). Düsseldorf, 1909.

Kraus, F. X., *Geschichte der christlichen Kunst,* II, 1. Freiburg i/B., 1897.

La Servière, J. de, *Charlemagne et l'église* (Science et religion, No. 289). Paris, 1904.

Lehmann, P., "Deutschland und die mittelalterliche Überlieferung der Antike" (Zeitschrift für deutsche Geistesgeschichte). 1935.

Lesne, E., *La hiérarchie épiscopale, provinces, métropolitains, primats en Gaule et Germanie, 742-882* (Mémoires et travaux des facultés cath. de Lille, Fasc. 1). Lille-Paris, 1905.

——, *Histoire de la propriété ecclésiastique en France:* II, *La propriété ecclésiastique et les droits régaliens à l'époque carolingienne;* III, *L'inventaire de la propriété* (ibid., Fasc. 19 and 44). Lille, 1922-36.

Lilienfein, H. See preceding chapter.

Lintzel, M., *Karl der Grosse und Widukind.* Hamburg, 1935.

Michel, A., *Histoire de l'art,* I, 1-2. Paris, 1915.

Müllenhofer, K., and Scherer, W., *Denkmäler deutscher Poesie und Prosa aus dem achten bis zwölften Jahrhundert.* 2 vols., 3rd ed., Berlin, 1892.

Ohr, W., *Der karolingische Gottesstaat in Theorie und Praxis* (dissertation). Leipzig, 1902.

Perels, E., *Die kirchlichen Zehnten im karolingischen Reiche* (dissertation). Berlin, 1914.

Pöschl, A., *Bischofsgut und mensa episcopalis,* I. Bonn, 1908.

Schönfeld, W., "Die Xenodochien in Italien und Frankreich im frühen Mittelalter" (Zeitschrift der Savigny-Stiftung für Rechtsgeschichte: Kanon. Abteilung, 43 [1922]).

Schubert, H. von, *Geschichte der christlichen Kirche im Frühmittelalter.* Tübingen, 1921.

Stachnik, K., *Die Bildung des Weltklerus im Frankenreich von Karl Martell bis auf Ludwig den Frommen.* Paderborn, 1926.

Steinmeyer, E., *Die kleineren althochdeutschen Sprachdenkmäler.* Berlin, 1916.

Steinmeyer, E., and Sievers, E., *Die althochdeutschen Glossen.* 5 vols., Berlin, 1879-1922.

Stutz, U., "Das karolingische Zehntgebot" (Zeitschrift der Savigny-Stiftung für Rechtsgeschichte: Germ. Abteilung, 29 [1908]).

Unwerth, W. von, and Siebs, T., *Geschichte der deutschen Literatur bis zur Mitte des elften Jahrhunderts.* Berlin, 1920.

Werminghoff, A., *Kirchenverfassung Deutschlands im Mittelalter.* Hanover, 1905.

Date Due